CONFLICT OR CONSENSUS
IN AMERICAN HISTORY

CONFLICT

OR

CONSENSUS

IN AMERICAN HISTORY

Edited with Introductions
by
Allen F. Davis and Harold D. Woodman
UNIVERSITY OF MISSOURI

D. C. HEATH AND COMPANY   *BOSTON*

For Roberta and Leonora

PREFACE

The perceptive student quickly discovers that the names and dates, facts and figures which he learns from his textbook are subject to varying interpretations. Two historians dealing with the same period and with the same general material often come to very different conclusions about the meaning of the period. It is the controversy over differing interpretations of the past which helps to lend excitement to the study of history. This collection of readings has been designed to introduce the beginning student of American history to this controversial literature of interpretation.

One theme unites all the selections in the book: Has there been real conflict in American history between classes, sections, and interest groups, or has the story of the American past been primarily one of general agreement or consensus? This theme, expressed either explicitly or implicitly, may be found in virtually all major interpretations of our country's past. The problem—conflict or consensus—then is real and meaningful in any attempt to understand the American past and, indeed, in efforts to evaluate the contemporary American scene.

We have attempted to avoid presenting only two extreme positions on each problem raised. Such an either/or approach tends to force the student to see things as either black or white, or else to conclude that truth always lies somewhere in between. To avoid this we have in every case included more than two selections dealing with each problem and have attempted to illustrate subtle disagreements as well as extreme differences of opinion.

Our main concern has not been with historiography. The beginning student is not (and should not be) especially interested in the shifting interpretations of history, with revisions and re-revisions. He should rather be interested in learning what happened and why it happened, in learning how it is possible to examine the same evidence and then arrive at different conclusions. In this volume, therefore, we have concentrated not on the evolution of historical writing but on historical problems. We hope to leave the student with a heightened understanding of the problems of interpretation of the various periods in American history and also to provide the ammunition for thoughtful and spirited discussions. For those who wish to pursue any matter further, we have provided a brief, annotated bibliography at the end of each problem, and a more general bibliography at the end of the book.

We have assumed that the book will supplement a textbook or a selection of paperbacks in the college level, introductory course in American history. More advanced students, already familiar with the basic chronology of events in the American past, will find the book to be a useful introduction to one of the main controversies in present day historical writing.

Columbia, Missouri   Allen F. Davis
                                            Harold D. Woodman

ACKNOWLEDGMENTS

The editing of this volume has put us in the debt of many. We wish to thank the various publishers and authors for permission to reprint copyrighted material. Former instructors in our introductory American history course at the University of Missouri will recognize many of the ideas in the book; we are grateful for their aid and recognize that in a real sense they have been collaborators. Several of our colleagues at the University of Missouri have made useful suggestions from which we benefited: Graham Adams, Jr., Thomas C. Barrow, and Richard S. Kirkendall. Robert L. Branyan and Lawrence H. Larsen (University of Missouri, Kansas City), Lyle W. Dorsett (University of Missouri, St. Louis), James F. Watts (City College of New York), John Burnham and J. Stanley Lemons (Ohio State University), and James Chase (University of Texas) also offered invaluable aid. Needless to say, we alone are responsible for the finished product.

Finally, we want to express a special debt to our wives, Roberta Davis and Leonora Woodman, who offered aid and encouragement at every step in the preparation of this book.

CONTENTS

CONFLICT OR CONSENSUS
IN AMERICAN HISTORY

INTRODUCTION

"Everything is in a state of metamorphosis," observed the Roman philosopher-statesman, Marcus Aurelius, about eighteen hundred years ago. And historians before and since have attempted to chronicle and to explain the everlasting change in human lives and institutions.

Nowhere does the historian find change more manifest than when he studies the United States. In a twinkling of an eye a vast, scarcely populated continent was transformed into a major industrial power of phenomenal complexity. Overnight, virgin forests became fertile farms, Indian trails became roads, highways, and railroads, and empty spaces became bustling cities. Matching this transformation of the physical face of the continent were equally momentous changes in politics, social relations, ideas, and attitudes. For most Americans change was inevitable simply because it was so obvious. "Ten years in America are like a century in Spain," wrote the German immigrant Francis Lieber soon after his arrival in the United States early in the nineteenth century. "The United States really change in some respects more within ten years than a country like Spain has within a hundred."

Yet if change seemed faster and more continuous in America than it did in Europe, only the ignorant and the naive would find the Old World to be stable and unchanging. Indeed, time after time, Americans watched Europe swept by rebellion and war as one group after another sought to revolutionize their lives and institutions.

Generations of American historians have tried to describe and explain the vast alterations which have taken place on the North American continent. As they have done so, many have kept one eye on the changes in European institutions and have sought to compare and contrast the nature and quality of changes in the Old World with those in the New.

As a result, despite all the complexities and variations among historians, two rather distinct traditions have emerged in American historical writing. Both are based on an acceptance of change, and both seek an explanation for it. For one tradition, change is the result of relatively smooth and orderly progression—rapid, perhaps, but always evolutionary. For the other, change is the result of sharp, bitter, and often violent conflict—at times so rapid as to be revolutionary.

The first tradition stresses a uniqueness in the American experience by emphasizing a basic continuity in American history. While there were changes of great significance, they were gradual, exhibiting no sharp breaks with the past. Nor were there sharp differences within American society at any time. According to this tradition, all Americans of whatever class or station shared what was essentially a common outlook. To be sure, Americans did not all live alike nor did they always agree with one another. But their disagreements, especially when compared with the dissensions which divided European society, were not fundamental. Americans had achieved a consensus on fundamentals; if they disagreed, their disagreements were minor differences within this basic consensus.

The second tradition does not ignore the unique features of American history, but by emphasizing abrupt changes and sharp differences, it finds the American experience to be more consonant with European history than does the first tradition. This tradition speaks in terms of revolution and of class and sectional conflict. It stresses differences among Americans—class differences, social differences, political differences. Change was the result of conflict among different groups and classes in American society. And changes, when they came, were fundamental. Not consensus and continuity, but conflict and discontinuity comprise the central theme of this tradition.

In the selections which follow, the reader is introduced to these two traditions through the words of their most able exponents. The selections are not designed simply to give alternative explanations for events, but rather to present two very different ways of looking at American history. Were the remarkable changes in American history the result of orderly development—of evolution—or were these changes the result of bitter disputes and of momentous and abrupt breaks with the past—of revolution?

Is the story of the American past the story of CONSENSUS OR CONFLICT?

I
THE ★
AMERICAN ★
REVOLUTION ★

The basic question which must be asked about the American Revolution is, "What was it?" At first glance, the answer to this question seems obvious; a more important problem, it would appear, would deal with the causes of the Revolution. Yet, the question is not so easy to answer as it might seem, and the causes of the Revolution cannot be dealt with without first seeking its answer.

Writing in 1909, the historian Carl Becker argued that the American Revolution was really two revolutions in one —a dual revolution: "The American Revolution was the result of two general movements: The contests for home-rule and independence, and the democratization of American politics and society. Of these movements, the latter was fundamental." In addition to the antagonism toward the British, Becker saw conflicts within America during the Revolutionary period, conflicts arising from sharp class cleavages in American society. The Revolution, then, arose from the desire to reform the British empire—by separating from it—*and* the desire to reform society at home—by instituting democratic and libertarian reforms and by undermining the power of the local aristocracy. Conflict, not consensus, is the theme of this interpretation.

Not all historians accept Becker's answer to the question, "What was the American Revolution?" While granting that there were differences among Americans before and during the Revolutionary period, some historians maintain that to emphasize these differences is to distort the true picture of American society in the eighteenth cen-

tury. Becker's stress on conflict, they argue, obscures the
fact that there was a general agreement among Americans
which was stronger and more significant than the differences which divided them. In a variety of ways the experience in the New World had created a new man with new
ideas and the Revolution was simply the attempt to maintain what Americans had already rather uniformly accepted. The Revolution was not revolutionary at all,
concludes historian Daniel J. Boorstin; it was merely a
"conservative colonial rebellion." Obviously, the theme of
this interpretation is consensus, not conflict.

The selections which follow illustrate the lack of agreement among historians concerning the nature of the
American Revolution. Quoting John Adams, Clinton Rossiter maintains that the "real American Revolution" took
place during the colonial period. The change was "in the
minds and hearts of the people" and it occurred before the
outbreak of hostilities. While Rossiter does not deny that
there were differences among the colonial Americans, he
finds that these very differences resulted in a general consensus in America.

Merrill Jensen also quotes John Adams and he too returns to the pre-Revolutionary period as a means of understanding the American Revolution. But Jensen sees conflict, not consensus, in the period. He argues that colonial
society was marked by vigorous class conflict and that the
agitation during the Revolutionary period allowed the
democratic, radical elements in America to achieve ascendancy over the aristocratic classes which had ruled
colonial society. For Jensen, the Declaration of Independence and the Articles of Confederation were the embodi-
ments of the radical philosophy which had become dominant.

The selections by Robert R. Palmer and Louis Hartz
deal with the same general problems in a wider context.
Both view the American Revolution in terms of European
revolutionary movements and ideas. Palmer finds that although the American Revolution had certain unique features it was, as was the French Revolution, a violent social
upheaval. Hartz disagrees sharply with this interpretation.
The American Revolution, he maintains, was not a social
upheaval simply because there was no feudal aristocracy
for it to overthrow. Thus while Palmer finds sharp class
divisions which lead to internal conflict, Hartz finds a con-

sensus stemming from the absence of these class differences.

It is evident that the American Revolution was a colonial rebellion resulting in the independence of thirteen of the English colonies in the New World. Had the colonial experience resulted in the creation of an American consensus, making the Revolution merely the culmination of generations of gradual change? If so, then perhaps the greatest significance of the American Revolution was that it was not revolutionary!

But such an interpretation may tell only half the story. Was the American Revolution also a bitter social conflict on the order of the French Revolution of 1789 or the Russian Revolution of 1917? Perhaps class conflict within the colonies transformed the colonial rebellion into a revolutionary turning point in American history.

In the year 1765 there lived along the American seaboard 1,450,000 white and 400,000 Negro subjects of King George III of England. The area of settlement stretched from the Penobscot to the Altamaha and extended inland, by no means solidly, to the Appalachian barrier. Within this area flourished thirteen separate political communities, subject immediately or ultimately to the authority of the Crown, but enjoying in fact large powers of self-government. Life was predominantly rural, the economy agrarian, religion Protestant, descent English, and politics the concern of men of property.

To the best of the average man's knowledge, whether his point of observation was in the colonies or England, all but a handful of these Americans were contented subjects of George III. It was hard for them to be continually enthusiastic about a sovereign or mother country so far away, yet there were few signs that the imperial bonds were about to chafe so roughly. Occasionally statements appeared in print or official correspondence accusing the colonists of republicanism, democracy, and a hankering for independence, but these could be written off as the scoldings of overfastidious travelers or frustrated agents of the royal will. Among the ruling classes sentiments of loyalty to the Crown were strongly held and eloquently expressed, while the attitude of the mass of men was not much different from that of the plain people of England: a curious combination of indifference and obeisance. Benjamin Franklin, who had more firsthand information about the colonies than any other man, could later write in all sincerity, "I never had heard in any Conversation from any Person drunk or sober, the least Expression of a wish for a Separation, or Hint that such a Thing would be advantageous to America."

Yet in the summer and fall of this same year the colonists shook off their ancient habits of submission in the twinkling of an eye and stood revealed as almost an alien people. The passage of the Stamp Act was greeted by an overwhelming refusal to obey, especially among colonial leaders who saw ruin in its provisions—lawyers, merchants, planters, printers, and ministers. Although the flame of resistance was smothered by repeal of the obnoxious act, the next ten years were at best a smoldering truce. In 1775 the policies of Lord North forced a final appeal to

From *The First American Revolution*, © 1953, 1956 by Clinton Rossiter. Reprinted by permission of Harcourt, Brace & World, Inc.

arms, and enough Americans answered it to bring off a successful war of independence.

Dozens of able historians have inquired into the events and forces that drove this colonial people to armed rebellion. Except among extreme patriots and equally extreme economic determinists, fundamental agreement now prevails on the immediate causes of the American Revolution. Less attention has been devoted to the question: What made this people ripe for rebellion, or, more exactly, what was there about the continental colonies in 1765 that made them so willing to engage in open defiance of a major imperial policy?

One answer, perhaps the best and certainly the best-known, was volunteered in 1818 by John Adams, himself a cause of the American Revolution: "The Revolution was effected before the war commenced. The Revolution was in the minds and hearts of the people. . . . This radical change in the principles, opinions, sentiments, and affections of the people, was the real American Revolution." What Adams seems to have argued was that well before Lexington and Concord there existed a collective outlook called the American mind, a mind whose chief characteristics, so we learn in other parts of his writings, were self-reliance, patriotism, practicality, and love of liberty, with liberty defined as freedom from alien dictation. It was the alien dictation of North, Townshend, Grenville, and the other shortsighted ministers of a shortsighted king that forced the American mind to assert itself boldly for the first time.

Adams did not find it necessary to describe in detail the long-range forces that had produced this mind, perhaps because that extraordinary student of political realities, Edmund Burke, had already given so perceptive a description. In his magnificent speech on conciliation with the colonies March 22, 1775, Burke singled out "six capital sources" to account for the American "love of freedom," that "fierce spirit of liberty" which was "stronger in the English colonies probably than in any other people of the earth": their English descent; their popular forms of government; "religion in the northern provinces"; "manners in the southern"; education, especially in the law; and "the remoteness of the situation from the first mover of government." Implicit in Burke's praise of the American spirit of liberty, as in Adams's recollection of it, was a recognition that this liberty rested on firm and fertile ground, that the colonists enjoyed in fact as well as in spirit a measure of opportunity and self-direction almost unique in the annals of mankind.

The grand thesis of American history toward which Adams and Burke were groping, not altogether blindly, was rounded off by Alexis de Tocqueville a half-century after the Revolution. With one of his most brilliant flashes of insight De Tocqueville revealed the unique nature of the American Republic: "The great advantage of the Americans is that they have arrived at a state of democracy without having to endure a democratic revolution" or, to state the thesis in terms of 1776, the Americans, unlike most revolutionists in history, already enjoyed the liberty for which they were fighting. The "real American Revolution" was over and done with before the Revolution began. The first revolution alone made the second possible.

My purpose . . . is to provide an extended commentary in support of Adams, Burke, and De Tocqueville—not that this glorious threesome needs support from anyone. I accept with practically no reservations the notion that the American Revolution was wholly different in character and purpose from the French, Russian, and almost all other revolutions, and I ascribe this difference largely to the plain truth that the Americans had no need and thus no intention to "make the world over." By 1765 their world had already been made over as thoroughly as most sensible men—most sensible white men, to be sure—could imagine or expect. Americans had never known or had long since begun to abandon feudal tenures, a privilege-ridden economy, centralized and despotic government, religious intolerance, and hereditary stratification. Americans had achieved and were prepared to defend with their blood a society more open, an economy more fluid, a religion more tolerant, and a government more popular than anything Europeans would know for decades to come. The goal of the rebellious colonists was largely to consolidate, then expand by cautious stages, the large measure of liberty and prosperity that was already part of their way of life. . . .

I think it necessary to point to four all-pervading features of the colonial experience that were hastening the day of liberty, independence, and democracy. Over only one of these massive forces did the colonists or English authorities have the slightest degree of control, and the political wisdom that was needed to keep it in tight rein simply did not exist in empires of that time.

I

The first ingredient of American liberty was the heritage from England. Burke acknowledged this "capital source" in words that his countrymen could understand but apparently not act upon.

> The people of the colonies are descendants of Englishmen. England, Sir, is a nation which still I hope respects, and formerly adored, her freedom. The colonists emigrated from you when this part of your character was most predominant; and they took this bias and direction the moment they parted from your lands. They are therefore not only devoted to liberty, but to liberty according to English ideas, and on English principles.

"Wee humbly pray," wrote the General Assembly of Rhode Island to the Board of Trade in 1723, "that their Lordships will believe wee have a Tincture of the ancient British Blood in our veines." The colonists had considerably more than a tincture: at least seven in ten were English in blood, and virtually all their institutions, traditions, ideas, and laws were English in origin and inspiration. The first colonists had brought over both the good and evil of seventeenth-century England. The good had been toughened and in several instances improved; much of the bad had been jettisoned under frontier conditions. As a result of this interaction of heredity and environment, the eighteenth-century American was simply a special brand of Englishman. When it pleased him he could be more English than the English, and when it pleased him most was any occurrence in which questions of liberty and self-government were at issue. In a squabble over the question of a fixed salary between Governor Joseph Dudley and the Massachusetts Assembly, the latter could state without any sense of pretension:

It hath been the Priviledge from Henry the third & confirmed by Edward the first, & in all Reigns unto this Day, granted, & is now allowed to be the just & unquestionable Right of the Subject, to raise when & dispose of how they see Cause, any Sums of money by Consent of Parliament, the which Priviledge We her Majesty's Loyal and Dutiful Subjects have lived in the Enjoym^t of, & do hope always to enjoy the same, under Our most gracious Queen Ann & Successors, & shall ever endeavour to discharge the Duty incumbent on us; But humbly conceive the Stating of perpetual Salaries not agreable to her Majesty's Interests in this Province, but prejudicial to her Majesty's good Subjects.

Southerners were, if anything, more insistent. In 1735 the South Carolina legislature resolved:

That His Majesty's subjects in this province are entitled to all the liberties and privileges of Englishmen . . . [and] that the Commons House of Assembly in South Carolina, by the laws of England and South Carolina, and ancient usage and custom, have all the rights and privileges pertaining to Money bills that are enjoyed by the British House of Commons.

And the men of the frontier, who were having the same trouble with assemblies that assemblies were having with governors, made the echo ring.

1st. We apprehend, as Free-Men and English Subjects, we have an indisputable Title to the same Privileges and Immunities with his Majesty's other Subjects, who reside in the interior Counties of Philadelphia, Chester and Bucks, and therefore ought not to be excluded from an equal Share with them in the very important Privilege of Legislation.

These were the words of men who made much of the English tie, even when, as in the last of these instances, most of them were Scotch-Irish or German. Their traditions—representative government, supremacy of law, constitutionalism, liberty of the subject—belonged to them as Englishmen. Their institutions, especially the provincial assembly, were often looked upon as sound to the extent that they conformed to English models, or at least to colonial interpretations or recollections of those models. The rights for which they contended were not the natural rights of all men but the ancient rights of Englishmen. "It is no Little Blessing of God," said Cotton Mather to the Massachusetts Assembly in 1700, "that we are a part of the *English Nation.*"

Throughout the colonial period the English descent and attitudes of the great majority of Americans gave impetus to their struggles for liberty. It is a momentous fact of American history that until 1776 it was a chapter in English history as well. Just as England in 1765 was ahead of the Continent in the struggle for law and liberty, so America, this extraordinary part of England, was even further ahead, not least because most of its leading inhabitants thought of themselves as Englishmen. Such men would not easily be cheated or argued out of their heritage—a truth that Burke did his best to advertise:

> The temper and character which prevail in our colonies are, I am afraid, unalterable by any human act. We cannot, I fear, falsify the pedigree of this fierce people, and persuade them that they are not sprung from a nation in whose veins the blood of freedom circulates. The language in which they would hear you tell them this tale would detect the imposition; your speech would betray you. An Englishman is the unfittest person on earth to argue another Englishman into slavery.

The clash of imperial policy and colonial self-reliance is almost always productive of the spirit of liberty. This is especially true if the policy of the parent state is conceived purely in its own interests, and if the colonists are men of high political aptitude and proud descent. Such was the pattern of Anglo-American relations in the colonial period. From the time of the earliest settlement, which like all the important settlements was the result of private initiative, English and American opinions on the political and economic status of the colonies were in sharp conflict.

The conduct of colonial affairs by the English government rested on these assumptions: The colonies were dependents of the parent state. Since their interests were subordinate to those of England, the welfare of the latter was to be the one concern of all agencies charged with governing them. They were therefore to serve, apparently forever, as a source of wealth and support for the land out of which their inhabitants had departed. If the English government had acted on these assumptions consistently throughout the colonial period, the contrasting ideas of the colonists would have had less chance to strike deep root. But confusion at the beginning, domestic troubles in the middle, and "salutary neglect" throughout most of this period permitted the colonists to build not only a theory but a condition of self-government. And it was this condition, of course, as some perceptive Englishmen were aware, that helped the colonies develop into prizes worth retaining by force of arms. The interests of England were, in this important sense, fatally self-contradictory.

The views of the colonists on their place in the imperial structure were somewhat mixed, ranging from the arrogant independence asserted by Massachusetts in the seventeenth century to the abject dependence argued by a handful of Tory apologists in the eighteenth. In general, the colonial attitude was one looking to near-equality in the present and some sort of full partnership in the future, all within the confines of a benevolent and protecting empire. The colonist acknowledged that for certain diplomatic and commercial purposes his destiny would rest for some time to come in the hands of men in London. But in all other matters, especially in that of political self-determination, he considered himself a "freeborn subject of the Crown of England." Theories of the origin and nature of the colonial assemblies are a good example of these divergent views. In English eyes the assemblies were founded by royal grant and existed at royal pleasure; in American eyes they existed as a matter of right. The Board of Trade looked upon them as inferior bodies enjoying rule-making powers under the terms of their charters; the men of Virginia and Massachusetts looked upon them as miniature Houses of Commons with power to make all laws they could get away with in practice. The struggle between these assemblies and the royal governors sent to control them was the focus of conflict of colonial and imperial interests.

Had Parliament not decided to intrude its authority into colonial affairs, the old-fashioned imperial views of the English authorities and the prophetic self-governing claims of the American colonists might have coexisted for decades without producing a violent break. The tardy policies of stern control initiated by the Grenville ministry brought this long-standing conflict fully into the open. In the years before 1765 the push-and-pull of imperialism and home rule had been a spur to the growth of liberty in the colonies. In the next decade it ignited a rebellion.

II

Let us hear again from the member for Bristol.

The last cause of this disobedient spirit in the colonies is hardly less powerful than the rest, as it is not merely moral, but laid deep in the natural constitution of things. Three thousand miles of ocean lie between you and them. No contrivance can prevent the effect of this distance in weakening government. Seas roll, and months pass, between the order and the execution; and the want of a speedy explanation of a single point is enough to defeat a whole system. . . . In large bodies, the circulation of power must be less vigorous at the extremities. Nature has said it. . . . This is the immutable condition, the eternal law, of extensive and detached empire.

This harsh fact of geography, the remoteness of the colonies, squared the difference between imperial purpose and colonial aspiration. The early colonists, thrown willy-nilly on their own devices, developed habits of self-government and passed them on to their descendants. The descendants, still just as far if not farther from London, fell naturally into an attitude of provincialism well suited to their condition but corrosive of empire. The lack of contact between one colony and another, the result of distance and unbelievably bad roads, allowed each to develop on its own. The diversity in character of the key colonies of Virginia, Massachusetts, New York, and Pennsylvania made a mockery of any notion of uniform imperial policy.

Worst of all from the imperial point of view, the ill effects of the inconsistency, inefficiency, corruption, stupidity, arrogance, and ignorance displayed to some degree at all times and to a perilous degree at some times by the English authorities were doubled and redoubled by the rolling seas and passing months. English laxity in enforcing the Navigation Acts and colonial habits of disobeying them were one instance of the extent to which three thousand miles of ocean could water down a policy of strict control. The technique of royal disallowance, which seemed so perfectly designed to keep the colonial assemblies in check, was likewise weakened by the mere fact of distance. For example, the disallowance in 1706 of two New Hampshire judiciary acts passed in 1699 and 1701 was never reported properly to the province, and the judiciary in that colony continued to function under these laws for a half century. And the royal governor, the linchpin of empire, was a far more accommodating fellow in Boston or Charleston than he appeared in his commissions and instructions issued from London. A governor like Sir Matthew Johnson of North Carolina, whose reports to the Board of Trade went astray four years in a row, could not have been much of a buffer against colonial urges to independence. When we realize that no regular mail-service of any kind existed until 1755, and that war disrupted communications more than one-third of the time between 1689 and 1763, we can understand how the ocean was at once a highway to freedom and a barrier to imperialism. Rarely in history have the laws of geopolitics worked so powerfully for liberty.

Had Burke ever lived in the colonies, he might have listed still another "capital source" to explain the rise of liberty in America, and thus have anticipated Frederick Jackson Turner and his celebrated thesis. We need not go all the way with Turner—"American democracy is fundamentally the outcome of the experiences of the American people in dealing with the West"—to acknowledge the significance of the frontier in early American history. Whatever the extent of that influence in the nineteenth century, in the seventeenth and eighteenth centuries—when America was one vast frontier and perhaps one in three Americans a frontiersman at some time in his life—it was clearly of the first importance. If we may take the word "frontier" to mean not only the line of farthest settlement to the west, but also the primitive conditions of life and thought which extended throughout the colonies in the seventeenth century and continued to prevail in many areas east of the Appalachians during most of the eighteenth, we may point to at least a half-dozen indications of the influence of the American environment.

First, the frontier impeded the transfer to America of outworn attitudes and institutions. The wilderness frustrated completely such attempts to plant feudalism in America as the schemes of Sir Ferdinando Gorges and the stillborn Fundamental Constitutio..s of Carolina, and everywhere archaic laws and customs were simplified, liberalized, or rudely abandoned. In the matter of church-state relations the frontier was especially influential as a decentralizing and democratizing force. The positive result of this process of sloughing off the old ways was an increase in mobility, experimentation, and self-reliance among the settlers.

The wilderness demanded of those who would conquer it that they spend their lives in unremitting toil. Unable to devote any sizable part of their energies to government, the settlers insisted that government let them alone and perform its severely limited tasks at the amateur level. The early American definition of liberty as freedom *from* government was given added popularity and meaning by frontier conditions. It was a new and invigorating experience for tens of thousands of Englishmen, Germans, and Scotch-Irish to be able to build a home where they would at last be "let alone."

The frontier produced, in ways that Turner and his followers have made clear, a new kind of individual and new doctrines of individualism. The wilderness did not of itself create democracy; indeed, it often encouraged the growth of ideas and institutions hostile to it. But it did help produce some of the raw materials of American democracy—self-reliance, social fluidity, simplicity, equality, dislike of privilege, optimism, and devotion to liberty. At the same time, it emphasized the importance of voluntary co-operation. The group, too, had its uses on the frontier, whether for defense or barn-raising or cornhusking. The phrases "free association," "mutual subjection," and "the consent of the governed" were given new content in the wilderness.

Next, the fact that wages were generally higher and working conditions better in the colonies than in England did much to advance the cause of liberty. The reason for this happy condition was a distinct shortage of labor, and a prime reason for the shortage was land for the asking. The frontier population was made up of thousands of men who had left the seaboard to toil for themselves in the great forest. The results of this constant migration were as important for the seaboard as they were for the wilderness.

From the beginning the frontier was an area of protest and thus a nursery of republican notions. Under-represented in assemblies that made a habit of overtaxing them, scornful of the privileges and leadership assumed by the tidewater aristocracy, resentful of attempts to saddle them with unwanted ministers and officials, the men of the back country were in fact if not in print the most determined radicals of the

colonial period. If their quaint and strangely deferential protests contributed very little to the literature of a rising democracy, they nevertheless
made more popular the arguments for liberty and self-government.

Finally, all these factors combined to give new force to the English
heritage of law, liberty, and self-government. The over-refined and often
archaic institutions that the settlers brought along as part of their intellectual baggage were thrust once again into the crucible of primitive conditions. If these institutions emerged in shapes that horrified royal governors, they were nevertheless more simple, workable, and popular than
they had been for several centuries in England. The laws and institutions
of early Rhode Island or North Carolina would not have worked in more
civilized societies, but they had abandoned most of their outworn features and were ready to develop along American lines. The hardworking,
long-suffering men and women of the frontier—"People a litle wilful
Inclined to doe when and how they please or not at al"—were themselves
a primary force in the rise of colonial self-government.

The English descent and heritage of the colonists, the conflict of imperial and colonial interests, the rolling ocean, the all-pervading frontier
—these were the "forces-behind-the-forces" that shaped the history of the
colonies and spurred the peaceful revolution that preceded the bloody
one of 1776. . . .

III

The colonists were not completely at the mercy of their environment. Much of the environment was of their own making; and if circumstances were favorable to the rise of liberty, they did not relieve the colonists of the formidable task of winning it for themselves. The condition
of liberty in 1765 was in large part the work of men determined to be
free, and the questions thus arise: Who were these men who talked so
much of their rights and privileges? Whence came they to America, and
how did they fare? . . .

It is now generally agreed that almost all immigrants to the colonies
came from the middle and lower classes. "The rich stay in Europe," wrote
Crèvecoeur; "it is only the middling and the poor that emigrate." The
myths of aristocratic lineage die hard, especially in Cavalier country, but
diaries, shipping lists, and court minutes tell us in no uncertain terms of
the simple origins of even the most haughty families of New York and
Virginia. This does not mean that early America was a land of rogues
and poor servant-girls. England and the Continent sent over thousands
upon thousands of substantial, intelligent, propertied men and women.
Yet fully half the people who came to the colonies could not pay their
own passage, and gentleman immigrants, even in the seventeenth century, were amazingly few.

As a matter of fact, those twentieth-century Americans who like to go searching for an ancestor among the gentry of East Anglia may wind up with three or four among the riffraff of Old Bailey. Probably thirty to forty thousand convicts were shipped from England to the colonies in the eighteenth century, a fact that inspired Dr. Johnson's famous growl: "Sir, they are a race of convicts, and ought to be content with anything we allow them short of hanging." Their behavior in the colonies, especially in unhappy Virginia and Maryland, moved Franklin to offer America's rattlesnakes to England as the only appropriate return. Not only did transported convicts commit a large proportion of the crimes in eighteenth-century America, but their presence did much to degrade the servant class and make a callous society even more callous. The mother country's insistence on dumping "the dregs, the excrescence of England" in the colonies was a major item in the catalogue of American grievances, especially since the Privy Council vetoed repeatedly the acts through which the colonies sought to protect themselves.

Well before 1765 the colonies had begun to take on a pattern of national origins that was "characteristically American": They looked to one country for their language, institutions, and paramount culture, but to many for their population. Americans were predominantly English in origin, but they were also Scotch, Irish, German, French, Swiss, Dutch, Swedish, and African. It is impossible to fix precisely the proportions of each nationality in the total white population of 1765; the necessary statistics are simply not available. These general percentages are about as accurate as can be expected: English, 65 to 70 per cent; Scots and Scotch-Irish, 12 to 15 per cent; Germans, 6 to 9 per cent; Irish, 3 to 5 per cent; Dutch 3 per cent; all others 3 to 5 per cent. Out of a total population of 1,850,000, probably 400,000 were Negroes and mulattoes. . . .

What was the total effect on society, culture, and government of this influx of nationalities into the American settlement? . . .

First, the melting pot had only just begun to heat up in the latter part of the eighteenth century. Crèvecoeur's example of the English-French-Dutch family "whose present four sons have now four wives of four different nations" was a phenomenon more prophetic of the Republic than typical of the colonies. The great process of national fusion had made little progress by 1765. Assimilation into the English stock rather than the creation of a new people was the result of such intermarriage as took place in colonial times. Nor were all the ingredients yet in the pot; the essential racial (Teutonic-Celtic) and religious (Protestant) unity of the population must not be overlooked.

The arrival of non-English immigrants did much to weaken the hold of the mother country. The newcomer wanted to be as loyal as anyone else, but his allegiance to the Crown could have little real emotional content. The Germans were inclined to be conservatively neutral about English dominion; the Scots and Irish were, for all the loyal humility that oozed from their petitions, innately hostile to the Georges and their agents. They lacked, as one traveler put it, the "same filial attachment" to England "which her own immediate offspring have."

Next, the influx of aliens did much to strengthen the Protestant, dissenting, individualistic character of colonial religion. The Presbyterian, Lutheran, Baptist, and German Pietist churches were the chief beneficiaries of this immigration. The numbers and enthusiasm of these dissenting groups gave a tremendous lift to the cause of religious liberty in the colonies south of Pennsylvania.

The eighteenth-century immigrants helped democratize the political institutions that had been brought over from England and put to work in the wilderness. This was especially true of the Scotch-Irish, whose only quarrel with the representative governments of their adopted colonies was that they were not representative enough. The Germans were inclined to be politically passive; their major contribution to the coming democracy was the support they brought to the middle-class creed of industry, frugality, and self-reliance. The Scotch-Irish, on the other hand, were more politically conscious. If the controlling groups of the coastal counties refused to honor their legitimate claims to participation in public life, this rebuff served only to make their radicalism more insistent. They had little intention of altering the English-American scheme of government, but they did mean to show the world how democratic it could be. The sentiments of "leveling republicanism" were especially active on the Scotch-Irish frontier; here the "real American Revolution" went on apace.

Finally, the mere volume of immigration from Germany and Ireland had a pronounced effect on colonial life. The swarming of these industrious peoples made possible the remarkable expansion in territory and population that marked the eighteenth century in America. If the Scotch-Irishman was America's typical frontiersman, the German was its typical farmer; and between them they made it possible for cities like Philadelphia and towns like Lancaster to grow and flourish. Though they were men of different natures, both sought the same blessing. "And what but LIBERTY, charming LIBERTY, is the resistless Magnet that attracts so many different Nations into that flourishing Colony?" . . .

THE SECOND AMERICAN REVOLUTION SUCCEEDS THE FIRST

On March 22, 1765, George III gave his royal assent to the Stamp Act, a stick of imperial dynamite so harmless in appearance that it had passed both houses of Parliament as effortlessly as "a common Turnpike Bill." Eleven years later, July 2, 1776, the Continental Congress resolved after "the greatest and most solemn debate":

That these United Colonies are, and, of right, ought to be, Free and Independent States; that they are absolved from all allegiance to the *British* crown, and that all political connexion between them, and the state of *Great Britain*, is, and ought to be totally dissolved.

In the tumultuous years between these two fateful acts the American colonists, at least a sufficient number of them, stumbled and haggled their way to a heroic decision: to found a new and independent nation upon political and social principles that were a standing reproach to almost every other nation in the world. Not for another seven years could they be certain that their decision had been sound as well as bold; only then would the mother country admit reluctantly that the new nation was a fact of life rather than an act of treason. The colonists were to learn at Brooklyn and Valley Forge that it was one thing to resolve for independence and another to achieve it.

Yet the resolution for independence, the decision to fight as a "separate and equal" people rather than as a loose association of remonstrating colonials, was as much the climax of a revolution as the formal beginning of one, and it is this revolution—the "real American Revolution"—that I have sought to describe. . . . By way of conclusion, I would think it useful to point briefly to those developments in the decade after 1765 that speeded up and brought to bloody conclusion "this radical change in the principles, opinions, sentiments, and affections" of the hitherto loyal American subjects of George III.

The progress of the colonies in these years was nothing short of astounding. Thanks to the fecundity of American mothers and the appeal of the American land, population increased from 1,850,000 in 1765 to more than 2,500,000 in 1776. America's troubles seemed only to make America more alluring; immigrants arrived in especially large numbers between 1770 and 1773. The westward pressure of 650,000 new colonists was, of course, enormous, and many new towns and settlements were planted in frontier lands east of the proclamation line of 1763. The sharp increase in population of the continental colonies lent support to arguments, especially popular after 1774, that Americans would some day outnumber Englishmen, and that there was "something absurd in supposing a continent to be perpetually governed by an island." Signs of increased wealth and well-being inspired other Americans to sing the glories of "a commerce out of all proportion to our numbers."

Far more significant than this material progress was the quickened influence of the "forces-behind-the-forces." . . . The English heritage, the ocean, the frontier, and imperial tension never worked so positively for political liberty as in this decade of ferment. Until the last days before independence the colonists continued to argue as Englishmen demanding English rights. The more they acted like Americans, the more they talked like Englishmen. Heirs of a tradition that glorified resistance to tyranny, they moved into political combat as English Whigs rather than American democrats, reminding the world that "it is the peculiar Right of Englishmen to complain when injured." The other basic forces were no less favorable to the swift advance of the spirit of liberty. In a situation that called desperately for accurate information, firm decisions, and resolute administration, the very distance between London and Boston frustrated the development of a viable imperial policy. In a situation that called no less desperately for colonial understanding of the imperial difficulties facing Crown and Parliament, the push to the frontier weakened the bonds of loyalty to an already too-distant land. And the Stamp Act and Townshend Acts forced most articulate colonists to reduce the old conflict of English and American interests to the simplest possible terms. Since some Englishmen proposed to consign other Englishmen to perpetual inferiority, was it not simply a question of liberty or slavery?

The forces that had long been working for political freedom underwent a sharp increase in influence. The ancient struggle between royal governor and popular assembly took on new vigor and meaning. The depths of ill feeling were plumbed in the maneuvers and exchanges of Governors Bernard and Hutchinson and the Massachusetts legislature. The colonial press engaged in more political reporting and speculation in the single year between June, 1765, and June, 1766, than in all the sixty-odd years since the founding of the *Boston News-Letter*. In early 1765 there were twenty-three newspapers in the colonies, only two or three of which were politically conscious; in early 1775 there were thirty-eight, only two or three of which were not. The spirit of constitutionalism and the demand for written constitutions also quickened in the course of the far-ranging dispute over the undetermined boundaries of imperial power and colonial rights. The word "unconstitutional," an essential adjunct of constitutionalism, became one of America's favorite words. Most important, the Stamp Act was a healthy spur to political awareness among all ranks of men. Wrote John Adams in 1766:

The people, even to the lowest ranks, have become more attentive to their liberties, more inquisitive about them, and more determined to defend them, than they were ever before known or had occasion to be; innumerable have been the monuments of wit, humor, sense, learning, spirit, patriotism, and heroism, erected in the several provinces in the course of this year. Their counties, towns, and even private clubs and sodalities have voted and determined; their merchants have agreed to sacrifice even their bread to the cause of liberty; their legislatures have resolved; the united colonies have remonstrated; the presses have everywhere groaned; and the pulpits have thundered.

The thundering pulpit, an old and faithful servant of American freedom, set out to demonstrate anew the affinity of religious and political liberty. Bumptious Protestantism vied with temperate rationalism as spurs to disestablishment and liberty of conscience. Conditions for the final triumph of unqualified religious liberty grew more favorable in this unsettled decade. So, too, did conditions of economic independence. The over-all state of the American economy lent impressive support to radical claims that the colonies would get along just as well, if not better, outside the protecting confines of British mercantilism. In wealth, resources, production, ingenuity, and energy the Americans were fast approaching the end of the colonial line. . . .

In every colony the middle class formed the nucleus of the patriot party, and in Boston it attained a position of commanding political influence. The aristocracy split into opposing camps, but the Lees of Virginia and Livingstons of New York are reminders that a decisive share of patriotic leadership fell to the American aristocrat. The political storms of the decade, which deposited power in new hands in almost every colony, did much to stimulate social mobility and class conflict. The career of the Sons of Liberty attests the growing fluidity of colonial society; the uprisings of the "Paxton Boys" in Pennsylvania and the Regulators in North Carolina attest the heightened tensions of class and section.

Finally, the colonial mind took rapid strides forward in this period, not alone in the field of political thought. Deism, rationalism, and the scientific spirit claimed increasing numbers of men in positions of leadership. The cult of virtue enjoyed a vogue even more intense than in the colonial period. The arts showed new signs of indigenous strength. The sharp increase in the number of newspapers was matched by an even sharper increase in the output of books and pamphlets. Three new colleges opened their doors to eager students, and King's and the Philadelphia Academy instituted the first American medical schools. Despite all the shouting about English rights and ways, the colonial mind was growing steadily less English and more American. By the standards of the old world, it was a mind not especially attractive, not least because it was setting out at last to find standards of its own.

The American colonies moved fast and far between 1765 and 1776. While the King fumed, the ministry blundered, assemblies protested, mobs rioted, and Samuel Adams plotted, the people of the colonies, however calm or convulsed the political situation, pushed steadily ahead in numbers, wealth, self-reliance, and devotion to liberty. The peaceful revolution that had been gathering momentum from the time of the first settlements moved irresistibly to conclusion, and the fighting revolution could now begin. It could begin, moreover, with high hopes for its success. Blessed by a way of life that knew much freedom and held the promise of much more, the Americans, like the Englishmen who unseated James II, could make their revolution "a parent to settlement, and not a nursery of future revolutions." This was one colonial people that went to war for liberty knowing in its bones what liberty was.

Merrill Jensen

The American Revolution was far more than a war between the colonies and Great Britain; it was also a struggle between those who enjoyed political privileges and those who did not. Yet the conclusions which may be drawn from the history of social conflict within the colonies and applied to such matters of mutual concern as the writing of a common constitution are seldom drawn and applied. Ordinarily the Revolution is treated as the end of one age and the beginning of another; a new country was born; political parties sprang into being; political leaders, full of wisdom learned during the Revolution, sought to save the new nation from the results of ignorance and inexperience. So runs the story.

But the story is true only in an external sense. The basic social forces in colonial life were not eliminated by the Declaration of Independence. There was no break in the underlying conflict between party and party representing fundamental divisions in American society. Those divisions had their roots in the very foundation of the colonies, and by the middle of the eighteenth century there had arisen broad social groupings based on economic and political conditions. More and more, wealth and political power were concentrated along the coast, in the hands of planters in the South and of merchants in the North. There were exceptions, of course, but by and large the colonial governments were in the hands of the economic upper classes. Exceedingly conscious of its local rights, the ruling aristocracy was willing to use democratic arguments to defeat the centralizing policies of Great Britain, but it had no intention of widening the base of political power within the colonies to accord with the conclusions which could be, and were, drawn from those arguments. On the contrary, it had kept itself in power through the use of a number of political weapons. As wealth accumulated and concentrated along the coast, as the frontier moved westward and became debtor and alien in character, and as the propertyless element in the colonial towns grew larger, the owners of property demanded "a political interpretation of their favored position"—that is, political supremacy—as a protection against the economic programs of debtor agrarians and the town poor. Encouraged by the British government, they gradually secured the political safeguards they demanded—property qualifications for participation

Reprinted with permission of the copyright owners, the Regents of the University of Wisconsin, from Merrill Jensen, *The Articles of Confederation*, 1959, the University of Wisconsin Press.

in government and representation disproportionate to their numbers. The imposition of property qualifications for the suffrage and of even higher qualifications for office effectively quelled the political ambitions of the greater part of the town population, and the denial of proportional representation to the newly settled areas prevented the growing West from capturing control of colonial governments. Laws of entail and primogeniture insured the economic basis of colonial society, so much so that Thomas Jefferson believed that their abolition in Virginia would annul the privileges of an "aristocracy of wealth."

But the economic-political aristocracy which Jefferson hoped to abolish had not always been characteristic of the American colonies. In early Virginia and Maryland every free man, whether holding property or not, could vote. The first serious attempt to impose a property qualification for the suffrage came with the Restoration and it met with bitter opposition. One of the significant acts of Bacon's Assembly in 1676 was the abolition of the property qualification imposed by the Berkeley regime. But the victory of the poorer elements was short-lived at best, and in Virginia, as elsewhere in the colonies by the end of the seventeenth century, the property qualification was an integral part of the political system. During the eighteenth century the tendency was in the direction of ever higher qualifications, and colonial assemblies continued to refuse adequate representation to the expanding West. By the middle of the century a small minority of the colonial population wielded economic and political powers which could not be taken from them by any legal means. This political oligarchy was able to ignore most of the popular demands, and when smoldering discontent did occasionally flare up in a violent outburst, it was forcibly suppressed. Thus democracy was decreasingly a characteristic of constitutional development in the American colonies.

Opposition to the oligarchical rule of the planters and merchants came from the agrarian and proletarian elements which formed the vast majority of the colonial population. Probably most of them were politically inert, but from their ranks nevertheless came some of the effective leadership and much of the support for revolutionary activity after 1763. In the towns the poorer people, although a small part of the colonial population, far outnumbered the large property-owners. Most of them—laborers, artisans, and small tradesmen—were dependent on the wealthy merchants, who ruled them economically and socially. Agrarian discontent, too, was the product of local developments: of exploitation by land speculators, "taxation without representation," and the denial of political privileges, economic benefits, and military assistance. The farmer's desire for internal revolution had already been violently expressed in Bacon's Rebellion and in the Regulator Movement, events widely separated in time but similar in cause and consequence.

To a large extent, then, the party of colonial radicalism was composed of the masses in the towns and on the frontier. In Charleston, Philadelphia, New York, and Boston the radical parties were the foundation of the revolutionary movement in their towns and colonies.[1] It was they who provided the organization for uniting the dispersed farming population, which had not the means of organizing, but which was more than ready to act and which became the bulwark of the Revolution once it had started. Located at the center of things, the town radicals were able to seize upon issues as they arose and to spread propaganda by means of circular letters, committees of correspondence, and provincial congresses. They brought to a focus forces that would otherwise have spent themselves in sporadic outbursts easily suppressed by the established order.

Colonial radicalism did not become effective until after the French and Indian War. Then, fostered by economic depression and aided by the bungling policy of Great Britain and the desire of the local governing classes for independence within the empire, it became united in an effort to throw off its local and international bonds. The discontented were given an opportunity to express their discontent when the British government began to enforce restrictions upon the colonies after 1763. The colonial merchants used popular demonstrations to give point to their more orderly protests against such measures as the Stamp Act, and it was only a step from such riots, incited and controlled by the merchants, to the organization of radical parties bent on the redress of local grievances which were of far more concern to the masses than the more remote and less obvious effects of British policy. Furthermore, there arose, in each of the colonies, leaders of more than ordinary ability, men who were able to create issues when none were furnished by Great Britain, and who seized on British acts as heaven-sent opportunities to attack the local aristocracy—too strongly entrenched to be overthrown on purely local issues—under the guise of a patriotic defense of American liberties. Thus, used as tools at first, the masses were soon united under capable

---

[1] The terms "radical" and "conservative" in this discussion are not synonymous with "revolutionist" and "loyalist." That they are not interchangeable is obvious from the easily demonstrable fact that there were in internal colonial politics radicals who became loyalists, and conservatives who became revolutionists.

The interpretation of the Revolution is too often confused by the insistence that all revolutionists were radicals. Probably most radicals were revolutionists, but a large number of revolutionists were not radicals. The conservatives were those who —whether they desired independence or not—wanted to maintain the aristocratic order in the American colonies and states. The radicals were those who wanted changes in the existing order, changes which can be best described as democratic, though the term is necessarily relative.

By and large the majority of the colonial aristocracy was opposed to independence. This attitude was due partly to training, partly to self-interest, and partly—increasingly after 1774—to the fear that independence would result in an internal revolution. The radicals, on the other hand, shifted from mere opposition to British measures to a demand for independence as they came to realize that only independence would make possible the internal revolution which radicalism in the colonies had come more and more to demand.

leadership in what became as much a war against the colonial aristocracy as a war for independence.

The American Revolution thus marks the ascendancy of the radicals
of the colonies, for the first time effectively united. True, this radical ascendancy was of brief duration, but while it lasted an attempt was made
to write democratic ideals and theories of government into the laws and
constitutions of the American states. Fulfillment was not complete, for
the past was strong and in some states the conservatives retained their
power and even strengthened it. And once independence was won, the
conservatives soon united in undoing, so far as they could, such political
and economic democracy as had resulted from the war. Nevertheless it is
significant that the attempt at democratization was made and that it was
born of colonial conditions. The participation of the radicals in the creation of a common government is all-important, for they as well as the
conservatives believed that a centralized government was essential to the
maintenance of conservative rule. Naturally the radicals who exercised
so much power in 1776 refused to set up in the Articles of Confederation
a government which would guarantee the position of the conservative
interests they sought to remove from power.

The conservatives gradually became aware that internal revolution
might be the result of continued disputes between themselves and Great
Britain, but they were not agreed on the measures necessary to retain
both "home rule" and the power to "rule at home." Some of them, like
Joseph Galloway, sought to tighten the bonds between the colonies and
the mother country and thus to consolidate the power and bulwark the
position of the colonial aristocracy. Other conservatives, like John Dickinson, denied that Parliament had any authority over the colonies and
cared little for a close tie with the mother country; what they demanded
was a status that was in effect home rule within the British Empire.
Complete independence was to be avoided if possible, for it was fraught
with the danger of social revolution within the colonies. As these men became aware that conservative rule had as much or more to fear from the
people of the colonies as from British restrictions, they sought more and
more for reconciliation with the mother country, in spite of her obvious
intention to enforce her laws by means of arms. But they made the fatal
yet unavoidable error of uniting with the radicals in meeting force with
force. They made themselves believe that it was neither traitorous nor
illegal to resist with arms the British measures they disliked.

When independence could no longer be delayed, the conservatives
were forced to choose between England and the United States. Some became "Tories," or "Loyalists." Others, the victims of circumstances partly
of their own creation, fearfully and reluctantly became revolutionists.
But in so doing they did not throw away their ideals of government. They
were too cool, too well versed in checkmating radicalism and in adminis-

tering governments in their own interest, to be misled by the democratic propaganda of the radicals. Not even John Adams, one of the few conservatives who worked for independence, was willing to stomach the ideas of Tom Paine when it came to the task of forming governments within the American colonies.

The continued presence of groups of conservatives in all the states, weakened though they were by the Revolution, is of profound importance in the constitutional history of the United States. They appeared in strength in the first Continental Congress. In it their ideas and desires were expressed. They were still powerful at the beginning of the second Continental Congress, but gradually their hold was weakened by the growing revolutionary movement in the various states. They were strong enough, however, to obstruct the radical program during 1775 and to delay a declaration of independence in 1776 until long after the radicals believed that independence was an accomplished fact. In the bitter controversies which occurred the conservatives stated their ideas of government. In its simplest form their objection to independence was that it involved internal revolution. When forced to accept independence, they demanded the creation of a central government which would be a bulwark against internal revolution, which would aid the merchant classes, which would control Western lands, which would, in short, be a "national" government. In this they were opposed by the radicals, who created a "federal" government in the Articles of Confederation and who resisted the efforts of the conservatives to shape the character of those Articles while they were in process of writing and ratification.

It is against such a background of internal conflict that the Articles of Confederation must be considered. Naturally any statement of the issues or principles of the Revolution, however broad the terminology, is likely to be misleading, for, as John Adams wrote, "the principles of the American Revolution may be said to have been as various as the thirteen states that went through it, and in some sense almost as diversified as the individuals who acted in it." There are inconsistencies and contradictions that cannot be forced into a logical pattern. Generalizations must therefore be understood as statements of tendencies and of presumed predominance rather than as unexceptionable statements of fact. Thus when the Revolution is interpreted in the following pages as predominantly an internal revolution carried on by the masses of the people against the local aristocracy, it is not without recognition of the fact that there were aristocratic revolutionists and proletarian loyalists; that probably the majority of the people were more or less indifferent to what was taking place; and that British policy after 1763 drove many conservatives into a war for independence.

Any interpretation of the American Revolution is subject to such qualifications, discomforting as it is to those who want complexities reduced to simple formulas. Any collection of facts must, however, be grouped around a theme, and particularly is this true of a movement having so many aspects as the American Revolution. Such grouping is unavoidable if one seeks to understand how the course of events, how the course of social revolution within the several states, often played a far more important role in determining political attitudes than did the more remote dangers of British policy.

In spite of the paradoxes involved one may still maintain that the Revolution was essentially, though relatively, a democratic movement within the thirteen American colonies, and that its significance for the political and constitutional history of the United States lay in its tendency to elevate the political and economic status of the majority of the people. The Articles of Confederation were the constitutional expression of this movement and the embodiment in governmental form of the philosophy of the Declaration of Independence.

The internal revolution

The Articles of Confederation were written by men many of whom rose to leadership as a result of the tempestuous local political battles fought in the years before the Revolution. Most of these new leaders gained power because they voiced the animosities and thus won the support of the discontented—the masses in the towns and the farmers of the back country—, who in most of the states won the right to express themselves politically, or were able to force concessions where the conservative element remained in control of the new governments created.

When it came to the formation of a common government for all the states, the radicals were guided by experience and by certain political ideas. Experience had taught them to dislike the colonial governing classes and to fear the concentration of wealth and political power. Their political philosophy taught that governments exercising power over wide areas were inherently undemocratic in action. This distrust of the concentration and centralization of unchecked political authority was deepened by the fact that most of the revolutionary leaders were essentially local leaders whom necessity had forced into an international movement for independence but who continued to be guided and controlled by the exigencies of local politics. It is necessary, therefore, to turn to the revolutionary history of the individual colonies for an explanation of the many exceptions one must make to any generalizations regarding the revolutionary movement as a whole and the constitution it produced.

*   *   *

Pennsylvania offers the clearest illustration of some of the basic issues upon which the course of the American Revolution turned. In no other colony were the racial-political-economic lines so sharply drawn, nowhere was the ruling class so opposed to change or to concession, and nowhere was the political revolution so complete in 1776.

As the colony had grown in wealth and population, political control had been retained by the three old counties of Philadelphia, Bucks, and Chester, and the city of Philadelphia. By the middle of the century an oligarchy of Quaker merchants and lawyers was dictating most of the policies of government. Their instrument was the colonial assembly, control of which they retained by denying representation to the ever-growing west. Even when new counties were created, they were made so vast in extent and were allotted so few representatives in the Assembly that the rule of the east was never endangered. In the east itself the masses were prevented from threatening oligarchical rule by suffrage laws which excluded all but a small minority of the population. The right to vote was contingent upon the possession of fifty pounds in personal property or a freehold. Neither was easy to secure, at least in the east. In Philadelphia in 1775 only 335 of 3,452 taxable males had estates large enough to give them the vote.

Opposition to the oligarchy was centered in the Susquehanna Valley and in the city of Philadelphia. The Susquehanna Valley, peopled largely by Scotch-Irish and Germans, was separated from the east by geography, by economic interest, by race, and by religion. Its natural market was the city of Baltimore, which very early improved roads to attract the trade of its northern neighbors, while the Pennsylvania Assembly refused to build roads or in any way to tie the west to the east.

Aside from racial and religious animosities, the grievances of the west against the east were very specific. It carried a burden of taxation without adequate representation, which in 1771, when an excise tax on hard liquor was instituted, was opposed in a manner prophetic of the later Whiskey Rebellion. The Presbyterian Scotch-Irish were driven to desperation by the refusal of the Quaker Assembly to aid them in their ever-continuing war with the Indians. The Proclamation line of 1763, which threatened to dispossess many westerners of lands already settled, was blamed on the Quakers. The pacifism of the Quaker merchants enraged frontiersmen, who suspected them of being moved more by a desire to maintain the fur trade than by humanitarian concern over the fate of the Indians.

The western farmer could meet the eastern merchant on terms of approximate equality only if he could secure adequate representation in the Assembly. This too was the demand of the populace of Philadelphia, where government was in the hands of the same wealthy class as controlled the colony. The sources of urban discontent were even more immediate than those of the west. All through the century the merchants had tried by various means to overthrow the system of markets and auctions in order to get a monopoly of the retail trade. Finally, in 1771, they devised a scheme which led to the most startling outburst of popular feeling that occurred before the Revolution. They agreed among themselves to buy from none but vendue masters who would agree to sell in large quantities. It was obvious that to continue in business the vendue masters would have to meet the demands of the big merchants. It was equally obvious that the poor could not afford to buy in large quantities and would thus be forced to buy from the merchants, who had long shown a disposition to take a more than "reasonable" profit in fixing retail prices. The merchants likewise tried to check the activity of wandering peddlers. Fishing rights in the navigable rivers were restricted, a measure which the poor felt to be aimed directly at them. In the face of such events it was natural that the lawyer-agents of the merchants should be bitterly attacked by the masses of the population.

The attempt of the Quaker element in the east to convert Pennsylvania from a proprietary into a crown colony was fought bitterly by the Presbyterians in both east and west. Though they had none too great a love for the Penn family, they knew full well that the creation of a crown colony would place them entirely at the mercy of the oligarchy. In this struggle John Dickinson led the proprietary party, which had the support of the west. Franklin, who, oddly enough, has since acquired a reputation as a democrat, was the agent of the oligarchy in England. A future loyalist, Joseph Galloway, led its forces in the Pennsylvania Assembly.

British policy was at once the occasion and the excuse for action in Pennsylvania. As in the other colonies, the propertied classes were strongly opposed to any acts of Parliament infringing upon their local independence or interfering with the profits of trade. But the arguments they advanced in support of their rights were a double-edged weapon that cut in favor of the unrepresented classes as well as colonial self-government. By 1775 the oligarchy began to realize that it was caught between the hammer and the anvil. This became increasingly clear as a revolutionary organization was developed wherein the old restrictions on the franchise and county representation no longer held. The creation of a provincial congress gave the west a dominance in the colony and deprived the three old counties of the hold they had had over the majority of the others. Yet the old Assembly continued to meet and to refuse concessions that would have weakened the radical program and enabled the Assembly to assume the leadership itself. By thus refusing either to lead or to guide, the conservative party was thrown from power in June, 1776. The radical party, temporarily unhampered, was able to write the most democratic constitution any American state has ever had.

The conservatives, led by James Wilson, Robert Morris, John Dickinson, and others, opposed the new order so bitterly that they very nearly wrecked the government of the state and did in fact render it largely ineffective in fighting the Revolution. The unicameral legislature, which they had considered satisfactory so long as it had been in their own control, they now criticized as the worst of all possible forms of government. Their proposal of a system of "checks and balances" as the remedy for all political ills was a thin disguise for their desire to regain control of the state. By 1779 they had made some political gains, but since they were a minority their control of a democratic government was bound to be precarious. Recognizing this to be so, they turned more and more to "nationalism" in the hope of gaining power and protection in another political sphere. They became more and more insistent upon the creation of a "national" government. Their program involved strengthening the Articles of Confederation, but when this failed they participated in a conservative political revolution which ignored the legal methods of constitutional change and created a government in harmony with conservative ideas and experiences. . . .

*   *   *

The calling of the first Continental Congress wrought a fundamental change in the growing revolutionary movement. No longer were the scattered revolutionary forces, feeding upon the vacillations of British policy and the exigencies of local politics, the center of the movement. When Congress outlined general policies which achieved the status of law as a result of popular support, it took the lead in the Revolution, although its effectiveness as a revolutionary organization was determined ultimately by the political character of the state organizations sending delegates to it. As the local radical parties gained power and sent radicals to Congress, it changed its policies. The history of those changing policies is the history of the outbreak of the American Revolution.

An ambivalent

revolution

Robert R. Palmer

THE REVOLUTION: WAS THERE ANY?

It is paradoxical . . . to have to begin by asking whether there was any American Revolution at all. There may have been only a war of independence against Great Britain. The British lid may have been removed from the American box, with the contents of the box remaining as before. Or there may have been a mechanical separation from En-

Reprinted from *The Age of Democratic Revolution*, Vol. I, by Robert R. Palmer. Copyright © 1959 by Princeton University Press. Reprinted by permission of Princeton University Press.

gland, without chemical change in America itself. Perhaps it was all a conservative and defensive movement, to secure liberties that America had long enjoyed, a revolt of America against Great Britain, carried through without fundamental conflict among Americans, by an "American consensus," in the words of Clinton Rossiter, or, as George Bancroft said a century ago, a revolution "achieved with such benign tranquillity that even conservatism hesitated to censure."

A populous country, much given to historical studies, has produced an enormous literature on the circumstances of its independence. Occupied more with European than with American history, I have been able only to sample this literature. It is apparent, however, that there is no agreement on what the American Revolution was. Differences reflect a different understanding of historical fact, a difference of attitude toward the concept of revolution, or a difference of feeling on the uniqueness, if it be unique, of the United States.

The old patriotic historians, like Bancroft, who fumed against British tyranny, had no doubt that there had been a real revolution in America, even if "benignly tranquil." Writers of a liberal orientation in a twentieth-century sense, admitting that all revolutions are carried through by minorities and by violence, have said that the American Revolution was no exception. Some have seen a kind of bourgeois revolution in America, in which merchants and planters made a few concessions to the lower classes, but then, at the Philadelphia convention of 1787, rallied to the defense of property in a kind of Thermidor. Still others, of conservative temperament, sympathizing with the American loyalists, have found the ruthlessness of a true revolution in the American upheaval. It must be admitted that, for the purposes of the present book, it would be convenient to present the American part of the story in this way, on the analogy of revolutions in Europe.

But there is the contrary school that minimizes the revolutionary character of the American Revolution. Some in this school hold that there was no "democratic revolution" in America because America was already democratic in the colonial period. Thus, it has recently been shown that, contrary to a common impression, as many as ninety-five per cent of adult males had the right to vote in many parts of colonial Massachusetts. Others find the Revolution not very revolutionary because the country was still far from democratic when it became independent. They point to the maintenance of property qualifications for voting and office-holding, or the fact that estates confiscated from loyalists found their way into the hands of speculators or well-to-do people, not of poor farmers. Those who discount the revolutionary character of the American Revolution seem to be gaining ground. For example, thirty years ago, J. F. Jameson in his little book, *The American Revolution Considered as a Social Movement,* suggested a variety of social changes that he said took place, in landholding and land law, in the disestablishment of churches and the democratizing tendencies in an aristocratic society. The book won followers and inspired research. F. B. Tolles described the aristocratic *ancien régime* of colonial Philadelphia, dominated by Quaker grandees whose social ascendancy, he said, came to an end in the American Revolution. But in 1954 the same Professor Tolles, reviewing the Jameson thesis and summarizing the research of recent decades, concluded that, while Jameson's ideas were important and fruitful, the degree of internal or social or revolutionary change within America, during the break with Britain, should not be unduly stressed.

Whether one thinks there was really a revolution in America depends on what one thinks a revolution is. It depends, that is to say, not so much on specialized knowledge or on factual discovery, or even on hard thinking about a particular time and place, as on the use made of an abstract concept. "Revolution" is a concept whose connotation and overtones change with changing events. It conveyed a different feeling in the 1790's from the 1770's, and in the 1950's from the 1930's.

No one in 1776, whether for it or against it, doubted that a revolution was being attempted in America. A little later the French Revolution gave a new dimension to the concept of revolution. It was the French Revolution that caused some to argue that the American Revolution had been no revolution at all. In 1800 Friedrich Gentz, in his *Historisches Journal* published at Berlin, wrote an essay comparing the French and American revolutions. He was an acute observer, whose account of the French Revolution did not suit all conservatives of the time, and would not suit them today; still, he made his living by writing against the French Revolution, and later became secretary to Metternich. He considered the French Revolution a bad thing, all the worse when compared to the American. He thought the American Revolution only a conservative defense of established rights against British encroachment. John Quincy Adams, then in Berlin, read Gentz's essay, liked it, translated it, and published it in Philadelphia in 1800. It served as a piece of high-toned campaign literature in the presidential election of that year, in which the elder Adams and the Federalist party were challenged by Jefferson and the somewhat Francophile democrats. The merit of Gentz's essay, said the younger Adams in his preface, was that "it rescues that revolution [the American] from the disgraceful imputation of having proceeded from the same principles as the French." In 1955 Adams' translation of Gentz was reprinted in America as a paper-back for mass distribution, with a foreword by Russell Kirk, known as a publicist of the "new conservatism." There was something in the atmosphere of 1955, as of 1800, which made it important, for some, to dissociate the American Revolution from other revolutions by which other peoples have been afflicted.

My own view is that there was a real revolution in America, and that it was a painful conflict, in which many were injured. I would suggest two quantitative and objective measures: how many refugees were there from the American Revolution, and how much property did they lose, in comparison to the French Revolution? It is possible to obtain rough but enlightening answers to these questions. The number of émigré loyalists who went to Canada or England during the American Revolution is set as high as 100,000; let us say only 60,000. The number of émigrés from the French Revolution is quite accurately known; it was 129,000, of whom 25,000 were clergy, deportees rather than fugitives, but let us take the whole figure, 129,000. There were about 2,500,000 people in America in 1776, of whom a fifth were slaves; let us count the whole 2,500,000. There were about 25,000,000 people in France at the time of the French Revolution. There were, therefore, 24 émigrés per thousand of population in the American Revolution, and only 5 émigrés per thousand of population in the French Revolution.

In both cases the revolutionary governments confiscated the property of counterrevolutionaries who emigrated. Its value cannot be known, but the sums paid in compensation lend themselves to tentative comparison. The British government granted £3,300,000 to loyalists as indemnity for property lost in the United States. The French émigrés, or their heirs, received a "billion franc indemnity" in 1825 during the Bourbon restoration. A sum of £3,300,000 is the equivalent of 82,000,000 francs. Revolutionary France, ten times as large as revolutionary America, confiscated only twelve times as much property from its émigrés, as measured by subsequent compensations, which in each case fell short of actual losses. The difference, even allowing for margins of error, is less great than is commonly supposed. The French, to be sure, confiscated properties of the church and other public bodies in addition; but the present comparison suggests the losses of private persons.

It is my belief also, John Quincy Adams notwithstanding, that the American and the French revolutions "proceeded from the same principles." The difference is that these principles were much more deeply rooted in America, and that contrary or competing principles, monarchist or aristocratic or feudal or ecclesiastical, though not absent from America, were, in comparison to Europe, very weak. Assertion of the same principles therefore provoked less conflict in America than in France. It was, in truth, less revolutionary. The American Revolution was, indeed, a movement to conserve what already existed. It was hardly, however, a "conservative" movement, and it can give limited comfort to the theorists of conservatism, for it was the weakness of conservative forces in eighteenth-century America, not their strength, that made the American Revolution as moderate as it was. John Adams was not much like Edmund Burke, even after he became alarmed by the French Revolution; and Alexander Hamilton never hoped to perpetuate an existing state of society, or to change it by gradual, cautious, and piously respectful methods. America was different from Europe, but it was not unique. The difference lay in the fact that certain ideas of the Age of Enlightenment, found on both sides of the Atlantic—ideas of constitutionalism, individual liberty, or legal equality—were more fully incorporated and less disputed in America than in Europe. There was enough of a common civilization to make America very pointedly significant to Europeans. For a century after the American Revolution, as is well known, partisans of the revolutionary or liberal movements in Europe looked upon the United States generally with approval, and European conservatives viewed it with hostility or downright contempt.

It must always be remembered, also, that an important nucleus of conservatism was permanently lost to the United States. The French émigrés returned to France. The émigrés from the American Revolution did not return; they peopled the Canadian wilderness; only individuals, without political influence, drifted back to the United States. Anyone who knows the significance for France of the return of the émigrés will ponder the importance, for the United States, of this fact which is so easily overlooked, because negative and invisible except in a comparative view. Americans have really forgotten the loyalists. Princeton University, for example, which invokes the memory of John Witherspoon and James Madison on all possible occasions, has been chided for burying in oblivion the name of Jonathan Odell, of the class of 1759, prominent as a physician, clergyman, and loyalist satirical writer during the Revolution, who died in New Brunswick, Canada, in 1818. The sense in which there was no conflict in the American Revolution is the sense in which the loyalists are forgotten. The "American consensus" rests in some degree on the elimination from the national consciousness, as well as from the country, of a once important and relatively numerous element of dissent.

ANGLO-AMERICA BEFORE THE REVOLUTION

The American Revolution may be seen as a conflict of forces some of which were old, others brought into being by the event itself.

The oldest of these forces was a tradition of liberty, which went back to the first settlement of the colonies. It is true that half of all immigrants into the colonies south of New England, and two-thirds of those settling in Pennsylvania, arrived as indentured servants; but indentured servitude was not a permanent status, still less a hereditary one; the indentures expired after a few years, and all white persons soon merged into a free population.

Politically, the oldest colonies had originated in a kind of *de facto* independence from the British government. Even after the British made their colonial system more systematic, toward the close of the seventeenth century, the colonies continued to enjoy much local self-determination. Only five per cent of the laws passed by colonial assemblies were disallowed in Great Britain, and, while these often concerned the most important subjects, the infrequency of the British veto was enough to make it the exception. The elected assemblies, as already noted, were the most democratically recruited of all such constituted bodies in the Western World. In general, it was necessary to own land in order to have the right to vote for a member of the assembly, but small owner-farmers were numerous, most of all in New England; and recent studies all tend to raise the estimates of the proportion of those enjoying the franchise before the Revolution. It seems to have been above eighty per cent of adult white males in Massachusetts, half or more in New Jersey, perhaps a little under half in Virginia. Many who had the right to vote did not often use it, and this was in part because the procedure of elections was not made convenient for the ordinary hard-working man; but non-voting also suggests an absence of grievances, or perhaps only that the common man neither expected much nor feared much from government. The elected assemblies enjoyed what in Europe would be thought a dangerously popular mandate. By 1760, decades of rivalry for power between the assemblies and the governors had been resolved, in most of the colonies, in favor of the assemblies. The idea of government by consent was for Americans a mere statement of fact, not a bold doctrine to be flung in the teeth of government, as in Europe. Contrariwise, the growing assertiveness of the assemblies made many in England, and some in America, on the eve of the Revolution, believe that the time had come to stop this drift toward democracy—or, as they would say, restore the balance of the constitution. In sum, an old sense of liberty in America was the obstacle on which the first British empire met its doom. Here the most sophisticated latest researches seem to return to the old-fashioned American patriotic historical school.

From the beginnings of British America there had also been a certain rough kind of equality. Except for slaves, the poor were less poor than in Europe, and the rich were not so wealthy. Almost a quarter of the population of England were classified as paupers in 1688; almost a tenth in 1801. There was no pauperism in America, accepted and institutionalized as such; anyone not hopelessly shiftless, or the victim of personal misfortune, could make a living. At the other extreme, on the eve of the Revolution, there were men who owned hundreds of thousands of acres, mostly vacant, the main values being speculative and in the future. It is hard to say how wealthy a wealthy colonial was. A fortune of £30,000 was thought very large in Massachusetts; Joseph Galloway of Pennsylvania was said to possess £70,000. In England in 1801 there were probably 10,000 families with an average income of £1,500 a year or more, of which the capital value would be about £30,000. There is ground for believing that in England at this time, as in the United States in 1929, five per cent of the population received over thirty-five per cent of the income. The distribution of wealth in colonial America was far more equal.

There were recognized inequalities of social rank. But rank somehow lacked the magic it enjoyed in Europe. In the migration from England and Europe, the well-situated and the high-born had been notably absent. There were Americans of aristocratic pretensions, but the most ambitious genealogy led only to some middling English gentleman's manor house; most Americans were conscious of no lineage at all, American genealogy being largely a nineteenth-century science. No American could truthfully trace his ancestry to the mists of time or the ages of chivalry— nor, indeed, could many British peers or French noblemen. It was the complaint of Lord Stirling, as the New Jersey revolutionary, William Alexander, was called, that he was *not* recognized as a lord in England. A Swedish clergyman arriving in New Jersey in 1770, to take over the old Swedish congregation on the Delaware, found that well-to-do farmers were like lesser gentry in Sweden, in their use of fine linen and fondness for good horses. The significant thing for America was that people of this style of life did not, as in Sweden, consider themselves nobles. Everyone worked, and to the Swedish newcomer it seemed that "all people are generally thought equally good."

Whether religion acted as a force in the conflict of the American Revolution is disputed. Since the Worship of Reason at Notre-Dame de Paris in November 1793, there have always been those who have stressed the religious principles of the founders of the United States. It is a way of showing how different they were from Jacobins or Communists. The truth is that the age was not notably religious, and that the sentiments that burst out violently in Paris in 1793 were, as sentiments, not uncommon. We read, for example, of an Anglican rector in England who, about 1777, so admired the writings of Catherine Macaulay that "he actually placed her statue, adorned as the Goddess of Liberty, within the altar railing" of his parish church. "It will never be pretended," wrote John Adams in 1786, that the men who set up the new governments in America "had interviews with the gods, or were in any degree under the inspiration of Heaven, more than those at work on ships or houses, or laboring in merchandise or agriculture; it will forever be acknowledged that these governments were contrived by reason and the senses, as Copley painted Chatham . . . [or] as Paine exposed the mistakes of Raynal. . . ." John Adams, while differing with him in detail, had not yet broken with Thomas Paine.

Aggressive anti-Christianity did not develop in America, to the great good fortune of the future United States. It failed to develop, however, not because American revolutionary leaders were warmly religious, but because no religious body seriously stood in their way. Here again it was the weakness of conservative forces, not their strength, that made the Revolution "conservative." No church seriously opposed the political aims of the Revolution. No church figured as a first estate in colonial America, none had its dignitaries sitting in the highest councils of government, and none lost vast tracts of material property, since none possessed any. The Anglican clergy generally opposed the Revolution, because of their close connection with British authority. Revolutionaries drove them out of their churches, for the same reason; worse would have happened to them had they not been so easily dislodged. In any case, even where the Anglican church was established, in New York and the South, Anglicans were not a majority of the population. At the opposite end of the religious spectrum the Quakers, because of their doctrine of non-resistance to established authority, were in effect a force to be reckoned on the British side. But they were unimportant politically outside of Pennsylvania. Over half the colonial Americans, and probably ninety per cent of New Englanders, were, vaguely or exactly, some species of Calvinists. No allegation was more common, from the British or the American loyalists, than that the whole Revolution had been stirred up by old Presbyterian disaffection. It is true that New England Congregationalists and Scotch-Irish Presbyterians did not admire some of the contemporary institutions of England, and that their ministers, when the time came, generally supported the Revolution. They probably infused, in a way hard to define, a certain religious atmosphere into the American patriot program.

A great many Americans, however, before and during the Revolution, belonged to no church at all. In conditions of constant movement, uprooting, settlement, and resettlement, probably a larger proportion of Americans were unchurched than in any European country. What aroused horror, when violently pursued as dechristianization in France a few years later, had gone pretty far, without violence, in America. As for the leaders of the American Revolution, it should be unnecessary to demonstrate that most of them were deists. They were strongly on the side of the best human virtues, or at least of those which were not ascetic; but they saw no connection between such virtues and religious practice. Like Jefferson in the Declaration of Independence, they appealed to the laws of Nature's God. They seem not to have felt, however, like Burke, that these laws placed serious limits upon their freedom of political action.

The simplicities in which British America had originated gave way to more complex forms of society in the eighteenth century. A liberty almost like that of the "state of nature," a liberty defined by the remoteness of government, gradually changed, especially after the British revolution of 1688, into the more organized and channelized liberty of British subjects under the British constitution. There was a bias toward equality in the foundations. The superstructure, as it was raised, exhibited palpable inequalities. As America became more civilized it began to have, like all civilized countries, a differentiation of social classes. Even the once un-manageable Quakers took on new social refinements. The Philadelphia Yearly Meeting of 1722 officially declared its "decent respect" for "ranks and dignities of men," and called for honor and obedience "from subjects to their princes, inferiors to superiors, from children to parents, and serv-ants to masters." Increasingly there was a kind of native American aris-tocracy. No question was of more importance for the future than the way in which this new aristocracy would develop.

The colonial aristocracy, as it took form in the eighteenth century, owed a good deal to close association with government. From New Hampshire to the far South . . . there were intermarried families which monopolized seats in the governors' councils, in some cases, now, to the third and fourth generation. There were Americans, close to the British authorities, who regarded themselves as the natural rulers of the coun-try. Sometimes, like Englishmen of the class to which they would com-pare themselves, they expected to draw a living from public offices, to which they need devote only part of their time. This practice has been most closely studied for Maryland, where there were a number of offices in which a man could live like a gentleman, with a good deal of leisure, for £150 a year.

More generally, the wealth of the growing American upper class came from early land grants, or from inheritance of land in a country where land values were always rising, or from mercantile wealth in the half-dozen seaboard cities, all of which except Charleston lay from Philadel-phia to the North, or from the ownership of plantations and Negro slaves in the South. New York and the Southern provinces, because of their sys-tems of landholding, were the most favorable to the growth of aristo-cratic institutions, but an upper class existed everywhere in the settled regions. In places where landed and mercantile wealth came together, as at New York and Charleston, people mixed easily with mutual regard; there was no standoffishness between "trade" and "gentry."

Without the rise of such a colonial aristocracy there could have been no successful movement against England. There had to be small groups of people who knew each other, who could trust each other in hazardous undertakings, who had some power and influence of their own, who could win attention and rally followers, and who, from an enlarged point of view, felt a concern for the welfare of the provinces as a whole. "While there are no noble or great and ancient families . . . they cannot rebel," as an observer of New England remarked in 1732. A generation later such "great" families, if not noble or very ancient, could be found everywhere in the colonies.

On the other hand, the rise of such an aristocracy brought class friction and internal tension. "In many a colony in 1764," according to Professor Rossiter (whose view of an "American consensus" I do not wish to misrepresent), "civil war seemed more likely than war with Britain." There was everlasting bickering over land titles, quitrents, debts, and paper money. There was complaint, in the western part of several provinces, at under-representation in the elected assemblies, or at the long distances it was necessary to go to cast a vote or to be present in a court of law. Rich and poor were not so far apart as in Europe, but they were far enough apart to cause trouble. Western Massachusetts, suspicious of Boston, was not hostile to Britain until 1774. There was a great rent riot in the Hudson valley in 1766, directed against the manorial system on which the Van Rensselaers and the Livingstons grew wealthy. A thousand angry western Pennsylvania farmers marched on Philadelphia in 1764, enraged that the over-represented East, and its opulent and pacifistic Quaker aristocracy, begrudged them military protection at the time of Pontiac's Indian war. The best example was afforded by the Regulators of North Carolina.

This province, though scarcely a century old, had developed a fine system of decayed boroughs on the British model. The five oldest coastal counties, thinly inhabited, enjoyed a dozen times as much representation in the assembly, per capita, as the newer uplands, so that the bulk of the people, while having the vote, could get little accomplished. Political life was most active at the county level, and in each county a few families named the judges and sheriffs, who are estimated to have embezzled over half the public funds. The governing elite, if one may so term it, unabashedly made a living off the legal business that small farmers could not avoid. A group of these farmers founded an "association" for "regulating public grievances," and these Regulators began to refuse to pay taxes. The governor finally called out the militia against them, chiefly a mounted troop of Gentlemen Volunteer Light Dragoons, in which 8 "generals" and 14 "colonels" led less than 1,300 enlisted men. The Regulators were routed in the Battle of Alamance in 1771. Seven of them were hanged. Later, when the gentry led the province into the Revolution, the British found many loyalist strongholds in the back country of Carolina.

Conflicting forces were therefore at work in America, when the Stamp Act added the conflict between America and Great Britain. Americans all but universally opposed the Stamp Act. Most of those who eventually became loyalists disapproved of British policy in the ten years before the Revolution. The doctrine of parliamentary supremacy was an innovation, accepted in England itself only since the revolution of 1689; the trend toward centralization of the empire under parliamentary authority, with attendant plans for reordering the colonial governments, was a modern development, a new force, much less old than the American liberties. On this Americans could agree. They began to disagree on the means used to

uphold the American position. It was one thing to sit in meetings or submit petitions to Parliament; it was another to persist stubbornly in defiance, to insult or intimidate the King's officers, stop the proceedings of
law courts, and condone the violence of mobs. Whether the British constitution really assured no taxation without representation was, after all,
uncertain. It was far more certain that the British constitution secured a
man against physical violence, against his having his house plundered
and wrecked by political adversaries, or against being tarred and feath-
ered for refusing to join a non-import agreement decided on by some unauthorized assembly which had no right to use force. As events unfolded,
men took sides, and Americans found themselves disputing with each
other on a new subject, the attitude to be taken to British law.

What happened to Plymouth Rock offers a parable. The stone on which
the Pilgrims of 1620 had supposedly first set foot already enjoyed a local
fame, as a symbol of what was most ancient and natively American in
the New World. In 1774 a party of patriots decided to use it as the base
for a liberty pole. They tried to haul it, with twenty oxen, from the shore
to the town square. Under the strain, it broke in two.

THE REVOLUTION: DEMOCRACY AND ARISTOCRACY

Fighting between the King's troops and the people of Massachusetts began at Lexington and Concord in April 1775. In the following December the British government put the insurgent colonists outside the
protection of the British crown. The Americans were now in what they
would call a state of nature, and what was in fact a condition of anarchy. Lawful authority melted away. Governors, unable to control their
assemblies, undertook to disband them, only to see most of the members
continue to meet as unauthorized congresses or associations; or conventions of counties, unknown to the law, chose delegates to such congresses
for provinces as a whole; or local people forcibly prevented the sitting of
law courts, or the enforcement of legal judgments by the sheriffs. Violence spread, militias formed, and the Continental Congress called into
existence a Continental army, placing General George Washington in
command.

In whose name were these armed men to act? To what civilian authority were they to be subordinated? How could the courts be kept open, or
normal court decisions and police protection be carried out? If American
ships, breaking the old navigation system, should enter the ports of Europe, in whose name should they appear? If diplomatic agents were
sent to Versailles or the Hague, whom were they to say that they represented? If aid was to be sought from France, would the French give it for
any purpose except to break up the British empire, and undo the British
victory of 1763? These practical needs, together with the inflaming of
feeling against England by war and bloodshed, and the extraordinary

success of Thomas Paine's pamphlet, *Common Sense,* induced the Congress, more than a year after the battle of Lexington, to announce the arrival of the United States of America "among the powers of the earth," able to do "all acts and things which independent states may of right do."

With the Declaration of Independence, and the new constitutions which most of the states gave themselves in 1776 and 1777, the revolutionary colonials began to emerge from the anarchy that followed the collapse or withdrawal of British power. They sought liberty, it need hardly be said; but they also sought authority, or a new basis of order. A revolution, it has been wisely observed, is an unlawful change in the conditions of lawfulness. It repudiates the old definitions of rightful authority, and drives away the men who have exercised it; but it creates new definitions of the authority which it is a duty to obey, and puts new men in a position to issue legitimate commands. The new lawfulness in America was embodied in the new constitutions, which will be considered shortly. Meanwhile, what happened in America was against the law.

The Revolution could be carried out, against British and loyal American opposition, only by the use of force. Its success "was impossible without a revolutionary government which could enforce its will." Let us look simply at the case of New Jersey. Late in 1776 the danger to the patriots became very pressing, as the British pursued Washington's army across the state. One of the New Jersey signers of the Declaration of Independence was forced to recant; the man who had presided over the convention which had proclaimed independence of the state went over to the British. The state was full of open and hidden enemies of the new regime. Taxes were neither levied nor collected with any regularity; the paper money which financed the Revolution flooded the state, swollen by counterfeits that poured from loyalist presses in New York. Prices soared; price controls were imposed, but were generally ineffective. The new government had no means of enforcing its authority except the thirteen county courts carried over from colonial times. These proved ineffectual under conditions of civil war. Revolutionary leaders thereupon created a Council of Safety as a temporary executive. Its twelve members were chosen by the state legislature. They toured the state to arouse local patriots and speed up action of the courts. They took the law into their own hands wherever they wished, hunted out suspects, ordered arrests, exacted oaths of allegiance, punished evasion of militia service, and instituted proceedings to confiscate the property of those who openly joined the British. One member of this Council of Safety was William Paterson, born in Ireland, son of a storekeeper. His career had been made by the Revolution, during which he became attorney-general to the state. He became a heated revolutionary, detesting more than all others, as he once said, that "pernicious class of men called moderates." His position allowed him to buy confiscated lands on advantageous terms; he became a

well-to-do man. He lived to be a justice of the United States Supreme
Court, and a terror to democrats in the days of the Alien and Sedition
laws.

Revolutionary government as a step toward constitutional government, committees of public safety, representatives on mission to carry
revolution to the local authorities, paper money, false paper money, price
controls, oaths, detention, confiscation, aversion to "moderatism," and
Jacobins who wind up as sober guardians of the law—how much it all
suggests what was to happen in France a few years later! With allowance
for differences of scale and intensity, there was foreshadowed in the
America of 1776 something of the *gouvernement révolutionnaire* and
even the Terror of France in 1793—except for the death sentences and
the horrors that went with them, and except for the fact that the victims
of these arbitrary proceedings never returned to political life as an organized force, to keep alive for all time an inveterate hatred of the Revolution.

It is not easy to say why some Americans warmly embraced the Revolution, or why others opposed it, or how many there were on each side.
Independence made it in principle necessary to choose between loyalty
and rebellion. But there were many who by isolation managed to avoid
commitment, or whose inclinations swayed with the course of battle, or
who, torn in their beliefs, prepared passively to accept whichever authority in the end should establish itself. Numbers therefore cannot be given.
It has often been repeated, as a remark of John Adams, that a third of
the American people were patriot, a third loyalist, and a third neutral;
but this neat summary has gone into the attic of historical fallacies; what
Adams meant, when he offered it in 1815, was that a third of the Americans in the 1790's had favored the *French* Revolution, a third had opposed it, and a third had not cared. The bulk of American opinion, after
July 1776, seems to have been actively or potentially for independence.
Positive and committed loyalists were a minority, but not therefore unimportant. They had the strength of the British empire on their side, and
much also in the American tradition to support them. They believed in
liberties for the colonies, and in old and historic rights under the British
constitution, which, however, they felt to be less threatened by Parliament than by unruly new forces in America itself.

It is not possible to explain the division between patriot and loyalist by
other or supposedly more fundamental divisions. The line coincided only
locally or occasionally with the lines of conflict that had appeared before
the war. Families divided, brothers often went different ways. Doubtless
many a man marked himself for a lifetime by the impulsive decision of a
moment. Economic and class motivations are unclear. The most firmly
established merchants and lawyers tended to loyalism, but there were re-
spected merchants and lawyers who embraced the revolution. New York

and Virginia were both full of great landowners, but New York was the most loyalist province, Virginia one of the most revolutionary. Ironmasters, who had reason to object to British controls on the American iron industry, wound up in both camps. Debtors had reason to object to British attempts, over the previous half century, to limit paper money in America and stop inflation; but people do not always act from reason, and indebtedness in any case was scarcely a class phenomenon, since it was characteristic of the free-spending southern aristocracy, the businessmen in the towns, and farmers whose land was mortgaged, as well as of such actually poor people as may have been able to borrow any money. Religion of the Calvinist type was a force working against England, but the Presbyterians of the Carolina frontier, not eager to be governed by their own gentry, supplied many soldiers to the King. National origin had no general influence, for the Middle Colonies, the least English in origin, were stronger centers of loyalism than New England or the South. The young men, if we may judge by the infinitesimal proportion who were in the colleges, were ardently patriot. The colleges, from Harvard to William and Mary, were denounced by loyalists as hotbeds of sedition.

An obvious explanation, quite on the surface, is as good as any: that the patriots were those who saw an enlargement of opportunity in the break with Britain, and the loyalists were in large measure those who had benefited from the British connection, or who had organized their careers, and their sense of duty and usefulness, around service to the King and empire. These would include the American-born governors, Thomas Hutchinson in Massachusetts and William Franklin in New Jersey. There were also the families that customarily sat on the governors' councils or held honorific or lucrative offices under the crown. There were some in the rising American upper class who admired the way of life of the aristocracy in England, and who would imitate it as best they could. Such was surely their right as British subjects, but it might alienate them from Americans generally, even many of the upper class, who were willing to have social distinctions in America develop in a new way.

It is estimated that from half to two-thirds of those who had sat on the governors' councils became loyalists. For New Jersey we know exactly what happened. Of the twelve members of the provincial council in 1775, five became active and zealous loyalists, two became cautious or neutral loyalists, one went into retirement for age, and four became revolutionaries, one of whom made his peace with the British when he thought they were going to win. Massachusetts had as few loyalists as any province, but when the British troops evacuated Boston in 1776 they took over 1,100 civilians with them. Of these, 102 had been councillors or officials and 18 were clergymen, mainly Anglican; but 382 were farmers, 213 were merchants "and others," and 105 came from country towns. The rest were probably women and children. Like the émigrés from the French Revolution, the émigrés from America came from all classes. But those connected with the English government or English church, and identifying themselves with English society and the values of the British governing class, were more numerous among loyalists than in the general population. On the other hand, lest any one thesis be carried too far, it should be pointed out that Virginia, a very English province in some ways, was so solidly patriotic that only thirteen natives of the Old Dominion ever applied to Britain for compensation for loyalist losses.

The war itself polarized the issues. Each side needed strength, and the revolutionary leaders looked for it in the mass of the population, the loyalists among the ruling circles of Great Britain. In legal form, the struggle was between the sovereignty of the former colonies and the sovereignty of the British King-in-Parliament. Rebellious leaders, however, clothed themselves in the sovereignty of the "people," both in form and to a large degree in content. The social content of Parliament in the eighteenth century needs no further elaboration. The struggle, whatever men said, and whatever has been said since, was inseparable from a struggle between democratic and aristocratic forces. If the rebellion was successful, democracy in America would be favored. If it failed, if Parliament and the loyal Americans had their way, development in America would move in an aristocratic direction. In this respect the American Revolution resembled the revolutions in Europe.

That the war favored democracy in America is apparent in many ways. In some places, notably Massachusetts, the suffrage was nearly universal before the Revolution; in others, notably Virginia, the Revolution did not extend it. But in Pennsylvania the pro-British leanings of the Quaker patriciate brought them into disrepute after hostilities began; and their aversion to military solutions, at a time when any solution was bound to be military, threw power into the hands of the western farmers, who by becoming soldiers made themselves indispensable to the infant state, so that Pennsylvania developed the most democratically organized government in the new union. In New Jersey the provincial congress, enjoying no legality and in rebellion against the legal authorities, sought to broaden its mandate by extending the voting franchise. In fact, petitions streamed into the Congress, urging that all householders or taxpayers should have the vote, the better to oppose enemies of the "American cause." The provincial congress in February 1776, five months before independence, granted the vote to all males at least twenty-one years old, resident in the state a year, and possessing goods worth £50 "proclamation money." With wartime depreciation of proclamation money, virtual universal manhood suffrage ensued. Voters also, after July 1776, were re-

quired to take an oath abjuring allegiance to George III, and some pur-
ists, pained by revolutionary illiberalism, have deprecated such restriction of political rights, as if the only feasible alternative would have been
more democratic, and as if oaths did not exist in Britain itself, where
men could still be obliged to abjure the House of Stuart.

An experience of Colonel Thomas Randolph of Virginia well illustrates
the same spread of democracy. Randolph, one of the many Virginia aristocrats who fought for the Revolution, was entertaining a captured British officer in his home. Three farmers came in, sat down, took off their
boots, did a little spitting, and talked business with the colonel. After they
left, Randolph commented to his guest on how "the spirit of independ-
ency was converted into equality, and everyone who bore arms esteemed
himself on a footing with his neighbor." He added, with distaste: "No
doubt, each of these men conceives himself, in every respect, my equal."
War, and a citizen army, had somewhat the same effects as in France after 1792. Leaders who did not fight for equality accepted it in order to
win.

On the other hand, the American loyalists, who were in any case the
Americans most inclined to favor hierarchic ideas, were made more so by
the necessities of their position. William Eddis of Maryland, as early as
1770, thought that noblemen and bishops should be established in America as soon as possible. The commonest of all loyalist ideas was that the
democratic branch, under the mixed British constitution in America,
had gotten out of control. Their commonest allegation, during the war,
was that the Revolution was the work of their social inferiors—"mechanics and country clowns," who had no right to dispute "what Kings, Lords,
and Commons had done," as a South Carolina clergyman expressed it.
He was driven out by his congregation.

The loyalists fully expected the British army to put down the rebellion
very soon. They believed that the whole disturbance had been caused by
a few troublemakers, from whom the bulk of the people in America were
patiently awaiting liberation. Hence, they had plans ready for the government of America after the restoration of order. These plans paral-
lelled some of the British ideas mentioned in the last chapter. Like them,
they called for the setting up in the colonies of something like a nobility.
They expressed the idea that I have tried to show was so common in the
eighteenth century, the idea of Blackstone and Gibbon and Montesquieu
and the French parlements and many others, that some sort of nobility
was a prerequisite to political liberty. There must be, in this view, an intermediate order of men having the personal right to take part in government, neither elected and hence under the influence of constituents, nor
yet too amenable to influence by a king, so that they should be hereditary
if possible, and at least hold office for life.

Loyal Americans congregated in New York, which was occupied by the

British during most of the war. Here, as they talked over the sad state of their country, they found much on which they could agree. David Ogden of New Jersey was typical. He had served for twenty-one years on the New Jersey governor's council. After he fled to New York in January 1777, the revolutionary government in New Jersey confiscated from him twenty-three pieces of real estate, which he himself later valued at £15,231. He was one of the more prominent of the fugitives in New York, becoming a member of the Board of Refugees established there in 1779. He proposed that, after suppression of the rebellion, an American parliament be set up for all the colonies, subordinate to that of Great Britain, to consist of three branches, as in Britain: namely, a lord lieutenant, certain "barons" created for the purpose, and a house of commons chosen by the several colonial assemblies. The new parliament, incidentally, was to supervise the colleges, those "grand nurseries of the late rebellion."

The case of Joseph Galloway is more fully known. In 1774 he had tried to restrain the First Continental Congress by submitting a plan of American union, which that body had rejected as too favorable to parliamentary claims. During the war, after spending some time in New York, where he convinced himself that all Americans of any standing agreed with him, Galloway proceeded in 1778 to England, where for ten years he submitted a series of plans on colonial government to various persons in authority in London. These plans built on the plan of 1774, retaining its proposal for an autonomous inter-colonial parliament subordinate to the Parliament of Great Britain; but they added new ideas of structural reform.

The revolutionary states in America, according to Galloway, would be dissolved by the coming British victory, and the old forms of government would be forfeited by rebellion. There would therefore be a "state of nature without a civil constitution," or what he also called a Chart Blanche, "a perfect blank upon which a new policy shall be established." Opportunity would thus be afforded for certain long-needed changes. Temporarily, because of the war, there were two parties in America, the party of independence, "actuated by views of ambition and private interest," and the party favoring perpetual union with Great Britain. The former was "a mere republican party firmly attached to democratical government"; it had "vested the powers of all their new states originally and ultimately in the People." The other party, favoring union with England, preferred a "mixed form of government," to guard against abuse of power by either the sovereign or the people. Most Americans, Galloway was persuaded, were tired of being pushed about by revolutionary cliques. Most of the colonists, and certainly most men of property, would therefore welcome his plan of reorganization.

In this reorganization, the old governments of the charter provinces

(Connecticut and Rhode Island) and of the proprietary provinces (Pennsylvania and Maryland) were to be abolished, and all the provinces made to conform to the same model, the balanced government of the British constitution. If Britain and America were to remain long together, it was imperative that they should have "the same customs, manners, prejudices and habits." These would then give "the same spirit to the laws." There should be an American union with a lord lieutenant or governor general representing the crown, an upper house appointed for life and with "some degree of rank or dignity above the Commons," and a lower house chosen by the various colonial assemblies. The "weight and influence" of the crown would be assured by making all offices, "civil and military, honorable and lucrative," depend on royal appointment. Thus a group of Americans would be built up, hostile to pure democracy and with an interest in mixed government and the British connection. The Americans also, declared Galloway, recurring to the almost forgotten origin of the whole controversy, would willingly pay an agreed-upon share toward military and imperial expenses, by taxing themselves through such a parliament as he outlined.

As among Americans themselves, it is clear that the Revolution involved a contest between men committed either to a more popular or a more aristocratic trend in government and society. Had the loyalists returned, received back their property, and resumed the positions of prestige and public influence which many of them had once enjoyed, it seems unlikely that the subsequent history of the United States would have been like the history that we know. . . .

AMBIVALENCE OF THE AMERICAN REVOLUTION

In conclusion, the American Revolution was really a revolution, in that certain Americans subverted their legitimate government, ousted the contrary-minded and confiscated their property, and set the example of a revolutionary program, through mechanisms by which the people was deemed to act as the constituent power. This much being said, it must be admitted that the Americans, when they constituted their new states, tended to reconstitute much of what they already had. They were as fortunate and satisfied a people as any the world has known. They thus offered both the best and the worst example, the most successful and the least pertinent precedent, for less fortunate or more dissatisfied peoples who in other parts of the world might hope to realize the same principles.

Pennsylvania and Georgia gave themselves one-chamber legislatures, but both had had one-chamber legislatures before the Revolution. All states set up weak governors; they had been undermining the authority of royal governors for generations. South Carolina remained a planter oligarchy before and after independence, but even in South Carolina

fifty-acre freeholders had a vote. New York set up one of the most conservative of the state constitutions, but this was the first constitution
under which Jews received equality of civil rights—not a very revolutionary departure, since Jews had been prospering in New York since
1654. The Anglican Church was disestablished, but it had had few
roots in the colonies anyway. In New England the sects obtained a little
more recognition, but Congregationalism remained favored by law. The
American revolutionaries made no change in the laws of indentured
servitude. They deplored, but avoided, the matter of Negro slavery. Quitrents were generally abolished, but they had been nominal anyway, and
a kind of manorial system remained long after the Revolution in New
York. Laws favoring primogeniture and entail were done away with, but
apparently they had been little used by landowners in any case. No general or statistical estimate is yet possible on the disposition of loyalist
property. Some of the confiscated estates went to strengthen a new propertied class, some passed through the hands of speculators, and some
either immediately or eventually came into the possession of small owners. There was enough change of ownership to create a material interest
in the Revolution, but obviously no such upheaval in property relations
as in France after 1789.

Even the apparently simple question of how many people received the
right to vote because of the Revolution cannot be satisfactorily answered.
There was some extension of democracy in this sense, but the more we
examine colonial voting practices the smaller the change appears. The
Virginia constitution of 1776 simply gave the vote to those "at present"
qualified. By one estimate the number of persons voting in Virginia actually declined from 1741 to 1843, and those casting a vote in the 1780's
were about a quarter of the free male population over twenty-one years of
age. The advance of political democracy, at the time of the Revolution,
was most evident in the range of officers for whom voters could vote. In
the South the voters generally voted only for members of the state legislatures; in Pennsylvania and New England they voted also for local officials, and in New England for governors as well.

In 1796, at the time of the revolution in Europe, and when the movement of Jeffersonian democracy was gathering strength in America,
seven of the sixteen states then in the union had no property qualification for voters in the choice of the lower legislative house, and half of
them provided for popular election of governors, only the seaboard South,
and New Jersey, persisting in legislative designation of the executive.
The best European historians underestimate the extent of political democracy in America at this time. They stress the restrictions on voting
rights in America, as in the French constitution of 1791. They do so because they have read the best American historians on the subject and
have in particular followed the school of Charles Beard and others. The

truth seems to be that America was a good deal more democratic than Europe in the 1790's. It had been so, within limits, long before the revolutionary era began.

Nor in broad political philosophy did the American Revolution require a violent break with customary ideas. For Englishmen it was impossible to maintain, in the eighteenth century or after, that the British constitution placed any limits on the powers of Parliament. Not so for Americans; they constantly appealed, to block the authority of Parliament or other agencies of the British government, to their rights as Englishmen under the British constitution. The idea of limited government, the habit of thinking in terms of two levels of law, of an ordinary law checked by a higher constitutional law, thus came out of the realities of colonial experience. The colonial Americans believed also, like Blackstone for that matter, that the rights of Englishmen were somehow the rights of all mankind. When the highest English authorities disagreed on what Americans claimed as English rights, and when the Americans ceased to be English by abjuring their King, they were obliged to find another and less ethnocentric or merely historical principle of justification. They now called their rights the rights of man. Apart from abstract assertions of natural liberty and equality, which were not so much new and alarming as conceptual statements as in the use to which they were applied, the rights claimed by Americans were the old rights of Englishmen—trial by jury, *habeas corpus*, freedom of the press, freedom of religion, freedom of elections, no taxation without representation. The content of rights was broadened, but the content changed less than the form, for the form now became universal. Rights were demanded for human beings as such. It was not necessary to be English, or even American, to have an ethical claim to them. The form also became more concrete, less speculative and metaphysical, more positive and merely legal. Natural rights were numbered, listed, written down, and embodied in or annexed to constitutions, in the foundations of the state itself.

So the American Revolution remains ambivalent. If it was conservative, it was also revolutionary, and vice versa. It was conservative because colonial Americans had long been radical by general standards of Western Civilization. It was, or appeared, conservative because the deepest conservatives, those most attached to King and empire, conveniently left the scene. It was conservative because the colonies had never known oppression, excepting always for slavery—because, as human institutions go, America had always been free. It was revolutionary because the colonists took the risks of rebellion, because they could not avoid a conflict among themselves, and because they checkmated those Americans who, as the country developed, most admired the aristocratic society of England and Europe. Henceforth the United States, in Louis Hartz's phrase, would be the land of the frustrated aristocrat, not of the frustrated democrat; for to be an aristocrat it is not enough to think of one-self as such, it is necessary to be thought so by others; and never again would deference for social rank be a characteristic American attitude. Elites, for better or for worse, would henceforth be on the defensive against popular values. Moreover the Americans in the 1770's, not content merely to throw off an outside authority, insisted on transmuting the theory of their political institutions. Their revolution was revolutionary because it showed how certain abstract doctrines, such as the rights of man and the sovereignty of the people, could be "reduced to practice," as Adams put it, by assemblages of fairly levelheaded gentlemen exercising constituent power in the name of the people. And, quite apart from its more distant repercussions, it was certainly revolutionary in its impact on the contemporary world across the Atlantic.

Democracy
without a
democratic
revolution

Louis Hartz

I

"The great advantage of the American," Tocqueville once wrote, "is that he has arrived at a state of democracy without having to endure a democratic revolution. . . ." Fundamental as this insight is, we have not remembered Tocqueville for it, and the reason is rather difficult to explain. Perhaps it is because, fearing revolution in the present, we like to think of it in the past, and we are reluctant to concede that its romance has been missing from our lives. Perhaps it is because the plain evidence of the American revolution of 1776, especially the evidence of its social impact that our newer historians have collected, has made the comment of Tocqueville seem thoroughly enigmatic. But in the last analysis, of course, the question of its validity is a question of perspective. Tocqueville was writing with the great revolutions of Europe in mind, and from that point of view the outstanding thing about the American effort of 1776 was bound to be, not the freedom to which it led, but the established feudal structure it did not have to destroy. He was writing too, as no French liberal of the nineteenth century could fail to write,

From *American Political Science Review* (Washington, D.C., June, 1952), Vol. XLVI, pp. 321–342. Reprinted by permission of the American Political Science Association.

with the shattered hopes of the Enlightenment in mind. The American revolution had been one of the greatest of them all, a precedent constantly appealed to in 1793. In the age of Tocqueville there was ground enough for reconsidering the American image that the Jacobins had cherished.

Even in the glorious days of the eighteenth century, when America suddenly became the revolutionary symbol of Western liberalism, it had not been easy to hide the free society with which it started. As a matter of fact, the liberals of Europe had themselves romanticized its social freedom, which put them in a rather odd position; for if Reynal was right in 1772, how could Condorcet be right in 1776? If America was from the beginning a kind of idyllic state of nature, how could it suddenly become a brilliant example of social emancipation? Two consolations were being extracted from a situation which could at best yield only one. But the mood of the Americans themselves, as they watched the excitement of Condorcet seize the Old World, is also very revealing. They did not respond in kind. They did not try to shatter the social structure of Europe in order to usher in a Tenth and Final Epoch in the history of man. Delighted as they were with the support that they received, they remained, with the exception of a few men like Paine and Barlow, curiously untouched by the crusading intensity we find in the French and the Russians at a later time. Warren G. Harding, arguing against the League of Nations, was able to point back at them and say, "Mark you, they were not reforming the world." And James Fenimore Cooper, a keener mind than Harding, generalized their behavior into a comment about America that America is only now beginning to understand: "We are not a nation much addicted to the desire of proselytizing."

There were, no doubt, several reasons for this. But clearly one of the most significant is the sense that the Americans had themselves of the liberal history out of which they came. In the midst of the Stamp Act struggle, young John Adams congratulated his colonial ancestors for turning their backs on Europe's class-ridden corporate society, for rejecting the "canon and feudal law." The pervasiveness of Adams' sentiment in American thought has often been discussed, but what is easily overlooked is the subtle way in which it corroded the spirit of the world crusader. For this was a pride of inheritance, not a pride of achievement; and instead of being a message of hope for Europe, it came close to being a damning indictment of it. It saturated the American sense of mission, not with a Christian universalism, but with a curiously Hebraic kind of separatism. The two themes fought one another in the cosmopolitan mind of Jefferson, dividing him between a love of Europe and fear of its "contamination"; but in the case of men like Adams and Gouverneur Morris, the second theme easily triumphed over the first. By the time the crusty Adams had gotten through talking to politicians abroad, he had buried the Enlightenment concept of an oppressed humanity so completely beneath the national concept of a New World that he was ready to predict a great and ultimate struggle between America's youth and Europe's decadence. As for Morris, our official ambassador to France in 1789, he simply inverted the task of the Comintern agent. Instead of urging the French on to duplicate the American experience, he badgered them by pointing out that they could never succeed in doing so. "They want an American constitution," he wrote contemptuously, "without realizing they have no Americans to uphold it."

Thus the fact that the Americans did not have to endure a "democratic revolution" deeply conditioned their outlook on people elsewhere who did; and by helping to thwart the crusading spirit in them, it gave to the wild enthusiasms of Europe an appearance not only of analytic error but of unrequited love. Symbols of a world revolution, the Americans were not in truth world revolutionaries. There is no use complaining about the confusions implicit in this position, as Woodrow Wilson used to complain when he said that we had "no business" permitting the French to get the wrong impression about the American revolution. On both sides the reactions that arose were well-nigh inevitable. But one cannot help wondering about something else: the satisfying use to which our folklore has been able to put the incongruity of America's revolutionary role. For if the "contamination" that Jefferson feared, and that found its classic expression in Washington's Farewell Address, has been a part of the American myth, so has the "round the world" significance of the shots that were fired at Concord. We have been able to dream of ourselves as emancipators of the world at the very moment that we have withdrawn from it. We have been able to see ourselves as saviours at the very moment that we have been isolationists. Here, surely, is one of the great American luxuries that the twentieth century has destroyed.

II

When the Americans celebrated the uniqueness of their own society, they were on the track of a personal insight of the profoundest importance. For the nonfeudal world in which they lived shaped every aspect of their social thought: it gave them a frame of mind that cannot be found anywhere else in the eighteenth century, or in the wider history of modern revolutions.

One of the first things it did was to breed a set of revolutionary thinkers in America who were human beings like Otis and Adams rather than secular prophets like Robespierre and Lenin. Despite the European flavor of a Jefferson or a Franklin, the Americans refused to join in the great Enlightenment enterprise of shattering the Christian concept of sin, replacing it with an unlimited humanism, and then emerging with an earthly paradise as glittering as the heavenly one that had been destroyed. The fact that the Americans did not share the crusading spirit of the French and the Russians, as we have seen, is already some sort of confirmation of this, for that spirit was directly related to the "civil religion" of Europe and is quite unthinkable without it. Nor is it hard to see why the liberal good fortune of the Americans should have been at work in the position they held. Europe's brilliant dream of an impending millennium, like the mirage of a thirst-ridden man, was inspired in large part by the agonies it experienced. When men have already inherited the freest society in the world, and are grateful for it, their thinking is bound to be of a solider type. America has been a sober nation, but it has also been a comfortable one, and the two points are by no means unrelated.

Sam Adams, for example, rejects the hope of changing human nature: in a mood of Calvinist gloom, he traces the tyranny of England back to "passions of Men" that are fixed and timeless. But surely it would be unreasonable to congratulate him for this approach without observing that he implicitly confines those passions to the political sphere—the sphere of Parliaments, ministers, and Stampmasters—and thus leaves a social side to man which can be invoked to hold him in check. The problem was a different one for Rousseau and Marx, who started from the view that the corruption of man was complete, as wide as the culture in which he lived, with the result that revolutions became meaningless unless they were based on the hope of changing him. Here, obviously, is a place where the conclusions of political thought breathe a different spirit from the assumptions on which they rest. Behind the shining optimism of Europe, there are a set of anguished grievances; behind the sad resignation of America, a set of implicit satisfactions.

One of these satisfactions, moreover, was crucially important in developing the sober temper of the American revolutionary outlook. It was the high degree of religious diversity that prevailed in colonial life. This meant that the revolution would be led in part by fierce Dissenting ministers, and their leadership destroyed the chance for a conflict to arise between the worldly pessimism of Christianity and the worldly ambitions of revolutionary thought. In Europe, especially on the Continent, where reactionary church establishments had made the Christian concept of sin and salvation into an explicit pillar of the *status quo*, liberals were forced to develop a political religion, as Rousseau saw, if only in answer to it. The Americans not only avoided this compulsion; they came close, indeed, to reversing it. Here, above all in New England, the clergy was so militant that it was Tories like Daniel Leonard who were reduced to blasting it as a dangerous "political engine," a situation whose irony John Adams caught when he reminded Leonard that "in all ages and countries" the church is "disposed enough" to be on the side of conservatism. Thus the American liberals, instead of being forced to pull the Christian heaven down to earth, were glad to let it remain where it was.

They did not need to make a religion out of the revolution because religion was already revolutionary.

Consider the case of Rev. William Gordon of Roxbury. In 1774, when
all of Boston was seething with resentment over the Port Bill, Gordon
opened one of his sermons by explicitly reminding his congregation that
there were "more important purposes than the fate of kingdoms" or the
"civil rights of human nature," to wit, the emancipation of men from the
"slavery of sin and Satan" and their preparation "for an eternal blessed-
ness." But the Sons of Liberty did not rise up against him; they accepted
his remarks as perfectly reasonable. For instead of trying to drug Bosto-
nians with a religious opiate, Gordon proceeded to urge them to prepare
for open war, delivering a blast against the British that the Tories later
described as a plea for "sedition, rebellion, carnage, and blood." When
Christianity is so explosive, why should even the most ardent revolutionary complain if heaven is beyond his grasp?

Of course, the Gordons and the Mayhews of America were quite unaware that their work had this significance—the indirect significance of
keeping political thought down to earth. If anything impressed them in
their role as religious figures, it was undoubtedly the crusade they were
carrying forward against the "popery" of the Anglican Tories—in other
words, what mattered to them was not that they were helping America to
avoid the eighteenth century, but that they were helping it to duplicate
the seventeenth. However, their achievement on the first count was actually far more important than their achievement on the second. The
revolutionary attack on Anglicanism, with its bogy of a Bishop coming to
America and its hysterical interpretation of the Quebec Act of 1774, was
half trumped up and half obsolete; but the alliance of Christian pessimism with liberal thought had a deep and lasting meaning. Indeed, the
very failure of the Americans to become seventeenth-century prophets
like the English Presbyterians enhances this point considerably. For
when we add to it the fact that they did not become latter-day prophets
like the Jacobins and the Marxists, they emerge, if we wish to rank them
with the great revolutionaries of modern history, as in a curious sense
the most secular of them all.

Perhaps it was this secular quality that Joel Barlow was trying to describe when he declared, in a Fourth of July oration in Boston in 1778,
that the "peculiar glory" of the American revolution lay in the fact that
"sober reason and reflection have done the work of enthusiasm and performed the miracles of Gods." In any case, there was something fateful
about it. For if the messianic spirit does not arise in the course of a country's national revolution, when is it ever going to arise? The post-revolu-
tionary age, as the experience of England, France, and even in some
sense Russia shows, is usually spent trying to recuperate from its effects.
The fact that the Americans remained politically sober in 1776 was, in

other words, a fairly good sign that they were going to remain that way during the modern age which followed; and if we except the religiosity of the Civil War, that is exactly what happened. There have been dreamers enough in American history, a whole procession of "millennial Christians," as George Fitzhugh used to call them; but the central course of our political thought has betrayed an unconquerable pragmatism.

Sir William Ashley, discussing the origins of the "American spirit," once remarked that "as feudalism was not transplanted to the New World, there was no need for the strong arm of a central power to destroy it." This is a simple statement, but, like many of Ashley's simple statements, it contains a neglected truth. For Americans usually assume that their attack on political power in 1776 was determined entirely by the issues of the revolution, when as a matter of fact it was precisely because of the things they were not revolting against that they were able to carry it through. The action of England inspired the American colonists with a hatred of centralized authority; but had that action been a transplanted American feudalism, rich in the chaos of ages, then they would surely have had to dream of centralizing authority themselves.

They would, in other words, have shared the familiar agony of European liberalism—hating power and loving it too. The liberals of Europe in the eighteenth century wanted, of course, to limit power; but confronted with the heritage of an ancient corporate society, they were forever devising sharp and sovereign instruments that might be used to put it down. Thus while the Americans were attacking Dr. Johnson's theory of sovereignty, one of the most popular liberal doctrines in Europe, cherished alike by Bentham and Voltaire, was the doctrine of the enlightened despot, a kind of political deism in which a single force would rationalize the social world. While the Americans were praising the "illustrious Montesquieu" for his idea of checks and balances, that worthy was under heavy attack in France itself because he compromised the unity of power on which so many liberals relied. Even the English Whigs, men who were by no means believers in monarchical absolutism, found it impossible to go along with their eager young friends across the Atlantic. When the Americans, closing their eyes to 1688, began to lay the axe to the concept of parliamentary sovereignty, most of the Whigs fled their company at once.

A philosopher, it is true, might look askance at the theory of power the Americans developed. It was not a model of lucid exposition. The trouble lay with their treatment of sovereignty. Instead of boldly rejecting the concept, as Franklin was once on the verge of doing when he said that it made him "quite sick," they accepted the concept and tried to qualify it out of existence. The result was a chaotic series of forays and retreats in which a sovereign Parliament was limited, first by the distinction between external and internal taxation, then by the distinction between rev-

enue and regulation, and finally by the remarkable contention that colonial legislatures were as sovereign as Parliament was. But there is a
limit to how much we can criticize the Americans for shifting their
ground. They were obviously feeling their way; and they could hardly be
expected to know at the time of the Stamp Act what their position would
be at the time of the first Continental Congress. Moreover, if they clung
to the concept of sovereignty, they battered it beyond belief, and no one
would confuse their version of it with the one advanced by Turgot or
even by Blackstone in Europe. The meekness of the American sovereign
testifies to the beating he had received. Instead of putting up a fierce and
embarrassing battle against the limits of natural law and the separation
of powers, as he usually did in the theories of Europe, he accepted those
limits with a vast docility.

If we look at what happened to America's famous idea of judicial control when the physiocrats advanced it in France, we will get an insight
into this whole matter. Who studies now the theory of legal guardianship
with which La Rivière tried to bind down his rational and absolute sovereign? Who indeed remembers it? American students of the judicial
power rarely go to Cartesian France to discover a brother of James Otis—
and the reason is evident enough. When the physiocrats appealed to the
courts, they were caught at once in a vise of criticism: either they were
attacked for reviving the feudal idea of the *parlements* or they were
blasted as insincere because they had originally advanced a despot to
deal with the feudal problem. They had to give the idea up. But in America, where the social questions of France did not exist and the absolutism
they engendered was quite unthinkable, the claim of Otis in the Writs of
Assistance Case, that laws against reason and the Constitution were
"void" and that the "Courts must pass them into disuse," met an entirely
different fate. It took root, was carried forward by a series of thinkers,
and blossomed ultimately into one of the most remarkable institutions in
modern politics.

The question, again, was largely a question of the free society in which
the Americans lived. Nor ought we to assume that its impact on their
view of political power disappeared when war and domestic upheaval
finally came. Of course, there was scattered talk of the need for a "dictator," as Jefferson angrily reported in 1782; and until new assemblies
appeared in most places, Committees of Public Safety had authoritarian
power. But none of this went deep enough to shape the philosophic mood
of the nation. A hero is missing from the revolutionary literature of
America. He is the Legislator, the classical giant who almost invariably
turns up at revolutionary moments to be given authority to lay the foundations of the free society. He is not missing because the Americans were
unfamiliar with images of ancient history, or because they had not read
the Harringtons or the Machiavellis and Rousseaus of the modern pe-

riod. Harrington, as a matter of fact, was one of their favorite writers. The Legislator is missing because, in truth, the Americans had no need for his services. Much as they liked Harrington's republicanism, they did not require a Cromwell, as Harrington thought he did, to erect the foundations for it. Those foundations had already been laid by history.

The issue of history itself is deeply involved here. On this score, inevitably, the fact that the revolutionaries of 1776 had inherited the freest society in the world shaped their thinking in a most intricate way. It gave them, in the first place, an appearance of outright conservatism. We know, of course, that most liberals of the eighteenth century, from Bentham to Quesnay, were bitter opponents of history, posing a sharp antithesis between nature and tradition. And it is an equally familiar fact that their adversaries, including Burke and Blackstone, sought to break down this antithesis by identifying natural law with the slow evolution of the past. The militant Americans, confronted with these two positions, actually took the second. Until Jefferson raised the banner of independence, and even in many cases after that time, they based their claims on a philosophic synthesis of Anglo-American legal history and the reason of natural law. Blackstone, the very Blackstone whom Bentham so bitterly attacked in the very year 1776, was a rock on which they relied.

The explanation is not hard to find. The past had been good to the Americans, and they knew it. Instead of inspiring them to the fury of Bentham and Voltaire, it often produced a mystical sense of Providential guidance akin to that of Maistre—as when Rev. Samuel West, surveying the growth of America's population, anticipated victory in the revolution because "we have been prospered in a most wonderful manner." The troubles they had with England did not alter this outlook. Even these, as they pointed out again and again, were of recent origin, coming after more than a century of that "salutary neglect" which Burke defended so vigorously. And in a specific sense, of course, the record of English history in the seventeenth century and the record of colonial charters from the time of the Virginia settlement provided excellent ammunition for the battle they were waging in defense of colonial rights. A series of circumstances had conspired to saturate even the revolutionary position of the Americans with the quality of traditionalism—to give them, indeed, the appearance of outraged reactionaries. "This I call an innovation," thundered John Dickinson, in his attack on the Stamp Act, "a most dangerous innovation."

Now here was a frame of mind that would surely have troubled many of the illuminated liberals in Europe, were it not for an ironic fact. America piled on top of this paradox another one of an opposite kind, and thus as it were, by misleading them twice, gave them a deceptive sense of understanding.

Actually, the form of America's traditionalism was one thing, its content quite another. Colonial history had not been the slow and glacial record of development that Bonald and Maistre loved to talk about. On the contrary, since the first sailing of the *Mayflower*, it had been a story of new beginnings, daring enterprises, and explicitly stated principles— it breathed, in other words, the spirit of Bentham himself. The result was that the traditionalism of the Americans, like a pure freak of logic, often bore amazing marks of anti-historical rationalism. The clearest case of this undoubtedly is to be found in the revolutionary constitutions of 1776, which evoked, as Franklin reported, the "rapture" of European liberals everywhere. In America, of course, the concept of a written constitution, including many of the mechanical devices it embodied, was the end-product of a chain of historical experience that went back to the Mayflower Compact and the Plantation Covenants of the New England towns: it was the essence of political traditionalism. But in Europe just the reverse was true. The concept was the darling of the rationalists—a symbol of the emancipated mind at work.

Thus Condorcet was untroubled. Instead of bemoaning the fact that the Americans were Blackstonian historicists, he proudly welcomed them into the fraternity of the illuminated. "American constitutionalism," he said, "had not grown, but was planned"; it "took no force from the weight of centuries but was put together mechanically in a few years." When John Adams read this comment, he spouted two words on the margin of the page: "Fool! Fool!" But surely the judgment was harsh. After all, when Burke clothes himself in the garments of Sieyès, who can blame the loyal rationalist who fraternally grasps his hand? The reactionaries of Europe, moreover, were often no keener in their judgment. They made the same mistake in reverse. Maistre gloomily predicted that the American Constitution would not last because it was created out of the whole cloth of reason.

But how then are we to describe these baffling Americans? Were they rationalists or were they traditionalists? The truth is, they were neither, which is perhaps another way of saying that they were both. For the war between Burke and Bentham on the score of tradition, which made a great deal of sense in a society where men had lived in the shadow of feudal institutions, made comparatively little sense in a society where for years they had been creating new states, planning new settlements, and, as Jefferson said, literally building new lives. In such a society a strange dialectic was fated to appear, which would somehow unite the antagonistic components of the European mind; the past became a continuous future, and the God of the traditionalists sanctioned the very arrogance of the men who defied Him.

This shattering of the time categories of Europe, this Hegelian-like revolution in historic perspective, goes far to explain one of the enduring secrets of the American character: a capacity to combine rock-ribbed traditionalism with high inventiveness, ancestor worship with ardent optimism. Most critics have seized upon one or the other of these aspects of the American mind, finding it impossible to conceive how both can go together. That is why the insight of Gunnar Myrdal is a very distinguished one when he writes: "America is . . . conservative. . . . But the principles conserved are liberal and some, indeed, are radical." Radicalism and conservatism have been twisted entirely out of shape by the liberal flow of American history.

III

What I have been doing here is fairly evident: I have been interpreting the social thought of the American revolution in terms of the social goals *it did not need to achieve.* Given the usual approach, this may seem like a perverse inversion of the reasonable course of things; but in a world where the "canon and feudal law" are missing, how else are we to understand the philosophy of a liberal revolution? The remarkable thing about the "spirit of 1776," as we have seen, is not that it sought emancipation but that it sought it in a sober temper; not that it opposed power but that it opposed it ruthlessly and continuously; not that it looked forward to the future but that it worshipped the past as well. Even these perspectives, however, are only part of the story, misleading in themselves. The "free air" of American life, as John Jay once happily put it, penetrated to deeper levels of the American mind, twisting it in strange ways, producing a set of results fundamental to everything else in American thought. The clue to these results lies in the following fact: the Americans, though models to all the world of the middle class way of life, lacked the passionate middle class consciousness which saturated the liberal thought of Europe.

There was nothing mysterious about this lack. It takes the contemptuous challenge of an aristocratic feudalism to elicit such a consciousness; and when Richard Price glorified the Americans because they were men of the "middle state," men who managed to escape being "savage" without becoming "refined," he explained implicitly why they themselves would never have it. Franklin, of course, was a great American bourgeois thinker; but it is a commonplace that he had a wider vogue on this score in Paris and London than he did in Philadelphia; and indeed there is some question as to whether the Europeans did not worship him more because he seemed to exemplify Poor Richard than because he had created the philosophy by which Poor Richard lived. The Americans, a kind of national embodiment of the concept of the bourgeoisie, have, as Mr. Brinkmann points out, rarely used that concept in their social thought, and this is an entirely natural state of affairs. Frustration produces the social passion, ease does not. A triumphant middle class, unassailed by the agonies that Beaumarchais described, can take itself for granted. This point, curiously enough, is practically never discussed, though the failure of the American working class to become class conscious has been a theme of endless interest. And yet the relationship between the two suggests itself at once. Marx himself used to say that the bourgeoisie was the great teacher of the proletariat.

There can, it is true, be quite an argument over whether the challenge of an American aristocracy did not in fact exist in the eighteenth century. One can point to the great estates of New York where the Patroons lived in something resembling feudal splendor. One can point to the society of the South where life was extraordinarily stratified, with slaves at the bottom and a set of genteel planters at the top. One can even point to the glittering social groups that gathered about the royal governors in the North. But after all of this has been said, the American "aristocracy" could not, as Tocqueville pointed out, inspire either the "love" or the "hatred" that surrounded the ancient titled aristocracies of Europe. Indeed, in America it was actually the "aristocrats" who were frustrated, not the members of the middle class, for they were forced almost everywhere, even in George Washington's Virginia, to rely for survival upon shrewd activity in the capitalist race. This compulsion produced a psychic split that has always tormented the American "aristocracy"; and even when wealth was taken for granted, there was still, especially in the North, the withering impact of a colonial "character" that Sombart himself once described as classically bourgeois. In Massachusetts Governor Hutchinson used to lament that a "gentleman" did not meet even with "common civility" from his inferiors. Of course, the radicals of America blasted their betters as "aristocrats," but that this was actually a subtle compliment is betrayed in the quality of the blast itself. Who could confuse the anger of Daniel Shays with the bitterness of Francis Place even in the England of the nineteenth century?

Thus it happened that fundamental aspects of Europe's bourgeois code of political thought met an ironic fate in the most bourgeois country in the world. They were not so much rejected as they were ignored, treated indifferently, because the need for their passionate affirmation did not exist. Physiocratic economics is an important case in point. Where economic parasites are few, why should men embark on a passionate search for the productive laborer? Where guild restrictions are comparatively slight and continental tariffs unknown, why should they embrace the ruthless atomism of Turgot? America's attack on the English Acts of Trade was couched in terms of Locke, not in terms of Quesnay; and though Franklin and Jefferson were much taken by the "modern economics," they did not, here as in certain other places, voice the dominant preoccupation of American thought. It had often been said, of course, that the Americans were passionately "laissez faire" in their thinking, but this is to confuse either bourgeois ease with bourgeois frustration or a hatred of absolute power with the very economic atomism which, in physiocratic terms, was allied to it. Turgot himself saw that the Americans did not long to smash a feudal world into economic atoms any more than they longed for a unified sovereign to accomplish this feat. A lover of the Americans who, like most European liberals, could not quite imagine life outside the *ancien regime,* he complained bitterly on both counts. His complaint on the count of sovereignty is legendary, but his complaint on the count of laissez faire has, alas, been entirely forgotten. This is because John Adams replied to the one in his *Defence of the Constitutions* but did not mention the other. And yet it appears in the same place, in Turgot's famous letter to Richard Price: *On suppose partout le droit de regler le commerce . . . tant on est loin d'avoir senti que la loi de la liberté entière de tout commerce est un corrollaire du droit de proprieté.*

The lament of Turgot reveals that America's indifference to the bourgeois fixations of Europe had in itself a positive meaning: the failure to develop a physiocratic conscience led to a quiet and pragmatic outlook on the question of business controls. This is the outlook that characterizes a whole mass of early economic legislation that American historians are now beginning to unearth in what should have been, reputedly, the most "laissez faire" country in the world. But it is in connection with materialism and idealism, utilitarianism and natural law, that the inverted position of the Americans comes out most clearly. There was no Bentham, no Helvetius among the superlatively middle-class American thinkers. On the contrary, they stuck with Puritan passion to the dogma of natural law, as if an outright hedonism were far too crass for consideration. In a purely political sense this may be interesting, for the Americans, at least during the Stamp Act phase of their struggle, were fighting that corrupt system of parliamentary representation which in England Benthamism later rose to assail. But it is in terms of the wider significance of utility as an attack on feudal norms, as an effort to make of "business a noble life," as Crane Brinton has put it, that America's indifference to it takes on its deepest meaning. Benjamin Franklins in fact, the Americans did not have to become Jeremy Benthams in theory. Unchallenged men of business, they did not have to equate morality with it. And this has been a lasting paradox in the history of American thought. The American tradition of natural law still flourishes after a century and a half of the most reckless material exploitation that the modern world has seen. A persistent idealism of mind, reflected in Emerson's remark that utilitarianism is a "stinking philosophy," has been one of the luxuries of a middle class that has never been forced to become class conscious.

But this is not all. If the position of the colonial Americans saved them from many of the class obsessions of Europe, it did something else as well: it inspired them with a peculiar sense of community that Europe had never known. For centuries Europe had lived by the spirit of solidarity that Aquinas, Bossuet, and Burke romanticized: an organic sense of structured differences, an essentially Platonic experience. Amid the "free air" of American life, something new appeared: men began to be held together, not by the knowledge that they were different parts of a corporate whole, but by the knowledge that they were similar participants in a uniform way of life—by that "pleasing uniformity of decent competence" which Crèvecoeur loved so much. The Americans themselves were not unaware of this. When Peter Thacher proudly announced that "simplicity of manners" was the mark of the revolutionary colonists, what was he saying if not that the norms of a single class in Europe were enough to sustain virtually a whole society in America? Richard Hildreth, writing after the levelling impact of the Jacksonian revolution had made this point far more obvious, put his finger directly on it. He denounced feudal Europe, where "half a dozen different codes of morals," often in flagrant contradiction with each other, flourished "in the same community," and celebrated the fact that America was producing "one code, one moral standard, by which the actions of all are to be judged. . . ." Hildreth knew that America was a marvellous mixture of many peoples and many regions, but he also knew that it was characterized by something more marvellous even than that: the power of the liberal norm to penetrate them all.

Now a sense of community based on a sense of uniformity is a deceptive thing. It looks individualistic, and in part it actually is. It cannot tolerate internal relationships of disparity, and hence can easily inspire the kind of advice that Professor Nettels once imagined a colonial farmer giving his son: "Remember that you are as good as any man— and also that you are no better." But in another sense it is profoundly anti-individualistic, because the common standard is its very essence, and deviations from that standard inspire it with an irrational fright. The man who is as good as his neighbors is in a tough spot when he confronts all of his neighbors combined. Thus William Graham Sumner looked at the other side of Professor Nettels's colonial coin and did not like what he saw: "public opinion" was an "impervious mistress. . . . Mrs. Grundy held powerful sway and Gossip was her prime minister."

Here we have the "tyranny of the majority" that Tocqueville later described in American life; here too we have the deeper paradox out of which it was destined to appear. Freedom in the fullest sense implies both variety and equality; but history, for reasons of its own, chose to separate these two principles, leaving the one with the old society of Burke and giving the other to the new society of Paine. America, as a kind of natural fulfillment of Paine, has been saddled throughout its history with the defect which this fulfillment involves, so that a country like England, in the very midst of its ramshackle class-ridden atmosphere, seems to contain an indefinable germ of liberty, a respect for the privacies of life, that America cannot duplicate. At the bottom of the American experience of freedom, not in antagonism to it but as a constituent element of it, there has always lain the inarticulate premise of conformity, which critics from the time of Cooper to the time of Lewis have sensed and furiously attacked. "Even what is best in America is compulsory," Santayana once wrote, "—the idealism, the zeal, the beautiful happy unison of its great moments." Thus while millions of Europeans have fled to America to discover the freedom of Paine, there have been a few Americans, only a few of course, who have fled to Europe to discover the freedom of Burke. The ironic flaw in American liberalism lies in the fact that we have never had a real conservative tradition.

One thing, we might suppose, would shatter the unprecedented sense of uniform values by which the colonial American was beginning to live: the revolution itself. But remarkably enough, even the revolution did not produce this result; John Adams did not confront Filmer, as Locke did, or Maistre, as the followers of Rousseau did. He confronted the Englishmen of the eighteenth century; and most of these men, insofar as the imperial struggle went, themselves accepted the Lockean assumptions that Adams advanced. Nor did the American Tories, with the fantastic exception of Boucher, who stuck to his thesis that Filmer was still "unrefuted," confront him with a vision of life completely different from his own. Samuel Seabury and Joseph Galloway accepted the Lockean principles, even sympathized with the American case, insisting only that peaceful means be used to advance it. Among their opponents, indeed, there were few who would fundamentally deny the "self-evident" truths the Americans advanced in 1776. The liberals of Europe always had a problem on their hands, which they usually neglected, to be sure, of explaining how principles could be "self-evident" when there were obviously so many people who did not believe them. Circumstance nearly solved this problem for the Americans, giving them, as it were, a national exemption from Hume's attack on natural law—which may be one of the reasons why they almost invariably ignored it. When one's ultimate values are accepted wherever one turns, the absolute language of self-evidence comes easily enough.

This then is the mood of America's absolutism: the sober faith that its norms are self-evident. It is one of the most powerful absolutisms in the world, more powerful even than the messianic spirit of the Continental liberals which, as we saw, the Americans were able to reject. That spirit arose out of contact with an opposing way of life, and its very intensity betrayed an inescapable element of doubt. But the American absolutism, flowing from an honest experience with universality, lacked even the passion that doubt might give. It was so sure of itself that it hardly needed to become articulate, so secure that it could actually support a pragmatism which seemed on the surface to belie it. American pragmatism has always been deceptive because, glacier-like, it has rested on miles of submerged conviction, and the conformitarian ethos which that conviction generates has always been infuriating because it has refused to pay its critics the compliment of an argument. Here is where the joy of a Dewey meets the anguish of a Fenimore Cooper; for if the American deals with concrete cases because he never doubts his general principles, this is also the reason he is able to dismiss his critics with a fine and crushing ease. But this does not mean that America's General Will always lives an easy life. It has its own violent moments—rare, to be sure, but violent enough. These are the familiar American moments of national fright and national hysteria when it suddenly rises to the surface with a vengeance, when civil liberties begin to collapse, and when Cooper is actually in danger of going to jail as a result of the Rousseauian tide. Anyone who watches it then can hardly fail to have a healthy respect for the dynamite which normally lies concealed beneath the free and easy atmosphere of the American liberal community.

When we study national variations in political theory, we are led to semantic considerations of a delicate kind, and it is to these, finally, that we must turn if we wish to get at the basic assumption of American thought. We have to consider the peculiar meaning that American life gave to the words of Locke.

There are two sides to the Lockean argument: a defense of the state that is implicit, and a limitation of the state that is explicit. The first is to be found in Locke's basic social norm, the concept of free individuals in a state of nature. This idea untangled men from the myriad associations of class, church, guild, and place, in terms of which feudal society defined their lives; and by doing so, it automatically gave to the state a much higher rank in relation to them than ever before. The state became the only association that might legitimately coerce them at all. That is why the liberals of France in the eighteenth century were able to substitute the concept of absolutism for Locke's conclusions of limited government and to believe that they were still his disciples in the deepest sense. When Locke came to America, however, a change appeared. Because the basic feudal oppressions of Europe had not taken root, the fundamental social norm of Locke ceased in large part to look like a norm and began, of all things, to look like a sober description of fact. The effect was significant enough. When the Americans moved from that concept to the contractual idea of organizing the state, they were not conscious of having already done anything to fortify the state, but were conscious only that they were about to limit it. One side of Locke became virtually the whole of him. Turgot ceased to be a modification of Locke, and became, as he was for John Adams, the destruction of his very essence.

It was a remarkable thing—this inversion of perspectives that made the social norms of Europe the factual premises of America. History was on a lark, out to tease men, not by shattering their dreams, but by fulfilling them with a sort of satiric accuracy. In America one not only found a society sufficiently fluid to give a touch of meaning to the individualist norms of Locke, but one also found letter-perfect replicas of the very images he used. There was a frontier that was a veritable state of nature. There were agreements, such as the Mayflower Compact, that were veritable social contracts. There were new communities springing up *in vacuis locis*, clear evidence that men were using their Lockean right of emigration, which Jefferson soberly appealed to as "universal" in his defense of colonial land claims in 1774. A purist could argue, of course, that even these phenomena were not enough to make a reality out of the pre-social men that liberalism dreamt of in theory. But surely they came as close to doing so as anything history has ever seen. Locke and Rousseau themselves could not help lapsing into the empirical mood when they looked across the Atlantic. "Thus, in the beginning," Locke once wrote, "all the world was America. . . ."

In such a setting, how could the tremendous, revolutionary social impact that liberalism had in Europe be preserved? The impact was not, of course, missing entirely; for the attack on the vestiges of corporate society in America that began in 1776, the disestablishment of the Anglican church, the abolition of quitrents and primogeniture, the breaking up of the Tory estates, tinged American liberalism with its own peculiar fire. Nor must we therefore assume that the Americans had wider political objectives than the Europeans, since even their new governmental forms were, as Becker once said, little more than the "colonial institutions with the Parliament and king left out." But after these cautions have been taken, the central point is clear. In America the first half of Locke's argument was bound to become less a call to arms than a set of preliminary remarks essential to establishing a final conclusion: that the power of the state must be limited. Observe how it is treated by the Americans in their great debate with England, even by original thinkers like Otis and Wilson. They do not lavish upon it the fascinated inquiry that we find in Rousseau or Priestley. They advance it mechanically, hurry through it, anxious to get on to what is really bothering them: the limits of the British Parliament, the power of taxation. In Europe the idea of social liberty is loaded with dynamite; but in America it becomes, to a remarkable degree, the working base from which argument begins.

Here, then, is the master assumption of American political thought, the assumption from which all of the American attitudes discussed in this essay flow: the reality of atomistic social freedom. It is instinctive to the American mind, as in a sense the concept of the polis was instinctive to Platonic Athens or the concept of the church to the mind of the middle ages. Catastrophes have not been able to destroy it, proletariats have refused to give it up, and even our Progressive tradition, in its agonized clinging to a Jeffersonian world, has helped to keep it alive. There has been only one major group of American thinkers who have dared to challenge it frontally: the Fitzhughs and Holmeses of the pre-Civil War South who, identifying slavery with feudalism, tried to follow the path of the European reaction and of Comte. But American life rode roughshod over them—for the "prejudice" of Burke in America was liberal and the positive reality of Locke in America transformed them into the very metaphysicians they assailed. They were soon forgotten, massive victims of the absolute temper of the American mind, shoved off the scene by Horatio Alger, who gave to the Lockean premise a brilliance that lasted until the crash of 1929. And even the crash, though it led to a revision of the premise, did not really shatter it.

It might be appropriate to summarize with a single word, or even with a single sentence, the political outlook that this premise has produced. But where is the word and where is the sentence one might use? American political thought, as we have seen, is a veritable maze of polar contradictions, winding in and out of each other hopelessly: pragmatism and absolutism, historicism and rationalism, optimism and pessimism, materialism and idealism, individualism and conformism. But, after all, the human mind works by polar contradictions; and when we have evolved an interpretation of it which leads cleanly in a single direction, we may be sure that we have missed a lot. The task of the cultural analyst is not to discover simplicity, or even to discover unity, for simplicity and unity do not exist, but to drive a wedge of rationality through the pathetic indecisions of social thought. In the American case that wedge is not hard to find. It is not hidden in an obscure place. We find it in what the West as a whole has always recognized to be the distinctive element in American civilization: its social freedom, its social equality. And yet it is true, for all of our Jeffersonian nationalism, that the interpretation of American political thought has not been built around this idea. On the contrary, instead of interpreting the American revolution in terms of American freedom, we have interpreted it in terms of American oppression, and instead of studying the nineteenth century in terms of American equality, we have studied it in terms of a series of cosmic Beardian and Parringtonian struggles against class exploitation. We have missed what the rest of the world has seen and what we ourselves have seen whenever we have contrasted the New World with the Old. But this is a large issue, which brings us not only to the Progressive historians but to the peculiar subjectivism of the American mind that they reflect, and it is beyond the scope of our discussion here.

IV

The liberals of Europe in 1776 were obviously worshipping a very peculiar hero. If the average American had been suddenly thrust in their midst, he would have been embarrassed by the millennial enthusiasms that many of them had, would have found their talk of classes vastly overdone, and would have reacted to the Enlightenment synthesis of absolutism and liberty as if it were little short of dishonest doubletalk. Bred in a freer world, he had a different set of perspectives, was animated by a different set of passions, and looked forward to different goals. He was, as Crèvecoeur put it, a "new man" in Western politics.

But, someone will ask, where did the liberal heritage of the Americans come from in the first place? Didn't they have to create it? And if they did, were they not at one time or another in much the same position as the Europeans?

These questions drive us back to the ultimate nature of the American experience, and, doing so, confront us with a queer twist in the problem of revolution. No one can deny that conscious purpose went into the making of the colonial world, and that the men of the seventeenth century who fled to America from Europe were keenly aware of the oppressions of European life. But they were revolutionaries with a difference, and the fact of their fleeing is no minor fact: for it is one thing to stay at home and fight the "canon and feudal law," and it is another to leave it far behind. It is one thing to try to establish liberalism in the Old World, and it is another to establish it in the New. Revolution, to borrow the words of T. S. Eliot, means to murder and create, but the American experience has been projected strangely in the realm of creation alone. The destruction of forests and Indian tribes—heroic, bloody, legendary as it was—cannot be compared with the destruction of a social order to which one belongs oneself. The first experience is wholly external and, being external, can actually be completed; the second experience is an inner struggle as well as an outer struggle, like the slaying of a Freudian father, and goes on in a sense forever. Moreover, even the matter of creation is not in the American case a simple one. The New World, as Lord Baltimore's ill-fated experiment with feudalism in the seventeenth century illustrates, did not merely offer the Americans a virgin ground for the building of a liberal system: it conspired itself to help that system along. The abundance of land in America, as well as the need for a lure to settlers, entered so subtly into the shaping of America's liberal tradition, touched it so completely at every point, that Sumner was actually ready to say, "We have not made America, America has made us."

It is this business of destruction and creation which goes to the heart of the problem. For the point of departure of great revolutionary thought everywhere else in the world has been the effort to build a new society on the ruins of an old society, and this is an experience America has never had. Tocqueville saw the issue clearly, and it is time now to complete the sentence of his with which we began this essay: "The great advantage of the American is that he has arrived at a state of democracy without having to endure a democratic revolution; *and that he is born free without having to become so.*"

Born free without having to become so: this idea, especially in light of the strange relationship which the revolutionary Americans had with their admirers abroad, raises an obvious question. Can a people that is born free ever understand peoples elsewhere that have to become so? Can it ever lead them? Or to turn the issue around, can peoples struggling for a goal understand those who have inherited it? This is not a problem of antitheses such, for example, as we find in Locke and Filmer. It is a problem of different perspectives on the same ideal. But we must not for that reason assume that it is any less difficult of solution; it may in the end be more difficult, since antitheses define each other and hence can understand each other, but different perspectives on a single value may, ironically enough, lack this common ground of definition. Condorcet might make sense out of Burke's traditionalism, for it was the reverse of his own activism, but what could he say about Otis, who combined both concepts in a synthesis that neither had seen? America's experience of being born free has put it in a strange relationship to the rest of the world.

SUGGESTIONS FOR FURTHER READING

Carl Becker's argument that the American Revolution was a conflict within the colonies as well as a struggle against England may be found in his *History of Political Parties in the Province of New York, 1760–1776* (Madison, 1909). Arthur M. Schlesinger, *Colonial Merchants and the American Revolution* (New York, 1918) gives support to Becker's position by showing how merchants sought to protect their interests against both England and other groups in colonial society. A classic little study showing the social upheaval resulting from the revolutionary struggle is J. Franklin Jameson, *The American Revolution Considered as a Social Movement* (Princeton, N.J., 1926). These views are generally upheld in a more recent study by Elisha P. Douglass, *Rebels and Democrats* (Chapel Hill, 1955).

Edmund S. Morgan, *The Birth of the Republic, 1763–89* (Chicago, 1956) disputes the contention that there were sharp divisions among the colonists and instead finds a basic consensus among the revolutionaries. Robert E. Brown,

* Books in paperback editions will be indicated with an asterisk.

*Middle-Class Democracy and the Revolution in Massachu-
setts, 1691–1780* (Ithaca, N.Y., 1955) supports Clinton Rossiter's argument that most Americans felt they had what they
wanted and were only fighting to preserve it. In Chapter III
of his **Genius of American Politics* (Chicago, 1953) Daniel
J. Boorstin uses very different evidence to come to conclusions
similar to those of Louis Hartz.

    Useful bibliographical articles surveying the litera-
ture on the Revolution are Edmund S. Morgan, "The American Revolution: Revisions in Need of Revising," *William and
Mary Quarterly*, XIV (January, 1957) and Frederick B. Tolles,
"The American Revolution Considered as a Social Movement:
A Re-Evaluation," *American Historical Review*, LX (October,
1954).

II
THE ★
CONSTITUTION ★

There was widespread unrest and dissatisfaction with government under the Articles of Confederation. With thirteen states often going thirteen different ways, many feared for the future of the new nation. Men of property lamented the inability of Congress to collect taxes, to regulate interstate commerce, and to negotiate a favorable trade treaty with England. Widespread depression following the end of the war compounded the difficulties. In the summer of 1786 a group of farmers in western Massachusetts, hard hit by depression and angered by the state legislature's failure to heed their demands for a paper money issue and debtors' stay laws, took matters into their own hands. Led by Daniel Shays, they organized an army, marched on several courthouses, and threatened to take over the government. The governor called out the militia which easily crushed the uprising, but the spectre of rebellion remained and had a significant influence on those who wanted a stronger, more centralized national government.

Even as rebellion raged in Massachusetts, a small group of delegates met at Annapolis to discuss the conflicting regulations regarding interstate commerce. The Annapolis Convention went beyond problems of trade, however, and issued a call for another convention to meet the following year in Philadelphia to consider remedies for the defects in the Articles of Confederation. Delegates to the Philadelphia convention quickly scrapped the idea of revising the Articles and instead drafted a new Constitution of the United States.

The American people have come to venerate, indeed,

almost to worship their constitution. For many, the founding fathers are god-like and their handiwork, almost divine. The student of history, however, quickly discovers that the Constitution was very controversial at the time it was drafted, and that its ratification was hotly contested. He also discovers that there has been a lively controversy among historians regarding the meaning and significance of the Constitution.

Some scholars have argued that the Constitution was the work of a political and economic minority striving to create a government which would limit the power of the majority. Opposed to this wealthy aristocracy of large property owners were the small farmers and artisans, men such as those who had followed Daniel Shays in Massachusetts. The struggle over the Constitution therefore was essentially a class struggle, exhibiting a basic conflict in American society.

Others have strongly contested this interpretation of the Constitution. Disputes over the ratification of the Constitution, they maintain, did not represent basic differences based on property and class. On fundamentals most Americans agreed. They knew why they had fought the Revolution and what kind of government they wanted. But they had no precedents to follow; they were feeling their way, searching for the best means to institutionalize the goals for which they had fought. Differences over means rested on the solid foundation of a basic consensus on ends.

These two interpretations are illustrated in the selections which follow. Carl Van Doren describes some of the compromises which produced the Constitution, and by emphasizing compromise, he minimizes the existence of fundamental conflict. Charles Beard and Robert Brown clash over the economic meaning of the Constitution. In a path-breaking study Beard argues that the Constitution was written by men of property who did not believe in democracy and who wanted to promote their own economic interests. Brown attacks Beard at every point and argues that it is wrong to assume that the new nation was marked by sharply delineated economic classes. In fact, Brown maintains, the country was largely middle class, and the overall aim of the framers of the Constitution was a middle-class democracy.

The last two selections view the problem from another

perspective. Richard Hofstadter depicts the founding fathers as realists who wanted a strong central government because they had little faith in human nature and democracy. They were anxious to protect property, yet they were not aristocratic tyrants. Stanley Elkins and Eric McKitrick, although they would agree that the founding fathers were realists with little faith in human nature, picture them as young men who came to power and prominence during the Revolution. In drafting a constitution they were working out some of the implications of their experiences, not reacting against the ideas of the Revolution. Elkins and McKitrick see few ideological differences dividing those who favored and those who opposed the Constitution. Once the debate over ratification was over, the opponents quickly accepted the new Constitution, illustrating that a basic consensus united both groups.

Few historians would deny that many of the founding fathers were brilliant men; the Philadelphia convention brought together perhaps the most remarkable group of men ever assembled. Yet when they probe further, historians begin to disagree. Whom did these men represent and what were they trying to accomplish? Were the men who gathered in Philadelphia in the summer of 1787 a representative cross section of the American people, or did they represent particular classes or property interests? Did the Constitutional Convention and the contest over ratification reveal fundamental conflict in America or fundamental agreement?

Early in the morning of July 3 Washington began sitting for his portrait by Charles Willson Peale, who wished to make the mezzotint soon to appear with the title lettered round the margin: "His Excel: G: Washington Esq: LLD. Late Commander in Chief of the Armies of the U.S. of America & President of the Convention of 1787." Washington was painted in a close-fitting wig and his famous uniform of blue and buff (taken over from the First Virginia Regiment which he had commanded when he was a soldier of the Crown) with three gold stars on his epaulets. That day, and perhaps other days, he went to the State House in uniform, general as well as president. Although this day's session was only a meeting of the grand committee of the states, of which Washington was not a member, he attended along with other delegates who were there as observers not debaters.

With Gerry as chairman, the committee took up the problem of conciliating the opposed views which were the same in the committee as they had been in the Convention. The majority favored proportional representation in both houses of the legislature of the United States; the minority favored equal representation in both. Sherman had earlier proposed that the states have proportional representation in the popular branch, but equal votes in the Senate. Franklin had proposed that the states be equally represented in the Senate, but that in money matters the Senate votes be based on the amount of contributions from the separate states. Now in the committee Sherman, who had taken the place of Ellsworth, offered a new compromise: that the states should have an equal vote in the Senate but that no decision could be final unless the states voting for it should comprise a majority of the inhabitants of the United States. None of these compromises suited the committee. At last, after debates of which there is no record, Franklin made the motion which, with "some modifications," was agreed to. As modified, it proposed that in the first branch each state be allowed one member for every 40,000 of its inhabitants (counting three-fifths of the slaves) and that any state with less than that number of inhabitants have one member; that all bills for raising or apportioning money and for paying salaries to federal officers originate in the first branch, without alteration or amendment by the Senate; and that in the Senate each state have an equal vote.

From *The Great Rehearsal* by Carl Van Doren. Copyright 1948 by Carl Van Doren. Reprinted by permission of The Viking Press, Inc.

This compromise combined and redefined Sherman's proposed compromise on different modes of representation in the two houses, and Franklin's on a special mode for allowing more votes to the states which paid more money for federal expenses. It was satisfactory to a majority of the members of the grand committee, though the large states were now in dissent because of the equal vote granted to all states in the Senate. The committee agreed to report their compromise to the Convention, with the condition that the provisions relating to both houses must be "generally adopted" together.

On Thursday July 5 Gerry reported for the committee to the Convention. Madison vigorously opposed the concession to the small states of equality in the Senate. It was, he thought, the surrender of a fundamental principle on the mere ground of expediency. It was conciliating a minority, by doing an injustice to the majority of the people of the United States. "It was in vain to purchase concord in the Convention on terms which would perpetuate discord among their constituents." He did not believe that Delaware "would brave the consequences of seeking her fortunes apart from the other States" or "pursue the rash policy of courting foreign support"; or that New Jersey "would choose rather to stand on its own legs, and bid defiance to events," than to accept a government which was absolutely necessary to protect the state from its overshadowing neighbors. "Harmony in the Convention was no doubt much to be desired. Satisfaction to all the States" from the first would be still more desirable. "But if the principal States comprehending a majority of the people of the United States should concur in a just & judicious plan, he had the firmest hopes that all the other States would by degrees accede to it."

Gouverneur Morris was rhetorical. "He came here as a Representative of America; he flattered himself he came here in some degree as a Representative of the whole human race; for the whole human race will be affected by the proceedings of this Convention." But it seemed to him, from some things he had heard, "that we were assembled to truck and bargain for our particular States." He believed that "this Country must be united. If persuasion does not unite it, the sword will." He spoke of the horrors of civil war. "The stronger party will then make traytors of the weaker; and the Gallows & Halter will finish the work of the sword." In the compromise report from the grand committee he saw prospects of confusion and conflict. "State attachments, and State importance have been the bane of this Country. We cannot annihilate; but we can perhaps take out the teeth of the serpents"—the jealousies of the states.

Bedford, who had let slip the unfortunate hint that the smaller states might turn to foreign alliances, again protested that he had not meant what he had said; that he had been speaking as a lawyer, for whom "warmth was natural & sometimes necessary." But no man could fore-

see "to what extremities the small States may be driven by oppression."
Paterson thought the talk about the sword and the gallows was "little
calculated to produce conviction." Both he and Bedford resented the
treatment the small states had endured from the large in the Convention.
Paterson was not entirely satisfied with the grand committee's compromise plan, but he agreed with Bedford that something must be done for
the United States. "Better that a defective plan should be adopted," Bedford said, "than that none should be recommended." Defects might be
remedied by later meetings.

Gerry had objections to the new plan, but he insisted that the United
States were "in a peculiar situation. We were neither the same Nation
nor different Nations. We ought not therefore to pursue the one or the
other of these ideas too closely." If that were done, some of the states
might secede from the Convention, and from the union. "If we do not
come to some agreement among ourselves some foreign sword will probably do the work for us." Mason thought there must be an accommodation between the opposing sides in the conflict. "It could not be more
inconvenient to any gentleman to remain absent from his private affairs, than it was for him; but he would bury his bones in this city
rather than expose his Country to the Consequences of a dissolution of
the Convention without anything being done."

Both Gouverneur Morris and Rutledge objected to basing representation in the lower house purely on numbers, one member for each 40,000
inhabitants. Life and liberty might be the first considerations of savages, Morris said, but in civilized conditions "property was the main object of Society." Property, Rutledge agreed, "was certainly the principal
object of Society." Here Rutledge was speaking for the slave-owners of
South Carolina and Morris for the large land-owners of New York. Moreover, they were both thinking of the new states in the Western territory
which might in time be admitted to the union. Any one of these, according to the grand committee's plan, might be entitled to one member even
though it had less than 40,000 inhabitants. Some arrangement must be
made to protect the rich maritime states from the lean voters of the backwoods.

Nothing was decided that day, and the debate went over to Friday the
6th. On Friday the Convention readily agreed that the proposal of one
member in the lower house for each 40,000 inhabitants called for further detailed study. The matter was referred to a smaller committee
made up of Gouverneur Morris, Gorham, Randolph, Rutledge, and King.
Then the debate continued on the clause providing that all money bills
should originate in the popular branch of the federal legislature.

The delegates from the small states were silent. They had won what
they wanted in the proposal that the states be equally represented in the

Senate, and were willing to let the larger states, with more votes in the lower house, have some advantage in raising revenues and fixing apportionments. The delegates from the large states failed to see that the small had made any real concession. What was the difference, Wilson asked, which house had the right to originate bills, since the other must concur? Mason explained that the committee had desired to put the voting of money as directly as possible into the hands of the people. If the members of the Senate should have "the power of giving away the people's money, they might soon forget the Source from whence they received it. We might soon have an aristocracy." He had been disturbed by certain aristocratic principles advanced in the Convention, but he was glad to find they did not prevail among the members.

Gouverneur Morris, to whom Mason had obviously referred, declared that he was sure "there never was, nor ever will be a civilized society without an Aristocracy. His endeavour was to keep it as much as possible from doing mischief." He assumed that the American aristocracy would dominate the Senate. If the sole right to originate money bills lay in the popular house, the country would lose the benefit of the superior abilities of the Senate in devising such bills; and the Senate, having no responsibility, would fall into disputes with the originating house, as in the British Parliament. Morris believed that the proposed restriction would be "either useless or pernicious."

Franklin summed up the argument with a clarity which enabled Madison, taking down the slow words, to make them sound almost like one of Franklin's written speeches. "It had been asked," the philosopher said, "what would be the use of restraining the second branch from medling with money bills. He could not but remark that it was always of importance that the people should know who had disposed of their money, & how it had been disposed of. It was a maxim that those who feel, can best judge." (It was a maxim of Franklin's own. He had used it as far back as February 1766 in his examination before the House cf Commons, when he said: "Those that feel can judge best.") "This end would, he thought, be best attained, if money affairs were to be confined to the immediate representatives of the people. This was his inducement to concur in the report. As to the danger or difficulty that might arise from a negative in the second [branch] where the people would not be proportionally represented, it might easily be got over by declaring that there should be no such Negative; or if that will not do, by declaring that there shall be no such branch at all"—which was what Franklin preferred in any case.

In the vote which followed, the Convention agreed by a narrow margin to let the clause relating to money bills stand for the present in the report. Connecticut, New Jersey, Delaware, Maryland, and North Carolina were now in the affirmative, with only Pennsylvania, Virginia, and South Carolina in the negative; and Massachusetts, New York, and Georgia divided.

If the popular branch of the legislature was to have the sole right to originate money bills, then the representation in that branch was bound to be of the greatest importance. On Saturday the 7th the Convention agreed that each state should "have an equal vote" in the Senate. There was some lively discussion, but the vote was not too close. Several of the delegates voted aye because they realized that this was only a part of the grand committee's report, and that another vote would later be taken on the whole of it. Before that could be done, there must be some settlement as to the actual number of representatives the people of the respective states would have to speak for them in the disposition of their money.

II

Gouverneur Morris, for the smaller committee, reported on Monday the 9th. His committee had been handicapped by lack of knowledge as to what the population of the states was. For want of better information, they had gone back to the estimates of 1774 with some guesses as to changes since then. They now proposed that at the first meeting of the lower house it should consist of fifty-six members, divided as follows: New Hampshire 2, Massachusetts 7, Rhode Island 1, Connecticut 4, New York 5, New Jersey 3, Pennsylvania 8, Delaware 1, Maryland 4, Virginia 9, North Carolina 5, South Carolina 5, Georgia 2. These figures were to be temporary. The legislature of the United States should be authorized "from time to time" to augment the number of representatives. "In case any of the States shall hereafter be divided, or any two or more States united, or any new State created within the limits of the United States," the legislature should have authority to regulate the number of the representatives of the new states "upon the principles of their wealth and number of inhabitants."

There had been talk in the Convention of the possible division of some of the larger states and the possible union of some of the smaller. The committee had provided for either possibility. But the proposal that new states should be granted representation according to their wealth as well as to their population roused fresh debate. Gorham, a member of the committee, explained the report. One member of the popular house to every 40,000 inhabitants, the committee thought, would make the house unworkably large as the population increased. Moreover, there was danger that new Western states, if admitted on those terms, might soon "out-vote the Atlantic." But if the Atlantic states kept the "Government in their own hands," they could take care of their own interest "by dealing out the right of Representation in safe proportions to the Western States. These were the views of the Committee."

Those were the views of several of the delegates who thought wealth no less than numbers should be represented in all the states. Butler of South Carolina "urged warmly the justice & necessity" of taking wealth into account. King of Massachusetts said that, as the Southern states were the richest, they must naturally hesitate to "league themselves with the Northern unless some respect were paid to their superior wealth." But the Northern states, which looked for commercial advantages from the union, had already consented to the representation of Southern wealth, which was slaves, by agreeing that three-fifths of them might be reckoned as inhabitants.

Nine states now agreed (New York and New Jersey dissenting) that the legislature of the United States should have authority in the future to regulate the representation of all the states "upon the principles of their wealth and number of inhabitants." As to the number of representatives for the present, that matter was referred to another committee of the states. The members were King, Sherman, Yates, Brearley, Gouverneur Morris, Read, Daniel Carroll (who had just taken his seat for Maryland), Madison, Williamson, Rutledge, and Houstoun.

They came in on July 10 with a proposal that the lower house begin with sixty-five members: New Hampshire 3, Massachusetts 8, Rhode Island 1, Connecticut 5, New York 6, New Jersey 4, Pennsylvania 8, Delaware 1, Maryland 6, Virginia 10, North Carolina 5, South Carolina 5, Georgia 3.

At once there was a scuffle of arguments over these figures. Butler and General Pinckney of South Carolina moved that New Hampshire be reduced from three representatives to two. "Her numbers did not entitle her to 3 and it was a poor State." King of Massachusetts, supporting the claim of New Hampshire to three members, made it plain that he was thinking less of New Hampshire in particular than of the Northern states in general. He had been willing to yield something to the Southern states for their security, but "no principle would justify giving them a majority." General Pinckney replied that the Southern states did not expect to have a majority, but he wished them "to have something like an equality." Otherwise, they would be "nothing more than overseers for the Northern states," since the regulation of trade would be in the hands of the central government. He was glad that one member had been added to Virginia, "as he considered her a Southern state. He was glad also that the members of Georgia were increased"—and he did not object to her being given a larger number than her population then entitled her to.

The motion to reduce New Hampshire from three to two members was lost by a vote of eight to two. Motions made by Southern delegates to increase the number of members for the Carolinas and Georgia by one each were lost by decisive votes.

Madison moved that the number of members be doubled, "A *majority* of a *Quorum of 65* members was too small a number to represent the whole inhabitants of the United States." Ellsworth and Sherman of Connecticut objected on the grounds of expense. Read of Delaware approved because the change would give Delaware two votes. Rutledge thought the state legislatures were at present too numerous, and the national legislature should not follow that bad example. The members would be forced by the interests of their states to attend regularly. He supposed "the General Legislature would not sit more than 6 or 8 weeks in the year."

Only two states, Delaware and Virginia, favored doubling the number of members. The number as fixed by the report of the committee of the states was approved by a vote of nine to two: only South Carolina and Georgia opposed.

Washington in the Chair, entertaining motions, putting questions, announcing votes, was troubled by the persistent conflicts. They were, he wrote that day to Hamilton in New York, worse than ever. "I *almost* despair of seeing a favourable issue to the proceedings of our Convention, and do therefore repent having had any agency in the business. The Men who oppose a strong and energetic government are, in my opinion, narrow minded politicians, or are under the influence of local views. The apprehension expressed by them that the *people* will not accede to the form proposed is the *ostensible,* not the *real* cause of the opposition. . . . I am sorry you went away. I wish you were back. The crisis is equally important and alarming, and no opposition under such circumstances should discourage exertions till the signature is fixed." Hamilton returned to the Convention three days later. His colleagues Yates and Lansing left it on the day Washington wrote.

The conflicts which troubled Washington went on for a week in a tangle of motions and motives. Randolph on the 10th moved that "in order to ascertain alterations in the population & wealth of the States the Legislature of the United States be required to cause a proper census and estimate to be taken" at regular intervals which were to be agreed on. Williamson of North Carolina on the 11th proposed an amendment to the effect that in the census enumeration the "free white inhabitants" be counted and three-fifths of "those of other descriptions"—that is, slaves. Butler and Charles Cotesworth Pinckney of South Carolina at once insisted that "blacks be included . . . equally with the Whites," and made a motion to that effect. The labor of a slave in South Carolina, Butler said, was as productive and valuable as that of a free man in Massachusetts. Wealth was the "great means of defence and utility to the Nation." Consequently wealth ought to be considered equal to numbers of free men "in a Government which was instituted principally for the protection of property, and was itself to be supported by property."

Mason of Virginia said that this principle of representation, however favorable it might be to Virginia, was unjust, and he could not vote for it. But since slaves by their labor raised the value of land, increased imports and exports and therefore revenues, "would supply the means of feeding & supporting an army, and might in cases of emergency become themselves soldiers," he believed they should not be wholly excluded from the estimates of population. He would be satisfied if three-fifths of them were counted. Like other Virginia delegates, Mason was opposed to slavery on principle, regretted the existence of it in their state, and desired to see slavery abolished if this could be done without destroying the economy of a society which had inherited its slaves as it had inherited its land and its laws.

Only three states, South Carolina, Georgia, and (for some reason) Delaware, voted to count slaves and free citizens equally in representation. The strength of the vote led the Convention to reconsider its earlier decision to reckon three-fifths of the slaves as inhabitants. Wilson did not see on what principle they could be so counted. "Are they admitted as Citizens? Then why are they not admitted on an equality with White Citizens? Are they admitted as property? Then why is not other property admitted into the computation?" Nevertheless he was willing to see them included as a necessary compromise. Gouverneur Morris said he found himself in the "dilemma of doing injustice to the Southern States or to human nature," and must decide in favor of human nature. To count slaves, in any ratio, as part of the population must encourage the slave trade, since the importing of slaves would increase not only the wealth but also the representation of the slave-holding states. He could not concur in that, even if the Southern states should refuse to "confederate" without it. On the question, six states voted against counting slaves at all in the estimate of population.

But on the 12th Morris made another motion to the effect that taxation should be proportioned according to representation. This naturally changed the position of the Southern states. South Carolina and Georgia were still willing to pay taxes on all their slaves if all of them could be counted as inhabitants. But the other states with large numbers of slaves were unwilling. Davie of North Carolina demanded, in the name of his state, merely that three-fifths of the slaves be included. Randolph of Virginia urged the same ratio. "He lamented that such a species of property existed. But as it did the holders of it would require this security." On another motion six states now favored the ratio of five to three, with Massachusetts and South Carolina divided, and only New Jersey and Delaware opposed.

On the 13th Randolph moved to alter the vote of July 9 which had said that representation should be based on wealth and population, by striking out wealth altogether. Gouverneur Morris objected. Suppose the population of the South should increase as it was expected to, and the South should make common cause with the Western states. Then between them they would have a majority which would overwhelm the Northern and Middle states. Butler replied that the South did not expect a majority, only an increase in relation to the other states, since "the people & strength of America are evidently bearing Southwardly & South-westwardly." But the Southern states did want to feel sure that "their negroes may not be taken from them, which some gentlemen within or without doors have a very good mind to do."

Wilson in one of his ablest speeches carried the house with him. "Conceiving," he said, "that all men wherever placed have equal rights and are equally entitled to confidence, he viewed without apprehension the period when a few States should contain the superior number of people. The majority of the people wherever found ought in all questions to govern the minority." Nor was he troubled by the fear that the "interior Country" might some time contain the majority of the population. If they became the majority, they would have a majority's rights, "whether we will or no." Did the delegates not remember that Great Britain had been jealous and apprehensive over the growth of the American colonies? That had led to rebellion and independence. The Atlantic states must avoid behaving toward the interior as Great Britain had once unwisely behaved toward them. The numbers of people had to be regarded as the proper rule of representation, since no better could be found. Congress in 1783, after long discussion, had been satisfied that "the rule of numbers does not differ much from the combined rule of numbers & wealth. Again he could not agree that property was the sole or the primary object of Government & Society. The cultivation & improvement of the human mind was the most noble object. With respect to this object, as well as to other *personal* rights, numbers were surely the natural & precise measure of Representation. And with respect to property, they could not vary much from the precise measure."

On the question of striking "wealth" out of the clause relating to representation in the popular house, all the states on July 13 voted aye except Delaware, which was divided. One of the most important decisions which ever came here to a vote found the Convention nearly unanimous in agreement.

By a memorable coincidence this decision was made on the very day when Congress in New York at last adopted the Ordinance of 1787 for the government of the Northwest Territory. The Ordinance provided that five new states (eventually named Ohio, Indiana, Illinois, Wisconsin, Michigan) from this Territory might be admitted to the union as soon as any of them should have 60,000 inhabitants, which was about the population of Delaware. Slavery was prohibited, thanks to an earlier suggestion of Jefferson, a bill of rights and freedom of religious worship guaranteed, and laws forbidden which might impair the obligations of private contracts. This was federal legislation over separate states-to-be of the sort contemplated by the constitution which the Convention was now trying to make.

The old Congress and the new Convention were in accord on a matter which was fundamental to the future. While Congress was arranging to admit Western states to the United States, the Convention was arranging that this should be on an equality in law with the original Thirteen. The states themselves had long shown partiality to the cities and counties on the seaboard. The "back counties" of Pennsylvania were now in resentful conflict with Philadelphia and the counties nearest it. In South Carolina the "up country," rebelling against the dominance of the "low country," had in 1786 voted the removal of the capital of the state from Charleston to Columbia, still almost in the primeval forest—though this had not yet been carried out. The seaboard shipowners, merchants, and planters all along the Atlantic had made every effort to protect themselves and their property against the rising demands of the frontier. Various delegates to the Convention, notably Gorham of Massachusetts, Gouverneur Morris of Pennsylvania, and Rutledge of South Carolina, had insisted that the Atlantic states must keep control of the government.

Gerry thought on July 14 that the Convention ought to limit the number of Western states to be admitted, so that there should never be more of them than of the Atlantic states. "There was a rage for emigration from the Eastern States to the Western Country," he said, "and he did not wish those remaining behind to be at the mercy of the Emigrants" once they had established themselves in new states. Sherman, with an odd mixture of shortsightedness and enlightenment, thought there was no probability that the Western states would ever outnumber the Eastern. "If the event should ever happen, it was too remote to be taken into consideration at this time." For the present, he said, "We are providing for our posterity, for our children & our grand Children, who would be as likely to be citizens of new Western States, as of the old States." They should not be discriminated against as Gerry proposed.

While deciding that wealth (except for three-fifths of the slaves) should not be represented in the legislature of the United States, the Convention decided also that the legislature must not be left free to regulate changes in representation at its own will. "From the nature of man," Mason said on July 11, "we may be sure, that those who have power in their hands will not give it up while they can retain it." He agreed with Randolph that alterations must be according to a regular census called for by a constitutional provision. Sherman, who was at first disposed to leave alterations to the discretion of the legislature of the United States, was convinced, he said, "by the observations of Mr. Randolph & Mr. Mason that the *periods* & the *rule* of revising the Representation ought to be fixt by the Constitution." After much discussion and numerous amendments proposed, it was decided on July 12 that representation ought to be "proportioned according to direct Taxation," and that the necessary revisions should be based on a census to be taken within six years after the first meeting of the legislature of the United States and again every ten years thereafter.

III

On the morning of July 14 Martin of Maryland called for the question on the whole report brought in by the grand committee of the states on the 5th. The Convention had now gone piecemeal through the compromise proposal and had accepted, or amended, its various clauses. Instead of one member in the legislature of the United States for every 40,000 inhabitants of a given state, as proposed, the Convention preferred for the present a fixed number of members for each state, subject to revision according to a decennial census as the population might change in the future. But money bills were to originate in the popular branch, and each state should have an equal vote in the Senate, as the committee had recommended. Since the committee had stipulated that the parts of their proposal were not to be adopted separately, the Convention must now either accept or reject it as a whole.

Some of the delegates were not yet ready to put the matter to a vote. Gerry moved that the new states to be admitted should never be allowed more representatives than the original members of the Confederation. Four states (Massachusetts, Connecticut, Delaware, and Maryland) voted aye, all the others no except Pennsylvania, which was divided. Charles Pinckney moved that instead of equal votes in the Senate the states have fixed numbers of representatives in that branch: New Hampshire 2, Massachusetts 4, Rhode Island 1, Connecticut 3, New York 3, New Jersey 2, Pennsylvania 3, Delaware 1, Maryland 3, Virginia 5, North Carolina 3, South Carolina 3, Georgia 2. Wilson seconded the motion. King approved, because he could see no better reason for equality of representation in one branch of the legislature than in the other. What they proposed to create was "a General and National Government over the people of America. There never will be a case," he said, "in which it will act as a federal Government on the States and not on the individual Citizens." Therefore the citizens through their representatives, and not the states as states, ought to influence the operations of the central authority. He thought that to consent to equality of votes in the Senate would be injustice, and worse than doing nothing. Better "a little more confusion & convulsion" than to submit to such an evil. Strong of Massachusetts believed that unless some accommodation could be agreed on, "the Union itself must soon be dissolved." If, as had been suggested, the principal states were to form and recommend a scheme of government without the others, there was no certainty that the smaller would ever be more likely than now to accede to it, or even that the people of the larger would "embrace and ratify it." Wilson thought nothing "so pernicious as bad first principles." If equality in the Senate were merely "an error that time would correct," he might accept it, being aware "that perfection was unattainable in any plan." But this was "a fundamental and a perpetual error." An evil in representation, like poison in a first potion, "must be followed by disease, convulsions, and finally death itself."

Charles Pinckney's motion for proportional votes in the Senate "passed in the negative," in the language of the time, with six states opposed. Massachusetts was among them, because Gorham was absent that day, and King was outvoted by Gerry and Strong.

On Monday the 16th the Convention voted on the compromise proposal as a whole. The vote was nearly as close as it could be, and as it had regularly been during all the recent deliberations. Connecticut, New Jersey, Delaware, Maryland, and North Carolina approved; Pennsylvania, Virginia, South Carolina, and Georgia opposed; Massachusetts was divided. Even if Massachusetts had voted with the larger states, the result would have been merely a tie. The Convention was at a standstill.

Randolph, original proposer of the Virginia plan over which they had been working for six weeks, said that the vote had "embarrassed the business extremely." He had come this morning with a series of suggestions which he thought might conciliate the smaller states. His suggestions provided for an enumeration of special cases in which the states might have equal votes in the Senate, proportional votes in all others. But since he now saw that the smaller states persisted in demanding equal votes in every case, he "could not but think we were unprepared to discuss this subject further. It will probably be in vain to come to any final decision with a bare majority on either side. For these reasons he wished the Convention might adjourn, that the large States might consider the steps proper to be taken in the present solemn crisis of the business, and that the small States might also deliberate on the means of conciliation."

Paterson thought it was high time to adjourn. The rule of secrecy ought to be rescinded, and the delegates ought to be free to consult their constituents. But the smaller states, he assured the Convention, would in no circumstances yield their absolute demand for equality in the Senate. If Randolph were willing to move that the Convention adjourn sine die, Paterson would second it "with all his heart." Whether or not Paterson was actually in favor of a permanent adjournment, he seized on this troubled moment to make a suggestion that amounted to a threat.

Randolph "had never entertained the idea of an adjournment sine die; & was sorry that his meaning had been so readily & strangely interpreted." He had meant merely to adjourn till the next day "in order that some conciliatory experiment might if possible be devised." If the smaller States should continue to hold back, then the larger might take "such measures, he would not say what, as might be necessary." Here Randolph too was hinting a threat.

Paterson seconded the adjournment for a day, since the larger states seemed to wish, as he reversed Randolph's terms to put it, "to deliberate further on conciliatory expedients."

In the following discussion nobody favored an adjournment sine die. Gerry said that Massachusetts was opposed to adjournment even for a day, since there appeared to be no "new ground of compromise," but the state could concur with the majority. Rutledge also thought there was no chance of a compromise, and no need of an adjournment. "The little states were fixt. They had repeatedly & solemnly declared themselves to be so. All that the large States then had to do, was to decide whether they would yield or not. For his part he conceiv'd that altho' we could not do what we thought best, in itself, we ought to do something. Had we not better keep the Government up a little longer, hoping that another Convention will supply our omissions, than abandon everything to hazard? Our Constituents will be very little satisfied with us if we take the latter course."

In such words, on the careful level of parliamentary courtesy, the delegates were saying that the Convention despaired of finding any just design for a government which the two parties could agree on, and doubted whether anything was to be gained by debating further. They had got nowhere in their plans for a new constitution. Perhaps the United States would never have a better constitution than the ineffectual old one. Perhaps there would not long be any United States.

The occasion might seem to call for the dramatic interchange of burning speeches, with angry and unhappy men on both sides, such as were in the Convention. There was more fire in the speeches than appears in Madison's quiet notes, which are the sole record of this crucial episode. But there is no missing, in his record, the essential drama of an immense decision being made by men who did not know how immense the decision was.

Nor is there less drama in his brief account of what happened on the morning of July 17. A number of delegates from the larger states, all unnamed in the record like heroes in masks, met "before the hour of the Convention." They believed that the smaller states were inflexible in their demand for equal representation in the Senate. That was what the delegates from the smaller states had said. Some of them were present at this meeting, and their faces today confirmed their words of yesterday.

The delegates from the larger states talked together. Nobody had a specific proposal. There was no agreement on any general principle. An equal vote in the Senate was anathema to some, to others an injustice, a mistake, or only an inconvenience. Some were willing to break off the Convention rather than yield to the smaller states' demand, but more were by no means sure it worth opposing further. Several insisted that the larger states, which meant a majority of the people of the United States, should make a constitution of their own, recommend it to Congress and any states that would accept it, and let the smaller states go their own way. Others were inclined to yield to the smaller states and to concur in some general plan or other. If there was none on which a large majority could agree, then continue, as lately, with a bare majority of the states and even now and then with only a minority of the people represented in the decisions.

The delegates from the smaller states, listening to this inconclusive discussion, were gradually reassured. There was no danger, they perceived, that their opponents would unite in any roughshod resistance to equal votes in the Senate. This was enough for the smaller states. They talked no more of withdrawing from the Convention. From the time of this morning caucus, this clash of drama without remembered words, they were active in support of the general plan for the new government which was to succeed the Confederation without abolishing the states as entities in one branch of the future legislature.

The Great Compromise, as this settlement is commonly called, or the Connecticut Compromise, was a federal compromise. The small states, by giving up their claim to equal representation in the popular branch of the legislature of the United States, had given up their attachment to a mere confederation. The large states, by giving up their claim to proportional representation in the Senate, had given up any hopes they may have had for a consolidated government. The states would now survive as states in a federal system to which they conceded the right to make, execute, and interpret federal laws, while themselves retaining the right to govern themselves within their own borders. The federal compromise was what Hamilton called a "motley measure," what Madison called a "novelty & a compound." Perhaps not a single delegate in the Convention was fully satisfied with the compromise. It was the creation of the corporate mind of the assemblage, reconciling differences, coming to such general agreement as was possible.

Naturally the desires of the conflicting parties in the Convention, or of the states they represented, were affected by their interests. The Southern states desired to be represented in part by their wealth, which was slaves, neither quite property nor quite population. They had been permitted to count three-fifths of the slaves in the estimate of their numbers. This gave them an anomalous advantage in the lower house of the legislature of the United States. The Northern states, averse to letting slaves be counted, nevertheless could realize that slaves would not be represented in the Senate if the votes of the states were there equal. As there were more Northern states than Southern, the North would have a majority in the Senate, and might look to it for security against the Southern votes in the lower house. These were compromises of interest which went with the compromises of political structure in the proposed government, entirely favorable neither to the several states nor to the United States. The individual states had special interests, as the individual delegates had. But the primary concern of all of them was for preservation of the union, defense against foreign aggression and domestic dissension, and the general prosperity of the American people. With these indispensable things provided for, the delegates believed, by the government they were devising, they could hope according to their interests for the particular blessings they might enjoy in the society which could develop under the guarantee of the new government.

At the end of these wrangling days which saw the federal compromise agreed on, a note appeared in the *Pennsylvania Packet* for July 19 which said: "So great is the unanimity, we hear, that prevails in the Convention, upon all great federal subjects, that it has been proposed to call the room in which they assemble—Unanimity Hall." It has been guessed, on no evidence, that this was deliberately given out by some delegate or delegates for the purpose of contradicting any rumors which might reach the public. The note was widely reprinted in newspapers in various states—there were then no national newspapers—and, while in general misleading, gave many readers a justified confidence that some progress was being made.

The constitution: a minority document

Charles Beard

At the close of this long and arid survey—partaking of the nature of catalogue—it seems worth while to bring together the important conclusions for political science which the data presented appear to warrant.

The movement for the Constitution of the United States was originated and carried through principally by four groups of personalty interests which had been adversely affected under the Articles of Confederation: money, public securities, manufactures, and trade and shipping.

The first firm steps toward the formation of the Constitution were taken by a small and active group of men immediately interested through their personal possessions in the outcome of their labors.

No popular vote was taken directly or indirectly on the proposition to call the Convention which drafted the Constitution.

A large propertyless mass was, under the prevailing suffrage qualifications, excluded at the outset from participation (through representatives) in the work of framing the Constitution.

The members of the Philadelphia Convention which drafted the Constitution were, with a few exceptions, immediately, directly, and personally interested in, and derived economic advantages from, the establishment of the new system.

The Constitution was essentially an economic document based upon the concept that the fundamental private rights of property are anterior to government and morally beyond the reach of popular majorities.

The major portion of the members of the Convention are on record as recognizing the claim of property to a special and defensive position in the Constitution.

In the ratification of the Constitution, about three-fourths of the adult males failed to vote on the question, having abstained from the elections at which delegates to the state conventions were chosen, either on account of their indifference or their disfranchisement by property qualifications.

The Constitution was ratified by a vote of probably not more than one-sixth of the adult males.

It is questionable whether a majority of the voters participating in the elections for the state conventions in New York, Massachusetts, New Hampshire, Virginia, and South Carolina, actually approved the ratification of the Constitution.

The leaders who supported the Constitution in the ratifying conventions represented the same economic groups as the members of the Philadelphia Convention; and in a large number of instances they were also directly and personally interested in the outcome of their efforts.

In the ratification, it became manifest that the line of cleavage for and against the Constitution was between substantial personalty interests on the one hand and the small farming and debtor interests on the other.

The Constitution was not created by "the whole people" as the jurists have said; neither was it created by "the states" as Southern nullifiers long contended; but it was the work of a consolidated group whose interests knew no state boundaries and were truly national in their scope.

A constitution
for all
the people

Robert E. Brown

At the end of Chapter XI Beard summarized his findings in fourteen paragraphs under the heading of "Conclusions." Actually, these fourteen conclusions merely add up to the two halves of the Beard thesis. One half, that the Constitution originated with and was carried through by personalty interests—money, public securities, manufactures, and commerce—is to be found in paragraphs two, three, six, seven, eight, twelve, thirteen, and fourteen. The other half—that the Constitution was put over undemocratically in an undemocratic society—is expressed in paragraphs four, five, nine, ten, eleven, and fourteen. The lumping of these conclusions under two general headings makes it easier for the reader to see the broad outlines of the Beard thesis.

Before we examine these two major divisions of the thesis, however, some comment is relevant on the implications contained in the first paragraph. In it Beard characterized his book as a long and arid survey, something in the nature of a catalogue. Whether this characterization was designed to give his book the appearance of a coldly objective study based on the facts we do not know. If so, nothing could be further from reality. As reviewers pointed out in 1913, and as subsequent developments have demonstrated, the book is anything but an arid catalogue of facts. Its pages are replete with interpretation, sometimes stated, sometimes implied. Our task has been to examine Beard's evidence to see whether it justifies the interpretation which Beard gave it. We have tried to discover whether he used the historical method properly in arriving at his thesis.

If historical method means the gathering of data from primary sources, the critical evaluation of the evidence thus gathered, and the drawing of conclusions consistent with this evidence, then we must conclude that Beard has done great violation to such method in this book. He admitted that the evidence had not been collected which, given the proper use of historical method, should have precluded the writing of the book. Yet he nevertheless proceeded on the assumption that a valid interpretation could be built on secondary writings whose authors had likewise failed to collect the evidence. If we accept Beard's own maxim, "no evidence, no history," and his own admission that the data had never been collected, the answer to whether he used historical method properly is self-evident.

Neither was Beard critical of the evidence which he did use. He was accused in 1913, and one might still suspect him, of using only that evidence which appeared to support his thesis. The amount of realty in the country compared with the personalty, the vote in New York, and the omission of the part of *The Federalist* No. 10 which did not fit his thesis are only a few examples of the uncritical use of evidence to be found in the book. Sometimes he accepted secondary accounts at face value without checking them with the sources; at other times he allowed unfounded rumors and traditions to color his work.

Finally, the conclusions which he drew were not justified even by the kind of evidence which he used. If we accepted his evidence strictly at face value, it would still not add up to the fact that the Constitution was put over undemocratically in an undemocratic society by personalty. The citing of property qualifications does not prove that a mass of men were disfranchised. And if we accept his figures on property holdings, either we do not know what most of the delegates had in realty and personalty, or we know that realty outnumbered personalty three to one (eighteen to six). Simply showing that a man held public securities is not sufficient to prove that he acted only in terms of his public securities. If we ignore Beard's own generalizations and accept only his evidence, we would have to conclude that most of the property in the country in 1787 was real estate, that real property was widely distributed in rural areas, which included most of the country, and that even the men who were directly concerned with the Constitution, and especially Washington, were large holders of realty.

Perhaps we can never be completely objective in history, but certainly we can be more objective than Beard was in this book. Naturally the historian must always be aware of the biases, the subjectivity, the pitfalls that confront him, but this does not mean that he should not make an effort to overcome these obstacles. Whether Beard had his thesis before he had his evidence, as some have said, is a question that each reader must answer for himself. Certain it is that the evidence does not justify the thesis.

So instead of the Beard interpretation that the Constitution was put over undemocratically in an undemocratic society by personal property, the following fourteen paragraphs are offered as a possible interpretation of the Constitution and as suggestions for future research on that document.

1. The movement for the Constitution was originated and carried through by men who had long been important in both economic and political affairs in their respective states. Some of them owned personalty, more of them owned realty, and if their property was adversely affected by conditions under the Articles of Confederation, so also was the property of the bulk of the people in the country, middle-class farmers as well as town artisans.

2. The movement for the Constitution, like most important movements, was undoubtedly started by a small group of men. They were probably interested personally in the outcome of their labors, but the benefits which they expected were not confined to personal property or, for that matter, strictly to things economic. And if their own interests would be enhanced by a new government, similar interests of other men, whether agricultural or commercial, would also be enhanced.

3. Naturally there was no popular vote on the calling of the convention which drafted the Constitution. Election of delegates by state legislatures was the constitutional method under the Articles of Confederation, and had been the method long established in this country. Delegates to the Albany Congress, the Stamp Act Congress, the First Continental Congress, the Second Continental Congress, and subsequent congresses under the Articles were all elected by state legislatures, not by the people. Even the Articles of Confederation had been sanctioned by state legislatures, not by popular vote. This is not to say that the Constitutional Convention should not have been elected directly by the people, but only that such a procedure would have been unusual at the time. Some of the opponents of the Constitution later stressed, without avail, the fact that the Convention had not been directly elected. But at the time the Convention met, the people in general seemed to be about as much concerned over the fact that they had not elected the delegates as the people of this

country are now concerned over the fact that they do not elect our delegates to the United Nations.

4. Present evidence seems to indicate that there were no "propertyless masses" who were excluded from the suffrage at the time. Most men were middle-class farmers who owned realty and were qualified voters, and, as the men in the Convention said, mechanics had always voted in the cities. Until credible evidence proves otherwise, we can assume that state legislatures were fairly representative at the time. We cannot condone the fact that a few men were probably disfranchised by prevailing property qualifications, but it makes a great deal of difference to an interpretation of the Constitution whether the disfranchised comprised ninety-five per cent of the adult men or only five per cent. Figures which give percentages of voters in terms of the entire population are misleading, since less than twenty per cent of the people were adult men. And finally, the voting qualifications favored realty, not personalty.

5. If the members of the Convention were directly interested in the outcome of their work and expected to derive benefits from the establishment of the new system, so also did most of the people of the country. We have many statements to the effect that the people in general expected substantial benefits from the labors of the Convention.

6. The Constitution was not just an economic document, although economic factors were undoubtedly important. Since most of the people were middle-class and had private property, practically everybody was interested in the protection of property. A constitution which did not protect property would have been rejected without any question, for the American people had fought the Revolution for the preservation of life, liberty, and property. Many people believed that the Constitution did not go far enough to protect property, and they wrote these views into the amendments to the Constitution. But property was not the only concern of those who wrote and ratified the Constitution, and we would be doing a grave injustice to the political sagacity of the Founding Fathers if we assumed that property or personal gain was their only motive.

7. Naturally the delegates recognized that the protection of property was important under government, but they also recognized that personal rights were equally important. In fact, persons and property were usually bracketed together as the chief objects of government protection.

8. If three-fourths of the adult males failed to vote on the election of delegates to ratifying conventions, this fact signified indifference, not disfranchisement. We must not confuse those who could *not* vote with those who *could* vote but failed to exercise their right. Many men at the time bewailed the fact that only a small portion of the voters ever exercised their prerogative. But this in itself should stand as evidence that the conflict over the Constitution was not very bitter, for if these people had felt strongly one way or the other, more of them would have voted.

Even if we deny the evidence which I have presented and insist that American society was undemocratic in 1787, we must still accept the fact that the men who wrote the Constitution believed that they were writing it for a democratic society. They did not hide behind an iron curtain of secrecy and devise the kind of conservative government that they wanted without regard to the views and interests of "the people." More than anything else, they were aware that "the people" would have to ratify what they proposed, and that therefore any government which would be acceptable to the people must of necessity incorporate much of what was customary at the time. The men at Philadelphia were practical politicians, not political theorists. They recognized the multitude of different ideas and interests that had to be reconciled and compromised before a constitution would be acceptable. They were far too practical, and represented far too many clashing interests themselves, to fashion a government weighted in favor of personalty or to believe that the people would adopt such a government.

9. If the Constitution was ratified by a vote of only one-sixth of the adult men, that again demonstrates indifference and not disfranchisement. Of the one-fourth of the adult males who voted, nearly two-thirds favored the Constitution. Present evidence does not permit us to say what the popular vote was except as it was measured by the votes of the ratifying conventions.

10. Until we know what the popular vote was, we cannot say that it is questionable whether a majority of the voters in several states favored the Constitution. Too many delegates were sent uninstructed. Neither can we count the towns which did not send delegates on the side of those opposed to the Constitution. Both items would signify indifference rather than sharp conflict over ratification.

11. The ratifying conventions were elected for the specific purpose of adopting or rejecting the Constitution. The people in general had anywhere from several weeks to several months to decide the question. If they did not like the new government, or if they did not know whether they liked it, they could have voted *no* and there would have been no Constitution. Naturally the leaders in the ratifying conventions represented the same interests as the members of the Constitutional Convention—mainly realty and some personalty. But they also represented their constituents in these same interests, especially realty.

12. If the conflict over ratification had been between substantial personalty interests on the one hand and small farmers and debtors on the other, there would not have been a constitution. The small farmers comprised such an overwhelming percentage of the voters that they could have rejected the new government without any trouble. Farmers and debtors are not synonymous terms and should not be confused as such.

A town-by-town or county-by-county record of the vote would show clearly how the farmers voted.

13. The Constitution was created about as much by the whole people as any government could be which embraced a large area and depended on representation rather than on direct participation. It was also created in part by the states, for as the *Records* show, there was strong state sentiment at the time which had to be appeased by compromise. And it was created by compromising a whole host of interests throughout the country, without which compromises it could never have been adopted.

14. If the intellectual historians are correct, we cannot explain the Constitution without considering the psychological factors also. Men are motivated by what they believe as well as by what they have. Sometimes their actions can be explained on the basis of what they hope to have or hope that their children will have. Madison understood this fact when he said that the universal hope of acquiring property tended to dispose people to look favorably upon property. It is even possible that some men support a given economic system when they themselves have nothing to gain by it. So we would want to know what the people in 1787 thought of their class status. Did workers and small farmers believe that they were lower-class, or did they, as many workers do now, consider themselves middle-class? Were the common people trying to eliminate the Washingtons, Adamses, Hamiltons, and Pinckneys, or were they trying to join them?

As did Beard's fourteen conclusions, these fourteen suggestions really add up to two major propositions: the Constitution was adopted in a society which was fundamentally democratic, not undemocratic; and it was adopted by a people who were primarily middle-class property owners, especially farmers who owned realty, not just by the owners of personalty. At present these points seem to be justified by the evidence, but if better evidence in the future disproves or modifies them, we must accept that evidence and change our interpretation accordingly.

After this critical analysis, we should at least not begin future research on this period of American history with the illusion that the Beard thesis of the Constitution is valid. If historians insist on accepting the Beard thesis in spite of this analysis, however, they must do so with the full knowledge that their acceptance is founded on "an act of faith," not an analysis of historical method, and that they are indulging in a "noble dream," not history.

The founding
fathers:

Richard Hofstadter   realists

WHEREVER *the real power in a government lies, there is the danger of oppression. In our Government the real power lies in the majority of the community.* . . . JAMES MADISON

POWER *naturally grows . . . because human passions are insatiable. But that power alone can grow which already is too great; that which is unchecked; that which has no equal power to control it.* JOHN ADAMS

Long ago Horace White observed that the Constitution of the United States "is based upon the philosophy of Hobbes and the religion of Calvin. It assumes that the natural state of mankind is a state of war, and that the carnal mind is at enmity with God." Of course the Constitution was founded more upon experience than any such abstract theory; but it was also an event in the intellectual history of Western civilization. The men who drew up the Constitution in Philadelphia during the summer of 1787 had a vivid Calvinistic sense of human evil and damnation and believed with Hobbes that men are selfish and contentious. They were men of affairs, merchants, lawyers, planter-businessmen, speculators, investors. Having seen human nature on display in the market place, the courtroom, the legislative chamber, and in every secret path and alleyway where wealth and power are courted, they felt they knew it in all its frailty. To them a human being was an atom of self-interest. They did not believe in man, but they did believe in the power of a good political constitution to control him.

This may be an abstract notion to ascribe to practical men, but it follows the language that the Fathers themselves used. General Knox, for example, wrote in disgust to Washington after the Shays Rebellion that Americans were, after all, "men—actual men possessing all the turbulent passions belonging to that animal." Throughout the secret discussions at the Constitutional Convention it was clear that this distrust of man was first and foremost a distrust of the common man and democratic rule. As the Revolution took away the restraining hand of the British government, old colonial grievances of farmers, debtors, and squatters against merchants, investors, and large landholders had flared up anew; the lower orders took advantage of new democratic constitutions in several states, and the possessing classes were frightened. The members of the Constitutional Convention were concerned to create a government that could not only regulate commerce and pay its debts but also prevent currency inflation and stay laws, and check such uprisings as the Shays Rebellion.

Cribbing and confining the popular spirit that had been at large since 1776 were essential to the purposes of the new Constitution. Edmund Randolph, saying to the Convention that the evils from which the country suffered originated in "the turbulence and follies of democracy," and that the great danger lay in "the democratic parts of our constitutions"; Elbridge Gerry, speaking of democracy as "the worst of all political evils"; Roger Sherman, hoping that "the people . . . have as little to do as may be about the government"; William Livingston, saying that "the people have ever been and ever will be unfit to retain the exercise of power in their own hands"; George Washington, the presiding officer, urging the delegates not to produce a document of which they themselves could not approve simply in order to "please the people"; Hamilton, charging that the "turbulent and changing" masses "seldom judge or determine right" and advising a permanent governmental body to "check the imprudence of democracy"; the wealthy young planter Charles Pinckney, proposing that no one be president who was not worth at least one hundred thousand dollars—all these were quite representative of the spirit in which the problems of government were treated.

Democratic ideas are most likely to take root among discontented and oppressed classes, rising middle classes, or perhaps some sections of an old, alienated, and partially disinherited aristocracy, but they do not appeal to a privileged class that is still amplifying its privileges. With a half-dozen exceptions at the most, the men of the Philadelphia Convention were sons of men who had considerable position and wealth, and as a group they had advanced well beyond their fathers. Only one of them, William Few of Georgia, could be said in any sense to represent the yeoman farmer class which constituted the overwhelming majority of the free population. In the late eighteenth century "the better kind of people" found themselves set off from the mass by a hundred visible, tangible, and audible distinctions of dress, speech, manners, and education. There was a continuous lineage of upper-class contempt, from pre-Revolutionary Tories like Peggy Hutchinson, the Governor's daughter, who wrote one day: "The dirty mob was all about me as I drove into town," to a Federalist like Hamilton, who candidly disdained the people. Mass unrest was often received in the spirit of young Gouverneur Morris: "The mob begin to think and reason. Poor reptiles! . . . They bask in the sun, and ere noon they will bite, depend upon it. The gentry begin to fear this." Nowhere in America or Europe—not even among the great liberated thinkers of the Enlightenment—did democratic ideas appear respectable to the cultivated classes. Whether the Fathers looked to the cynically illuminated intellectuals of contemporary Europe or to their own Christian heritage of the idea of original sin, they found quick confirmation of the notion that man is an unregenerate rebel who has to be controlled.

And yet there was another side to the picture. The Fathers were intellectual heirs of seventeenth-century English republicanism with its opposition to arbitrary rule and faith in popular sovereignty. If they feared the advance of democracy, they also had misgivings about turning to the extreme right. Having recently experienced a bitter revolutionary struggle with an external power beyond their control, they were in no mood to follow Hobbes to his conclusion that any kind of government must be accepted in order to avert the anarchy and terror of a state of nature. They were uneasily aware that both military dictatorship and a return to monarchy were being seriously discussed in some quarters—the former chiefly among unpaid and discontented army officers, the latter in rich and fashionable Northern circles. John Jay, familiar with sentiment among New York's mercantile aristocracy, wrote to Washington, June 27, 1786, that he feared that "the better kind of people (by which I mean the people who are orderly and industrious, who are content with their situations, and not uneasy in their circumstances) will be led, by the insecurity of property, the loss of confidence in their rulers, and the want of public faith and rectitude, to consider the charms of liberty as imaginary and delusive." Such men, he thought, might be prepared for "almost any change that may promise them quiet and security." Washington, who had already repudiated a suggestion that he become a military dictator, agreed, remarking that "we are apt to run from one extreme to the other."

Unwilling to turn their backs upon republicanism, the Fathers also wished to avoid violating the prejudices of the people. "Notwithstanding the oppression and injustice experienced among us from democracy," said George Mason, "the genius of the people is in favor of it, and the genius of the people must be consulted." Mason admitted "that we had been too democratic," but feared that "we should incautiously run into the opposite extreme." James Madison, who has quite rightfully been called the philosopher of the Constitution, told the delegates: "It seems indispensable that the mass of citizens should not be without a voice in making the laws which they are to obey, and in choosing the magistrates who are to administer them." James Wilson, the outstanding jurist of the age, later appointed to the Supreme Court by Washington, said again and again that the ultimate power of government must of necessity reside in the people. This the Fathers commonly accepted, for if government did not proceed from the people, from what other source could it legitimately come? To adopt any other premise not only would be inconsistent with everything they had said against British rule in the past but would open the gates to an extreme concentration of power in the future. Hamilton saw the sharp distinction in the Convention when he said that "the members most tenacious of republicanism were as loud as any in declaiming the vices of democracy." There was no better expression of the dilemma of a man who has no faith in the people but insists that government be based upon them than that of Jeremy Belknap, a New England clergyman, who wrote to a friend: "Let it stand as a principle that government originates from the people; but let the people be taught . . . that they are not able to govern themselves."

II

If the masses were turbulent and unregenerate, and yet if government must be founded upon their suffrage and consent, what could a Constitution-maker do? One thing that the Fathers did not propose to do, because they thought it impossible, was to change the nature of man to conform with a more ideal system. They were inordinately confident that they knew what man always had been and what he always would be. The eighteenth-century mind had great faith in universals. Its method, as Carl Becker has said, was "to go up and down the field of history looking for man in general, the universal man, stripped of the accidents of time and place." Madison declared that the causes of political differences and of the formation of factions were "sown in the nature of man" and could never be eradicated. "It is universally acknowledged," David Hume had written, "that there is a great uniformity among the actions of men, in all nations and ages, and that human nature remains still the same, in its principles and operations. The same motives always produce the same actions. The same events always follow from the same causes."

Since man was an unchangeable creature of self-interest, it would not do to leave anything to his capacity for restraint. It was too much to expect that vice could be checked by virtue; the Fathers relied instead upon checking vice with vice. Madison once objected during the Convention that Gouverneur Morris was "forever inculcating the utter political depravity of men and the necessity of opposing one vice and interest to another vice and interest." And yet Madison himself in the *Federalist* number 51 later set forth an excellent statement of the same thesis:

Ambition must be made to counteract ambition. . . . It may be a reflection on human nature that such devices should be necessary to control the abuses of government. But what is government itself, but the greatest of all reflections on human nature? If men were angels, no government would be necessary. . . . In framing a government which is to be administered by men over men, the great difficulty lies in this: you must first enable the government to control the governed; and in the next place oblige it to control itself.

Political economists of the laissez-faire school were saying that private vices could be public benefits, that an economically beneficent result would be providentially or "naturally" achieved if self-interest were left free from state interference and allowed to pursue its ends. But the Fathers were not so optimistic about politics. If, in a state that lacked constitutional balance, one class or one interest gained control, they believed, it would surely plunder all other interests. The Fathers, of course, were especially fearful that the poor would plunder the rich, but most of them would probably have admitted that the rich, unrestrained, would also plunder the poor. Even Gouverneur Morris, who stood as close to the extreme aristocratic position as candor and intelligence would allow, told the Convention: "Wealth tends to corrupt the mind and to nourish its love of power, and to stimulate it to oppression. History proves this to be the spirit of the opulent."

What the Fathers wanted was known as "balanced government," an idea at least as old as Aristotle and Polybius. This ancient conception had won new sanction in the eighteenth century, which was dominated intellectually by the scientific work of Newton, and in which mechanical metaphors sprang as naturally to men's minds as did biological metaphors in the Darwinian atmosphere of the late nineteenth century. Men had found a rational order in the universe and they hoped that it could be transferred to politics, or, as John Adams put it, that governments could be "erected on the simple principles of nature." Madison spoke in the most precise Newtonian language when he said that such a "natural" government must be so constructed "that its several constituent parts may, by their mutual relations, be the means of keeping each other in their proper places." A properly designed state, the Fathers believed, would check interest with interest, class with class, faction with faction, and one branch of government with another in a harmonious system of mutual frustration.

In practical form, therefore, the quest of the Fathers reduced primarily to a search for constitutional devices that would force various interests to check and control one another. Among those who favored the federal Constitution three such devices were distinguished.

The first of these was the advantage of a federated government in maintaining order against popular uprisings or majority rule. In a single state a faction might arise and take complete control by force; but if the states were bound in a federation, the central government could step in and prevent it. Hamilton quoted Montesquieu: "Should a popular insurrection happen in one of the confederate states, the others are able to quell it." Further, as Madison argued in the *Federalist* number 10, a majority would be the most dangerous of all factions that might arise, for the majority would be the most capable of gaining complete ascendancy. If the political society were very extensive, however, and embraced a large number and variety of local interests, the citizens who shared a common majority interest "must be rendered by their number and local situation, unable to concert and carry into effect their schemes of oppression." The chief propertied interests would then be safer from "a rage for paper money, for an abolition of debts, for an equal division of property, or for any other improper or wicked project."

The second advantage of good constitutional government resided in the mechanism of representation itself. In a small direct democracy the unstable passions of the people would dominate lawmaking; but a representative government, as Madison said, would "refine and enlarge the public views by passing them through the medium of a chosen body of citizens." Representatives chosen by the people were wiser and more deliberate than the people themselves in mass assemblage. Hamilton frankly anticipated a kind of syndical paternalism in which the wealthy and dominant members of every trade or industry would represent the others in politics. Merchants, for example, were "the natural representatives" of their employees and of the mechanics and artisans they dealt with. Hamilton expected that Congress, "with too few exceptions to have any influence on the spirit of the government, will be composed of landholders, merchants, and men of the learned professions."

The third advantage of the government the Fathers were designing was pointed out most elaborately by John Adams in the first volume of his *Defence of the Constitutions of Government of the United States of America*, which reached Philadelphia while the Convention was in session and was cited with approval by several delegates. Adams believed that the aristocracy and the democracy must be made to neutralize each other. Each element should be given its own house of the legislature, and over both houses there should be set a capable, strong, and impartial executive armed with the veto power. This split assembly would contain within itself an organic check and would be capable of self-control under the governance of the executive. The whole system was to be capped by an independent judiciary. The inevitable tendency of the rich and the poor to plunder each other would be kept in hand.

III

It is ironical that the Constitution, which Americans venerate so deeply, is based upon a political theory that at one crucial point stands in direct antithesis to the main stream of American democratic faith. Modern American folklore assumes that democracy and liberty are all but identical, and when democratic writers take the trouble to make the distinction, they usually assume that democracy is necessary to liberty. But the Founding Fathers thought that the liberty with which they were most concerned was menaced by democracy. In their minds liberty was linked not to democracy but to property.

What did the Fathers mean by liberty? What did Jay mean when he spoke of "the charms of liberty"? Or Madison when he declared that to destroy liberty in order to destroy factions would be a remedy worse than the disease? Certainly the men who met at Philadelphia were not interested in extending liberty to those classes in America, the Negro slaves and the indentured servants, who were most in need of it, for slavery was recognized in the organic structure of the Constitution and indentured servitude was no concern of the Convention. Nor was the regard of the delegates for civil liberties any too tender. It was the opponents of the Constitution who were most active in demanding such vital liberties as freedom of religion, freedom of speech and press, jury trial, due process, and protection from "unreasonable searches and seizures." These guarantees had to be incorporated in the first ten amendments because the Convention neglected to put them in the original document. Turning to economic issues, it was not freedom of trade in the modern sense that the Fathers were striving for. Although they did not believe in impeding trade unnecessarily, they felt that failure to regulate it was one of the central weaknesses of the Articles of Confederation, and they stood closer to the mercantilists than to Adam Smith. Again, liberty to them did not mean free access to the nation's unappropriated wealth. At least fourteen of them were land speculators. They did not believe in the right of the squatter to occupy unused land, but rather in the right of the absentee owner or speculator to pre-empt it.

The liberties that the constitutionalists hoped to gain were chiefly negative. They wanted freedom from fiscal uncertainty and irregularities in the currency, from trade wars among the states, from economic discrimination by more powerful foreign governments, from attacks on the creditor class or on property, from popular insurrection. They aimed to create a government that would act as an honest broker among a variety of propertied interests, giving them all protection from their common enemies and preventing any one of them from becoming too powerful. The Convention was a fraternity of types of absentee ownership. All property should be permitted to have its proportionate voice in government. Individual property interests might have to be sacrificed at times, but only for the community of propertied interests. Freedom for property would result in liberty for men—perhaps not for all men, but at least for all worthy men. Because men have different faculties and abilities, the Fathers believed, they acquire different amounts of property. To protect property is only to protect men in the exercise of their natural faculties. Among the many liberties, therefore, freedom to hold and dispose property is paramount. Democracy, unchecked rule by the masses, is sure to bring arbitrary redistribution of property, destroying the very essence of liberty.

The Fathers' conception of democracy, shaped by their practical experience with the aggressive dirt farmers in the American states and the urban mobs of the Revolutionary period, was supplemented by their reading in history and political science. Fear of what Madison called "the superior force of an interested and overbearing majority" was the dominant emotion aroused by their study of historical examples. The chief examples of republics were among the city-states of antiquity, medieval Europe, and early modern times. Now, the history of these republics—a history, as Hamilton said, "of perpetual vibration between the extremes of tyranny and anarchy"—was alarming. Further, most of the men who had overthrown the liberties of republics had "begun their career by paying an obsequious court to the people; commencing demagogues and ending tyrants."

All the constitutional devices that the Fathers praised in their writings were attempts to guarantee the future of the United States against the "turbulent" political cycles of previous republics. By "democracy," they meant a system of government which directly expressed the will of the majority of the people, usually through such an assemblage of the people as was possible in the small area of the city-state.

A cardinal tenet in the faith of the men who made the Constitution was the belief that democracy can never be more than a transitional stage in government, that it always evolves into either a tyranny (the rule of the rich demagogue who has patronized the mob) or an aristocracy (the original leaders of the democratic elements). "Remember," wrote the dogmatic John Adams in one of his letters to John Taylor of Caroline, "democracy never lasts long. It soon wastes, exhausts, and murders itself. There never was a democracy yet that did not commit suicide." Again:

If you give more than a share in the sovereignty to the democrats, that is, if you give them the command or preponderance in the . . . legislature, they will vote all property out of the hands of you aristocrats, and if they let you escape with your lives, it will be more humanity, consideration, and generosity than any triumphant democracy ever displayed since the creation. And what will follow? The aristocracy among the democrats will take your places, and treat their fellows as severely and sternly as you have treated them.

Government, thought the Fathers, is based on property. Men who have no property lack the necessary stake in an orderly society to make stable or reliable citizens. Dread of the propertyless masses of the towns was all but universal. George Washington, Gouverneur Morris, John Dickinson, and James Madison spoke of their anxieties about the urban working class that might arise some time in the future—"men without property and principle," as Dickinson described them—and even the democratic Jefferson shared this prejudice. Madison, stating the problem, came close to anticipating the modern threats to conservative republicanism from both communism and fascism:

> In future times, a great majority of the people will not only be without landed but any other sort of property. These will either combine, under the influence of their common situation—in which case the rights of property and the public liberty will not be secure in their hands—or, what is more probable, they will become the tools of opulence and ambition, in which case there will be equal danger on another side.

What encouraged the Fathers about their own era, however, was the broad dispersion of landed property. The small land-owning farmers had been troublesome in recent years, but there was a general conviction that under a properly made Constitution a *modus vivendi* could be worked out with them. The possession of moderate plots of property presumably gave them a sufficient stake in society to be safe and responsible citizens under the restraints of balanced government. Influence in government would be proportionate to property: merchants and great landholders would be dominant, but small property-owners would have an independent and far from negligible voice. It was "politic as well as just," said Madison, "that the interests and rights of every class should be duly represented and understood in the public councils," and John Adams declared that there could be "no free government without a democratical branch in the constitution."

The farming element already satisfied the property requirements for suffrage in most of the states, and the Fathers generally had no quarrel with their enfranchisement. But when they spoke of the necessity of founding government upon the consent of "the people," it was only these small property-holders that they had in mind. For example, the famous Virginia Bill of Rights, written by George Mason, explicitly defined those eligible for suffrage as all men "having sufficient evidence of permanent common interest with and attachment to the community"— which meant, in brief, sufficient property.

However, the original intention of the Fathers to admit the yeoman into an important but sharply limited partnership in affairs of state could not be perfectly realized. At the time the Constitution was made, Southern planters and Northern merchants were setting their differences aside in order to meet common dangers—from radicals within and more powerful nations without. After the Constitution was adopted, conflict between the ruling classes broke out anew, especially after powerful planters were offended by the favoritism of Hamilton's policies to Northern commercial interests. The planters turned to the farmers to form an agrarian alliance, and for more than half a century this powerful coalition embraced the bulk of the articulate interests of the country. As time went on, therefore, the main stream of American political conviction deviated more and more from the antidemocratic position of the Constitution-makers. Yet, curiously, their general satisfaction with the Constitution together with their growing nationalism made Americans deeply reverent of the founding generation, with the result that as it grew stronger, this deviation was increasingly overlooked.

There is common agreement among modern critics that the debates over the Constitution were carried on at an intellectual level that is rare in politics, and that the Constitution itself is one of the world's masterpieces of practical statecraft. On other grounds there has been controversy. At the very beginning contemporary opponents of the Constitution foresaw an apocalyptic destruction of local government and popular institutions, while conservative Europeans of the old regime thought the young American Republic was a dangerous leftist experiment. Modern critical scholarship, which reached a high point in Charles A. Beard's *An Economic Interpretation of the Constitution of the United States,* started a new turn in the debate. The antagonism, long latent, between the philosophy of the Constitution and the philosophy of American democracy again came into the open. Professor Beard's work appeared in 1913 at the peak of the Progressive era, when the muckraking fever was still high; some readers tended to conclude from his findings that the Fathers were selfish reactionaries who do not deserve their high place in American esteem. Still more recently, other writers, inverting this logic, have used Beard's facts to praise the Fathers for their opposition to "democracy" and as an argument for returning again to the idea of a "republic."

In fact, the Fathers' image of themselves as moderate republicans standing between political extremes was quite accurate. They were impelled by class motives more than pietistic writers like to admit, but they were also controlled, as Professor Beard himself has recently emphasized, by a statesmanlike sense of moderation and a scrupulously republican philosophy. Any attempt, however, to tear their ideas out of the eighteenth-century context is sure to make them seem starkly reactionary. Consider, for example, the favorite maxim of John Jay: "The people who own the country ought to govern it." To the Fathers this was simply a swift axiomatic statement of the stake-in-society theory of political rights, a moderate conservative position under eighteenth-century conditions of property distribution in America. Under modern property relations this maxim demands a drastic restriction of the base of political power. A large portion of the modern middle class—and it is the strength of this class upon which balanced government depends—is propertyless; and the urban proletariat, which the Fathers so greatly feared, is almost one half the population. Further, the separation of ownership from control that has come with the corporation deprives Jay's maxim of twentieth-century meaning even for many propertied people. The six hundred thousand stockholders of the American Telephone & Telegraph Company not only do not acquire political power by virtue of their stock-ownership, but they do not even acquire economic power: they cannot control their own company.

From a humanistic standpoint there is a serious dilemma in the philosophy of the Fathers, which derives from their conception of man. They thought man was a creature of rapacious self-interest, and yet they wanted him to be free—free, in essence, to contend, to engage in an um-pired strife, to use property to get property. They accepted the mercan-tile image of life as an eternal battleground, and assumed the Hobbesian war of each against all; they did not propose to put an end to this war, but merely to stabilize it and make it less murderous. They had no hope and they offered none for any ultimate organic change in the way men conduct themselves. The result was that while they thought self-interest the most dangerous and unbrookable quality of man, they necessarily underwrote it in trying to control it. They succeeded in both respects: under the competitive capitalism of the nineteenth century America con-tinued to be an arena for various grasping and contending interests, and the federal government continued to provide a stable and acceptable me-dium within which they could contend; further, it usually showed the wholesome bias on behalf of property which the Fathers expected. But no man who is as well abreast of modern science as the Fathers were of eighteenth-century science believes any longer in unchanging human nature. Modern humanistic thinkers who seek for a means by which society may transcend eternal conflict and rigid adherence to property rights as its integrating principles can expect no answer in the philoso-phy of balanced government as it was set down by the Constitution-makers of 1787.

The founding
fathers:

Stanley Elkins and Eric McKitrick   activists

The Anti-Federalists . . . were transfixed by the specter of power. It was not the power of the aristocracy that they feared, but power of any kind, democratic or otherwise, that they could not control for themselves. Their chief concern was to keep governments as limited

Reprinted with permission from *Political Science Quarterly*, Vol. LXXVI, No. 2, pp. 200–216.

and as closely tied to local interests as possible. Their minds could not embrace the concept of a national interest which they themselves might share and which could transcend their own parochial concerns. Republican government that went beyond the compass of state boundaries was something they could not imagine. Thus the chief difference between Federalists and Anti-Federalists had little to do with "democracy" (George Clinton and Patrick Henry were no more willing than Gouverneur Morris to trust the innate virtue of the people), but rather in the Federalists' conviction that there was such a thing as national interest and that a government could be established to care for it which was fully in keeping with republican principles. To the Federalists this was not only possible but absolutely necessary, if the nation was to avoid a future of political impotence, internal discord, and in the end foreign intervention. So far so good. But still, exactly how did such convictions get themselves generated?

Merrill Jensen has argued that the Federalists, by and large, were reluctant revolutionaries who had feared the consequences of a break with England and had joined the Revolution only when it was clear that independence was inevitable. The argument is plausible; few of the men most prominent later on as Federalists had been quite so hot for revolution in the very beginning as Patrick Henry and Samuel Adams. But this may not be altogether fair; Adams and Henry were already veteran political campaigners at the outbreak of hostilities, while the most vigorous of the future Federalists were still mere youngsters. The argument, indeed, could be turned entirely around: the source of Federalist, or nationalist, energy was not any "distaste" for the Revolution on these men's part, but rather their profound and growing involvement in it.

Much depends here on the way one pictures the Revolution. In the beginning it simply consisted of a number of state revolts loosely directed by the Continental Congress; and for many men, absorbed in their effort to preserve the independence of their own states, it never progressed much beyond that stage even in the face of invasion. But the Revolution had another aspect, one which developed with time and left a deep imprint on those connected with it, and this was its character as a continental war effort. If there is any one feature that most unites the future leading supporters of the Constitution, it was their close engagement with this continental aspect of the Revolution. A remarkably large number of these someday Federalists were in the Continental Army, served as diplomats or key administrative officers of the Confederation government, or, as members of Congress, played leading roles on those committees primarily responsible for the conduct of the war.

Merrill Jensen has compiled two lists, with nine names in each, of the men whom he considers to have been the leading spirits of the Federalists and Anti-Federalists respectively. It would be well to have a good look at this sample. The Federalists—Jensen calls them "nationalists" —were Robert Morris, John Jay, James Wilson, Alexander Hamilton, Henry Knox, James Duane, George Washington, James Madison, and Gouverneur Morris. Washington, Knox, and Hamilton were deeply involved in Continental military affairs; Robert Morris was Superintendent of Finance; Jay was president of the Continental Congress and minister plenipotentiary to Spain (he would later be appointed Secretary for Foreign Affairs); Wilson, Duane, and Gouverneur Morris were members of Congress, all three being active members of the war committees. The Anti-Federalist group presents a very different picture. It consisted of Samuel Adams, Patrick Henry, Richard Henry Lee, George Clinton, James Warren, Samuel Bryan, George Bryan, George Mason, and Elbridge Gerry. Only three of these—Gerry, Lee, and Adams—served in Congress, and the latter two fought consistently against any effort to give Congress executive powers. Their constant pre-occupation was state sovereignty rather than national efficiency. Henry and Clinton were active war governors, concerned primarily with state rather than national problems, while Warren, Mason, and the two Bryans were essentially state politicians.

The age difference between these two groups is especially striking. The Federalists were on the average ten to twelve years younger than the Anti-Federalists. At the outbreak of the Revolution George Washington, at 44, was the oldest of the lot; six were under 35 and four were in their twenties. Of the Anti-Federalists, only three were under 40 in 1776, and one of these, Samuel Bryan, the son of George Bryan, was a boy of 16.

This age differential takes on a special significance when it is related to the career profiles of the men concerned. Nearly half of the Federalist group—Gouverneur Morris, Madison, Hamilton, and Knox—quite literally saw their careers launched in the Revolution. The remaining five —Washington, Jay, Duane, Wilson, and Robert Morris—though established in public affairs beforehand, became nationally known after 1776 and the wide public recognition which they subsequently achieved came first and foremost through their identification with the continental war effort. All of them had been united in an experience, and had formed commitments, which dissolved provincial boundaries; they had come to full public maturity in a setting which enabled ambition, public service, leadership, and self-fulfillment to be conceived, for each in his way, with a grandeur of scope unknown to any previous generation. The careers of the Anti-Federalists, on the other hand, were not only state-centered but—aside from those of Clinton, Gerry, and the young Bryan —rested heavily on events that preceded rather than followed 1776.

As exemplars of nationalist energy, two names in Professor Jensen's sample that come most readily to mind are those of Madison and Hamilton. The story of each shows a wonderfully pure line of consistency. James Madison, of an influential Virginia family but with no apparent career plans prior to 1774, assumed his first public rôle as a member of the Orange County Revolutionary Committee, of which his father was chairman. As a delegate from Orange County he went to the Virginia convention in 1776 and served on the committee that drafted Virginia's new constitution and bill of rights. He served in the Virginia Assembly in 1776 and 1777 but failed of re-election partly because he refused to treat his constituents to whisky. (He obviously did not have the right talents for a state politician.) In recognition of Madison's services, however, the Assembly elected him to the Governor's Council, where he served from 1778 to 1780. Patrick Henry was then Governor; the two men did not get on well and in time became bitter political enemies. At this period Madison's primary concern was with supplying and equipping the Continental Army, a concern not shared to his satisfaction by enough of his colleagues. It was then, too, that he had his first experience with finance and the problems of paper money. He was elected to the Continental Congress in 1780, and as a member of the Southern Committee was constantly preoccupied with the military operations of Nathanael Greene. The inefficiency and impotence of Congress pained him unbearably. The Virginia Assembly took a strong stand against federal taxation which Madison ignored, joining Hamilton in the unsuccessful effort to persuade the states to accept the impost of 1783. From the day he entered politics up to that time, the energies of James Madison were involved in continental rather than state problems—problems of supply, enlistment, and finance—and at every point his chief difficulties came from state parochialism, selfishness, and lack of imagination. His nationalism was hardly accidental.

The career line of Alexander Hamilton, *mutatis mutandis*, is functionally interchangeable with that of James Madison. Ambitious, full of ability, but a young man of no family and no money, Hamilton arrived in New York from the provinces at the age of 17 and in only two years would be catapulted into a brilliant career by the Revolution. At 19 he became a highly effective pamphleteer while still a student at King's College, was captain of an artillery company at 21, serving with distinction in the New York and New Jersey campaigns, and in 1777 was invited to join Washington's staff as a lieutenant-colonel. He was quickly accepted by as brilliant and aristocratic a set of youths as could be found in the country. As a staff officer he became all too familiar with the endless difficulties of keeping the Continental Army in the field from 1777 to 1780. With his marriage to Elizabeth Schuyler in 1780 he was delightedly welcomed into one of New York's leading families, and his sage advice to his father-in-law and Robert Morris on matters of finance and paper money won him the reputation of a financial expert with men who knew an expert when they saw one. He had an independent command at York-town. He became Treasury representative in New York in 1781, was elected to Congress in 1782, and worked closely with Madison in the fruitless and discouraging effort to create a national revenue in the face of state particularism. In the summer of 1783 he quit in despair and went back to New York. Never once throughout all this period had Alexander Hamilton been involved in purely state affairs. His career had been a continental one, and as long as the state-centered George Clinton remained a power in New York, it was clear that this was the only kind that could have any real meaning for him. As with James Madison, Hamilton's nationalism was fully consistent with all the experience he had ever had in public life, experience whose sole meaning had been derived from the Revolution. The experience of the others—for instance that of John Jay and Henry Knox—had had much the same quality; Knox had moved from his bookstore to the command of Washington's artillery in little more than a year, while Jay's public career began with the agitation just prior to the Revolution and was a story of steady advancement in continental affairs from that time forward.

The logic of these careers, then, was in large measure tied to a chronology which did not apply in the same way to all the men in public life during the two decades of the 1770's and 1780's. A significant proportion of relative newcomers, with prospects initially modest, happened to have their careers opened up at a particular time and in such a way that their very public personalities came to be staked upon the national quality of the experience which had formed them. In a number of outstanding cases energy, initiative, talent, and ambition had combined with a conception of affairs which had grown immense in scope and promise by the close of the Revolution. There is every reason to think that a contraction of this scope, in the years that immediately followed, operated as a powerful challenge.

The stages through which the constitutional movement proceeded in the 1780's add up to a fascinating story in political management, marked by no little élan and dash. That movement, viewed in the light of the Federalist leaders' commitment to the Revolution, raises some nice points as to who were the "conservatives" and who were the "radicals." The spirit of unity generated by the struggle for independence had, in the eyes of those most closely involved in coördinating the effort, lapsed; provincial factions were reverting to the old provincial ways. The impulse to arrest disorder and to revive the flame of revolutionary unity may be pictured in "conservative" terms, but this becomes quite awkward when we look for terms with which to picture the other impulse, so different in nature: the urge to rest, to drift, to turn back the clock.

Various writers have said that the activities of the Federalists during this period had in them a clear element of the conspiratorial. Insofar as this refers to a strong line of political strategy, it correctly locates a key element in the movement. Yet without a growing base of popular dissatisfaction with the status quo, the Federalists could have skulked and plotted forever without accomplishing anything. We now know, thanks to recent scholarship, that numerous elements of the public were only too ripe for change. But the work of organizing such a sentiment was quite another matter; it took an immense effort of will just to get it off the ground. Though it would be wrong to think of the Constitution as something that had to be carried in the face of deep and basic popular opposition, it certainly required a series of brilliant maneuvers to escape the deadening clutch of particularism and inertia. An Anti-Federalist "no" could register on exactly the same plane as a Federalist "yes" while requiring a fraction of the energy. It was for this reason that the Federalists, even though they cannot be said to have circumvented the popular will, did have to use techniques which in their sustained drive, tactical mobility, and risk-taking smacked more than a little of the revolutionary.

By 1781, nearly five years of intimate experience with the war effort had already convinced such men as Washington, Madison, Hamilton, Duane, and Wilson that something had to be done to strengthen the Continental government, at least to the point of providing it with an independent income. The ratification of the Articles of Confederation early in the year (before Yorktown) seemed to offer a new chance, and several promising steps were taken at that time. Congress organized executive departments of war, foreign affairs, and finance to replace unwieldy and inefficient committees; Robert Morris was appointed Superintendent of Finance; and a 5 per cent impost was passed which Congress urged the states to accept.

By the fall of 1782, however, the surge for increased efficiency had lost the greater part of its momentum. Virginia had changed its mind about accepting the impost, Rhode Island having been flatly opposed all along, and it became apparent that as soon as the treaty with England (then being completed) was ratified, the sense of common purpose which the war had created would be drained of its urgency. At this point Hamilton and the Morrises, desperate for a solution, would have been quite willing to use the discontent of an unpaid army as a threat to coerce the states out of their obstructionism, had not Washington refused to lend himself to any such scheme. Madison and Hamilton thereupon joined forces in Congress to work out a revenue bill whose subsidiary benefits would be sufficiently diffuse to gain it general support among the states. But in the end the best that could be managed was a new plan for a 5 per cent impost, the revenues of which would be collected by state-appointed officials. Once more an appeal, drafted by

Madison, was sent to the states urging them to accept the new impost, and Washington wrote a circular in support of it. The effort was in vain. The army, given one month's pay in cash and three in certificates, reluctantly dispersed, and the Confederation government, with no sanctions of coercion and no assured revenues, now reached a new level of impotence. In June, 1783, Alexander Hamilton, preparing to leave Congress to go back to private life, wrote in discouragement and humiliation to Nathanael Greene:

There is so little disposition either in or out of Congress to give solidity to our national system that there is no motive to a man to lose his time in the public service, who has no other view than to promote its welfare. Experience must convince us that our present establishments are Utopian before we shall be ready to part with them for better.

Whether or not the years between 1783 and 1786 should be viewed as a "critical period" depends very much on whose angle they are viewed from. Although it was a time of economic depression, the depressed conditions were not felt in all areas of economic life with the same force, nor were they nearly as damaging in some localities as in others; the interdependence of economic enterprise was not then what it would become later on, and a depression in Massachusetts did not necessarily imply one in Virginia, or even in New York. Moreover, there were definite signs of improvement by 1786. Nor can it necessarily be said that government on the state level lacked vitality. Most of the states were addressing their problems with energy and decision. There were problems everywhere, of course, many of them very grave, and in some cases (those of New Jersey and Connecticut in particular) solutions seemed almost beyond the individual state's resources. Yet it would be wrong, as Merrill Jensen points out, to assume that no solutions were possible within the framework which then existed. It is especially important to remember that when most people thought of "the government" they were not thinking of Congress at all, but of their own state legislature. For them, therefore, it was by no means self-evident that the period through which they were living was one of drift and governmental impotence.

But through the eyes of men who had come to view the states collectively as a "country" and to think in continental terms, things looked altogether different. From their viewpoint the Confederation was fast approaching the point of ruin. Fewer and fewer states were meeting their requisition payments, and Congress could not even pay its bills. The states refused to accept any impost which they themselves could not control, and even if all the rest accepted, the continued refusal of New York (which was not likely to change) would render any impost all but valueless. Local fears and jealousies blocked all efforts to establish uniform regulation of commerce, even though some such regulation seemed indispensable. A number of the states, New York in particular, openly ignored the peace treaty with England and passed discriminatory legislation against former Loyalists; consequently England, using as a pretext Congress' inability to enforce the treaty, refused to surrender the northwest posts. Morale in Congress was very low as members complained that lack of a quorum prevented them most of the time from transacting any business; even when a quorum was present, a few negative votes could block important legislation indefinitely. Any significant change, or any substantial increase in the power of Congress, required unanimous approval by the states, and as things then stood this had become very remote. Finally, major states such as New York and Virginia were simply paying less and less attention to Congress. The danger was not so much that of a split with the Confederation—Congress lacked the strength that would make any such "split" seem very urgent—but rather a policy of neglect that would just allow Congress to wither away from inactivity.

These were the conditions that set the stage for a fresh effort—the Annapolis Convention of 1786—to strengthen the continental government. The year before, Madison had arranged a conference between Maryland and Virginia for the regulation of commerce on the Potomac, and its success had led John Tyler and Madison to propose a measure in the Virginia Assembly that would give Congress power to regulate commerce throughout the Confederation. Though nothing came of it, a plan was devised in its place whereby the several states would be invited to take part in a convention to be held at Annapolis in September, 1786, for the purpose of discussing commercial problems. The snapping-point came when delegates from only five states appeared. The rest either distrusted one another's intentions (the northeastern states doubted the southerners' interest in commerce) or else suspected a trick to strengthen the Confederation government at their expense. It was apparent that no serious action could be taken at that time. But the dozen delegates who did come (Hamilton and Madison being in their forefront) were by definition those most concerned over the state of the national government, and they soon concluded that their only hope of saving it lay in some audacious plenary gesture. It was at this meeting, amid the mortification of still another failure, that they planned the Philadelphia Convention.

The revolutionary character of this move—though some writers have correctly perceived it—has been obscured both by the stateliness of historical retrospection and by certain legal peculiarities which allowed the proceeding to appear a good deal less subversive than it actually was. The "report" of the Annapolis meeting was actually a call, drafted by Hamilton and carefully edited by Madison, for delegates of all the states to meet in convention at Philadelphia the following May for the purpose

of revising the Articles of Confederation. Congress itself transmitted the
call, and in so doing was in effect being brought to by-pass its own constituted limits. On the one hand, any effort to change the government
within the rules laid down by the Articles would have required a unanimous approval which could never be obtained. But on the other hand,
the very helplessness which the several states had imposed upon the
central government meant in practice that the states were sovereign and
could do anything they pleased with it. It was precisely this that the nationalists now prepared to exploit: this legal paradox had hithertho prevented the growth of strong loyalty to the existing Confederation and
could presently allow that same Confederation, through the action of
the states, to be undermined in the deceptive odor of legitimacy. Thus
the Beardian school of constitutional thought, for all its errors of economic analysis and its transposing of ideological semantics, has called
attention to one element—the element of subversion—that is actually
entitled to some consideration.

But if the movement had its plotters, balance requires us to add that
the "plot" now had a considerable measure of potential support, and
that the authority against which the plot was aimed had become little
more than a husk. Up to this time every nationalist move, including the
Annapolis Convention, had been easily blocked. But things were now
happening in such a way as to tip the balance and to offer the nationalists for the first time a better-than-even chance of success. There had
been a marked improvement in business, but shippers in Boston, New
York, and Philadelphia were still in serious trouble. Retaliatory measures against Great Britain through state legislation had proved ineffective and useless; there was danger, at the same time, that local manufacturing interests might be successful in pushing through high state
tariffs. In the second place, New York's refusal to reconsider a national
impost, except on terms that would have removed its effectiveness, cut
the ground from under the moderates who had argued that, given only a
little time, everything could be worked out. This did not leave much alternative to a major revision of the national government. Then there
were Rhode Island's difficulties with inflationary paper money. Although that state's financial schemes actually made a certain amount of
sense, they provided the nationalists with wonderful propaganda and
helped to create an image of parochial irresponsibility.

The most decisive event of all was Shays' Rebellion in the fall and
winter of 1786-1787. It was this uprising of hard-pressed rural debtors
in western Massachusetts that frightened moderate people everywhere
and convinced them of the need for drastic remedies against what
looked like anarchy. The important thing was not so much the facts of
the case as the impression which it created outside Massachusetts. The
Shaysites had no intention of destroying legitimate government or of

redistributing property, but the fact that large numbers of people could very well imagine them doing such things added a note of crisis which was all to the Federalists' advantage. Even the level-headed Washington was disturbed, and his apprehensions were played upon quite knowingly by Madison, Hamilton, and Knox in persuading him to attend the Philadelphia Convention. Actually the Federalists and the Shaysites had been driven to action by much the same conditions; in Massachusetts their concern with the depressed state of trade and the tax burden placed them for all practical purposes on the same side, and there they remained from first to last.

Once the balance had been tipped in enough states, to the point of a working consensus on the desirability of change, a second principle came into effect. Unless a state were absolutely opposed—as in the extreme case of Rhode Island—to any change in the Articles of Confederation, it was difficult to ignore the approaching Philadelphia Convention as had been done with the Annapolis Convention: the occasion was taking on too much importance. There was thus the danger, for such a state, of seeing significant decisions made without having its interests consulted. New York, with strong Anti-Federalist biases but also with a strong nationalist undercurrent, was not quite willing to boycott the convention. Governor Clinton's solution was to send as delegates two rigid state particularists, John Yates and Robert Lansing, along with the nationalist Hamilton, to make sure that Hamilton would not accomplish anything.

We have already seen that nineteenth-century habits of thought created a ponderous array of stereotypes around the historic Philadelphia conclave of 1787. Twentieth-century thought and scholarship, on the other hand, had the task of breaking free from them, and to have done so is a noteworthy achievement. And yet one must return to the point that stereotypes themselves require some form of explanation. The legend of a transcendent effort of statesmanship, issuing forth in a miraculously perfect instrument of government, emerges again and again despite all efforts either to conjure it out of existence or to give it some sort of rational linkage with mortal affairs. Why should the legend be so extraordinarily durable, and was there anything so special about the circumstances that set it on its way so unerringly and so soon?

The circumstances *were*, in fact, special; given a set of delegates of well over average ability, the Philadelphia meeting provides a really classic study in the sociology of intellect. Divine accident, though in some measure present in men's doings always, is not required as a part of this particular equation. The key conditions were all present in a pattern that virtually guaranteed for the meeting an optimum of effectiveness. A sufficient number of states were represented so that the delegates could, without strain, realistically picture themselves as thinking, acting, and making decisions in the name of the entire nation. They themselves, moreover, represented interests throughout the country that were diverse enough, and they had enough personal prestige at home, that they could act in the assurance of having their decisions treated at least with respectful attention. There had also been at work a remarkably effective process of self-selection, as to both men and states. Rhode Island ignored the convention, and as a result its position was not even considered there. There were leading state particularists such as Patrick Henry and Richard Henry Lee who were elected as delegates but refused to serve. The Anti-Federalist position, indeed, was hardly represented at all, and the few men who did represent it had surprisingly little to say. Yates and Lansing simply left before the convention was over. Thus a group already predisposed in a national direction could proceed unhampered by the friction of basic opposition in its midst. This made it possible for the delegates to "try on" various alternatives without having to remain accountable for everything they said. At the same time, being relieved from all outside pressures meant that the only way a man could expect to make a real difference in the convention's deliberations was to reach, through main persuasion, other men of considerable ability and experience. Participants and audience were therefore one, and this in itself imposed standards of debate which were quite exacting. In such a setting the best minds in the convention were accorded an authority which they would not have had in political debates aimed at an indiscriminate public.

Thus the elements of secrecy, the general inclination for a national government, and the process whereby the delegates came to terms with their colleagues—appreciating their requirements and adjusting to their interests—all combined to produce a growing esprit de corps. As initial agreements were worked out, it became exceedingly difficult for the Philadelphia delegates not to grow more and more committed to the product of their joint efforts. Indeed, this was in all likelihood the key mechanism, more important than any other in explaining not only the peculiar genius of the main compromises but also the general fitness of the document as a whole. That is, a group of two or more intelligent men who are subject to no cross-pressures and whose principal commitment is to the success of an idea, are perfectly capable—as in our scientific communities of today—of performing what appear to be prodigies of intellect. Moving, as it were, in the same direction with a specific purpose, they can function at maximum efficiency. It was this that the historians of the nineteenth century did in their way see, and celebrated with sweeping rhetorical flourishes, when they took for granted that if an occasion of this sort could not call forth the highest level of statesmanship available, then it was impossible to imagine another that could.

Once the Philadelphia Convention had been allowed to meet and the delegates had managed, after more than three months of work, to hammer out a document that the great majority of them could sign, the political position of the Federalists changed dramatically. Despite the major battles still impending, for practical purposes they now had the initiative. The principal weapon of the Anti-Federalists—inertia—had greatly declined in effectiveness, for with the new program in motion it was no longer enough simply to argue that a new federal government was unnecessary. They would have to take positive steps in blocking it; they would have to arouse the people and convince them that the Constitution represented a positive danger.

Moreover, the Federalists had set the terms of ratification in such a way as to give the maximum advantage to energy and purpose; the key choices, this time, had been so arranged that they would fall right. Only nine states had to ratify before the Constitution would go into effect. Not only would this rule out the possibility of one or two states holding up the entire effort, but it meant that the Confederation would be automatically destroyed as an alternative before the difficult battles in New York and Virginia had to be faced. (By then, Patrick Henry in Virginia would have nothing but a vague alliance with North Carolina to offer as a counter-choice.) Besides, there was good reason to believe that at least four or five states, and possibly as many as seven, could be counted as safe, which meant that serious fighting in the first phase would be limited to two or three states. And finally, conditions were so set that the "snowball" principle would at each successive point favor the Federalists.

As for the actual process of acceptance, ratification would be done through state conventions elected for the purpose. Not only would this circumvent the vested interests of the legislatures and the ruling coteries that frequented the state capitals, but it gave the Federalists two separate chances to make their case—once to the people and once to the conventions. If the elected delegates were not initially disposed to do the desired thing, there was still a chance, after the convention met, of persuading them. Due partly to the hampering factor of transportation and distance, delegates had to have considerable leeway of choice and what amounted to quasi-plenipotentiary powers. Thus there could be no such thing as a fully "instructed" delegation, and members might meanwhile remain susceptible to argument and conversion. The convention device, moreover, enabled the Federalists to run as delegates men who would not normally take part in state politics.

The revolutionary verve and ardor of the Federalists, their resources

of will and energy, their willingness to scheme tirelessly, campaign everywhere, and sweat and agonize over every vote meant in effect that
despite all the hairbreadth squeezes and rigors of the struggle, the Anti-
Federalists would lose every crucial test. There was, to be sure, an Anti-
Federalist effort. But with no program, no really viable commitments,
and little purposeful organization, the Anti-Federalists somehow always
managed to move too late and with too little. They would sit and watch
their great stronghold, New York, being snatched away from them despite a two-to-one Anti-Federalists majority in a convention presided
over by their own chief, George Clinton. To them, the New York Federalists must have seemed possessed of the devil. The Federalists' convention men included Alexander Hamilton, James Duane, John Jay, and
Robert Livingston—who knew, as did everyone else, that the new government was doomed unless Virginia and New York joined it. They insisted
on debating the Constitution section by section instead of as a whole,
which meant that they could out-argue the Anti-Federalists on every sub-
stantive issue and meanwhile delay the vote until New Hampshire and
Virginia had had a chance to ratify. (Madison and Hamilton had a horse
relay system in readiness to rush the Virginia news northward as quickly
as possible.) By the time the New York convention was ready to act, ten
others had ratified, and at the final moment Hamilton and his allies
spread the chilling rumor that New York City was about to secede from
the state. The Anti-Federalists, who had had enough, directed a chosen
number of their delegates to cross over, and solemnly capitulated.

In the end, of course, everyone "crossed over." The speed with which
this occurred once the continental revolutionists had made their point,
and the ease with which the Constitution so soon became an object of
universal veneration, still stands as one of the minor marvels of American history. But the document did contain certain implications, of a
quasi-philosophical nature, that make the reasons for this ready consensus not so very difficult to find. It established a national government
whose basic outlines were sufficiently congenial to the underlying commitments of the whole culture—republicanism and capitalism—that
the likelihood of its being the subject of a true ideological clash was
never very real. That the Constitution should mount guard over the rights
of property—"realty," "personalty," or any other kind—was questioned
by nobody. There had certainly been a struggle, a long and exhausting
one, but we should not be deceived as to its nature. It was not fought on
economic grounds; it was not a matter of ideology; it was not, in the
fullest and most fundamental sense, even a struggle between nationalism and localism. The key struggle was between inertia and energy;
with inertia overcome, everything changed.

There were, of course, lingering objections and misgivings; many of
the problems involved had been genuinely puzzling and difficult; and

there remained doubters who had to be converted. But then the perfect bridge whereby all could become Federalists within a year was the addition of a Bill of Rights. After the French Revolution, anti-constitutionalism in France would be a burning issue for generations; in America, an anti-constitutional party was undreamed of after 1789. With the Bill of Rights, the remaining opponents of the new system could say that, ever watchful of tyranny, they had now got what they wanted. Moreover, the Young Men of the Revolution might at last imagine, after a dozen years of anxiety, that *their* Revolution had been a success.

SUGGESTIONS FOR FURTHER READING

Those interested in exploring the controversy over the constitution further should begin by reading Charles Beard, *An Economic Interpretation of the Constitution* (New York, 1913); only the conclusions are reprinted in this volume. In many ways the best of the books that attack Beard is Forrest McDonald, *We The People: The Economic Origins of the Constitution* (Chicago, 1958). Basing his conclusions on a great deal of research, McDonald tries to show that Beard was wrong in many particulars and that he grossly over-simplified the story. Merrill Jensen, however, in *The New Nation: A History of the United States During the Confederation, 1781–89* (New York, 1950) and Jackson T. Main in *The Anti-Federalists: Critics of the Constitution* (Chapel Hill, 1961) follow Beard in seeing real economic conflict in the period and in the idea that the constitution was a repudiation of the Articles of Confederation and of the Revolution. That the constitution is still controversial can be seen by reading Jackson T. Main's review of *We The People* and McDonald's reply in *William and Mary Quarterly*, XVII (January, 1960), 86–102. For a brief general account of the Confederation and the Constitution period see, Edmund S. Morgan, *The Birth of the Republic, 1763–1789* (Chicago, 1956), a book that plays down the importance of conflict in the period.

III

JEFFERSONIAN ★

AND ★

JACKSONIAN ★

DEMOCRACY ★

The ratification and general acceptance of the Constitution did not eliminate all disagreements in the new nation. Indeed, strong differences of opinion arose within George Washington's cabinet, differences which soon spread to the Congress and, through the public press, to the country at large. The economic program proposed by Washington's strong-willed secretary of the treasury, Alexander Hamilton, was soon opposed by the secretary of state, Thomas Jefferson. In less than a decade after the inauguration of the first administration under the new Constitution disagreements had led to the formation of the nation's first organized political parties. The election of 1800 was clearly a party battle, and Jefferson's newly organized Republican party emerged victorious.

Certainly this was a time of sharp debate and furious party struggle. Yet how significant were the differences which divided the country? In his old age, looking back on the event, Thomas Jefferson called his first election "the revolution of 1800," obviously an assessment which implied vast differences separating him from his opponents. Yet in his first inaugural address, Jefferson minimized the importance of the party conflict from which the country had just emerged. "We are all Republicans, we are all Federalists," he said.

Because Jefferson himself entertained two seemingly

contradictory evaluations of his victory, later historians have been able to agree with him and still disagree among themselves. For some, Jefferson's victory was indeed a revolution; his administration is said to have ushered in a period of agrarian democracy; his victory signalled the defeat of an aristocratic moneyed power. Others argue that Jefferson changed little of the inheritance from the Federalists he had defeated; in truth, they maintain, Jefferson continued the Federalist program.

The Federalist party never recovered from the defeat administered by the Jeffersonians. Perhaps the reason for this was the completeness of the "revolution" of 1800; on the other hand, perhaps the Federalists disappeared because the Republicans had absorbed their program. Yet if almost everyone in the years following the administration of Thomas Jefferson called himself a Jeffersonian, this did not mean that disagreements disappeared. Conflict between parties gave way to strife within the party. The efforts of influential leaders to win a following in the Party led to factions and factions soon developed into new parties. The leader of one such party, calling itself the Democracy, was Andrew Jackson of Tennessee. Elected in 1828, Jackson claimed to be the people's choice and not the candidate of King Caucus. His opponents charged that Jackson was a tyrant, dubbed him "King Andrew I," and organized the Whig party to oppose the Democrats.

How significant were the disagreements which divided Democrats from Whigs? For some scholars the differences were profound, reflecting class conflict between the rich and the poor, the aristocrats and the democrats. For other scholars, the differences were largely rhetorical, mere political bickering against the background of an essentially equalitarian society.

Varying interpretations of Jeffersonian and Jacksonian democracy may be seen in the following selections. Vernon Parrington pictures Jefferson as the philosopher of agrarian democracy. Jefferson feared the development of cities and of urban "mobs" and believed the future of the country should be in the hands of the yeoman farmers. He had faith in the ability of the common man to rule himself and favored decentralized government. As such, Jeffersonianism was the antithesis of Hamiltonianism. Clearly to Parrington, conflict is the central theme of this period. Morton Borden sees a much different Jefferson.

Writing primarily about Jefferson the president, Borden finds him to be a compromiser, a man who on the most important issues was not in any fundamental disagreement with his opponents. Indeed, to Borden, the genius of Jefferson was that he was able to achieve an American consensus.

Arthur Schlesinger, Jr. describes Jacksonian democracy as a part of "that enduring struggle between the business community and the rest of society." There is no doubt in Schlesinger's mind that there was real and important conflict in the Age of Jackson. Bray Hammond does not agree; he decides that there was little dividing the Jacksonians from their opponents. Rather than an ideological struggle between business and the rest of society, the Age of Jackson was marked by a wild scramble of "expectant capitalists" for a place in the economic sun.

The British historian, Marcus Cunliffe, surveys the entire period and seeks to discover an emerging American character. In so doing he finds an American consensus amidst party and sectional differences.

The separation of Americans into different parties and factions matched by sharp and often abusive exchanges among leaders in the newspapers of the day leaves no doubt of differences among Americans during the Age of Jefferson and Jackson. But how significant were these difences? Did they arise from basic economic and social cleavages in American society and reflect fundamental class conflict based on real ideological differences? Or did they reflect only minor disagreements within a general context of fundamental agreement or consensus?

Thomas Jefferson: agrarian reformer

Vernon L. Parrington

The years following the great defeat were disastrous to the party of agrarian democracy. Under the brilliant leadership of Hamilton the Federalists went forward confidently, gaining daily a firmer grip on the machinery of government, and establishing their principles in far-reaching legislative enactments. Their appeal to the wealthy classes, to those who made themselves audible above the clamor, was electrical. Hamilton was the hero of the hour, and the effusive approval that augmented with every added profit to the money brokers, seemed to indicate that the country was enthusiastically behind the Federalist policy. To what despondency the democrats were reduced is revealed in Maclay's *Journal,* with its caustic comment on political measures and motives. But the tide was already at the turn. The ideas let loose by the French Revolution were running swiftly through America, awakening a militant spirit in the democracy. Antagonism to the aristocratic arrogance of Federalism, and disgust at its coercive measures, were mounting fast. If that inchoate discontent were organized and directed by a skillful leader, it might prove strong enough to thrust the Hamiltonian party from power. To that work Thomas Jefferson devoted himself with immense tact and untiring patience. A master of political strategy, he spun his webs far and wide, quietly awaiting the time when the bumbling Federalist bees should range too carelessly in search of their honey. Accepted at once as the leader of agrarian America, he was to prove in the course of a long life the most original and native of the political leaders of the time.

Despite the mass of comment that has gathered about Jefferson, the full reach and significance of his political philosophy remains too little understood. Uncritical praise and censure have obscured or distorted his purpose, and allied his principles with narrow and temporary ends. Detraction will not let him alone. The hostility of his enemies, as a recent biographer has remarked, has frequently taken "the peculiar form of editing his works or writing his life." For this distortion there is, perhaps, more than usual excuse. Certainly Jefferson is the most elusive of our great political leaders. Apparently inconsistent, changing his program with the changing times, he seemed to his enemies devoid of principle, a shallow demagogue who incited the mob in order to dupe the people. One of the most bitterly hated and greatly loved men in the day when love and hate were intense, he was the spokesman of the new order at a time of transition from a dependent monarchical state, to an independent republican state. Back of the figure of Jefferson, with his aristocratic head set on a plebeian frame, was the philosophy of a new age and a new people—an age and a people not yet come to the consistency of maturity, but feeling a way through experiment to solid achievement. Far more completely than any other American of his generation he embodied the idealisms of the great revolution—its faith in human nature, its economic individualism, its conviction that here in America, through the instrumentality of political democracy, the lot of the common man should somehow be made better.

From the distinguished group of contemporary political thinkers Jefferson emerges as the preëminent intellectual, widely read, familiar with ideas, at home in the field of speculation, a critical observer of men and manners. All his life he was a student, and his devotion to his books, running often to fifteen hours a day, recalls the heroic zeal of Puritan scholars. He was trained in the law, but he was too much the intellectual, too curious about all sorts of things, to remain a lawyer. For such a man the appeal of political speculation was irresistible, and early in life he began a wide reading in the political classics that far outweighed Coke and Blackstone in creative influence on his mind. He was equally at home with the English liberals of the seventeenth century and the French liberals of the eighteenth; and if he came eventually to set the French school above the English, it was because he found in the back-to-nature philosophy, with its corollary of an agrarian economics and its emphasis on social well-being, a philosophy more consonant with Virginian experience and his own temperament than Locke's philosophy of property. But he was very far from being a narrow French partisan, as has been often charged; rather he judged old-world theory in the light of its applicability to existing American conditions, and restrained his love of speculation by immediate practical considerations. The man of affairs kept a watchful eye on the philosopher in his study.

In the major doctrines of his political philosophy Jefferson was an amalgam of English and French liberalisms, supplemented by the conscious influence of the American frontier. That fusion early took place in his mind. The first bill that he introduced into the Virginia Assembly, at the age of twenty-six, was a bill to permit slave-owners to manumit their slaves; and his first published pamphlet, issued in 1774, rejected the legal reasoning of John Dickinson and Daniel Dulaney—supporting the parliamentary right to impose external taxation—and took its stand on the doctrine of natural right to local self-government and freedom of trade. When two years later he drafted the Declaration of Independence the fusion was complete. The strong influence of French humanitarianism is revealed in the passage on slavery that was stricken out on the floor of Congress, and more significantly in the change in the familiar phrasing of the several natural rights. Samuel Adams and other followers of Locke had been content with the classical enumeration of life, liberty, and property; but in Jefferson's hands the English doctrine was given a revolutionary shift. The substitution of "pursuit of happiness" for "property" marks a complete break with the Whiggish doctrine of property rights that Locke had bequeathed to the English middle class, and the substitution of a broader sociological conception; and it was this substitution that gave to the document the note of idealism which was to make its appeal so perennially human and vital. The words were far more than a political gesture to draw popular support; they were an embodiment of Jefferson's deepest convictions, and his total life thenceforward was given over to the work of providing such political machinery for America as should guarantee for all the enjoyment of those inalienable rights. If the fact that he set the pursuit of happiness above abstract property rights is to be taken as proof that Jefferson was an impractical French theorist, the critic may take what comfort he can from his deduction.

That Jefferson was an idealist was singularly fortunate for America; there was need of idealism to leaven the materialistic realism of the times. It was a critical period and he came at the turn of a long running tide. He watched the beginnings of the political shift in America from isolated colonial commonwealths to a unitary sovereign state; and his wide reading and close observation had convinced him that the impending change was fraught with momentous issues for the common man. He had meditated much on the social results of the slow oscillations in western civilization between social decentralization and centralization, with their contrasting political and economic structures; and he understood how the movement from simplicity to complexity—from freedom to regimentation—creates a psychology and an institutionalism that conducts straight to the leviathan state, controlled by a ruling caste, serving the demands of exploitation, heedless of the well-being of the regimented mass. This great lesson in social drifts he brought home to America. There had been created here the psychology and institutions of a decentralized society, with a corresponding exaltation of the individual and the breakdown of caste. In the broad spaces of America the old-world coercive state had dwindled to a mere police arrangement for parochial duties; the free citizen refused to be regimented; the several communities insisted on managing their affairs by their own agents. Such was the natural consequence of free economics; but with the turning of the tide would not the drift towards centralization nullify the results of earlier American experience and repeat here the unhappy history of European peoples?

To the philosophic mind of Jefferson, such a question was not academic, but urgent and vital. He had been bred in that older world, he believed passionately in the excellence of its virtues, and his political and social philosophy was determined by that experience. He sprang from a society deep-rooted in an agrarian economy, and he wished to preserve that society. Born on the Virginia frontier, he had never seen a hamlet so large as twenty houses before his eighteenth year; his neighbors and associates were capable and vigorous frontier democrats, who managed the affairs of local government with the same homespun skill that went to their farming. "It is not difficult," remarks an acute critic, "to see how the great principle of Jefferson's life—absolute faith in democracy—came to him. He was the product of the first West in American history; he grew up with men who ruled their country well, who fought the Indians valiantly. . . . Jefferson loved his backwoods neighbors, and he, in turn, was loved by them." This early conviction of the excellence of a freehold order was confirmed by later experience; wide observation and much travel convinced him that no other people was so favored by circumstance as the American, or so vigorously self-reliant. That such well-being resulted from a plastic economics, he regarded as self-evident; and from this economic freedom came political freedom. In his European travels he saw everywhere want and wretchedness dwelling in the shadow of the aristocratic state, and he could not dissociate the two. Political tyranny was the outward and visible sign of greater tyrannies that ran down to the very roots of society; the leviathan state was the convenient instrument through which those tyrannies took their heavy toll of the common well-being. America was a land of free men; it was exploited neither by an aristocracy nor a plutocracy. Surely there could be no greater or nobler ambition for an American than to assist in preserving his country from the misery that must attend a change from the present happy condition of democratic industry, to the serfdom of the European wage-taker and peasant.

To a mind imbued with such conceptions the appeal of the Physiocratic theory of social economics would be irresistible. The ground was prepared for the sowing of the seeds of the liberal French thought. With its emphasis laid upon agriculture, its doctrine of the *produit net,* its principle of *laissez faire,* and its social concern, the Physiocratic theory accorded exactly with his familiar experience, and it must have seemed to Jefferson that it was little other than a deduction from the open facts of American life. He had read much in the works of the Physiocratic group, and was intimately acquainted with DuPont de Nemours; and the major principles of the school sank deep into his mind and creatively determined his thinking, with the result that Jeffersonian democracy as it spread through Virginia and west along the frontier assumed a pronounced Physiocratic bias. The sharp struggle between Jefferson and Hamilton must be reckoned, in part at least, a conflict between the rival principles of Quesnay and Adam Smith, between an agrarian and a capitalistic economy. Much as Jefferson feared the ambitions of an aristocracy, he feared quite as much the creation of a proletariat. As he looked into the future he saw great cities rising to breed their Roman mobs, duped and exploited by demagogues, the convenient tools of autocracy; and counting the cost in social well-being, he set his face like flint against the rising capitalism. A free yeomanry he regarded as the backbone of every great people, the producers of the real wealth, the guardians of manly independence; and the number of factory workers measured for him the extent of social disease. It is this Physiocratic conception that explains his bitter hostility to protective tariffs, national banks, funding manipulations, the machinery of credit, and all the agencies of capitalism which Hamilton was skillfully erecting in America. Not to have hated such things Jefferson must first have emptied his mind of the teachings of experience and the lessons of the social philosophers.

In the *Notes on Virginia* there is a well-known passage that amplifies his favorite thesis that a sound American economy was an agrarian economy:

The political economists of Europe have established it as a principle, that every State should endeavor to manufacture for itself; and this principle, like many others, we transfer to America. . . . But we have an immensity of land courting the industry of the husbandman. Is it best then that all our citizens should be employed in its improvement, or that one half should be called off from that to exercise manufactures and handicraft arts for the other? Those who labor in the earth are the chosen people of God, if ever he had a chosen people, whose breasts he has made his peculiar deposit for substantial and genuine virtue. It is the focus in which he keeps alive that sacred fire, which otherwise might escape from the face of the earth. Corruption of morals in the mass of cultivators is a phenomenon of which no age nor nation has furnished an example. It is the mark set on those, who not looking up to heaven, to their own soil and industry, as does the husbandman, for their subsistence, depend for it on casualties and caprice of customers. Dependence begets subservience and venality, suffocates the germ of virtue, and prepares fit tools for the designs of ambition. . . . Generally speaking the proportion which the aggregate of the other classes of citizens bears in any state to that of its husbandmen, is the proportion of its unsound to its healthy parts, and is a good enough barometer whereby to measure its degree of corruption. While we have land to labor then, let us never wish to see our citizens occupied at a work-bench, or twirling a distaff . . . for the general operations of manufacture, let our work-shops remain in Europe. It is better to carry provisions and materials to work-men there, than bring them to the provisions and materials, and with them their manners and principles. . . . The mobs of great cities add just so much to the support of pure government, as sores do to the strength of the human body. It is the manners and spirit of a people which preserve a re-

public in vigor. A degeneracy in these is a canker which soon eats to the heart
of its laws and constitution.

Such was his attitude in 1782, an attitude identical with Franklin's.
Thirty-four years later he had modified his views of industrialism. The
bitter experience of the Napoleonic wars, with the hardships and losses
visited upon neutral shipping, had convinced him of the need of domestic manufactures, and he was then deeply interested in improved machinery, new methods, original ventures. "We must now place the manufacturer by the side of the agriculturist," he conceded, or remain in
economic dependence. But how much further the country should be industrialized, whether it "shall be proposed to go beyond our own supply"
to compete in foreign markets, was not yet clear to him; the problem remained still to be determined whether "the *surplus* labor" would be
"most beneficially employed in the culture of the earth, or in the fabrica-
tions of art." In such commentary Jefferson failed to measure the thrust
of economic determinism that drives every people to go through with the
industrial revolution, once it is begun; but if we recall the primary principle of his political philosophy, that the "care of human life and happiness, and not their destruction, is the first and only legitimate object of
good government," we may perhaps judge what would have been his attitude towards a centralized industrialism. He would have judged its desirability, not by the balance sheet of corporate business, but by the social ledger. As a social economist he could not think in terms of the
economic man, nor simplify human beings to labor commodity, nor reduce the social tie to the cash nexus. It is inconceivable that he should
have shared Hamilton's satisfaction at the contemplation of women and
children—and many of the latter "of tender age"—wasting away in the
mills; he was too social-minded for that, too much an idealist, too human
in short. Though necessity might force him away from a simple agrarian
economy, it does not follow that he would become partisan to a centralizing industrialism, with control vested in banking credit.

It is a common charge that Jefferson was consumed with suspicion,
and it is set down against him as the mark of a mean and ungenerous nature. That in later years he was suspicious of fair spoken advocates and
plausible programs was as true of Jefferson as of Sam Adams; he had
learned like the Boston democrat the virtue of the saying, *felix qui cau-
tus*, and with so much at stake he would practice caution. He feared
many things, for he was acutely aware of the incapacity of the heedless
majority to defend itself against an able and instructed minority. As a
child of an aristocratic age he fell into the mistake of visualizing that
minority in the guise of a landed gentry, rather than in the guise of
plutocracy; but in his quick fear of a minority he had all history as counselor. When he took his seat in Washington's cabinet his suspicions of
the Hamiltonian program were quickly aroused. He believed that a

monarchy was aimed at, and if that proved unattainable, then a highly centralized state designed to hold in check the democratic tendencies. His line of reasoning may be summarized thus: In consequence of the republican enthusiasm of the early years of the Revolution, democratic reorganization of the several state governments had been successfully achieved. Very great progress towards democracy had been made. Certain legislative acts of agrarian assemblies were now being turned against democracy, to invalidate it as a working system of government. But if agrarian majorities had used their power to enact laws beneficial to their interests, they were only applying a lesson learned from long experience with aristocratic legislatures. Such acts were no serious indictment of the democratic principle, and to make partisan use of them to justify curtailing the powers of the majority, was a betrayal of popular rights. And this, Jefferson believed, was the deliberate purpose of the Federalist leaders. Unable to stem the popular tide in the several commonwealths, the wealthy minority had devised a plan to superimpose upon the sovereign commonwealths a centralized federal government, so hedged about as to lie beyond the reach of local majorities, and hence able to override and nullify the democratic will. Once safely established, this federal government would gather fresh powers into its hands, until there emerged a rigorous machine, modeled after the British system, and as little regardful of the common interests. If this were not the Federalist purpose, why all the praise of the British system as the ripe product of experience, exactly adapted to the political genius of the English race?

In the matter of appeal to past experience, which provided the staple of Federalist argument, Jefferson discovered fresh grounds of fear. The past he looked upon as evil, and the record of experience was a tale of injustice and bitter wrong. He would not have America follow the trodden paths, for whither they led he knew too well. He would countenance no entangling alliances with old-world upper-class systems of statecraft, for such systems would reproduce in America the evils it should be the chief business of America to prevent. There must be erected here no counterpart of the European state; there must be no king, no aristocracy, no plutocracy; but a new democratic organization of government, in which the welfare of the whole people should be the sole concern.

> When I left Congress in '76 [he wrote as an old man] it was in the persuasion that our whole code must be revised, adapted to our republican form of government, and now that we had no negatives of Councils, Governors and Kings to restrain us from doing right, that it should be corrected in all its parts with a single eye to reason and the good of those for whose government it was planned.

Not past experience but present need should instruct America in drawing the plans of a new system of government and a new code of law. In

analyzing the evils of European systems Jefferson came to certain conclusions that dominated all his later thinking, and that may be phrased
thus: The political state tends inevitably to self-aggrandizement, the
logical outcome of which is a political leviathan, too big and too complex
for popular control. With sovereign powers vested in the hands of governmental agents, those agents lie under a constant temptation to corruption and tyranny, and in the end they align the powers of the state on
the side of the most ambitious and capable. The greater the power of
government, the ampler its revenues, the more energetic its administration, the more dangerous it may become to the rights of men; for where
the prize is greatest, men struggle most ruthlessly, and what prize could
be greater than the privilege of exploiting society in the name of the
state? History knows no objective more tempting to the will to power,
than the control of the absolute state. A government adequately socialized, intent solely upon furthering the common well-being, Jefferson
would have been unanxious about. But such governments existed only in
the dreams of Sir Thomas More and the Utopians; he could discover
none such either in the past or present. Everywhere strong governments
were little more than efficient tax-machines to support armies and provide subsidies and places for the minority. Against such forces of corruption the people struggle in vain.

If such was the common testimony of old-world experience—and no
man who knew the inner workings of government there would deny
it—what reason was there to expect that like causes would work unlike
results in America? To what purpose was the talk of strong government
encouraged amongst the holders of the public debt? To what end had
lobbyists for the funding bill invaded the floor of Congress? It was idle to
expect in America a nullification of the law, that where power sits
within, corruption waits without. The love of power is universal. Most
men are potential autocrats, the strong and capable may become actual
autocrats. No man is good enough, no group of men, to be trusted with
unrestrained powers—in America any more than in Europe. A centralized government in control of the tax-machine, and secure from popular
restraint, would undo the results of the Revolutionary War. The movement to consolidate power, Jefferson asserted, was "but Toryism in disguise." "The generalizing and concentrating all cares and powers into
one body . . . has destroyed the liberty and the rights of men in every
government which has ever existed under the sun."

Our country is too large to have all its affairs directed by a single government. Public servants at such a distance, and from under the eye of their constituents, must, from the circumstance of distance, be unable to administer and
overlook all the details necessary for the good government of the citizens; and
the same circumstance, by rendering detection impossible to their constituents,
will invite the public agents to corruption, plunder and waste.

The practice of local home rule had grown up in America in response to native conditions; it had resulted from democratic needs; and Jefferson was too thoroughly American, too instinctively democratic, to overlook the significance of local sovereignties in a democratic philosophy. From the sharp contrast between American and European practice he deduced a cardinal principle, namely, that good government springs from a common interest in public affairs, and that such common interest is possible only when the field of activities is circumscribed. Set government apart from the people, or above them, and public interest is lost in a sense of futility. The danger of an encroaching tyranny by a superimposed sovereignty, is made easy by the public lethargy in respect to distant and unfamiliar things, and establishes itself through the psychology of custom. Jefferson was never greatly concerned about stable government; he was very much more concerned about responsive government—that it should faithfully serve the majority will. He made no god of the political state. He had no conventional reverence for established law and order; he inquired rather what sort of law and order he was asked to accept, was it just or unjust. Changing conditions make ancient good uncouth, and established institutions tend to fall into dry-rot, or to become tyrannical. Men are more important than constitutions, and the public well-being is more sacred than statutes. An occasional revolution, he commented grimly apropos of the hue and cry over Shays's Rebellion, is salutary; if it does not come of itself it might well be brought about. Progress in government results from experiment; and it is easier and safer to experiment on a small scale than on a great. Inertia increases with size, and the more consolidated the government, the more unyielding it becomes. The longest delayed revolutions are the gravest.

In asserting the principle of the majority will, Jefferson like other democratic thinkers of the time, found himself countered by the argument of abstract justice. Vehement denunciation had greeted Paine's doctrine that what a nation chooses to do, it has a right to do. There can be no rights, it was confidently asserted, superior to the right. The people may legislate, but it remains to determine the validity of statutes in the light of justice; that which is unjust is *ipso facto* null and void. It was Coke's doctrine of judicial review, set up in America after its repudiation in England, and Jefferson's hostility to it was bitter. As an intellectual he had none of the lawyer's complacency with legal principles, or conceit of the law's sufficiency; and as a democrat he would not yield sovereignty into the hands of the judiciary. He had no veneration for the Common Law of England: it had grown up by slow accretions during centuries of absolutism; how should it be expected to answer the needs of a freer age? It must be purged of outworn elements, imbued with democratic sympathies. The Revolution had been fought in defense of rights that are broader and more human than legal principles; and to hand over those rights to be interpreted away by lawyers, seemed to him moonstruck madness. It was the law of Blackstone rather than of Coke that he feared most—that "elegant" canonization of the malign influences of Tory reaction, and that was so cried up by the smatterers and "ephemeral insects of the law" in America; whereas Coke "was as good a Whig as ever wrote":

Blackstone and Hume have made tories of all England, and are making tories of those young Americans whose native feelings of independence do not place them above the wily sophistries of a Hume or a Blackstone. These two books, and especially the former [Blackstone], have done more towards the suppression of the liberties of man, than all the million of men in arms of Bonaparte, and the millions of human lives with the sacrifice of which he will stand loaded before the judgment seat of his Maker.

As Jefferson grew older his fear of judicial encroachment on the popular will became acute, but it shifted from distrust of the Common Law to concern over the Supreme Court. A strong and outspoken hatred of the Federal judiciary runs through all his later writings, and he lost no opportunity to popularize the thesis—"It is a misnomer to call a government republican, in which a branch of the supreme power is independent of the nation."

The great object of my fear is the Federal Judiciary. That body, like gravity, ever acting, with noiseless foot, and unalarming advance, gaining ground step by step, and holding what it gains, is engulfing insidiously the special governments into the jaws of that which feeds them.

It is a very dangerous doctrine to consider the judges as the ultimate arbiters of all constitutional questions. It is one which would place us under the despotism of an oligarchy. . . . The Constitution has erected no such single tribunal, knowing that to whatever hands confided, with the corruptions of time and party, its members would become despots.

As Jefferson watched Chief Justice John Marshall gathering all things within the purview of the Federal judiciary, preparing future strongholds by the skillful use of *obiter dicta*, legislating by means of judicial interpretation, nullifying the will of the majority, and with the power of repeal made nugatory by the complexity of the process, he saw clearly what the outcome would be. Surely that was no democracy where judge-made laws were enforced by bench warrants, and where the sovereign power lay beyond the immediate reach of the popular will. The government that he desired would not rest on the legal fiction of an abstract justice above statutes and constitutions, whereof a group of judicial gentlemen were the repositories and guardians. It would be like Paine's, "a plain thing, and fitted to the capacity of many heads"; for "where the law of the majority ceases to be acknowledged, there government ends; the law of the strongest takes its place."

Granted the truth of Jefferson's premises that power tends to contract to the hands of a few, and that all government of the few is vicious, then

democracy is the only form of government under which an approxima-
tion to justice can be realized. A class will serve class interests. Government by an aristocracy is government in the interest of the aristocracy.
For the staple argument of the Federalists, that gentlemen of principle
and property alone may be intrusted with affairs of state, Jefferson had
a quiet contempt. "I have never observed men's honesty to increase with
their riches," he remarked. On the contrary, he regarded the "better sort
of people" as a chief hindrance to the spread of social justice. The past
had been evil because the past had been exploited by gentlemen of principle and property. They had kept government away from the people,
and with their secret councils and secret diplomacy they had plundered
the taxpayers and drenched nations in blood. Their selfish rivalries
everywhere exacted a heavy toll of society and left behind a trail of poverty and wretchedness. The future would be better in the degree that
mastery passed into common hands.

From the conclusions of his democratic premise he did not shrink. If
it were indeed true that the people were beasts, then the democratic government of the future would be a bestial government—and even that
might be better than the old arrangement of masters and slaves. But the
American people whom Jefferson trusted were very far from beasts; he
was convinced that they were honest and well-meaning; and if government were brought close to them, kept responsive to their will, a new and
beneficent chapter in human history would open. The populistic laws
passed by the legislatures of Rhode Island and New Hampshire, about
which such an uproar was raised by fearful creditors, and which were
urged as an argument against popular government, gave him no concern. He understood the ways of propaganda, and he never accepted
judgment of the American people from the mouths of their enemies. The
cure for the evils of democracy, he believed, was more democracy. The
whole are far less likely to be unjust than the few; and if sovereignty
does not rest in the majority will, where shall it lodge?

Hume, the great apostle of toryism, says "the Commons established a principle, which is noble in itself, and seems specious [*i.e.* pleasing], but is belied
by all history and experience, *that the people are the origin of all just power.*"
And where else will this degenerate son of science, this traitor to his fellow
men, find the origin of *just* power, if not in the majority of the society? Will it
be in the minority? Or in the individual of that minority?

The America of Jefferson's day was a simple world, with a simple
domestic economy. More than ninety per cent were plain country folk,
farmers and villagers, largely freeholders, managing their local affairs
in the traditional way. There were no great extremes of poverty and
wealth, no closely organized class groups. With its sharp restrictions on
suffrage and the prestige accorded the gentry, it was still far from a political democracy; but it was hastening towards a more democratic order.

Remote from the cesspools of European diplomacy, and not yet acquainted with imperialism, it had no need for a leviathan state. Economic conditions sanctioned a *laissez-faire* government, simple and unambitious. In such a world the well-known words of Jefferson's first inaugural address, justified themselves to all who did not seek to use the state for personal advantage.

A wise and frugal government, which shall restrain men from injuring one another, which shall leave them otherwise free to regulate their own pursuits of industry and improvement, and shall not take from the mouth of labor the bread it has earned. This is the sum of good government, and this is necessary to close the circle of our felicities.

In one significant direction he would extend the scope of government—the encouragement of education. An intelligent people is necessary to a democracy; free schools are a sign of a free society. Tyranny thrives on ignorance and superstition, and every exploiting group fears popular education. Free himself in thought and action, believing in the unshackled commerce of ideas, hating all censorships, Jefferson accounted the founding of the University of Virginia his largest contribution to the well-being of his native commonwealth.

To all who profess faith in the democratic ideal Jefferson is a perennial inspiration. A free soul, he loved freedom enough to deny it to none; an idealist, he believed that the welfare of the whole, and not the prosperity of any group, is the single end of government. He was our first great leader to erect a political philosophy native to the economics and experience of America, as he was the first to break consciously with the past. His life was dedicated to the service of freedom, and later generations may well recall his words, "I have sworn upon the altar of God eternal hostility against every form of tyranny over the mind of man." Europe made Jefferson wholly American. From his studies in France he came to see that where men enjoy free access to the sources of subsistence, government is likely to be simple and honest, and society free and content; but where a policy of preëmption has run its course, the function of government is seduced from its social purpose to perpetuate the inequalities which spring from the progressive monopolization of natural resources, with augmenting corruption and injustice. To preserve government in America from such degradation, to keep the natural resources open to all, were the prime desire and object of his life. That such an effort was foredoomed to failure, in presence of imperious forces that shape society beyond the capacity of political means to change or prevent, cannot detract from the nobility of his ideal, or the inspiration of his life. Among the greater thinkers of the constitutional period Jefferson remains by far the most vital and suggestive, the one to whom later generations may return most hopefully.

Morton Borden

For twelve years the Constitution worked, after a fashion. From its inception the new document had been subjected to severe trials and divisive strains. A rebellion in Pennsylvania, a naval war with France, a demand for states' rights from Virginia and Kentucky, and various Western schemes of disunion—all had been surmounted. Had it not been for the great prestige of George Washington and the practical moderation of John Adams, America's second attempt at a federal union might have failed like the first. Partisan passions had run high in the 1790's, and any single factor on which men disagreed—Hamilton's financial plans or the French Revolution or the Sedition Act—might easily have caused a stoppage of the nation's political machinery.

The two-party system emerged during this decade, and on each important issue public opinion seemed to oscillate between Federalist and Democratic-Republican. Perhaps this was to be expected of a young nation politically adolescent. Year by year Americans were becoming more politically alert and active; if there was little room for middle ground between these two factions, yet opinions were hardly fixed and irrevocable. The culmination of partisan controversy and the test of respective strengths took place in the monumental election of 1800.

Jefferson was feared, honestly feared, by almost all Federalists. Were he to win the election, so they predicted, all the hard constructive gains of those twelve years would be dissipated. Power would be returned to the individual states; commerce would suffer; judicial power would be lessened; and the wonderful financial system of Hamilton would be dismantled and destroyed. Jefferson was an atheist, and he would attack the churches. Jefferson was a hypocrite, an aristocrat posing as democrat, appealing to the baser motives of human beings in order to obtain votes. Jefferson was a revolutionary, a Francophile and, after ruining the Army and Navy under the guise of economy measures, might very well involve the nation in a war with England. In short, it was doubtful

From *America's Ten Greatest Presidents*, edited by Morton Borden (Chicago, 1961), pp. 57–67. Copyright © 1961 by Rand McNally & Company. Reprinted by permission of Rand McNally & Company.

if the Constitution could continue its successful course under such a
president.

In like manner the Republicans feared another Federalist victory. To
be sure, John Adams had split with Hamilton and had earned the enmity
of the Essex Junto. But would he not continue Hamilton's "moneyed system"? Did not Adams share the guilt of every Federalist for the despicable Alien and Sedition Acts? Was it not true that "His Rotundity" so
admired the British system that he was really a monarchist at heart? Republicans were not engaging in idle chatter, nor were they speaking
solely for effect, when they predicted many dire consequences if Adams
were elected. A typical rumor had Adams uniting "his house to that of his
majesty of Britain" and "the bridegroom was to be king of America."

Throughout the country popular interest in the election was intense,
an intensity sustained over months of balloting. When the Republicans
carried New York City, Alexander Hamilton seriously suggested that the
results be voided. And when the breach between Adams and Hamilton
became public knowledge, Republicans nodded knowingly and quoted
the maxim: "When thieves fall out, honest men come by their own."

The Federalists were narrowly defeated. But the decision was complicated by a result which many had predicted: a tied electoral vote between
the two Republican candidates, Aaron Burr and Thomas Jefferson. (Indeed, the Twelfth Amendment was adopted in 1804 to avoid any such
recurrence.) A choice between the two would be made by the House of
Representatives. At this moment, February, 1801, the Constitution
seemed on the verge of collapse. Federalist members of the lower house
united in support of Burr; Republicans were just as adamant for Jefferson. After thirty-five ballots, neither side had yet obtained the necessary
majority. The issue seemed hopelessly deadlocked. What would happen
on March 4, inauguration day?

One representative from Maryland, sick with a high fever, was literally carried into Congress on a stretcher to maintain the tied vote of his
state. The Republican governor of Pennsylvania, Thomas McKean,
threatened to march on Washington with troops if the Federalists persisted in thwarting the will of the people. Hamilton was powerless; his
advice that Jefferson was the lesser evil went unheeded. So great was
their hatred of the Virginian that most Federalists in Congress would
have opposed him regardless of the consequences. After all, they reasoned, Jefferson would dismantle the Federal government anyway. In
the end, however, patriotism and common sense prevailed. For the choice
was no longer Jefferson or Burr, but Jefferson or no president at all. A
few Federalists, led by James A. Bayard of Delaware, could not accept
the logic of their party, and threw the election to Jefferson.

What a shock it was, then, to read Jefferson's carefully chosen words
in his inaugural address:

But every difference of opinion is not a difference of principle. We have called by different names brethren of the same principle. We are all republicans—we are all federalists. If there be any among us who would wish to dissolve this Union or to change its republican form, let them stand undisturbed as monuments of the safety with which error of opinion may be tolerated where reason is left free to combat it. I know, indeed, that some honest men fear that a republican government cannot be strong; that this government is not strong enough. But would the honest patriot, in the full tide of successful experiment, abandon a government which has so far kept us free and firm, on the theoretic and visionary fear that this government, the world's best hope, may by possibility want energy to preserve itself? I trust not. I believe this, on the contrary, the strongest government on earth. I believe it is the only one where every man, at the call of the laws, would fly to the standard of the law, and would meet invasions of the public order as his own personal concern. Sometimes it is said that man cannot be trusted with the government of himself. Can he, then, be trusted with the government of others? Or have we found angels in the form of kings to govern him? Let history answer this question.

The words were greeted with applause—and confusion. It was obvious that Jefferson wanted to salve the wounds of bitter factionalism. While many Federalists remained distrustful and some even regarded it as hypocritical, most men approved the tone of their new president's message.

But what did Jefferson mean? Were there no economic principles at stake in his conflicts with Hamilton? Were there no political and constitutional principles implicit in the polar views of the respective parties? And, in the last analysis, did not these differences reflect a fundamental philosophical quarrel over the nature of human beings? Was not the election of 1800 indeed a revolution? If not, then what is the meaning of Jeffersonianism?

For two terms Jefferson tried, as best he could, to apply the standards of his inaugural address. Naturally, the Alien and Sedition Acts were allowed to lapse. The new secretary of the treasury, Albert Gallatin, was instructed to devise an easily understood program to erase the public debt gradually. Internal taxes were either abolished or reduced. Frugality and economy were emphasized to an extreme. Elegant and costly social functions were replaced by simple and informal receptions. The expense of maintaining ambassadors at the courts of Portugal, Holland, and Prussia was erased by withdrawing these missions. The Army and Navy were pared down to skeleton size. To be sure, Jefferson had to reverse himself on the matter of patronage for subordinate Government posts. Originally he planned to keep these replacements to a minimum, certainly not to permit an individual's partisan opinions to be a basis for dismissal unless the man manifestly used his office for partisan purposes. This position was politically untenable, according to Jefferson's lieutenants, and they pressed him to accept a moderate number of removals. Indeed, Jefferson's handling of patronage is symbolic of what Hamilton once called his "ineradicable duplicity."

The Federalist leaders cried out in anguish at every one of these pol-

icy changes. The lowering of the nation's military strength would increase the danger of invasion. It was a rather risky gamble to assume
that peace could be maintained while European war was an almost constant factor, and the United States was the major neutral carrier. The
abolition of the excises, especially on distilled spirits, would force the
Government to rely on tariffs, an unpredictable source of revenue depending on the wind and waves. It was charged that several foreign ambassadors were offended by Jefferson's rather affected and ultrademo-
cratic social simplicity. Most important, the ultimate payment of the
public debt would reduce national power.

This time, however, the people did not respond to the Federalist lament of impending anarchy. After all, commerce prospered throughout
most of Jefferson's administration. Somehow the churches remained
standing. No blood baths took place. The Bank of the United States still
operated. Peace was maintained. Certainly, some Federalist judges were
under attack, but the judicial power passed through this ordeal to
emerge unscathed and even enhanced. Every economic indicator—urban
growth, westward expansion, agricultural production, the construction
of canals, turnpikes and bridges—continued to rise, undisturbed by the
political bickering in Washington.

At first the Federalists were confident that they would regain power.
Alexander Hamilton's elaborate scheme for an organization to espouse
Christianity and the Constitution, as the "principal engine" to restore
Federalist power, was rejected out of hand. He was told that "our adversaries will soon demonstrate to the world the soundness of our doctrines and the imbecility and folly of their own." But hope changed to
despair as the people no longer responded; no "vibration of opinion"
took place as in the 1790's. Federalism was the party of the past, an an-
tiquated and dying philosophy. "I will fatten my pigs, and prune my
trees; nor will I any longer . . . trouble to govern this country," wrote
Fisher Ames: "You federalists are only lookers-on." Jefferson swept the
election of 1804, capturing every state except Connecticut and Delaware
from the Federalist candidate, Charles C. Pinckney. "Federalism is dead,"
wrote Jefferson a few years later, "without even the hope of a day of
resurrection. The quondam leaders indeed retain their rancour and
principles; but their followers are amalgamated with us in sentiment,
if not in name."

It is the fashion of some historians to explain the Federalist demise
and Republican ascendancy in terms of a great change in Jefferson. A
radical natural law philosopher when he fought as minority leader, he
became a first-rate utilitarian politician as president. The Virginian became an American. Revolutionary theory was cast aside when Jefferson
faced the prosaic problem of having to run the country. He began to

adopt some of the techniques and policies of the Federalists. Indeed, it is often observed that Jefferson "outfederalized the Federalists."

There is much to be said for this view. After all, less than three months after he assumed the presidency, Jefferson dispatched a naval squadron to the Mediterranean on a warlike mission, without asking the permission of Congress. Two members of his Cabinet, Levi Lincoln and Albert Gallatin, thought the action unconstitutional, and so advised the President. Almost from the moment of its birth the young nation had paid tribute, as did every European power, rather than risk a war with the Barbary pirates. But Jefferson could not abide such bribery. No constitutional scruples could delay for a moment his determination to force the issue. Later, Congress declared war, and in four years Barbary power was shattered. The United States under Jefferson accomplished an object that England, France, Spain, Portugal, and Holland had desired for more than a century—unfettered commerce in the Mediterranean. Here, then, in this episode, is a totally different Jefferson—not an exponent of states' rights and strict interpretation of the Constitution, but an American nationalist of the first order.

Perhaps the most frequently cited example of Jefferson's chameleon quality, however, was on the question of whether the United States should or should not purchase the Louisiana Territory from France. On this question the fundamental issue was squarely before Jefferson, and a choice could not be avoided. The purchase would more than double the size of the United States. Yet the Constitution did not specifically provide for such acquisition of foreign territory. Further, the treaty provided that this area would eventually be formed into states, full partners in the Union. Again, the Constitution did not specifically cover such incorporation. A broad interpretation of Article IV, Section III, however, might permit United States' ratification of the treaty. Should theory be sacrificed and an empire gained? Or were the means as important as the ends?

Broad or loose construction of the Constitution was the key to the growth of Federal power. Federalists had argued in this vein to justify most of their legislation in the 1790's. To Jefferson, individual liberty and governmental power were on opposite ends of a see-saw, which the Federalists had thrown off balance. He believed that government, especially the central government, must be restricted within rather narrow and essential limits. Only by continually and rigidly applying strict construction to the Constitution could this tendency to overweening power be controlled and individual liberty be safeguarded. As early as 1777, Jefferson, then governor of Virginia, had warned that constitutions must be explicit, "so as to exclude all possible doubt; . . . [lest] at some future day . . . power[s] should be assumed."

On the other hand, the purchase of Louisiana would fulfill a dream and solve a host of problems. Jefferson envisioned an American empire covering "the whole northern, if not the southern continent, with a people speaking the same language, governed in similar forms, and by similar laws." The purchase would be a giant step in the direction of democracy's inevitable growth. "Is it not better," asked Jefferson, "that the opposite bank of the Mississippi should be settled by our own brethren and children, than by strangers of another family?"

Of more immediate interest, Westerners would be able to ship their goods down the Mississippi without fear that New Orleans might be closed. Indian attacks undoubtedly would taper off without the Spanish to instigate them. Uppermost in Jefferson's mind, however, was the freedom from England that the purchase would assure. He did not fear Spanish ownership. A feeble, second-rate nation like Spain on the frontier offered little threat to America's future security. The continued possession of Louisiana by an imperialistic France led by the formidable Napoleon, however, might force the United States into an alliance with England. At first Jefferson thought a constitutional amendment specifically permitting the purchase might solve the dilemma. But Napoleon showed signs of wavering. The treaty had to be confirmed immediately, with no indication of constitutional doubt. Jefferson asked the Republican leaders in the Senate to ratify it "with as little debate as possible, and particularly so far as respects the constitutional difficulty."

In still other ways Jefferson's presidency was marked by Federalist policies which encouraged the growth of central power. Internal improvements loomed large in Jefferson's mind. While many turnpikes and canals were financed by private and state capital, he realized that Federal support would be necessary, especially in the western part of the nation. With the use of Federal money obtained from the sale of public lands, and (later) aided by direct congressional appropriations, the groundwork for the famous Cumberland road was established during Jefferson's administration. He enthusiastically supported Gallatin's plan to spend twenty million dollars of Federal funds on a network of national roads and canals. Other more pressing problems intervened, however, and it was left to later administrations to finance these local and interstate programs. If Hamilton had pressed for internal improvements in the 1790's (he suggested them in the *Report on Manufactures*), Jefferson probably would have raised constitutional objections.

Finally, is not Jefferson's change of tack further reflected in the political history of that era? Over the span of a few years it seemed as if each party had somehow reversed directions. In 1798–99 Jefferson and Madison penned the Virginia and Kentucky Resolutions as an answer to the Federalists' infamous Alien and Sedition Acts. In 1808–9 more radical but comparable rumblings of dissatisfaction emanated from some New England Federalists over Jefferson's Embargo Act. For the embargo, says one of Jefferson's biographers, was "the most arbitrary, inquisitorial, and confiscatory measure formulated in American legislation up to the period of the Civil War." Further, both parties splintered during Jefferson's administration. Many moderate Federalists, like John Quincy Adams, found themselves in closer harmony with Administration policy than with Essex Junto beliefs. And Jefferson's actions alienated old comrades, like John Randolph, Jr., whose supporters were called the Tertium Quids. It is interesting to note that there is no historical consensus of why, when, how, or what precipitated the break between Randolph and Jefferson. Randolph is always referred to as brilliant but erratic; and whatever immediate reason is alleged, the cause somehow has to do with Randolph's personality and Jefferson's betrayal of the true doctrines.

It is part of Jefferson's greatness that he could inspire a myth and project an image. But one must not confuse myth and reality, shadow and substance. Thomas Jefferson as he was, and Thomas Jefferson as people perceived him, are quite different. While both concepts of course, are of equal value in understanding our past, it is always the historian's task to make the distinction. Too often, in Jefferson's case, this has not been done. Too often the biographers have described the myth—have taken at face value the popular view of Jefferson and his enemies, contained in the vitriolic newspaper articles and pamphlets, the passionate debates and fiery speeches of that period—and missed or misconstrued the reality.

This is understandable. Even the principals inevitably became involved and helped to propagate the exaggerated images of the 1790's and thus misunderstood one another's aims and motives. Jefferson, according to his grandson, never considered Federalist fulminations "as abusing him; they had never known him. They had created an imaginary being clothed with odious attributes, to whom they gave his name; and it was against that creature of their imaginations they had levelled their anathemas." John Adams, reminiscing in a letter to Jefferson, wrote: "Both parties have excited artificial terrors and if I were summoned as a witness to say upon oath, which party had excited . . . the most terror, and which had really felt the most, I could not give a more sincere answer, than in the vulgar style 'Put them in a bag and shake them, and then see which comes out first.' "

On March 4, 1801, following a decade of verbal violence, many Americans were surprised to hear that "We are all republicans—we are all federalists." Some historians act as if they, too, are surprised. These historians then describe Jefferson's administration as if some great change took place in his thinking, and conclude that he "outfederalized the Federalists." This is a specious view, predicated on an ultraradical Jefferson of the 1790's in constant debate with an ultraconservative

Hamilton. Certainly Jefferson as president had to change. Certainly at times he had to modify, compromise, and amend his previous views. To conclude, however, that he outfederalized the Federalists is to miss the enormous consistency of Jefferson's beliefs and practices.

Jefferson was ever a national patriot second to none, not even to Hamilton. He always conceived of the United States as a unique experiment, destined for greatness so long as a sharp line isolated American civilization from European infection. Thus he strongly advised our youth to receive their education at home rather than in European schools, lest they absorb ideas and traits he considered "alarming to me as an American." From "Notes on Virginia" to his advice at the time of Monroe's doctrine, Jefferson thought of America first. It matters not that Hamilton was the better prophet; Jefferson was the better American. The French minister Adet once reported: "Although Jefferson is the friend of liberty . . . although he is an admirer of the efforts we have made to cast off our shackles . . . Jefferson, I say, is an American, and as such, he cannot sincerely be our friend. An American is the born enemy of all the peoples of Europe."

Jefferson's nature was always more practical than theoretical, more common-sensical than philosophical. Certainly the essence of his Declaration of Independence is a Lockean justification of revolution; but, said Jefferson, "It was . . . an expression of the American mind," meant "to place before mankind the common sense of the subject." Jefferson always preferred precision to "metaphysical subtleties." The Kentucky and Virginia Resolutions can be understood only as a specific rebuttal of the Sedition Act. "I can never fear that things will go far wrong," wrote Jefferson, "where common sense has fair play."

One must also remember that Hamilton's power lessened considerably in the last four years of Federalist rule. He had a strong coterie of admirers, but the vast body of Federalists sided with John Adams. Despite all Hamilton did to insure Adams' defeat, and despite the split in Federalist ranks, the fact that Jefferson's victory in 1801 was won by a narrow margin indicated Federalist approval of Adams' actions. Certainly the people at that time—Jefferson and Adams included—regarded 1801 as the year of revolution. But if historians must have a revolution, perhaps Adams' split with the Hamiltonians is a better date. "The mid-position which Adams desired to achieve," writes Manning Dauer, "was adopted, in the main, by Jefferson and his successors."

To be sure, the two men disagreed on many matters of basic importance. Jefferson placed his faith in the free election of a virtuous and talented natural aristocracy; Adams did not. Within the constitutional balance, Jefferson emphasized the power of the lower house; Adams would give greater weight to the executive and judiciary. Jefferson, as a general rule, favored a strict interpretation of the Constitution; Adams did not

fear broad construction. Both believed that human beings enjoyed inalienable rights, but only Jefferson had faith in man's perfectability.
Jefferson could say, "I like a little rebellion now and then. It is like a
storm in the atmosphere"; Adams had grown more conservative since
1776. Jefferson always defended and befriended Thomas Paine; Adams
found Edmund Burke's position on the French Revolution more palat-
able.

Yet, the sages of Quincy and Monticello were both moderate and practical men. Despite the obvious and basic contrasts, both Adams and Jefferson stood side by side on certain essentials: to avoid war, to quiet
factionalism, to preserve republican government. Their warm friendship, renewed from 1812 to 1826 in a remarkable and masterful correspondence, was based on frankness, honesty, and respect. "About facts,"
Jefferson wrote, "you and I cannot differ, because truth is our mutual
guide; And if any opinions you may express should be different from
mine, I shall receive them with the liberality and indulgence which I ask
for my own." Jefferson and Adams represent, respectively, the quint-
essence of the very best in American liberalism and conservatism. Their
indestructible link, then, was "a keen sense of national consciousness," a
realization that America's destiny was unique. This is the meaning of
Jefferson's words: "We are all republicans—we are all federalists."

Jacksonian democracy vs. the business community

Arthur M. Schlesinger, Jr.

The Jacksonian revolution rested on premises which the struggles
of the thirties hammered together into a kind of practical social philosophy. The outline of this way of thinking about society was clear. It was
stated and restated, . . . on every level of political discourse from presidential messages to stump speeches, from newspaper editorials to private
letters. It provided the intellectual background without which the party
battles of the day cannot be understood.

I

The Jacksonians believed that there was a deep-rooted conflict in
society between the "producing" and "non-producing" classes—the farm-

From *The Age of Jackson* by Arthur M. Schlesinger, Jr., by permission of Little,
Brown, and Co. Copyright 1945 by Arthur M. Schlesinger, Jr.

ers and laborers, on the one hand, and the business community on the other. The business community was considered to hold high cards in this conflict through its network of banks and corporations, its control of education and the press, above all, its power over the state: it was therefore able to strip the working classes of the fruits of their labor. "Those who produce all wealth," said Amos Kendall, "are themselves left poor. They see principalities extending and palaces built around them, without being aware that the entire expense is a tax upon themselves."

If they wished to preserve their liberty, the producing classes would have to unite against the movement "to make the rich richer and the potent more powerful." Constitutional prescriptions and political promises afforded no sure protection. "We have heretofore been too disregardful of the fact," observed William M. Gouge, "that social order is quite as dependent on the laws which regulate the distribution of wealth, as on political organization." The program now was to resist every attempt to concentrate wealth and power further in a single class. Since free elections do not annihilate the opposition, the fight would be unceasing. "The struggle for power," said C. C. Cambreleng, "is as eternal as the division of society. A defeat cannot destroy the boundary which perpetually separates the democracy from the aristocracy."

The specific problem was to control the power of the capitalistic groups, mainly Eastern, for the benefit of the noncapitalist groups, farmers and laboring men, East, West and South. The basic Jacksonian ideas came naturally enough from the East, which best understood the nature of business power and reacted most sharply against it. The legend that Jacksonian democracy was the explosion of the frontier, lifting into the government some violent men filled with rustic prejudices against big business, does not explain the facts, which were somewhat more complex. Jacksonian democracy was rather a second American phase of that enduring struggle between the business community and the rest of society which is the guarantee of freedom in a liberal capitalist state.

Like any social philosophy, Jacksonian democracy drew on several intellectual traditions. Basically, it was a revival of Jeffersonianism, but the Jeffersonian inheritance was strengthened by the infusion of fresh influences; notably the antimonopolistic tradition, formulated primarily by Adam Smith and expounded in America by Gouge, Legett, Sedgwick, Cambreleng; and the pro-labor tradition, formulated primarily by William Cobbett and expounded by G. H. Evans, Ely Moore, John Ferral.

II

The inspiration of Jeffersonianism was so all-pervading and fundamental for its every aspect that Jacksonian democracy can be properly regarded as a somewhat more hard-headed and determined version of Jeffersonian democracy. But it is easy to understate the differences. Jef-

ferson himself, though widely revered and quoted, had no personal influence on any of the leading Jacksonians save perhaps Van Buren.
Madison and Monroe were accorded still more vague and perfunctory
homage. The radical Jeffersonians, Taylor, Randolph and Macon, who
had regarded the reign of Virginia as almost an era of betrayal, were
much more vivid in the minds of the Jacksonians.

Yet even Taylor's contributions to the later period have been exaggerated. His great work, the *Inquiry into the Principles and Policy of the
Government of the United States,* published in 1814 just before the Mad-
isonian surrender, had no significant contemporary vogue except among
the faithful; and its difficult style, baffling organization and interminable length prevented it ever from gaining wide currency. By Jackson's
presidency it was long out of print. In 1835 it was reported unobtainable
in New York and to be procured only "with great difficulty" in Virginia.
There is little trace of its peculiar terminology in the Jacksonian literature.

While the *Inquiry* properly endured as the most brilliant discussion of
the foundations of democracy, many of its details were in fact obsolete
by 1830. It was oriented to an important degree around the use of the national debt as the mechanism of aristocracy; in Jackson's day the debt
had been extinguished but the aristocracy remained. Moreover, Taylor's
arguments against executive power, against the party system and for a
revivified militia had lost their point for the Jacksonians. George Bancroft voiced a widely felt need when he called, in 1834, for a general
work on American society. "Where doubts arise upon any point relating
to the business of government," one radical wrote in response, "no dependence can be placed upon any treatise that has yet appeared which
professes to discuss this subject. You must draw upon your own resources, you must think,—and think alone."

The obsolescence of Taylor was caused by the enormous change in the
face of America. The period of conservative supremacy from 1816 to
1828 had irrevocably destroyed the agricultural paradise, and the Jacksonians were accommodating the insights of Jefferson to the new concrete situations. This process of readjustment involved a moderately
thorough overhauling of favorite Jeffersonian doctrines.

The central Jefferson hope had been a nation of small freeholders,
each acquiring thereby so much moral probity, economic security and
political independence as to render unnecessary any invasion of the
rights or liberties of others. The basis of such a society, as Jefferson
clearly recognized, was agriculture and handicraft. What was the status
of the Jeffersonian hope now that it was clear that, at best, agriculture
must share the future with industry and finance?

Orestes A. Brownson exhausted one possibility in his essay on "The

Laboring Classes." He reaffirmed the Jeffersonian demand: "we ask that every man become an independent proprietor, possessing enough of the goods of this world, to be able by his own moderate industry to provide for the wants of his body." But what, in practice, would this mean? As Brownson acknowledged years later, his plan would have "broken up the whole modern commercial system, prostrated the great industries, . . . and thrown the mass of the people back on the land to get their living by agricultural and mechanical pursuits." Merely to state its consequences was to prove its futility. The dominion of the small freeholder was at an end.

The new industrialism had to be accepted: banks, mills, factories, industrial capital, industrial labor. These were all distasteful realities for orthodox Jeffersonians, and, not least, the propertyless workers. "The mobs of great cities," Jefferson had said, "add just so much to the support of pure government, as sores do to the strength of the human body." The very ferocity of his images expressed the violence of his feelings. "When we get piled upon one another in large cities, as in Europe," he told Madison, "we shall become corrupt as in Europe, and go to eating one another as they do there." It was a universal sentiment among his followers. "No man should live," Nathaniel Macon used to say, "where he can hear his neighbour's dog bark."

Yet the plain political necessity of winning the labor vote obliged a change of mood. Slowly, with some embarrassment, the Jeffersonian preferences for the common man were enlarged to take in the city workers. In 1833 the *New York Evening Post,* declaring that, if anywhere, a large city of mixed population would display the evils of universal suffrage, asked if this had been the case in New York and answered: No. Amasa Walker set out the same year to prove that "great cities are not *necessarily,* as the proverb says, 'great sores,'" and looked forward cheerily to the day when they would be "great fountains of healthful moral influence, sending forth streams that shall fertilize and bless the land." The elder Theodore Sedgwick added that the cause of the bad reputation of cities was economic: "it is the sleeping in garrets and cellars; the living in holes and dens; in dirty, unpaved, unlighted streets, without the accommodations of wells, cisterns, baths, and other means of cleanliness and health"—clear up this situation, and cities will be all right.

Jackson himself never betrayed any of Jefferson's revulsion to industrialism. He was, for example, deeply interested by the mills of Lowell in 1833, and his inquiries respecting hours, wages and production showed, observers reported, "that the subject of domestic manufactures had previously engaged his attentive observation." His presidential allusions to the "producing classes" always included the workingmen of the cities. . . .

III

In several respects, then, the Jacksonians revised the Jeffersonian faith for America. They moderated that side of Jeffersonianism which talked of agricultural virtue, independent proprietors, "natural" property, abolition of industrialism, and expanded immensely that side which talked of economic equality, the laboring classes, human rights and the control of industrialism. This readjustment enabled the Jacksonians to attack economic problems which had baffled and defeated the Jeffersonians. It made for a greater realism, and was accompanied by a general toughening of the basic Jeffersonian conceptions. While the loss of "property" was serious, both symbolically and intellectually, this notion had been for most Jeffersonians somewhat submerged next to the romantic image of the free and virtuous cultivator; and the Jacksonians grew much more insistent about theories of capitalist alienation. Where, for the Jeffersonians, the tensions of class conflict tended to dissolve in vague generalizations about the democracy and the aristocracy, many Jacksonians would have agreed with A. H. Wood's remark, "It is in vain to talk of Aristocracy and Democracy—these terms are too variable and indeterminate to convey adequate ideas of the present opposing interests; the division is between the rich and the poor—the warfare is between them."

This greater realism was due, in the main, to the passage of time. The fears of Jefferson were now actualities. One handled fears by exorcism, but actualities by adjustment. For the Jeffersonians mistrust of banks and corporations was chiefly a matter of theory; for the Jacksonians it was a matter of experience. The contrast between the scintillating metaphors of John Taylor and the sober detail of William M. Gouge expressed the difference. Jefferson rejected the Industrial Revolution and sought to perpetuate the smiling society which preceded it (at least, so the philosopher; facts compelled the President toward a different policy), while Jackson, accepting industrialism as an ineradicable and even useful part of the economic landscape, sought rather to control it. Jeffersonian democracy looked wistfully back toward a past slipping further every minute into the mists of memory, while Jacksonian democracy came straightforwardly to grips with a rough and unlovely present.

The interlude saw also the gradual unfolding of certain consequences of the democratic dogma which had not been so clear to the previous generation. Though theoretically aware of the relation between political and economic power, the Jeffersonians had been occupied, chiefly, with establishing political equality. This was their mission, and they had little time to grapple with the economic questions.

But the very assertion of political equality raised inevitably the whole range of problems involved in property and class conflict. How could political equality mean anything without relative economic equality among the classes of the country? This question engaged the Jacksonians. As Orestes A. Brownson said, "A Loco-foco is a Jeffersonian Democrat, who having realized political equality, passed through one phase of the revolution, now passes on to another, and attempts the realization of social equality, so that the actual condition of men in society shall be in harmony with their acknowledged rights as citizens." This gap between Jeffersonian and Jacksonian democracy enabled men like John Quincy Adams, Henry Clay, Joseph Story and many others, who had been honest Jeffersonians, to balk at the economic extremities to which Jackson proposed to lead them.

The Jacksonians thus opened irrevocably the economic question, which the Jeffersonians had only touched halfheartedly. Yet, while they clarified these economic implications of democracy, the Jacksonians were no more successful than their predecessors in resolving certain political ambiguities. Of these, two were outstanding—the problem of the virtue of majorities, and the problem of the evil of government....

IV

The radical democrats had a definite conception of their relation to history. From the Jeffersonian analysis, fortified by the insights of Adam Smith and Cobbett, they sketched out an interpretation of modern times which gave meaning and status to the Jacksonian struggles.

Power, said the Jacksonians, goes with property. In the Middle Ages the feudal nobility held power in society through its monopoly of land under feudal tenure. The overthrow of feudalism, with the rise of new forms of property, marked the first step in the long march toward freedom. The struggle was carried on by the rising business community— "commercial, or business capital, against landed capital; merchants, traders, manufacturers, artizans, against the owners of the soil, the great landed nobility." It lasted from the close of the twelfth century to the Whig Revolution of 1688 in Britain.

The aristocracy of capital thus destroyed the aristocracy of land. The business classes here performed their vital role in the drama of liberty. The victory over feudalism, as the *Democratic Review* put it, "opened the way for the entrance of the democratic principle into the Government." But the business community gained from this exploit an undeserved reputation as the champion of liberty. Its real motive had been to establish itself in power, not to free mankind; to found government on property, not on the equal rights of the people. "I know perfectly well what I am saying," cried George Bancroft, "and I assert expressly, and challenge contradiction, that in all the history of the world there is not to be found an instance of a commercial community establishing rules for self-government upon democratic principles." "It is a mistake to suppose commerce favorable to liberty," added Fenimore Cooper. "Its tendency is to a monied aristocracy." "Instead of setting man free," said Amos Kendall, it has "only increased the number of his masters."

The next great blow for liberty was the American Revolution, "effected not in favor of men in classes; . . . but in favor of men." But the work of Hamilton halted the march of democracy. "He established the money power," wrote Van Buren, "upon precisely the same foundations upon which it had been raised in England." The subsequent history of the United States was the struggle to overthrow the Hamiltonian policy and fulfill the ideals of the Revolution.

What of the future? The Jacksonians were sublimely confident: history was on their side. "It is now for the yeomanry and the mechanics to march at the head of civilization," said Bancroft. "The merchants and the lawyers, that is, the moneyed interest broke up feudalism. The day for the multitude has now dawned." "All classes, each in turn, have possessed the government," exclaimed Brownson; "and the time has come for all predominance of class to end; for Man, the People to rule."

This was not simply a national movement. It was a movement of all people, everywhere, against their masters, and the Jacksonians watched with keen interest the stirrings of revolt abroad. Jackson and his cabinet joined in the celebrations in Washington which followed the Revolution of 1830 in France; and Van Buren, as Secretary of State, ordered the new government informed that the American people were "universally and enthusiastically in favor of that change, and of the principle upon which it was effected." (The Whigs, on the other hand, in spite of Clay's support of national revolutions in Greece and South America, remained significantly lukewarm.) Lamennais, the eloquent voice of French popular aspirations, was read in Jacksonian circles. The *Paroles d'un Croyant* influenced Orestes A. Brownson, and in 1839 *Le Livre du Peuple* was published in Boston under the title of *The People's Own Book,* translated by Nathaniel Greene, postmaster of Boston, brother of Charles Gordon Greene of the *Post* and intimate of David Henshaw.

Democrats followed with similar enthusiasm the progress of the Reform Bill in England, while the Whigs sympathized with the Tories. The Chartist uprisings at the end of the decade were greeted with delight by the Democratic press. British reformers returned this interest. Not only Cobbett and Savage Landor but the veteran radical Jeremy Bentham observed Jackson's administration with approval. Bentham, a friend of John Quincy Adams, had been disappointed at the triumph in 1828 of this military hero; but early in 1830, as he huddled by his hissing steam radiator, he heard read aloud Jackson's first message to Congress. The old man was highly pleased to discover greater agreement with the new President than with the old. Later he wrote that lengthy and cryptic memorandum entitled *Anti-Senatica,* intended to aid Jackson in the problems of his administration.

Jacksonians everywhere had this faith in the international significance of their fight. For this reason, as well as from a desire to capture their votes, Democratic leaders made special appeals to newly naturalized citizens. Where many Whigs tended to oppose immigration and demand sanctions against it, Democrats welcomed the newcomers with open arms and attacked the nativist agitation. The United States must remain a refuge from tyranny. "The capitalist class," said Samuel J. Tilden, "has banded together all over the world and organized the *modern dynasty of associated wealth,* which maintains an unquestioned ascendency over most of the civilized portions of our race." America was the proving-ground of democracy, and it was the mission of American Democrats to exhibit to the world the glories of government by the people. They were on the spearhead of history. They would not be denied. "With the friends of freedom throughout the world," declared Theophilus Fisk, "let us be co-workers." "The People of the World," cried Fanny Wright, "have but one Cause."

The jacksonians: expectant capitalists

Bray Hammond

During the half century that ended with General Jackson's election, America underwent changes perhaps the most radical and sweeping it has ever undergone in so short a time. It passed the climacteric separating a modern industrial economy from an older one of handicraft; it passed from colonial weakness through bare independence to actual power and from an unjostled rural culture to the complexities of populousness, sectionalism, urban slums, mechanized industry, and monetary credit. Men who had spent their childhood in a thin line of seaboard colonies, close even in their little cities to the edge of the westward continental wilderness, spent their late years in a tamed and wealthy land spread already to the Missouri and about to extend beyond it. They lived to ride on railways and steamships, to use the products of steam-driven machinery, to dwell in metropolitan centers, and to feel within

Reprinted from *Banks and Politics in America from the Revolution to the Civil War* by Bray Hammond. Copyright © 1957 by Princeton University Press. Reprinted by permission of Princeton University Press.

their grasp and the grasp of their sons more potential and accessible wealth than had ever before excited the enterprise of man.

An outstanding factor in the changes that came about was the flow of immigration from Europe. Between 1790 and 1840 the population grew from 4,000,000 to 17,000,000. In the latter year an average of 230 immigrants entered the country daily. Ten years later it was over 1,000 daily. The area of settlement and exploitation expanded swiftly under the pressure of this movement. While General Jackson was President the federal union came to include twice as many states as it had begun with and held territory that recently had belonged to Spain and France. It was shortly to add regions in the South and West taken from Mexico and regions in the Northwest that Great Britain claimed. Its expansion seemed irresistible.

The changes in social outlook were profound. Steam was generating conceptions of life, liberty, and the pursuit of happiness that were quite alien to Thomas Jefferson's; and the newcomers pushing into the country from Europe had more impatient economic motives than their 18th-century predecessors. People were led as they had not been before by visions of money-making. Liberty became transformed into *laisser faire*. A violent, aggressive, economic individualism became established. The democracy became greedy, intolerant, imperialistic, and lawless. It opened economic advantages to those who had not previously had them; yet it allowed wealth to be concentrated in new hands only somewhat more numerous than before, less responsible, and less disciplined. There were unenterprising and unpropertied thousands who missed entirely the economic opportunities with which America was thick. There was poverty in the eastern cities and poverty on the frontier. Those who failed to hold their own in the struggle were set down as unfit.

Wealth was won and lost, lost and won. Patient accumulation was contemned. People believed it was not what they saved but what they made that counted. Jay Cooke, one of America's future millionaires, who was scarcely born poor on a farm but primitively at least, in a frontier settlement, was already on his way to fortune in a private banking firm before the age of twenty and writing home about his work with enthusiasm. This was in the winter of 1839–1840. "My bosses are making money fast," he said. "This business is always good, and those who follow it in time become rich. . . . Among our customers are men of every age and every position in society, from the hoary miser to the dashing buck who lives upon his thousands. Through all grades I see the same all-pervading, all-engrossing anxiety to grow rich." Something of the same sort, to be sure, was taking place in western Europe and especially in Great Britain. Half the people and most of the money for America's transformation came from there. But though industrial and technological revolution occurred also in the Old World, in the New, where vast

resources awaited exploitation, it produced a dazzling, democratic expansion experienced nowhere else. The situation was such that the
rallying cry, *"Laissez nous faire!"* expressed the views of Americans
perfectly, when translated.

Socially, the Jacksonian revolution signified that a nation of democrats
was tired of being governed, however well, by gentlemen from Virginia
and Massachusetts. As Professor Sumner observed, what seems to have
enchanted people with General Jackson when he became a candidate for
President was not any principles or policies he advocated but his
breaches of decorum, real or alleged. Economically, the revolution signified that a nation of potential money-makers could not abide traditionary, conservative limitations on business enterprise, particularly by capitalists in Philadelphia. The Jacksonian revolution was a consequence of
the Industrial Revolution and of a farm-born people's realization that
now anyone in America could get rich and through his own efforts, if he
had a fair chance. A conception of earned wealth arose which rendered
the self-made man as superior morally to the hereditary well-to-do as
the agrarian had been. It was like the conception which led Theodoric
the Great to boast that he held Italy solely by right of conquest and without the shadow of legal, that is, hereditary right. The humbly born and
rugged individualists who were gaining fortunes by their own toil and
sweat, or wits, were still simple Americans, Jeffersonian, anti-monop-
olistic, anti-governmental, but fraught with the spirit of enterprise and
fired with a sense of what soon would be called manifest destiny. They
envied the social and economic advantages of the established urban
capitalists, mercantile and financial; and they fought these aristocrats
with far more zeal and ingenuity than the agrarians ever had. They
resented the federal Bank's interference with expansion of the monetary
supply. They found it bestriding the path of enterprise, and with Apol-
lyon's brag but Christian's better luck they were resolved to spill its soul.
They democratized business under a great show of agrarian idealism
and made the age of Jackson a festival of *laisser faire* prelusive to the
age of Grant and the robber barons.

In their attack on the Bank of the United States, the Jacksonians still
employed the vocabulary of their agrarian backgrounds. The phraseology
of idealism was adapted to money-making, the creed of an earlier generation becoming the cant of its successor. Their terms of abuse were
"oppression," "tyranny," "monied power," "aristocracy," "wealth," "privilege," "monopoly"; their terms of praise were "the humble," "the poor,"
"the simple," "the honest and industrious." Though their cause was a
sophisticated one of enterpriser against capitalist, of banker against
regulation, and of Wall Street against Chestnut, the language was the
same as if they were all back on the farm. Neither the President, nor his
advisers, nor their followers saw any discrepancy between the concept

of freedom in an age of agrarianism and the concept of freedom in one of enterprise. Only the poets and philosophers were really aware that a discrepancy existed and though troubled by it their vision was far from clear. Notwithstanding their language, therefore, the Jacksonians' destruction of the Bank of the United States was in no sense a blow at capitalism or property or the "money power." It was a blow at an older set of capitalists by a newer, more numerous set. It was incident to the democratization of business, the diffusion of enterprise among the mass of people, and the transfer of economic primacy from an old and conservative merchant class to a newer, more aggressive, and more numerous body of business men and speculators of all sorts.

The Jacksonians were unconventional and skillful in politics. In their assault on the Bank they united five important elements, which, incongruities notwithstanding, comprised an effective combination. These were Wall Street's jealousy of Chestnut Street, the business man's dislike of the federal Bank's restraint upon bank credit, the politician's resentment at the Bank's interference with states' rights, popular identification of the Bank with the aristocracy of business, and the direction of agrarian antipathy away from banks in general to the federal Bank in particular. Destruction of the Bank ended federal regulation of bank credit and shifted the money center of the country from Chestnut Street to Wall Street. It left the poor agrarian as poor as he had been before and it left the money power possessed of more and more power than ever.

By the term "Jacksonian" I mean not merely the President's Democratic supporters, whom he still called Republican, but in particular his closest advisers and sharers in responsibility. These included most of his "Kitchen Cabinet," some of his official Cabinet, and a number of others. Those most responsible for the destruction of the Bank, without whose urgency and help it might not have been undertaken or achieved, were all either business men or closely concerned with the business world. Named in the approximate order of their appearance, they were Duff Green, Samuel Ingham, Isaac Hill, Martin Van Buren, Amos Kendall, Francis Preston Blair, Churchill C. Cambreleng, Roger B. Taney, and David Henshaw—all but Taney being or becoming men of wealth. They did not include Major William B. Lewis, a Tennessee planter, one of the General's oldest friends and the only one of his intimates not openly hostile to the Bank. Others of importance were Thomas Hart Benton, James K. Polk, Levi Woodbury, Benjamin F. Butler, Jacob Barker, Reuben M. Whitney, William Gouge, and James A. Hamilton.

*   *   *

With the business interests and objectives of the Jacksonians I have no quarrel save for the cant which made the conflict over the Bank of the United States appear to be one of idealism against lucre and of human rights against property rights. The Jacksonians were no less drawn by lucre than the so-called conservatives, but rather more. They had no greater concern for human rights than the people who had what they were trying to get. The millionaires created by the so-called Jacksonian revolution of "agrarians" against "capitalists"—of the democracy against the money-power—were richer than those they dispossessed, they were more numerous, they were quite as ruthless; and *laisser faire*, after destroying the monopolies and vested rights the Jacksonians decried, produced far greater ones. There was nothing sacred about the federal Bank. The defense of it is simply that it was very useful and if not perfect it could have been improved, had its enemies felt any interest in improving it. The Jacksonians paid no heed to its merits but canted virtuously about the rich and the poor, hydras, and other irrelevancies. This was good politics. But it cannot conceal the envy and acquisitiveness that were their real motives. What the Jacksonians decided on, they directed their propaganda toward, and got. What they went for, they fetched, like Amos Kendall. An unusual number of them were not only business men but journalists, and gained both profit and influence through the press—notably Duff Green, Amos Kendall, Francis Preston Blair, Isaac Hill, and David Henshaw. They told the world it was governed too much. They vied with their great contemporary James Gordon Bennett in a glib and vigorous style. The Washington *Globe,* the organ of the administration, was attractively printed on good paper, every active Jacksonian had to take it, and, its contents aside, even the best people could feel satisfied to have it lying on the parlor table. It relied otherwise on unashamed, repetitious adulation of Andrew Jackson and defamation of his enemies. It presented matters in black and white, Bank and President, hydra and hero. "Many a time," Amos Kendall is made to say in John Pendleton Kennedy's satire, *Quod-libet,* "have I riveted by diligent hammering, a politic and necessary fabrication upon the credulity of the people—so fast that no art of my adversary could tear it away to make room for the truth. Therefore, I say to you and our democratic friends—hammer without ceasing."

Andrew Jackson himself had been lawyer, legislator, jurist, merchant, and land speculator, but principally planter and soldier. His origin was humble and agrarian. He was a self-made man. He belonged to an aristocracy of a frontier sort peculiar to the Southwest of his day—landed, proud, individualistic, slave-owning, and more bound by the cruder conventions than the politer ones. Cock-fighting, betting, horse-racing, and the punctilio of the duel seem to have satisfied its cultural needs. It was without the education and discipline of the older aristocracies of the sea-board. It possessed more of the aristocrat's assertive and obnoxious vices than his gentler, liberal virtues and stood on property and pretension rather than birth and breeding. In a quarrel General Jackson would resort to the field of honor if his enemy were a "gentleman" but merely beat him with a stick on sight if he were not. Such distinctions seem to have been lost on Albert Gallatin, an aristocrat of a different water, in whose fastidious judgment President Jackson was "a pugnacious animal."

Yet the distinction and courtesy of the General's manners took by surprise those who knew him first as President; he was by then unwell, grieving over the death of his wife, and softened besides by what age will sometimes do to men. He was not now the brawler in taverns and at racetracks. "I was agreeably disappointed and pleased," wrote William Lyon Mackenzie of Upper Canada in 1829—a man of considerable violence himself in word and deed—"to find in General Jackson great gentleness and benevolence of manner, accompanied by that good natured affability of address which will enable persons who wait upon him to feel at ease in his presence. . . ." When he chose, however, the General still could storm outrageously enough. He could simulate bursts of passion that terrified strangers, who shrank from having the President of the United States burst a blood vessel on their account, even though they were not fond of him. But his tongue seldom slipped. No one profited from blunders of his. What mistakes he made arose from a child-like trust in his friends and not from carelessness with his adversaries.

He was exceptionally susceptible to the flattery and suggestion of his friends. This did not impair his maintaining a forceful, determined leadership. He listened to his advisers individually and chose his plan of action himself. His native views were agrarian and Jeffersonian, though of Jefferson himself he could entertain very low opinions, and no one—not Alexander Hamilton himself—ever went further from the constitutional principles of Jefferson than Jackson did in his nullification proclamation of December 1832. With him, moreover, as with other self-made men of his time, agrarian and Jeffersonian views faded into *laisser faire*. He was a rugged individualist in all directions. He was no friend to the shiftless and indigent who got into debt and then could not get out. He paid his own debts, no matter how hard he found it to do so, and he expected others to pay theirs.

"Andrew Jackson was on the side of the capitalists," writes Mr Marquis James of his earlier career. "His first case in Nashville in 1788 had landed him as champion of the creditors against the debtors. Jackson desired wealth." He had been opposed to western relief measures taken on behalf of debtors in the ten years preceding his election to the Presidency. They were wicked, pernicious, profligate, and unconstitutional. Opinions like this put him logically on the side of the Bank of the United States, which was the pivotal creditor, and opposed him to the banks made of paper, such as the Bank of the Commonwealth of Kentucky, over which his kitchen adviser, Francis Preston Blair, had presided. But solecisms embarrassed the General very little. On the frontier more than elsewhere, the modification of an agrarian economy into an industrial and financial one was such, in William Lyon Mackenzie's words, as to "make speculation as extensive as life, and transform a Jeffersonian democracy into a nation of gamesters and our land into one great gaming house where all are forced to play, while but few can understand the game." General Jackson's prejudices were stronger than his convictions, and he was himself among the least consistent and stable of the Jacksonians. "Not only was Jackson not a consistent politician," says Professor Thomas P. Abernethy, "he was not even a real leader of democracy. He had no part whatever in the promotion of the liberal movement which was progressing in his own state. . . . He was a self-made man . . . he always believed in making the public serve the ends of the politician. Democracy was good talk with which to win the favor of the people and thereby accomplish ulterior objectives. Jackson never really championed the cause of the people; he only invited them to champion his. He was not consciously hypocritical in this. It was merely the usual way of doing business in these primitive and ingenuous times." Of his election to the Presidency Professor Richard Hofstadter writes that it was not "a mandate for economic reform; no financial changes, no crusades against the national Bank, were promised. . . . Up to the time of his inauguration Jackson had contributed neither a thought nor a deed to the democratic movement, and he was elected without a platform."

What counts is that Jackson was popular. He was a picturesque folk character, and it does his memory an injustice to make him out a statesman. "All the remodelling and recoloring of Andrew Jackson," says Professor Abernethy, "has not created a character half so fascinating as he was in reality." To the dissatisfied, whether through distress or ambition, Andrew Jackson offered a distinct and attractive change from the old school of leaders the country had had—and not the least by his want of real ideas. He became the champion of the common man, even though the latter might be no longer either frontiersman or farmer but speculator, capitalist, or entrepreneur of a new, democratic sort, who in every village and township was beginning to profit by the Industrial Revolution, the growth of population, and the expanding supply of bank credit. This new common man was manufacturer, banker, builder, carrier, and promoter. He belonged to the "active and enterprising," in the luminous contrast put by Churchill C. Cambreleng, as against the "wealthier classes." And his conflict was not the traditionary one between the static rich and the static poor but a dynamic, revolutionary one between those who were already rich and those who sought to become rich.

General Jackson was an excellent leader in the revolt of enterprise

against the regulation of credit by the federal Bank. Though the inferior
of his associates in knowledge, he was extraordinarily effective in combat. And as a popular leader he combined the simple agrarian principles
of political economy absorbed at his mother's knee with the most up-to-
date doctrine of *laisser faire*. Along with several of the best constitutional
authorities of his day—but not Mr Taney —General Jackson believed
that the notes issued by state banks were unconstitutional. In 1820 he
wrote to his friend Major Lewis: "You know my opinion as to the banks,
that is, that the constitution of our state as well as the Constitution of
the United States prohibited the establishment of banks in any state.
Sir, the tenth section of the first article of the federal Constitution is
positive and explicit, and when you read the debates in the convention
you will find it was introduced to prevent a state legislature from passing
such bills." Seventeen years later, in 1837, he wrote to Senator Benton:
"My position now is and has ever been since I have been able to form an
opinion on this subject that Congress has no power to charter a Bank and
that the states are prohibited from issuing bills of credit or granting a
charter by which such bills can be issued by any corporation or order."
Yet in effect he did as much as could be done to augment the issue of
state bank notes and was proud of what he did. Most statesmen would
feel some embarrassment in such a performance.

The Jacksonians were anything but rash. Once decided that they
should fight the Bank rather than wed with it, they developed their attack patiently, experimentally, shrewdly, probing the aristocratic victim
and teasing public interest into action. The President himself took no unnecessary chances, but those he had to take he took without fear. He was
a man of "sagacious temerity," in the words of one of his contemporaries.
His attack on the Bank was like his careful slaying of Charles Dickinson
in a duel thirty years before. His opponent had been formidable—much
younger than he and an expert marksman, which he himself was not.
Each was to have one shot. Jackson and his second had gone over the
prospects carefully and decided it would be best to wait for Dickinson to
fire first. For though Jackson would probably be hit, "he counted on the
resource of his will to sustain him until he could aim deliberately and
shoot to kill, if it were the last act of his life." So he awaited his adversary's fire and, as he had expected, he was hit. But his coat, buttoned
loosely over his breast, as was his wont, had presented a deceptive sil-
houette, and the ball had missed his heart. He concealed his hurt and
concentrated on his helpless enemy, whose life he now could take. "He
stood glowering at him for an instant, and then his long pistol arm came
slowly to a horizontal position." He aimed carefully and pulled the trig-
ger. But the hammer stopped at half-cock. The seconds consulted while
the principals stood, and Jackson was allowed to try again. Once more

he took deliberate aim, his victim waiting in evident horror, and fired. Dickinson fell, mortally hurt. "I should have hit him," Jackson asserted later, "if he had shot me through the brain." The same mystical will power, the same canny and studious appraisal of probabilities and of relative advantages and disadvantages, weighed in the conflict with the Bank. The President tantalized the frank and impatient Mr Biddle, he waited for him to make the appropriate mistakes, and then with care and effectiveness he struck. His adversaries' weaknesses were no less at his command than his own skill. . . .

Despite the fact of a strong and determined rebellion within the business world against the Bank of the United States, the fiction that the attack on the Bank was on behalf of agrarians against capitalists, of humanity against property, of the poor against the rich, and of "the people" against "the money power," has persisted. There was, to be sure, an extremely respectable minority comprising the more conservative and thoughtful men of business, Mr Gallatin, for example, and Nathan Appleton, who defended the Bank till near the end, but it will scarcely do to say that they represented the business world while C. C. Cambreleng, David Henshaw, and Reuben Whitney did not.

It is obvious that New York, besides gaining most from a successful attack on the Bank, risked the least; for it did not need, as the South and West did, the capital brought in by the Bank's branches. The West's aversion for the federal Bank was like the nationalistic resentment in a 20th-century under-developed economy which wants and needs imported capital but growls at the "imperialism" of the country that is expected to provide it. The western enemies of the Bank were moved by complex psychological and political considerations—including past distress and present dependence—while its New York enemies were moved, much more simply, by covetousness and rivalry. This was the decisive new ingredient provided in the Jacksonian attack. The agrarian prejudice had been alive since 1791 and most dangerous to the Bank a few years past during its critical days and the distress in the Ohio valley. The state bank opposition was almost as old as the agrarian. And the relative importance of the two varied with the decline of agrarianism and the growth of enterprise. New York, now the center of enterprise, added to the long-lived antagonism a hearty and acute self-interest. That Andrew Jackson proved to be the instrument of her interest was the happy result of Mr Van Buren's skill and devotion.

It goes without saying that Andrew Jackson himself did not understand what was happening. He had started with a vague, agrarian prejudice against banking which on occasion cropped up throughout his life but never led him to deny himself the service of banks or the friendship

and support of bankers.* It was no great task for his advisers to arouse
this dormant distrust, nourished on what he had read about the South
Sea Bubble, and focus it upon the Bank in Philadelphia, a city whence he
had suffered years before, at the hands of a bankrupt merchant and speculator, a harsh financial misfortune. Nor was an elaborate plot required
to be agreed upon among conspirators. The first harassment of the Bank
from the administration group was evidently spontaneous and simply
aimed at making the Bank Jacksonian. Some time elapsed before it got
under directed control. Even then there is no reason to suppose that the
program was not mainly opportunistic. In the early stages the object
need have been only to make sure that the charter be not renewed. To
this end the General's mind must be fixed against the Bank, and the
proper improvement of opportunities could be left to the discretion of
those in whose path the opportunities appeared. The adviser who influenced the General most directly or who perhaps left the best record of
what he did was Roger B. Taney, though he joined the Jacksonian circle
late. He succeeded in filling the General's mind with a vindictiveness
that Martin Van Buren or Amos Kendall would probably not have produced. They too would have killed the Bank but with less emotion and
less cant. "When a great monied institution," Mr Taney told the General,
"attempts to overawe the President in the discharge of his high constitutional duties, it is conclusive evidence that it is conscious of possessing
vast political power which it supposes the President can be made to feel."
The Taney reasoning is sound, but the premises are misrepresented, and
the effect was to fill the President with bitter suspicion of the Bank;
though the alleged "attempts to overawe the President"—this was written
in June 1832—were the reasonable attempts of Mr Biddle to gain support
for the Bank, find out what the scowls and rumblings from Washington
signified, and remove the doubts that he thought were troubling the
President.

But thanks to the sort of thing Mr Taney kept telling him, the President by now had few doubts such as Mr Biddle imagined. He was merely
considering how best to proceed against the Bank. Replacement, he realized, was necessary, and for a long time he was fumbling over unintel-
ligible projects to that end. One of these projects, which may be intelli-
gible to those whose understanding has not been corrupted by some
knowledge and experience of the subject, was described to James A.
Hamilton, 3 June 1830. The President had in mind "a national bank
chartered upon the principles of the checks and balances of our federal
government, with a branch in each state, the capital apportioned agree-

* He did not cease transacting personal and family business with the Nashville office of the Bank of the United States, which he presumably dissociated from the
main office in Philadelphia. The view was reasonable. Gravitation of the branches
toward independence was a perennial source of weakness to the Bank; and eventually they became local banks in fact.

ably to representation and to be attached to and be made subject to supervision of the Secretary of the Treasury." He recalls having shown
Mr Hamilton "my ideas on a bank project, both of deposit (which I
think the only national bank that the government ought to be connected
with) and one of discount and deposit, which from the success of the
State Bank of South Carolina I have no doubt could be wielded profitably
to our government with less demoralizing effects upon our citizens than
the Bank that now exists. But a *national* Bank, entirely *national* Bank
of deposit is all we ought to have: but I repeat a national Bank of discount and deposit may be established upon our revenue and national
faith pledged and carried on by salaried officers, as our revenue is now
collected, with less injury to the morals of our citizens and to the destruction of our liberty than the present hydra of corruption and all the emol-
uments accrue to the nation as part of the revenue." But these rumina-
tions belonged merely to a period of waiting. As soon as a promising
arrangement offered, the President acted. He ordered the federal funds
removed from the Bank and put in the banks of his friends.

Besides contributing mainly, by this course, to a shift of the money
market from Chestnut Street to Wall Street, the General contributed to
the inflation, the speculation, and the various monetary evils which,
with a persistent agrarian bias, he blamed on banks and paper money.
There were plenty of men in his own party, among them better agrarians
than himself, who would have cleared his vision and tried to, but the old
gentleman preferred the sycophantic advisers who stimulated his suspicions and prejudices, blinded him to facts, confused him about the
nature of the federal Bank's usefulness, diverted his attention from the
possibility that it be amended and corrected instead of being destroyed,
and allowed him to declaim the most ignorant but popular clap-trap.

The nation
takes
shape

Marcus Cunliffe

In summing up the quality of the period 1789–1837 two tempta-
tions should be avoided. One is that of investing it with a false aura of
tranquillity. In some respects, especially up to 1815, it was a time of
prolonged crisis, full of regret and foreboding, hostility and confusion.

The other danger is of assuming that the period constitutes an "era" of its own, separate from what came before and after, instead of being merely a half-century removed from the continuum of American history.

There is nevertheless some point in regarding the period as an entity and in trying to identify its special features. After all, its terminal dates have a certain force. At least 1789 has, as the beginning of the United States under a new Constitution. The working-out of that Constitution, in its various governmental, judicial, political, economic, social, and patriotic implications, is in large part the story of the period. As for 1837, it or its near neighbors in the decade of the 1830's can be argued to mark the inauguration of another era. . . .

. . . Granted that there are some features of the time that disappear subsequently—its homogeneity of population and its pre-industrial economy are two of the chief examples—nevertheless, the American character seems to have been formed in essence within a generation of George Washington's accession to the presidency. How else are we to account for the remarkable freshness, even for the present day, of Alexis de Tocqueville's *Democracy in America,* which was based on a visit to the United States in 1831–32? "National character" is a hazy expression. But for our approximate purposes we may think of it as an assemblage of beliefs and patterns of behavior which are widely recognized, inside and outside the country in question, as being more common among its citizens than among those of other nations. If this clumsy description is acceptable, then we may go on to suggest that Tocqueville's diagnosis of American attitudes to commerce, to social class, to politics, to literature, and a dozen other matters could be applied with surprising relevance to the America of 1870 or even 1950.

One might object that Tocqueville was not really writing about the United States but about the social and political phenomenon of democracy, and that his book is therefore not a guide to American character but a brilliant piece of intellectual prophecy relating to the whole Western world. The criticism cannot be altogether brushed aside. Now and then, in the interests of his thesis, he did overstress the "democratic" ethos of America and the correspondingly "aristocratic" nature of Europe, making the one stand schematically for tomorrow and the other for yesterday. However, the objection can be answered in large part by pointing out that Tocqueville's diary of his American travels—a day-to-day record—embodies the same observations. So, broadly speaking, do the travel narratives of other contemporary European visitors, and so do the commentaries by Americans of the period when they discuss their native qualities. Then, as now, the South was held to be an exception to the prevailing American mood of egalitarian bustle. Then, as now, the more recently settled western areas were praised by some witnesses for their additional informality or "democracy" and criticized by others for their excessive uncouthness. But on the whole, whether favorable or not, the picture drawn by Tocqueville and by lesser men was consistent and is still recognizable. . . .

To observers in the early nineteenth century, then, Americans seem restless, competitive, "go-ahead" (another revealing Americanism coined in Jackson's time), egalitarian, naïve, serious, coarse and importunate yet in some ways prim and moralistic, matter-of-fact and yet imbued with vague, soaring notions of American futurity. This last point was wittily made by Tocqueville, in the comment that the American mind is either concentrated upon the practical and parochial or else diffused in vast and formless reverie, and that in between lies a vacuum. One could go on adding almost indefinitely to the list of American characteristics identified during the period, and nearly all would support the assertion that American "national character" has not altered fundamentally since its early definitions. Similarly, if we glance at the conflicting elements in the picture and at the actual controversies that have separated individual from individual and section from section in American history, there appear to be certain enduring features in the record.

However, . . . it is extremely difficult to analyze American experience in satisfactory terms. Some Europeans and a few disillusioned Americans during the period 1789–1837 gave up the effort or concluded that the effort was not worth making. The United States, they felt, was an unstable experiment, hopelessly divided within itself, lacking in all the necessary safeguards of true nationhood, like some badly designed Mississippi steamboat whirling downriver until the irrevocable collision or explosion shattered her. Even Tocqueville, immeasurably more judicious than most spectators, doubted whether the Union could long hold together—and of course it did not.

By contrast, a number of recent American historians have dwelt upon the essential soundness of their country's early disposition. Seizing like Tocqueville on the absence of feudalism as the basic clue to American national development—on the fact that she was "born in broad daylight," unhampered by the past, dating the origin of her own national epic no farther back than 1776 and therefore able to carry the national legend around with her, so to speak, as a portable heritage—seizing on this truth, these historians have interpreted America's past as an organic affair. American politics were to a considerable degree a matter of *ad hoc* local or sectional bargaining. American ideology was an affair of fine shades, qualifications, ambiguities, contradictions. Perhaps, in such a view, it could be held that Emerson came near to grasping a subtle truth. In his unsystematic, perceptive way he typified the American intellect. He may have touched the heart of American reality with his doctrine of "compensation," according to which dualities are friendly rather than inimical, since they cancel one another out and thus lead to a kind of equilibrium:

> Foolish hands may mix and mar;
> Wise and sure the issues are.
> Round they roll till dark is light.

Some of these newer interpretations are highly sophisticated, so much so that they come full circle and are able to make good use of the old cynical-contemptuous, European view of the United States as a mere shapeless agglomerate. Thus they might fasten upon and extract significance from a casual remark made by the British visitor Mrs. Trollope as she watched a Methodist camp meeting in Ohio. The passage as a whole, from her book *Domestic Manners of the Americans* (1832) is censorious. But she also admits, "I . . . experienced a strange vibration between tragic and comic feeling." In such an *aperçu* a modern commentator might find much food for thought, for it hints at the tantalizing oddity of some sides of American history that could mean little or could mean far more than appears at first glimpse. The revivalist frenzy Mrs. Trollope witnesses is cheap, banal, erotic. Yet it has a pathos, a novelty, a colloquial vigor, a directness of emotion that go deeper than the occasion—like that of a Negro spiritual (the word "spiritual" being both neologist noun and poignant adjective).

Between the sweeping disapproval of a Frances Trollope and the refined insights of a study like R. W. B. Lewis' *The American Adam: Innocence, Tragedy, and Tradition in the Nineteenth Century* (1955) come a quantity of attempts to interpret American history in terms of some bold polarity. In the widest terms of all, the division is seen as that of America versus Europe, which can be taken to imply democracy versus aristocracy, adaptability versus rigidity, innocence versus experience, and so on. Or, in the influential thesis of Frederick Jackson Turner, as West versus East, which represents a not-too-different polarity. Some scholars, for instance, now expound American history within an "Atlantic community," within which in turn there is a boundary between West and East—a boundary that shifts steadily inland across America, so that during part of the nineteenth century the eastern seaboard of the United States is linked economically and culturally with Europe rather than with the trans-Appalachian West.

Or again, there is the familiar polarity of Jefferson versus Hamilton, which can be visualized as a contest between Republicanism and Federalism, or agrarianism and capitalism, or rural life and urbanism, or debtor and creditor, or free trade and the tariff, or Jacksonianism and the "Monster Bank," or state rights and centralization in government, or

—by extension—North and South, which can be again stylized as a division between Massachusetts and Virginia or between freedom and slavery. Present in some interpretations is a theory of class conflict or of sectional controversy as being principally economic in origin.

There is much to be said for these polarities. They have the merit of clarity. They satisfy our ingrained habit of thinking dualistically, in terms of body and soul, god and devil, and so on; we respond readily, for example, to Emerson's idea of an American schism between "the party of the Past and the party of the Future" or to George Bancroft's statement of an immemorial feud between "the capitalist and laborer, the house of Have and the house of Want." They escape the current tendency in historiography to explain away conflicts as mere smoke screens behind which men maneuver and chaffer for "real" benefits.

The arguments epitomized in the string of contests cited above *were* important to those involved in them. Apart from the slavery dispute, perhaps no American controversy was as implacable as some in Europe. They often seem almost pastorally mild after one has looked at the mortal enmities of the Old World during the period. But though in this sense they might be circumscribed quarrels, some of them implied profound differences of viewpoint on how to shape the future. Americans under their new Constitution were gravely conscious that their decisions would be imprinted upon and enlarged in the lives of successive generations. Theirs, they wished to believe, was *tabula rasa*—the clean slate.

But current historiography has nevertheless made some of these polarities seem blurred and dubious; Americans even more than the rest of mankind have been described as likelier to choose "and . . . and" than "either . . . or." . . . Republicanism versus Federalism and Jackson versus the B.U.S. are instances of contests that are by no means clear cut. It is not just that we are uncertain which side is hero and which villain, but that we are not always able to say with confidence which side is which, so confusing and sudden are the shifts in allegiance. Moreover, though some of the polarities seem nearly synonymous and though all are to some extent linked with one another, it is not possible to arrange them meaningfully by parceling them into teams, like this:

America	Europe
West	East
Democracy	Aristocracy
Agrarianism	Capitalism
State Rights	Centralization
South	North

There is a rough correspondence, perhaps, in each of the two groups. But it is so rough as to be almost worthless. Worse than that, it is positively misleading. Overly simple groupings of this kind have led some American historians to attach a spurious dynamism to geography (for such men, one feels, if Bishop Berkeley had never written his celebrated line,"Westward the course of empire," it would have been necessary to invent it. How fitting that the line was stamped on the cover of the first volume of Bancroft's sonorously patriotic history, published in 1834). Others have exaggerated the difference between Europe and the United States, making Europe more tyrannical and obsolescent than it really was and the United States more freedom-loving and progressive than any nation could be under heaven. One can but maintain that Turner's frontier thesis, while "true" and "useful" within limits, suffers from being so simplistic in shape. In his day there were cogent reasons for attempting a synthesis of geography-*cum*-idealism. And in European history, partly because one is dealing with fixed geographical/ethnic areas, partly because of the severity of European controversies and their relation to a well-defined class and occupational structure, it *is* possible to make up quite coherent "teams" of the sort shown above.

For the United States, the thing cannot be done. As some recent neo-conservative writings reveal, the teams will not line up properly. What is "South" doing in the left-hand table if "Aristocracy" is in the right-hand column? One cannot construct an American "conservative" or "liberal" genealogy by any straightforward method. The result is full of illegitimacies, adoptions, divorces, remarriages.

If two teams cannot be chosen, is there any other way of representing the issues of American history for the period (which, to reiterate, embodies or foreshadows most of the major problems in American domestic experience)? The word "polarity" suggests a slightly less obvious diagram, by reminding us of a compass. So let us construct a diagram of polarities set out as a kind of compass and using the same twelve labels as before. North, South, East, and West, though standing for states of mind as well as actual geographical areas of the United States, can be left in their conventional places, as if they were compass points.

This is a more plausible representation. If we regard each of the twelve "points" as a concept or a cluster of attitudes, then this diagram suggests better than the two-team listing the complexities of the American situation. In fact, the diagram could be thought of more fitly as a spectrum of continuous and continuously modified color, each "point" shading off into those adjacent. Neighboring attitudes are shown to bear a sympathetic relationship to one another—like that between "centralization" and "capitalism." In fact, so do any four attitudes within a quadrant—say "aristocracy," "South," "state rights," "agrarianism." The polar opposites can be seen as mutually antagonistic. Here is a pictorial representation that avoids some of the oversimplifications we have alluded to.

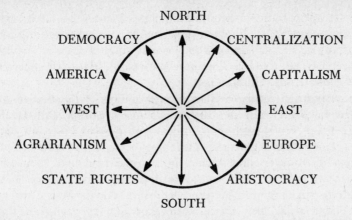

NORTH

DEMOCRACY — CENTRALIZATION

AMERICA — CAPITALISM

WEST — EAST

AGRARIANISM — EUROPE

STATE RIGHTS — ARISTOCRACY

SOUTH

However, the diagram is still not really satisfactory, and no reshuffling of the points will altogether remedy its weaknesses. One trouble is that it perpetuates the notion that the West is more innately "American" than the East and that the West is almost diametrically opposed to "capitalism." Also, of course, the diagram is static. It does not take into account the fluctuations of American development: the process, for instance, by which North and West were drawn together, instead of West to South, or that by which "state rights" became a southern instead of a New England doctrine.

Like the effort to compile two rival teams, it overlooks a basic truth about America. This is the truth grasped by Tocqueville, though he missed some of the historical factors that underlay it and though he emphasized the Europe-America polarity a little too much: in comparison with at any rate the Europe of his father's day, the United States was an amazingly unformed and unfettered society. What was already formed, thanks to the British heritage and to the happy outcome of the Revolutionary War, was acquisitive, Protestant, libertarian, reasonably law-abiding. The rest was a matter for posterity to determine or, rather, for the Americans themselves to impose upon posterity, since they were free agents to a unique degree.

In this whole context rather than in preoccupation with the frontier, the United States was differentiated from Europe (though, in relation to the European continent, Britain itself was a more open and flexible society).

This is not to contend that America had no problems during the period or that she solved them. She was haunted by colonialism and wracked with dissension at the same time that she grew and thrived and exulted. But the point to stress, if we are searching for interpretations, is this: There are ideological polarities of real import. The nature and mission of the United States, the struggle to make it in a new likeness without reference to the Old World, constituted a vital quest, and the continuing influence of Europe posed a genuine dilemma. The wrangle over the balance between the federal government and the states, while it later lost much of its gravity, was during the period a weighty matter. The mutual hostilities of North and South embraced profound issues of government, political economy, and human nature.

These are all significant, and so are other issues. . . . Moreover, Americans alive between 1789 and 1837 took them seriously. But—and here we reach the crux—though the polarities are more or less fixed, the personnel are not. The arguments stand fast, rooted in permanent considerations of law, order, and society, heavy and dignified (if not, as we have seen, speculative in the sense of academic philosophy). The men who employ the arguments, however, constantly change their own standpoints. They change their minds and their political parties, and the parties likewise reverse names and strategies. In 1815 New England and its "godlike" Daniel Webster adopt the extreme state-rights position, while the South and its spokesman John C. Calhoun breathe the spirit of nationalism. Fifteen years later, Calhoun and the South are sectionalist; Webster and his region stand for the federal Union. Similar examples can be found, not merely in politics, throughout the land and throughout the half-century.

Why? Not because politicians were all rogues or because Americans were all vulgar opportunists. But for two reasons. First, that since the United States was inchoate, there were no permanent sectional, political, economic, religious, or occupational groupings of the kind which are immediately recognizable in Europe and which impart a degree of coherence to European affairs even when these affairs include revolutions or other violent upheavals. American society was not entirely fluid; all sorts of rules and associations affected its operation. But they did not form inviolable taboos and imperatives. American society was tentative. Its rules could be modified; "joiners" could be and were "leavers," moving from one societal institution to another at will, and sometimes abruptly from one polar extreme to the other. Such looseness perhaps encouraged cynicism and corruptness of purpose, as permissive situations tend to. But expediency was not an inherent vice.

The second reason has already been suggested. It is that the range of possible choices was, by European standards, extraordinarily wide. Not merely was the American at liberty to change his occupation, his religious and political affiliations, his home and state; he saw before him all sorts of more solemn alternatives on which he was required by the nature of American democracy to have an opinion. His vote was endlessly solicited, his brain teased by conundrums about internal improvements, interstate commerce, the limits of suffrage, policy on land settlement, new states, tariffs. What he decided might make or mar his country. But how on such complex questions *could* he decide? No wonder that the average American changed his mind or did not bother to have an opinion or voted according to calculations of how his pocket would feel—and heavy financial stakes were frequently involved. Again, he was not being inherently irresponsible.

To recapitulate, the polarities are more or less fixed, the personnel are not. The people choose the position that matches their need or conviction of the moment and will shift to another if pressed. Some verities or some symbols of nationality—the Christian church, the Declaration of Independence, the Constitution, the memory of George Washington—are unchallenged in their broad generality; they are in the possession of virtually all Americans. The rest are a common heritage that may be repudiated or accepted as the situation dictates. The comedy of the situation is not lost upon Americans; one side of their nature, in the eyes of European visitors, is a cliché-ridden pomposity that makes them talk all too often like Supreme Court justices or like Independence Day orators. But the other side is a glorious irreverence; they coin big, nonsensical words like "splendiferous," revel in mock solemnity, delight in puncturing the national self-image, for the disparity between the unchanging pieties of nationhood and the nimble uses to which they are put is rich material for the humorist.

A diagram that sought to convey something of this would be too complicated to depict here. In part, though, it could still be conceived of as a fixed compass card of concept polarities, except that we might remove the four geographical labels—North, South, East, West—from the card and perhaps substitute other polarities. On top of the fixed card we might visualize another, floating dial. The superimposed dial would represent various sectional, political, and occupational groups pivoted loosely above the permanent card, defining positions in relation to it: a dial fluctuating, swayed, so cynical-righteous that Tocqueville shuddered a little at the intellectual slovenliness of America, so unsteady that he foresaw the dismemberment of the Union, so buoyant that he rightly marveled at the fortuitous miracle of American democracy.

Such a device may serve to elucidate much that is characteristic and puzzling in American experience. From George Washington to Andrew Jackson (and since), it is the symbol of a people at once erratic and straightforward, self-conscious and demonstrative, friendly and suspicious, tolerant and bigoted, radical and conservative, confident and nostalgic. "Inconsistencies cannot both be right," says the philosopher Imlac in Samuel Johnson's *Rasselas;* "but, imputed to man, they may both be true." His comment hints that one might enter similar claims on behalf of other peoples. Even so, as the events of the formative half-century from 1789 to 1837 may have made plain, it is no accident that while the American language abounds in such words and expressions as "footloose" and "every which way," many of America's national and state mottoes emphasize unity, sameness, perpetuity. Not all these expressions and mottoes were coined during the period but nearly all were anticipated then.

SUGGESTIONS FOR FURTHER READING

Two provocative interpretative essays on Jefferson and Jackson may be found in Richard Hofstadter, *The American Political Tradition* (New York, 1948). Hofstadter plays down the differences between Hamilton and Jefferson and pictures the followers of Jackson as expectant capitalists, rather than as disgruntled farmers and workers seeking more democracy. Claude Bowers in *Jefferson and Hamilton: The Struggle for Democracy in America* (Boston, 1925) has written the classic interpretation of the Jefferson-Hamilton struggle as a "clear-cut fight between democracy and aristocracy." On the other hand Nathan Schachner in *The Founding Fathers* (New York, 1954), is one of several recent historians who is sympathetic to Hamilton. Merrill D. Peterson, *The Jeffersonian Image in the American Mind* (New York, 1960) is a fascinating study of the shifting interpretations of Jefferson.

The most controversial recent book on Jacksonian democracy is Arthur Schlesinger, *The Age of Jackson* (Boston, 1945), a portion of which is reprinted here. But for a critical analysis see, Bray Hammond's review in *Journal of Economic History*, VI (May, 1946), 79–84. Hammond and Hofstadter, unlike Schlesinger, see little conflict in the Jackson period. John Ward in *Andrew Jackson: Symbol for an Age* (New York, 1955) sees conflict, but Jackson becomes a symbol that provided direction for social advance. Marvin Meyers, on the other hand, in *Jacksonian Persuasion* (Stanford, 1957) sees the followers of Jackson trapped by the past, trying desperately to recapture an agrarian dream in an age of expanding industrialism.

IV
THE ★
CIVIL ★
WAR ★

Americans have found their Civil War to be more interesting than any other event in their history. Even the Revolution which marked the birth of the republic cannot compete in popularity with the bloody fratricidal conflict of 1861–1865. The popular imagination has been fed by thousands of books and articles, movies and television performances. Commemorative monuments, museums, parks, and cemeteries dot every state which saw battle. No skirmish, however minor, lacks at least one historical marker to remind visitors of the event, and every state which raised troops has its mementos—flags, uniforms, guns, and equipment—which it treasures. And it is only in recent years that anniversary dates were not marked by the appearance of an old veteran, willing to recount his experiences—real and imagined—in the war.

The historian has not been immune to this fascination with our Civil War. He has recounted the battles many times over and has described, defended, and attacked the actions of the important actors (and many not so important) on both sides of the conflict.

Hundreds of thousands of casualties and millions of dollars in destroyed property are ample evidence that the Civil War marked a sharp conflict in American history. But, how significant were the differences which led to war between North and South in 1861? In October, 1858 William H. Seward, a prominent New York Republican leader, declared that the struggle over slavery which divided North and South was "an irrepressible conflict." Ear-

lier that same year an Illinois Republican politician, Abraham Lincoln, had enunciated similar beliefs: "A house
divided against itself cannot stand. I believe this government cannot endure permanently, half-slave and half-
free."

Taking their lead from such statements some historians
have argued that the Civil War revealed deep and abiding
differences in American society. So significant were the
disagreements between North and South that compromise
became impossible. The gulf which separated the sections
had become so wide that a bridge of consensus could not
be built and conflict in the form of organized warfare was
inevitable. Moreover, the defeat and subjugation of the
South, many of these scholars argue, marked a fundamental turning point in American history. The victory of the
Northern troops led to the victory of the Northern point of
view; compromise, which had been impossible, now had
become unnecessary.

Other historians dispute this interpretation. The nation
had lived with slavery for many generations, they argue,
and when disputes arose between the sections they had
repeatedly been resolved through compromise. While Lincoln made it clear he did not like slavery, he also made it
clear that he would not interfere with it in the South. War
was not inevitable; on the contrary it could have been prevented. That it was not prevented was not the result of
fundamental differences between North and South, but
rather the result of what one historian has called the failures of a "blundering generation."

The three selections which follow give very different
evaluations of the significance of the Civil War. For
Charles and Mary Beard the Civil War was a struggle for
political power waged by representatives of two economic
systems. The War was an "irrepressible conflict" between
the industrial North and the agricultural South; the prize
for which they contended was political domination of the
nation. When the North won on the battlefields, the industrialists won in Congress. The domination of the country
by the agricultural interests was at an end and as such the
Civil War, the Beards conclude, was "a Second American
Revolution."

Both Avery Craven and Daniel J. Boorstin strongly dispute this interpretation. Craven argues that war became
inevitable only after blind emotionalism based on preju-

dice and ignorance had fettered the minds of the people of both sections. What were minor differences which could have been settled became moral absolutes which could no longer be amicably resolved. Boorstin is struck by what he considers to be an essential "continuity" of American thought through the period of the Civil War. He finds both sides more alike than different in their arguments about institutions and politics.

It would seem that the American people would turn to war as a way to settle their differences only after every other means of settlement had proved ineffective. Can we say, then, that the Civil War arose because the differences between North and South were so great and so fundamental that compromise became impossible? If so, the Civil War, however tragic, was inevitable and was only a continuation on the battlefield of a basic conflict which divided the sections. On the other hand, few modern social scientists would deny the existence of irrational sources of human behavior. Can such sources explain the Civil War? Did war come because Americans ignored the roads to compromise and accommodation, roads available to them and utilized by them many times before 1861? If so, the war was a double tragedy and could have been avoided had the participants acted more wisely.

The
second
american
revolution

Charles and Mary Beard

Had the economic systems of the North and the South remained static or changed slowly without effecting immense dislocations in the social structure, the balance of power might have been maintained indefinitely by repeating the compensatory tactics of 1787, 1820, 1833, and 1850; keeping in this manner the inherent antagonisms within the bounds of diplomacy. But nothing was stable in the economy of the United States or in the moral sentiments associated with its diversities.

Within each section of the country, the necessities of the productive system were generating portentous results. The periphery of the industrial vortex of the Northeast was daily enlarging, agriculture in the Northwest was being steadily supplemented by manufacturing, and the area of virgin soil open to exploitation by planters was diminishing with rhythmic regularity—shifting with mechanical precision the weights which statesmen had to adjust in their efforts to maintain the equilibrium of peace. Within each of the three sections also occurred an increasing intensity of social concentration as railways, the telegraph, and the press made travel and communication cheap and almost instantaneous, facilitating the centripetal process that was drawing people of similar economic status and parallel opinions into cooperative activities. Finally the intellectual energies released by accumulating wealth and growing leisure—stimulated by the expansion of the reading public and the literary market—developed with deepened accuracy the word-patterns of the current social persuasions, contributing with galvanic effect to the consolidation of identical groupings.

As the years passed, the planting leaders of Jefferson's agricultural party insisted with mounting fervor that the opposition, first of the Whigs and then of the Republicans, was at bottom an association of interests formed for the purpose of plundering productive management and labor on the land. And with steadfast insistence they declared that in the insatiable greed of their political foes lay the source of the dissensions which were tearing the country asunder.

"There is not a pursuit in which man is engaged (agriculture excepted)," exclaimed Reuben Davis of Mississippi in 1860, "which is not demanding legislative aid to enable it to enlarge its profits and all at the expense of the primary pursuit of man—agriculture. . . . Those interests, having a common purpose of plunder, have united and combined to use the government as the instrument of their operation and have thus virtually converted it into a consolidated empire. Now this combined host of interests stands arrayed against the agricultural states; and this is the reason of the conflict which like an earthquake is shaking our political fabric to its foundation." The furor over slavery is a mere subterfuge to cover other purposes. "Relentless avarice stands firm with its iron heel upon the Constitution." This creature, "incorporated avarice," has chained "the agricultural states to the northern rock" and lives like a vulture upon their prosperity. It is the effort of Prometheus to burst his manacles that provokes the assault on slavery. "These states struggle like a giant," continued Davis, "and alarm these incorporated interests, lest they may break the chain that binds them to usurpation; and therefore they are making this fierce onslaught upon the slave property of the southern states."

The fact that free-soil advocates waged war only on slavery in the territories was to Jefferson Davis conclusive proof of an underlying conspiracy against agriculture. He professed more respect for the abolitionist than for the freesoiler. The former, he said, is dominated by an honest conviction that slavery is wrong everywhere and that all men ought to be free; the latter does not assail slavery in the states—he merely wishes to abolish it in the territories that are in due course to be admitted to the Union.

With challenging directness, Davis turned upon his opponents in the Senate and charged them with using slavery as a blind to delude the unwary: "What do you propose, gentlemen of the Free-Soil party? Do you propose to better the condition of the slave? Not at all. What then do you propose? You say you are opposed to the expansion of slavery. . . . Is the slave to be benefited by it? Not at all. It is not humanity that influences you in the position which you now occupy before the country. . . . It is that you may have an opportunity of cheating us that you want to limit slave territory within circumscribed bounds. It is that you may have a majority in the Congress of the United States and convert the Government into an engine of northern aggrandizement. It is that your section may grow in power and prosperity upon treasures unjustly taken from the South, like the vampire bloated and gorged with the blood which it has secretly sucked from its victim. . . . You desire to weaken the political power of the southern states; and why? Because you want, by an unjust system of legislation, to promote the industry of the New England states, at the expense of the people of the South and their industry."

Such in the mind of Jefferson Davis, fated to be president of the Confederacy, was the real purpose of the party which sought to prohibit slavery in the territories; that party did not declare slavery to be a moral disease calling for the severe remedy of the surgeon; it merely sought to keep bondage out of the new states as they came into the Union—with one fundamental aim in view, namely, to gain political ascendancy in the government of the United States and fasten upon the country an economic policy that meant the exploitation of the South for the benefit of northern capitalism.

But the planters were after all fighting against the census returns, as the phrase of the day ran current. The amazing growth of northern industries, the rapid extension of railways, the swift expansion of foreign trade to the ends of the earth, the attachment of the farming regions of the West to the centers of manufacture and finance through transportation and credit, the destruction of state consciousness by migration, the alien invasion, the erection of new commonwealths in the Valley of Democracy, the nationalistic drive of interstate commerce, the increase of population in the North, and the southward pressure of the capitalistic glacier all conspired to assure the ultimate triumph of what the orators were fond of calling "the free labor system." This was a dynamic thrust far too powerful for planters operating in a limited territory with incompetent labor on soil of diminishing fertility. Those who swept forward with it, exulting in the approaching triumph of machine industry, warned the planters of their ultimate subjection.

To statesmen of the invincible forces recorded in the census returns, the planting opposition was a huge, compact, and self-conscious economic association bent upon political objects—the possession of the government of the United States, the protection of its interests against adverse legislation, dominion over the territories, and enforcement of the national fugitive slave law throughout the length and breadth of the land. No phrase was more often on the lips of northern statesmen than "the slave power." The pages of the Congressional Globe bristled with references to "the slave system" and its influence over the government of the country. But it was left for William H. Seward of New York to describe it with a fullness of familiar knowledge that made his characterization a classic.

Seward knew from experience that a political party was no mere platonic society engaged in discussing abstractions. "A party," he said, "is in one sense a joint stock association, in which those who contribute most direct the action and management of the concern. The slaveholders contributing in an overwhelming proportion to the capital strength of the Democratic party, they necessarily dictate and prescribe its policy. The inevitable caucus system enables them to do this with a show of fairness and justice." This class of slaveholders, consisting of only three hundred and forty-seven thousand persons, Seward went on to say, was spread from the banks of the Delaware to the banks of the Rio Grande; it possessed nearly all the real estate in that section, owned more than three million other "persons" who were denied all civil and political rights, and inhibited "freedom of speech, freedom of press, freedom of the ballot box, freedom of education, freedom of literature, and freedom of popular assemblies. . . . The slaveholding class has become the governing power in each of the slaveholding states and it practically chooses thirty of the sixty-two members of the Senate, ninety of the two hundred and thirty-three members of the House of Representatives, and one hundred and five of the two hundred and ninety-five electors of the President and Vice-President of the United States."

Becoming still more concrete, Seward accused the President of being "a confessed apologist of the slave-property class." Examining the composition of the Senate, he found the slave-owning group in possession of all the important committees. Peering into the House of Representatives he discovered no impregnable bulwark of freedom there. Nor did respect for judicial ermine compel him to spare the Supreme Court. With irony he exclaimed: "How fitting does the proclamation of its opening close with the invocation: 'God save the United States and this honorable court'. . . . The court consists of a chief justice and eight associate justices. Of these five were called from slave states and four from free states. The opinions and bias of each of them were carefully considered by the President and Senate when he was appointed. Not one of them was found wanting in soundness of politics, according to the slaveholder's exposition of the Constitution, and those who were called from the free states were even more distinguished in that respect than their brethren from the slaveholding states."

Seward then analyzed the civil service of the national government and could descry not a single person among the thousands employed in the post office, the treasury, and other great departments who was "false to the slaveholding interest." Under the spoils system, the dominion of the slavocracy extended into all branches of the federal administration. "The customs-houses and the public lands pour forth two golden streams—one into the elections to procure votes for the slaveholding class; and the other into the treasury to be enjoyed by those whom it shall see fit to reward with places in the public service." Even in the North, religion, learning, and the press were under the spell of this masterful class, frightened lest they incur its wrath.

Having described the gigantic operating structure of the slavocracy, Seward drew with equal power a picture of the opposing system founded on "free labor." He surveyed the course of economy in the North—the growth of industry, the spread of railways, the swelling tide of European immigration, and the westward roll of free farmers—rounding out the country, knitting it together, bringing "these antagonistic systems" continually into closer contact. Then he uttered those fateful words which startled conservative citizens from Maine to California—words of prophecy which proved to be brutally true—"the irrepressible conflict."

This inexorable clash, he said, was not "accidental, unnecessary, the work of interested or fanatical agitators and therefore ephemeral." No. "It is an irrepressible conflict between opposing and enduring forces." The hopes of those who sought peace by appealing to slave owners to reform themselves were as chaff in a storm. "How long and with what success have you waited already for that reformation? Did any property class ever so reform itself? Did the patricians in old Rome, the noblesse or clergy in France? The landholders in Ireland? The landed aristocracy in England? Does the slaveholding class even seek to beguile you with such a hope? Has it not become rapacious, arrogant, defiant?" All attempts at compromise were "vain and ephemeral." There was accordingly but one supreme task before the people of the United States—the task of confounding and overthrowing "by one decisive blow the betrayers of the Constitution and freedom forever." In uttering this indictment, this prophecy soon to be fulfilled with such appalling accuracy, Seward stepped beyond the bounds of cautious politics and read himself out of the little group of men who were eligible for the Republican nomination in 1860. Frantic efforts to soften his words by explanations and additions could not appease his critics.

Given an irrepressible conflict which could be symbolized in such unmistakable patterns by competent interpreters of opposing factions, a transfer of the issues from the forum to the field, from the conciliation of diplomacy to the decision of arms was bound to come. Each side obdurately bent upon its designs and convinced of its rectitude, by the fulfillment of its wishes precipitated events and effected distributions of power that culminated finally in the tragedy foretold by Seward. Those Democrats who operated on historic knowledge rather than on prophetic insight, recalling how many times the party of Hamilton had been crushed at elections, remembering how the Whigs had never been able to carry the country on a cleancut Webster-Clay program, and counting upon the continued support of a huge array of farmers and mechanics marshaled behind the planters, imagined apparently that politics—viewed as the science of ballot enumeration—could resolve the problems of power raised by the maintenance of the Union.

And in this opinion they were confirmed by the outcome of the presidential campaign in 1852, when the Whigs, with General Winfield Scott, a hero of the Mexican war, at their head, were thoroughly routed by the Democratic candidate, General Franklin Pierce of New Hampshire. Indeed the verdict of the people was almost savage, for Pierce carried every state but four, receiving 254 out of 296 electoral votes. The Free-Soil party that branded slavery as a crime and called for its prohibition in the territories scarcely made a ripple, polling only 156,000 out of more than three million votes, a figure below the record set in the previous campaign.

With the Whigs beaten and the Free-Soilers evidently a dwindling handful of negligible critics, exultant Democrats took possession of the Executive offices and Congress, inspired by a firm belief that their tenure was secure. Having won an overwhelming victory on a definite tariff for revenue and pro-slavery program, they acted as if the party of Hamilton was for all practical purposes as powerless as the little band of abolitionist agitators. At the succeeding election in 1856 they again swept the country—this time with James Buchanan of Pennsylvania as their candidate. Though his triumph was not as magisterial as that of Pierce it was great enough to warrant a conviction that the supremacy of the Democratic party could not be broken at the polls.

During these eight years of tenure, a series of events occurred under Democratic auspices, which clinched the grasp of the planting interest upon the country and produced a correlative consolidation of the opposition. One line of development indicated an indefinite extension of the slave area; another the positive withdrawal of all government support from industrial and commercial enterprise. The first evidence of the new course came in the year immediately following the inauguration of Pierce. In 1854, Congress defiantly repealed the Missouri Compromise and threw open to slavery the vast section of the Louisiana Purchase which had been closed to it by the covenant adopted more than three decades before. On the instant came a rush of slavery champions from Missouri into Kansas determined to bring it into the southern sphere of influence. Not content with the conquest of the forbidden West, filibustering parties under pro-slavery leaders attempted to seize Cuba and Nicaragua and three American ministers abroad flung out to the world a flaming proclamation, known as the "Ostend Manifesto," which declared that the United States would be justified in wresting Cuba from Spain by force—acts of imperial aggression which even the Democratic administration in Washington felt constrained to repudiate.

Crowning the repeal of the Missouri Compromise came two decisions of the Supreme Court giving sanction to the expansion of slavery in America and assuring high protection for that peculiar institution even in the North. In the Dred Scott case decided in March, 1857, Chief Justice Taney declared in effect that the Missouri Compromise had been void from the beginning and that Congress had no power under the Constitution to prohibit slavery in the territories of the United States anywhere at any time. This legal triumph for the planting interest was followed in 1859 by another decision in which the Supreme Court upheld the fugitive slave law and all the drastic procedure provided for its enforcement. To the frightened abolitionists it seemed that only one more step was needed to make freedom unconstitutional throughout the country.

These extraordinary measures on behalf of slavery were accompanied by others that touched far more vitally economic interests in the North. In 1859, the last of the subsidies for trans-Atlantic steamship companies was ordered discontinued by Congress. In 1857, the tariff was again reduced, betraying an unmistakable drift of the nation toward free trade. In support of this action, the representatives of the South and Southwest were almost unanimous and they gathered into their fold a large number of New England congressmen on condition that no material reductions should be made in duties on cotton goods. On the other hand, the Middle States and the West offered a large majority against tariff reduction so that the division was symptomatic.

Immediately after the new revenue law went into effect an industrial panic burst upon the country, spreading distress among business men and free laborers. While that tempest was running high, the paper money anarchy let loose by the Democrats reached the acme of virulence as the notes of wildcat banks flooded the West and South and financial institutions crashed in every direction, fifty-one failing in Indiana alone within a period of five years. Since all hope of reviving Hamilton's system of finance had been buried, those who believed that a sound currency was essential to national prosperity were driven to the verge of desperation. On top of these economic calamities came Buchanan's veto of the Homestead bill which the impatient agrarians had succeeded in getting through Congress in a compromise form—an act of presidential independence which angered the farmers and mechanics who regarded the national domain as their own inheritance. . . .

The amazing acts of mastery—legislative, executive, judicial—committed by the federal government in the decade between 1850 and 1860 changed the whole political climate of America. They betrayed a growing consolidation in the planting group, its increased dominance in the Democratic party, and an evident determination to realize its economic interests and protect its labor system at all hazards. In a kind of doom, they seemed to mark the final supremacy of the political army which had swept into office with Andrew Jackson. During the thirty-two years between that event and the inauguration of Lincoln, the Democrats controlled the Presidency and the Senate for twenty-four years, the Supreme Court for twenty-six years, and the House of Representatives for twenty-two years. By the end of the period, the old farmer-labor party organized by Jackson had passed under the dominion of the planting interest and the farming wing of the North was confronted with the alternative of surrender or secession.

In this shift of power the Whigs of the South, discovering the tendencies of the popular balloting, moved steadily over into the Democratic camp. Though unavoidable, the transfer was painful; the planting Whigs, being rich and influential, had little affection for the white farmers who rallied around the Jacksonian banner. According to the estimate of a southern newspaper in 1850, the Whigs owned at least three-fourths of all the slaves in the country and it was a matter of common knowledge that leaders among them disliked wildcat banking as much as they hated high duties on the manufactured goods they bought. Indeed to a southern gentleman of the old school the radical agrarianism of Andrew Jackson was probably more odious than the tariff schedules devised by Daniel Webster. It was said that one of them, when asked whether a gentleman could be a Democrat, snapped back the tart reply: "Well, he is not apt to be; but if he is, he is in damned bad company."

But the rich planters were relatively few in numbers and virtue was subject to the law of necessity; the populace had the votes, northern manufacturers were demanding protection, abolitionists were agitating, and in the end all but the most conservative remnant of the southern Whigs had to go over to the party that professed the dangerous doctrines of Jackson. The achievements of the years that lay between 1850 and 1860 seemed to justify the sacrifice.

Though the drift toward the irrepressible conflict was steady and strong, as events revealed, the politics of the decade had the outward semblances of dissolution. The abolitionists and free-soilers, while a mere minority as we have seen, were able to worry the politicians of both parties in the North. Largely deserted by their southern cohorts, the Whigs, whose organization had always been tenuous at best, could discover no way of mustering a majority of votes on the bare economic policies of Hamilton and Webster. Their two victories—in 1840 and 1848—had been dubious and their only hope for a triumph at the polls lay in a combination with other factors. . . .

The signal for a general realignment of factions and parties was given by the passage of the Kansas-Nebraska bill of 1854 repealing the Missouri Compromise. In fact, while that measure was pending in Congress a coalescing movement was to be observed: northern Whigs persuaded that their old party was moribund, Democrats weary of planting dominance, and free-soilers eager to exclude slavery from the territories began to draw together to resist the advance of the planting power. In February of that year, a number of Whigs and Democrats assembled at Ripon, Wisconsin, and resolved that a new party must be formed if the bill passed.

When the expected event occurred, the Ripon insurgents created a fusion committee and chose the name "Republican" as the title of their young political association. In July, a Michigan convention composed of kindred elements demanded the repeal of the Kansas-Nebraska act, the repeal of the fugitive slave law, and the abolition of slavery in the District of Columbia. This convention also agreed to postpone all differences "with regard to political economy or administrative policy" and stay in the field as a "Republican" party until the struggle against slavery extension was finished. All over the country similar meetings were mustered and the local cells of the new national party rose into being. Meanwhile the old Whigs who wanted peace and prosperity were floating about looking for any drifting wreckage that might hold them above the waves. . . .

"The Government has fallen into the hands of the Slave Power completely," wrote Wendell Phillips in 1854. "So far as national politics are concerned, we are beaten—there's no hope. We shall have Cuba in a year or two, Mexico in five, and I should not wonder if efforts were made to revive the slave trade, though perhaps unsuccessfully, as the northern slave states, which live by the export of slaves, would help us in opposing that. Events hurry forward with amazing rapidity; we live fast here. The future seems to unfold a vast slave empire united with Brazil and darkening the whole West. I hope I may be a false prophet, but the sky was never so dark."

Three years later, when the inauguration of Buchanan had turned discouragement into despair, the only strategic stroke that Phillips and his colleagues could invent was to hold an abolition convention in Massachusetts and adopt a solemn slogan calling for the disruption of the Union with the slave states. And the events of the swiftly flowing months that followed, as we have already indicated, merely seemed to confirm the belief of Phillips in the supremacy of the Democratic party led by the indomitable planting interest; events such as the downward revision of the tariff, the withdrawal of the ship subsidies, and the Dred Scott decision opening the territories to slavery.

All the while the conflict was growing more furious. Advocates of protection, taking advantage of the panic which followed the tariff revision, organized a stirring campaign to wean workingmen from their allegiance to a free-trade Democracy. Advocates of a sound currency protested against the depreciated notes and the wildcat banks that spread ruin through all sections of the land. The abolitionists maintained their fusillade, Garrison and Phillips, despite their pessimism, resting neither day nor night. Going beyond the bounds of mere agitation, the slavery faction of Missouri in its grim determination to conquer Kansas for bondage and northern abolitionists in their equally firm resolve to seize it for freedom convulsed the country by bloody deeds and then by bloody reprisals. In a powerful oration, "The Crime against Kansas," done in classical style but bristling with abuse of the slavery party, Charles Sumner threw Congress into a tumult in 1856 and provided a text for the free-soilers laboring to wrest the government from the planting interest. Before the public excitement caused by this speech had died away, the attention of the nation was arrested by a series of debates between Lincoln and Douglas held in Illinois in 1858—debates which set forth in clear and logical form the program for excluding slavery from the territories and the squatter-sovereignty scheme for letting the inhabitants decide the issue for themselves.

Then came the appalling climax in 1859 when John Brown, after a stormy career in Kansas, tried to kindle a servile insurrection in the South. In the spring of that year, Brown attended an anti-slavery convention from which he went away muttering: "These men are all talk; what we need is action—action!" Collecting a few daring comrades he made a raid into Harper's Ferry for the purpose of starting a slave rebellion. Though his efforts failed, though he was quickly executed as a "traitor to Virginia," the act of violence rocked the continent from sea to sea.

In vain did the Republicans try to treat it as the mere work of a fanatic and denounce it as "among the gravest of crimes." In vain did Lincoln attempt to minimize it as an absurd adventure that resulted in nothing noteworthy except the death of Brown. It resounded through the land with the clangor of an alarm bell, aggravating the jangling nerves of a people already excited by fears of a race war and continued disturbances over the seizure of slaves under the fugitive slave act—disorders which sometimes assumed the form of menacing riots.

The turmoil in the country naturally found sharp echoes in the halls of Congress. Buchanan's policy of aiding the slavery party in its efforts to get possession of Kansas and the taunting action of the free-soilers in their determination to save it for liberty, gave abundant occasions for debates that grew more and more acrimonious. Indeed the factions in Congress were now almost at swords' points, passion in argument and gesture becoming the commonplace of the day.

When Senator Sumner made a vehement verbal attack on Senator Butler of South Carolina in 1856, Preston Brooks, a Representative from the same state and a relative of the latter, replied in terms of physical force, catching Sumner unawares and beating his victim senseless with a heavy cane. Though the act was not strictly chivalrous—for Sumner, wedged in between his chair and his desk, could not defend himself—admiring South Carolinians gave Brooks a grand banquet and presented him with a new cane bearing the words: "Use knockdown arguments." On both sides of the Senate chamber all the arts of diplomacy were discarded, and the meanest weapons of personal abuse brought into play. Douglas called Sumner a perjurer who spat forth malignity upon his colleagues. The prim, proud Senator from Massachusetts, conscious of possessing a mellow culture, replied by likening Douglas to a "noisome, squat and nameless animal" that filled the Senate with an offensive odor.

Things were even worse in the lower house. Again and again debate was on the verge of physical combat, for which members equipped themselves with knives and revolvers. A Representative from Pennsylvania and another from North Carolina had to be put under bonds to keep the peace. A general mêlée occurred in the spring of 1860 when Lovejoy, whose brother had been shot by a pro-slavery mob in Illinois, made an unbridled attack on slave owners and Democrats, advanced to their side of the house shaking his fists in a terrible rage, and threw the whole chamber into such a confusion that all the resources of experienced leaders were needed to prevent bloodshed then and there. Without exaggeration did Jefferson Davis exclaim that members of Congress were more like the agents of belligerent states than men assembled in the interest of common welfare—an utterance that was startlingly accurate—born of prophetic certainty. After a few fleeting days, the irrepressible conflict that had so long been raging was actually to pass from the forum to the battlefield, to that court where the only argument was the sword and where the one answer that admitted of no appeal was death.

Every shocking incident on the one side only consolidated the forces on the other. By 1860 leaders of the planting interest had worked out in great detail their economic and political scheme—their ultimatum to the serried opposition—and embodied it in many official documents. The economic elements were those made familiar to the country through twenty years of agitation: no high protective tariffs, no ship subsidies, no national banking and currency system; in short, none of the measures which business enterprise deemed essential to its progress. The remaining problem before the planting interest, namely, how to clinch its grip and prevent a return to the Hamilton-Webster policy as the industrial North rapidly advanced in wealth and population, was faced with the same penchant for definition.

Plans for accomplishing that purpose were mapped out by able spokesmen from the South in a set of Senate resolutions adopted on May 24–25, 1860: slavery is lawful in all the territories under the Constitution; neither Congress nor a local legislature can abolish it there; the federal government is in duty bound to protect slave owners as well as the holders of other forms of property in the territories; it is a violation of the Constitution for any state or any combination of citizens to intermeddle with the domestic institutions of any other state "on any pretext whatever, political, moral, or religious, with a view to their disturbance or subversion"; open or covert attacks on slavery are contrary to the solemn pledges given by the states on entering the Union to protect and defend one another; the inhabitants of a territory on their admission to the Union may decide whether or not they will sanction slavery thereafter; the strict enforcement of the fugitive slave law is required by good faith and the principles of the Constitution.

In brief, the federal government was to do nothing for business enterprise while the planting interest was to be assured the possession of enough political power to guarantee it against the reënactment of the Hamilton-Webster program. Incidentally the labor system of the planting interest was not to be criticized and all runaway property was to be returned. Anything short of this was, in the view of the planting statesmen, "subversive of the Constitution."

The meaning of the ultimatum was not to be mistaken. It was a demand upon the majority of the people to surrender unconditionally for all time to the minority stockholders under the Constitution. It offered nothing to capitalism but capitulation; to the old Whigs of the South nothing but submission. Finally—and this was its revolutionary phase —it called upon the farmers and mechanics who had formed the bulk of Jacksonian Democracy in the North to acknowledge the absolute sovereignty of the planting interest. Besides driving a wedge into the nation, the conditions laid down by the planters also split the Democratic party itself into two factions.

Soon after the Democratic convention assembled at Charleston in April, 1860, this fundamental division became manifest. The northern wing, while entirely willing to indorse the general economic program of the planters, absolutely refused to guarantee them sovereignty in the party and throughout the country. Rejecting the proposal of the southern members to make slavery obligatory in the territories, it would merely offer to "abide by the decisions of the Supreme Court on all questions of constitutional law." Since the Dred Scott case had opened all the territories to slavery, that tender seemed generous enough but the intransigent representatives of the planting interest would not accept it as adequate. Unable to overcome the majority commanded in the convention by the northern group, they withdrew from the assembly, spurning the pleas of their colleagues not to break up the union of hearts on "a mere theory" and countering all arguments with a declaration of finality: "Go your way and we will go ours."

After balloting for a time on candidates without reaching a decision under the two-thirds rule, the remaining members of the Charleston conference adjourned to meet again at Baltimore. When they reassembled, they nominated Stephen A. Douglas of Illinois, the apostle of "squatter sovereignty," who was ready to open the territories to slavery but not to guarantee the planting interest unconditional supremacy in the Democratic party and the Union. Determined to pursue their separate course to the bitter end, the Charleston seceders adopted the platform rejected by the Douglas faction and chose as their candidate, John C. Breckinridge of Kentucky, an unyielding champion of planting aristocracy and its labor system. The union of farmers and slave owners was thus severed: the Republicans had carried off one large fragment of the northern farmers in 1856; Douglas was now carrying off another.

During the confusion in the Democratic ranks, the Republicans, in high glee over the quarrels of the opposition, held their convention in Chicago—a sectional gathering except for representatives from five slave states. Among its delegates the spirit of opposition to slavery extension, which had inspired the party assembly four years before, was still evident but enthusiasm on that ticklish subject was neutralized by the prudence of the practical politicians who, sniffing victory in the air, had rushed to the new tent. Whigs, whose affections were centered on Hamilton's program rather than on Garrison's scheme of salvation, were to be seen on the floor. Advocates of a high protective tariff and friends of free homesteads for mechanics and farmers now mingled with the ardent opponents of slavery in the territories. With their minds fixed on the substance of things sought for, the partisans of caution were almost able to prevent the convention from indorsing the Declaration of Independence. Still they were in favor of restricting the area of slavery; they had no love for the institution and its spread helped to fasten the grip of the planting interest on the government at Washington. So the Republican convention went on record in favor of liberty for the territories, free homesteads for farmers, a protective tariff, and a Pacific railway. As the platform was read, the cheering became especially loud and prolonged when the homestead and tariff planks were reached. Such at least is the testimony of the stenographic report.

Since this declaration of principles was well fitted to work a union of forces, it was essential that the candidate should not divide them. The protective plank would doubtless line up the good old Whigs of the East but tender consideration had to be shown to the Ohio Valley, original home of Jacksonian Democracy, where national banks, tariffs, and other "abominations" still frightened the wary. Without Ohio, Indiana, and Illinois, the Republican managers could not hope to win and they knew that the lower counties of these states were filled with settlers from the slave belt who had no love for the "money power," abolition, or anything that savored of them. In such circumstances Seward, idol of the Whig wing, was no man to offer that section; he was too radical on the slavery issue and too closely associated with "high finance" in addition. "If you do not nominate Seward, where will you get your money?" was the blunt question put by Seward's loyal supporters at Chicago. The question was pertinent but not fatal.

Given this confluence of problems, a man close to the soil of the West was better suited to the requirements of the hour than a New York lawyer with somewhat fastidious tastes, obviously backed by fat purses. The available candidate was Abraham Lincoln of Illinois. Born in Kentucky, he was of southern origin. A son of poor frontier parents, self-educated, a pioneer who in his youth had labored in field and forest, he appealed to the voters of the backwoods. Still by an uncanny genius for practical affairs, he had forged his way to the front as a shrewd lawyer and politician. In his debates with Douglas he had shown himself able to cope with one of the foremost leaders in the Democratic party. On the tariff, bank, currency, and homestead issues he was sound. A local railway attorney, he was trusted among business men.

On the slavery question Lincoln's attitude was firm but conservative. He disliked slavery and frankly said so; yet he was not an abolitionist and he saw no way in which the institution could be uprooted. On the contrary, he favored enforcing the fugitive slave law and he was not prepared to urge even the abolition of slavery in the District of Columbia. His declaration that a house divided against itself could not stand had been counterbalanced by an assertion that the country would become all free or all slave—a creed which any southern planter could have indorsed. Seward's radical doctrine that there was a "higher law" than the Constitution, dedicating the territories to freedom, received from the Illinois lawyer disapproval, not commendation.

Nevertheless Lincoln was definite and positive in his opinion that slavery should not be permitted in the territories. That was necessary to satisfy the minimum demands of the anti-slavery faction and incidentally it pleased those Whigs of the North who at last realized that no Hamiltonian program could be pushed through Congress if the planting interest secured a supremacy, or indeed held an equal share of power, in the Union. Evidently Lincoln was the man of the hour: his heritage was correct, his principles were sound, his sincerity was unquestioned, and his ability as a speaker commanded the minds and hearts of his auditors. He sent word to his friends at Chicago that, although he did not indorse Seward's higher-law doctrine, he agreed with him on the irrepressible conflict. The next day Lincoln was nominated amid huzzas from ten thousand lusty throats.

A large fraction of Whigs and some fragments of the Know Nothing, or American, party, foreseeing calamity in the existing array of interests, tried to save the day by an appeal to lofty sentiments without any definitions. Assuming the name of Constitutional Unionists and boasting that they represented the "intelligence and respectability of the South" as well as the lovers of the national idea everywhere, they held a convention at Baltimore and nominated John Bell of Tennessee and Edward Everett of Massachusetts for President and Vice-President. In the platform they invited their countrymen to forget all divisions and "support the Constitution of the country, the union of the states, and the enforcement of the laws." It was an overture of old men—men who had known and loved Webster and Clay and who shrank with horror from agitations that threatened to end in bloodshed and revolution—a plea for the maintenance of the status quo against the whims of a swiftly changing world.

A spirited campaign followed the nomination of these four candidates for the presidency on four different platforms. Huge campaign funds were raised and spent. Beside pursuing the usual strategy of education, the Republicans resorted to parades and the other spectacular features that had distinguished the log-cabin crusade of General Harrison's year. Emulating the discretion of the Hero of Tippecanoe, Lincoln maintained a judicious silence at Springfield while his champions waged his battles for him, naturally tempering their orations to the requirements of diverse interests. They were fully conscious, as a Republican paper in Philadelphia put it, that "Frémont had tried running on the slavery issue and lost." So while they laid stress on it in many sections, they widened their appeal.

In the West, a particular emphasis was placed on free homesteads and the Pacific railway. With a keen eye for competent strategy, Carl Schurz carried the campaign into Missouri where he protested with eloquence against the action of the slave power in denying "the laboring man the right to acquire property in the soil by his labor" and made a special plea for the German vote on the ground that the free land was to be opened to aliens who declared their intention of becoming American citizens. Discovering that the homestead question was "the greatest issue in the West," Horace Greeley used it to win votes in the East. Agrarians and labor reformers renewed the slogan: "Vote yourself a farm."

In Pennsylvania and New Jersey, protection for iron and steel was the great subject of discussion. Curtin, the Republican candidate for governor in the former state, said not a word about abolishing slavery in his ratification speech but spoke with feeling on "the vast heavings of the heart of Pennsylvania whose sons are pining for protection to their labor and their dearest interests." Warming to his theme, he exclaimed: "This is a contest involving protection and the rights of labor. . . . If you desire to become vast and great, protect the manufactures of Philadelphia. . . . All hail, liberty! All hail, freedom! freedom to the white man! All hail freedom general as the air we breathe!" In a fashion after Curtin's own heart, the editor of the Philadelphia *American* and *Gazette,* surveying the canvass at the finish, repudiated the idea that "any sectional aspect of the slavery question" was up for decision and declared that the great issues were protection for industry, "economy in the conduct of the government, homesteads for settlers on the public domain, retrenchment and accountability in the public expenditures, appropriation for rivers and harbors, a Pacific railroad, the admission of Kansas, and a radical reform in the government."

With a kindred appreciation of practical matters, Seward bore the standard through the North and West. Fully conversant with the Webster policy of commercial expansion in the Pacific and knowing well the political appeal of Manifest Destiny, he proclaimed the future of the American empire—assuring his auditors that in due time American outposts would be pushed along the northwest coast to the Arctic Ocean, that Canada would be gathered into our glorious Union, that the Latin-American republics reorganized under our benign influence would become parts of this magnificent confederation, that the ancient Aztec metropolis, Mexico City, would eventually become the capital of the United States, and that America and Russia, breaking their old friendship, would come to grips in the Far East—"in regions where civilization first began." All this was involved in the election of Lincoln and the triumph of the Republican party. Webster and Cushing and Perry had not wrought in vain.

The three candidates opposed to Lincoln scored points wherever they could. Douglas took the stump with his usual vigor and declaimed to throngs in nearly every state. Orators of the Breckinridge camp, believing that their extreme views were sound everywhere, invaded the North. Bell's champions spoke with dignity and warmth about the dangers inherent in all unwise departures from the past, about the perils of the sectional quarrel. When at length the ballots were cast and counted, it was found that the foes of slavery agitation had carried the country by an overwhelming majority. Their combined vote was a million ahead of Lincoln's total; the two Democratic factions alone, to say nothing of Bell's six hundred thousand followers, outnumbered the Republican army. But in the division and uproar of the campaign Lincoln, even so, had won the Presidency; he was the choice of a minority—a sectional minority at that—but under the terms of the Constitution, he was entitled to the scepter at Washington.

From what has just been said it must be apparent that the forces which produced the irrepressible conflict were very complex in nature and yet the momentous struggle has been so often reduced by historians to simple terms that a re-examination of the traditional thesis has become one of the tasks of the modern age. On the part of northern writers it was long the fashion to declare that slavery was the cause of the conflict between the states. Such for example was the position taken by James Ford Rhodes and made the starting point of his monumental work.

Assuming for the moment that this assertion is correct in a general sense, it will be easily observed even on a superficial investigation that "slavery" was no simple, isolated phenomenon. In itself it was intricate and it had filaments through the whole body economic. It was a labor system, the basis of planting, and the foundation of the southern aristocracy. That aristocracy, in turn, owing to the nature of its economic operations, resorted to public policies that were opposed to capitalism, sought to dominate the federal government, and, with the help of free farmers also engaged in agriculture, did at last dominate it. In the course of that political conquest, all the plans of commerce and industry for federal protection and subvention were overborne. It took more than a finite eye to discern where slavery as an ethical question left off and economics—the struggle over the distribution of wealth—began.

On the other hand, the early historians of the southern school, chagrined by defeat and compelled to face the adverse judgment of brutal fact, made the "rights of states"—something nobler than economics or the enslavement of Negroes—the issue for which the Confederacy fought and bled. That too like slavery seems simple until subjected to a little scrutiny. What is a state? At bottom it is a majority or perhaps a mere plurality of persons engaged in the quest of something supposed to be beneficial, or at all events not injurious, to the pursuers. And what are rights? Abstract, intangible moral values having neither substance nor form? The party debates over the economic issues of the middle period answer with an emphatic negative. If the southern planters had been content to grant tariffs, bounties, subsidies, and preferences to northern commerce and industry, it is not probable that they would have been molested in their most imperious proclamations of sovereignty.

But their theories and their acts involved interests more ponderable than political rhetoric. They threatened the country with secession first in defying the tariff of abominations and when they did secede thirty years later it was in response to the victory of a tariff and homestead party that proposed nothing more dangerous to slavery itself than the mere exclusion of the institution from the territories. It took more than a finite eye to discern where their opposition to the economic system of Hamilton left off and their affection for the rights of states began. The modern reader tossed about in a contrariety of opinions can only take his bearings by examining a few indubitable realities.

With reference to the popular northern view of the conflict, there stands the stubborn fact that at no time during the long gathering of the storm did Garrison's abolition creed rise to the dignity of a first-rate political issue in the North. Nobody but agitators, beneath the contempt of the towering statesmen of the age, ever dared to advocate it. No great political organization even gave it the most casual indorsement.

When the abolitionists launched the Liberty party in the campaign of 1844 to work for emancipation, as we have noted, the voters answered their plea for "the restoration of equality of political rights among men" in a manner that demonstrated the invincible opposition of the American people. Out of more than two and a half million ballots cast in the election, only sixty-five thousand were recorded in favor of the Liberty candidate. That was America's answer to the call for abolition; and the advocates of that policy never again ventured to appeal to the electorate by presenting candidates on such a radical platform.

No other party organized between that time and the clash of arms attempted to do more than demand the exclusion of slavery from the territories and not until the Democrats by repealing the Missouri Compromise threatened to extend slavery throughout the West did any party poll more than a handful of votes on that issue. It is true that Van Buren on a free-soil platform received nearly three hundred thousand votes in 1848 but that was evidently due to personal influence, because his successor on a similar ticket four years afterward dropped into an insignificant place.

Even the Republican party, in the campaign of 1856, coming hard on the act of defiance which swept away the Missouri compact, won little more than one-third the active voters to the cause of restricting the slavery area. When transformed after four more years into a homestead and high tariff party pledged merely to liberty in the territories, the Republicans polled a million votes fewer than the number cast for the opposing factions and rode into power on account of the divided ranks of the enemy. Such was the nation's reply to the anti-slavery agitation from the beginning of the disturbance until the cannon shot at Sumter opened a revolution.

Moreover not a single responsible statesman of the middle period committed himself to the doctrine of immediate and unconditional abolition to be achieved by independent political action. John Quincy Adams, ousted from the presidency by Jacksonian Democracy but returned to Washington as the Representative of a Massachusetts district in Congress, did declare that it was the duty of every free American to work directly for the abolition of slavery and with uncanny vision foresaw that the knot might be cut with the sword. But Adams was regarded by astute party managers as a foolish and embittered old man and his prophecy as a dangerous delusion.

Practical politicians who felt the iron hand of the planters at Washington—politicians who saw how deeply intertwined with the whole economic order the institution of slavery really was—could discover nothing tangible in immediate and unconditional abolition that appealed to reason or came within the range of common sense. Lincoln was emphatic in assuring the slaveholders that no Republican had ever been detected in any attempt to disturb them. "We must not interfere with the institution of slavery in the states where it exists," he urged, "because the Constitution forbids it and the general welfare does not require us to do so."

Since, therefore, the abolition of slavery never appeared in the platform of any great political party, since the only appeal ever made to the electorate on that issue was scornfully repulsed, since the spokesman of the Republicans emphatically declared that his party never intended to interfere with slavery in the states in any shape or form, it seems reasonable to assume that the institution of slavery was not the fundamental issue during the epoch preceding the bombardment of Fort Sumter.

Nor can it be truthfully said, as southern writers were fond of having it, that a tender and consistent regard for the rights of states and for a strict construction of the Constitution was the prime element in the dispute that long divided the country. As a matter of record, from the foundation of the republic, all factions were for high nationalism or low provincialism upon occasion according to their desires at the moment, according to turns in the balance of power. New England nullified federal law when her commerce was affected by the War of 1812 and came out stanchly for liberty and union, one and inseparable, now and forever, in 1833 when South Carolina attempted to nullify a tariff act. Not long afterward, the legislature of Massachusetts, dreading the overweening strength of the Southwest, protested warmly against the annexation of Texas and resolved that "such an act of admission would have no binding force whatever on the people of Massachusetts."

Equally willing to bend theory to practical considerations, the party of the slavocracy argued that the Constitution was to be strictly and narrowly construed whenever tariff and bank measures were up for debate; but no such piddling concept of the grand document was to be held when a bill providing for the prompt and efficient return of fugitive slaves was on the carpet. Less than twenty years after South Carolina prepared to resist by arms federal officers engaged in collecting customs duties, the champions of slavery and states' rights greeted with applause a fugitive slave law which flouted the precious limitations prescribed in the first ten Amendments to the Constitution—a law which provided for the use of all the powers of the national government to assist masters in getting possession of their elusive property—which denied to the alleged slave, who might perchance be a freeman in spite of his color, the right to have a jury trial or even to testify in his own behalf. In other words, it was "constitutional" to employ the engines of the federal authority in catching slaves wherever they might be found in any northern community and to ignore utterly the elementary safeguards of liberty plainly and specifically imposed on Congress by language that admitted of no double interpretation.

On this very issue of personal liberty, historic positions on states' rights were again reversed. Following the example of South Carolina on the tariff, Wisconsin resisted the fugitive slave law as an invasion of her reserved rights—as a violation of the Constitution. Alarmed by this action, Chief Justice Taney answered the disobedient state in a ringing judicial decision announcing a high nationalism that would have delighted the heart of John Marshall, informing the recalcitrant Wisconsin that the Constitution and laws enacted under it were supreme; that the fugitive slave law was fully authorized by the Constitution; and that the Supreme Court was the final arbiter in all controversies over the respective powers of the states and the United States. "If such an arbiter had not been provided in our complicated system of government, internal tranquility could not have been preserved and if such controversies were left to the arbitrament of physical force, our Government, State and National, would cease to be a government of laws, and revolution by force of arms would take the place of courts of justice and judicial decisions." No nullification here; no right of a state to judge for itself respecting infractions of the Constitution by the federal government; federal law is binding everywhere and the Supreme Court, a branch of the national government, is the final judge.

And in what language did Wisconsin reply? The legislature of the state, in a solemn resolution, declared that the decision of the Supreme Court of the United States in the case in question was in direct conflict with the Constitution. It vowed that the essential principles of the Kentucky doctrine of nullification were sound. Then it closed with the rebel fling: "that the several states . . . being sovereign and independent, have the unquestionable right to judge of its [the Constitution's] infraction and that a positive defiance by those sovereignties of all unauthorized acts done or attempted to be done under color of that instrument is the rightful remedy."

That was in 1859. Within two years, men who had voted for that resolution and cheered its adoption were marching off in martial array to vindicate on southern battlefields the supremacy of the Union and the sovereignty of the nation. By that fateful hour the southern politicians who had applauded Taney's declaration that the Supreme Court was the final arbiter in controversies between the states and the national government had come to the solemn conclusion that the states themselves were the arbiters. Such words and events being facts, there can be but one judgment in the court of history; namely, that major premises respecting the nature of the Constitution and deductions made logically from them with masterly eloquence were minor factors in the grand dispute as compared with the interests, desires, and passions that lay deep in the hearts and minds of the contestants.

Indeed, honorable men who held diametrically opposite views found warrant for each in the Constitution. All parties and all individuals, save the extreme abolitionists, protested in an unbroken chant their devotion to the national covenant and to the principles and memory of the inspired men who framed it. As the Bible was sometimes taken as a guide for theologians traveling in opposite directions, so the Constitution was the beacon that lighted the way of statesmen who differed utterly on the issues of the middle period. . . .

When the modern student examines all the verbal disputes over the nature of the Union—the arguments employed by the parties which operated and opposed the federal government between the adoption of the Constitution and the opening of the Civil War—he can hardly do otherwise than conclude that the linguistic devices used first on one side and then on the other were not derived from inherently necessary concepts concerning the intimate essence of the federal system. The roots of the controversy lay elsewhere—in social groupings founded on differences in climate, soil, industries, and labor systems, in divergent social forces, rather than varying degrees of righteousness and wisdom, or what romantic historians call "the magnetism of great personalities."

In the spring of 1861 the full force of the irrepressible conflict burst upon the hesitant and bewildered nation and for four long years the clash of arms filled the land with its brazen clangor. For four long years the anguish, the calamities, and the shocks of the struggle absorbed the energies of the multitudes, blared in the headlines of the newspapers, and loomed impressively in the minds of the men and women who lived and suffered in that age.

Naturally, therefore, all who wrote of the conflict used the terms of war. In its records, the government of the United States officially referred to the contest as the War of the Rebellion, thus by implication setting the stigma of treason on those who served under the Stars and Bars. Repudiating this brand and taking for his shield the righteousness of legitimacy, one of the leading southern statesmen, Alexander H. Stephens, in his great history of the conflict, called it the War between the States. This, too, no less than the title chosen by the federal government, is open to objections; apart from the large assumptions involved, it is not strictly accurate for, in the border states, the armed struggle was a guerrilla war and in Virginia the domestic strife ended in the separation of several counties, under the aegis of a new state constitution, as West Virginia. More recently a distinguished historian, Edward Channing, entitled a volume dealing with the period The War for Southern Independence—a characterization which, though fairly precise, suffers a little perhaps from abstraction.

As a matter of fact all these symbols are misleading in that they overemphasize the element of military force in the grand denouement. War there was unquestionably, immense, wide-sweeping, indubitable, as Carlyle would say. For years the agony of it hung like a pall over the land. And yet with strange swiftness the cloud was lifted and blown away. Merciful grass spread its green mantle over the cruel scars and the gleaming red splotches sank into the hospitable earth.

It was then that the economist and lawyer, looking more calmly on the scene, discovered that the armed conflict had been only one phase of the cataclysm, a transitory phase; that at bottom the so-called Civil War, or the War between the States, in the light of Roman analogy, was a social war, ending in the unquestioned establishment of a new power in the government, making vast changes in the arrangement of classes, in the accumulation and distribution of wealth, in the course of industrial development, and in the Constitution inherited from the Fathers. Merely by the accidents of climate, soil, and geography was it a sectional struggle. If the planting interest had been scattered evenly throughout the industrial region, had there been a horizontal rather than a perpendicular cleavage, the irrepressible conflict would have been resolved by other methods and accompanied by other logical defense mechanisms.

In any event neither accident nor rhetoric should be allowed to obscure the intrinsic character of that struggle. If the operations by which the middle classes of England broke the power of the king and the aristocracy are to be known collectively as the Puritan Revolution, if the series of acts by which the bourgeois and peasants of France overthrew the king, nobility, and clergy is to be called the French Revolution, then accuracy compels us to characterize by the same term the social cataclysm in which the capitalists, laborers, and farmers of the North and West drove from power in the national government the planting aristocracy of the South. Viewed under the light of universal history, the fighting was a fleeting incident; the social revolution was the essential, portentous outcome.

To be sure the battles and campaigns of the epoch are significant to the military strategist; the tragedy and heroism of the contest furnish inspiration to patriots and romance to the makers of epics. But the core of the vortex lay elsewhere. It was in the flowing substance of things limned by statistical reports on finance, commerce, capital, industry, railways, and agriculture, by provisions of constitutional law, and by the pages of statute books—prosaic muniments which show that the so-called civil war was in reality a Second American Revolution and in a strict sense, the First. . . .

An outburst
of emotion

Avery Craven

When Lee surrendered at Appomattox a tall gaunt North Carolinian stolidly stacked arms and fell back into line. He was worn, hungry, and dirty. The insistent Yankees had granted him little time during the past weeks for relaxation. Food had been scarce; the opportunities for cleanliness lacking. He had gone on fighting more from habit than purpose. He had quit because the orders were to that effect. Suddenly, with a sharp realization of what was taking place around him, he turned to his neighbor and drawled: "Damn me if I ever love another country!"

In these words the disheartened Tarheel passed judgment on a generation.

Up to 1825 there had been no "United South" nor no "self-conscious North." There were some recognizable differences between these larger sections, in climate, in economic interests, in ideals, and in those intangible things which go to make "a way of life." But these differences were of long standing and were no more acute than those existing between other geographic regions within the nation. With a population ever on the move toward the West or the city, new and old societies constantly found themselves bound together under the same political organization. With highly diversified natural resources, conflicting types of economic endeavor grew up, side by side, to contend for favorable legislation. Social patterns brought into new lands from different sources fought for dominance. The struggle for control in governments, where majorities ruled, forms the central theme in more than one era of the nation's history.

Nor were the sections units. The careful scholar must ever recognize the cleavage between Upper and Lower New England; between the Ohio Valley and the lake region of the Old Northwest; between the mountains and the bluegrass of Kentucky and Tennessee. He must understand the basic differences between the "tidewater districts" and the "upcountry" in the Old South. He must know that before 1860 every issue which later divided North and South had been fought out and reduced to a workable compromise by Southern men struggling against Southern men in Virginia and the Carolinas—the rights of minorities, the distribution of power between local and central governments, the relative values of a single economic effort as against diversification secured by tariffs and other legislative aids, even the problem of free and slave labor!

Differences—economic, social, and political—did not then or afterwards portend an "irrepressible conflict" between North and South, to be settled only by bloodshed. The War Between the States in 1861–1865 did not come simply because one section was agricultural and the other industrial; because one exploited free labor and the other slaves; or because a sectional majority refused to respect the constitutional rights of the minority! The Northwest was as thoroughly agricultural as the South; the Republican party was vigorous in disclaiming abolition tendencies and was willing to leave slavery alone where it was; the minority has never found the constitution of much value in the face of "manifest destinies." The problem of why these sections went to war lies deeper. It is one of emotions, cultivated hostilities, and ultimately of hatred between sections. Bloodshed was "necessary" because men associated their rivals with disliked and dishonorable symbols, and crowned their own interests with moral sanctions. Differences were but the materials with which passions worked. Each side, in the end, fought the

other for principles and the glory of God, for the preservation of civiliza-
tions, for the maintenance of honor. The conflict was the work of politicians and pious cranks! The peoples knew little of each other as realities. They were both fighting mythical devils.

The steps by which sectional differences were emotionalized are highly
involved and often obscure. Of one thing only can we be reasonably
certain: The first apprehensions and resentments which stirred the people in each section were the product of purely local conditions. We can
understand the national situation only when we have grasped the vital
forces at work in each locality. Men react to what they know—they
create their symbols from such experiences. But they shed blood for and
against abstractions which better carry all the good and all the evils
which they imagine possible from their limited experiences. We must
begin with everyday affairs in each section.

The general period in American history from 1825 to 1860 was one
of vast material growth and expansion. But it was also one in which the
wealth and power of the few grew disproportionately to that of the many.
Democracy was not functioning properly. *Liberty* was putting an end to
equality. If some were content, others felt deepest resentments and
dreamed of a more perfect society as the political and moral right of an
American. It is sometimes difficult to discover whether this claim rested
on the Constitution, the Scriptures, or the Declaration of Independence.
Perhaps they did not make such unimportant distinctions. But at any
rate injustice, lack of material prosperity, loss of equality or failure to
achieve American purposes—all became matters of moral significance
and evidence of God's plan thwarted. It was on the one hand, a day of
pulling down aristocrats, fighting devils, saving democratic institutions,
acquiring material things as a natural and moral right; and on the other,
of checking harebrained movements which threatened social security,
private rights, and private property.

In the Northeast the Industrial Revolution was in full swing. Old commercial centers and fishing villages found themselves overshadowed by
a new life which grew up at the fall line. The city became a land of opportunity—the center of a varied and attractive life. Wealth shifted into
new hands and new places. Labor became dependent on capital. Dominance in legislative halls passed from farmers, merchants, and fisher-
men to industrial leaders and the lawyers they sent to do their bidding.
Daniel Webster's conversion from free trade to protection was only a
larger manifestation of a common phenomenon. The harbor was passing
into eclipse.

Along side of these urban changes went an agricultural revolution as
significant in effects. For the first time the farmers of this region had
expanding markets of their own. Opportunities for specialized crops
which could feed both men and machines brought capital into farming,

crowded out the less efficient, and often set sheep, as in Old England, "to gobbling up" their farms and villages. Thousands, unwilling or unable to make the required adjustments, turned cityward or toward the New West from which they soon poured floods of agricultural produce to plague those who remained behind. Every decade held a crisis for those who tilled the soils of New England and Upper New York. The abandoned farm became the symbol of permanent decline.

Meanwhile a series of Wests were rising one after the other in the great region which stretched from New York to the Mississippi—"a greater New England," the Ohio Valley, the Old Northwest. Each began as a frontier but hurried on as rapidly as exploitation of natural resources could accomplish the task toward a more perfect and complex society. Their citizens had sacrificed the present for future returns which depended on easy access to rich lands and open ways to profitable markets. Their hopes ever outran their realizations but their faith in the dividends of democracy did not decline. They were American pioneers and they had a right to prosper and would do so if democracy functioned properly. But the Panic of '37 spread wreck and ruin among them; land legislation lagged behind their demands; internal improvements came all too slowly; prices slumped as home markets broke and "overproduction" glutted the few outside markets they had developed. Throughout the "middle period" this was a region of half-realized purposes, of extravagant dreams checked by hard raw realities; of plain men who sought consolation and found emotional outlet in evangelical churches; of earnest souls who, here and there, even talked with God. All things, economic as well as social, were either "right" or "wrong." And too many things in this period were "wrong."

The rural North, therefore, throughout the era, was a region of potential and actual unrest. The "average farmer," for whose welfare the American system had been established, resented bitterly the growing importance of the city and the mounting wealth of those engaged in what he considered "minor pursuits." Securing the support of the lesser folk of the towns, only recently come from nearby farms, he launched his protests in various forms, but all in the name of a faltering democracy. The labor movements of the period, says Commons, were "not so much the modern alignment of wage-earner against employer" as they were the revolts of "the poor against the rich, the worker against the owner." Professor Darling has shown that the "Workingmen's Movement" in Massachusetts was almost exclusively a farmers' effort—"a protest against the 'accumulations' in Bostonian society, the assault of 'country folk' on the 'exclusive privileges' of the wealthy." The bitter New England farmer who declared he would "sooner, infinitely sooner, follow [his] daughters to the grave than see them 'go out to service'" in the kitchens of those "who by successful industry, by good luck, or possibly fraud were in a situation to make hewers of wood and drawers of water of their less fortunate sisters and brethren," was merely expressing a very prevalent attitude.

The Locofoco groups were even more concerned about inequality and privilege. An Upper New York convention in 1836, "appointed by the farmers, mechanics and others friendly in their views," struck at the "Banking System" because it "filled the coffers of the already wealthy and took from the earnings of the poor." It denounced the practices of "the courts of law" for being "aristocratic"; it declared in form consciously modeled after the Declaration of Independence that "the foundations of Republican Government are in the equal rights of every citizen, in his person and property, and in their management." This group talked much of the "aristocracy of wealth" and "the odious distinctions betwixt the rich and the poor." They would restore democracy by public education and by granting to every man his "inalienable right to a share of the bounties of our Common Father"—meaning the public domain.

It should also be noted that the transcendental protest against materialism took point from the new urban-industrial growth; that Brook Farm, Hopedale, and Fruitlands represented a return to rural-agricultural living; that the well-being of common men in a democracy formed a basic argument for temperance, peace, women's rights, and abolition. Both the misfortunes and the hopes of a disgruntled people were moving under the banners of *democracy*.

To this glorification was soon added another. The cause of the oppressed was also the cause of "righteousness." Rural folk, whose one social center was the church and whose great spokesman was the preacher, could hardly have escaped this conclusion. The great revivals which burned through the back country and in which Charles Grandison Finney was the leader, shifted the emphasis in Calvinism from "a painful quest for a safe escape from life" to the transforming of this world into the Kingdom of Heaven. Salvation was no longer the "end of all human desire"; it was but the beginning of *being useful in the highest degree possible*." Not only was social reform an obligation but social evils had to do with morality; and the purposes of religion, society, and democratic politics were one and the same. "It is a departure, in our representatives and judges, from the laws of nature and laws of the Creator, which has produced the derangement in the affairs of our State," declared the Locofoco convention referred to above. "To a Believer who has rejoiced in the light of Locofocoism, as an outward sign of the inward light of Christianity," was the dedication in F. Byrdsall's history of the movement. The *Democratic Review* echoed this sentiment by insisting that ". . . Democracy is the cause of Humanity. . . . It is essentially involved in Christianity, of which it has been well said that its pervading spirit of democratic equality among men is its highest fact." Gerrit Smith's congregation at Peterboro in December, 1840, resolved among other things, that:

> Whereas there is, ever amongst professors of religion, a prevailing opinion that it is wrong to preach politics on the Sabbath. *Resolved,* That the correctness of this opinion turns wholly on the character of the politics which are preached; for whilst it is clearly wrong to preach anti-Bible or unrighteous politics on the Sabbath or on any other day, nothing can be clearer than that no day is too holy to be used in preaching the politics which are inculcated in the Bible.

Smith himself declared that "No man's religion is better than his politics." He believed that righteous civil governments depended on "the prevalence of [a] Christianity," which kept from office "anti-abolitionists, and land-monopolists and other enemies of human rights." To leave God out of "a moral reformation" was like enacting "the play of Othello" and leaving "out the part of Othello." To him "Civil Government" was "of God." And Jeffersonian Democracy was God's chosen form of civil government.

In the Northwest the sublimation of local resentments in terms of democracy and morality was even more pronounced. The addition of men and ideas from the Northeast played some part in the formation of attitudes but the expression was largely native. Western men began with the naïve assumption voiced by the members of the Missouri assembly that "Our country is peculiarly the asylum of the oppressed, and emphatically the poor man's home." They were certain that "Every law . . . which opens to the poor man the way to independence . . . not only subserves the cause of Humanity but advances and maintains the fundamental principles of our Government." They believed that "persons . . . disposed to live out of the labors of others" (meaning land speculators) were establishing "a petty aristocracy" which would "choke the tree of Liberty and cause her leaves to wither so that her sons . . . [could] no more recline under her balmy shadows, but . . . [would] be compelled to endure the scorching rays and blasting influences of the slavery making idol of money tyrants." In early days the danger arose from " 'Eastern *millionaires* . . . who like the flies that come upon the borders of Egypt' " caused " 'the land to stink' " but their resentments were vague enough to be lodged in any direction as occasion required. Senator Lewis Cass of Michigan climaxed the argument in favor of settlers by insisting that "we shut our eyes upon the seven hundred per cent., and look to our duty as a Christian people." And a colleague in the House argued that the public lands should go "as God intended, and as good governments and good men desire they should go, into the hands *of the people.*" The significant fact was that here were men who believed in the natural right of settlers to lands and who felt that the failure to secure that right constituted an infringement on democracy and on God's purposes.

The Jacksonian war against "the money power" in an earlier period was "from this same cloth." It represented far more the deep resentments of a "grasping" people than it did a belief in abstract ideals. The same holds, in a degree, for the so-called "free-soil" movement. Historians have largely overlooked the fact that the "liberty groups" with a single human rights appeal failed to gain any great following in the Northwest —but that when Salmon P. Chase, the Democrat, broadened the platform to one in which homesteads, internal improvements at Federal expense, and home markets by tariffs, were included, the moral indignation against slavery rose to a burning flame. A local convention in Chicago in 1848 resolved that the Wilmot Proviso "is now and ever has been the doctrine of the Whigs of the free States" and added hastily, "the Whig party has ever been the firm, steady, and unchanging friend of harbor and river appropriations." Lincoln himself would keep slavery from the territories because God had intended them "for the homes of free white people." The Wisconsin farmer, whose interest in Negroes was slight, did not further heckle this great Commoner when the assurance was given that the prime purpose behind his program was a 160-acre farm for all interested persons. Thus the halo of democracy and morality, in part borrowed from the abolitionist, was placed upon the brow of all vital Western needs, and its bitterness from unrealized ambitions became a holy sentiment.

The next step in the process was one of transferring the resentment, generated out of local conditions, to the Southern planter, and fashioning him into the great symbol of aristocracy, of immorality, and of disloyalty to the democratic government. It began when the evangelical churches accepted slavery as a sin rather than an evil; it reached its climax in the triumph of a political party, purely sectional and openly hostile on moral grounds to the institutions of another section.

The antislavery movement was, in the beginning, part and parcel of the larger humanitarian impulse which got going in the early nineteenth century and which sought to be rid of injustice and to establish a more wholesome social order. It was closely related to the peace movement, the effort for women's rights, the temperance crusade, prison and Sabbath reforms, the improvement of education, and many other efforts of the kind. It rose to particular dominance only gradually and among certain well-defined groups. It was fortunate in leadership but more fortunate in its appeal. Human slavery more clearly violated democratic institutions than any other evil of the day; it was close enough to be touched now and then, yet far enough removed to give widest scope to the imagination; it violated most completely the moral senses of a people whose ideas of sin were largely in terms of self-indulgence and whose purposes in religious expression were toward the social betterment of the downtrodden; and, what was as important, it constituted the most talked-of feature in the life of a rival section long contending for control in a government of majorities. Garrison, who, if living today, could profitably consult a psychiatrist, early denounced slavery as a crime and the slaveholder as a criminal. But, of more reaching consequences were the teachings of Theodore Weld and his type, who as W. C. Preston said, made "the anti-slavery cause identical with religion" and urged men "by all the high and exciting obligations of duty of man to God, by all that can warm the heart and inflame the imagination, to join the pious work of purging the sin of slavery from the land."

It was but a step from such attitudes to the condemnation of Southern men for holding slaves or permitting others to hold them. By 1841 Garrison was speaking of "The desperadoes from the South, in Congress" and declaring that "We would sooner trust the honor of the country . . . in the hands of the inmates of our penitentiaries and prisons, than in their hands . . . they are the meanest of thieves and the worst of robbers. . . . We do not acknowledge them to be within the pale of Christianity, of republicanism, of humanity." And then finding his hatred not entirely spent he lamented the poverty of the English language which prevented doing full justice to the infamy of the South.

This conception of the slaveholder opened the way for abolition imaginations to create much needed symbols. In a surprisingly short time *all* Southerners, except a few "poor whites," were planters, living in great white-pillared mansions, drinking intemperately, consorting with female slaves, and selling "down river" their own blood without the trace of a civilized blush. "A million and a half slave women, some of them without a tinge of African blood, are given up, a lawful prey to the unbridled lusts of their masters," declared an antislavery tract. A whole section of the nation living upon the toil of a downtrodden race. Here was the aristocrat *par excellence;* the perfection in licentiousness and self-indulgence! Harriet Beecher Stowe in *Uncle Tom's Cabin* pictured a way of life which would have done credit to the romancing of a Thomas Nelson Page; novels, and there were scores of them, like *Our World: or the Slaveholder's Daughter*, pictured a society of licentiousness which must have disturbed the dreams of many an abstemious Puritan. The South had begun to do service for all aristocrats and all sinners in an era of democracy and morality!

Garrison and his kind, of course, were few; his violence was shared by only a handful of antislavery men, who in turn formed a very, very small minority in the North. His attitudes are important only because they were *extreme*, and by their extremeness reveal in clearest fashion something of what was gradually to seep into the subconsciousness of a whole people. One day, only a few decades off, the moral weaknesses of slaveholding would form a vital part of the understanding of a whole section and hatred of Southerners be so near the surface that "the shedding of a little blood" would set them savagely at the throats of their neighbors.

The next step in the process was one of directly associating the slave-holding South with the economic and social ills from which men of North and West suffered. The "hard times" of the late 1830's, they said, were due to the fact that Northern capital had been loaned to "prodigal" Southern planters who could not and would not repay. "Slavery," said the report of the American Anti-Slavery Society in 1837, "is the rule of violence and arbitrary will. . . . It would be quite in character both with its theory and practice . . . if the slave-drivers should refuse to pay their debts and meet the sheriff with dirk and pistol." Three years later the Society resolved "That the existence of Slavery is the grand cause of the pecuniary embarrassments of the Country; and that no real permanent relief is to be expected . . . until the total abolition of that execrable system." One writer estimated that within five years the South had taken "more than $100,000,000 by notes which will never be paid."

This period saw also the rise of the idea of a "slave-power" or "slave-ocracy" which had seized control of the Federal government to shape its policies in the interests of slavery. It had already destroyed "the protective system 'at the hazard, if not with the intention' of breaking up the manufacturing interests of the free states." It had developed and protected markets for cotton "in all parts of the known world, while it studiously avoided doing anything to procure a market for the free products of the grain growing Northwest."

The aggressive opposition of Southern leaders to pre-emption and homestead legislation in the period from 1840 to 1860 added to the growing belief that slave interests were hostile to Western development. A typical point of view was that of Senator James M. Mason of Virginia who declared that he had "not yet known . . . a bill so fraught with mischief, and mischief of the most demoralizing tendency, as the homestead bill." *The Columbus* [Mississippi] *Democrat* insisted that settlers on homesteads would be abolitionists" and declared that it would be "better for us that these territories should remain a waste, a howling wilderness, trod only by red hunters than be so settled." Robert Y. Hayne of South Carolina added insult to injury by implying that a homesteader was a "drone," a man unworthy "of protection in a country where every man goes ahead who has any strength of will, or any firmness, or any character."

Northwestern reaction to such attitudes was sharp and direct. "When did the Senator from Georgia ever vote anything for Iowa or the West?" growled Augustus Caesar Dodge at one who opposed his measures. "I, sir, have inherited my Democracy," said James M. Cavanaugh, member of the House from Minnesota, "have been attached to the Democratic party from my boyhood. . . . But, sir, when I see southern gentlemen come up . . . and refuse . . . to aid my constituents, refuse to place the actual tiller of the soil, the honest, industrious laborer, beyond the grasp and avarice of the speculator, I tell you, sir, I falter and hesitate." The Dubuque (Iowa) *Herald* revealed the emotional extent reached in 1860 in these words: "Last Saturday the old reprobate, who now sits in the Presidential chair at Washington *vetoed the Homestead Bill*. . . . The slave propagandists demanded that the Bill should be vetoed, and their pliant tool was swift to obey them. Let the pimps and hirelings of the old sinner defend this last act of his, if they dare."

Even more bitter was the complaint against Southern opposition to river and harbor improvements. "This harbor question," said the Chicago *Democrat* after Polk's veto of a favorable bill, "is not a political one, but a sectional one. It is one between the North and the South. The iron rod wielded over her [the North] by Southern despots must be broken." Another Chicago paper declared:

The North can and will be no longer hoodwinked. If no measure of protection and improvement of anything North or West are to be suffered by our Southern masters, if we are to be downtrodden and all our cherished interests crushed by them, a signal revolution will eventually ensue. The same spirit and energy that forced emancipation for the whole country from Great Britain will throw off the Southern Yoke. . . . The power to oppress shall not again be entrusted to men who have shown themselves to be slave-holders, but not Americans.

A final charge against the so-called "slaveocracy" was the corruption of the Democratic party. When James K. Polk was elected president in 1844, certain old leaders such as Martin Van Buren, Francis Preston Blair, and Thomas H. Benton were pushed aside. Each in turn blamed John C. Calhoun and the slave interests; each in a different way added to the impression that the party was no longer a fit place for those who followed the immortal Andrew Jackson. The antislavery groups darkened the picture, and Whig and Republican partisans completed it. Distrust thus created ended in a widespread belief that the annexation of Texas, the Mexican War, the Kansas-Nebraska Act, and the Dred Scott Decision were steps in a well-worked out scheme for the extension of slavery and the rule of the slaveholder. Scholars have revealed the falsity of such opinions; yet in the years before the war they served all the purposes of fact, and Seward and Lincoln used them as deliberately as did the recognized demagogues. Even John Wentworth, a staunch Northern Democrat, accused his Southern colleagues of always acting as slaveholders, never as party men. By 1860 Wyndham Robertson, looking back at the recent Republican victory, could say: "The possession of the power of the Federal Government by the Democratic party . . . furnished the pretext . . . to confound the whole slave-holding interest as identical with democracy, and thus to turn and direct opposition, for whatever cause, to the policy and acts of the Democratic party, into opposition to the slave-holding interests."

Thus by 1860 the apprehensions and resentments of the North had deepened as they had been sanctified by democracy and morality. That section, striving as it believed, for things truly American, had fallen short of realization because of opposition from aristocratic and ignoble enemies. The time for being firm had arrived. The right to hate had been achieved. And what was as important the South had been fashioned into the perfect symbol of all they feared and all they despised. The extreme abolition picture of what slaveholders might be had been given legal currency by the bombast of politicians in verbal conflict for place and power and favors. They pictured an aggressive interest, wringing great wealth from unwilling and overworked Negroes, bent on extending its system to the ends of the land. They talked of "a house divided against itself"; of "a higher law" of "the aristocratic lords of slavery." The ends they sought were immediate, but common folk back home, under the sway of unimaginative evangelical clergymen could think only in terms of the eternal verities. In 1854 they created the Republican party which in six short years passed from an expression of the moral indignation of a limited group to the position of carrier of all the material aspirations of a section and the political hopes of most of those not under the Democratic roof. It was the party of homestead legislation—the culmination of America's greatest democratic effort, the fruition of God's purpose, as Senator John P. Hale put it, to have His lands inhabited (and it might be added, a policy made more democratic and more holy by relieving poor settlers from competition with slaveholders). It was the party of internal improvements with Federal aid— a policy now embracing a Pacific Railroad along the central route for the upbuilding of Chicago and St. Louis. Lincoln's railroad support in 1860 rivaled that of Douglas and came from lines better placed for future trends than his. It was the party of protective tariffs—a policy lifted by the logic of William H. Seward into the very cornerstone of democratic society. Free farmers and industrialists at last united for common accomplishment! Satisfactory markets and new prosperity for all, including Pennsylvania and Cameron! Here was a program making the Union worth saving; the experiment in democracy would pay sound dividends.

But this was not all. The great ideals of an evangelistic Calvinistic society had not been sacrificed in the turn toward "respectability." In opposing the extension of slavery, the party skillfully capitalized on all the moral indignation long generating against the institution itself. Its leaders disavowed all the political implications of abolition sentiment yet openly announced their personal abhorrence of slaveholding. They even took profit from the few who went further. Charles Sumner's bitter invectives, aimed "to keep alive that old Puritan hatred of wickedness, which must overthrow slavery," were carefully distributed by the machine throughout the rural North. Seward permitted his "higher law" and "irrepressible conflict" doctrines to become "all things to all men."

And Lincoln's "ultimate extinction" policy was used to satisfy all but the most extreme abolitionists. The Republican "stock in trade" was indeed, as Caleb Cushing said, "the insolent assumption, in some of them, perhaps, the stupid mental delusion, that whatever view they take of the measures of government *is the only moral side of public questions.*"

It was this situation which produced a crisis in the party when Douglas' squatter sovereignty, in practice, yielded only free territory. The danger of slave extension, on which the party was founded, was over. And by 1858 even Republican leaders understood this fact. Some said the party had fulfilled its mission and should join with Stephen A. Douglas in the formation of a new party for wider sectional and national ends. Some talked of a "broad base" by which the Republicans could attack the old Southern Whigs. But Abraham Lincoln, in his "House Divided" speech, prevented himself and his party from being thrust aside by a desperate appeal to old moral foundations. Though *his* own policy and that of "Judge" Douglas gave identical results, the latter was not born of moral conviction. And until the issue was conceived in terms of "the eternal struggle between two principles—right and wrong—throughout the world" the fight must go on. That is why a man who was willing to save the Union at the cost of a bloody civil war, even with slavery untouched, would not save it by a compromise which yielded party principle but which did not sacrifice a single material thing. The party was one with God and the world's great experiment in Democracy.

The Southern side of the story needs only to be suggested. Rural and lacking in means for the easy creation and expression of public opinion, the section was ever peculiarly susceptible to the ideas and oratory of a few leaders. As a result the focal point of consciousness was, in the beginning, generally an abstract and theoretical right which logic deduced from some traditional source. In the ante-bellum period, when farmers, who lived by staple crops, felt the sting of poverty, these spokes·men, under the influence of Old World agrarian thinking, voiced protest in terms of local government versus central government made strong by the power to grant economic favors. Specifically, industry and commerce, largely centering in the North, were, by tariffs and centralization, profiting at the expense of the nation's real producers. Before long Southerners were calculating the millions of dollars tribute paid to this "Lord North" and were talking of being in a state of colonial dependence.

The remedy was found in a strict adherence to the Constitution. Yankee traits could be controlled and Southern rights be preserved by a series of phrases, on the meaning of which not even the framers could agree. The section had begun to chop logic; it was the champion of things as they were,—a conscious minority in a republican system. Yet in its own eyes, the South was the defender of democratic government against the onslaughts of those who would distort sacred institutions in order to promote their own material interests. All that the Revolution had won, all that "the Fathers" had achieved, was involved in the struggle.

When opposition to slavery developed, a new threat of economic loss, now joined with fear of racial conflict and social unrest, was added. When that drive became a moral attack on the whole Southern way of life, the defense broadened in proportion and emotions deepened. The Constitution was not enough against those who would not respect its provisions; the whole South must become unified for political efficiency. The section must have that security which the Constitution guaranteed and an equal right to expand with its institutions *as a matter of principle*. Keen minds set to work to reveal the virtues in slavery and the life it permitted in the South. When they had finished a stratified society, with Negro "mud-sills" at the bottom, alone permitted genuine republican government, escaped the ills of labor and race conflict, gave widest opportunity for ability and culture, and truly forwarded the cause of civilization. The stability and quiet under such a system were contrasted with the restless strife of the North which was developing socialism and threatening the destruction of security in person and in property. The Southern way of life was the way of order and progress.

Here was something else worth fighting to preserve. The old struggle against "King Numbers," which in large part had been won at home, must go on. But the field had broadened and the struggle was against a foe more base and self-seeking. Both the system of republican government and the cause of civilization were bound up in the struggle.

Early efforts at unified defense proved futile because the masses, with cotton and the hopes it gave, could not muster the emotional response to leaders sufficient for action. They neither felt the inferiority suggested by economic dependence nor the compelling force of rights which gave no practical returns. They gladly accepted compromise in 1850, and were surprisingly unmoved throughout the next eight years. Leaders might support the fruitless Kansas-Nebraska Bill, as the Richmond *Enquirer* said, "solely for the reason that it would vindicate the equality and sovereignty of the states." But the masses, to quote one individual, were "not a particle" excited. They knew, as this writer put it, that the struggle was over "a shadow." Their outlook was as yet practical.

But the John Brown raid was another matter. It put reality into the much discussed program of Yankee "money-changers," "peasant farmers," and the "long haired men and short haired women" of the North. The sharpest resentments and deepest fears of which a people were capable broke loose. A race war was impending. And that was a poor man's problem. Albert G. Brown of Mississippi put it this way.

The rich will flee the country. . . . Then the non-slaveholder will begin to see what his real fate is. The Negro will intrude into his preserve . . . insist on being treated as an equal . . . that he shall go to the white man's bed, and the white man his . . . that his son shall marry the white man's daughter, and the white man's daughter his son. In short that they shall live on terms of perfect social equality. The non-slaveholder will, of course, reject the terms. Then will commence a war of races such as has marked the history of San Domingo.

The triumph of the Republican party, sectional and containing, as it did, men as rabid as Sumner and as vague and shifting as Seward and Lincoln, drove the more inflamed Southerners to secession. Lincoln's refusal of compromise and his handling of Fort Sumter forced conservatives to follow. War had become inevitable. Fear and hate had taken charge.

By May, 1861, that staunch lover of the Union, Jonathan Worth, could write from peaceable old Randolph County in North Carolina: "The voice of reason is silenced. Furious passion and thirst for blood consume the air. . . . Nobody is allowed to retain and assert his reason. The cartridge box is preferred to the ballot box. The very women and children are for war."

A little later the New York *Herald* solemnly reported from the battlefield of Bull Run that Southern "fiends in human shape have taken the bayonets and knives of our wounded and dying soldiers and thrust them into their hearts and left them sticking there, and some of the Louisiana Zouaves have severed the heads of our dead from their bodies, and amused themselves by kicking them as footballs."

The old Carolinian at Appomattox was right. It is a serious thing to love a country!

The civil war and the spirit of compromise

Daniel J. Boorstin

As the American Revolution had been a struggle within a long-established colonial framework, so the Civil War was a struggle within a working federal system. The two events were to have analogous consequences in hedging in our political reflection, and in identifying the special institutions of this country with the normal conditions of life on

this continent. Whatever theoretical debate went on, with few exceptions, was concerned not with the nature of governments but rather with
the nature of this particular government.

That the Civil War was a federal conflict, like the colonial character
of our Revolution, seems, perhaps, too obvious to require elaboration.
But some of our ablest recent historians have given currency to an emphasis which has tended to obscure, or even to displace, the obvious.

In their brilliant *Rise of American Civilization,* Charles A. and Mary
R. Beard christened the Civil War "The Second American Revolution."
The phrase and the idea have had wide appeal. It has suited our current
attitudes to suspect that the actual subject of debate was not the real
cause of the conflict. The battle itself, supposedly, was but a symptom of
deeper forces: "the social cataclysm in which the capitalists, laborers,
and farmers of the North and West drove from power in the national
government the planting aristocracy of the South . . . the social revolution was the essential, portentous outcome." Without denying that such
a social revolution was taking place, we can recall that there was another
side to the conflict. If we turn our attention from inevitable forces to
human debate, we must look primarily at a different aspect of the struggle. This is only appropriate, since we are concerned with the place of
theory in our conscious political life.

The name "The Second American Revolution" given by the Beards
and their disciples, is misleading. They (and others who find the center
of change in economic events) would thus emphasize the *dis*continuity
of our history: the Civil War as a hiatus in our development, a gulf between an agricultural-commercial and an industrial society. But to those
students who, like me, are impressed by the extraordinary continuity of
our history, such an emphasis seems distortion. As we all know, the
great economic developments are slow, evolutionary, and sometimes im-
perceptible; their triumphs are not self-announced in manifestoes. The
Industrial Revolution was a matter of centuries, and the kind of revolution to which the Beards refer must also have been a matter of decades.

But *political* history (such events as go by the name of "revolution"
and "civil war") has the abruptness of mutation. It is therefore in this
area that it would be especially significant to note that what is called a
great gulf in our history may not be so great as has been supposed. One
of the remarkable characteristics of our Civil War, as contrasted with
civil wars of recent European history (excepting possibly the English
Civil War), is that ours did *not* significantly interrupt the continuity of
our thinking about institutions.

From the point of view of political and constitutional thought, we
might do better to call our Civil War "The Second War of Independence."
I have already mentioned Guizot's remark that the English Revolution

succeeded twice, once in England in the seventeenth century and a second time in America in the eighteenth. We might go further and say that, from the point of view of constitutional law and political theory, the Revolution occurred a third time, namely, in the middle of the nineteenth century. For the relation of the ancient rights of Englishmen to federalism, which was only partly redefined in the course of the American Revolution, was more extensively explored and settled during the Civil War.

That continuity of our political thought which, as we have seen, had been expressed in the legalistic character of the American Revolutionary debate was also expressed later in much of the argument over the Civil War. There is even less evidence here for the pattern which Carl Becker saw in the Revolution. The main current did not seem to rise above the "provincial" level of constitutionalism to the more "cosmopolitan" atmosphere of natural law. Indeed, we find something of the opposite of what Becker remarks as the increasing abstractness of Revolutionary debate. In the South at least, as the crisis proceeded the debate seemed to become more and more legalistic, reaching its climax actually after the war was over. The legal debate never rose to the realm of natural law, not even to the extent found in the American Revolution.

The North and the South each considered that it was fighting primarily for its legal rights under the sacred federal Constitution. A man like Thoreau probably stood only for himself and a few fire-eating abolitionists. On neither side do we hear much of the sort of argument familiar in European civil wars: that the existing federal constitution was bad and ought to be changed, and that was what one should fight for. On the contrary, each side purported to represent the authentic original doctrine, to be *defending* the Constitution.

Calhoun, who was by far the most profound of the southern writers on the subject, shows this peculiarity. His major theoretical work, not published until after his death in 1850, consists of two parts: "A Disquisition on Government" and "A Discourse on the Constitution and Government of the United States." It is on these that his growing reputation as a political philosopher largely depends. These works taken together (as Calhoun intended that they should be) admirably illustrate the point of view I have been describing.

The "Disquisition," an essay of about a hundred pages, though starting from some general principles of psychology and political theory, is primarily a defense of Calhoun's principle of the "concurrent majority" and an exposition of his objections to governments based on the "numerical majority." In a closely reasoned argument, Calhoun points out the dangers of uncontrolled majority rule. The only safeguard, he insists, is a system of constitutionalism which will allow each separate interest a veto on all legislation to which it objects. Such a system, he urges, results in moderation and compromise and still can leave government strong enough to combat enemies from without. He supports his argument by the experience of Rome, Poland, and Great Britain.

"A Discourse on the Constitution and Government of the United States," a work about three times the length of the "Disquisition," is the sequel. In it Calhoun tries to show that "it was the object of the framers of the constitution, in organizing the government, to give to the two elements [the states as units and the voting population], of which it is composed, separate, but concurrent action; and, consequently, a veto on each other, whenever the organization of the department, or the nature of the power would admit: and when this could not be done, so to blend the two, as to make as near an approach to it, in effect, as possible. It is, also, apparent, that the government, regarded apart from the constitution, is the government of the concurrent, and not of the numerical majority" (*Works*, I, 181).

By reference to the proceedings of the Philadelphia convention and of the ratifying conventions, Calhoun demonstrates that, through a happy coincidence, the true and original conception of the federal Constitution was actually nothing but a design for the attainment of his ideal government. The departure from his ideal, the gradual growth of a consolidated national government, and the development of means by which one section could dominate another were all to be explained as departures from the true intent of the Framers.

> To the one, or to the other,—to monarchy, or disunion it must come, if not prevented by strenuous and timely efforts. And this brings up the question,— How is it to be prevented? How can these sad alternatives be averted? For this purpose, it is indispensable that the government of the United States should be restored to its federal character. Nothing short of a perfect restoration, as it came from the hands of its framers, can avert them [*Works*, I, 381].

This restoration was to be effected by getting rid of certain perversions which had been introduced after the adoption of the Constitution. Calhoun urges, for example, the repeal of Section 25 of the Judiciary Act of 1789, and of the Act of 1833; "the repeal of all acts by which the money power is carried beyond its constitutional limits"; the confining of the president to those powers expressly conferred on him by the Constitution and by acts of Congress; the return in practice to the original way of electing the president and vice-president.

Such means as these—together with a few reforms like the introduction of a plural executive—would, in Calhoun's phrase, "complete the work of restoration." We are never allowed to forget that what Calhoun aims at is not revolution but *restoration*.

A CONFLICT OF ORTHODOXIES

Here, once again, was a competition between constitutional orthodoxies. As often in American history, a great political conflict was taking the form not of a struggle between essentially different political theories but between differences of constitutional emphasis. There was a striking, if obvious, parallel to the epoch of the Revolution. But the South was now even more conservative than the Revolutionaries had been. It found no reason to issue a Declaration of Independence. The colonists had set themselves up as defenders of the British constitution and contended that it was not they but the parliament who were actually the revolutionaries. So now, champions of the South could—and did—argue that it was not they, but the northerners, who were, properly speaking, the revolutionaries. Each accused the other of seeking to overthrow the established doctrine of the federal Constitution, the ideas of the Founding Fathers.

The Civil War secessionist argument—like that of the Revolution—could be carried on in such a conservative vocabulary because both events were, theoretically speaking, only surface breaches in a firm federal framework. Because of this, they both implied, win or lose, the continued acceptance of the existing structure of local government. Thus in the Civil War southern partisans, like the Americans in the Revolution, could continue to profess loyalty to the theory of the Union. As a New Yorker championing the Southern cause declared in 1860:

> The South views the matter in the spirit of Patrick Henry. "The object is now, indeed, small, but the shadow is large enough to darken all this fair land." They can have no faith in men who profess what they think a great moral principle, and deny that they intend to act upon it. It was the principle of taxation without representation that the colonies resisted, and it is the principle of the "irrepressible conflict," based avowedly on a "higher law," that the South resists. She is now in the position of the Colonies eighty-four years ago, and is adopting the same measures that they adopted. . . . A prompt retreat from this dangerous agitation within the shadow of the Constitution, is the only means of realizing the rich future, which will be the reward only of harmony, good faith, and loyalty to the Constitution [Thomas P. Kettell, *Southern Wealth and Northern Profits* (New York, 1860), p. 5].

On the other side, Lincoln, in nearly every one of his principal speeches, appealed to the authentic Revolutionary tradition. His most succinct statement was, of course, in the familiar opening of the Gettysburg Address, to which I have already referred in another connection. But he rang all the rhetorical changes on this appeal, as, for example, in his speech at Peoria in 1854:

> Our republican robe is soiled and trailed in the dust. Let us repurify it. Let us turn and wash it white in the spirit, if not the blood, of the Revolution. Let us turn slavery from its claims of "moral right" back upon its existing legal rights and its argument of "necessity." Let us return it to the position our fathers gave it, and there let it rest in peace. Let us readopt the Declaration of Independence, and with it the practices and policy which harmonize with it.

Statesmen of the North were perhaps more inclined to appeal to the Declaration of Independence, while those of the South leaned more heav-

ily on the Constitution. But both had in common the assumption that
the pretty homogeneous philosophy of the Founding Fathers was what
they were being called upon to vindicate. Fitzhugh did, to be sure,
characterize the Declaration as "exhuberantly false, and arborescently
fallacious." Yet even the Declaration of Independence was by no means
generally rejected by southern advocates. Some southerners, for example, Chief Justice Taney in the Dred Scott decision, even argued that
their position had been well stated in the Declaration. They adduced
historical proof (in my opinion convincing) that the authors of the
sacred document had intended that Negroes be excluded from their
professions of "equality." Another remarkable feature of the Dred Scott
decision for us is the frankness with which it takes a preformation or a
static view of the Constitution. Chief Justice Taney seemed to assume
that the legal question of Negro status could be resolved by accurate historical definition of the original meaning of the Declaration of Independence and the Constitution, considered together.

Few documents could be more interesting in this connection than one
which nowadays is almost never read. For there is probably no more authentic index to the theoretical conservatism of the "rebel" cause than
the Constitution of the Confederate States of America. President Jefferson Davis boasted that the document proved the "conservative" temper
of the people of the Confederate States. Alexander Stephens, his vice-
president, declared that the form of the document showed that "their
only leading object was to sustain, uphold, and perpetuate the fundamental principles of the Constitution of the United States." Closely following the original in organization, the Confederate constitution is almost a verbatim copy of the federal Constitution.

Its differences consist mainly in that it incorporates into the body of
the document some of the principal amendments to the federal Constitution (the Bill of Rights, for example, being absorbed into Art. I, sec. 9);
and it explicitly resolves certain ambiguities (for example, those concerning slavery and the federal principle generally) in the sense which
the South believed to have been the original intent of the authors. The
Preamble, for example, reads:

> We, the People of the Confederate States, each State acting in its sovereign
> and independent character, in order to form a permanent Federal Government,
> establish justice, insure domestic tranquility, and secure the blessings of
> liberty to ourselves and our posterity—invoking the favor and guidance of Al-
> mighty God—do ordain and establish this Constitution for the Confederate
> States of America.

It is of great significance that in our bloody Civil War the so-called
"rebel" side produced, through two of its best minds, treatises on the
origin and nature of our Constitution which deserve to stand, alongside
The Federalist and Adams' *Defence of the Constitutions*, on the small

shelf of basic books about the American political system. The first, of course, is Calhoun's "Discourse on the Constitution and Government of the United States" (1851), which I have already described. The second is Alexander H. Stephens' *Constitutional View of the Late War between the States* (1868–70).

We cannot be surprised that the South, weaker in economy and in arms, found an incentive to be stronger in legal debate. But it remains a curiosity of political thought, as well as a pregnant fact of American history, that the principal theoretical defense of the southern position should have been a treatise on the origin of the federal Constitution, produced actually *after* the South had lost the last battle. Stephens' work was dedicated to "All true friends of the Union under the Constitution of the United States, throughout their entire limits, without regard to present or past party associations." The conflict, Stephens emphasized, was not basically over slavery but over two "different and opposing ideas as to the nature of what is known as the General Government. The contest was between those who held it to be strictly Federal in its character, and those who maintained that it was thoroughly National." The work is historical: a documented demonstration that the Constitution was intended to set up a *federal* government.

We can begin to grasp the true proportions of what I have called the continuity of the history of the United States, as contrasted with that of the countries of western Europe, if we try to imagine the leader of a defeated party in any of the recent European civil wars producing a heavy scholarly treatise proving that he had been in the right *strictly from the point of view of constitutional theory*. George Fitzhugh in 1857 and Jefferson Davis in 1881 both earnestly wished for the "strength and perpetuity" of the Union.

In virtually every one of the recent domestic struggles in Europe, the conflict has been so basic that only one side could conceivably have set itself up as the champion of existing legal institutions. The other has proudly stood for a new concept of government, for a new constitution, and another basis of law. Hitler's cynicism toward the German constitution is typical of this frame of mind. Yet in the American Civil War, after hundreds of thousands of lives had been lost, both sides were still thinking on similar constitutional assumptions. An intelligent and realistic critic like Alexander Stephens still after the war considered it possible that his image of the original doctrine (that the Union was a federal and not a national government) might eventually prevail. This hope would have been hardly conceivable, had not both parties to the conflict accepted the same premises of political theory, had they not preserved a common devotion to a hypothetically perfect original theory. This is what I mean by the idea of "preformation."

For the reasons which I have mentioned, the legacy of the Civil War to American thought has been one of sectionalism and constitutional debate rather than of dogmatic nationalism and "return to fundamentals." The tendency of sectionalism has been to reinforce our awareness of variety within our national culture and of the desirability and inevitability of preserving it. The tendency of the continuous constitutional tradition has been to give the defeated cause, the South, a legitimate theoretical position within the federal system.

The South, except in its romantic literature of chivalry and mint juleps, is now no champion of a different concept of life but rather of a different constitutional emphasis. The South remains, as it is desirable that someone should always be, champion of the states'-rights, local-autonomy principle of our federal Constitution. The South can still debate about what it once gave its lives to defend, for it has never lost essential devotion to the constitutional spirit and its pure original image. What Lincoln called "the spirit of concession and compromise, that spirit which has never failed us in past perils, and which may be safely trusted for all the future"—that spirit can survive precisely because the Civil War was poor in political theory. Notwithstanding the abolitionists and people like Garrison who wished to burn the Constitution, the war did not represent a quest for a general redefinition of political values.

Whatever the crimes, the senseless bitterness, that were visited on the South in the era of reconstruction, they were committed in a vindictive or narrowly provincial spirit. The triumph of the national emphasis in the federal structure did not carry with it victory of a nationalist philosophy. In Lincoln's phrase, "the Union"—not any self-conscious national culture—was what was to be preserved. This distinguished him sharply from his contemporaries like Bismarck and Cavour. The remarkable reintegration of the South into our constitutional system is the best evidence of the community of certain assumptions. The Civil War emerged, then, as a struggle over complicated matters, on which everyone knew there had been a long series of compromises, beginning with the Declaration of Independence and the Constitution themselves. Such a controversy could have happened only within the framework of going federal institutions.

Not the least remarkable feature of the Civil War—apart from the fact that it occurred at all—is that it was so unproductive of political theory. This, the bloodiest single civil war of the nineteenth century, was also perhaps the least theoretical. The sectional character of the conflict had tended to make sociology—the description of things as they were—take the place of the uncharted exploration of things as they ought to be. It also prevented the crisis from propagating panaceas. This was another example of the recurrent tendency in American history to identify the "is" with the "ought," to think of values and a theory of society as implicit in facts about society. The era was strikingly lacking in romanticism of the Rousseauistic brand. The romantics of the day were the Thaddeus Stevenses—the bearers of fire and sword.

At the same time, the federal character of the struggle, the fact that it took place within a functioning federal order, confined much of the theoretical discussion within the area of constitutional law, of the search for the true original image of the Constitution. This, too, discouraged American thinkers of the age (excepting a vagrant Thoreau) from making confusion in the market place an excuse for going off into the solitude of the woods to rethink the whole problem of institutions. The sense of "givenness" was reinforced. In this case it meant the empirical tradition, the reliance on constitutionalism, and an unwillingness to remake institutions out of whole cloth.

The continuity of American political thought—which included the American way of *not* philosophizing about politics—was to stay. The mere fact that the nation had survived the ordeal of civil war seemed itself to prove the strength of the thread which bound the present to the past and to confirm the common destiny of the nation.

SUGGESTIONS FOR FURTHER READING

Avery Craven's point of view may be found in greater detail in his *The Coming of the Civil War* (Chicago, 1942) and *The Growth of Southern Nationalism, 1848–1861* (Baton Rouge, 1953). A similar viewpoint is described in an influential article by James G. Randall, "The Blundering Generation," *Mississippi Valley Historical Review*, XXVII (June, 1940).

Charles and Mary Beard's description of the Civil War as a "revolution" is supported by Louis M. Hacker, *The Triumph of American Capitalism* (New York, 1940). Arthur C. Cole finds the Civil War to be *The Irrepressible Conflict, 1850–1865* (New York, 1934), and Robert R. Russell describes some Southern economic grievances in his *Economic Aspects of Southern Sectionalism, 1840–61* (Urbana, Ill., 1924).

David Donald has argued perceptively against both the Craven and the Beard points of view in his "An Excess of Democracy: The American Civil War and the Social Process," Chapter XI of *Lincoln Reconsidered (New York, 1961).

No subject has received more attention than the Civil War; the bibliography is endless. Those wishing to delve into the literature may start with Thomas J. Pressly, *Americans Interpret Their Civil War* (Princeton, 1954). A convenient collection of primary and secondary sources on the war may be found in Edwin C. Rozwenc, ed., *The Causes of the American Civil War* (Boston, 1961).

V
FARMERS ★
IN AN ★
INDUSTRIAL ★
AGE ★

"Those who labor in the earth are the chosen people of God," wrote Thomas Jefferson. Virtue resides in the
hearts of the agriculturists, he explained. "Corruption of
morals in the mass of cultivators is a phenomenon of
which no age nor nation has furnished an example." To
this day many Americans have the vague feeling that
farming is the most natural, the most virtuous occupation, that somehow those who work the land are especially
important to the survival of American democracy.

Yet farmers are rarely mentioned in American history
except in discussions of farmers' problems. And, indeed,
over the years the American farmer has had many serious
problems. In the colonial period, when most of the nation's citizens tilled the soil, the small farmers along the
frontier bore the brunt of the Indian raids and lamented
the lack of adequate protection for their families and
lands. They complained that they were under-represented
in the assemblies, over-taxed, and given too few of the
bridges and roads they demanded. Occasionally, when
they felt that their problems had gone unheeded too long,
they rebelled against colonial authorities.

Independence did not end the small farmers' difficulties. Shays' Rebellion in Massachusetts, the Whiskey Rebellion in Pennsylvania, both put down quickly, represented
the unhappiness and the discontent of some farmers.

Working the land may have seemed an ideal occupation to those living in the cities, but many farmers knew better. The everyday struggle to eke out a living from the soil, often without the cooperation of the elements, was hard and frequently frustrating. Nor did the passage of time solve the farmers' problems; more often new problems were added to the old.

From the colonial period to the early nineteenth century, most of those who worked the land were subsistence farmers, that is, they produced the greatest part of what they ate and wore. A few had a cash crop—potash or grain (often distilled into whiskey) or cotton or tobacco, depending on the area—but most sold very little of what they raised. With the rise of industrialism in the mid-nineteenth century, and the improvement of transportation, first through the canal and then the railroad, subsistence farming gave way in many areas to commercial farming. Farmers concentrated on cash crops, wheat or cotton or pork, and used the proceeds to buy the food and clothing and the other items they needed. With the rise of commercial farming, the farmer lost his economic independence. He became increasingly dependent on the bankers, who lent him money to buy more land and machinery needed to increase production, and upon the railroad, which was often the only way he could get his crop to market. Moreover, his income, and hence his well-being, depended upon the vicissitudes of the world-wide market for his crop.

The spread of commercial farming and the expansion of industrialism, especially in the years after the Civil War, raised the standard of living of many farmers, who were able to purchase some of the luxuries enjoyed by the city-dweller. Often, however, the price of higher living standards was great. Many went deeply in debt as they sought to increase production through the purchase of new lands and machinery. As production rose, prices went down; efforts to increase income through further increases in production compounded the problem. Fluctuations of the business cycle, as well as the natural disasters of droughts, floods, hail, and wind added to the farmers' woes. Increasingly in the years after the Civil War, the farmer felt victimized, and often he blamed the railroad or the banker for his plight. To improve his situation he attempted to organize. He joined the Patrons of Husbandry, more commonly known as the Grange. At first primarily a social organization, inevitably the Grange became involved in politics in several mid-western states and successfully pressured for laws regulating railroads. Most of the laws proved inadequate and the farmers continued to agitate, joining societies like the Agricultural Wheel in Arkansas, the Farmers' Union in Louisiana, and the Farmers' Alliances in various other states. All of this organizing came to a climax in 1892 when many farmers bolted the two regular parties and formed the Peoples' or Populist Party.

The Populists regarded their movement as a massive struggle against "the interests," the bankers, railroad owners, and big businessmen generally. For many of their opponents, the movement was fraught with danger, for it smacked of revolution. Some historians have accepted this evaluation and have concluded that the farmers' movements represented a fundamental class conflict in American society. Other scholars disagree. The farmers were not revolutionary, they insist, but merely wanted a bigger slice of the economic pie and therefore differed little from the other classes in society. Both these viewpoints are represented in the following selections.

In the first selection Thomas Cochran and William Miller describe farmers essentially as businessmen, and these authors see the farmers' main difficulty developing because they were not very good businessmen. Richard Hofstadter agrees essentially with Cochran and Miller that the farmers' problems resulted from their inability to adapt themselves to the modern world of industry. He also suggests that the Populists really wanted to turn the clock back, to return to the age of subsistence agriculture, the small family farm, and the pastoral village. The Populists, according to Hofstadter, thought there was real conflict in American society, indeed that there was a conspiracy and that they were the victims. But the conspiracy, according to Hofstadter, was a product of their own imagination. Norman Pollack, on the other hand, sees the conflict between farmers and businessmen as real and important. He sees the Populists as realists and radicals, who were not trying to return to the past, but instead looked forward to a time when the businessmen would no longer be able to exploit the farmers and workers.

There can be no doubt that the farmer's life was often difficult and that his complaints were real and justified.

But did the farmer's problems stem from fundamental differences in American society? Was he a victim, as he claimed, of the businessmen and bankers who controlled the country? Did his efforts to organize to improve his condition signal class war between farmer and businessman? Or were the farmers simply the victims of overproduction which drove their prices down? If so, then perhaps their complaints and their organizational efforts, despite the rhetoric involved, were merely efforts to adapt to the new industrial age.

Commercial farmers in an industrial age

Thomas Cochran and
William Miller

Men are in business, according to Gras and Larson, when they "make a living *chiefly* out of providing goods and services for exchange with others." On this basis early American farmers living on nearly self-sufficient farms, relying on local services for milling, smithing, tanning, and lumbering, were not businessmen. But even in the colonial period the great southern plantations were business ventures. In addition, many wheat, corn, and cattle farms in the valleys of the Chesapeake, Susquehanna, Delaware, and Hudson rivers and truck farms near big towns were business enterprises. The shift from local self-sufficiency to specialization and distant marketing, therefore, particularly in new western areas after 1850, was simply an extension of business agriculture in the United States. Sometimes, when a railroad or canal brought new transportation to the back country, specialization took place rapidly; more often it occurred gradually as industrialism built up surrounding cities, and lower shipping costs widened markets.

While specialization in cash crops meant higher living standards, it also meant increased dependence upon stable weather conditions and greater vulnerability to market fluctuations. Individual farmers, however, had little choice in determining whether or not to run these new risks. As expanding industries sent factory products into rural areas, local services upon which farmers depended were killed off. Local fulling, weaving, and flour mills closed down, local foundries and smithies that made farm and household implements were abandoned. Unless farmers could buy the new city goods in the market, therefore, their economic and social positions deteriorated, and for those who would at least maintain their standard of living there was nothing to do but grow *cash* crops.

Many farmers to be sure, especially in some hilly areas of the South, East, and older Middle West, did not take this alternative; and in these regions, as the soil was exhausted and local enterprises shut down, the population and the standard of living declined. In 1920 about 25 per cent of American farms were in these retrogressive areas, and they maintained the original self-sufficient system with only slight changes. The settlement of the prairie states and the Great Plains following the Civil War, however, opened up enormous new areas that were cultivated on a business basis practically from the start, and thus made the great majority of American farmers business farmers with many business problems in common. It is in the story of this majority, therefore, that we are chiefly interested. The cattlemen, who were the first producers to occupy the Plains, were usually large business enterprisers investing substantial amounts of capital, often foreign capital, in the conversion of the prairie grass into beef to feed the rapidly growing urban populations of Europe and the United States. But it was not long before large portions of the cattle ranges were enclosed and put under cultivation by farmers who were brought West by the railroads. These farmers bought farms on credit from land companies. They were in debt for mortgages to local lenders and banks. And they devoted their energies to raising wheat for world markets. Thus they were as completely subject to the agencies of industrial business as a Minneapolis merchant or manufacturer.

Though farming, especially in the West, became a great business, the commercial farmers themselves—their characteristic individualism heightened by their dispersion over the prairies and the Plains—almost always came off second best in their financial jousts with industrialists and financiers. Almost continuously after the Civil War, therefore, large numbers of discontented cultivators were seeking ways and means to check their growing indebtedness. Through political regulation of elevator and railroad rates, and through cooperation among themselves in marketing and banking, they sought to reduce their costs. Through diversification of crops they sought to increase their incomes. None of these stratagems, however, brought relief to the whole farm community or to those most in need of assistance. And even in the twentieth century, when new conditions made agrarian prosperity possible, the staple farmers failed to reduce their burdensome debt.

Up to 1933, at least, the farmer remained one of the few true competitors in a business society that steadily was becoming less and less competitive. Hence, he almost alone was subject to the classic laws of the *laissez faire* market to which those around him paid lip service only. If he could not solve the problems of production and distribution under rigorous competition, he was doomed as a property owner. He might then become a tenant or a wage laborer, or abandon farming altogether, and one of these courses was the fate of the majority of Americans born on the farm.

PLANNING AND PLANTING

The failure of the farmer after the Civil War permanently to improve his position was due mainly to the complexities of his business problems. From the very start he had to plan his crops carefully, in relation to soil, rainfall, and temperature. Corn, for example, needed at least eight inches of rain during the growing season, and a mean summer temperature of over 65 degrees. Even the hardiest varieties of wheat need a certain minimum depth of subsurface moisture at planting. Yet these conditions are not constant, and in dry areas like western Kansas or Oklahoma they were present in some years and absent in others, present in one township and lacking in the next. In well watered, fertile areas like Illinois and Iowa, on the other hand, the cultivator was faced with even greater problems in selecting the particular crops which would yield the maximum cash returns without impairing the fertility of the soil.

The mechanization of cereal production after 1850 introduced also the problem of buying new machinery if new crops were to be attempted, and hence the necessity for careful calculation of the initial cost of equipment, its probable earning power, and its length of life. Obviously it would not pay to purchase a reaper, twine binder, or complete harvester if only a few acres of wheat were to be planted; yet if they were not purchased reliable arrangements had to be made for renting such equipment when it was needed for the harvest. And in addition to the problems of new equipment, there were those of new skills and new information.

These difficulties led directly to a third general consideration: the proper apportionment of labor and machinery to acreage. What should be done by hand? When should horses be replaced by a tractor, a team and wagon by a motor truck? The heaviness of yield per acre, and the subsidiary activities that could be carried on in the time saved by machine cultivation had a direct bearing on the solution to these problems. So elusive were the answers, however, that, historically, probably more American farmers went bankrupt from overmechanization than from undermechanization.

The value of the land was in some respects the key factor controlling adjustments in all the others, and, like rainfall, it was subject to continual change. The able farmer did not cultivate crops that failed to show a reasonable return on the money the farm would bring if offered for sale. If he wished to continue to grow his usual crop despite rising land values, therefore, he would sell out and go to an area where land prices were lower. The inefficient farmer on the other hand, failing to recognize the cause of his difficulties, might compensate for unsuccessful seasons by increasing his mortgage. Ultimately, with the proceeds from his poorly planned crops, he would find himself unable to meet the high taxes and interest, and he also would be forced to migrate. It was indeed very difficult to be efficient in determining the best adjustment of crops to land values in fertile areas, so complicated were the factors involved. The problems of rotation, availability of certain types of markets, competition within the market area, availability of equipment and labor, all were variables that had to be considered each year. Wheat, for example, would not be a good major crop on most $200-an-acre land; yet, grown in limited quantities in rotation with corn, it had its place.

The problems of the commercial farmer were still far from solved even when he made a success of the year's *production* by harvesting excellent crops, for then he had to sell his produce in a market subject to wide fluctuations from year to year from forces over which he as an individual had no control. This was the final obstacle to his success.

MARKETING AND CREDIT

In the latter half of the nineteenth century, as the legend of America spread among the freed serfs and peasants of Europe and colonizing agents of railroad and land companies began to offer transportation and credit to farmers at home and abroad, an endless stream of Scandinavian, German, Hungarian, and Polish immigrants and easterners poured across the Mississippi, seeking their fortunes on the prairies and the plains. With horses, wagons, tools, and stock, they embarked on their interminable trek. Those who survived settled down at last on railroad or speculator land, only a few being lucky enough to find free homesteads near water, transportation, or towns.

Starting with mortgages on their quarter-sections, many of these settlers had to get additional credit for seed, machinery, and fencing. To raise funds for the first year's sustenance, for barns and houses to replace sod huts thrown up against the first year's weather, they had to pledge their chattels and initial crops. Only local moneylenders would accept such pledges, for the settlers had no direct access to eastern financial institutions and no standing in them. And the only cash crops which they could easily grow with the resulting funds, because of labor and marketing conditions, were wheat and corn in the more southerly regions and wheat alone to the north. Thus the average commercial farmer encountered his first dilemma in relation to the problem of credit. Without credits at high rates he could not grow wheat for the market. Burdened with such rates, he could not make wheat pay.

The farther west the wheat farmers went, the more acute became the problem presented by this dilemma, sheer distance from the Atlantic coast not only aggravating credit difficulties, but adding new obstacles as well. As the center of wheat production in America was pushed steadily toward the Rockies, wheat farmers were removed farther from the great cities of Europe, farther from the manufacturing centers of the East, farther from the capitals and booming mill towns of the Ohio and Mississippi valleys, where they were destined to find their ultimate markets. The farther they moved from such centers of population, the more dependent they became upon sources of information available only in their vicinity. As the price of grain fluctuated in Liverpool, New York, Chicago, or Minneapolis, the international broker knew about it immediately; the exporter, the jobber, the commission man, and the local merchant would soon learn of it; but the farmer in North Dakota or Montana, for instance, as late as 1890 had access to no such information, just as he had no access to news of his competitors' crops in every wheat-growing part of the world. The more he needed easy access to county seats and community churches where he might talk with his neighbors, the more distant were these centers of civilization. The more he needed newspapers, magazines, and regular mail routes through which he might learn of market conditions at home and abroad, the more inaccessible they were.

On the same fall day in 1874, there was a spread of twenty cents in the price of wheat between Minneapolis and Breckenridge, one hundred seventy-five miles to the northwest. The conditions which permitted this spread were repeated in subsequent decades as new wheat lands were occupied. The remote farmer's ignorance of his market was responsible for part of this difference. Much of the rest could be charged to transportation costs. Just as distance from organized communities reduced the farmer's familiarity with his ultimate market, so it reduced also his means of access to that market, leaving him in the end in a sparsely settled region where a single line of river boats or a single railroad company had no competition for freight. The farmer himself rarely shipped his wheat on such lines, his transportation problem ending when he sold his wagonloads to the local merchant. The price he received, however, was profoundly influenced by the rates such merchants had to pay for monopolistic short hauls to the nearest shipping terminals. As distance from these terminals increased, the price at the local merchant's fell proportionately, leaving many farmers, after their work was done, once again a little more deeply in debt than they had been when the new season began.

Of course, not every wheat farmer in the American West was doomed to failure by this combination of high credit and transportation charges and ignorance of world markets. And even for the majority who could not make a net profit from crops alone, there seemed always a way out. As the younger sons in large farm families matured, the more ambitious among them joined with the majority of the 13,000,000 immigrants who arrived between 1865 and 1900 to seek western lands for themselves. Augmenting the ranks of these eager land seekers was a continuous stream of discontented eastern farmers and their own ambitious off-spring. And all of them together created in the trans-Mississippi a persistent land boom which ebbed only in drought or depression years, and reached in 1886 the frantic proportions of the earlier days of western speculation. The result was that, while prices of all commodities were falling in the decades after the Civil War and prices for farm products were falling faster than the rest, the demand for farms steadily increased and the farmer's equity in his land increased proportionately. While they were forced periodically to the verge of bankruptcy by their dealings with the organized businessmen in the wheat and money markets, many farmers thus were able to save themselves by negotiating new mortgages or by selling their farms at good prices. In a typical Nebraska township, twenty years after its initial settlement, more than 50 per cent of the original cultivators had sold out; 77 per cent of the remaining *resident* owners owed mortgages. By 1890, there were on the farms of Kansas, Nebraska, the Dakotas, and Minnesota as many mortgages as there were families in the five states.

Faced with the necessity of paying cash for his family's food and clothing, for wagons, horses, and harness, for installments and interest on his machinery and other fixed charges on his land, the wheat farmer was fortunate in thus being able, in poor crop years, to raise money outside the wheat market. In the end, however, such good fortune only postponed the day of reckoning for many cultivators; and when that day came the costs of the postponement were onerous indeed. For eight years before 1886, the Great Plains had had such extraordinary rainfall that responsible geologists predicted a permanent moistening of the climate of the region. And so optimistic had farmers become that, encouraged by abundant eastern capital, they had steadily increased their mortgages in order to buy more land and machines. In the winter of 1886, however, the wet weather ended. Extreme cold and violent blizzards decimated the cattle on the overstocked ranges. And the following summer intense heat and parching drought killed the wheat and forage. To the hopeful farmers who had poured over the plains in the years of plenty and paid land speculators as much as $6,000 for quarter-sections, this was a fateful summer. To the railroads that had issued new bonds to finance extensions of their lines across the booming plains, it meant the beginning of retrenchment. To the banks and insurance companies that were charging high commissions and 8 to 10 per cent interest for land loans, it marked the end of a profitable branch of their business. And when this year 1886 was followed by a decade of intermittent drought and extreme changes of temperature, panic ran across the smitten area. The rush to the West soon was sharply reversed. Thousands who only a few years before had hopefully sought imagined wealth in central Kansas and similar areas, now retreated from the scorched or frozen earth.

Equity in land disappeared. Farms mortgaged to the limit were fore-closed. Settlers who had tided themselves over lean years by expensive borrowing, lost their homesteads. Literally the Middle Border had shriv-eled up, had withered and turned to dust.

To the ranks of those defeated by Nature soon were added those who were crushed by their ties with eastern business institutions and their dependence upon world business conditions. For in 1893 to drought and frost was added financial panic and, for the next five years, business de-pression. During these years wheat fell to its lowest price in our history, and homesteads fell with it. Truly the business of farming seemed too complicated, too dependent for success upon the caprices of man and Nature.

POLITICS AND SELF-HELP

Paralleling the great dispersion of grain farmers over the prairies and the plains, was the enormous extension of cotton areas in the Gulf states and the Mississippi valley as far as the northern boundary of Arkansas. And paralleling the problems of the wheat farmer were those of the cotton cultivator. Aside from the complexities of farm manage-ment the troubles of both could be traced to large crops, rising fixed charges, especially for land, and falling prices, the nadir in wheat com-ing in 1894 when a bushel that yielded $1.05 in 1870 brought 49 cents, the bottom in cotton being reached in 1896 when a crop nearly six times that of 1866 brought $51,000,000 less. North and east of the cotton lands were tobacco planters, and south and east of wheat areas were corn and hog farmers. All of them had become businessmen devoting their ener-gies to the cultivation of staples for sale at a profit. While corn farmers had not surrendered entirely the self-sufficiency that was once typical of American rural life, and tobacco planters were too few in number to be of special national interest, the new wheat and cotton farmers consti-tuted large groups, unorganized, highly individualistic, inexperienced in business, ignorant of the vagaries of organized national and interna-tional markets and absolutely dependent upon them. Among no other groups was credit so necessary and so dear, among no others was dis-tribution so complicated and so costly. By the middle nineties, the prob-lems of these wheat and cotton farmers had come to be of national im-portance. Before that time, especially in the West, many local attempts to ameliorate their condition had been undertaken.

The earliest of these attempts revolved about the Granges, secret so-cieties formed after 1867 to break down the farmer's insularity and to educate him in scientific farming. In some states, in order to alleviate capital and credit shortages, the Granges set up cooperative banks, life and fire insurance companies. To reduce the prices of tariff-protected commodities manufactured by "trusts," they set up cooperative stores and cooperative farm machine factories. To reduce middlemen's profits and the fees of monopolistic elevators, they organized cooperative marketing agencies, some of which shipped wheat directly to Chicago, New York, and Liverpool. But perhaps most important were the efforts of the Granges to reduce transportation and storage charges. Having mortgaged their farms to invest in railroad bonds and having paid taxes and assessments to help the states make similar investments, the wheat farmers especially felt they deserved cheap and efficient service. As early as 1869 these farmers won in Illinois the promise of such service through a maximum rate law and a railroad commission to administer it. Though originally without a political program, the Granges soon became engaged in seeking similar laws in other states and improvements in existing legislation. So efficient were they that, despite strong railroad opposition, they elected enough governors and legislators in Illinois, Wisconsin, Minnesota, Missouri, California, and Iowa to enact between 1871 and 1878 laws regulating railroad rates, nominally ending discrimination between long competitive hauls and short monopolistic ones, between great shippers and small.

In the chain of productive activities which create out of the raw materials of the soil the finished commodity for the ultimate consumer, that group which is least efficiently organized always gets the smallest share of the profit. That was true of the master craftsman in his relations with merchant capitalists; it was true of the small manufacturer in relation to the railroads; and it was preeminently true of the isolated cereal farmer in his relation to the town merchant, the jobber, the commission man, the railroad and elevator operator, the great broker in the primary market and the processor who turned his product into the world's food. The activities of the Grange constituted the grain farmer's first organized effort to remedy his unenviable position. And on the whole this effort proved futile. For want of sufficient working capital, most of the western cooperative stores and factories soon shut down. Through superior political experience, superior knowledge of the law, superior financial means, and adept bribery and corruption, the railroads were able to emasculate the laws seeking to end rate discrimination. And through the continuance of such discrimination, private elevator operators were able easily to defeat their cooperative marketing competitors. The history of the Granges is the history of the failure of makeshift organizations among independent agricultural enterprisers, in their fight against other business forces, richer, more closely integrated, more accustomed to cooperating until their objectives were attained.

In sympathy with a secular decline in prices in every part of the occidental world, American railroad rates in the late seventies had also begun to decline, and the construction in the eighties of competitive roads

in most parts of the old wheat belt accelerated this reduction. Simultaneously, however, unfair grading systems, speculative trading in grain
futures in the Chicago "Pit," and increasing monopoly among elevator
operators combined to deprive the wheat farmer of as great a percentage
of the consumer's price as before. While the average corn farmer received about 40 per cent of this price, the dairy farmer about 50 per
cent, and the cattleman nearly as much, the wheat farmer, according to
one estimate, received on the average no more than 17 per cent. The
Granges had failed to increase this proportion by reducing railroad
charges. In the eighties, new attempts at cooperative marketing also
failed substantially to increase this percentage. In the meantime, the
farmer's money income fell steadily as wheat prices sagged, and the
price of improved farm land rose steadily as settlement thickened. The
result was that problems of management became more complex, cheap
land became more and more difficult to acquire, and tenancy increased.

Though the cotton South after the Civil War had always had a much
larger percentage of tenants than the West, southern tenancy also increased steadily in the eighties because of falling crop prices and mounting credit charges. And for farmers in both areas, after the failure of
political or cooperative devices, there seemed to be only one way to preserve their lands. That was to diversify their crops. Since wheat and cotton could no longer sustain the heavily mortgaged land upon which they
grew, wheat and cotton farmers were urged to try other products which,
through more intensive cultivation, would yield a greater return per
acre. They were urged especially to try dairying and truck farming to
supply near-by industrial towns. There was, however, one hitch; the shift
to new products required new capital, and new skills. Since those who
most needed diversification were those most heavily in debt and presumably least skillful, it offered no solution to them. Besides, there were
other obstacles. Much wheat land in the West was unsuitable for other
cash crops and was already too expensive for cattle and sheep raising.
In the South, the average farmer owed a great deal to the merchant of
the "country store." Since the merchant wanted real, hard cash above
all, and since cotton at whatever price was the only sure bringer of cash,
the planter was not permitted to speculate in the cultivation of the other
products about which he presumably knew nothing.

Cooperative, political, and technical devices thus failed to ameliorate
the condition of the debtor wheat and cotton farmers. But as they shifted
to cheaper and cheaper land on the moving western frontier they left
available for men with more money or credit great areas in the Mississippi valley. Here, north of Tennessee, especially in Wisconsin, Illinois, and Indiana, dairy farmers moved in. Equipped with adequate capital for intensive farming, they were also sufficiently few in number to
cooperate successfully among themselves and sufficiently strong to resist

the impositions of monopolistic railroads or monopolistic marketing
agencies. Early they organized their own trade associations, the first
being the Illinois & Wisconsin Dairymen's Association of 1867. They
also organized cooperative cheese factories, creameries, and milk distributing companies, all of them successful in expanding local markets.
In the meantime, for those who continued to specialize in grain, conditions got increasingly worse, rising fixed charges and falling prices
reaching their widest spread between 1896 and 1897.

THE MISUSE OF PROSPERITY, 1897–1920

Impoverished by drought and depression and defeated in politics,
the staple farmer, late in 1896, was confronted with a bleak and ominous prospect. All his devices had failed to alleviate his increasingly difficult position, and now he was bankrupt not only of funds but of ideas.
At the very nadir of his dejection, however, his position had begun to
change. The seemingly interminable aridity on the western plains ended
in 1897. At the same time, the world depression had run its course. In
addition, American population was beginning to increase faster than improved farm acreage, and the producer of grain staples thus became less
and less dependent upon foreign markets. Prices for produce and land
began to rise, and the differential between income and fixed charges
began to be more comfortable. For the first time in thirty years, by this
sudden turn of events, staple farmers were enjoying the prospect of a
prolonged period of prosperity.

During the first fifteen years of the new era these favorable trends
continued. Even Nature smiled upon the cultivator as generally good
rainfall helped raise the per-acre yield of wheat despite the movement
to poorer land. In addition, the mature industrial economy offered the
western farmer new luxuries and conveniences such as telephones, automobiles, phonographs, attractive magazines, and household appli-
ances for which to spend his larger cash income. The spread of country
trolley lines made the cities and their educational facilities, better markets, and exciting amusements available to many farmers for the first
time. Had the cereal farmer diversified production to the greatest possible extent he might have enjoyed these favorable trends indefinitely
and been able to break away from dependence on export altogether. Nor
would this achievement have been bad for the economy as a whole. The
United States no longer needed the foreign purchasing power that cereal
and meat exports had provided in the nineteenth century. In addition,
the decline of competition from our own agricultural products would
have helped build up our *industrial* exports, which returned far greater
profits to the nation.

But this wholesome diversification failed to take place prior to the
First World War. As long as export markets existed for wheat, pork, cot-

ton, and tobacco, farmers adhered to the traditional routines rather than risk new crops with their greater rewards but more exacting demands upon thought, skill, and labor. The prevalence of farm tenancy was in no small degree responsible for this failure. For both economic and psychological reasons tenants are naturally loath to work hard to improve land they do not own, and as long as rents are paid under existing conditions, landlords are equally unwilling to have tenants experiment with crops that may be beyond their skill as cultivators. With 50 to 65 per cent of the farms in the cotton belt tilled by cash tenants or share-croppers in 1910 this inertia was particularly noticeable in the South. But even in Illinois and the northwest central states over 30 per cent of the farmers were tenants, and the effect there was more pronounced than the figures reveal. For it was in the rich fertile sections, where land values were high and the land best suited to varied cultivation, that tenancy was most frequent. This situation goes far to explain why, during the prewar years, the increase in the sale of eggs, milk, and vegetables fell 20 to 50 per cent behind population growth. It explains why a commentator surveying the scene in 1910 could write: "American agriculture must develop enormously along new lines if it is to save the nation from hunger."

The failure of the new lines to develop rapidly was in part a result of the World War and its immediate aftermath. Even before the war, however, more liberal homestead laws, higher crop prices, heavier rainfall, and plentiful mortgage money had started hectic real estate booms that spread wheat production into the grass lands of western Kansas, Oklahoma, and northern Texas while prospective cotton planters moved as far west as the Rio Grande. Thus months before the shot at Serajevo a wheat crop had been planted that was to produce a harvest surpassing all previous records by a hundred million bushels. The war, of course, with its blockade of Russia, and devastation of farming areas in France, gave impetus to acreage extension, while high labor costs and soaring prices for wheat and corn removed the stimulus to diversification in the more fertile areas. The United States government also played an active part in the expansion. The Smith-Lever Act of 1914 brought county agents of the Department of Agriculture right to the farmer's door with scientific information on how to increase production, and the Farm Loan Act of 1916 brought government lending agents close on their heels. Unfortunately, the mortgages easily negotiated with these lending agents were based upon costs and prices that were not to be maintained in the following years of peace. In 1918 wheat farming returned, on the average, thirty-two dollars an acre. But the resumption of normal production in Europe and the limited buying power of the Continent in the twenties sharply curtailed the market for American wheat, and the western farmer soon found himself once again confronted with the problems of the nineties. The rudely awakened cultivator found his mortgage payments 200 per cent higher than before the war, his taxes about 140 per cent higher and his income only 75 per cent higher.

THE END OF AN ERA

In 1920 slightly more than half of our western farms were unmortgaged, and life on such farms during the boom years of the twenties was more comfortable and interesting than ever before. Improved free education, radios, moving pictures, and automobiles ended the cultural isolation of remote farms. Electricity and gasoline motors supplied running water and lightened household tasks. The tractor made possible the cultivation of big acreages with less labor in field or barn. Farm bureaus, marketing cooperatives, and farm clubs not only gave cultivators a larger part of the food dollar but also a more interesting social life.

The brighter outlook of the more fortunate, however, could not compensate for the many dark aspects of the farm picture after 1921. Immigration restriction, the disappearing export market, and the decline in all commodity prices began to reduce land values in specialized wheat areas. Farm economists had for the first time fully to realize the extent to which the prosperity of American agriculture had been based upon profits from real estate rather than from crops. Agricultural enterprisers had for the first time to adjust their plans to constantly falling land values. The price of farm land in South Dakota fell 55 per cent in the twenties, and prices in surrounding states were hardly more stable. At the same time, mortgages and taxes continued to mount. Thus the mortgaged farmer, accustomed in earlier days to seeing his equity increase, now saw it rapidly decline. He no longer had the chance to sell out at a profit and to try again to make farming pay in some cheaper area farther west. The inevitable result was the conversion of owners into tenants at a more alarming rate than ever. In Louisiana, Arkansas, Oklahoma, and Texas, the most recent boom areas, by 1930 almost two-thirds of the cultivators were tenants, and many remaining "owners" continued in possession of their land only at the pleasure of local banks or lending agencies. In the Dakotas, a 50 per cent increase in tenancy occurred during these "good" years.

While rising fixed charges for land thus oppressed the small or marginal farmer, the widespread use of the gasoline tractor after the World War made his competitive position still more unfavorable. Either he had to compete without machinery, and thus with higher labor costs, against mechanized farms, or else he had to use his tractor on smaller plots of cheap land and thus still have higher costs per bushel.

The commercial farmer obviously was a businessman in a highly complicated line, and prior to 1933 he was in the most fiercely competitive of all major businesses. Whereas industrial prices after 1929 were to a considerable degree controlled by the mechanics of limited competition, the farmer's price structure disintegrated and the essentially unstable farm situation exploded. With farm prices in 1932 at half the already unsatisfactory levels of 1926, taxes and mortgage payments could no longer be met in large sections of the farm area. As early as 1929 the government had embarked upon a policy of supporting prices by temporarily removing cereal surpluses from the market; but the victory of the more advanced agrarian reformers in the elections of 1932 brought about much wider government activity. The Agricultural Adjustment Acts and crop loan legislation really ended the era of free and unrestrained competition among farm enterprisers, and introduced the kind of limitations on production and prices that trade associations had always aimed at in industry and Big Business had finally achieved.

Richard Hofstadter

Populism: nostalgic agrarianism

THE TWO NATIONS

For a generation after the Civil War, a time of great economic exploitation and waste, grave social corruption and ugliness, the dominant note in American political life was complacency. Although dissenting minorities were always present, they were submerged by the overwhelming realities of industrial growth and continental settlement. The agitation of the Populists, which brought back to American public life a capacity for effective political indignation, marks the beginning of the end of this epoch. In the short run the Populists did not get what they wanted, but they released the flow of protest and criticism that swept through American political affairs from the 1890's to the beginning of the first World War.

Where contemporary intellectuals gave the Populists a perfunctory and disdainful hearing, later historians have freely recognized their achievements and frequently overlooked their limitations. Modern liberals, finding the Populists' grievances valid, their programs suggestive, their motives creditable, have usually spoken of the Populist episode in the spirit of Vachel Lindsay's bombastic rhetoric:

> *Prairie avenger, mountain lion,*
> *Bryan, Bryan, Bryan, Bryan,*
> *Gigantic troubadour, speaking like a siege gun,*
> *Smashing Plymouth Rock with his boulders from the West.*

There is indeed much that is good and usable in our Populist past. While the Populist tradition had defects that have been too much neglected, it does not follow that the virtues claimed for it are all fictitious. Populism was the first modern political movement of practical importance in the United States to insist that the federal government has some responsibility for the common weal; indeed, it was the first such movement to attack seriously the problems created by industrialism. The complaints and demands and prophetic denunciations of the Populists stirred the latent liberalism in many Americans and startled many conservatives into a new flexibility. Most of the "radical" reforms in the Populist program proved in later years to be either harmless or useful. In at least one important area of American life a few Populist leaders in the South attempted something profoundly radical and humane—to build a popular movement that would cut across the old barriers of race—until persistent use of the Negro bogy distracted their following. To discuss the broad ideology of the Populists does them some injustice, for it was in their concrete programs that they added most constructively to our political life, and in their more general picture of the world that they were most credulous and vulnerable. Moreover, any account of the fallibility of Populist thinking that does not acknowledge the stress and suffering out of which that thinking emerged will be seriously remiss. But anyone who enlarges our portrait of the Populist tradition is likely to bring out some unseen blemishes. In the books that have been written about the Populist movement, only passing mention has been made of its significant provincialism; little has been said of its relations with nativism and nationalism; nothing has been said of its tincture of anti-Semitism.

The Populist impulse expressed itself in a set of notions that represent what I have called the "soft" side of agrarianism. These notions, which appeared with regularity in the political literature, must be examined if we are to re-create for ourselves the Populist spirit. To extract them from the full context of the polemical writings in which they appeared is undoubtedly to oversimplify them; even to name them in any language that comes readily to the historian of ideas is perhaps to suggest that they had a formality and coherence that in reality they clearly lacked. But since it is less feasible to have no labels than to have somewhat too facile ones, we may enumerate the dominant themes in Populist ideology as these: the idea of a golden age; the concept of natural harmonies; the dualistic version of social struggles; the conspiracy theory of history; and the doctrine of the primacy of money. The last of these I will touch upon in connection with the free-silver issue. Here I propose to analyze the others, and to show how they were nurtured by the traditions of the agrarian myth.

The utopia of the Populists was in the past, not the future. According to the agrarian myth, the health of the state was proportionate to the degree to which it was dominated by the agricultural class, and this assumption pointed to the superiority of an earlier age. The Populists looked backward with longing to the lost agrarian Eden, to the republican America of the early years of the nineteenth century in which there were few millionaires and, as they saw it, no beggars, when the laborer had excellent prospects and the farmer had abundance, when statesmen still responded to the mood of the people and there was no such thing as the money power. What they meant—though they did not express themselves in such terms—was that they would like to restore the conditions prevailing before the development of industrialism and the commercialization of agriculture. It should not be surprising that they inherited the traditions of Jacksonian democracy, that they revived the old Jacksonian cry: "Equal Rights for All, Special Privileges for None," or that most of the slogans of 1896 echoed the battle cries of 1836. General James B. Weaver, the Populist candidate for the presidency in 1892, was an old Democrat and Free-Soiler, born during the days of Jackson's battle with the United States Bank, who drifted into the Greenback movement after a short spell as a Republican, and from there to Populism. His book, *A Call to Action,* published in 1892, drew up an indictment of the business corporation which reads like a Jacksonian polemic. Even in those hopeful early days of the People's Party, Weaver projected no grandiose plans for the future, but lamented the course of recent history, the growth of economic oppression, and the emergence of great contrasts of wealth and poverty, and called upon his readers to do "All in [their] power to arrest the alarming tendencies of our times."

Nature, as the agrarian tradition had it, was beneficent. The United States was abundantly endowed with rich land and rich resources, and the "natural" consequence of such an endowment should be the prosperity of the people. If the people failed to enjoy prosperity, it must be because of a harsh and arbitrary intrusion of human greed and error. "Hard times, then," said one popular writer, "as well as the bankruptcies, enforced idleness, starvation, and the crime, misery, and moral degradation growing out of conditions like the present, being unnatural, not in accordance with, or the result of any natural law, must be attributed to that kind of unwise and pernicious legislation which history proves to have produced similar results in all ages of the world. It is the mission

of the age to correct these errors in human legislation, to adopt and establish policies and systems, in accord with, rather than in opposition to
divine law." In assuming a lush natural order whose workings were being deranged by human laws, Populist writers were again drawing on
the Jacksonian tradition, whose spokesmen also had pleaded for a proper
obedience to "natural" laws as a prerequisite of social justice.

Somewhat akin to the notion of the beneficence of nature was the idea
of a natural harmony of interests among the productive classes. To the
Populist mind there was no fundamental conflict between the farmer
and the worker, between the toiling people and the small businessman.
While there might be corrupt individuals in any group, the underlying
interests of the productive majority were the same; predatory behavior
existed only because it was initiated and underwritten by a small parasitic minority in the highest places of power. As opposed to the idea that
society consists of a number of different and frequently clashing interests—the social pluralism expressed, for instance, by Madison in the
Federalist—the Populists adhered, less formally to be sure, but quite
persistently, to a kind of social dualism: although they knew perfectly
well that society was composed of a number of classes, for all practical
purposes only one simple division need be considered. There were two
nations. "It is a struggle," said Sockless Jerry Simpson, "between the
robbers and the robbed." "There are but two sides in the conflict that is
being waged in this country today," declared a Populist manifesto. "On
the one side are the allied hosts of monopolies, the money power, great
trusts and railroad corporations, who seek the enactment of laws to
benefit them and impoverish the people. On the other are the farmers,
laborers, merchants, and all other people who produce wealth and bear
the burdens of taxation. . . . Between these two there is no middle
ground." "On the one side," said Bryan in his famous speech against the
repeal of the Sherman Silver Purchase Act, "stand the corporate interests of the United States, the moneyed interests, aggregated wealth and
capital, imperious, arrogant, compassionless. . . . On the other side stand
an unnumbered throng, those who gave to the Democratic party a name
and for whom it has assumed to speak." The people versus the interests,
the public versus the plutocrats, the toiling multitude versus the money
power—in various phrases this central antagonism was expressed. From
this simple social classification it seemed to follow that once the techniques of misleading the people were exposed, victory over the money
power ought to be easily accomplished, for in sheer numbers the people
were overwhelming. "There is no power on earth that can defeat us,"
said General Weaver during the optimistic days of the campaign of
1892. "It is a fight between labor and capital, and labor is in the vast majority."

The problems that faced the Populists assumed a delusive simplicity:

the victory over injustice, the solution for all social ills, was concentrated in the crusade against a single, relatively small but immensely strong interest, the money power. "With the destruction of the money power," said Senator Peffer, "the death knell of gambling in grain and other commodities will be sounded; for the business of the worst men on earth will have been broken up, and the mainstay of the gamblers removed. It will be an easy matter, after the greater spoilsmen have been shorn of their power, to clip the wings of the little ones. Once get rid of the men who hold the country by the throat, the parasites can be easily removed." Since the old political parties were the primary means by which the people were kept wandering in the wilderness, the People's Party advocates insisted, only a new and independent political party could do this essential job. As the silver question became more prominent and the idea of a third party faded, the need for a monolithic solution became transmuted into another form: there was only one *issue* upon which the money power could really be beaten and this was the money issue. "When we have restored the money of the Constitution," said Bryan in his Cross of Gold speech, "all other necessary reforms will be possible; but . . . until this is done there is no other reform that can be accomplished."

While the conditions of victory were thus made to appear simple, they did not always appear easy, and it would be misleading to imply that the tone of Populistic thinking was uniformly optimistic. Often, indeed, a deep-lying vein of anxiety showed through. The very sharpness of the struggle, as the Populists experienced it, the alleged absence of compromise solutions and of intermediate groups in the body politic, the brutality and desperation that were imputed to the plutocracy—all these suggested that failure of the people to win the final contest peacefully could result only in a total victory for the plutocrats and total extinction of democratic institutions, possibly after a period of bloodshed and anarchy. "We are nearing a serious crisis," declared Weaver. "If the present strained relations between wealth owners and wealth producers continue much longer they will ripen into frightful disaster. This universal discontent must be quickly interpreted and its causes removed." "We meet," said the Populist platform of 1892, "in the midst of a nation brought to the verge of moral, political, and material ruin. Corruption dominates the ballot-box, the Legislatures, the Congress, and touches even the ermine of the bench. The people are demoralized. . . . The newspapers are largely subsidized or muzzled, public opinion silenced, business prostrated, homes covered with mortgages, labor impoverished, and the land concentrating in the hands of the capitalists. The urban workmen are denied the right to organize for self-protection, imported pauperized labor beats down their wages, a hireling standing army, unrecognized by our laws, is established to shoot them down, and they are rapidly degenerating into European conditions. The fruits of the toil

of millions are boldly stolen to build up colossal fortunes for a few, unprecedented in the history of mankind; and the possessors of these, in
turn, despise the Republic and endanger liberty." Such conditions fore-
boded "the destruction of civilization, or the establishment of an absolute
despotism." . . .

HISTORY AS CONSPIRACY

. . . There was . . . a widespread Populist idea that all American history since the Civil War could be understood as a sustained conspiracy of the international money power.

The pervasiveness of this way of looking at things may be attributed to
the common feeling that farmers and workers were not simply oppressed
but oppressed deliberately, consciously, continuously, and with wanton
malice by "the interests." It would of course be misleading to imply that
the Populists stand alone in thinking of the events of their time as the results of a conspiracy. This kind of thinking frequently occurs when political and social antagonisms are sharp. Certain audiences are especially
susceptible to it—particularly, I believe, those who have attained only a
low level of education, whose access to information is poor, and who are
so completely shut out from access to the centers of power that they feel
themselves completely deprived of self-defense and subjected to unlimited manipulation by those who wield power. There are, moreover, certain types of popular movements of dissent that offer special opportunities to agitators with paranoid tendencies, who are able to make a
vocational asset out of their psychic disturbances. Such persons have an
opportunity to impose their own style of thought upon the movements
they lead. It would of course be misleading to imply that there are no
such things as conspiracies in history. Anything that partakes of political
strategy may need, for a time at least, an element of secrecy, and is thus
vulnerable to being dubbed conspiratorial. Corruption itself has the character of conspiracy. In this sense the Crédit Mobilier was a conspiracy,
as was the Teapot Dome affair. If we tend to be too condescending to the
Populists at this point, it may be necessary to remind ourselves that they
had seen so much bribery and corruption, particularly on the part of the
railroads, that they had before them a convincing model of the management of affairs through conspiratorial behavior. Indeed, what makes conspiracy theories so widely acceptable is that they usually contain a
germ of truth. But there is a great difference between locating conspiracies *in* history and saying that history *is*, in effect, a conspiracy, between singling out those conspiratorial acts that do on occasion occur
and weaving a vast fabric of social explanation out of nothing but skeins
of evil plots.

When conspiracies do not exist it is necessary for those who think in
this fashion to invent them. Among the most celebrated instances in

modern history are the forgery of the Protocols of the Elders of Zion and the grandiose fabrication under Stalin's regime of the Trotzkyite-Bukharinite-Zinovievite center. These inventions were cynical. In the history of American political controversy there is a tradition of conspiratorial accusations which seem to have been sincerely believed. Jefferson appears really to have believed, at one time, that the Federalists were conspiring to re-establish monarchy. Some Federalists believed that the Jeffersonians were conspiring to subvert Christianity. The movement to annex Texas and the war with Mexico were alleged by many Northerners to be a slaveholders' conspiracy. The early Republican leaders, including Lincoln, charged that there was a conspiracy on the part of Stephen A. Douglas to make slavery a nationwide institution. Such pre-Civil War parties as the Know-Nothing and Anti-Masonic movements were based almost entirely upon conspiratorial ideology. The Nye Committee, years ago, tried to prove that our entry into the first World War was the work of a conspiracy of bankers and munitions-makers. And now not only our entry into the second World War, but the entire history of the past twenty years or so is being given the color of conspiracy by the cranks and political fakirs of our own age.

Nevertheless, when these qualifications have been taken into account, it remains true that Populist thought showed an unusually strong tendency to account for relatively impersonal events in highly personal terms. An overwhelming sense of grievance does not find satisfactory expression in impersonal explanations, except among those with a well-developed tradition of intellectualism. It is the city, after all, that is the home of intellectual complexity. The farmer lived in isolation from the great world in which his fate was actually decided. He was accused of being unusually suspicious, and certainly his situation, trying as it was, made thinking in impersonal terms difficult. Perhaps the rural middle-class leaders of Populism (this was a movement of farmers, but it was not led by farmers) had more to do than the farmer himself with the cast of Populist thinking. At any rate, Populist thought often carries one into a world in which the simple virtues and unmitigated villainies of a rural melodrama have been projected on a national and even an international scale. In Populist thought the farmer is not a speculating businessman, victimized by the risk economy of which he is a part, but rather a wounded yeoman, preyed upon by those who are alien to the life of folkish virture. A villain was needed, marked with the unmistakable stigmata of the villains of melodrama, and the more remote he was from the familiar scene, the more plausibly his villainies could be exaggerated.

It was not enough to say that a conspiracy of the money power against the common people was going on. It had been going on ever since the Civil War. It was not enough to say that it stemmed from Wall Street. It was international: it stemmed from Lombard Street. In his preamble to the People's Party platform of 1892, a succinct, official expression of Populist views, Ignatius Donnelly asserted: "A vast conspiracy against mankind has been organized on two continents, and it is rapidly taking possession of the world. If not met and overthrown at once it forebodes terrible social convulsions, the destruction of civilization, or the establishment of an absolute despotism." A manifesto of 1895, signed by fifteen outstanding leaders of the People's Party, declared: "As early as 1865–66 a conspiracy was entered into between the gold gamblers of Europe and America. . . . For nearly thirty years these conspirators have kept the people quarreling over less important matters while they have pursued with unrelenting zeal their one central purpose. . . . Every device of treachery, every resource of statecraft, and every artifice known to the secret cabals of the international gold ring are being made use of to deal a blow to the prosperity of the people and the financial and commercial independence of the country."

The financial argument behind the conspiracy theory was simple enough. Those who owned bonds wanted to be paid not in a common currency but in gold, which was at a premium; those who lived by lending money wanted as high a premium as possible to be put on their commodity by increasing its scarcity. The panics, depressions, and bankruptcies caused by their policies only added to their wealth; such catastrophes offered opportunities to engross the wealth of others through business consolidations and foreclosures. Hence the interests actually relished and encouraged hard times. The Greenbackers had long since popularized this argument, insisting that an adequate legal-tender currency would break the monopoly of the "Shylocks." Their demand for $50 of circulating medium per capita, still in the air when the People's Party arose, was rapidly replaced by the less "radical" demand for free coinage of silver. But what both the Greenbackers and free-silverites held in common was the idea that the contraction of currency was a deliberate squeeze, the result of a long-range plot of the "Anglo-American Gold Trust." Wherever one turns in the Populist literature of the nineties one can find this conspiracy theory expressed. It is in the Populist newspapers, the proceedings of the silver conventions, the immense pamphlet literature broadcast by the American Bimetallic League, the Congressional debates over money; it is elaborated in such popular books as Mrs. S. E. V. Emery's *Seven Financial Conspiracies which have Enslaved the American People* or Gordon Clark's *Shylock: as Banker, Bondholder, Corruptionist, Conspirator.*

Mrs. Emery's book, first published in 1887, and dedicated to "the enslaved people of a dying republic," achieved great circulation, especially among the Kansas Populists. According to Mrs. Emery, the United States had been an economic Garden of Eden in the period before the Civil War. The fall of man had dated from the war itself, when "the money kings of

Wall Street" determined that they could take advantage of the wartime necessities of their fellow men by manipulating the currency. "Controlling it, they could inflate or depress the business of the country at pleasure, they could send the warm life current through the channels of trade, dispensing peace, happiness, and prosperity, or they could check its flow, and completely paralyze the industries of the country." With this great power for good in their hands, the Wall Street men preferred to do evil. Lincoln's war policy of issuing greenbacks presented them with the dire threat of an adequate supply of currency. So the Shylocks gathered in convention and "perfected" a conspiracy to create a demand for their gold. The remainder of the book was a recital of a series of seven measures passed between 1862 and 1875 which were alleged to be a part of this continuing conspiracy, the total effect of which was to contract the currency of the country further and further until finally it squeezed the industry of the country like a hoop of steel.

Mrs. Emery's rhetoric left no doubt of the sustained purposefulness of this scheme—described as "villainous robbery," and as having been "secured through the most soulless strategy." She was most explicit about the so-called "crime of 1873," the demonetization of silver, giving a fairly full statement of the standard greenback-silverite myth concerning that event. As they had it, an agent of the Bank of England, Ernest Seyd by name, had come to the United States in 1872 with $500,000 with which he had bought enough support in Congress to secure the passage of the demonetization measure. This measure was supposed to have greatly increased the value of American four per cent bonds held by British capitalists by making it necessary to pay them in gold only. To it Mrs. Emery attributed the panic of 1873, its bankruptcies, and its train of human disasters: "Murder, insanity, suicide, divorce, drunkenness and all forms of immorality and crime have increased from that day to this in the most appalling ratio."

"Coin" Harvey, the author of the most popular single document of the whole currency controversy, *Coin's Financial School,* also published a novel, *A Tale of Two Nations,* in which the conspiracy theory of history was incorporated into a melodramatic tale. In this story the powerful English banker Baron Rothe plans to bring about the demonetization of silver in the United States, in part for his own aggrandizement but also to prevent the power of the United States from outstripping that of England. He persuades an American Senator (probably John Sherman, the *bête noire* of the silverites) to co-operate in using British gold in a campaign against silver. To be sure that the work is successful, he also sends to the United States a relative and ally, one Rogasner, who stalks through the story like the villains in the plays of Dion Boucicault, muttering to himself such remarks as "I am here to destroy the United States—Cornwallis could not have done more. For the wrongs and insults, for the glory of my own country, I will bury the knife deep into the heart of this nation." Against the plausibly drawn background of the corruption of the Grant administration, Rogasner proceeds to buy up the American Congress and suborn American professors of economics to testify for gold. He also falls in love with a proud American beauty, but his designs on her are foiled because she loves a handsome young silver Congressman from Nebraska who bears a striking resemblance to William Jennings Bryan!

One feature of the Populist conspiracy theory that has been generally overlooked is its frequent link with a kind of rhetorical anti-Semitism. The slight current of anti-Semitism that existed in the United States before the 1890's had been associated with problems of money and credit. During the closing years of the century it grew noticeably. While the jocose and rather heavy-handed anti-Semitism that can be found in Henry Adams's letters of the 1890's shows that this prejudice existed outside Populist literature, it was chiefly Populist writers who expressed that identification of the Jew with the usurer and the "international gold ring" which was the central theme of the American anti-Semitism of the age. The omnipresent symbol of Shylock can hardly be taken in itself as evidence of anti-Semitism, but the frequent references to the House of Rothschild make it clear that for many silverites the Jew was an organic part of the conspiracy theory of history. Coin Harvey's Baron Rothe was clearly meant to be Rothschild; his Rogasner (Ernest Seyd?) was a dark figure out of the coarsest anti-Semitic tradition. "You are very wise in your way," Rogasner is told at the climax of the tale, "the commercial way, inbred through generations. The politic, scheming, devious way, inbred through generations also." One of the cartoons in the effectively illustrated Coin's Financial School showed a map of the world dominated by the tentacles of an octopus at the site of the British Isles, labeled: "Rothschilds." In Populist demonology, anti-Semitism and Anglophobia went hand in hand.

The note of anti-Semitism was often sounded openly in the campaign for silver. A representative of the New Jersey Grange, for instance, did not hesitate to warn the members of the Second National Silver Convention of 1892 to watch out for political candidates who represented "Wall Street, and the Jews of Europe." Mary E. Lease described Grover Cleveland as "the agent of Jewish bankers and British gold." Donnelly represented the leader of the governing Council of plutocrats in Cæsar's Column, one Prince Cabano, as a powerful Jew, born Jacob Isaacs; one of the triumvirate who lead the Brotherhood of Destruction is also an exiled Russian Jew, who flees from the apocalyptic carnage with a hundred million dollars which he intends to use to "revive the ancient splendors of the Jewish race, in the midst of the ruins of the world." One of the more elaborate documents of the conspiracy school traced the power of the Rothschilds over America to a transaction between Hugh McCulloch, Secretary of the Treasury under Lincoln and Johnson, and Baron James Rothschild. "The most direful part of this business between Rothschild and the United States Treasury was not the loss of money, even by hundreds of millions. It was the resignation of the country itself INTO THE HANDS OF ENGLAND, as England had long been resigned into the hands of HER JEWS."

Such rhetoric, which became common currency in the movement, later passed beyond Populism into the larger stream of political protest. By the time the campaign of 1896 arrived, an Associated Press reporter noticed as "one of the striking things" about the Populist convention at St. Louis "the extraordinary hatred of the Jewish race. It is not possible to go into any hotel in the city without hearing the most bitter denunciation of the Jews as a class and of the particular Jews who happen to have prospered in the world." This report may have been somewhat overdone, but the identification of the silver cause with anti-Semitism did become close enough for Bryan to have to pause in the midst of his campaign to explain to the Jewish Democrats of Chicago that in denouncing the policies of the Rothschilds he and his silver friends were "not attacking a race; we are attacking greed and avarice which know no race or religion."

It would be easy to misstate the character of Populist anti-Semitism or to exaggerate its intensity. For Populist anti-Semitism was entirely verbal. It was a mode of expression, a rhetorical style, not a tactic or a program. It did not lead to exclusion laws, much less to riots or pogroms. There were, after all, relatively few Jews in the United States in the late 1880's and early 1890's, most of them remote from the areas of Populist strength. It is one thing, however, to say that this prejudice did not go beyond a certain symbolic usage, quite another to say that a people's choice of symbols is of no significance. Populist anti-Semitism does have its importance—chiefly as a symptom of a certain ominous credulity in the Populist mind. It is not too much to say that the Greenback-Populist tradition activated most of what we have of modern popular anti-Semitism in the United States. From Thaddeus Stevens and Coin Harvey to Father Coughlin, and from Brooks and Henry Adams to Ezra Pound, there has been a curiously persistent linkage between anti-Semitism and money and credit obsessions. A full history of modern anti-Semitism in the United States would reveal, I believe, its substantial Populist lineage, but it may be sufficient to point out here that neither the informal connection between Bryan and the Klan in the twenties nor Thomas E. Watson's conduct in the Leo Frank case were altogether fortuitous. And Henry Ford's notorious anti-Semitism of the 1920's, along with his hatred of "Wall Street," were the foibles of a Michigan farm boy who had been liberally exposed to Populist notions.

Norman Pollack

Did Populism accept industrialism and social change, basing its protest on what it believed to be the realities of the 1890's? Or did it seek instead to restore pre-industrial society, comprehending neither the major trends of its age nor the solutions necessary to cope with these altered circumstances? Was Populism therefore a progressive or retrogressive, a forward- or backward-looking, social force? The disparity noted above is nowhere better seen than in the conclusion reached by historians on these questions. Whatever their personal view of the movement, itself important because Populism has had its critics as well as supporters, and whatever their field of specialization, historians agree in regarding it, in the words of Professor John D. Hicks, as "beginning the last phase of a long and perhaps losing struggle—the struggle to save agricultural America from the devouring jaws of industrial America."

That this retrogressive framework can be supported through the examples of numerous industrial revolutions is undeniable; clearly, agrarians often aligned with conservative groups in the vain attempt to turn back history. Nor do the results appear different when agrarian movements acted alone and in a radical direction, for they seemed generally incapable of combining with industrial labor to promote a society both democratic *and* industrial. Thus, whether radical or conservative, agrarianism in a world perspective takes on the shape of a retrogressive social force. It would, however, be a serious mistake merely to assume that all industrial transformations follow the same pattern. I submit that while the generalization is not without foundation, the American experience proves a notable exception. For three reasons, this difference has not been sufficiently appreciated: The belief that agrarianism must act retrogressively, deduced usually from situations of abrupt transition from feudalism to capitalism, is no longer questioned; Americanists have followed suit, accepting this view and then confining their research to more specific problems; and most important, the actual evidence on the agrarian response to industrialism has not hitherto been presented. . . .

. . . Proponents of this framework adopt the following line of reasoning: Populism did not adjust to industrialism; hence, the movement occupied an untenable historical position. And because it looked backward, its long-range solutions were, by definition, unrealistic. This meant that by not comprehending the basis for its discontent, Populism was forced to search for simplistic explanations and, ultimately, scapegoats. The result is a cumulatively deteriorating position; as protest becomes more emotional, it bears less resemblance to reality. The final image is that of a movement of opportunists, crackpots, and anti-Semites, whose perception of the world conforms to the dictates of a conspiracy theory of history. The over-all consequence of this image is that Populism has been denied its traditional place as a democratic social force. Rather, its significance for American history is altered so greatly that it has come to stand as the source for later proto-fascist groups, McCarthyism, anti-Semitism, xenophobia, and anti-intellectualism. One senses the proportions of this denigration process when it is seen that the very term "populistic" has passed into the working vocabulary of many intellectuals as an epithet, signifying the traits just enumerated.

The final dissociation of this image from previous scholarship occurs over the question of social conditions during the 1890's. Earlier writers never challenged the fact of hard times. Rather, they took Populist protest seriously as a direct response to economic grievances. It would be well to recall the situation facing Populism, as found in Hicks and other standard accounts: the serious decline in farm prices during the period 1870–1897; the railroad rate structure and, perhaps as important, railroad land and tax policies; high mortgage indebtedness within a financial context of contracting currency; actual dispossession from the land; adverse marketing arrangements, particularly the power of elevator companies to fix prices and establish grading standards; and consumption in a monopolistic framework.

The new image of Populism, by emphasizing irrationality, shifts the responsibility for discontent away from society and to Populism itself: The movement was more rhetorical than radical; hence, its protest was grossly exaggerated. Following this through, proponents of this view held that Populism was not a trustworthy barometer for reflecting actual conditions. The result was that the extent of oppression became increasingly minimized, and finally glossed over. And because the basis for discontent was almost totally denied, Populism then became subject to the charge of double irrationality: Not only was it retrogressive, but it responded to nonexistent grievances. Meanwhile, the society which gave birth to the protest was forgotten or exonerated. . . .

I propose, then, the following historical definition of midwestern Populism: While primarily an agrarian movement, it also contained significant support from industrial labor, social reformers, and intellectuals. The interaction between these groups was expressed not in terms of pre-industrial producer values, but of a common ideology stemming from a

shared critique of existing conditions. In a word, Populism regarded itself as a class movement, reasoning that farmers and workers were assuming the same material position in society. Thus, it accepted industrialism but opposed its capitalistic form, seeking instead a more equitable
distribution of wealth. But Populism went further in its criticism: Industrial capitalism not only impoverished the individual, it alienated and
degraded him. The threat was not only subsistence living, but the destruction of human faculties. According to Populism, there was an in-
verse relation between industrialism and freedom, because the machine
was being made to exploit rather than serve man. Is Populism, then, a
socialist movement? Here labels become unimportant; it was far more
radical than is generally assumed. Had Populism succeeded, it could
have fundamentally altered American society in a socialist direction.
Clearly, Populism was a progressive social force.

Populism had a peculiar notion of freedom: Man was free only when
society encouraged the fullest possible development of human potential-
ity. Addressing the mammoth Tattersall rally, which climaxed the 1894
People's party campaign in Chicago, Henry Demarest Lloyd declared:
"The people's party is more than the organized discontent of the people.
It is the organized aspiration of the people for a fuller, nobler, richer,
kindlier life for every man, woman, and child in the ranks of humanity."
Seeking to enhance human self-fulfillment, it could not be a temporary
phenomenon: "The people's party is not a passing cloud on the political
sky. It is not a transient gust of popular discontent caused by bad crops
or hard times." Rather, "It is an uprising of principle, and the millions
who have espoused these principles will not stop until they have become
incorporated into the constitution of the government and the framework
of society." Thus, the goal of Populism was "the hope of realizing and in-
carnating in the lives of the common people the fullness of the divinity
of humanity."

Here, then, was a standard for judging industrial America in the
1890's: Did it promote "the divinity of humanity," or merely produce de-
humanized and impoverished men? While human rights is an abstraction admirably suited to campaign rhetoric, the theme recurs with sufficient frequency and intensity to indicate that Populists took it seriously.
As Hamlin Garland stated to James B. Weaver, in the midst of the latter's
1892 presidential campaign: "Don't confine the fight to any one thing
money or land. Let's make the fight for *human liberty* and for the rights
of man." Ignatius Donnelly, in a circular prepared for party members in
the 1896 campaign, defined the task at hand as "the preservation of humanity in the highest estate of which it is capable on earth." And Senator
Allen of Nebraska similarly held that Populism "rests on the cause of
labor and the brotherhood of man."

Populists further clarified their conception of human rights by distinguishing it from property rights. Governor Lorenzo D. Lewelling of Kansas, in a major speech, reminded his Kansas City audience that "we have so much regard for the rights of property that we have forgotten the liberties of the individual." A Broken Bow, Nebraska, paper saw the conflict as that of the "rights of man" and the "rights of capital." And one in Nelson, Nebraska, characterized it as between "the wealthy and powerful classes who want the control of the government to plunder the people" and "the people" themselves, who are "contending for equality before the law and the rights of man."

More concretely, human rights are a sham unless predicated upon an equitable distribution of wealth. An editorial in the Lincoln, Nebraska, *Farmers' Alliance* expressed the view in these words: "The people's party has sprung into existence not to make the black man free, but to emancipate all men; not to secure political freedom to a class, but to gain for all *industrial* freedom, without which there can be no political freedom; no lasting people's government." Making "industrial freedom" the precondition for political freedom, it further asserted that the People's party "stands upon the declaration that 'all men are created equal,' having equal right to live, labor and enjoy the fruits of their labor. It teaches that none should have power to enjoy without labor." On the contrary, Populism "demands equal opportunities and exact justice in business for each individual and proposes to abolish all monopolistic privileges and power." Thus, the perspective is refined still further: Monopoly poses the principal threat to human rights. Significantly, the editorial immediately added that the People's party "is the first party that has comprehended the great question of injustice and proposed an adequate remedy for the evils of society." Its closing sentence reveals that, while opposing monopoly, Populism accepted industrialism: Populists "shall make of this nation an industrial democracy in which each citizen shall have an equal interest."

At the same Tattersall rally where Lloyd spoke, Clarence Darrow also called for a more democratic industrial system: "We of the People's party believe that the men who created our wonderful industrial system have the right to enjoy the institution which they have created." A Columbus, Nebraska, paper voiced the same sentiment: "The people do not want to tear up the railroads nor pull down the factories." Instead, "they want to build up and make better everything." And social protest became necessary to secure these conditions, for "even a worm will writhe and struggle when stepped upon, and surely, if Americans cannot be anything higher, they can be a nation of worms." As the Populist organ in Wahoo, Nebraska, simply observed: "There should be no want." Thus, industrial America could, but did not, provide greater material benefits for the total society. The technological potential was present for overcoming poverty, the results otherwise. A correspondent to Lloyd summarized this feeling when he wrote: "The whole ideal of our civilization is wrong."

But privation was not inevitable; measures *could* be taken to create a more equitable distribution of wealth. Here the essential rationality of Populism becomes clear: Man could rationally control his society, particularly by harnessing the productive forces already in existence. But this could not occur under the existing form of social organization, for industrial capitalism was not responsive to human needs. Society, in a word, had to be changed. And while the means selected were moderate—working through the political system—this should not obscure the radical conception Populists maintained of politics. The same Columbus paper defined politics as the ability to control "the distribution of wealth." Politics no longer meant seeking office, still less preserving the status quo. Rather, this paper added, "Politics can cause this country to bloom and blossom like the rose; it can make our people, generally speaking, prosperous, happy and contented, or it can stagnate every kind of enterprise, reduce the masses to want and misery and cause our people to become restless, desperate and blood-thirsty."

Frank Doster, a Populist leader in Kansas, spelled out in detail this demand for political action to achieve the benefits of technology. Speaking at Topeka on Labor Day of 1894, Doster pointed out that although "steam, electricity, compressed air, are utilized to do the work of man," the expected gains failed to materialize. These productive forces, which are "the common property of all," have not benefited the total society because they "have been made the monopoly of the few." Through this monopoly structure they "have been turned aside from the beneficent ends for which designed, to serve the selfish purposes of avarice and greed." Moreover, Populism was, according to Doster, the only major political force which sought to control economic concentration in the interests of the larger society: "In the face of the power exerted by the monopolists of these tremendous engines of industry and commerce the republican and democratic parties stand paralyzed—hypnotized, as it were, unable to control it or give direction and shape for common good." Here the traditional charge is reversed; a Populist holds that the major parties have been overwhelmed by these rapid changes. "The failure to adapt the legislation of the country to the strange conditions which this new life has forced upon us is the cause in greater part of our industrial ills." The statement suggests the attempt to confront, not retreat from, the new situation. Accordingly, Doster closed with a presentation of "two political formulae," serving as the "philosophic bases" for reliance upon governmental action: Government must "do that for the individual which he can not successfully do for himself, and which other individuals will not do for him upon just and equitable terms." And more comprehensively, "the industrial system of a nation, like its political system, should be a government of and for and by the people alone."

Stepping back momentarily to view Populist thought in a wider ideological spectrum, one immediately recognizes its challenge to what are generally considered the prevailing ideologies of the period—the success myth, social Darwinism, and laissez faire. Governor Lewelling's Kansas City speech clearly states the Populist case for paternalism: "It is the business of the Government to make it possible for me to live and sustain the life of my family." Further, "It is the duty of government to protect the weak, because the strong are able to protect themselves." This is totally at variance with the success-myth faith in individual self-help through character development, industry, and perseverance. An article in the *Farmers' Alliance* suggests why Populists could not subscribe to the success myth: It contradicted their actual experiences, denied their grievances, and led to markedly different conclusions regarding the operation of the economic system. Hence, "No effort of the people, no degree of economy, no amount of industry in their several avocations could have averted these results. The people are as powerless as though they were actually in a state of bondage." A change in the nature of society, not a reliance on individual self-help, was necessary: "While the cause exists the evils *must* and *will* remain."

But Populism rejected the success myth, and indeed laissez faire and social Darwinism, for a more basic reason. Unbridled individualism, it contended, destroyed rather than promoted the general welfare. Its own counter-formulation, simply, was that cooperation and mutual help, not competition and self-help, led to true individualism.

An editorial in the *Farmers' Alliance* stated the argument as follows: "The plutocracy of to-day is the logical result of the individual freedom which we have always considered the pride of our system." In fact, "The theory of our government has been and is that the individual should possess the very greatest degree of liberty consistent, not with the greatest good of the greatest number, but with the very least legal restraint compatible with law and order. Individual enterprise was allowed unlimited scope." Thus, individualism creates monopoly capitalism, where "the corporation has absorbed the community." Instead, the reverse must take place: "The community must now absorb the corporation—must merge itself into it. Society must enlarge itself to the breadth of humanity." The editorial closed with an unmistakable repudiation of these other value systems: "A stage must be reached in which each will be for all and all for each. The welfare of the individual must be the object and end of all effort." And three years later, this paper (under its new name, *Alliance-Independent*) succinctly noted that "a reigning plutocracy with the masses enslaved, is the natural development and end of individualism." It remained for the Topeka *Advocate* to add a final, somewhat ironic, comment: "The horror of 'paternalism' hangs like a black pall over the burried hopes of the helpless poor."

Populism was even more unsparing in its criticism of social Darwinism, especially the latter's sanction of competition and survival of the fittest. Governor Lewelling, again in the Kansas City speech, warned that unless the government exerted greater control over industrial capitalism there would be "a state of barbarism and everywhere we slay, and the slayer in turn is slain and so on the great theatre of life is one vast conspiracy all creatures from the worm to the man in turn rob their fellows." For him, social Darwinism meant "the law of natural selection the survival of the fittest—Not the survival of the fittest, but the survival of the strongest." Lewelling concluded: "It is time that man should rise above it."

George H. Gibson, in a letter to the *Alliance-Independent* (he later became its editor), expressed a similar view of competition. Arguing that the type of social reform represented by Jane Addams was futile, he observed: "Uplifting the masses is all right, but it would be much better to put a stop to the beastly struggle which crowds them down." Nor did Gibson reason abstractly; he denied the wisdom of competition by what was daily taking place in American society. "There are tens of thousands in this city [Chicago] all the time out of work, fighting for positions and the low wages which enable capitalists to rake off dividends for idle and scheming stockholders." Writing later to Henry D. Lloyd, Gibson outlined his counter-proposal to competition: "We must put together our property, labor, economic wisdom, knowledge, varying talents, Christianizing or democratizing what we have and are . . . We feel that it is wrong to continue the selfish struggle, even with charitable or philanthropic intent, as many noble souls are doing."

Using for his standard "political and economic equality," a Walnut Grove, Minnesota, editor judged competitive society in these terms: "The calamities that have heretofore and that now are upon us—as a nation— are but the measure or indicator of the extent that this standard has been departed from in the practice of the competitive system." Nor did Populists admire those who were presumably the fittest. Ignatius Donnelly characterized them as follows: "Shallow-pated, sordid, unintellectual, they stand there, grabbing and grinning, while their brethren march past them to destruction." The Columbus, Nebraska, paper was less charitable, describing "the so-called great men" as "moral cowards and public plunderers who have "reversed the code of morals and stand up like hypocrites of olden times and thank god they are not like other men are." And it opposed these men, again not on abstract grounds, but because it regarded competition as destroying all but the victors: "They have the power to impoverish the farmers, make millions of good men tramps; to reduce their employees to silent slaves; to ruin great cities; to plunge a happy and prosperous nation into sorrow and bankruptcy."

These criticisms do not, however, reflect a conspiracy theory of history; Populists were concerned with the consequences of power, not the personalities or motivations of successful men. Referring to Rockefeller, Henry D. Lloyd noted that personal questions are extraneous because "the main point is the simple issue of monopoly." Even if "they are angels," he continued, the problem remains critical so long as they "have obtained the power of controlling the markets." Lloyd argued somewhat earlier in this same fashion against Carnegie, "I have no sort of feeling" against the man, but he is nonetheless "one of the worst representatives of our mercenary system of ordering industry which is perverting it from the supply of demand and the production and distribution of the wealth in nature for the use of all men, and making it an instrument of personal aggrandisement and cannibalistic selfishness."

Nor did Populism concede the more attractive side of social Darwinism, the latter's belief that society evolved into progressively higher stages. Technological progress was one matter—its translation into material well-being quite another. "While we think, brag of it, how far we are ahead of any former civilization," wrote a Minnesota state senator to Donnelly, "I for one am disgusted of the bragging and boasting and simply believe it is not true." Surely, through improvements in communications, "we are making history a little faster than when those elements were lacking in the world's affairs." But, he added, "I disdain to call it progress when, considering what it eventually . . . will lead to." This position is exceedingly interesting, for it starts from the recognition that technology provides the means for the liberation of man: "I have heard it asserted that the printing Press, telegraph, etc. have educated the masses, that the direful relapse will not come again as in the past." Yet, he then reaches a decidedly unexpected conclusion. While it can serve man, technology can also be used to insure a greater domination over man. In a word, progress is not only meaningless for a defective society; it actually becomes harmful by intensifying these defects. For Populism, then, progress was not an unmixed blessing: "Bosh, our would be masters have a corner on the whole outfit of the inventions, and they are now just as much employed to the destruction of human rights as formerly in the absence of those inventions the peoples ignorance was used as a means."

Yet, Populism denied not the idea of progress but its realization in existing society. Optimistic in reforming zeal, Populism was still essentially pessimistic in its awareness of the ensuing obstacles. Not surprisingly, the result was an ambivalence with pessimism the overriding factor. A letter to Bryan after the 1896 election stated that an "appeal to reason may elevate the human race to a point we dream not of." But the same letter tempered this optimistic outburst with a sobering reminder: "A social system which permits puny children to toil in grimy factories and foul sweatshops while brawny men walk the streets vainly begging for work . . . is damnable!" How, then, could the net balance be otherwise than on the pessimistic side when Populists continually asked themselves such questions as this: "And for what object has this tremendous slaughter of the human family and this unparalleled suffering of the living been inflicted upon mankind?"

SUGGESTIONS FOR FURTHER READING

Two excellent books which view the farmers' problems through the eyes of the farmers are Fred A. Shannon, *The Farmers' Last Frontier: Agriculture, 1860–1897* (New York, 1945) and John D. Hicks, *The Populist Revolt* (Minneapolis, 1931). In the 1950's Richard Hofstadter's *The Age of Reform* (a portion of which is reprinted here) began a re-examination of the Populists. He and others charged the Populists with some degree of responsibility for the anti-semitism, isolationism, and anti-intellectualism in American life. C. Vann Woodward discusses some of this anti-Populist literature in "The Populist Heritage and the Intellectual," *American Scholar*, XXIX (Winter, 1959–60), 55–72, also reprinted in Woodward, *The Burden of Southern History* (Baton Rouge, 1960). The attack on the Populists has also produced a vigorous defense. In addition to the book by Norman Pollack (reprinted here in part) see, Walter T. K. Nugent, *The Tolerant Populists* (Chicago, 1963).

VI

ORGANIZED ★

LABOR ★

IN AN ★

INDUSTRIAL ★

AGE ★

Organized labor has a long tradition in American history. The earliest organizations of labor may be found in the colonial period and the early national period witnessed increased activity among laboring groups. In the early nineteenth century printers, shoemakers, tailors, and other workers joined together in unions as they attempted to improve working conditions and wages. At times these unions tried to combine forces by forming city and even national associations or, seeking to advance themselves in the political arena, workingmen's parties. But it was not until after the Civil War that the trade-union movement became a significant and lasting·influence in American society.

The most casual glance at the history of labor-management relations in the United States reveals a story of conflict, at times violent and bloody. Striking workers were often greeted at plant gates by armed guards hired by factory owners determined to disperse pickets and to maintain production with non-union labor. Workers regularly armed themselves and were equally determined to keep the struck factory closed by preventing "scabs" from entering the shops. When these two determined and armed groups met, the result was invariably a bloody clash.

Historians, of course, cannot ignore the many instances of conflict and every labor history bristles with accounts of violent struggles between labor and management. From this many scholars conclude that there is no tradition of consensus in this aspect of American history.

Yet others argue that conflict is not the basic underlying feature in American labor history. Without attempting to ignore the conflicts, they point to other aspects of the American labor movement. They argue that only a few American unionists have been radicals and that never has the trade-union movement followed a program designed to overthrow the existing social and economic system. Those unions which have adopted a radical or revolutionary program have always been in the distinct minority and the major portion of organized labor has consistently repudiated the radical sections of the movement.

In a word, then, these historians point to consensus as the basic theme in American labor history. Labor and management, they argue, have often disagreed over wages and working conditions and these disagreements often led to strikes and conflicts, but behind these disagreements there existed an underlying unity based upon an acceptance of the sanctity of private property as well as the most important features of American democratic government.

Just as those historians who emphasize consensus cannot ignore the violent conflicts which often characterized labor-management relations, those who stress conflict cannot ignore the fact that the major portions of the American labor movement have not been radical and revolutionary. Still they continue to insist that conflict is the basic theme. Some argue that although the labor movement is not socialistic, it has always adopted goals which would fundamentally alter our social and economic system even if they would not completely destroy it. Others argue that the American labor movement will soon become socialistic, like its European counterparts.

In the selections which follow the reader is given the opportunity to see examples of both points of view. Leo Huberman finds a basic conflict between the "Have-nots" and the "Haves" and traces the different means labor adopted for "fighting capital." Edward Kirkland deals with substantially the same period of time as does Huberman but he concludes that there was "a harmony of interests" between labor and capital.

Selig Perlman approaches the problem in a somewhat different manner. Looking for a general theory of the labor movement, he finds American labor unions, for the most part, rejecting class conscious radicalism and adopting instead an emphasis on what he calls job consciousness. American workers are concerned with wages and working conditions and not with the overthrow of private property, and this, he concludes, is the only policy possible in America. William Z. Foster, a worker, union organizer, and in his later life a leader and historian of the American Communist party, comes to completely different conclusions, although he begins with premises similar to those of Perlman. For Foster it is only a matter of time until the American worker recognizes his true interests and adopts a militant, socialistic point of view which will lead to the overthrow of the capitalist system in America.

It is clear that the evaluation of the organized labor movement, including the many instances of strikes and violence, rests upon an assessment of the nature of the divisions between worker and employer. Do the activities of organized labor reflect fundamental class conflict in American society? Are the aims and interests of each group so different and opposed that sharp and bitter conflict has been and will continue to be inevitable? Or do workers and employers in the United States accept the fundamentals of the system? Are workers interested in no more than to increase their share of the nation's wealth?

What of the future? Radicals place great emphasis on the role of the working class in the overthrow of private property, in the replacement of capitalism by socialism. Does the history of American labor point in this direction?

Leo Huberman

Through their trade-unions the men who did the actual work of operating the railroads, mining the coal and iron, building the great cities, and running the machines in the factories—in short, the working class—came to grips with the capitalists.

Nor were they merely battles of words alone. Quite frequently dynamite, bombs, and machine-guns were used. There were murders on both sides. It was a fierce struggle.

Woodrow Wilson hit upon one of the reasons. "Did you never think of it,—men are cheap and machinery is dear; many a superintendent is dismissed for over-driving a delicate machine who wouldn't be dismissed for over-driving an over-taxed man. You can discard your man and replace him; there are others ready to come into his place; but you can't, without great cost, discard your machine and put a new one in its place. . . . It is time that property, as compared with humanity, should take second place, not first place."

Property was first, human life second—that was one reason for the conflict.

Capitalists were interested in making money—the more the better. The smart businessman was the one who paid as little as possible for what he bought, and received as much as possible for what he sold. The first step on the road to high profits was to reduce expenses.

One of the expenses of production was wages to labor. It was therefore to the interest of the employer to pay as low wages as possible. It was likewise to his interest to get as much work out of his laborers as he could. Accordingly, he tried to make the working day as long as possible.

The Industrial Revolution had put the worker at the mercy of the capitalist. The employer owned the factory and the expensive machinery in it. The worker could no longer produce his own food and do his own work. He no longer owned the tools of production. He had to become a wage earner in another man's factory. If that factory was an unhealthful, ill-lighted, poorly ventilated place with no safeguards on its dangerous machinery, he had to work there, nevertheless. If the hours were very long, and the wages so low that he could not support himself and his

From *We, the People* by Leo Huberman (New York, 1940) chap. XIII, pp. 223–240. Reprinted by permission of the author.

254

family, he had to work there just the same. There was no way out—work or starve.

That the laborer was not a *thing* like coal or cotton, but a person—a human being like himself—made no difference to the profit seeker. Labor, machinery, raw materials, they were all alike to him—the less they cost him the better. He was interested in profits.

Workers stood this as long as they could. Then they tried to fight back. What could they do?

Alone they could do nothing. Organized together as one group, they could exert pressure on their employers. They banded together and formed unions.

What kind of unions did they form? Were they organized on the basis of craft or industry? Were they local, state, or national? Were they concerned with the here and now or with the utopias of tomorrow? Were they content with the capitalist system, or did they fight to overthrow it? There is no short answer to these questions. Unions arise out of the necessities of the situation and take the form best suited to that situation. They never develop as something separate from the way in which people live and earn their living. There may be a lag—there often is—but in the long run the kind of labor organization that emerges and grows is the one that is forced by the industrial setup. As changes come in the industrial development of a country, so changes come in the workers' organizations.

That is what happened in the United States. The Declaration of Independence which announced our separation from England was followed soon after by one declaration after another of workmen announcing their separation of interests from the employing class. So, in 1817, the New York printers announced, "This is a society of journeymen printers; and as the interests of the journeymen are separate and in some respects opposite to those of the employers, we deem it improper that they should have any voice or influence in our deliberations."

This was a break with what had prevailed before. In earlier years it had been quite proper that the employers should have a voice in the deliberations of the men who worked for them. It had been proper because the gulf between the master craftsmen and his journeymen had not been very wide. Journeymen could become masters fairly easily. The masters worked side by side with the journeymen, believed the same things, and had the same ideas. Their interests both social and economic were practically the same. So long as that was true, the employer and the journeymen could belong to the same society. Because in 1817 it was no longer true, the New York printers said so and expelled a member who had become an employer.

In some respects this was similar to what had happened to the guild system in western Europe centuries ago. It was the expansion of the market which was the major factor in the breakdown of the guild system; and it was the expansion of the market which brought the change here.

To meet the needs of the expanding market in the early nineteenth century, the merchant-capitalist made his entrance on the American scene. He brought in large quantities of cheap manufactured goods from England, stored them in warehouses which dotted the whole country, and undersold the master craftsmen in the different local communities. Gradually he took away from the master craftsmen their marketing function, and before long he was in a position to force their prices down. Faced with this competition, the master craftsmen had to find ways and means of cutting their costs. They tried to lower the wages of their journeymen; they hired young men to do the skilled jobs before their term of apprenticeship was over; they sought out and employed workers who would take less than the old scale of wages. The workers resisted these attempts to lower their standards. Shoemakers, carpenters, coopers, tailors, and printers fought back through their own local craft societies. The interests of employers and workers grew farther apart.

The earliest American unions, then, were not those of oppressed factory workers: They were unions of highly skilled craftsmen who were forced to combine in self-defense—to keep their wages up and hours down, and to prevent the breakdown of the old regulated conditions of work. Their tactics were the familiar ones of collective bargaining, the strike, the closed shop, and the boycott. A series of separate struggles by the separate craft unions made their next step plain—and before long they took it.

In 1827 fifteen trade societies in Philadelphia joined together to form the Mechanics' Union of Trade Associations. It was the first city-wide union of unions in the world. One year later, the year that Andrew Jackson, "the people's choice," became President, the first Workingmen's party in the world was launched in Philadelphia. It was followed by the formation of other workingmen's parties in almost every state, and the beginning of a labor press—over fifty labor papers were founded at this time. In their political platforms the workers demanded the restriction of child labor, direct election of public officials, abolition of imprisonment for debt, the universal ten-hour day, and free and equal public education (the labor movement was largely responsible for the free public school system in the United States).

The next forty years was a story of ups and downs; first, a period of reaction against political activity, and an increase in the number of trade-unions; more city centrals, further growth—then sudden collapse with the paralysis of industry in the panic of 1837; return to political activity and participation in humanitarian movements of every description —co-operative societies, land reform, utopian communities, etc.; then revival of business, further expansion of the market, further development of transportation and communication, and the formation of craft unions on a national scale; followed the crisis of 1857—a check to industrial enterprise and a general destruction of trade-unions; then the Civil War—expansion of business and revival of old and formation of new unions; establishment again of a labor press—over one hundred daily, weekly, and monthly journals published; after the war, attempts to unite the national unions into a lasting single federation—at first failure, then finally, success.

The growth of Big Business after the Civil War meant that trade unionism would take tremendous strides. This had to happen because industrial expansion brought with it further concentration of workers into cities, further improvements in transportation and communication so essential to a nationwide organization, and the conditions which made a worker's movement so necessary. Working-class organization grew with capitalist development, which produced both the class and the class sentiment, as well as the physical means of co-operation and communication. At the same time, the difficulties were great; facing the working class in its struggle for unionization was a capitalist class which increased its ruthlessness as it increased its wealth. Capital in the United States after the Civil War did not stand by idly while workers organized; it was fierce in its opposition.

Labor union leaders were not agreed among themselves on the best way of fighting capital. The Knights of Labor, the American Federation of Labor, and the Industrial Workers of the World went at the problem from different angles. The approach of the first was welfare or "uplift" unionism; of the second, business unionism; and of the third, revolutionary unionism.

The Noble Order of the Knights of Labor was a secret society founded in Philadelphia in 1869, by a small group of clothing cutters. Their leader was Uriah S. Stephens, a tailor, who had been trained for the ministry. Since it was a secret society it was able to grow in a period when open unions were going to pieces because of the depression (there was a "panic" in 1873), or because of the bitter attacks of the employers. Glass workers, iron workers, printers, shoemakers, and other craftsmen who found themselves without a union formed new locals within the Knights of Labor.

But not only skilled workers became members of the Knights—the organization was open to all workers, white and black, men and women, unskilled as well as skilled. Farmers, and even some employers, were eligible for membership. Any person over eighteen "working for wages or who at any time worked for wages" could join. The Knights of Labor was an all-inclusive labor organization to which even members of the middle class could belong. Not, however, all middle-class people—there were some interesting exceptions: "No person who either sells or makes a living, or any part of it, by the sale of intoxicating drink, either as manufacturer, dealer, or agent, or through any member of the family, can be admitted to membership in this order, and no lawyer, banker, professional gambler, or stockbroker can be admitted."

Because the Knights was "one big union" accepting the unskilled as well as the skilled, it is frequently thought of as an industrial union. That is not true. Though it was not organized on craft lines, neither was it organized on the basis of industry. Its local assemblies were of two kinds, trade and mixed. The members of the first were usually those engaged in a single craft; the members of the second were everybody, regardless of occupation. It was not set up to help any single group within labor, but to bring about the union of all labor.

To what end? The Noble Order of the Knights of Labor had the kind of program which one would expect from an organization with such a name. Its leaders announced as their purpose the idealistic aim of elevating the whole laboring class through organization, education, and co-operation. The set of instructions given every new member contained the following:

> Labor is noble and holy. To defend it from degradation; to divest it of the evils to body, mind, and estate which ignorance and greed have imposed; to rescue the toiler from the grip of the selfish—is a work worthy of the noblest and best of our race. . . . We mean no conflict with legitimate enterprise, no antagonism to necessary capital; but men, in their haste and greed, blinded by self-interests, overlook the interests of others and sometimes violate the rights of those they deem helpless. We mean to uphold the dignity of labor, to affirm the nobility of all who earn their bread by the sweat of their brows. . . . We shall, with all our strength, support laws made to harmonize the interests of labor and capital, and also those laws which tend to lighten the exhaustiveness of toil. . . .

Thus early were the new members given their dose of sentimental uplift which was characteristic of the speeches and writings of the leaders of the Knights. Here was no declaration of war on capital, no ringing challenge to the existing order. Nor was there even a recognition of the opposing interests of labor and capital. The creed of the Knights was not employers vs. workers, but employers *and* workers together advancing the cause of humanity. There was "no conflict with legitimate enterprise." Only the selfish—in other writings they are identified as the "money power"—were to be curbed. The way to uphold the dignity of labor was for it to employ itself through "co-operation, of the order, by the order, and for the order"—the Knights believed in and organized producers' co-operatives. The milestones on their path to social reform were to be co-operation, education, and organization.

Their co-operative ventures—some two hundred mines, iron foundries, cooperage works, nail mills, shoe factories, etc.—failed; but they did educate the American workers—largely through their agitation for political reforms such as the income tax, the abolition of child labor, workmen's compensation, labor exchanges for the unemployed, payment of wages by the week and in lawful money, social insurance, the eight-hour day, public ownership of railroads and utilities; and they did succeed, for a time, in organizing the most truly representative labor organization that had yet appeared in America. In 1879, Terence V. Powderly succeeded Stephens as Grand Master Workman of the Order. In 1881, the Knights gave up secrecy. In 1886, the organization had grown from the initial membership of eleven tailors in Assembly No. 1 in Philadelphia, to over seven hundred thousand members in most of the United States.

The chief cause of that growth, however, could not be traced to the leaders' idealistic sentimental program of social uplift. It was to be found, rather, in the fact that the rank and file was militant—it forced strikes and boycotts in spite of the leadership. While Powderly dreamed dreams and talked endlessly of the brotherhood of man, the rank and file translated the slogan of the order, "an injury to one is the concern of all," into concrete action. While Powderly believed that "strikes are deplorable in their effect and contrary to the best interests of the order," and said openly, "I shudder at the thought of a strike and I have good reason," the rank and file did not shudder at strikes, but became more and more aggressive. Had the leadership been less bewildered, had it devoted less time to preaching the principles of the good society and more to perfecting the principles of militant union organization, then its grand conception of one big union embracing all wage earners, skilled and unskilled, of every creed, nationality, race, sex, and craft, might have had even greater success than it did have. As it was, where the Knights of Labor succeeded, it did so largely in spite of its constitution, program, and leadership; where it failed, it did so largely because of them.

The year 1886 was an eventful one in American labor history. In that year the Noble Order of the Knights of Labor reached the height of its power—and began its decline. In that year, out of the Federation of Trades and Labor Unions of the United States and Canada, organized in 1881, the American Federation of Labor was founded.

The Noble Order of the Knights had lost out to an organization entirely opposite in aim, program, membership, and method of struggle. The business unionism of the American Federation of Labor was totally unlike the uplift unionism of the Knights. Where the K. of L. had been idealistic—dreaming of a utopia to come, the A.F. of L. was practical—thinking of better conditions now; where the K. of L. had been unselfish—concerning itself with the interest of all the working class, unskilled as well as skilled, the A.F. of L. was selfish—concerning itself only with the interest of the skilled workers who were in the organization; where the K. of L. had been unbusinesslike—run by the humanitarian Stephens and the windbag Powderly, the A.F. of L. was businesslike—run by the shrewd, matter-of-fact Samuel Gompers.

Three years before the A.F. of L. was finally launched, Adolph Strasser, president of the Cigar Makers' Union and founder, with Gompers and P. J. McGuire, of the A.F. of L., was on the stand before the Senate Committee upon Relations between Capital and Labor. His testimony on the aim of his organization was a forerunner of the program of the A.F. of L. "We have no ultimate ends. We are going on from day to day. We are fighting for immediate objects—objects that can be realized in a few years."

The immediate objects for which the A.F. of L. fought were higher wages, shorter hours, better conditions. It was that simple. Though Gompers had flirted with socialism in the past, he was ever anxious to keep reform out of the A.F. of L. picture. The only uplift that was to come to the workers through the A.F. of L. was the uplift that came with higher wages, shorter hours, and better conditions.

The A.F. of L. was essentially a craft organization, a loose federation of national and international (so called because some of them had locals in Canada) craft unions. It was a union of many separate unions, each of them composed of skilled workers and all of them fighting to obtain higher wages, shorter hours, and better conditions. The unskilled workers who had flocked by the thousands to the banner of the Knights of Labor could not obtain admittance into the A.F. of L. The attitude of the leaders of the A.F. of L. toward the unskilled who were left out in the cold was best expressed by one of them who said, as recently as 1934, "We do not want to charter the riffraff or good-for-nothings, or those for whom we cannot make wages or conditions, unless we are compelled to do so by other organizations offering to charter them under any condition."

In membership and aim, then, the A.F. of L. differed from the Knights of Labor. There was an important difference, too, in the structure of the two organizations. "To understand completely the structure and function of the Knights of Labor, it is necessary to read but one constitution. To understand fully the functions and structure of the American Federation of Labor, over a hundred constitutions must be read. The Knights of Labor is a sovereignty, the American Federation of Labor is a federation of sovereignties." Where power in the Knights was centralized in the permanent officers of the General Assembly, in the A.F. of L. power was centralized in the leaders of the various national unions that made up the federation.

While the A.F. of L. unions believed in bargaining with employers to obtain higher wages, shorter hours, and better conditions, while they bent all their efforts to win collective bargaining agreements peaceably, they did not hesitate to fight when it was necessary. But they made certain, whenever possible, that they were entering the fray well armed. Their dues were high enough to enable them to build up a strong fighting fund to be used when they had to resort to strikes or boycotts. The A.F. of L. was aware of the realities of the capitalist system—they knew that there was a struggle going on between capitalists and laborers. But they kept their eyes on immediate goals. They did not plan to overthrow the system. They were quite content to continue in a master-and-servant relationship with capital, but they wanted a bigger share for themselves as servants. Their motto was "a fair day's wage for a fair day's work."

In the "pure and simple trade unionism" philosophy of Samuel Gompers there was no room for the creation by the A.F. of L. of a political party which would represent labor. Despite repeated efforts by some of the members of the A.F. of L. to have the organization form a labor party, Gompers' policy of working within the existing political parties won out. In politics the A.F. of L. has played the game of "rewarding its friends, and punishing its enemies."

By 1900 what was the position of the A.F. of L.? From one point of view it had not done well at all. Despite its practical program of fighting for immediate gains which were the first concern of most American workers, it had grown slowly. The powerful Railway Brotherhoods had not affiliated with it; the unskilled workers had not been invited into its ranks, so they were unorganized; and many, even of the skilled workers whom it had sought out, had not joined up.

From another point of view it had done remarkably well. True, the largest percentage of skilled workers remained outside its ranks, but, nevertheless, its five hundred and fifty thousand members represented more than three times the one hundred and fifty thousand it had begun with in 1886. That was less than the total reached by the Knights of Labor at the height of its power, but it was a different kind of membership—more lasting, more powerful, better disciplined. Its decentralized organization of independent national member unions, following the tactics of business unionism, had stood the test; in a period of fierce opposition by a ruthless employer class, it had managed to hold its own. It had managed to do what no other nonsecret national labor organization had been able to do before in American history—successfully weather the storm of a depression (that of 1893). For its defenders, that it had survived at all was proof of the correctness of its policies.

The Industrial Workers of the World, organized in 1905 with "Big Bill" Haywood as their leader, stood for revolutionary unionism. They did not believe in the A.F. of L. method of fighting capital. The preamble to their constitution declared that:

The working class and the employing class have nothing in common. There can be no peace so long as hunger and want are found among millions of the working-people, and the few, who make up the employing class, have all the good things of life. Between these two classes a struggle must go on until the workers of the world organize as a class, take possession of the earth and the machinery of production and abolish the wage system. . . . The trade unions foster a state of affairs which allows one set of workers to be pitted against another set of workers in the same industry, thereby helping to defeat one another in wage wars. Moreover, the trade unions aid the employing class to mislead the workers into the belief that the working class have interests in common with their employers.

Instead of the conservative motto, "a fair day's pay for a fair day's work," we must inscribe on our banner the revolutionary watchword "abolition of the wage system."

It is the historic mission of the working class to do away with capitalism.

The leaders of the I.W.W., unlike those of the A.F. of L., were opposed to making agreements with capitalists. They pointed to the fact that in several A.F. of L. strikes, one group of workmen in an industry—say, the cooks—would be out on strike, while the waiters in the same industry had to continue working because of an agreement with the employer. The I.W.W. leaders held that when one set of workers went out on strike, all the workers in that industry should support them by striking also. They were against contracts with capital because they wanted to get rid of capital entirely. They were not interested in immediate gains, but in the final and complete victory of labor over capital. They stood for one big union of all the workers, instead of division into craft unions. They made the dues to their organization very low so that all workers, the unskilled as well as the skilled, could join. They hated the A.F. of L. only a little less than they hated capital. The main points in their program are contained in their song:

PAINT 'ER RED

By RALPH CHAPLIN

(*Tune:* "Marching through Georgia")

Come with us, you working-men, and join the rebel band;
Come, you discontented ones, and give a helping hand,
We march against the parasite to drive him from the land
    With One Big Industrial Union!
Chorus:
    Hurrah! Hurrah! we're going to paint 'er red!
    Hurrah! Hurrah! the way is clear ahead—
    We're gaining shop democracy and liberty and bread
        With One Big Industrial Union!
We hate their rotten system more than any mortals do.
Our aim is not to patch it up, but build it all anew,
And what we'll have for government, when finally we're through
        Is One Big Industrial Union!

The influence of the I.W.W. was much greater than the total of its membership at the peak would lead one to believe. At no time, probably, did it ever have more than seventy-five thousand members, but in the course of its militant activities it reached hundreds of thousands of other workers. The unorganized and unskilled, the many migratory workers who largely made up its rank and file, were infected with the revolutionary ardor of the leaders. Strikes were not worrisome to the I.W.W.—on the contrary, it welcomed them. Its leaders were fearless and magnetic and showed marked ability in conducting many bitter struggles.

In the course of those struggles oppressed workers received from them the help which they sorely needed. But the revolutionary program of the I.W.W. did not, in the first quarter of the twentieth century, attract a permanent following. The government cracked down on the "wobblies" during World War I, and in 1918 over one hundred of their leaders were clapped into jail for conspiracy. By 1924 they were practically out of existence.

Unionists, whether members of the Knights of Labor, the A.F. of L., or the I.W.W., found the going hard. The employing class saw in labor unions a challenge to its power. It was, accordingly, opposed to unions, and it used every means, fair or foul, to destroy them. Some of the most bitter struggles in American history—struggles in which thousands of dollars worth of property was destroyed and scores of lives were lost—were the result, in the last analysis, of the refusal by the employers to recognize labor unions and bargain collectively with them. That this truth is not more widely accepted is due to the simple fact that the employers have had control of the opinion-making forces—the press, the schools, the church, etc. The newspapers have printed, the teachers have taught, and the clergymen have preached, in the main, the capitalist side of the struggle.

In addition, in their direct dealings with organized workers, many employers made effective use of their economic power. They formed unions of their own—employers' associations—to present a united front in opposition to unions of workers; they imposed the "iron-clad oath" ("yellow-dog" contract), which exacted a promise from the worker that he would not join a union—under penalty of losing his job; they openly discriminated against and discharged known unionists; they made extensive use of the black list against "troublemakers"—i.e., union men—they employed spies to report on the organizing efforts of their employees and to smash the unions; they stuck badges on men, thus converting them into "company police," then gave them clubs and guns to be used on strikers. (It was this ability to obtain workers to fight against their fellow workers that led Jay Gould, a famous capitalist, to boast, "I can hire one-half of the working class to kill the other half.") These employer methods were all very effective—unions had a difficult time.

It was made more difficult for unions when employers discovered that what they could not do for themselves by their own direct economic pressure, they could often get the courts to do for them. The courts could do the most surprising things—so surprising as to excite the envy of a magician.

Congress, in 1890, had put into the legislative hat an antitrust act. Lo, and behold! The courts pulled out an antilabor act! Look, for example, at the government batting average in the courts for the years 1892–1896:

Cases Brought under the Sherman Antitrust Act:

	Total	Won	Lost	Percentage
Against trusts	5	1	4	.200
Against labor	5	4	1	.800

In the list of Sherman Act antilabor cases of this period was the Pullman strike, one of the most famous of labor disputes. Mr. Pullman had built the town of Pullman, in Illinois, for Pullman workers. Pullman was a very appropriate name for it. The factories belonged to the Pullman Company, the stores belonged to the Pullman Company, the workmen's homes belonged to the Pullman Company, the school belonged to the Pullman Company, the church belonged to the Pullman Company, and the theater belonged to the Pullman Company.

In the spring of 1894 the management of the Pullman Company discharged about one third of its workers and announced a 25 to 40 per cent cut in wages for the others. Did Mr. Pullman also reduce the rent in his houses? Did he lower the prices in his stores? He did not.

In May, 1894, the Pullman workers went out on strike.

Immediately the company shut down its plant and the workers' credit at the stores was stopped. By June, many of the workers' families were starving.

The American Railway Union, organized by Eugene V. Debs, a railway fireman, tried to act as peacemaker, but the Pullman Company management would not see its leaders.

The Railway Union then ordered its members to boycott all Pullman cars attached to the trains on which they worked. In a few days, railway men on roads running west from Chicago refused to handle Pullman cars. The railroad managers refused to allow these cars to be detached and discharged the boycotters.

Then the American Railway Union called all its men out on strike and the trains were stopped. Railway labor all over the country had rallied behind Debs, its standard-bearer. The strike was well organized, and it grew more effective day by day. Trains in every part of the country stood still.

The Pullman Company was not alone in its war on the American Railway Union. The General Managers' Association, whose membership consisted of twenty-four railroad companies, joined forces with the Pullman Company against the union. Debs, in his appeal to the railroad workers to support the boycott of Pullman cars, told them what had happened: " . . . Then the railway corporations, through the General Managers' Association, came to the rescue, and in a series of whereases declared to the world that they would go into partnership with Pullman, so to speak, and stand by him in his devilish work of starving his employees to death. The American Railway Union accepted the gauge of war, and thus the contest is now on between the railway corporation united solidly upon the one hand and the labor forces upon the other. . . ."

So united were the labor forces in the struggle, so effective was their strike against the General Managers' Association, one of the most powerful combinations of capital in the United States, that it looked for a time as though they might win. If they had had to fight the General Managers' Association by itself they might have succeeded. But the combination of the General Managers' Association and the courts and Federal troops was too much for them.

The capitalists appealed to President Cleveland for troops. On July 4, 1894, two thousand United States soldiers moved into Chicago. John Altgeld, then Governor of Illinois, immediately sent a letter of protest to the President, saying that the state of Illinois could handle its own affairs. Cleveland replied that the soldiers were there to protect and move the United States mails. Following the arrival of the troops, trouble started. What had been a comparatively peaceful strike situation became a warring one. Bricks were thrown, trains were overturned, scabs were dragged from their posts and beaten, and railroad property was burned. Though the union officials had begged their men not to break loose—a request which the strikers had heeded up to this time—there was little doubt that union men were responsible for some of the destruction. On the other hand, the strikers claimed that much of the violence was caused by *agents provocateurs*, men hired by the railroad officials who wanted in this way to give the strikers a black eye with the public. There was little doubt that this was true as well. At any rate, the wrecking and burning continued and twelve people were killed.

The man most responsible for the sending of the troops was Mr. Edwin Walker. He was one of the lawyers for the General Managers' Association, and the attorney general of the United States had very obligingly appointed him special counsel for the government as well. Mr. Walker found that he could serve both his clients at the same time quite easily.

He had the troops sent in. And he appeared before the courts and was able to convince the judges that the railroad strike was an unlawful conspiracy *in violation of the Sherman Act*. Then the judges, at his request, issued an injunction, or order, prohibiting the officials of the union from interfering in any way with trains engaged in interstate commerce; or from compelling, or even persuading, the workers on the railways not to do their jobs. It was a "blanket" injunction which meant it covered everybody—not only Debs and the other union officers, but "all other persons whomsoever"; and it forbade practically every activity which the strikers had to engage in to keep the strike effective—even peaceful picketing was now a crime. And all this was based on the law passed to curb the trusts!

Debs and the other leaders carried on in defiance of the injunction. In the middle of July they were arrested for contempt of court. The backbone of the strike was broken. The railway companies, triumphant, refused to take back some of the strikers. Others they hired again on their own terms.

With the help of the government and the courts the capitalists had won a great victory.

They had won more than that. The Pullman strike showed them the effectiveness of a weapon which they had used before but had never really sharpened to a cutting edge. Now they polished it up in great style. The injunction was swift and deadly. From 1895 on the capitalists used it with telling effect. It was a wonderfully efficient strikebreaker.

Employers had only to march into federal or state courts and persuade the judges that unless they restrained the strikers horrible things were about to happen. Irreparable damage was going to be done to their property. Not to their tangible property alone—stuff you could lay your hands on, like the factory, machinery, material, etc.; but to their intangible property as well—stuff you couldn't lay your hands on, like the right to do business, the good will of the public toward the employer and his product, the right to make a profit. The judges were very easily persuaded. There was a deluge of injunctions. They forbade acts which were crimes (which could have been handled by the criminal courts) and acts which were not crimes (which the strikers had a constitutional right to do). Judges have issued injunctions which have prohibited strikers from parading, picketing, assembling near the place where the strike was going on, or distributing pamphlets; strikers have even been prohibited from attending certain churches, or praying and singing on the public highways!

Small wonder that labor spent years in agitating for a law to limit the use of the injunction in labor disputes. In 1932, thirty-eight years after the Pullman strike, such a law was passed—the Norris-La Guardia Act. It read as though it might do the trick, but realist friends of labor were not certain—they remembered that it still remained for the courts to interpret the law. And so long as that was true, then it was wise not to be too optimistic.

They remembered that Sam Gompers had been too optimistic in 1914. In that year a new antitrust act, one supposedly designed to exempt labor unions from the provisions of the Sherman Act, was passed. The Clayton Antitrust Act was hailed by Gompers as labor's "Magna Charta upon which the working people will rear their constitution of industrial freedom." He based his hopes on Section 6, which said in part: "The labor of a human being is not a commodity or article of commerce . . . nor shall such [labor] organizations, or the members thereof, be held or construed to be illegal combinations or conspiracies in restraint of trade, under the anti-trust laws."

Mr. Gompers' enthusiasm was short lived. The Clayton Act, as construed by the courts, did not do what it was supposed to do. On the contrary. There were more suits brought against labor under the Sherman Act in the twenty-four years following the passage of the Clayton Act in 1914, than in the twenty-four years following the passage of the law in 1890!

It had become increasingly clear that laws designed to prevent the growth of trusts were, by court interpretation, being used to prevent the growth of organized labor. It often happened that when a combination of employers was on trial the Supreme Court applied the "rule of reason"— and the employers went free; but when a combination of workers was on trial, then the Supreme Court applied a rule of unreason—and the workers were penalized.

It was all very strange. That was what Justice Brandeis thought in his celebrated dissenting opinion in the Bedford Stone case:

The Sherman Law was held in United States v. United States Steel Corporation . . . to permit capitalists to combine in a single corporation 50 per cent. of the steel industry of the United States, dominating the trade through its vast resources. The Sherman Law was held in United States v. United Shoe Machinery Co. . . . to permit capitalists to combine in another corporation practically the whole shoe machinery industry of the country. . . . It would indeed be strange if Congress had by the same act willed to deny to members of a small craft of working men the right to co-operate in simply refraining from work when that course was the only means of self-protection against a combination of militant and powerful employers. I cannot believe that Congress did so."

But this was a dissenting opinion. The majority of the justices of the Supreme Court thought otherwise. In the long and bitter struggle of the haves v. the have-nots, the courts of the country were on the side of the haves.

Edward C. Kirkland

HAZARDS AND CHARMS OF POLITICAL ACTION

Labor had always had an alternative to boycotts and strikes—
politics. There was much to recommend it. Some issues—prison-made
goods, immigration restriction, child labor—could only be handled by
legislation, if at all. Economic pressure against employers could not repeal statutes hampering labor organizations or strike the blinders from
the eyes of judges. Politics was a means of action as useful in a falling as
in a rising market. It did not call for the men to leave their tools and
machines; it simply asked them to go to the ballot box and vote their interests. This had the consecration of being the democratic and the American way. The auguries of success were favorable. As employers were
all too well aware, there were more workers than there were managers,
and, besides, the former could call on reformers sympathetic to labor's
cause. From Massachusetts, where an old pillar of anti-slavery, Wendell
Phillips, maintained the momentum of agitation in behalf of labor, to
Illinois, where the members of Hull House, a Chicago settlement house,
conducted investigations and drew up legislation, such outsiders lent
aid.

As in the case of economic pressure, resort to political action involved
decisions by the union as to when to act and as to the methods employed.
Through logic and pressing necessity, labor came quickly to see that it
must aid in the defense of its oppressed members before the courts, especially since judicial decisions concerned larger issues than the fate of
individuals at the bar. Such occasional stabs at political action did not
involve complex organization; appeals could be made for funds through
existing labor journals and through correspondence. Legislation was a
more subtle matter, for the simple constitutional right of petition required the maintenance of a lobby. Among other things, this was expensive. Though the National Labor Union demanded a lobby, it was not until the mid-eighties that Powderly was proposing that the Knights set up
a lobby in every state capital and in Washington to push labor bills and
keep tabs on legislators.

But lobbies faced much the same difficulty as strike pickets; somehow
they were more "educative" and "persuasive" when they represented
strength and could promise rewards and threaten reprisals. One way to

achieve this effectiveness was to vote for trade union members who ran for public office; a second was to vote for the friends and punish the enemies of labor, no matter on what ticket they were running, a procedure quaintly termed non-partisanship. The Knights adopted both these measures. In 1886 the General Assembly resolved: "We will hold responsible at the ballot box all members of Congress who neglect or refuse to vote in compliance" with the Knights' demands. Thirdly labor could go it alone by establishing its own political party or combine with others to do so. The National Labor Union had done this in 1870–1872. At the end of the seventies the Knights of Labor were half way in the Greenback-Labor Party and seemed likely to repeat the commitment in 1886, but the next year Powderly reverted to his fundamental non-partisan stand.

The leaders of the American Federation of Labor and its constituent unions were generally non-political, though they were less vacillating than Powderly and more forceful verbally. In 1885 P. J. McGuire of the Carpenters was expressing his disillusionment with labor legislation. Such laws Democrats and Republicans made to fool the workers, not to be enforced. "We have come to the conclusion that wherever we can help ourselves we will do it, without asking the aid of the Government, and if we want to make a law we will make it in our own trades unions and try to enforce it through them by contracts with our employers." Years later, Samuel Gompers summarized what history had taught him: "An independent labor and progressive movement was inaugurated by the National Labor Union and David Davis of Illinois was nominated for the Presidency in 1872. The National Labor Union never held another convention. It had spent its force; it had nominated a candidate for president."

It required conviction, courage and parliamentary skill for Gompers to keep the Federation on the non-political course, for the Socialist-Labor Party, boring from within the union ranks, sought direct representation at the Federation's meetings and, in the mid-nineties, presented an eleven-point political program introduced with a preamble proposing, as in Great Britain, "the principle of independent labor politics as an auxiliary to their economic action." The depression of 1893 and the hard knocks union organization had taken, as at Homestead, gave the Socialists their chance. In the main battle Gompers put down the insurgents, but at the Denver Convention of 1894 he lost the presidency of the Federation for the only time during his life as labor leader. In Socialist eyes the defeat of their program committed the Federation to an "opportunistic political line." Such episodes also convinced believers in pure and simple trade unionism that association with reformers was not a one-way street.

While such evidence would seem to demonstrate that the conspicuous national organizations were moving from political to industrial weapons, other labor groupings provide evidence for a contrary conclusion. Since the structure of American political action was not corporate but geographical, political activity by organized labor naturally clustered about organizations on a geographical basis, state or urban aggregations. Since urban labor unions were apt to embrace more foreign or Socialist members, their influence helped to push central labor unions along the path of politics. Thus in New York City the call for the establishment of the Central Labor Union was issued in 1881 by a member of a Socialist local assembly of the Knights of Labor, and the Central's Declaration of Principles re-echoed Socialist slogans about the class struggle and the desirability of political action. Its constitution included the precautionary provisions that the union should have no permanent president lest he "sell out the union to any political party" and no public official or lawyer could be a delegate to the union. By 1886 the Central Labor Union was debating in an abstract fashion whether labor should take independent political action or try to swing its followers from party to party in a balance-of-power policy.

A famous boycott case in New York City in which the judge sentenced the boycotters to Sing Sing for "extortion" (they had collected $1,000 from the employer through arbitration) gave urgency to a program of participation in politics and seemed to reenforce the necessity of independent political action. Through a series of accommodations, the Central Labor Union nominated the single tax reformer, Henry George, for mayor. The Democrats under Tammany Hall nominated Abram S. Hewitt, the philanthropist employer, and the Republicans, young Theodore Roosevelt. The excitement of the campaign and the criticalness of the issue so infected the high command of labor that Terence Powderly and Samuel Gompers spoke and worked for Henry George. Hewitt won, George was second, Roosevelt third. On their roles as participants, both Powderly and Gompers had sober second thoughts. The former wrote of 1887, "I am glad I didn't talk [for George] this year," and the latter characterized the 1886 campaign as "this curious determination to disregard experience."

The New York campaign of 1886 did not have to surmount all the customary handicaps to labor's political action. The George candidacy had a campaign chest, an *ad hoc* journal, a roster of speakers and a force of volunteer workers. But it collided with some powerful advantages of the established parties. This was a period of intense political loyalties, partly inherited from the Civil War days; the habit of independent voting was not widespread. Nor were all political issues aligned along the axis of the labor-capital controversy. Workers were citizens and party members before they were workers. Politics, like religion, was a divisive factor and astute labor leaders tried to keep it out of the labor organizations. That was why lawyers were not allowed in the Knights of Labor. This was a period when politics became a business, the period of the machine. Neither a successful lobby nor a third party could be improvised; politics required full-time, sophisticated attention, and labor leaders in politics were part-time amateurs who lacked know-how and staying power. Curiously enough their political ideology reflected that of the employers. Politics was dishonest, a dirty business. The labor union cause, like private business enterprise, became a sort of holy grail, above or beyond politics. Furthermore, like their business counterparts, some union leaders thought government action was really futile and wrong. P. J. McGuire affirmed, "I believe the Government had better keep its hands off private business as much as possible."

LABOR LEGISLATION

Although labor legislation in extent and enforcement fell short of the expectations of the more hopeful, the record was not one of absolute failure. At the end of the century an agent of the Industrial Commission surveyed the status of protective legislation. Just over half the states had legislation prohibiting the labor of children in factories; the age limitation was ordinarily fourteen but some additional years were added if the children lacked education. The states which did not have child labor laws were generally in the trans-Mississippi West or in the South. Nearly every Eastern state had passed legislation regulating the hours of labor for women and minors of both sexes in factories and mercantile establishments. The general limitation was to ten hours a day and sixty hours a week, though Massachusetts had a fifty-eight hour week and Wisconsin a forty-eight. About half the states had factory acts, so called after the great English factory act of 1831, enforcing certain standards of safety and sanitation in factories and sometimes other establishments. There were almost no factory acts in the South or beyond the Mississippi. In the chief industrial states of the East and Midwest there were generally laws providing for the licensing, inspection and, in Pennsylvania, the prohibition of sweatshops. Such establishments usually produced clothing, artificial flowers, and cigars in tenements or houses. Practically all the states "in which mines of any character are located" had mining laws providing for mining inspectors to see that operators obeyed provisions for escape shafts, ventilation, safety lamps, and for care in carrying and hoisting products and personnel and in handling explosives. Laws on the statute books were not self-enforcing and much of this legislation perforce dealt with definitions and details of administration.

That the trans-Mississippi West in general stood aloof from this movement was due to its agricultural preoccupations; that the South did so was due, in part, to its desire to establish industries and not handicap their advance. In truth, the cutthroat competition among states for industrial growth was one reason for the general slowness in passing this legislation and laxness in enforcing it. The difficulty of securing uniform legislation, where the central government had limited powers within a federal system, exasperated both employers and employees, and, among other things, explained the latter's disillusionment with political activity.

Some ascribed the movement for legislation to employers or to government officials, such as commissioners of statistics for labor, who had come to look upon themselves as the guardians of labor's interests. Others, like McNeill of Massachusetts, felt that the "initiative" for such legislation came "in every instance" from labor men. More commonly the state of mind of the community was felt to be responsible. "I do not believe Massachusetts would have accomplished what she has done in the way of factory legislation unless there had been enough sense of justice in the leisure class and the educated class to uphold the work of the workingman, and not only uphold it but aid it actively." As usual Gompers had the common sense of the matter: "What is everybody's business is nobody's business, and organized labor makes it its business and then has the sympathy of the general public to come in and aid."

THE VALUE OF LABOR

Whether wrung at first instance from employers or realized at second hand in legislation, the program of organized labor took off from certain assumptions. Perhaps these are best summarized in the bald assertion of the Grand Secretary of the Knights of Labor: "We know we have produced the wealth." The theory that labor was the source of all value was as commonplace with the Federation of Labor as it was with the Knights. It followed that unions were concerned with attaining an acknowledgment of labor's nobility and dignity by community and employer. The reason the Central Labor Union of New York advocated in 1882 an annual Labor Day distinct from other national holidays was that labor alone had no day which it could call its own. Though at least one employer thought this holiday hardly attained its lofty objectives ("drunken rabble, harvest for saloon keepers"), its implied tribute to work certainly ought to have won popular sympathy in a generation which worshipped work and suspected leisure. It did. In 1893 the committee of the Senate investigating Homestead casually remarked in an obiter dictum: "It should not be forgotten that labor is the source of all wealth."

Even wider approval might have been forthcoming if labor's thoughts about its own value had been somewhat less exclusive and somewhat less oblivious of other factors in the productive process. Labor on the whole grudgingly allowed capital a place. After all, capital was "the fruit of labor" and interest "may probably be right." Labor's blind spot was management. "Do not let the man who has no money hire capital to build the factory and to buy the raw material, and pay interest on that money, and then hire money to pay his labor, and make a profit above all that, and hire a superintendent at a good salary to manage the business, and be himself one of the lords of the land—so-called." Paradoxically Gompers preferred the capitalist with an inherited status to the self-made man. It was the fortunes of this latter group—Jay Gould was usually the example—that seemed to be made by some dishonesty or magic; they could not be accounted for by "the natural increase of capital." Parasitic employers should "go into a workshop and earn an honest living instead of undertaking to make money from nothing, absolutely nothing."

THE WAGES SYSTEM

No specific phase of labor union policy was more interpenetrated by the theory that labor created all wealth than was wages; for "the wage question is the labor question." At first organized labor hoped to avoid the complexities, injustice, and industrial strife engendered by the wages system. They would abolish it. In his own Moulders' Union and in the National Labor Union William Sylvis became the prophet of producers' cooperation. The moulders would build and operate their own factories and divide all the returns, be they profits or wages. Ultimately such cooperation would end poverty and elevate the workers spiritually and morally. This did not mean that producers' cooperation had solely an idealistic motive; in periods of business depression or after strikes had failed, producers' cooperatives served the practical end of putting people to work.

From time to time the Knights of Labor were enthusiastic over cooperation. In 1885 its Grand Secretary, for instance, was rather impatient with his unions' concern with wages. This was a mere short-time matter "while we remain wage workers." Instead the Knights desired to solve the problem of just distribution "by going into business for ourselves, contributing our own money, and starting a business of our own." Uriah Stephens, like Sylvis, was a zealot for cooperation, and Terence V. Powderly in his first annual address to the General Assembly in 1880 summoned the Knights to abolish the wage system and embark upon a crusade for cooperation "which will eventually make every man his own master—every man his own employer; a system which will give the laborer a fair proportion of the products of his toil. . . . There is no good reason why labor cannot, through cooperation, own and operate mines, factories and railroads." There were always some among the Knights who dragged their feet on this issue; and by the end of the eighties the Order was retreating on this front as on most others.

Though, as a central organization, the Knights of Labor undertook but one cooperative enterprise, a coal mine, its constituent assemblies or trades embarked upon several experiments. Their number in the mid-eighties may have reached 135. They were most numerous in mining, coopering, and shoe-making, occupations in which individual skill continued to play a considerable part. Most cooperative ventures were small, the average amount of investment per establishment being $10,000. Most cooperatives failed, and those that did not assumed an organizational form far from flawless. The original investors among the workingmen became a directoral élite interested in profits; they employed other workers at wages, sometimes low ones, and they cut the price of their products to compete with unionized rivals. Surveying these failures and deviations, one observer came to the conclusion that they were due to the effort "to get rid of the *entrepreneur* or manager." In spite of labor's blind spot on this score, managerial talent was necessary and it was rare.

Few experiments by organized labor have stirred so much interest as producers' cooperation and won so much approval, particularly among intellectuals. At one extreme E. L. Godkin of the *Nation* beat the drum for cooperation with the zeal of a Sylvis or a Stephens, and for much the same reasons. At the other extreme a group of reformers like R. T. Ely and E. W. Bemis, for whom Godkin would have had only contempt, undertook a study of cooperative enterprises on a regional basis. According to R. T. Ely, who wrote an introduction for the essays published by the *Johns Hopkins Studies in Historical and Political Science*, the investigators found more significant examples of cooperation in the United States than in England and demonstrated that one of "the prime conditions of success of cooperation is moral integrity of the cooperators. The cause of failure is more frequently ethical than intellectual weakness. This is true of all popular movements and for the mass of men. . . . Christ uttered a scientific truth, confirmed by every careful and intelligent observation of economic phenomena when he said, 'Seek ye first the kingdom of God and His righteousness, and all these things [economic goods] shall be added unto you.' "

The practical men heading the A.F. of L. who had to face the day-to-day problems of labor while expecting that "ultimately" after the passage of ages workers would become their own capitalists and their own employers, in general accepted the wage system and sought to make the best of it rather than to escape to utopia on the installment plan. Since they still adhered to the labor theory of value, they naturally thought labor should have a "prior" claim to the results of the wealth-producing process and that wages should not be determined by profits or dividends. Employers who could not make a profit and pay workers their rightful share should be driven out of industry by the stern rule of the survival of the fittest. As to the proper share for workers, labor leaders were apt to resort to generalities: it should be "just" and "reasonable" and "fair." Since these terms, however useful as slogans, were not self-defining, labor leaders advanced equivalents: a "living" wage, a "decent" wage, enough "to live comfortably." To objectives, so stated, few could take exception;

they were, however, a sort of time bomb planted beneath the wage policy of employers. Organized labor, for instance, was not greatly interested in real wages. Their conclusion that cheap goods meant cheap labor revealed a distaste for tying wages to the cost of living. "I believe in high wages and high prices for commodities. . . . When a man has good wages he can save something even if prices are high." Organized labor looked forward to a wage level which would give them a surplus above mere living.

Another complaint of employers was that the unions hoped to set all workers' wages at a uniform standard and thus hampered the paying of wages based on differences in skill and industry. Although Gompers acknowledged that he preferred time to piecework for its "excellence and perfection," he nonetheless felt that superior workers should and would get higher wages. All the union insisted upon was the "life-line" of a minimum wage. Actually the search for definitively just wages has the static quality of most formulas. The economy was dynamic; labor's wage theory was fluid and pragmatic. Said Gompers: "I know we are living under the wage system, and so long as that lasts, it is our purpose to secure a continually larger share for labor, for the wealth producers. Whether the time shall come, as this constantly increasing share to labor goes on, when profits shall be entirely eliminated, and the full product of labor, the net result of production, go to the laborer . . . I am perfectly willing that the future shall determine and work out."

THE EIGHT HOUR DAY

While labor's wage policy was for more and more, its policy on hours was for less and less. On this question, to an exceptional degree in labor history, the unions operated on the basis of a thought-out creed, which, coming early in the period, resembled a theological doctrine. In the sixties, Ira Steward, a self-educated machinist of Boston, began propagandizing the advantages of the eight-hour day. This was daring, for two decades later at least one manufacturer thought "ten hours a day is about right for a day's labor." Steward's visionary concept went further than a minor improvement in the status quo. He felt that the workers, having attained greater leisure, would look around and see how others spent it—even the exhibitionist expenditures of the rich had utility—and thus develop their own cultural and social interests. As a result of their uplifted status, they would demand higher wages. As Steward's wife, an able woman, put it in a jingle:

> Whether you work by the piece or work by the day
> Decreasing the hours increases your pay.

When workers had wants and the means to satisfy them, there would be an end to the underconsumption responsible for unemployment and for business depression. The shortening of the work day need not reduce production, for improved methods and machinery would compensate.

While these happy outcomes might appeal to employers, Steward's further inference that eventually his system would so erode profits that the glory of the cooperative commonwealth would come in could hardly reassure them. Quite clearly Steward's ideas, like those of Henry George and Edward Bellamy, involved a new order of society. Luckily they had the advantage of combining a short-range objective and a long-range cure-all. The latter, like most panaceas, was almost too easy and automatic. Since the shortened day fitted in with reformist optimism, with the efforts of practical men to cope with the unemployment of depression, and with the natural human desire to cut down hours of labor, the eight-hour program in one gloss or another colored the thinking of labor organizations for decades. Originally workers expected to realize the program through agitation and legislation. The diversity of state jurisdictions and the consequent fear in each state lest producers in another get an advantage pointed to the desirability of Congressional legislation. Nearly everyone agreed, however, that the Constitution had given the central government no power directly to regulate hours in private industry.

Within the limited area of its own workers, Federal legislation was possible. In 1868 a Federal statute declared, "That eight hours shall constitute a day's work for all laborers, workmen, and mechanics now employed . . . by or on behalf of the government of the United States." For this measure it is hard to unearth any immediate political explanation. The National Labor Union under William Sylvis had made the eight-hour day an important part of its program, and on its behalf Sylvis and others lobbied with the President and with Congress. A Senator also acknowledged that the "experiment" had "been discussed before the country." Perhaps a stronger wave than usual in the ebb tide of Civil War reform carried the measure to safety on the beach. However murky the background, the act naturally aroused expectations, for the phrasing was explicit and it covered wage earners in private establishments working under government contracts. These factors, along with the example of the nation as a "model employer," could have had great weight. Actually administrative officials and the courts made the act a nullity. They held it was directive and not mandatory, that wages would have to be reduced with a reduction of hours. Workers had little choice but to continue under previous stipulations.

This experience, along with their general hesitancy about politics, turned organized labor to the alternative weapon of economic pressure. It had always been their chief means against private employers. General campaigns for the eight-hour day, as contrasted with sporadic demands in particular establishments or occupations, were waged on an urban

basis, for instance in New York City in 1872, but the national movement
for the same purpose waited until the mid-eighties. Even then there was
an atmosphere of the accidental about the drive. That stumbling forerunner of the A.F. of L., the Federation of Organized Trades and Labor
Unions, in order to recoup its waning strength resolved in 1884, "that
eight hours shall constitute a legal day's labor from and after May 1,
1886, and that we recommend to labor organizations throughout this
jurisdiction that they so direct their laws as to conform to this resolution
by the time named." Persuasion or the threat of action or a general strike
might bring employers to compliance.

The resolution did not necessarily enlist the support of the larger and
rival Knights of Labor. Although the course of Powderly and other leaders was certainly equivocal, the membership of the Knights, according to
the evidence, was enthusiastic for the eight-hour drive. Thus, as it turned
out, there was a widespread rank-and-file support for action. Politicians
and even a portion of the press gave approval. The momentum thus generated carried furthest in metropolitan areas. Even before the date set
workers were striking for and securing a shorter day's work. Chicago,
with 80,000 participants and strikers, mounted the biggest drive. Then
the Haymarket episode, as we have seen, shattered the movement. In the
nineties the American Federation of Labor attempted to put together
again the pieces of the eight-hour philosophy but in a different frame.
Such constituent unions as were eager for a reduction of hours and well-
heeled enough to undertake a strike were to be backed by the Federation
and financially supported by it. A series of galloping strikes would thus
attain eight hours for organized workers. This tactic met with both success and failure, but by the end of the century the Federation discarded
even this effort. Though the movement had shortened hours, it had not
attained, except in special instances, the eight-hour optimum. To Gompers the issue in 1901 was still a "burning" one, and for reasons which
Ira Steward would have commended.

A HARMONY OF BELIEFS

We have noted that the philosophy of labor frequently resembled
that of managers and employers. A belief in natural law and in practical
measures are cases in point. Also labor tended to accept the values of the
society about it and wished simply to share in them more generously.
Nor was there much divergence in group attitudes over the fundamentals
of the economic order or the features currently attending its hasty and
disturbing development. For labor as for capital, production was a goal;
the former relished the fact that "we are producing wealth to-day at a
greater ratio than ever in the history of mankind."

One means to this end was machinery, and labor, instead of smashing
machines, admired the inventive genius which created them and advo-

cated their introduction. The eight-hour day program was postulated upon the introduction of machinery which would, in spite of fewer hours, maintain production. Labor's complaint was that it did not get its share of the advantages of machinery. The solution, most often commended for its ideology and ingenuity, was the one the International Typographical Union followed when the Merganthaler linotype machine threatened in 1887 and after to destroy the old-fashioned type-setting by hand. The president of the International Union shrewdly observed, "Those familiar with the productiveness of machines are agreed that hand work cannot begin to compete with them, and it is therefore futile to attempt to stay the tide of their introduction." The union accepted the machine. However, by its insistence that they be operated by already skilled operatives it prevented extensive technological unemployment and it used the productiveness of the machines to facilitate a shorter working day. The union also insisted on a minimum wage. For the industrial picture as a whole Gompers was explicit: "In the great race for the production of wealth we do not want to go back to the primitive methods; no sane man wants that."

The collective action of the labor union was, according to its leaders, an evolution in response to circumstance. Were they able to apply a similarly benevolent judgment to parallel developments—the business combination, big business, the trust? Hostility to the trust on the part of the Knights smacked more of agrarian than industrial criticism. Gompers was unwilling to embark upon a "general proposition." "We view the trust from the standpoint that they are our employers, and the employer who is fair to us, whether an individual, or a collection of individuals, an aggregation of individuals in the form of a corporation or a trust, matters little to us so long as we obtain the fair conditions." The general opinion of labor leaders added up to a tentative willingness to tolerate combinations, for the latter seemed to hold out the promise of more stable wages, a better guarantee of continuous work, and also an easier way to establish common conditions of labor than by dealing with hosts of small competitors. On the asserted lowering of prices by big business, Gompers pointed out labor was not greatly interested in this accomplishment—"I am not a cheap man, anyway"—and that prices tended to decline largely because of mechanization. He did fear that trusts had a tendency and ability "to prevent the will of the people by buying up legislators." As for trust policy, the government had better leave combinations alone, for the "State is not capable of preventing development or natural concentration of industry." Instead of regulating business, the Interstate Commerce Act and the Sherman Anti-Trust Act had been turned against labor to deprive it "of the benefit of organized effort."

When anti-business statutes were dismissed as "panaceas" by labor's spokesmen, it was unlikely that its high command would be enthusiastic over proposals seriously challenging an owner's right to manage his property. The cooperative enthusiasms of the Knights contained no threat of confiscation nor idea of government direction. Within the A.F. of L. an energetic socialist minority differed from the officers on the fundamental issue of private enterprise. In the nineties this faction sponsored a program calling for the municipal ownership of public utilities, the nationalization of telegraphs, telephones, railroads and mines, and the "collective ownership by the people of all means of production and distribution." Against this last proposal, article 10, Gompers and his allies fought with skill, determination and success. After the failure of the A.F. of L. to endorse public ownership, socialist influence fell off. Perhaps no point illustrated better the tolerance of the unions for private enterprise than the consistent refusal of their leaders to count among its failures the panics and depressions of these years. "I think that panics come, not through those men's [employers'] idiocy or incompetency, but are attributable to causes not generally understood."

Since the expressed thought of the leaders of organized labor was at bottom conservative and empirical and becoming more so and treasured the same scheme of values as did ownership-management, it would seem that the latter group might well vouchsafe the dearly-sought recognition the former strove for. Increasingly it did. Every great labor crisis, which in theory should have closed the ranks of employers, produced at least one capitalist of purest ray serene with courage and insight enough to look beyond doctrinaire partisanship. After the great railroad strikes of the seventies, culminating in the destructive Pittsburgh rioting of 1877, Congress investigated the alarming situation. The chairman of the committee was Abram S. Hewitt, a Representative and a noted ironmaster. In 1878 Hewitt was observing in an address, "A new power has entered into the industrial world, which must be recognized. . . . It must be heard. Its just demands must be heeded. . . . The great result achieved is that capital is ready to discuss. It is not to be disguised that till labor presented itself in such an attitude as to compel a hearing capital was unwilling to listen; but now it does listen. The results already attained are full of encouragement."

Again after Haymarket, when the air quivered with hysteria, Andrew Carnegie cut down the danger of revolution to pygmy size, and concluded: "The right of the working-men to combine and to form trades-unions is no less sacred than the right of the manufacturer to enter into associations and conferences with his fellows, and it must be sooner or later conceded. . . . My experience has been that trades-unions upon the whole are beneficial both to labor and to capital." Carnegie went so far as to doubt the wisdom of the conventional belief that an employer should hire strikebreakers. And in the labor disturbances of the 1890's, Marcus Alonzo Hanna derided the philanthropic façade of the town of Pullman and exploded: "A man who won't meet his men half-way is a God-damn fool!" The suspicion that Hanna only inferentially advocated union recognition soon vanished when he became the chief participant in the efforts of the National Civic Federation, whose members included labor leaders and capitalists, to abate industrial conflict by persuasion and mediation. And it was practical men in "the upper" and "lower classes," not economists, who led the way to the acceptance of unionism. At least that would seem to be the gravamen of an address delivered in 1888 to his fellow economists by their president, Francis A. Walker.

In truth, it is as misleading to write the history of labor between 1860 and 1900 in terms of labor upheavals or uprisings as it is to detect in every local breakdown of orderly development the pattern of a general strike or any other form of proto-revolutionary action. This was a period when the immense productive powers of the country were in transition from one system to another. The great problem was adjustment. Some turbulence was bound to attend the search for answers to the questions of what was fair and just and to the even more searching query of what was feasible and possible. That labor did not crystallize into a permanent party of discontent, nor come to regard itself as a group apart from the community with no responsibility for the common welfare, was a tribute to the discernment, foresight and flexibility of both labor and capital.

Labor
and capitalism
in America

Selig Perlman

The most distinctive characteristic of the development of the labor movement in America has not been, as in Germany, a slow but certain shedding of the philosophy originally imparted by an intellectual leadership. No intellectuals, in the true sense of the word, presided at its birth. The main feature of its development has been rather a perpetual struggle to keep the organization from going to pieces for want of inner cohesiveness. For, it has had to cope with two disruptive tendencies: First, American labor has always been prone, though far more in the past than now, to identify itself in outlook, interest, and action, with the great lower middle class, the farmers, the small manufacturers and business men, in a word, with the "producing classes" and their periodic "anti-monopoly" campaigns. Second, and here is a tendency of a rising rather than diminishing potency, the American employer has, in general, been able to keep his employees contented with the conditions, determined by himself, on which they individually accepted employment. Both these tendencies have seriously hindered the efforts of trade unionism towards stability and solidarity. The first tendency proved inimical because the organized wage earners would periodically be drawn into the whirlpool of politics under the banner of the "anti-monopoly" parties, so, under the American system of party politics, invariably suffering dissension, and ultimately disintegration. The second of the tendencies mentioned has balked unionism because the employer, wielding the initiative, has been able successfully to carry his own individualistic competitive spirit into the ranks of his employees. Moreover, both factors making for disintegration go back to a common cause. For whether the labor organization has succumbed to the lure of a political reform movement aiming to shield the "small man" and the "man on the make," and has broken up in political dissension; or whether it has failed to get started because the individual laborer has accepted the incentive of a bonus wage and of a better opportunity for advancement within the framework of a non-union bargain, the ultimate explanation, at all events, lies in the basic conditions of life in the American community—economic, political, ethnic, mental, and spiritual. Some of these are a heritage from the past, others of more recent origin, but all are closely interwoven with the present and the future of American labor.

THE BASIC CHARACTERISTICS OF THE AMERICAN COMMUNITY

1. The Strength of the Institution of Private Property

A labor movement must, from its very nature, be an organized campaign against the rights of private property, even where it stops short of embracing a radical program seeking the elimination, gradual or abrupt, "constitutional" or violent, of the private entrepreneur. When this campaign takes the political and legislative route, it leads to the denial of the employer's right to absolute control of his productive property. It demands and secures regulatory restrictions which, under American constitutional practice, are within the province of the "police power" vested in the states and granted by specific authority to Congress; only they must, in every case, square with "public purpose," as that term is interpreted in the last analysis by the United States Supreme Court. When the same campaign follows the economic route, the route of unionism, strikes, boycotts, and union "working rules," the restrictions on the rights of property are usually even more thoroughgoing and far-reaching, since unions are less amenable to judicial control than are legislatures and Congress. A third form of the labor movement seeks to promote cooperative production and distribution, neither of which is practiced appreciably in this country. This co-operative movement sets out to beat private capitalism by the methods of private business: greater efficiency and superior competitive power. To the advocates of the rights of private property, this third mode of the labor movement is the least offensive.

Because the labor movement in any form is a campaign against the absolute rights of private property, the extent to which the institution of private property is intrenched in the community in which a labor movement operates is of overwhelming importance to it. . . .

The enormous strength of private property in America, at once obvious to any observer, goes back to the all-important fact that, by and large, this country was occupied and settled by laboring pioneers, creating property for themselves as they went along and holding it in small parcels. This was the way not only of agriculture but also of the mechanical trades and of the larger scale industries. Thus the harmony between the self-interest of the individual pursuing his private economic aim and the general public interest proved a real and lasting harmony in the American colonies and states. This Adam Smith saw in 1776, his eye on the frugal and industrious class of masters of workshops still on the threshold of their elevation by the industrial revolution yet to come. Every addition to the total of the privately held wealth was at the same time an addition to the productive equipment in the community, which meant a fuller satisfaction of its wants and a higher level of the general welfare. Moreover, being held in small parcels, wealth was generally accessible to whomever would pay the price in industry, frugality, and ingenuity. Furthermore, this condition had not been destroyed even with the coming in of modern "big business," combinations, mergers, and "trusts." For, too often does the grandeur of business on its modern gigantic scale, the magnitude of billion dollar corporations completely hide from one's view those other millions of small businesses. These, here and now, may be forced to struggle hard for existence, perhaps only to fail in the end. But failing, still others will take their place and continue to form a social layer firm enough to safeguard against even a possible revolutionary explosion from below. The earnestness with which judges will rush to stand between legislatures and menaced property rights; the rigor of their application of the injunction to keep unionists and strikers from interfering with those rights in their own way; the ease with which a typically American middle-class community may work itself up, or be worked up, into an anti-radical hysteria, when Soviet missionaries or syndicalist agitators are rumored to be abroad in the land; and the flocking to the election polls of millions to vote for the "safe" candidate—all are of one piece, and are to be explained by the way in which the American community originated and grew.

This social and economic conservatism, bred in the American community from the beginning, has been tested repeatedly by sections of the American labor movement, now wittingly, now unwittingly, and invariably the test has evoked the same and identical reaction. It began in 1829, when the Workingman's Party of New York, moved by the desire to frighten employers lest they add to the recently won ten-hour day, officially endorsed the crude communistic "Equal Division" program of Thomas Skidmore. A whole generation had to pass before the recollection of this brief indiscretion had faded from the public memory and ceased to plague the labor movement. Another such test of the public mind was the unplanned, but virtual anarchy of the destructive great railway strikes of 1877, from Baltimore to San Francisco. It was then that the judiciary, watching the paralysis which had seized the democratically chosen sheriffs and governors, and remembering well the Commune of Paris of 1871, resolved to insure society against a labor revolution by dint of the injunction, the outlawing of the boycott, and like measures. Nine years later, the Chicago "Anarchists," with a full-blown program of revolutionary syndicalism in all but the name itself, were made to feel the ferocious self-defense of a gigantically growing and self-satisfied community against those who would import the methods of the class struggle of Russia and of Spain. Still later, in the Pullman strike of 1894, the labor movement saw how the courts, the Federal Executive, and the ruling forces in the country could be counted on to act as one in crushing any real or fancied industrial rebellion. The treatment of the Industrial Workers of the World in the Western States, the anti-"Red" hysteria of 1919 and 1920, and the great godsend which the syndicalist past of William Z. Foster proved to the employers in defeating the great steel strike in 1919, which he led, are of too recent occurrence to necessitate detailed discussion. The state of Kansas, a representative American farming and middle-class community, furnishes perhaps the most telling illustration of the typical American reaction to industrial radicalism. That state, which was in 1912 a stamping ground for Roosevelt progressivism, just as it had been the heart of the "Populism" of the nineties, showed no hesitancy, in 1919, when the coal miners' strike had endangered the comfort of its citizenry, at enacting a law depriving of the right to strike, labor in public utilities and in other industries supplying food, fuel, and clothing, which the law classed as public utilities for that purpose.

Briefly, if the century-long experience of American labor as an organized movement holds any great lesson at all, that lesson is that under no circumstances can labor here afford to arouse the fears of the great middle class for the safety of private property as a basic institution. Labor needs the support of public opinion, meaning the middle class, both rural and urban, in order to make headway with its program of curtailing, by legislation and by trade unionism, the abuses which attend the employer's unrestricted exercise of his property rights. But any suspicion that labor might harbor a design to do away altogether with private property, instead of merely regulating its use, immediately throws the public into an alliance with the anti-union employers. . . .

2. *The Lack of a Class Consciousness in American Labor*

The overshadowing problem of the American labor movement has always been the problem of staying organized. No other labor movement has ever had to contend with the fragility so characteristic of American labor organizations. In the main, this fragility of the organization has come from the lack of class cohesiveness in American labor. . . .

The cause of this lack of psychological cohesiveness in American labor is the absence, by and large, of a completely "settled" wage earning class. Sons of wage earners will automatically follow their fathers' occupations in the mining districts, which, because of their isolation, are little worlds in themselves. The Negroes in industry are, of course, a hereditary wage earning group. And apparently such a class has developed also in the textile centers. To be sure, the great mass of the wage earners in American industry today, unless they have come from the farm intending to return there with a part of their wages saved, will die wage earners. However, many of these do not stay in a given industry for life, but keep moving from industry to industry and from locality to locality, in search for better working conditions. Moreover, the bright son of a mechanic and factory hand, whether of native or immigrant parentage, need not despair, with the training which the public schools give him free of charge and with whatever else he may pick up, of finding his way to this or that one of the thousand and one selling "lines" which pay on the commission basis; or, if his ambition and his luck go hand in hand, of attaining to some one of the equally numerous kinds of small businesses, or, finally, of the many minor supervisory positions in the large manufacturing establishments, which are constantly on the lookout for persons in the ranks suitable for promotion. It is, therefore, a mistake to assume that, with the exhaustion of the supply of free public land, the wage earner who is above the average in ambition and ability, or at least his children, if they are equally endowed (and the children's opportunities color the parents' attitude no less than do their own), have become cooped up for good in the class of factory operatives. For today, the alternative opportunities to being a lowly factory hand are certainly more varied and entail less hardship than the old opportunity of "homesteading" in the West and "growing up with the country."

But, in a sense, the opportunity of the "West" has never ceased. In this vast country, several historical industrial stages are found existing side by side, though in demarcated areas. There is, therefore, the opportunity to migrate from older to newer and less developed sections, in which a person without much or any inherited property may still find the race for economic independence a free and open race. The difference between a section in the United States which is still underdeveloped economically and a similar one in a European country, is the difference between a navigable stream with some obstacles in its bed still waiting to be removed, and a stagnant pool without an outlet. In the former, opportunities are plentiful, multipliable by effort, and only waiting to be exploited; in the latter, the few extant opportunities are jealously monopolized by their incumbents.

If the characteristically American fluidity of economic society has preserved and created opportunities for the non-propertied individual of not much more than average ability, those with a higher ability and a gift for leadership have found their upward progression smoother still. Participation in political life in America has never been reserved to the upper classes, as until recently in England, nor to those with a higher education, as in France, but is open to all who can master the game. In the past, before the trade unions became stabilized, capable of holding both their leaders and their membership, considerable leadership material drained away from labor into politics. However, at that time industry had not yet come to appreciate the "political" talent of handling men as a valuable business asset. But in the present era of "personnel management" and "industrial relations" departments, of "Welfare capitalism," and of efficiency by "inducement" and "leadership," there is room for that sort of talent, at least in the largest establishments. For the present, businessmen look to college trained men to fill these positions. But it is not at all precluded that what otherwise might have been union leadership talent, is being drawn into this sort of activity.

Another cause of the lack of "class-consciousness" in American labor was the free gift of the ballot which came to labor at an early date as a by-product of the Jeffersonian democratic movement. In other countries, where the labor movement started while the workingmen were still denied the franchise, there was in the last analysis no need of a theory of "surplus value" to convince them that they were a class apart and should therefore be "class conscious." There ran a line like a red thread between the laboring class and the other classes. Not so, where that line is only an economic one. Such a line becomes blurred by the constant process of "osmosis" between one economic class and another, by fluctuations in relative bargaining power of employer and employee with changes in the business cycle, and by other changing conditions.

Next to the abundant economic opportunities available to wage earners in this country, and to their children, immigration has been the factor most guilty of the incohesiveness of American labor. To workers employed in a given industry, a new wave of immigrants, generally of a new
nationality, meant a competitive menace to be fought off and to be kept
out of that industry. For, by the worker's job consciousness, the strongest
animosity was felt not for the employer who had initiated or stimulated
the new immigrant wave, but for the immigrants who came and took the
jobs away. When immigrants of a particular nationality acquired higher
standards and began rebuilding the unions which they destroyed at their
coming, then a new nationality would arrive to do unto the former what
these had done unto the original membership. The restriction of immigration by the quota system has at last done away with this phenomenon,
which formerly used to occur and recur with an inevitable regularity.

American labor remains the most heterogeneous laboring class in existence—ethnically, linguistically, religiously, and culturally. With a
working class of such a composition, to make socialism or communism
the official "ism" of the movement, would mean, even if the other conditions permitted it, deliberately driving the Catholics, who are perhaps in
the majority in the American Federation of Labor, out of the labor movement, since with them an irreconcilable opposition to socialism is a matter of religious principle. Consequently the only acceptable "consciousness" for American labor as a whole is a "job consciousness," with a
"limited" objective of "wage and job control"; which not at all hinders
American unionism from being the most "hard hitting" unionism in any
country. Individual unions may, however, adopt whatever "consciousness" they wish. Also the solidarity of American labor is a solidarity with
a quickly diminishing potency as one passes from the craft group,—
which looks upon the jobs in the craft as its common property for which
it is ready to fight long and bitterly,—to the widening concentric circles
of the related crafts, the industry, the American Federation of Labor, and
the world labor movement. . . .

. . . The future builders of the American Federation of Labor, like
Strasser and Gompers of the Cigar Makers and McGuire of the Carpenters, studied the labor question both theoretically and experimentally.
They studied Marx and the other European socialists, but they were also
constantly testing to see what appeals were "taking" with the workingmen so that they came in as permanent members, and what appeals had
only an ephemeral effect. It was in this unusual school, in which theory
was mixed with direct experience, that they discovered that the union
card was the only real bond that held wage earners together, not politics,
whether "greenback" or socialist. They found that a labor movement became proof against disintegration only when it was built around the job.
These discoveries did not at first estrange them from socialism as a pro-

gram for the future. But as time went on and they became engrossed in their "job unionism," which eschewed politics and every other quick social panacea; as they watched their organizations grow from nothing to something like the large and stable British "Amalgamated" unions, from which the International Cigar Makers' Union, reorganized by Strasser and Gompers, copied its comprehensive benefit features and centralized financial management; and as they observed with pride how their organizations, small though they still were, held together and grew steadily, in defiance of the alternating tides in business conditions so fatal to the labor organizations which had preceded theirs; then the original socialistic class-consciousness of these "philosophers-organizers" gradually paled if not shriveled, and in its place flourished a robust trade unionist "job and wage consciousness."

It was indeed a new species of trade unionism that was thus evolved. It differed from the trade unionism that the native American labor movement had evolved earlier, in that it grasped the idea, supremely correct for American conditions, that the economic front was the only front on which the labor army could stay united. From this it followed that when a business depression or a powerful combination of employers made the chances for advance on that front unlikely for the time being, the correct strategy was not, as the unions before them had done, to shift the main strength to the political front, because that front seemed weakly held by the enemy. On the contrary, this unionism reasoned that, during depression, labor's strategy should be thoroughly to dig in on the same economic front, awaiting the next opportunity, which was certain to come, for advancing further; in the meantime using every device, like benefit features, to keep the membership from dropping out. For the American labor movement, which, during the first half century of its existence, had been doing exactly the opposite, that is, abandoning trade unionism for the lure and excitement of "anti-monopoly" politics, this discovery was as pivotal a discovery as that by the Rochdale pioneers was for the world co-operative movement. But this discovery, it should not be forgotten, could neither have been hit upon nor later exalted into the cardinal principle of the American labor movement, if the class-consciousness of these "philosopher-organizers" had not, from the beginning, rendered them immune against being swept off their feet by the "producer consciousness" of the individualistic panaceas of the native American labor movement, and thus kept them at their "study-experiment" in their own trade unions. In this circuitous way, therefore, the class-conscious International of Marx was the cause of the least class-conscious labor movement in the world today.

In the evolution of the psychology of the American wage earner, the fruition of this "job and wage conscious" unionism and its eventual mastery of the whole field meant a final and complete rupture with the old

"producing classes" point of view, which saw the road to economic democracy in a restoration to the individual, or to intimately associated
groups of individuals, of access to economic opportunity in land, marketing, and credit; this opportunity once restored, competition alone
would suffice to preserve it all around. This philosophy, as already
noted, had issued from the typically American premise of an existing
abundance of opportunity for every industrious person, an abundance,
however, which conspiring monopolists have artificially converted into
scarcity. The predominance of the "anti-monopoly" point of view in the
American labor movement down to this time actually denoted a mental
subordination of the wage earner to the farmer, a labor movement in the
grip of a rural ideology. In contrast, the ideology of the American Federation of Labor was both an urban and a wage earner's ideology. It was
based on a consciousness of limited job opportunities, a situation which
required that the individual, both in his own interest and in that of a
group to which he immediately belonged, should not be permitted to occupy any job opportunity except on the condition of observing the "common rule" laid down by his union. The safest way to assure this group
control over opportunity, though also a way so ideal that only a union as
favored as the printers' was able to actualize it entirely, was for the
union, without displacing the employer as the owner of his business and
risk taker, to become the virtual owner and administrator of the jobs.
Where such an outright "ownership" of the jobs was impossible, the union would seek, by collective bargaining with the employers, to establish
"rights" in the jobs, both for the individual and for the whole group, by
incorporating, in the trade agreement, regulations applying to overtime,
to the "equal turn," to priority and seniority in employment, to apprenticeship, to the introduction and utilization of machinery, and so forth.
Thus the industrial democracy envisaged by this unionism descended
from Marxism was not a democracy of individualistic producers ex-
changing products under free competition, with the monopolist ban-
ished, but a highly integrated democracy of unionized workers and of
associated employer-managers, jointly conducting an industrial government with "laws" mandatory upon the individual.

How far the unionism of the American Federation of Labor had traveled from the "anti-monopoly" philosophy of the old American labor
movement was clearly revealed in its attitude on the "trust" question.
Early in the present century, while almost the whole nation was insisting
that the government should break up the trusts, or at least regulate them
with most stringent legislation, many going so far as to demand price fixing by government, the American Federation of Labor declared unequiv-
ocally that the "trusts" were an inevitable economic development before
which the law was completely helpless, but the power of which could be
controlled by another economic power, the organized trade union move-

ment. Is it, therefore, a mere coincidence that the German trade unions, thirty years later, facing the "trustified" Germany of today, should equally have despaired of the political state as an instrument for curbing the "trusts," and should, like the American unionists in the late nineties, have seen that the main road to industrial democracy lies within the economic sphere?

STABLE UNIONISM AT WORK

The American Federation of Labor entered upon a triumphant possession of the field of organized labor about 1890, with the virtual disappearance of its rival, the Knights of Labor. It survived in the struggle with the Knights because it was the product of continuous experimentation ever since the early seventies, when Gompers' "Ten Philosophers" first developed their "theory-practice" method of self-instruction. This experimentation by the trade unions went on through alternating periods of depression and prosperity, avoiding the most serious political excitements, like the "Populist" in the early nineties; but going through with the mistaken attempt to copy the British Trades Union Congress in their first federation, the Federation of Organized Trades and Labor Unions of the United States and Canada, 1881–1886. And all the while the trade union organizations were being hammered into shape in the struggles with employers, and especially in the life and death struggle with the Knights of Labor. The resultant unionism had therefore the merit that it "fitted" both the external environment and the American workman's psychology. For otherwise, beset on all sides, without and within the labor movement, it could neither have survived, nor attained a stability thitherto unknown in American labor history. The unionism of the American Federation of Labor "fitted," first, because it recognized the virtually inalterable conservatism of the American community as regards private property and private initiative in economic life. It, too, accordingly arrayed itself on the same side, demanding only that the employers should concede the union's right to control the jobs through "recognition" embodied in the trade agreement; and in this attitude it remained unperturbed in the face of all the charges by socialist intellectuals of treason to labor or even of corruption.

This unionism "fitted," secondly, because it grasped the definite limitations of the political instrument under the American Constitution and under American conditions of political life. It therefore used the political weapon only sparingly and with great circumspection. It went into politics primarily to gain freedom from adverse interference by judicial authority in its economic struggles;—it did not wish to repeat former experiences when trade unions standing sponsor for a labor party found themselves dragged down to the ground by internecine political strife. The American Federation of Labor made itself felt politically by exercising pressure on the old parties; but it kept politics at arm's length from its own cherished trade union organization. It must be acknowledged, however, that the American movement, led by leaders risen from the ranks, could withstand the political temptation with so much greater ease than the European movements, because it saw little to choose between an autocratic capitalist management of industry and a bureaucratic one by "experts" appointed by the state.

Thirdly, the unionism of the Federation was a fit unionism to survive because it was under no delusion as to the true psychology of the workingman in general and of the American workingman in particular. It knew that producers' co-operation was a beautiful but a really harmful dream, since it only caused labor to fritter away its spiritual and material resources by shouldering itself with an impossible task of winning in the unequal competition between the capitalist-managed business undertakings, which marched like an army, and co-operatively managed ones, which were governed more by debating clubs.

This unionism was also without illusions with regard to the actual extent of labor solidarity. It knew that where wage earners were held together by the feeling that their jobs came out of a common job reservoir, as did those in the same or in closely related crafts, their fighting solidarity left nothing to be desired; provided that their unity was safeguarded by vigilantly uprooting "dual" unions as so many noxious weeds and by enforcing a military discipline against "outlaw" actions within the union itself. The leaders of this unionism also knew, however, that they had to go slow in pressing on to greater solidarity. Where conditions made co-operation between different craft groups urgent, it was best obtained through free co-operation in "departments" of unions in the same industry, each union reserving the right to decide for itself in every situation whether to co-operate or not. Thus, as with allied sovereign states, solidarity in action remained dependent on the sense of honor of each ally instead of on compulsion. . . .

This "stable unionism," from the nineties to the present, has undergone many vicissitudes: alternating prosperity and depression; employers' belligerency in many industries and conciliatoriness in others; the heaping up of legal disabilities by court decisions, and the "removal" of these disabilities by legislation under friendly administrations. This unionism entered upon a new day in the emergency of the World War period, when it phenomenally expanded in thitherto barred industries, the membership skyrocketing up to 4,000,000. Then followed an "open shop" and wage deflation campaign of equally unheard of intensity, in which most of the wartime gains were lost. Nevertheless, unionism has emerged as a permanent national force, though no more than a minority interest in the American community. As a minority interest, viewed askance by the majority, unionism has been under the necessity, if its influence and numbers were not to diminish but to grow, of exercising constant care lest by radical action on its part, the middle-class public should be thrown into an alliance with the reactionaries. For this necessary caution, unionism has been attacked as passionately from the "left," as the "open shop" employers and conservative interests have, for the opposite reason, assailed it from the "right."

The American
working
class
William Z. Foster   # and socialism

Spokesmen of American capitalism, both inside and outside the labor movement, shout tirelessly that there is no basis for socialism in the United States. They maintain that ours is a special type of economy, not really capitalism at all, and that it progresses in an endless upward spiral of development. This is "American exceptionalism." Such reactionaries declare, with a voice of dogmatic finality, that the American working class, as well as the rest of the nation, neither needs nor wants socialism; that the workers have the highest wage standards in the world; that they elect capitalist-minded officials to head their trade unions; that they have no mass labor party, that they are not class-conscious, that they have no revolutionary perspective. From all of which the capitalist spokesmen conclude that the American workers, living in a basically different economy from the workers of other lands, are immune to Marxism-Leninism and are permanently dedicated to the capitalist system.

All this is nothing more than whistling in the dark on the part of the ruling class in a capitalist world that is decaying. In reality, American capitalism is fundamentally the same as the system in every capitalist country, although . . . certain historical factors have favored its greater growth and strength. In the United States, as everywhere else under capitalism, the industries and the land are privately owned and are operated for the profit of their owners. Production, based upon competition at home and abroad, is carried on chaotically, without plan. Through the wage system, the workers are systematically exploited and

From *History of the Communist Party of the United States* by William Z. Foster (New York, 1952), pp. 541–549. Reprinted by permission of International Publishers Co., Inc.

robbed by their employers. Consequently, this country also suffers from overproduction and cyclical economic crises. The United States too, possesses the same classes—capitalists, middle classes, and workers— that are characteristic of capitalist economies generally. And, as else- where, among these rival classes, the class struggle has raged with greater or less intensity ever since the foundation of the Republic. The American economy has typically produced monopoly and imperialism and, as we remarked previously, like all other capitalist countries, the United States is definitely involved in the general crisis of the world capitalist system.

FACTORS RETARDING THE IDEOLOGICAL DEVELOPMENT OF THE WORKERS

Although the great bulk of the American working class has long lacked a Socialist ideology, this condition is only temporary. The workers in this country have an extensive and militant record of class struggle. During their struggle against the employers for over a century, they have built up a vast trade union movement, they have carried on many huge and bitter strikes and political fights, and they have evolved an ever- stronger class spirit. Although, in the main, they have not yet developed the degree of class consciousness and Socialist perspective common to the workers in Europe and elsewhere, they are on the way to doing so.

The ideological development of the American working class has been retarded by the effects, over a long period, of a number of important, but secondary, features in the development of capitalism in this country. These factors have tended to cultivate petty-bourgeois illusions among the workers and to lead them to believe that they can solve their eco- nomic and political problems within the framework of the capitalist sys- tem. These specific American economic and political characteristics are the fruitful soil out of which grows "American exceptionalism" in its var- ious forms of Gompersism, Hillquitism, Lovestoneism, Browderism, Wallaceism, and the like. Chief among these characteristics are the fol- lowing:

First: Owing to the lack of feudal political hangovers and to the more thorough-going bourgeois revolutions of 1776 and 1861, the workers in this country, but not the Negro people, won broader civil liberties than existed in Continental Europe. Particularly important in this respect was the more extensive right to vote. This situation tended to cultivate among workers in the United States widespread and deep-seated illusions about the possibilities of bourgeois democracy in this country, despite their long struggle for the right to organize unions, for woman suffrage, for popular education, for social security, and for other popular liberties. By contrast to the situation in the United States, in many European countries franchise rights of the workers were severely limited by the so-called class system of voting, right up to the revolutionary aftermath of World War I. Hence, they built their big Social-Democratic parties primarily by two generations of struggle for "equal, direct, secret, and general" manhood suffrage, acquiring a high degree of class consciousness in the process. The American working class in general, during these decades, did not have to make such an elementary fight for the vote.

Second: The long-continued lack of uniformity in the composition of the American working class has been, historically, another important factor militating against the growth of proletarian class consciousness and a Socialist outlook in this country. For generations huge masses of the workers were immigrants, of two score or more nationalities and possessing widely varying languages, religions, cultures, and historical backgrounds. These factors obviously made it more difficult for them to organize economically and politically, and to develop ideologically.

Third: For the first century of the Republic's life there existed immense tracts of government-owned land, small parcels of which could be had without great difficulty, especially after the passage of the Homestead Act of 1862. This free land served for decades as a sort of safety valve for the class struggle and a deterrent to the growth of class consciousness. It gave the workers the goal of a farm, and all the early trade unions interested themselves keenly in the land question. As we have seen, this "free land" even gave birth to special forms of "American exceptionalism." In actual fact, however, comparatively few workers ever got "free land," most of it being grabbed by the railroads, coal companies, lumber and cattle kings, and big farmers and planters.

Fourth: Another long-term deterrent to the growth of class consciousness in the American working class was the fact that, in the vast and swift growth of industry and agriculture, numbers of workers were able to acquire property and to pass into the ranks of the middle class. Not a few even became big capitalists. The expectation of one day establishing little businesses of their own was common among the workers, and it operated to keep them thinking in terms of capitalism.

Fifth: The most powerful element, tending traditionally to slow down the development of a Socialist ideology among the workers in this country, has been the big shortage of labor power, due to the unusually favorable conditions under which American capitalism has developed. This enabled the workers, especially the skilled among them, to achieve wage rates considerably higher than those prevailing in other major capitalist countries. These "high" wages were offset, however, by such factors as a greater intensification of labor, more danger of unemployment, far more hazardous working conditions, a total lack of social insurance, and so on. While the central fact of the higher money wages in this country did not prevent the workers from forming trade unions and waging bitter strikes to defend and improve their living conditions, it nevertheless militated against their becoming fully class-conscious and revolutionary-minded.

Sixth: There grew a very big labor aristocracy, those workers whom Engels called "bourgeoisified," to whom the employers conceded relatively high wages at the expense of the unskilled, the Negro toilers, and the people of colonial lands. Especially with the development of imperialism, a corrupt labor bureaucracy grew up on the basis of this labor aristocracy. This reactionary officialdom, the characteristic American counterpart of European Social-Democracy, repeated the slogans of the employers and dominated the economic and political activities of the workers. Historically, it has been a potent weapon in retarding the ideological development of the working class. The employers have always helped this bureaucracy to gain and hold power in the trade unions.

FACTORS MAKING FOR CLASS CONSCIOUSNESS

Today, however, the foregoing factors, hindering the development of class consciousness and a Socialist perspective among the workers, have either wholly disappeared or are on the eve of so doing. First, the United States, with the growth of monopoly and imperialism, has long since lost its democratic leadership among the nations and is now veering toward fascism—a degeneration of capitalist democracy which is fast undermining bourgeois illusions among the workers. Second, the working class is swiftly becoming more homogeneous. The immigrant masses have largely learned the English language and domestic customs; the second and third generations of their descendants, while not ignoring their national backgrounds, are quite American; and the Negro and white workers are developing a real solidarity in organization and action. Third, the free land has been gone now for at least sixty years, and the prospect of getting a real farm has been practically forgotten by the working class. Fourth, with the growth of the trusts, the traditional hope of the workers eventually to become small tradesmen or industrialists has steadily faded, until now, among the bulk of the working class, little remains of this expectation except illusory speculation here and there about one day "opening up a gas station." Today the great mass of actual workers, although hoping "to do better for their children," themselves expect to live and die as workers—which is obviously a long stride toward developing class consciousness. Fifth, the wages of American workers, while still generally above those in Europe, are now resting precariously upon a very treacherous quicksand, and this chief barrier to the development of a Socialist perspective among the workers is steadily being undermined. The imperiling of American wage rates threatens the privileged position of the labor aristocracy and also that of the reactionary labor bureaucracy, which bases itself upon this aristocracy.

The impoverishment of the workers

The primary factor undermining the traditionally higher American wage standards is what Marx called the *relative* impoverishment of the workers. This is taking place to an ever-increasing degree in this country, as in all capitalist economies. That is, taking all elements together—wages, prices, and productivity—American workers are more deeply exploited and are getting a smaller proportion of what they produce than they did half a century ago. "By 1939," says Perlo, "the employers were not only getting twice as much production from each worker as forty years earlier, but they were keeping a much larger share of the production for themselves; their real profits had increased by much more than 100 percent." The Labor Research Association states, too, that "the 'relative position' of the worker in manufacturing in 1949 was 34 percent below the level of the last century. . . . The index fell from 100 in 1899 to 66 in 1948, even on the basis of inadequate government statistics." And the U.S. Department of Labor, in trying to make a favorable case for American capitalism, unwittingly substantiates the above conclusions of Perlo and the L.R.A. by stating that whereas real wages in the United States have about doubled since 1900 (a gross misstatement), the productivity of the workers has increased four to five times during the same period. Kuczynski says, "The relative position of the American industrial worker has deteriorated very considerably during the last seventy years."

In fact, in no other country in the world is the *relative* impoverishment of the workers so pronounced as it is in the United States. Nowhere are the workers so heavily exploited, for all their alleged "high wages," as they are in this country. And from this deep exploitation and *relative* impoverishment inevitably grow the roots of overproduction, cyclical economic crises, mass unemployment, lowered living standards, class consciousness, and the eventual breakdown of the capitalist system.

The second factor to consider regarding the decline of the traditionally higher real wages of the workers in the United States is that the *relative* impoverishment under capitalism inexorably brings about *absolute* impoverishment of the workers. This is clearly to be seen all over the rest of the capitalist world, where the workings of the capitalist system—its exploitation, economic crises, and wars—have plunged the toiling masses into deepest poverty. The workings of this economic law are also very much in evidence in the United States, where huge masses of the workers, despite recent enormous increases in production, are living in a state of destitution.

Only a few years ago, Roosevelt spoke of "one-third of a nation ill-housed, ill-clad, ill-nourished"—in a country with the greatest productive capacity in the world. The widely accepted Heller Budget, in 1948, called for a weekly wage of $79.04, in order to provide an average-sized worker's family with a decent living. However, only 67 percent of the people were actually getting an income equal to this budget, the average wage in manufacturing being but $54.48. In 1939 the top one percent of the population received 12 percent of the national income. The widespread poverty now existing in the United States was dramatically indicated recently by a Congressional report which showed that 10,500,000 families —about one-fourth of all families—are now living upon incomes of $2,000 a year or less; that is to say, at poverty levels. At present, of 17 million women employed in industry, 50 percent are married, which means that in the greater part of these cases at least two persons must work in order to support the family adequately.

The worst sufferers in the widespread *absolute* impoverishment are the Negro people and the great armies of unskilled workers, whose plight is obscured by the government's generalized statistics and Pollyanna interpretations. This widespread poverty among the masses is accentuated by new insecurities and difficulties from the industrial speed-up, disruption of normal family life, early obsolescence of workers, fears of economic crises and wars, loss of popular freedoms, and so on.

The U.S. Census Bureau recently reported on wealth ownership in the United States. It stated that the top one-fifth of the population now owns 47 percent of the wealth and the lower one-fifth only 3 percent. Of the total national savings (banks, insurance, etc.) the lower 40 percent of American families owns nothing at all, whereas the upper 10 percent owns 65 percent. Actually, 200 super-wealthy families dominate the industries and organized wealth of the United States. Such polarization of great wealth and deep poverty is characteristic of capitalism the world over.

With the continuation of capitalism and the deepening of its general crisis the perspective is one of great intensification and extension of mass *absolute* impoverishment in the United States. Although the wages of American workers are on the average higher than those prevalent in Europe, they now rest upon a most insecure basis. Today they are dependent on a feverish arms economy, instead of, as in former years, on the normal growth of the industries. Present-day American "prosperity" is artificial, drawing its sustenance from munitions production and war, and from imperialist exploitation of peoples all over the world. The present American gross national output of $324 billion ($180 billion in 1939 dollars) is tremendously overswollen from war production. Those sections of the American people, including many top labor leaders, who believe that "full" employment and "high" wages can be continued on this basis are living in a fool's paradise and are due for a sad awakening.

Already the huge armaments program, with its inflation, high taxes, gigantic profits, and wage freeze, is sending American living standards tobogganing. The continuation of this program will eventually climax in either a deep economic breakdown or a catastrophic war, either of which will spread *absolute* mass impoverishment over the country like a plague. The great economic crisis of 1929–33, when living standards were cut in half, millions of jobless walked the streets, and mass starvation stalked the country, was the result of the normal workings of the American capitalist economy. The present arms production cannot possibly avert a similar disaster in the near future; but instead, it will produce an even greater economic smash-up. The existing mass destitution in capitalist Europe is only a foretaste of what is eventually in store for American workers, if they do not succeed in putting a halt to Wall Street's war-fascism plans and adopting the fundamental programs, making toward socialism, necessary to conserve their own well-being and to create a healthy economic system.

The condition of the American working class fully confirms the correctness of the general law of capitalist accumulation, discovered by Marx; namely, "that in proportion as capital accumulates, the lot of the laborer, be his payment high or low, must grow worse. . . . It establishes an accumulation of misery, corresponding with accumulation of capital. Accumulation of wealth at one pole is, therefore, at the same time, accumulation of misery, agony of toil, slavery, ignorance, brutality, mental degradation at the opposite pole."

THE WORKERS WILL TURN TO SOCIALISM

Achieved at the expense of the unskilled, the Negro people, and the exploited of other lands, the relatively higher American living standards, especially among the skilled workers, are a phenomenon of the upswing of American imperialism. Capitalism here will no longer be able to furnish these wages when it goes into decline, as it surely will through the workings of its own internal contradictions and of the general crisis of the world capitalist system. When in its prime and on the upgrade, British imperialism could and did corrupt the labor aristocracy with relatively high wages, at the expense of the colonial peoples and the unskilled at home, as Marx and Engels pointed out. At that time the British workers as a class, bemused by this hollow imperialist "prosperity," were also not interested in socialism. The British capitalists boasted that even though workers on the Continent might be Marxist, this could never be in Britain.

But with British imperialism now far on the downgrade, those times are gone forever. Consequently, the British working class, with lowered living standards, is now irresistibly heading toward socialism, despite its opportunist Social-Democratic leadership. The general political development in the United States, although not so far advanced as in Great Britain, is going inevitably in the same direction. The American working class is facing a situation in which, in developing crisis and destitution, it will also surely learn that the only way it can protect and improve its living standards is by taking the road that eventually leads to socialism.

Because of the relatively strong position of American imperialism there is at present comparatively little demand for socialism among the broad working class. The specific type of bourgeois illusions now predominant among the bulk of American workers and their conservative leaders amounts to Rooseveltism, or Keynesism. This is the false theory that a "progressive capitalism," capable of full employment, can be created by government subsidies to industry and agriculture, plus doles to the workers. Keynesism in the United States plays approximately the political role of right-wing Social-Democracy in Europe in keeping the workers tied to the capitalist system. Although the European right-wing Social-Democrats, who deal with more radical workers, pepper their reformist dish with pseudo-nationalization of industry, seeming independent political action, and much talk about socialism, actually they, too, base their economic and political programs upon a framework of Keynesian "progressive capitalism."

American Social-Democracy has surrendered outright to bourgeois reformism, of which Keynesism is the latest expression, and it has abandoned completely the propaganda for socialism that it once carried on. This surrender was marked by the gradual acceptance of the succeeding forms of so-called progressive capitalism—Theodore Roosevelt's "Square Deal" (1912), Woodrow Wilson's "New Freedom" (1916), and Franklin D. Roosevelt's "New Deal" (1932), and during the current period, Truman's demagogic "Fair Deal." Nowadays such "Socialists" as Dubinsky and Reuther are practically indistinguishable from Green and Murray in their general political outlook. The fighters for socialism are the Communists.

The capitalist system in this country is a colossus with feet of clay. American imperialism will lose ideological and organizational control of the workers as its dominant world position weakens. And because of the inevitable deepening of the general crisis of capitalism, this decline is bound to come. The political advance of the working class will then become very rapid, as Engels remarked long ago. The workers will speedily throw off their bourgeois illusions and reactionary leaders, as they have already done in many countries.

During the past twenty years the workers in this country, despite lingering capitalist "prosperity" illusions among them, have made real progress in political understanding and organization. This was evidenced by the great mass unemployed struggles, the building of the C.I.O. and the independent unions, the organization of the large body of Negro workers, the development of the program for social insurance, the increasing movements for independent political action, and the continued struggle against fascism and war. These major political developments, in which the Communist Party played a very important part, are so many sure signs of developing class consciousness among the workers of the United States.

With the deepening general crisis of capitalism and its involvement of American imperialism in growing economic difficulties, the near future will produce an ever swifter political development of the working class. More advanced economic and political demands, a great independent party with labor as its base, a broad people's front movement, a progressive trade union leadership, and the growth of a Socialist ideology and a mass Communist Party—these developments are also inevitable for the American working class, even as they have been for the workers in other capitalist countries. They will arrive upon the political scene in this country far sooner than the power-drunk capitalist ruling class now even dreams. In these vital developments, the Communist Party, in the very nature of things, will be more and more of a leading factor.

SUGGESTIONS FOR FURTHER READING

Selig Perlman was a student of John R. Commons of the University of Wisconsin and his point of view reflects that of the so-called Wisconsin School. Other studies from this group are the four-volume *History of Labor in the United States* by Commons and others (New York, 1918–35); and Philip Taft's massive two-volume history of the A. F. of L.: *The A. F. of L. in the Time of Gompers* (New York, 1957); *The A. F. of L. from the Death of Gompers to the Merger* (New York, 1959). The influence of the Wisconsin school may be seen in a recent survey history of *American Labor* by the British historian, Henry Pelling (Chicago, 1960).

Strongly opposed to the Wisconsin group is Philip S. Foner whose Marxist interpretation of the *History of the Labor Movement in the United States* (three volumes to date; New York, 1947–1964) emphasizes class struggle and conflict. Violent labor conflict can be seen in studies of specific strikes: Almont Lindsay, *The Pullman Strike* (Chicago, 1942) and Henry David, *History of the Haymarket Affair* (New York, 1936). Louis Adamic's theme is expressed in the title of his book, *Dynamite, The Story of Class Violence in America* (New York, 1931).

VII
THE ★
PROGRESSIVE ★
MOVEMENT ★

Progressivism was a broad and diverse reform movement that had its roots in the 1890's, but came to a climax on the national level during the administrations of Theodore Roosevelt and Woodrow Wilson. Although it affected all areas of American life, including art, literature, religion, and education, it was essentially a political movement founded on the idea that the problems arising in an industrialized America could be solved only by expanding democracy and social justice. Reformers in the cities sought to promote clean, honest, efficient government, and often to throw the bosses out. Reformers in the states paraded under the banner of "give the government back to the people," seeking the initiative, the referendum, the recall, the direct election of senators and many other planks which had been supported by the Populists. Muckrakers sought to expose corruption in the world of business and politics. Social workers and other reformers fought to regulate child labor, clean up the slums, and promote better working conditions for both men and women. On the national level, leaders of both political parties sought ways to deal with the giant industrial combinations and turned to regulation, control, and "trust busting." Everywhere progressives were concerned with solving the many problems created by industrialism.

Not all progressives agreed on the objectives of the movement or even the best methods for reform; similarly historians have also disagreed about the essential nature of progressivism. To some historians the progressive era was a time of fundamental conflict between reformers on one side and businessmen and political bosses on the other. Their emphasis is usually on the Populist origins of progressivism. These scholars agree with William Allen White, a leading mid-western progressive, who remarked that the progressives "caught the Populists in swimming and stole all their clothing except the frayed underdrawers of free silver." They see the movement as drawing its chief support from the mid-western farmer and small businessman who were engaged in a bitter struggle for survival with the eastern bankers and corporation presidents.

Another group of historians interpret the progressive movement as much more than an extension of Populism; indeed, its dominant spirit becomes not "rural and provincial" but "urban, middle-class and nationwide." These historians often explain the movement in terms of what Richard Hofstadter has called "the status revolution." This thesis attempts to show that a group of middle-class, well-educated citizens including lawyers, doctors, preachers, educators, and small businessmen who had usually held positions of leadership were being displaced in the late nineteenth century by the rising power of labor union leaders, corporation executives, and political bosses. Frustrated by their loss of status and power, driven by a sense of responsibility or guilt when confronted by the problems of urbanism and industrialism, they became reformers not so much to improve society as to give themselves a feeling of importance.

Regardless of how the historian explains the motivation of the reformers, he usually sees the progressive era as a time of great exuberance and optimism when a lot of people thought they could make the world a better place in which to live. But would progress come because there was nothing fundamentally wrong in the world, or would it come through bitter conflict with the forces of evil? The progressives themselves were not sure, and historians have not been able to agree on an answer.

In the selections that follow Russell Nye sees the progressives building on the Populist anti-business heritage. Indeed, he defines the progressive period as the time when business control and dominance was drawing to a close. George Mowry, on the other hand, finds the secret to understanding the progressives in the failure of most of them to adjust to an industrial age, rather than in a real conflict between reformers and businessmen. Mowry, unlike Nye, sees very little continuity between Populism and progressivism. He emphasizes the anti-urban, and anti-labor and nostalgic aspects of the movement but at the same time notes the urban and middle-class origins of the reformers. Eric Goldman, however, sees progressivism as a part of a long and sincere attempt to promote social justice in America. He pictures the progressives as having a real concern for labor and the immigrant. Goldman inevitably finds some conflict; to him the progressive era was a time when there was a "condition of excitement" because there were real problems to be solved and many people stood ready with the solutions. John Chamberlain represents those historians and progressives disillusioned with the meager results of the movement. Looking at the wreckage of progressivism from the vantage point of the early 1930's, he sees no fundamental conflict between the reformers and the business civilization they thought they were regulating. In a different way than Mowry, Chamberlain sees the progressive period as essentially one of consensus rather than of conflict. The progressive solutions, he argues, were not fundamentally different from the goals of their opponents. He suggests that ultimately the real solution to the problems that bothered the progressives would lie with revolution not reform.

How important were the differences which divided reformers and their opponents during the progressive period? Was there a widespread agreement on fundamentals which led progressives merely to seek minor adjustments in a basically sound society? Or did progressive reformers recognize deep-seated problems and seek major changes?

Russell Nye

The wave of agrarian protest washed itself away in Bryan's defeat. The crusade of 1896, and the "dull and colorless reign of privilege" (Altgeld's phrase) that followed it, settled nothing. The issues of the eighties and nineties were driven underground by the Spanish war and militarism, the upsurge of prosperity, the to-be-or-not-to-be of imperialism. But the old difficulties were still unsolved—the trust, the "plutocrat," the twin problems of good government and representative government. What were the economic and political functions of wealth? What were the social and economic functions of government? What of Big Business? What of the farmer and the worker? They all boiled down to a single question, what is democracy?

The plain fact was (and many saw it clearly) that the American dream was simply not coming true. America, "the hope of the human race" as Turgot had called it, was not realizing its promise. The difference between what was and what might be was very great. The nineteenth-century Midwestern radicals tried to change the system and, with Bryan, lost "the first battle." The twentieth-century leaders reformed the army and mapped new offensives. They were a new kind of captain, trained in the West Point of state politics, with the same objectives as the tattered militia who preceded them.

The initial blow of the twentieth century was struck by the "muckrakers," who provided a sort of cutting edge to a three-pronged reform movement in politics, society, and economics at the turn of the century. Henry D. Lloyd, and before him Bellamy and George, warned of the dangers of wealth and corporate power. B. O. Flower, an Illinois-born editor who imbibed Midwest radicalism at its source, ran energetic attacks on business and privilege in his magazine, the *Arena,* and shared with Lloyd the credit for pioneering in the journalism of exposure. Flower (who edited the *Arena* from 1889 to 1896, then the Chicago *New Time,* and then rejoined the *Arena*) was undoubtedly one of the most influential of the early reform editors before 1900. His magazines published articles by such well-known dissenters as Henry George, Hamlin Garland, Eugene Debs, George Herron, Frances Willard, and Frank Parsons and were filled with discussions of railroads and trusts, the Australian ballot, municipal ownership, and co-operatives.

The real upswing of muckraking journalism came, however, with the appearance of the cheap popular magazine. The four old standards (*Scribner's, Harper's,* the *Century,* and the *Atlantic*—all sedate, literate, and Eastern controlled)—were hardly the proper outlets for exposure of

From *Midwestern Progressive Politics* by Russell Nye (East Lansing, 1951), pp. 169–73, 180–81, 184–87, 190, 208–9, 224–25, 233–35, 242. Reprinted by permission of The Michigan State University Press.

corruption and graft. The newer inexpensive ones (*Munsey's, Cosmopol-itan, Colliers,* the *American, Everybody's, McClure's*) and the more radical intellectual ones (the *Arena, Review of Reviews,* the *Outlook*) suited the purpose admirably. The ten-cent magazine quadrupled the magazine-reading public after 1893.

"Muckraking" (as Theodore Roosevelt later named it) came into being after 1900. Lloyd, Flower, and the editors of *Everybody's* and the *Independent* started it, but when S. S. McClure in 1901 put Lincoln Steffens on the trail of the grafting politicians and later sent Ida M. Tarbell after Standard Oil, the lid was off. Every politician, every corporation, every executive was under suspicion, every public and private citizen open to investigation. Most of the writers were newspapermen rather than political scientists or economists, sentimental rather than doctrinaire liberals, but they all hated social and political injustice and pursued it relentlessly in print.

Steffens found political corruption of the grimiest sort in St. Louis, Minneapolis, Pittsburgh, New York, Philadelphia, and Chicago, and wrote it up in *The Shame of the Cities.* Next he inspected Ohio, Rhode Island, New Jersey, California, and Wisconsin; except for Wisconsin, he did not like what he saw and said so in *The Struggle for Self-Government.* As the time came to draw some generalizations from his observations of democracy in action, Steffens turned into less of a muckraker and more of a political philosopher. The trail of boodle, he discovered, led from city hall to state capitol to Washington itself—corruption was simply characteristic of the American political system on all levels. Reluctantly he was forced to the conclusion that the people themselves preferred "bad" to "good" government, that machines and corruption existed because the voter wished them to. America was so involved in business, and business so in need of special privileges, that it was more satisfactory to wink at someone else's "pull" while getting your own than to live under rigidly honest government. The remedy lay, Steffens decided, not in reforming politics but in reforming the voter (a point already noted by Jane Addams in *Democracy and Social Ethics*), by entirely removing privilege from politics, and by reverting to a co-operative economic system—a path that eventually led Steffens straight to Russia.

Steffens' articles set the journals afire. McClure himself took to the road; C. E. Russell, Ben Lindsey, C. P. Connolly, George Kernan, Burton Hendrick, and others found Pennsylvania, Montana, Colorado, and Delaware as "corrupt and contented" as the states on Steffens' beat. When Steffens trained his sights on Washington, as did David Graham Phillips, Ernest Crosby, Alfred Lewis, and Benjamin Hampton, he found corruption rife in the Congress itself.

Meanwhile, others put big business under the microscope. Ida Tarbell's scholarly and damning study of Standard Oil set the pattern for

Russell's study of the beef trust, Ray Stannard Baker's of the railroads, Welliver's of General Electric, Lewis' of International Harvester, Hendricks' of life insurance, Lawson's of Wall Street, and a dozen more. Muckraking moved on to other fields, too. Gentle Jake Riis wrote on the slums; Samuel Hopkins Adams investigated pure food; Will Irwin, Upton Sinclair, and others probed journalism. Churches were scrutinized for commercialism and connections with wealth, and the journals went to work on Belgian rule in the Congo, prison reform, loan sharks, prostitution, literary immorality, various sects—the thing was getting out of hand by 1910 when the public began to tire of it. It became harder to find new muck to rake, and big business discovered that withholding advertising from unco-operative magazines robbed them of a great deal of reforming zeal. Business also launched a counter-offensive of its own, beginning when the anthracite coal industry hired Ivy Lee in 1906 as publicity agent (he later was hired by the Pennsylvania Railroad and Standard Oil), a practice followed by other corporations until the "public relations counselor" became standard business equipment.

Muckraking, both good and bad, was part of a wider political, social, and intellectual reaction to industrial expansion and political corruption, a result of the same forces that produced Bryan, Theodore Roosevelt, Wilson, and La Follette. It was an exposure of fraudulent, misrepresentative government, of monopoly, of industrial immorality, of the trust—essentially the same tendencies in political, social, and economic life criticized by the agrarian radicals of the 1870's. The Grangers, and their descendants the Populists, had said the same things in a general way. The muckrakers offered proof and gave dates, names, places. The Grangers and Populists turned to government for help with little success. Now it was clear why. Government itself was under the thumb of the very forces they were fighting, as the Midwestern farmer and small businessman suspected all along. Like Populism and later progressivism, muckraking was an attack on privilege, on the exploitation of the many by the few, on social and economic malpractice. Steffens' conclusions were not so far removed from those of Jerry Simpson, nor Ida Tarbell's from General Weaver's.

The investigations of the muckrakers into city governments accelerated a trend toward municipal reform that reached back to the nineties and the Populist tradition. The Populists, and their agrarian predecessors, demanded clean, efficient, and representative government on a state and national scale; their urban counterparts demanded the same thing in the city....

The movement for civic reform knew no regional boundaries (though perhaps it was strongest in the West), for municipal corruption was not specifically a regional problem. But certainly the Grangers and the Populists paved the way for it. Like them, the civic reformers had one aim—

to make government more representative and more efficient—and they encountered (as the agrarians did) the monopoly, the corporation, and the machine. All intended to abolish privilege in government, whether it be the corporation working against the farmer or the traction tycoon against the city dweller. The personnel of the two movements showed some similarities and later greater differences. The early reform mayors —Pingree, Jones, and Johnson—came from Populist trust busting, Georgism, and Christian socialism, whereas the later reformers of the muckraker era were academic, well-schooled, urbane young attorneys, not crusaders but efficiency experts. The city reformers would no doubt have arrived had no Grangers or Populists existed, but the Grange, Farmers' Alliance, and People's party awakened the public conscience, drew the lines of conflict, and started the argument. Civic reform tied in with the Midwest agrarian radical tradition, doing locally what the Populists wished to do nationally. The cities, said Brand Whitlock, were really "working models of the larger democracy" that earlier Populists and later progressives visioned.

The twentieth-century progressive movement was, like its predecessors, deeply rooted in the social and economic soil of the times. American politics has been usually a direct reflection of current patterns of thought—embracing attitudes in business, science, education, economics, the church, and the home—and a manifestation of contemporary ideas that expresses itself among other ways in platforms and candidates. Thus the Grangers, the Farmers' Alliance, and the Populists were compounds of many elements, expressions of what the people (or a considerable segment of it) believed at a particular time. The elements themselves were concentrated for the most part in the agrarian Midwest, where the conflict between the old and new economics was most apparent, where the traditions of frontier discontent were strongest. . . .

Despite the dozens of young leaders it developed after 1900, the Midwest never really produced a politician of major stature (with the exception of La Follette) who might have tied Midwest progressivism into one neat bundle and delivered it bound and sealed on the White House doorstep. Neither did the Granger or Populist movements, whose leaders were colorful, astute, and sincere, but none of whom possessed the qualities needed to organize a political movement on a national rather than a regional scale. Bryan, the best of them, had neither the gifts to begin with nor the ability to develop them. Excepting La Follette, the later progressives—honest and skillful men all—were no more than good noncommissioned officers, while La Follette himself was too inflexible, too rigid, too much the lone wolf to become the prairie Jackson that the Midwest progressive tradition demanded. The reason for the Midwest's failure to produce a national leader lay in the fact that the movement itself was a distinctively Midwestern thing that developed regional

politicians who were chiefly concerned with regional problems. Progressivism in its Eastern phase—as represented by Theodore Roosevelt and
Woodrow Wilson—attained national power and dealt with national issues, but it was not the same thing.

The drift of Midwestern progressive thought in the early 1900's was
away from its Jeffersonian-Jacksonian-frontier sources. The ends remained the same, but the methods changed. As the frontier faded, the
old eighteenth-century idea of untrammeled individualism and decentralized political power disappeared with it, for in the industrial nineteenth century individualism by itself was hardly enough to secure democracy. Jefferson thought he had secured it when he established the
principle that there should be no political or legal check upon the individual's life, liberty, and pursuit of happiness. But the feudalism and
royal tyranny he feared might threaten his democracy were replaced in
the industrial age by the lords of the trusts, the knights of transportation, the corporate kings, the ministerial bosses. The Jacksonian period
believed that in spoils, in the ability of the ordinary man, in the complex
safeguards of intricate governmental machinery—there lay safety for
the common people; but the boss and the corporation took over the
machinery and bought the office. The Granger and the Populist dimly
realized that the goals of the old democratic tradition could be attained
only by modifications of the old methods and principles. Paradoxically,
he found that the preservation of individualism required the introduction of certain restraints upon it. He could restrain it through the only
agency—the government—that lay more or less under his direct control.

The most distinctive tendency in twentieth-century Midwestern progressivism, therefore, was its shift away from pure individualism toward social control, a trend already noticeable in the agrarian radicalism of the nineteenth century. Here was an effort to fit the individualism
of the old frontier (and of Darwinism) to the new circumstances of an
industrial society, an adjustment designed to give the citizen the same
advantages under new social and economic conditions that he had enjoyed under the old. . . . "[We must stop] trying to apply a logic, true
and proper for an individualistic era, to a new socialistic era," C. L. Deyo
wrote in the *Public*. "All our fundamental conceptions will have to be ex-
changed for new ones in which the *social* side shall have due emphasis."
If the individual's welfare—his pursuit of happiness—was the object
of democracy, how might one, in trying to evolve a democratic capitalistic society, avoid the perils of a dog-eat-dog individualism on the one
hand or the regimentation of socialism or communism on the other? The
progressives chose a middle path between the two extremes. Their aim
was not simply to restrict individualism, but to restrict in order to conserve the values of democracy.

This course was called by Charles McCarthy of Wisconsin "The New Individualism." It was not socialism, nor was it close to it. True, the Midwest progressive was occasionally willing to accept a so-called "socialistic" method to gain his desired objective. But the progressive, McCarthy explained, believed he could fulfill the promises of socialism without losing the essentials of private ownership and private enterprise. As Jane Addams remarked, since no political party or economic school possessed exclusive right to any device for eradicating poverty or obtaining political and social justice, the progressive had a right to borrow from socialism if he wished. Restrictions on laissez faire were, to the progressive, merely effective ways of preserving laissez faire itself.

Another major principle, a bequest of Populism, was the progressive's faith in and trust of the popular majority. The assumption was that every normal citizen who was mentally and morally qualified had both the right and the duty to participate directly in his government. "The composite judgment is always safer and wiser and stronger and more unselfish than the judgment of any one individual mind," wrote La Follette. "The people have never failed in any great crisis in history." The real cure for the ills of democracy, the Midwest progressive believed, was more democracy. His aim in politics therefore was simply to make government responsible and representative. Or as La Follette put it, "The very backbone of true representative government is the direct participation in the affairs of government by the people."

To insure a government that was both responsible and representative, Midwestern progressives believed it vitally necessary that the people control their government, both before and after elections. Machines and bosses controlled it only when they were allowed to steal the political machinery—something that pre-election measures such as the short ballot, the direct primary, the corrupt-practices act, and revised registration and voting systems were intended to prevent. As post-election controls they suggested the initiative, referendum, recall, and city home rule. Special influence must be removed, the structure of government so modified as to allow a greater direct participation by the citizen in the conduct of public business. The whole purpose of progressivism, said La Follette, was "to uphold the fundamental principles of representative government." It was an attempt to adapt the old democratic system to the needs of a new society, "a movement of a new generation toward more democracy in human relationships."

A third major principle of progressivism was its belief that the functions of government should be extended to meet the growing needs of the people. The state was not to be simply a negative factor in society, its influence happiest when least, but a positive factor, doing some things that no other agency could do, and others that no other agency could do so well. "He is really a Progressive," wrote Walter Owen in *La*

Follette's Magazine, "who first discovers any wrongs and suggests the appropriate governmental action to prevent further abuse." Progressivism represented the culmination of an old frontal attack (the Grangers were its vanguard) on the laissez-faire concept of governmental donothingism, an assault seconded by economists like Ely and sociologists like Ward. It was the last phase of a movement away from the agrarian-Jeffersonian idea that government was merely a way to keep the individual's pursuit of life, liberty, and happiness within bounds, that government was "anarchy plus the street constable." The earlier agrarians never foresaw that the new industrial capitalism would find that "hands-off" concept of government exactly to its liking. The Populists realized, and the post-1900 progressives knew it more surely, that the tradition of government noninterference defeated the ends of democratic government itself. It had to be modified and adapted to secure democracy and extend it—hence the name "progressive.". . .

The real leader of Midwestern progressivism, and its greatest, was Robert Marion La Follette. The Midwest had been laboring to produce a leader for thirty years when he appeared on the scene in 1900. Under him progressivism captured a state and in turn furnished the pattern for the capture of the region; he carried it himself into the Senate and up to the doors of the White House. He had what the others lacked, expressed the tradition best, gave it its wisest and clearest direction, and when he died, it died with him. . . .

La Follette was closer to the people and closer to the Midwest than any politician after Bryan. Unlike Bryan's, his appeal to the public was rational, rather than emotional. He had none of Bryan's crowd-swaying hypnosis, speaking instead in a rapid, intense fashion, flooding his audience with statistics, figures, and examples. The fact that he could keep a crowd of farmers on the edge of their seats for three hours by reciting tariff schedules and tax rates (as he once did on Chautauqua) is a tribute to a skill less flamboyant than Bryan's but one certainly equally effective. He once spoke for fifty-three consecutive nights, without the slightest flagging of his own energy or the audience's interest, a political feat only Bryan himself could equal.

La Follette was a small, wiry man, with a shock of black (later iron-gray) hair and a tendency toward swift and sharp gesture. He was honest, serious, almost inhumanly intense, and thoroughly uncompromising. He was perfectly willing to jeopardize his career, as he did a dozen times, to keep his principles, and the hate and vituperation that often came his way affected him not one iota. "I can no more compromise, or seem to compromise . . . ," he said, "than I could by wishing it add twenty years to my life." His principles were always clear, his course equally so. Cold, severe, almost austere in manner, La Follette did not invite easy friendship. He never had fun in politics (as Theodore Roosevelt did), nor did he inspire the devotion that Bryan did. It would be difficult to choose, from the group of men who knew him best and followed him, one who was a really close friend, for his complete and selfless dedication to his cause wrapped him about like armor. In truth, with his solid, lined face, his tremendous idealism, his rigid indifference to any blandishments of friendship, party, place, profit, or power, La Follette was a trifle frightening. No one ever took Bob La Follette lightly or disinterestedly. "The politician cannot exist without absolute, unyielding, uncompromising honesty," he said, and he lived it out to the letter.

La Follette's Wisconsin cut the pattern, and the whole Midwest copied it. Progressivism after 1900 at one time or another had complete control of every state but Illinois, Michigan, Ohio, and Indiana. For that matter, it spread elsewhere under the leadership of men like Hiram Johnson in California, Charles Evans Hughes in New York, Woodrow Wilson in New Jersey, Bass in New Hampshire, and so on. But in the Middle West, where it started, progressivism was considerably more than simply a swing toward honest government. It was a definite and coherent political philosophy, a concept of democracy that grew naturally out of Grangerism and Populism. Behind it were Weaver and Bryan, Donnelly and Lloyd, Altgeld, and Simpson, and a distinctively Midwestern, agrarian, Jeffersonian, frontier tradition. . . .

The assassin's bullet that cut down McKinley put a man already committed to progressivism into the White House. Both the political leaders of the Midwest and the city and state reformers of the East had begun their work, and T. R. seemed to be the national leader they all prayed for. No man ever stepped into the Presidency with a greater following or more personal power than Theodore Roosevelt. Not quite forty-three, vigorous, and energetic, with a sharp intellect, a quick mind, and a thirst for information, Roosevelt certainly possessed superb equipment for a politician. He was an experienced administrator, with a genius for personal contracts and a good sense of public relations, his appeal wide and his personal charm devastating. He could, as John Hay once said, "organize the unorganizable" by sheer personality.

Roosevelt was also a wizard at group diplomacy. He had an ambidextrous ability to please everybody, to have something for everyone, to catch the prevailing tone of any time or the temper of any group—cowboy, war hero, stern prosecutor of graft and crime, brilliant (though superficial) scholar, and so on. When the country went to war, T.R. was there with the Rough Riders and in the headlines. How many knew or cared that he was second in command, and who heard of Colonel Wood, his superior? If the public criticized college football, there was T.R. with a carefully balanced statement on the matter. If the public liked cowboys, T.R. owned a ranch, had cowboys to lunch, and wore a cowboy hat and a red bandanna to the 1900 Republican convention. He knew Bat

Nelson, Bob Fitzsimmons, John L. Sullivan, President Eliot of Harvard, Booker T. Washington, Confederate soldiers (his uncle fought for the South), college professors, stockbrokers—name a prominent man in any walk of life and Roosevelt probably knew him. With his gift for phrases —the "big stick," the "square deal," the "malefactors of great wealth"— he said dramatically and concisely what people thought and wanted to hear. "Teddy" was a familiar face peering out of the newspaper and a familiar name in the headlines before he even went to Washington to serve as Vice-President under McKinley. He seemed in 1901 to be the heaven-sent answer to the progressive prayer for a national leader. . . .

Whether or not Roosevelt was really a progressive during his two terms as President is an open question. It is doubtful that he possessed, during the years 1900 to 1908, a coherent and organized theory of politics beyond his general desire to institute honest and efficient government. It was not until after he had retired from the Presidency that he developed, under the influence of Eastern intellectuals such as Herbert Croly, a more distinctively progressive political philosophy. From 1900 to 1908 Roosevelt's three chief interests, as shown in his speeches and actions, were regulation of corporations, conservation, and the extension of governmental power in social and economic areas, all of them in agreement with Midwestern progressive aims. Yet his policy toward corporations was certainly not that of Bryan and the Populists, nor that of La Follette and the post-1900 Midwesterners. "As a matter of fact," he confided to a friend in 1908, "I have let up in every case where I have had any possible excuse for so doing." He took a middle road between the Populist-Granger principle of destroying trusts and the La Follette policy of regulating them to insure competition. Roosevelt chose to take his stand on the principle of *establishing* the right to regulate, a wholly different emphasis. He considered the "rural Tories" of the Midwest, who wished to curb the trust or smash it, as no progressives at all, but simply wreckers. Conservation and social legislation, as La Follette pointed out, were progressive issues indeed, but significantly they were not controversial party issues either. Roosevelt's progressivism, it was suspected, stopped where party politics began. The Midwestern states, said La Follette, had done much more on all counts than T.R. had done in seven and one-half years.

In other words, certain Midwestern progressives felt in 1908 that Roosevelt was either not a progressive at all or (more charitably) a progressive of decidedly limited aims and enthusiasms. He talked a great deal, but failed to produce. "This cannonading," wrote La Follette of T.R.'s crusades, "first in one direction and then the other, filled the air with noise and smoke, which confused and obscured the line of action, but when the battle cloud drifted by and quiet was restored, it was always a matter of surprise that so little had really been accomplished."

Louis Post, somewhat to the left of La Follette, thought Roosevelt "incapable of cooperation . . . and generally irresponsible," concluding that "progressivism would be stronger without him." Eugene Debs, on the socialist left and one of the gentlest of men, could barely speak or write of him with restraint. But a good many progressives held their tongues, content to accept what minor progress T.R. had undoubtedly made and to hope for more under Taft.

Roosevelt's real contribution to Midwestern progressivism did not come from the fact that he was part of it (for he was not) nor from what he accomplished for it, for he accomplished little. It lay instead in the leadership he assumed in the progressive movement at large—a leadership that the Midwest accepted with reservations, but nevertheless accepted. There was in the nation in 1900 a vague but powerful drift toward honest, efficient, and representative government. Roosevelt became its spearhead. Whether he led the way or whether he stepped in at the head of a procession that had already formed (Roosevelt believed the latter) is beside the question. He was important to progressivism because he was the first President after the Civil War who understood what had happened to the nation socially, politically, and economically since 1865. He dramatized the conflict between progressivism and conservatism, made it alive and important, and caught the imagination of the people with it, even though he did not resolve it. For reasons of temperament he was unable to resolve it, since his principles dissolved too often into glittering generalities. "We are neither for the rich man nor the poor man as such, but for the upright man, rich or poor," is a cheeringly liberal statement, but one difficult to put into law books. Yet his contributions to the rising wave of progressivism were not inconsiderable. The teeth, the eyeglasses, the bouncing vitality, the "big stick" and the "strenuous life," the St. George-like sallies against the trusts—all of these were trademarks of a muscular, youthful, aggressive, optimistic democracy that captured the nation's fancy. . . .

Though there was a tendency to establish tighter governmental regulation of industry during the period 1900 to 1908, the trend toward consolidation and combination in business slowed down, but it did not stop. "It really seems hard . . . ," said Jim Hill, thinking of the old freebooting days, "that we should now be compelled to fight for our lives against political adventurers who have never done anything but pose and draw a salary." But the plain fact was that the public, which had long watched business running politics, could see no reason why politics should not run business. For decades the railroads and other business combinations had bought the people's legislators and packed the people's conventions. It was not much use for businessmen to cry after 1900 that business was private business, removed from politics, for it never had been removed from politics.

The truth was that the era of the businessman was drawing to a close. The temper of national life had changed since 1870, the philosophy of democracy was no longer so popularly nor so solidly based on Darwin and Adam Smith. The issues of 1870 were by no means fully settled— indeed, the real settlement had hardly begun—but the alliance between government and business was not so strong as before, the trust under closer rein, the financier not quite so firmly certain of his ground.

Progressivism: middle-class disillusionment

George Mowry

As a group, the reform mayors and governors, their prominent supporters, and the muckrakers were an interesting lot. Considering the positions they held, they were very young. Joseph W. Folk was only thirty-five when elected governor, Theodore Roosevelt forty, Charles Evans Hughes and Hiram Johnson forty-four, and Robert La Follette forty-five. The average age of the important progressive leaders who up- set the Southern Pacific Railroad machine in California was a little over thirty-eight. The tale of a rather typical young reformer was that of Joseph Medill Patterson of the Chicago *Tribune* family. Patterson's grandfather founded the *Tribune*, his father was general manager of the paper, and his cousin was Robert McCormick, who controlled the paper for over thirty years. Patterson sharply reacted against the reigning con- servatism by winning a seat in the Illinois legislature at the age of twenty-four on a platform advocating the municipal ownership of all city utilities in the state. Two years later he resigned from the Chicago Com- mission of Public Works to become a Socialist because, he announced, it was impossible to reform the city and the country under capitalism. In 1906 he published a diatribe against wealth in the *Independent* entitled "The Confessions of a Drone," and followed it two years later with a book of similar tone.[1] Obviously, this was a period, like the ones after the War of 1812 and in the 1850's, when energetic and incautious youth took

[1] George E. Mowry, *The California Progressives* (Berkeley and Los Angeles, 1952), p. 87; *The Public*, April 8, 1905; *Independent*, LXI (1906), 493–495; Joseph Medill Patterson, *Little Brother of the Rich* (Chicago, 1908).

Pp. 85–93, 98–105 *The Era of Theodore Roosevelt, 1900–1912* by George Mowry. Copyright © 1958 by George E. Mowry. Reprinted with the permission of Harper & Row, Publishers.

command. And in each instance the departure of the elder statesmen portended great changes.

Some of these reformers, like Golden Rule Jones, Charles Evans Hughes, and Tom Johnson, were self-made men, although Hughes's father was a minister, and Johnson's, a Confederate colonel, had come from the upper stratum of Kentucky society. A surprising number of them came from very wealthy families, with names like du Pont, Crane, Spreckels, Dodge, Morgenthau, Pinchot, Perkins, McCormick, and Patterson. The quip was made that this was a "millionaire's reform movement." But the great majority of the reformers came from the "solid middle class," as it then was called with some pride. That their families had been of the economically secure is indicated by the fact that most of them had had a college education in a day when a degree stamped a person as coming from a special economic group. It is interesting to note that most of the women reformers and social workers had gone to college. Occupationally also the reformers came from a very narrow base in society. Of a sample of over four hundred a majority was lawyers, as might be expected of politicians, and nearly 20 per cent of them newspaper editors or publishers. The next largest group was from the independent manufacturers or merchants, with the rest scattered among varied occupations, including medicine, banking, and real estate. A statistical study of sixty of the wealthier reformers reveals that the largest single group of twenty-one was manufacturers or merchants, ten lawyers, six newspaper publishers, while nineteen more had inherited their wealth. Quite a few among the latter group had no definite occupation save that of preserving their family fortune and indulging in reform. Of the sixty only about half attended college, a figure much lower than that for the entire group of reformers. Of this number just 50 per cent came from three institutions, Harvard, Princeton, and Yale.[2]

If names mean anything, an overwhelming proportion of this reform group came from old American stock with British origins consistently indicated. Except for the women, who were predominantly Midwestern, the reformers' places of origin were scattered over the country roughly in proportion to population densities. Practically all of them by 1900, however, lived in northern cities, most of the Southerners having left their section during early manhood. Religious affiliations were surprisingly difficult to get, and no really trustworthy national sample was obtained. The figures collected were not at all consonant with national church membership statistics. Representatives of the Quaker faith bulked large among the women reformers, as did members of the Jewish religion among the very wealthy. But for the group as a whole the religious descendants of Calvin and Knox predominated, with the Congre-

[2] These statistics and the ones following came from a series of studies in the writer's seminar. The figures were rechecked and are in the author's possession.

gationalists, Unitarians, and Presbyterians in the vast majority. Thus it seems likely that the intellectual and religious influence of New England was again dominating the land.

Whether Democrats or Republicans, the overwhelming number of this group of twentieth-century reformers had been conservatives in the nineties. If Republican, they had almost to a man followed the way of Theodore Roosevelt, Robert La Follette, Lincoln Steffens, and William Allen White to support William McKinley. Most of the progressive Democrats had not been supporters of Bryan, but, like Woodrow Wilson, John Johnson, and Hoke Smith of Georgia, had either followed the Gold Democratic ticket or had remained silent during the election of 1896. Yet from four to six years later most of these men were ardent advocates of municipal gas and water socialism, and were opposed to their regular party machines to the extent of leading either nonpartisan movements in the municipalities or rebellious splinter groups in the states. Moreover, the new century found most of them, except on the currency issue, supporting many of the 1896 Populist and Bryanite demands. Before the Progressive years were finished they and their kind had not only secured the inception of a host of the Populists' reforms, but had contributed a few of their own.

Obviously, a good many questions arise about the motivation of this economically secure, well-educated, middle-class group. On the surface it looked as if the progressive movement was simply a continuation under different leadership of the Populist cause. According to William Allen White, Populism had "shaved its whiskers, washed its shirt, put on a derby, and moved up into the middle class. . . ." But White's remark scarcely probed beneath the surface. Populism arose from farmer distress in a period of acute depression. Its reforms were belly reforms. The movement was led by angry men and women not too far removed from the Grange hall. Except for the western silver men, they were incensed at the mounting figures of farm foreclosures and a withering countryside. To the contrary, progressivism arose in a period of relative prosperity. Its reforms were more the results of the heart and the head than of the stomach. Its leaders were largely recruited from the professional and business classes of the city. A good many were wealthy men; more were college graduates. As a group they were indignant at times, but scarcely ever angry. What caused them to act in the peculiar way they did? A part of the answer lies in the peculiar economic and social position in which this middle-class group found itself at about the turn of the century, a part in the intellectual and ethical climate of the age, a part in the significant cluster of prejudices and biases that marked the progressive mind.

"The world wants men, great, strong, harsh, brutal men—men with purpose who let nothing, nothing, nothing stand in their way," Frank

Norris wrote in one of his novels. This worship of the strong man, so characteristic of the age, produced a cult of political leadership with ominous overtones for later years. Tempered at this time with the ethics of the social gospel, the cult produced an image far less frightening: an image of men dedicated to the social good, an image approximating the hope of Plato for his guardians. These strong good men, "the change-makers," Harold Frederic wrote, were the protectors of morality, the originators of progress. They were ambitious men and ruthless, but only ruthless in their zeal for human advancement. They were supremely alone, the causative individuals. Far from being disturbed when isolated, David Graham Phillips's hero Scarborough was only concerned when he was "propped up" by something other than his own will and intelligence. "I propose," he commented, "never to 'belong' to anything or anybody."[3]

In 1872 a future progressive, Henry Demarest Lloyd, confessed that he wanted power above all things, but "power unpoisoned by the presence of obligation." That worship of the unfettered individual, the strong pride of self, the strain of ambition, and the almost compulsive desire for power ran through progressive rhetoric like a theme in a symphony. From Frank Norris's strong-minded heroes to Richard Harding Davis's men of almost pure muscle these feelings were a badge of a restless, sensitive, and troubled class. They were never far below the surface in the character of Theodore Roosevelt. Robert La Follette knew them, and Woodrow Wilson had more than his share of them. While still a scholar and teacher, Wilson poured out his frustration with the contemplative life: "I have no patience with the tedious world of what is known as 'research,' " he wrote to a friend. "I should be complete if I could inspire a great movement of opinion. . . ."[4]

A few progressive leaders like William Jennings Bryan and Golden Rule Jones really thought of themselves as servants of the people,[5] and almost completely identified themselves with their constituents. But most progressives set themselves apart from the crowd. Mankind was basically good and capable of progress, but benign change scarcely issued from the masses. Rather it was only accomplished through the instrumentality of a few great and good men. Woodrow Wilson believed that efficient government could come only from "an educated elite," William Kent thought that progress never came from the bottom, and Roosevelt often spoke of government as the process of "giving justice from above." Occasionally, when the electorate disagreed with them, the

---

[3] Frank Norris, *A Man's Woman* (New York, 1900), p. 71; David Graham Phillips (Indianapolis, 1904), *The Cost*, p. 17.
[4] Quoted in Daniel Aaron, *Men of Good Hope* (New York, 1951), p. 139; Richard Hofstadter, *The American Political Tradition and the Men Who Made It* (New York, 1948), p. 243.
[5] Frances G. Newlands, *Public Papers* (New York, 1932), p. 311.

progressives contented themselves with the thought that truth "was always in the minority" and a possession alone of the "few who see." In 1912 Walter Lippmann wrote that since men could do anything but govern themselves, they were constantly looking for some "benevolent guardian." To the progressive politician that guardian, of course, was patterned after his image of himself.[6] . . .

A small reform-minded minority in 1900 was outspoken in defense of the large industrial and commercial city as the creator of the good life. Some of them saw the city as a place of refuge from an ugly countryside and from a hostile natural environment. Remembering his own bleak and lonely boyhood on an upstate New York farm, the novelist Harold Frederic condemned a daily communion with nature that starved the mind and dwarfed the soul. Theodore Dreiser bluntly described the natural processes as inimical to man as a species. Others felt the fascination of the city, a place of excitement and of opportunity. Lincoln Steffens recalled that he felt about the concrete canyons of New York as other youths felt about the wild West. For people like Jane Addams, Jacob Riis, and Hutchins Hapgood the city offered a place to work and an avenue to opportunity.

For the great majority of the new century's reformers, however, the city contained almost the sum of their dislikes. It was a "devilsburg of crime" sucking into its corrupt vortex the "young, genuine, strong and simple men from the farm." There, if successful, they became "financial wreckers" who made their money strangling legitimate enterprises and other human beings. If they were failures—that is, if they remained factory workers—they gradually became like the machine they tended, "huge, hard, brutal, strung with a crude blind strength, stupid, unreasoning." At the worst such unfortunates became the flotsam of the slums, making the saloon their church and the dive their home. The native American lost not only his morals in the city but also his talent for creative work and his sense of beauty. "Sometimes, I think, they'se poison in th' life in a big city," Mr. Dooley remarked, "the flowers won't grow there. . . ." If a man stayed in the city long enough, one of David Graham Phillips' characters remarked, he would almost inevitably lose those qualities that made him an American: one had to go West to see a "real American, a man or a woman who looks as if he or she would do something honest or valuable. . . ."[7]

With such intense antiurban feelings, it is small wonder that the

[6] Theodore Roosevelt, "Who Is a Progressive?" *The Outlook*, C (1912), 2; *The Public*, April 18, 1903; Walter Lippmann, *Drift and Mastery* (New York, 1914), p. 189.
[7] For varied expressions of this antiurbanism, see Irving Bacheller, *Eben Holden* (Boston, 1900), p. 336; Alice H. Rice, *Mrs. Wiggs of the Cabbage Patch* (New York, 1901), p. 29; Winston Churchill, *The Dwelling-Place of Light* (New York, 1917), p. 79; Finley Peter Dunne, *Mr. Dooley in Peace and War* (Boston, 1898), p. 125; D. G. Phillips, *Golden Fleece* (New York, 1903), pp. 57–58.

United States began to romanticize its pioneer past and its agrarian background. Following the Spanish War historical novels fairly poured from the publishers. The public appetite for western stories had one of its periodic increases, and the virtues of the countryside were extolled in even the best literature. In one of Ellen Glasgow's first novels the country, "with its ecstatic insight into the sacred plan of things," is contrasted with the city's "tainted atmosphere." Almost repeating William Jennings Bryan in 1896, Miss Glasgow wrote that the country was the world as God had planned it, the city as man had made it. The cult of the frontier, first introduced into historical scholarship by Frederic Jackson Turner in 1890, and the new emphasis upon agrarian virtues were zealously reflected by the more sensitive politicians. William Jennings Bryan, Theodore Roosevelt, Robert La Follette, and Woodrow Wilson all showed to varying degrees this national nostalgia, this reactionary impulse. Roosevelt in particular saw the great city as the creator of national weakness and possible disintegration, and the countryside as the nation's savior. It was the man on the farm, he wrote, who had consistently done the nation the "best service in governing himself in time of peace and also in fighting in time of war." Dangerous elements to the commonwealth lurked in every large city, but among the western farmers of the West "there was not room for an anarchist or a communist in the whole lot." What Professor Richard Hofstadter has called the agrarian myth, but which might better be called the agrarian bias, was one of the more important elements that went into the making of the progressive mind.[8]

A part of the progressive's romantic attraction to the countryside at this particular time can be explained by the alien character of the urban population. In 1903 the Commissioner of Immigration reported that the past year had witnessed the greatest influx of immigrants in the nation's history. But far from being pleased, the Commissioner was plainly worried. An increasing percentage of these newcomers, he pointed out, belonged to an "undesirable foreign element," the "indigestible" aliens from south Europe. The public was neither surprised at the figures of the report nor shocked by its adjectives. It had been made increasingly sensitive to the changing patterns of immigration by numerous periodical articles and newspaper items calling attention to the alien nature of the eastern seaboard cities. As the immigrant tide welled stronger each year, the nativist spirit that had been so obviously a part of the mental complex leading to the Spanish War increased in intensity. Throughout the decade editors, novelists, and politicians competed with each other in singing the praises of the "big-boned, blond, long-haired" Anglo-Saxon with the blood of the berserkers in his veins, and in denigrating Jack

[8] Ellen Glasgow, *The Descendant* (New York, 1897), p. 254; Roosevelt to George Otto Trevelyan, March 9, 1905, and to Kermit Roosevelt, January 1, 1907, Roosevelt MSS.; *The Public*, November 14, 1903.

London's "dark pigmented things, the half castes, the mongrel bloods, and the dregs of long conquered races. . . ." In Frank Norris's novels the really despicable characters run all to a type. Braun, the diamond expert in *Vandover;* Zerkow, the junk dealer in *McTeague;* the flannel-shirted Grossman in *The Pit;* and Behrman in *The Octopus* were all of the same religion and approximately from the same regions in Europe. One of the themes in Homer Lea's *The Vermillion Pencil* was the extranational loyalty of the Catholic bishop who intrigued endlessly for the Church and against the State. Although Chester Rowell frankly admitted that California needed "a class of servile labor," he was adamantly opposed to the admission of Orientals, who were dangerous to the state and to "the blood of the next generation."[9]

The progressives, of course, had no monopoly of this racism. Such conservatives as Elihu Root, Henry Cabot Lodge, and Chauncey Depew, and even radicals like Debs, shared their views to a degree. But for one reason or another neither conservative nor radical was as vocal or as specific in his racism as was the reformer. No more eloquent testimony to the power of racism over the progressive mind is evident than in the writings of the kindly, tolerant Middle Westerner William Allen White. In a book published in 1910 White explained nearly all of America's past greatness, including its will to reform, in terms of the nation's "race life" and its racial institutions, "the home and the folk moot." Nor would this genius, this "clean Aryan blood," White promised, be subjected to a debilitating admixture in the future despite the incoming hordes. "We are separated by two oceans from the inferior races and by an instinctive race revulsion to cross breeding that marks the American wherever he is found."[10] Such diverse reformers as Theodore Roosevelt, Albert J. Beveridge, Chester Rowell, Frank Parsons, Hoke Smith, Richard W. Gilder, and Ray Stannard Baker, with more or less emphasis, echoed White's sentiments. . . .

Since the progressive usually came from a comfortable part of society and a general attack upon property was usually furthest from his mind, this assault upon great wealth put him in a rather ambiguous position. The one way out of the paradox was to draw a line between good and bad wealth. For some the limit of private fortunes was the total that man could "justly acquire." For others the measurement was made in terms of service to society. Tom Johnson, for example, believed that the law could be so drawn that men would be able "to get" only the amount "they earned." Still others argued that there must be a point where additional money ceased to be salubrious for a man's character and became instead

[9] *Literary Digest,* XXVII (1903), 158; Jack London, *The Mutiny of the Elsinore* (New York, 1914), pp. 197–198. See also John Higham, *Strangers in the Land, Patterns of American Nativism, 1860–1925* (New Brunswick, N.J., 1955), pp. 131 ff.
[10] William Allen White, *The Old Order Changeth* (New York, 1910), pp. 128, 197, 253.

a positive evil force. Wayne MacVeagh, Garfield's Attorney General, suggested that all people could be divided into three classes: those who had
more money than was good for them, those who had just enough, and
those who had much less than was morally desirable. Just where the exact lines should be drawn, most progressives would not say. But the imputation that the state ought to redivide wealth on a morally desirable
basis found a receptive audience. To George F. Baer's claim that coal
prices should be the sum of "all the traffic will bear," the editors of *The
Outlook* replied that property was private not by any natural right but by
an "artificial arrangement made by the community." "If under those artificial arrangements," the editorial continued, "the community is made
to suffer, the same power that made them will find a way to unmake
them." Thus in the progressive mind the classical economic laws repeatedly described in the past as natural had become artificial arrangements
to be rearranged at any time the community found it morally or socially
desirable. Admittedly the formulations of new ethical standards for a
division of national wealth were to be extremely difficult. But once the
progressive had destroyed the popular sanction behind the "laws" of
rent, prices, and wages, there was to be no complete turning back. A
revolution in human thought had occurred. Man, it was hoped, would
now become the master and not the creature of his economy. And the
phrases punctuating the next fifty years of history—the "square deal,"
the New Deal, the Fair Deal, the just wage, the fair price—attested to his
efforts to make the reality square with his ambitions.[11]

After revisiting the United States in 1905, James Bryce, the one-time
ambassador from Great Britain, noted that of all the questions before the
public the ones bearing on capital and labor were the most insistent and
the most discussed. Certainly for many a progressive the rise of the labor
union was as frightening as the rise of trusts. True, he talked about them
less because nationally they were obviously not as powerful as were the
combines of capital. But emotionally he was, if anything, more opposed
to this collectivism from below than he was to the collectivism above him
in the economic ladder.[12]

"There is nothing ethical about the labor movement. It is coercion
from start to finish. In every aspect it is a driver and not a leader. It is
simply a war movement, and must be judged by the analogues of belligerence and not by industrial principles." This statement by a Democratic
progressive illustrates the ire of the small and uncertain employer who
was being challenged daily by a power he often could not match. In their
lawlessness and in their violence, remarked another, unions were "a

[11] *The Public*, September 23, 1905, and February 3, 1906; Wayne MacVeagh, "An
Appeal to Our Millionaires," *North American Review*, June, 1906; *The Outlook*,
LXXVI (1904), 240.
[12] James Bryce, "America Revisited," *The Outlook*, LXXIX (1905), 848.

menace not only to the employer but to the entire community."[13] To the small employer and to many middle-class professionals unions were just another kind of monopoly created for the same reasons and having the same results as industrial monopoly. Unions, they charged, restricted production, narrowed the available labor market, and raised wages artificially in the same manner that trusts were restricting production, narrowing competition, and raising their own profits. "Every step in trade unionism has followed the steps that organized capital has laid down before it," Clarence Darrow observed in a speech before the Chicago Henry George Association. The ultimate direction of the two monopolies was as clear to the individual entrepreneur as it was to Darrow. Either trade unionism would break down, a Midwestern editor argued, or it would culminate in "a dangerously oppressive partnership" with the stronger industrial trusts. The end result was equally obvious to such men: a steady decrease in opportunity for the individual operating as an individual, an economy of statics, an end to the open society. The burden of the industrial evolution, Darrow said in concluding his speech, "falls upon the middle class."[14] And Howells' traveler from Altruria put the case even more graphically: "the struggle for life has changed from a free fight to an encounter of disciplined forces, and the free fighters that are left get ground to pieces between organized labor and organized capital." . . .

" 'I am for labor,' or 'I am for capital,' substitutes something else for the immutable laws of righteousness," Theodore Roosevelt was quoted as saying in 1904. "The one and the other would let the class man in, and letting him in is the one thing that will most quickly eat out the heart of the Republic." Roosevelt, of course, was referring to class parties in politics. Most progressives agreed with Herbert Croly that a "profound antagonism" existed between the political system and a government controlled by a labor party.[15] In San Francisco in 1901, in Chicago in 1905, and in Los Angeles in 1911, when labor used or threatened direct political action, the progressive reacted as if touched by fire. Chicago was a "class-ridden" city, remarked one progressive journal, which would not redeem itself until the evil pretensions of both organized capital and labor had been suppressed. In Los Angeles, where a Socialist labor group came within a hair's breadth of controlling the city, the progressives combined with their old enemies, the corporation-dominated machine, to

---

[13] *The Public*, June 13, 1903; *The Outlook*, LXVIII (1901), 683.
[14] Chicago *Record Herald*, June 26, 1903; *The Public*, June 11, 1903.
[15] Charles H. Cooley, *Human Nature and the Social Order* (New York, 1902), p. 72; Ray Stannard Baker, "The Rise of the Tailors," *McClure's*, XXIV (1904), 14. For other expressions of the same spirit, see Simon Patten, *The New Basis of Civilization* (New York, 1907), p. 84; John N. McCormick, *The Litany and the Life* (Milwaukee, 1904), p. 93; H. B. Brown, "Twentieth Century," *Forum* XIX (1895), 641; *The Public*, November 26, 1914; Jacob A. Riis, "Theodore Roosevelt, The Citizen," *The Outlook*, LXXVI (1904), 649; Croly, *Promise*, p. 129.

fight off the challenge, and as a result never again exerted the power they once had in the city. Apropos of that struggle punctuated by a near general strike, dynamite, and death, the leading California progressive theorist, Chester Rowell, expostulated that no class as a class was fit to rule a democracy; that progress came only from the activities of good citizens acting as individuals. Class prejudice and class pride excused bribery, mass selfishness, lawlessness, and disorder. This class spirit emanating from both business and labor was "destroying American liberty." When it became predominant, Rowell concluded, American institutions would be dead, for peaceful reform would no longer be possible, and "nothing but revolution" would remain.[16]

At various times and places the progressive politician invited the support of organized labor, but such co-operation was almost invariably a one-way street. Somewhat reminiscent of the early relations between the British Liberal and Labor parties, it worked only if the progressive rather than the labor politician was in the driver's seat. In Maine, for example, when labor attempted to lead a campaign for the initiative and referendum, it was defeated in part by progressives, who two years later led a successful campaign on the same issues.[17] In the progressive literature the terms "captain of industry" and "labor boss" were standard, while "labor statesman" was practically unknown. Roosevelt's inclination to try labor lawbreakers in a criminal court is well known; his administration's failure to indict criminally one corporation executive is eloquent of the limits of his prejudice. Progressive literature contained many proposals for permitting corporations to develop until they had achieved quasimonopoly status, at which time federal regulation would be imposed. No such development was forecast for labor. Unions were grudgingly recognized as a necessary evil, but the monopolistic closed shop was an abomination not to be tolerated with or without government regulation. In the Chicago teamsters' strike of 1905 Mayor Dunne ordered the city police to be "absolutely impartial" toward both capital and labor. But he also insisted that the strikers not be allowed to block the teams of nonunion men or the delivery of nonunion-marked goods.[18]

A few progressives, of course, hailed the rise of labor unions as an advance in democracy. But the majority, while sincerely desirous of improving the plight of the individual workingman, was perhaps basically more hostile to the union than to corporate monopoly. If the progressive attention was mostly centered on the corporation during the decade, it was largely because the sheer social power of the corporation vastly overshadowed that of the rising but still relatively weak unions. When

[16] *The Public*, May 13, 1905, and June 17, 1905; Fresno *Republican*, November 20, 1911.
[17] J. William Black, "Maine's Experience with the Initiative and Referendum," *Annals of the American Academy of Political Science*, XLII, 164–165.
[18] *The Public*, April 15, 1905.

confronted with a bleak either-or situation, progressive loyalties significantly shifted up and not down the economic ladder.

Emotionally attached to the individual as a causative force and to an older America where he saw his group supreme, assaulted economically and socially from above and below, and yet eager for the wealth and the power that flowed from the new collectivism, the progressive was at once nostalgic, envious, fearful, and yet confident about the future. Fear and confidence together for a time inspired this middle-class group of supremely independent individuals with a class consciousness that perhaps exceeded that of any other group in the nation. This synthesis had been a long time developing. Back in the early 1890's Henry George had remarked that the two dangerous classes to the state were "the very rich" and "the very poor." Some years afterward a Populist paper referred to the "upper and lower scum" of society. At about the same time the acknowledged dean of American letters had inquired just where the great inventions, the good books, the beautiful pictures, and the just laws had come from in American society. Not from the "uppermost" or "lowermost" classes, Howells replied. They had come mostly from the middle-class man. In the first decade of the twentieth century the progressive never questioned where ability and righteousness resided. Nor was he uncertain of the sources of the nation's evils. "From above," one wrote, "come the problems of predatory wealth. . . . From below come the problems of poverty and pigheaded and brutish criminality."[19]

As the progressive looked at the sharply differentiated America of 1900, he saw "pyramids of money in a desert of want." For William Allen White the world was full of "big crooks" and the "underprivileged." The polar conditions of society assaulted the progressive conscience and threatened progressive security. Supremely individualistic, the progressive could not impute class consciousness, or, as he would have phrased it, class selfishness, to himself. His talk was therefore full of moral self-judgments, of phrases like "the good men," "the better element," "the moral crowd." From the Old Source, he paraphrased, "Thou shalt not respect the person of the poor, nor honor the person of the great; in righteousness shalt thou judge thy neighbor." His self-image was that of a "kind-hearted man" dealing in justice. William Kent publicly stated that he could not believe in the class struggle because every great reform of the past had been wrought by men who were not "selfishly interested." "I believe," he concluded, "altruism is a bigger force in the world than selfishness."[20]

Since the progressive was not organized economically as was the cap-

[19] Aaron, *Men of Good Hope*, pp. 84, 193; Jackson (Michigan) *Industrial News*, March 8, 1894; *California Weekly*, December 18, 1908.
[20] William Allen White to Henry J. Allen, July 28, 1934, in Walter Johnson (ed.), *Selected Letters of William Allen White, 1899–1943* (New York, 1947), p. 348; San Francisco *Bulletin*, September 8, 1911.

italist and the laborer, he chose to fight his battles where he had the most power—in the political arena. And in large terms his political program was first that of the most basic urge of all nature, to preserve himself, and secondly to refashion the world after his own image. What the nation needed most, wrote a Midwestern clergyman, was an increase in the number of "large-hearted men" to counteract the class organization of both capital and labor. "Solidarity," Herbert Croly stated, "must be restored." The point of reconcentration around which the hoped-for solidarity was to take place, of course, was the middle class. It was to "absorb" all other classes, thought Henry Demarest Lloyd. It was to be both the sum and substance of the classless state of the future.[21]

The progressive mentality was a compound of many curious elements. It contained a reactionary as well as a reform impulse. It was imbued with a burning ethical strain which at times approached a missionary desire to create a heaven on earth. It had in it intense feelings of moral superiority over both elements of society above and below it economically. It emphasized individual dynamism and leadership. One part of it looked backward to an intensely democratic small America; another looked forward to a highly centralized nationalistic state. And both elements contained a rather ugly strain of racism.

The progressive mentality was generated in part from both a fear of the loss of group status and a confidence in man's ability to order the future. Had progressive militancy come in a more despondent intellectual and ethical climate and in a bleaker economic day, group fear might have won over group hope. Its more benign social ends might then have been transmuted into something more malignant. But in the warm and sunny atmosphere of 1900 the optimistic mood prevailed. . . .

A condition of excitement

Eric Goldman

At first the new reformers had no special name for themselves. "Liberal" was too closely associated with Clevelandism. "Populist" called up the dour radicalism of the Nineties. Gradually the term "progressiv-

[21] William J. McCaughan, *Love, Faith and Joy* (Chicago, 1904), p. 206; Croly, *Promise of American Life*, p. 139; Aaron, *Men of Good Hope*, p. 160.

ism" took its place after "liberalism" and "Populism" as the label for another, quite different attempt to reform post-Civil War America.

In many fundamentals progressivism continued Populism. For both movements, the central problem was opportunity and they aimed to "restore" opportunity by quite similar programs. Government was to be democratized in order to make it more amenable to reform. Reform meant primarily the ending of governmental interventions that benefited large-scale capital and a rapid increase in the interventions that favored men of little or no capital. Many of progressivism's specific proposals came straight from Populism, including the direct election of United States senators, the initiative and the referendum, anti-trust action, a federal income tax, the encouragement of trade-unions, and an eight-hour day. In the spirit of Populism, progressives took up new proposals for direct democracy or the advancement of lower-income groups, most notably popular primaries, the recall of elected officials, workmen's compensation legislation, and minimum-wage and maximum-hour laws. The new reform also continued Populism's political recognition of women. The cities were producing their own female activists, and these women, for the most part talented and well educated, made effective advocates of feminism in the eyes of progressives.

Yet progressivism was not simply the Populist buggy rolled out for a new century. More urban in its base, progressivism was much more genuinely concerned with the problems of labor and was far more inclined to include small businessmen and white-collar workers in the groups it wanted to help. Equally important, progressivism was developing its own special attitude toward the immigrant.

The progressives did not entirely drop Populism's anti-immigrant feeling. One of the country's best-known progressive spokesmen, the sociologist Edward Ross, provided the era's most effective formula for fear of immigration by arguing that the "squalid" newcomers bred rapidly while the old stock, "struggling to uphold a decent standard of living," stopped at two or three children. Many progressives also carried over the Populist fear that unlimited immigration kept wage scales down and consequently they continued the Populist demand for restriction of the influx. But progressivism as a movement was far more friendly than Populism to the immigrants who had already arrived. It was tending toward a genuine acceptance of the newcomer, even toward espousal of an important role for him.

Progressives made up the dominant element in the settlement houses that were undertaking the first systematic "Americanization" work, and the Americanization they advocated was no one-way street. The immigrant was not only to learn, settlement workers emphasized; he was to teach. While assimilating, he was to preserve the parts of his heritage which did not conflict with adjustment to the United States and he was

to enrich American culture by bringing to it desirable ideas or customs
from his old-country background. This type of Americanization was enthusiastically approved by Israel Zangwill, a British Jew who had become familiar with American settlement work by serving as head of an
organization that helped Russian Jews flee the pogroms to the United
States. In 1908 Zangwill wrote his enthusiasm into *The Melting Pot*, one
of those occasional literary works that both express and further a social
movement.

The chief characters of Zangwill's play were all immigrants in New
York City—an Irish Catholic, a Jew-hating nobleman who had personally
conducted pogroms in Russia, his daughter, and a young Russian Jew
whose parents had been murdered at the order of the nobleman. The
theme was the general benefit to be derived from what Zangwill called
an "all-around give-and-take," between the various groups of immigrants
and between all the newcomers and the old stock. At the end of the play,
as the Jew and the Jew-killer's daughter prepared to marry, the young
man looked out to a sunset and proclaimed it "the fires of God round His
crucible."

DAVID: There she lies, the great Melting Pot—listen! Can't you hear the
roaring and the bubbling? (*he points east*). There gapes her mouth—
the harbour where a thousand mammoth feeders come from the ends
of the world to pour in their human freight. . . . Celt and Latin, Slav and
Teuton, Greek and Syrian,—black and yellow—
VERA: Jew and Gentile—
DAVID: Yes, East and West, and North and South, the palm and the pine, the
pole and the equator, the crescent and the cross—how the great alchemist
melts and fuses them with his purging flame! . . . Ah, Vera, what is the
glory of Rome and Jerusalem where all nations and races come to worship
and look back, compared with the glory of America, where all races and
nations come to labour and look forward!

"Romantic claptrap," the *New York Times* critic snorted, and Zangwill's gushing prose is certainly hard to read today without wincing. But
in a more sentimental era, the play provided for thousands of progressives an exciting expression of their desire for an attitude toward the immigrant that was more generous and hopeful than Populist snarling.

In the political field, progressivism was altering Populism by the
greater degree to which it sought centralization. The Populists may not
have been afraid of pyramided power, and the progressives certainly did
not ignore reform possibilities on the municipal and state levels. But the
increasing urge to centralize was showing itself in a number of ways, of
which the two most important were greater dependence on federal rather
than state action and on executives rather than legislatures.

The progressives were men in a hurry, and even at their best legislatures must always seem slow and cumbersome. The legislatures of the
turn of the century, reformers constantly learned in additional ways,
were hardly legislatures at their best. At the same time, able individuals

were showing the prodigies that could be performed by one skillful reformer in an executive position. Under the circumstances, progressives
relied increasingly on the "good man" who would bring to reform the de-
cisiveness of a Carnegie and would maneuver, drive, or skirt around a
legislature. The desire to provide efficient by-passes heightened progressive enthusiasm for the administrative commission, the device which
gave long-time, quasi-legislative powers to a few men appointed by the
executive.

Simultaneously progressives were becoming discouraged about the
potentialities of action by the states. The problem with which the reformers were most concerned, the large corporation, did not yield readily
to state action. No one of the huge businesses operated in only one state,
and state regulations usually ended up in creating a maze of conflicting
statutes that hindered the efficiency of corporations without exacting
from them any real social responsibility. Worse yet, state social legislation was being thrown out by state courts almost as fast as it was
passed. Quite obviously, Washington was no perfect base for reform. But
the federal Constitution did explicitly empower Congress to regulate interstate commerce and national action did seem the logical way to regulate corporations operating on a national scale. In the early 1900's, much
more than in the Populist era, reform eyes were focusing on Washington.

If progressivism was going beyond Populism in its attitude toward
centralization, it was pulling back in another important respect. Progressivism virtually gave up the Populist attempt to make the Southern Negro an equal citizen. It paid little attention to the Negro problem as a
whole and, to the extent that it worried over the black man at all, gave
its support to the program of a Negro whose whole life had been a preparation for compromise.

Born to slavery and to poverty so great that his bed was a bundle of
rags, Booker T. Washington had been helped to his education by a series
of kindly whites. The Negro school he was invited to run, Tuskegee Institute, was founded on the initiative of Southern whites, and continued
white aid permitted Washington to build Tuskegee from a dilapidated
shanty for thirty students to forty-six substantial buildings offering
thirty trades to fourteen hundred pupils. It is possible to exaggerate the
amount of faith in the white man which this background gave Booker
Washington. His was a practical, canny mind, operating in a situation
that suggested bargaining Negro equality for some Negro advances.
("Actually," W.E.B. Du Bois once remarked, "Washington had no more
faith in the white man than I do," which was saying that he had little
faith indeed.) But whatever was going on behind that calm, pleasant
face of Booker Washington, he spoke no belligerence toward the white
man and no call for immediate equality.

When he was asked to address the Atlantic Cotton Exposition in 1895, Washington put his philosophy into sentences that immediately became famous as the "Atlanta Compromise." The Negro should accept political inequality, Washington said, provided he was given the opportunity to advance economically and educationally; in time, having prepared himself for the wise use of the vote, he would be granted the privilege. Washington bluntly repudiated any drive for social equality. "In all things that are purely social," he declared in his most widely quoted sentence, "we can be as separate as the fingers, yet one as the hand in all things essential to mutual progress."

In the early 1900's Washington's argument had the force of apparent success. His program was the first to promise any substantial advance for the Negro which the nation as a whole seemed willing to accept. Tuskegee Institute and similar schools were rapidly turning out trained Negroes who could train others and, by supporting themselves in decency, win respect for the whole race. In the decade between 1900 and 1910, Negro illiteracy throughout the country declined from forty-four to thirty per cent, while the number of farms owned by Southern Negroes increased at a rate four times more swiftly than the growth of the Negro population. Progressives interested in the Negro observed all this and remembered the violence and quick failure that had come with Populist attempts at equality. They were inclined to become enthusiastic, to help make Booker T. Washington the first Negro national hero—and to let well enough alone.

In other, less important details, progressivism also moved away from Populism, but the core of the differences between the movements lay in a consideration that no discussion of specific variations would adequately reveal. Agrarian-dominated Populism, with its desperate sense of being left behind, its doubts whether anyone could be both a businessman and a decent citizen, its inclination to suspect the man with well-fitted clothes or polished grammar, was not the only base of progressivism. The new reform was a product of the cities as much as of the farms, an amalgam of the Best People's liberalism and of the nobody's Populism, a middle doctrine for a nation rapidly committing itself to middle-class ways of thinking.

Progressivism accepted business America, even was enthusiastic about it, and aimed merely to correct abuses. It prized cultivation, manner, and efficiency; quite characteristically, progressivism restored liberalism's emphasis on civil-service reform. Above all, progressivism replaced Populist grimness with a gusty, dawn-world confidence, worrying about America but not worrying about it enough to turn to extremes. The ominous Populist distinction between "producing" and "nonproducing" classes fast disappeared from reform terminology. To the progressive, America was never farmers or industrial workers locked in a class struggle with big capital. America was always "the people," some of whom were richer and more powerful than others, but all of whom could be given back their birthright of opportunity by moderate, practical moves.

The restoration of opportunity by giving stronger powers to more democratized governments, a businesslike restoration with no disreputable caterwauling—such was the least common denominator of the thinking that was rising out of the union of liberalism and Populism. It was a denominator to which each progressive added his own integers; it had its confusions, its vagaries, and its dodges. But it was a sweepingly appealing program, the most national one since the Republican platform that rode Lincoln into the White House, and for most progressives it carried the kind of emotional intensity that whirls political movements ahead.

"In fact," the progressive journalist Ray Stannard Baker has remembered his mood in the early 1900's, "I used to be sure reform would sweep the country, that is, I always used to be sure until I talked to the man next to me on the street car." Throughout progressive America a growing confidence in the program was accompanied by a growing awareness that the program alone was not enough. Progressivism was face to face with a potent set of hostile ideas, ideas that had been tangled up with the middle-class rejection of Populism and that did not quickly wither as the middle-class attitude moved toward dissent. Somehow the progressives had to dissolve away the argument that their whole program was unscientific, contrary to human nature, antidemocratic, unconstitutional, and immoral. . . .

Blurrings, tendencies, trends—but in the first decade of the twentieth century the main current of progressivism was the one on which Teddy Roosevelt bobbed along so gaily. He might scourge minority nationalists, but Du Bois and Brandeis were both admirers as his Administrations drew to a close. He might suddenly turn on the muckrakers, even, on occasion, thwack the unions or help the United States Steel trust, but for the overwhelming number of American reformers Roosevelt was progressivism incarnate, and that progressivism was bringing an all-excusing sense of achievement. The new reform not only ruled the White House and hundreds of state and local governments. Progressives could take deeper satisfaction in the way that economic and social change was becoming the central subject of the day, the exciting, even the glamour subject, replacing the older generation's awed discussions of captains of industry with ebullient talk about the goodness, the inevitability, the sheer fun of re-doing America.

Late in 1904 Mrs. Sarah P. Decker took her ample self to the rostrum of the General Federation of Women's Clubs, turned a carefully coiffured head to the delegates, and said: "Ladies, you have chosen me your leader. Well, I have an important piece of news to give you. Dante

is dead. He has been dead for several centuries, and I think it is time
that we dropped the study of his *Inferno* and turned our attention to our
own." It was that way everywhere in the country, on all social levels. In
Chicago an immigrant worker walked up to her boss and demanded better toilet facilities with the statement: "Old America is gone. There is
new times." In middle-class New York, pretty young Frances Perkins
was reading the reform books the President was always recommending,
and vowing that "the pursuit of social justice would be my vocation."
In Baltimore a socialite horseman turned the city upside down with
full-page advertisements preaching Rauschenbusch's dictum that "the
greatest thing a millionaire can do is to make the rise of future millionaires impossible." Thirty-three Protestant denominations joined in a
Federal Council dedicated to Reform Darwinian Christianity, Walter
Lippmann proudly took over the presidency of the Harvard Socialist Club,
a muckraking novelist, Winston Churchill, led both Rex Beach and *The
Trail of the Lonesome Pine* on the best-seller lists, and Clarence Darrow
was invited to address the Ulysses S. Grant Chapter of the Daughters of
the American Revolution in Ashtabula, Ohio.

There was, said Theodore Roosevelt in the only understatement of his
entire career, "a condition of excitement and irritation in the public
mind. . . ."

Farewell to reform

John Chamberlain

And so we come to the end of the Progressive trail. What have
the years left with us? Their reverberations have bequeathed to us what
might be called, with proper obeisance to Lewis Mumford, a Little Golden
Day of general culture, with satire at its base. This culture has been the
more adventurous because of the spirit of general dissent and inquiry
that begot it. But since this book is concerned only with that culture
which, on the plane of ideas, has served as carrier of the notions shaping the direct development of the politics of the Progressive epoch, the
end-product of the Little Golden Day need not concern us here.

The results, or lack of results, of the Progressive years in government
and interrelated business are, however, our direct concern. There are
some—such as the good William Allen White, and Charles Edward Russell—who consider that American industry has been suffused with Pro-

gressive shibboleths; we have been saved, they aver, from a harsh industrial tyranny by the stirrings of the Rooseveltian and Wilsonian years.
This is not an opinion to be dismissed with a sneer. Al Smith's factory
legislation, the pure food laws, workmen's compensation, and so on,
have done some humanizing. The Morgan trick of taking in the public as
investors, the idea of which had a grand burgeoning after the success of
the government in floating the Liberty Loan bond issues, is beneficent in
one sense, although in a larger sense it is unfortunate, since it paralyzes
the will to radical action when radical action is needed. There have been
honest efforts directed toward instituting a humane science of industrial
management, notably in the Procter and Gamble Company, the Hart,
Schaffner and Marx Company, the Baltimore and Ohio railroad equipment shops, the manufacturing company of Henry Dennison of Fra-
mingham, Mass. Mr. E. A. Filene, given his way, could, no doubt, do
much to integrate the spirit of humane rationalism with the spirit of
business.

But the ghost of the Veblen who knew, better than Lippmann, the import of the phrase, "well-meaning but un-meaning," will not down; the
very nature of business, which is, fundamentally, based on the desire
for profits, works to undermine the advance guard of the Filenes and
the Dennisons. Faced with a loss, only the most Quixotic man of business can indulge in positive humanitarian tactics. Consciences may be
salved by the practice of hiring outside efficiency experts to do firing
and wage cutting, but the results are the same. Work may be "shared"
and staggered, but sharing on the basis of stationary or diminished total
wages per week does not increase purchasing power. The Progressive
business man, individually humane, is caught in a complicated net of
aggregate weave. He cannot cut clear by himself. In business, in time
of trouble, the most unscrupulous inevitably set the pace for the whole
machine, just as in good times the ones out for the immediate gain set
the pace.

As for Progressive government, the results of the three decades of strife
antecedent to 1919 are, perhaps, minimal. Oswald Garrison Villard
thinks we are no further along the road than we were in 1900. This, I
think, is susceptible of proof—and, to boot, we are on the wrong road. If
you think the tariff is at the bottom of our troubles, it is to be noted that
the tariff is still sky-high. But even if we had a low tariff, it is doubtful
that it could have stemmed the down-thrust of depression. The Under-
wood tariff of 1913 did not prevent us from limping industrially until
the War created a market for American goods. Free trade, in the long
run, cannot prevent a dynamic capitalistic industrial machine from glut-
ting markets as the upcurve of greed succeeds the downcurve of fear in
the psychological cycle that is the concomitant of the business cycle.

The pet political solutions of the Progressives, designed to make government more responsible to the will of the electorate, have notoriously been weak reeds. The initiative and the referendum have produced nothing. Women suffrage has only added, in direct proportion, to Republican and Democratic totals. Direct primaries have proved not even a palliative; they have worked against strong labor and independent party organization, which is the only hope of labor and the consumer in the political field. As Paul Douglas says, where parties are closed organizations, as in England, nominations are made by local nuclei of party workers who know what they want. If a group dislikes the candidates of existing party machines, the only recourse is to put a candidate of its own in the field. The direct primary seemingly weakens the necessity for this; it creates the illusion that an inert "people," spasmodically led, can be aroused to holding the machine politician in line by the threat that they may turn on him at the primary polls. The result is . . . the machine politician promises much, does little . . . and the people are let down. During a two, or four, or six, year period of office-holding, there is much time for an electorate to forget.

The popular election of Senators, instituted in 1913, has made very little actual difference. The real difference between the type of Senator that flourished in the days of the McKinley plutocracy and the type of the present is one of demagoguery; the modern Senator, representing the same interests as his legislature-elected predecessor, is compelled to be a master of the art of obfuscation. Senator Nelson Aldrich, in the 1890 dispensation, could afford to leave the obfuscation to his local manipulator, General Brayton, who kept the legislature in line while his master attended to more important business.

The real human gain of Woodrow Wilson's Administration was the domestication of the eight-hour day in many areas of industry, made possible by the Adamson Law rendering it compulsory on the railroads. The Federal Reserve system is, beyond doubt, better than the previous banking system. It is flexible, it is an instrument which, through its control of the rediscount rate, can take up the slack between productive activity, and speculation at any time *if it is properly run*. But, in setting down these gains, we have about exhausted the really important positive legislation of thirty years. The business cycle remains; until that is done away with, all legislation looking to the welfare of the common man must appear in the light of small, temporary oscillations along the course of a major graph.

This brings us to the definition of "reform," and its alternative, revolution. Now, revolution (change of structure and aims) inevitably carries with it connotations of untoward happenings, of barricades or whatever may be their twentieth-century equivalent, of whatever modern ingenuity can devise as substitute for the guillotine, of the reign of terror induced by the menace of counter-revolution. To Stuart Chase, it means a sudden sharp disruption of the distributive mechanism of an entire nation.

Personally, I experience none of the psychological thrill which hopes of "the revolution" send tingling through the born radical. I am as timorous in the face of physical violence as Mr. Bernard Shaw. Because of this fact, it may be that I am indulging in wishful thinking when I say that I am not persuaded that votes will not do. It seems to me that, in a nation of forty-eight organized State governments, with forty-eight militias, votes *must* do. I am mindful of the good old revolutionary axiom that no owning class ever gave up its property and preferred position without a struggle. Yet there are revolutions *and* revolutions; and there are ways *and* ways of confiscation, even in the face of the Fifth and Fourteenth Amendments. There is the revolution advocated (but not worked out in its implications) by Mr. Kenneth Burke—the revolution by indirection. An income of six per cent may be shaved to the vanishing point by a five per cent system of taxation, as will be necessary if the toll of technological unemployment in agriculture and industry grows. Such a system of taxation would sorely cripple the re-investment process— which, in turn, would help bring closer the day of total legal confiscation of productive private property (with the exception of small farm holdings). In the light of the possibilities which the Sixteenth (Income Tax) Amendment, one of the negative triumphs of the Progressive epoch, has opened up for bloodless revolution in this country, I affirm the hope, in bidding farewell to reform, that parliamentary processes will not fail in the interim leading up to the necessary class shifts in control.

But, one fancies the reader asking, are not parliamentary methods the very essence of reform? This depends upon the definition of the word. In the United States, "reform"—apart from the meaning pumped into it by the Anti-Saloon Leaguers and other specifically "moral" reformers, who are beyond the scope of this inquiry—has always had a "return" connotation. By "reform," a host of political leaders, Bryan, La Follette, Wilson, Theodore Roosevelt at times, and Franklin D. Roosevelt to-day, have hoped to "return" to the ways of their fathers—to the methods and possibilities of a more primitive capitalism. As Walter Lippmann remarked of the Wilson of *The New Freedom*, they have seen the laborer as a possible shopkeeper. That is why Progressivism and Liberalism in this country are, at the moment, preparing the ground for an American Fascism; they have been identified with the shopkeeper instincts of the common citizen, who is willing to make his trade with the "big fellow" if he can retain a privilege or two.

The curbing of the "money power," the abolition of "privilege," the opening up of opportunity by the Single Tax, the redemption of the promises of the New Freedom, all of these have been made the basis for a "return" demand—a demand for the evocation and reëstablishment of a vanished, and somehow more "moral" and "honest" *status quo*. And all economic reforms that have been undertaken in the spirit of Bryan, of La Follette, of Wilson, have worked in a way precisely against the grain of Progressive or neo-democratic hopes; instead of "freeing" the common man within the capitalistic system, these reforms have made the system, as a long-run proposition, more difficult of operation; and this, in turn, has reacted upon the common man as employee, as small bondholder, as savings-account depositor, as insurance-policy owner. The value of reforms, as I see it, is that they fail to achieve what they are sanguinely intended to achieve; and in so failing they help make the system which they are intended to patch up only the more unpatchable. In other words, every vote for reform, entered upon intelligently, is a Jesuitical vote for revolution. Conservatives like Nicholas Murray Butler know this; that is why they fear the growth of a bureaucracy intended to administer a "return"; that is why they fear the retention of the anti-trust acts.

Illustration is called for. Let us begin by taking the first of the "return" reforms that resulted from the agitation of the Farm Border: the Interstate Commerce Commission. This Commission was instituted at the repeated request of the shippers, who had their own capitalistic economic interest in getting the railroads "down." The Commission has had whatever real success it can claim because two wary, strongly entrenched economic classes have fought for its control. If the fight had been merely consumer versus exploiter, the latter would inevitably have won by superiority of pressure. As things have worked out, what with the development of motor transportation, the shipper has been able to bring pressure a little stronger than that of the railroad owners. I do not question the shipper's "right" to the victory; in fact, my sympathy is all with the shipper, since he has represented the underdog in the game of grab to which William Graham Sumner so strenuously objected. But—as a long-run proposition—the efforts of the shipper will be defeated, for, indirectly, they have worked to undermine the system of which the shipper is a part.

What is now left to the railroad capitalists after three or four decades of "reform" is a limited right to management, a limited right to profits. Under the present dispensation, as Walter J. Shepard has pointed out, the railroad shareholder (often synonymous with the shipper and the small business man, either directly or through the ownership of insurance policies) is reduced to the position of a mere investor in securities, indistinguishable from the bondholder, save that his right is contingent within limits instead of being fixed. Directors and managers, again as Professor Shepard says, function within the limits of a circumscribed plan that leaves little scope for initiative. Because of the partial control involved in the supervision of the railroads, the howl of "unfair" discrimination goes up. We are faced with either a general weakening of the railroads or the extension of control to bus lines, trucking companies and airplanes in the interests of "fairness" to all. Beyond this looms the control of electric power and of gasoline, or the substitutes for gasoline, inasmuch as they supply the dynamic food of the carriers. The result—a general limitation of profits, a cutting of dividends, less money to reinvest. The shipper will win—and lose. He will transport his goods the more cheaply, but cutthroat competition in his own field will inevitably work to squeeze out the weakling, and the investment structure open to the big fellow will be impaired by the very legislation he has brought into effect. A congealing capitalism, I suspect, is of no benefit, ultimately, to any capitalist, no matter what his immediate interest may be. It produces the racketeer, brought in to maintain the *status quo* against extension of competition. It limits the scope of possible profit; it thereby limits new enterprise. It creates business bureaucracy, which is more horrible to contemplate than political bureaucracy.

More illustration is called for. Let us take the second of the reforms that grew out of the agitation sired on the Farm Border—the anti-trust legislation. Under capitalism, we are damned if we accept this legislation, and damned if we don't. If we accept it, and endeavor to enforce it, the resources of business in a technological age are crippled. If we remove the restrictions, there is no assurance that open trustification will result in a benefit to labor and the consumer. In any case, the Sherman and the Clayton Acts have served only as a latent threat; they have notoriously failed to break up large units. Anti-trust legislation failed in all but name when the Northern Securities Company was ordered dissolved; it failed to halt the ingestion of the Tennessee Coal and Iron Company by United States Steel; it has failed to halt the inevitable push toward railroad consolidation; and it has failed, recently, to prevent radio trustification. The "genius" of the machine is clearly against anti-trust laws. . . .

The situation begs for a "demand" politics along socialist lines, with propaganda playing a prominent part in the necessary political organization. The "social planners," who are for a "planned society" under capitalism can help; but not in the way they think they can. If they succeed in embodying their proposals for a control and "management" of money, for a regulated investment, for publicity of business processes and account books (as William Z. Ripley advocates), for a supercabinet to correlate industry, something may be gained; but it will not be the gain along the "third road" that Mr. Chase expects. The gain will be—a further congealing of capitalism, a further check upon the system. Prosperity, it must not be forgotten, is a function of a rising market. Because the issue between preservation of individual profits and fulfillment of mass desires would not be clear, a national economic council under capitalism would tend to waver, depending upon the strength of relative pressures brought to bear on it. Thus such a council would do the work of the Rooseveltian and Wilsonian reforms; it would make the system upon which it is grafted so much the more unpredictable and unpatchable. Regulated investment, for example, would create more graft. At first it would make capital timid, conduce to hoarding, send money abroad. For, under regulation, withdrawal of capital would be as difficult as investment of capital; otherwise it would not be regulation. And who would be willing to tie up a fortune—unless that fortune is to be guaranteed by the government that ties it up, an intolerable situation for the tax payer? That is, who would be willing to tie up a fortune unless the men to be controlled are to do their own controlling? And if they are to do the controlling to make profits for themselves, what sort of social control would it be?

Buying into control would, as a political corollary, follow inevitably, just as buying into control of our political parties—even our Progressive political parties—has followed inevitably in a democracy. This would, I think, work to kill new enterprise—perhaps a desirable thing, but hardly contemplated by Mr. Chase in his prospectus for the Investment Board of his New Jerusalem. Inevitably the men whose money is tied up in a *status quo* would tend to cut off competition in the form of new industries that might threaten the income of their regulated capital. A Board with the power to control investment could, by easy alliance through politics with the top economic planning board, also control obsolescence. A new alloy—"lighter than aluminum and stronger than steel"—would find it hard sledding to get a chance from a Board whose money connections were with either aluminum or steel. A favored class would be created, a class interested in maintaining itself on a certain favored plane. The Rockefellers and the Carnegies of the future would find themselves faced by an intrenched priesthood of investors.

Here Mr. Chase, if he is to run true to form, would step in to reply to Mr. Redbonnet. The system could not be humanly disastrous, he would say, because under machine technology and mass production, the masses must be paid sufficient money to buy back the goods they turn out. A *status quo* would have a proprietary interest in paying high wages and in spending all high salaries and incomes. This sounds very enticing. But is it psychologically sound? Does it take into consideration the emulative factor? A group of favored spenders, an inner circle of Lorenzos, gorgeous in their open-handed welcome to the arts, would be the object of the invidious comparison which Veblen has so urbanely satirized in *The Theory of the Leisure Class.* The worker, naturally, would tend to save some of his high wages, that he might the better seize the elusive opportunity to buy his way into the favored group. The hierarchy of owners, human nature being what it is, would let him in, increasing the capitalization of existing industries in order that more money might be made to spend. Short of police-dictated consumption to infinity, the system, running on spending power, would thus be thrown out of kilter, its life-blood partially withdrawn. Inflation would be the remedy, as now. And inflation is the very dislocation that Mr. Chase wants, really, to avoid. It fails to consider the sections of society that have made no provision for it in their calculations.

So planned capitalism, being a contradiction in terms, seems no permanent way out. Mr. Chase is valuable only insofar as his efforts to point out the desirability of a planned society tend to show up the inner inconsistencies of capitalism. Political organization looking towards a socialist America, or an "industrial democracy," as Oscar Ameringer, with his sound instinct for the telling Americanism, prefers to call it, is the *sine qua non* of any alternative to the present chaotic order. This does not mean a reliance upon strict Marxist doctrine; for, as Mr. Soule has so cogently pointed out in his analysis of theories of social revolution, the group of men whom the Marxians are in the habit of regarding as the "industrial proletariat" (those who work with their hands and receive wages) is tending to decrease. The advance of industrial technique means more and more products turned out with less and less physical labor. Workers in factories, mills, railroads and mines fail to keep pace with the increase in population, or even decrease in relation to a static population. And at the same time sales and office forces grow, or did grow before 1930. As direct labor goes down, overhead rises. In good times, amusement occupations increase. And the result is that a group of human material which is not good "revolutionary" material in the original Marxist sense tends to grow up at the base of society. The increase in unemployment, too, is not material for the classic Marxist revolution. Marx expected as little from the "rotting" masses of the unemployed as he did from employees with a petty bourgeois psychology. The unemployed man is usually a potential scab. And a dole buys him.

Mr. Soule regards all this as very damaging to the Marxian hopes—that is, unless a war or a catastrophe occurs which would give a small determined inner circle the opportunity which Lenin and Trotsky had in Russia. But, in a larger sense, is it as damaging as he thinks? Does it not call for a redefinition of the phrases of the class struggle, a reapplication of Marxian dogma to American conditions? If Marx is any good, he can stand the tampering. If capitalism cannot get back to its pre-1915 basis on a world stage (and who believes that it can?), is not the field open in America for a decade of reapplication? A *milieu*, a climate of opinion, is being created. Literature, after a decade of pure individualism split off from any "social consciousness," is returning to its function of 1902–17, and with its return, the whole general field of pamphleteering and propaganda will be re-opened to discussion of these matters and possibly advanced beyond the state of 1902–17.

Somewhere, within the jostling alignment of the disaffected of America, whether within the ranks of the striking farmers, the forces of Foster or Thomas, or the 11,000,000 unemployed who have made experiments with councils of their own, there is the nucleus of an American party which will include not only the traditional "industrial proletariat," which tends to diminish, but the groups which Mr. Soule has singled out for mention, and the groups which have, traditionally, followed the star of Bryanism. The course of the present depression will determine the chances for the immediate cohesion and the rise of this party. The danger is, of course, that the American set-up will tend to force a division of the disaffected into the Fascist and socialist camps, with Ku Kluxism, American Legion "buddy" patriotism, and bloody intolerance congregating under the device of the fasces. I venture no prophecies here, but fear the worst.

However, any development of American radicalism, whether Red or Black, to impressive proportions must depend on the course of the depression. If capitalism survives the crisis and moves on toward another upgrade, the coming to grips will be postponed. You cannot talk to a man with hopes. Socialism, as W. E. Woodward says, is based on pessimism; it assumes that human nature cannot change. It assumes, too, that man cannot work the complicated credit structure he has reared without getting fingers caught in the machinery. It is a last-ditch refuge, stormed by hungry men who prefer to live on terms of economic equity rather than starve on terms of hopes for economic superiority. Its mass appeal, as distinct from its individual appeal, like the appeal of all other political systems, is a belly appeal.

But the next half-century should witness the convergence of forces. There may be, as the economic parrot says, new markets to be uncovered, new wants to be exploited, new famines to create new farmer-purchasing power, even new sources of gold.

But . . . there is Russia. The hopes for eternal capitalism are all predicated on the course of events in the Soviet Union. What will be the rôle of Russia in the forthcoming years? A nation whose industries have no six per cents to pay to investors will, inevitably, become a favored nation in some quarters; it can undersell. And underselling that you don't just happen to like is dumping. The menace of Russian dumping will lead to the adoption of the quota system of imports and exports in many countries. Is this propitious for capitalist expansion?

No, however we look at it, eventual constriction stares us in the face. And that is why a contemplation of "reform" in America—the reform that has talked, endlessly, about going back to the primitive capitalism of our fathers while an economic revolution has been beating about our ears—is productive of no further hopes in its tenets. The situation, looked upon with intelligence and considered as a long-range proposition, can lead to but one of two personal conclusions: it can make one either a cynic or a revolutionist. Even if an American Fascist régime intervenes in the future, one, two or ten years from now, it can only postpone the inevitable day when one must decamp into cynicism, facing endless trouble, with the assurance that we are born to trouble, or concur. For Fascism implies the development of the labor-syndicate idea; and it would be only a question of opportunity before the syndicates attempted their own march to power.

SUGGESTIONS FOR FURTHER READING

Much of the writing on American History in the Twentieth Century has been influenced by the progressive movement. Beard and Parrington, of course, felt the impact directly while later writers like Eric Goldman in *Rendezvous With Destiny* (New York, 1952) are also sympathetic to the progressive point of view. Richard Hofstadter in the *Age of Reform* (New York, 1955) tried to interpret the impulse behind the movement in terms of a "status revolution" and in so doing takes a more objective look at the progressives. Samuel P. Hays in his book, *The Response to Industrialism* (Chicago, 1957) attempts to get outside the progressive framework; adjustment rather than conflict is the key to his interpretation. Robert Wiebe in *Businessmen and Reform: A Study of the Progressive Movement* (Cambridge, 1962) shows that many businessmen were participants in the movement and not opponents. George E. Mowry, *The Era of Theodore Roosevelt, 1900–1912* (New York, 1958) and Arthur S. Link, *Woodrow Wilson and the Progressive Era, 1910–1917* (New York, 1954) are balanced attempts that fit the two major progressive politicians into the larger progressive movement and in the process reduce some of the conflict that earlier writers emphasized.

VIII
THE ★
NEW ★
DEAL ★

The depression following the stock market crash in the fall of 1929 revealed important weaknesses in the American economic system, weaknesses that had not been corrected by earlier reforms of the Populists and progressives, weaknesses only suspected by a few during the 1920's. Hungry men and women fought over garbage dumped in the street. Farmers, forced to burn their corn for fuel, watched sullenly as their creditors came to evict them from their farms, and some of them talked of revolution. A group of unemployed Army veterans marched on Washington in the summer of 1932 to demand immediate payment of their bonus, only to be driven out of town by troops and tanks and tear gas.

"Only a foolish optimist can deny the dark realities of the moment," declared the newly elected president of the United States, Franklin Delano Roosevelt, in his inaugural address. Roosevelt went on to announce that he interpreted his victory in the elections of the previous November as a "mandate" for "direct, vigorous action" under active leadership. This leadership he promised to give.

The result was the New Deal, a period of intensive legislative activity lasting roughly from 1933 to 1938. Virtually no part of the economy failed to feel the effects of the New Deal Legislation. The unemployed received aid and work; farmers were helped with measures to cut production and support prices; working people organized unions under the protection of federal law. The banks and the stock exchange came under strict government supervision and the government used its money to institute flood control, rural electrification, and other forms of natural resource conservation.

The goals of the New Deal legislation, it has been said, were the Three R's: Relief, Recovery, and Reform. Some opponents insisted that a fourth "R" be added: Revolution. Roosevelt, these critics charged, had brought about a radical break with the traditions of the American past; some said that he had turned the country toward socialism. Others, however, argued that the New Deal was in reality conservative, that the legislation passed in the early thirties was really designed to conserve the American system. The New Deal was neither radical in intent nor in method, having borrowed its techniques, its personnel, and its goals from a long tradition of American reform.

In the first selection, Frank Freidel, the biographer of Franklin Roosevelt, views the New Deal in historical perspective, and decides that it borrowed much from the progressive era. In total, Freidel concludes, the New Deal represents a conservative solution to the problems of the thirties. Some businessmen, of course, thought that Roosevelt was endangering the American way of life and leading the country toward socialism, but, Freidel argues, most of the businessman's problems were of his own making; Roosevelt certainly preferred to be, and usually was, conciliatory rather than hostile toward the business community. To Freidel the fact that in recent years the opposition party as well as the business community have accepted most of the New Deal measures proves that the Roosevelt reforms were in the tradition of the American consensus.

Carl Degler, like Freidel, views the New Deal sympathetically, but he finds Roosevelt's reforms revolutionary. In fact he sees a fundamental political reorientation because of the depression and the New Deal. While Freidel finds continuity and a conservative consensus, Degler sees a sharp break with the past and a radical consensus. Edgar Robinson, who is very critical of Roosevelt and the New Deal, agrees with Degler that the New Deal was revolutionary; for him the altered nature and role of the federal government represent a distinct departure from previous American tradition. As a result there was harsh and bitter conflict between Roosevelt and the business community.

The far-reaching effects of New Deal legislation cannot

be denied. But how is this legislation to be evaluated? Did it mark a radical change in American society? Did the problems of the depression bring about a revolutionary break with the past? Or was the New Deal really the culmination of a reform movement going as far back as the immediate post-Civil War period?

By placing the problems in this way the historian attempts to put the New Deal in the context of American reform. Yet even if one accepts the contention of those who see the New Deal as marking a sharp break with the past, the question remains: How fundamental were the changes brought about by the New Deal? Did the reforms usher in a new system or did they merely serve to adapt the old system to new conditions? In short, were the reforms essentially conservative or were they revolutionary?

The new deal:

conservative

reform

movement

Frank Freidel

In less than a generation, the New Deal has passed into both popular legend and serious history. The exigencies of American politics long
demanded that its partisans and opponents paint a picture of it either
in the most glamorous whites or sinister blacks. Long after the New Deal
was over, politicians of both major parties tried at each election to reap a
harvest of votes from its issues.

Gradually a new generation of voters has risen which does not remember the New Deal and takes for granted the changes that it wrought.
Gradually too, politicians have had to recognize that the nation faces
new, quite different problems since the second World War, and that campaigning on the New Deal has become as outmoded as did the "bloody
shirt" issue as decades passed after the Civil War. At the same time,
most of the important manuscript collections relating to the New Deal
have been opened to scholars so rapidly that careful historical research
has been possible decades sooner than was true for earlier periods of
United States history. (The Franklin D. Roosevelt papers and the Abraham Lincoln papers became available for research at about the same
time, just after the second World War.)

It has been the task of the historians not only to analyze heretofore
hidden aspects of the New Deal on the basis of the manuscripts, but also
to remind readers of what was once commonplace and is now widely forgotten. A new generation has no firsthand experience of the depths of
despair into which the depression had thrust the nation, and the excitement and eagerness with which people greeted the new program. Critics
not only have denied that anything constructive could have come from
the New Deal but they have even succeeded in creating the impression
in the prosperous years since 1945 that the depression really did not
amount to much. How bad it was is worth remembering, since this is a
means of gauging the enormous pressure for change.

Estimates of the number of unemployed ranged up to thirteen million
out of a labor force of fifty-two million, which would mean that one

From *The New Deal in Historical Perspective*, Service Center #25, by Frank Freidel
(Washington, D.C., 1959) pp. 1–20. Reprinted by permission of the American Historical Association.

344

wage-earner out of four was without means of support for himself or his family. Yet of these thirteen million unemployed, only about a quarter were receiving any kind of assistance. States and municipalities were running out of relief funds; private agencies were long since at the end of their resources. And those who were receiving aid often obtained only a pittance. The Toledo commissary could allow for relief only 2.14 cents per person per meal, and the Red Cross in southern Illinois in 1931 was able to provide families with only seventy-five cents a week for food. It was in this crisis that one of the most flamboyant members of the Hoover administration suggested a means of providing sustenance for the unemployed: restaurants should dump left-overs and plate scrapings into special sanitary cans to be given to worthy unemployed people willing to work for the food. It was a superfluous suggestion, for in 1932 an observer in Chicago reported:

Around the truck which was unloading garbage and other refuse were about thirty-five men, women, and children. As soon as the truck pulled away from the pile, all of them started digging with sticks, some with their hands, grabbing bits of food and vegetables.

The employed in some instances were not a great deal better off. In December 1932 wages in a wide range of industries from textiles to iron and steel, averaged from a low of 20 cents to a high of only 30 cents an hour. A quarter of the women working in Chicago were receiving less than 10 cents an hour. In farming areas, conditions were equally grim. In bitter weather on the Great Plains, travelers occasionally encountered a light blue haze that smelled like roasting coffee. The "old corn" held over from the crop of a year earlier would sell for only $1.40 per ton, while coal cost $4 per ton, so many farmers burned corn to keep warm. When Aubrey Williams went into farm cellars in the Dakotas in the early spring of 1933 farm wives showed him shelves and shelves of jars for fruits and vegetables—but they were all empty. Even farmers who could avoid hunger had trouble meeting payments on their mortgages. As a result a fourth of all farmers in the United States lost their farms during these years.

Despairing people in these pre-New Deal years feared President Herbert Hoover had forgotten them or did not recognize the seriousness of their plight. As a matter of fact he had, more than any other depression president in American history, taken steps to try to bring recovery. But he had functioned largely through giving aid at the top to prevent the further collapse of banks and industries, and the concentric rings of further collapses and unemployment which would then ensue. Also he had continued to pin his faith upon voluntary action. He felt that too great federal intervention would undermine the self-reliance, destroy the "rugged individualism" of the American people, and that it would create federal centralization, thus paving the way for socialism.

President Hoover was consistent in his thinking, and he was humane. But it would have been hard to explain to people like those grubbing on the Chicago garbage heap, why, when the Reconstruction Finance Corporation was loaning $90,000,000 to a single Chicago bank, the President would veto a bill to provide federal relief for the unemployed, asserting, "never before has so dangerous a suggestion been seriously made in this country." It was not until June 1932 that he approved a measure permitting the RFC to loan $300,000,000 for relief purposes.

It seems shocking in retrospect that such conditions should have existed in this country, and that any president of either major party should so long have refused to approve federal funds to alleviate them. It adds to the shock when one notes that many public figures of the period were well to the right of the President—for instance, Secretary of the Treasury Andrew Mellon—and that almost no one who was likely to be in a position to act, including Governor Roosevelt of New York, was ready at that time to go very far to the left of Hoover.

Roosevelt, who was perhaps the most advanced of the forty-eight governors in developing a program to meet the depression, had shown little faith in public works spending. When he had established the first state relief agency in the United States in the fall of 1931, he had tried to finance it through higher taxes, and only later, reluctantly, abandoned the pay-as-you-go basis. He was, and he always remained, a staunch believer in a balanced budget. He was never more sincere than when, during the campaign of 1932, he accused the Hoover administration of having run up a deficit of three and three-quarters billions of dollars in the previous two years. This, he charged, was "the most reckless and extravagant past that I have been able to discover in the statistical record of any peacetime Government anywhere, any time."

Governor Roosevelt's own cautious record did not exempt him from attack. In April 1932, seeking the presidential nomination, he proclaimed himself the champion of the "forgotten man," and talked vaguely about raising the purchasing power of the masses, in part through directing Reconstruction Finance Corporation loans their way. This little was sufficient to lead many political leaders and publicists, including his Democratic rival, Al Smith, to accuse Roosevelt of being a demagogue, ready to set class against class.

Smith and most other public figures, including Roosevelt, favored public works programs. A few men like Senators Robert F. Wagner of New York and Robert M. La Follette of Wisconsin visualized really large-scale spending on public construction, but most leaders also wanted to accompany the spending with very high taxes which would have been deflationary and thus have defeated the program. None of the important political leaders, and none of the economists who had access to them, seemed as yet to visualize the decisive intervention of the government into the economy of the sort that is considered commonplace today. The term "built-in stabilizers" had yet to be coined.

The fact was that Roosevelt and most of his contemporaries, who like him were products of the Progressive Era, were basically conservative men who unquestioningly believed in the American free enterprise system. On the whole, they were suspicious of strong government, and would indulge in it only as a last resort to try to save the system. This was their limitation in trying to bring about economic recovery. On the other hand, part of their Progressive legacy was also a humanitarian belief in social justice. This belief would lead them to espouse reforms to improve the lot of the common man, even though those reforms might also take them in the direction of additional government regulation. Roosevelt as governor had repeatedly demonstrated this inconsistency in his public statements and recommendations. He had ardently endorsed states rights and small government in a truly Jeffersonian way. Then in quite contrary fashion (but still in keeping with Jeffersonian spirit applied to twentieth-century society) he had pointed out one or another area, such as old age security, in which he believed the government must intervene to protect the individual.

At this time, what distinguished Governor Roosevelt from his fellows were two remarkable characteristics. The first was his brilliant political skill, which won to him an overwhelming proportion of the Democratic politicians and the general public. The second was his willingness to experiment, to try one or another improvisation to stop the slow economic drift downward toward ruin. During the campaign of 1932, many a man who had observed Roosevelt felt as did Harry Hopkins that he would make a better president than Hoover, "chiefly because he is not afraid of a new idea."

Roosevelt's sublime self-confidence and his willingness to try new expedients stood him in good stead when he took over the presidency. On that grim March day in 1933 when he took his oath of office, the American economic system was half-paralyzed. Many of the banks were closed; the remainder he quickly shut down through presidential proclamation. Industrial production was down to 56 per cent of the 1923–25 level. Yet somehow, Roosevelt's self-confidence was infectious. People were ready to believe, to follow, when he said in words that were not particularly new, "The only thing we have to fear is fear itself." He offered "leadership of frankness and vigor," and almost the whole of the American public and press—even papers like the Chicago *Tribune* which soon became bitter critics—for the moment accepted that leadership with enthusiasm.

For a short period of time, about one hundred days, Roosevelt had behind him such overwhelming public support that he was able to push through Congress a wide array of legislation which in total established the New Deal. It came in helter-skelter fashion and seemed to go in all directions, even at times directions that conflicted with each other. There was mildly corrective legislation to get the banks open again, a slashing of government costs to balance the budget, legalization of 3.2 beer, establishment of the Civilian Conservation Corps, of the Tennessee Valley Authority, and of a wide variety of other agencies in the areas of relief, reform, and, above all in those first months, of recovery.

What pattern emerged in all of this legislation? How sharply did it break with earlier American political traditions? The answer was that it represented Roosevelt's efforts to be president to all the American people, to present something to every group in need. And it was based squarely on American objectives and experience in the Progressive Era and during the first World War. It went beyond the Hoover program in that while the word "voluntary" remained in many of the laws, they now had behind them the force of the government or at least strong economic incentives.

It has been forgotten how basically conservative Roosevelt's attitudes remained during the early period of the New Deal. He had closed the banks, but reopened them with relatively little change. Indeed, the emergency banking measure had been drafted by Hoover's Treasury officials. What banking reform there was came later. His slashing of the regular government costs was something he had promised during his campaign, and in which he sincerely believed and continued to believe. He kept the regular budget of the government low until the late thirties. While he spent billions through the parallel emergency budget, he did that reluctantly, and only because he felt it was necessary to keep people from starving. He was proud that he was keeping the credit of the government good, and never ceased to look forward to the day when he could balance the budget. For the first several years of the New Deal he consulted frequently with Wall Streeters and other economic conservatives. His first Director of the Budget, Lewis Douglas, parted ways with him, but late in 1934 was exhorting: "I hope, and hope most fervently, that you will evidence a real determination to bring the budget into actual balance, for upon this, I think, hangs not only your place in history but conceivably the immediate fate of western civilization." (Douglas to FDR, November 28, 1934)

Remarks like this struck home with Roosevelt. Douglas's successors as Director of the Budget held much the same views, and Henry Morgenthau, Jr., who became Secretary of the Treasury at the beginning of 1934, never failed to prod Roosevelt to slash governmental expenditures.

We should add parenthetically that Roosevelt always keenly resented the untrue newspaper stories that his parents had been unwilling to entrust him with money. As a matter of fact he was personally so thrifty when he was in the White House that he used to send away for bargain mail-order shirts, and when he wished summer suits, switched from an expensive New York tailor to a cheaper one in Washington. This he did despite the warning of the New York tailor that he might thus lose his standing as one of the nation's best-dressed men.

Financial caution in governmental affairs rather typifies Roosevelt's economic thinking throughout the entire New Deal. He was ready to go much further than Hoover in construction of public works, but he preferred the kind which would pay for themselves, and did not think there were many possibilities for them in the country. His estimate before he became president was only one billion dollars worth. In 1934, he once proposed that the government buy the buildings of foundered banks throughout the nation and use them for post-offices rather than to construct new buildings. This is how far he was from visualizing huge public works expenditures as a means of boosting the country out of the depression. His course in this area was the middle road. He wished to bring about recovery without upsetting the budget any further than absolutely necessary. He did not launch the nation on a program of deliberate deficit financing.

When Roosevelt explained his program in a fireside chat at the end of July 1933, he declared:

"It may seem inconsistent for a government to cut down its regular expenses and at the same time to borrow and to spend billions for an emergency. But it is not inconsistent because a large portion of the emergency money has been paid out in the form of sound loans . . . ; and to cover the rest . . . we have imposed taxes. . . .

"So you will see that we have kept our credit good. We have built a granite foundation in a period of confusion."

It followed from this that aside from limited public works expenditures, Roosevelt wanted a recovery program which would not be a drain on governmental finances. Neither the Agricultural Adjustment Administration nor the National Recovery Administration were. He had promised in the major farm speech of his 1932 campaign that his plan for agricultural relief would be self-financing; this was achieved through the processing tax on certain farm products. The NRA involved no governmental expenditures except for administration.

Both of these programs reflected not the progressivism of the first years of the century, but the means through which Progressives had regulated production during the first World War. This had meant regulation which would as far as possible protect both producers and consumers, both employers and employees. Here the parallel was direct. The rest of Roosevelt's program did not parallel the Progressives' wartime experience, for during the war, in terms of production regulation had meant channeling both factories and farms into the maximum output of what was needed to win the war. Now the problem in the thirties was one of reducing output in most areas rather than raising it, and of getting prices back up rather than trying to hold them down.

Certainly the nation badly needed this sort of a program in 1933. The products of the fields and mines and of highly competitive consumers' goods industries like textiles were being sold so cheaply that producers and their employees alike were close to starvation. The overproduction was also wasteful of natural resources. In an oilfield near Houston, one grocer advertised when 3.2 beer first became legal that he would exchange one bottle of beer for one barrel of oil. They were worth about the same. In other heavy industries like automobiles or farm machinery, production had been cut drastically while prices remained high. One need was to bring prices throughout industry and agriculture into a more equitable relationship with each other, and with the debt structure.

The NRA scheme in theory would help do this. Its antecedents were in the regulatory War Industries Board of the first World War, and indeed it was run by some of the same men. The War Industries Board had functioned through industrial committees; in the twenties these committees had evolved into self-regulatory trade associations. Unfortunately, as Roosevelt had found when he headed the association created to discipline one of the largest and most chaotic of industries, the American Construction Council, self-regulation without the force of law behind it, had a tendency to break down. When the depression had hit, some businessmen themselves had advocated the NRA scheme, but Hoover would have none of it. Roosevelt was receptive.

The theory was that committees in a few major fields like steel, textiles, bituminous coal and the like, would draw up codes of fair practice for the industry. These would not only stabilize the price structure, but also protect the wages and working conditions of labor. Even consumers would benefit, presumably through receiving more wages or profits, and thus enjoying larger purchasing power with which to buy goods at somewhat higher prices.

In practice, the NRA program went awry. Too many committees drew up too many codes embodying many sorts of unenforceable provisions. There was a code even for the mopstick industry. What was more important, some manufacturers rushed to turn out quantities of goods at the old wage and raw material level before the code went into effect, hoping then to sell these goods at new higher prices. Consequently during the summer of 1933 there was a short NRA boom when industrial production jumped to 101 per cent of the 1923–25 level, and wholesale prices rose from an index figure of 60.2 in March to 71.2 by October. The crop reduction program of the AAA led to a corresponding rise in agricultural prices.

Had consumers at the same time enjoyed a correspondingly higher purchasing power, the recovery scheme might well have worked. Some of its designers had visualized pouring the additional dollars into consumers' pockets through a heavy public works spending program. Indeed the bill which created the NRA also set up a Public Works Administration with $3,300,000,000 to spend. This money could have been poured here and there into the economy where it was most needed to "prime the pump." But Roosevelt and his most influential advisers did not want to give such an enormous spending power to the administrator of the NRA, nor had they really accepted the deficit spending school of thought. Hence while some of the money being spent by the New Deal went for immediate relief of one form or another, it went to people so close to starvation that they were forced to spend what they received on bare necessities. This was of little aid in priming the pump. The public works fund, which could have served that purpose, went to that sturdy old Progressive, "Honest Harold" Ickes. He slowly went about the process of allocating it in such a way that the government and the public would get a return of one hundred cents (or preferably more) on every dollar spent. Raymond Moley has suggested that if only the cautious Ickes had headed the NRA and the impetuous Johnson the Public Works Administration the scheme might have worked.

Without a huge transfusion of dollars into the economy, the industrial and agricultural recovery programs sagged in the fall of 1933. Roosevelt turned to currency manipulation to try to get prices up. He explained to a critical Congressman, "I have always favored sound money, and do now, but it is 'too darned sound' when it takes so much of farm products to buy a dollar." Roosevelt also accepted a makeshift work relief program, the Civil Works Administration, to carry the destitute through the winter.

Already the New Deal honeymoon was over, and in 1934 and 1935 a sharp political struggle between Roosevelt and the right began to take form. To conservatives, Roosevelt was shattering the constitution with his economic legislation. Al Smith was attacking the devalued currency as "baloney dollars," and was writing articles with such titles as "Is the Constitution Still There?" and "Does the Star-Spangled Banner Still Wave?" Former President Hoover published his powerful jeremiad, *The Challenge to Liberty*.

Many businessmen complained against the NRA restrictions, the favoritism allegedly being shown to organized labor, and the higher taxes. Although some of them had advocated the NRA, the significant fact was that the thinking of most businessmen seems to have remained about what it had been in the 1920's. They were eager for aid from the government, as long as it involved no obligations on their part or restrictions against them. They wanted a government which could protect their domestic markets with a high tariff wall, and at the same time seek out foreign markets for them, a court system which could discipline organized labor with injunctions, and a tax structure which (as under Secretary of the Treasury Mellon) would take no enormous bite of large profits, and yet retain disciplinary levies on the lower-middle income groups. All these policies they could understand and condone. The New Deal, which would confer other benefits upon them, but require corresponding obligations, they could not.

This hostile thinking which began to develop among the business community was sincere. Businessmen genuinely believed that under the New Deal program too large a share of their income had to go to organized labor, and too much to the government. They freely predicted federal bankruptcy as the deficit began to mount. If they had capital to commit, they refused to expend it on new plants and facilities (except for some introduction of labor-saving machinery). They were too unsure of the future, they complained, because they could not tell what that man in the White House might propose next. Business needed a "breathing spell," Roy Howard wrote Roosevelt, and the President promised one. Nevertheless, the legislative requests continued unabated.

All this, important though it is in delineating the ideology of businessmen, is not the whole story. The fact is that during the long bleak years after October 1929 they had slipped into a depression way of thinking. They regarded American industry as being over-built; they looked upon the American market as being permanently contracted. By 1937 when industrial production and stock dividends were up to within ten percent of the 1929 peak, capital expenditures continued to drag along the depression floor. Industrialists did not engage in the large-scale spending for expansion which has been a significant factor in the boom since 1945. As late as 1940 to 1941, many of them were loathe to take the large defense orders which required construction of new plants. Unquestionably the pessimism of businessmen during the thirties, whether or not linked to their hatred of Roosevelt and fear of the New Deal, was as significant a factor in perpetuating the depression, as their optimism since the war has been in perpetuating the boom.

The paradox is that some of the New Deal measures against which the businessmen fought helped introduce into the economy some of the stabilizers which today help give businessmen confidence in the continuation of prosperity. These came despite, not because of, the businessmen. Roosevelt long continued to try to co-operate with the leaders of industry and banking. Their anger toward him, and frequently-expressed statements that he had betrayed his class, at times bewildered and even upset him. For the most part he laughed them off. He hung in his bedroom a favorite cartoon. It showed a little girl at the door of a fine suburban home, apparently tattling to her mother, "Johnny wrote a dirty word on the sidewalk." And the word, of course, was "Roosevelt."

To some of his old friends who complained to him, he would reply with patience and humor. Forever he was trying to point out to them the human side of the problem of the depression. Perhaps the best illustration is a witty interchange with a famous doctor for whom he had deep affection. The doctor wired him in March 1935:

"Pediatricians have long been perplexed by difficulty of weaning infant from breast or bottle to teaspoon or cup. The shift often establishes permanent neurosis in subsequent adult. According to report in evening paper twenty-two million citizen infants now hang on federal breasts. Can you wean them doctor and prevent national neurosis?"

Roosevelt promptly replied:

"As a young interne you doubtless realize that the interesting transitional process, which you describe in your telegram, presupposes that the bottle, teaspoon, or cup is not empty. Such vehicles of feeding, if empty produce flatulence and the patient dies from a lack of nutrition.

"The next question on your examination paper is, therefore, the following:

"Assuming that the transitional period has arrived, where is the Doctor to get the food from to put in the new container?"

As time went on, and the attacks became virulent from some quarters, at times even passing the bounds of decency, Roosevelt struck back vigorously. During his campaign in 1936 he excoriated the "economic royalists." When he wound up the campaign in Madison Square Garden, he declared:

"We had to struggle with the old enemies of peace—business and financial monopoly, speculation, reckless banking, class antagonism, sectionalism, war profiteering. They had begun to consider the Government of the United States as a mere appendage to their own affairs. And we know now that Government by organized money is just as dangerous as Government by organized mob.

"Never before in all our history have these forces been so united against one candidate as they stand today. They are unanimous in their hate for me—and I welcome their hatred."

To these sharp words Roosevelt had come from his position early in the New Deal as the impartial arbiter of American economic forces. He had come to them less because of what he considered as betrayal from the right than through pressure from the left. How had this pressure applied between 1934 and the campaign of 1936?

Back in 1934, while the economic temperature chart of the near frozen depression victim had fluctuated up and down, still dangerously below normal, the dispossessed millions began to look at the New Deal with despair or even disillusion. Those workers going on strike to obtain the twenty-five or thirty-five cents an hour minimum wage or the collective bargaining privileges promised by the NRA began to wisecrack that NRA stood for the National Run-Around. Some of them and of the unemployed millions in northern cities still dependent upon meager relief handouts, began to listen to the stirring radio addresses of Father Charles Coughlin. Old people began to pay five cents a week dues to Dr. Francis Townsend's clubs, which promised them fantastically large benefits. Throughout the South (and even in parts of the North) the dispossessed small farmers listened with enthusiasm to the exhortations of the Louisiana Kingfish, Huey Long, that he would share the wealth to make every man a king.

Many Democratic politicians were surprisingly oblivious to these rumblings and mutterings. Much of the private conversation of men like Vice President John Nance Garner sounded like the public demands of the Liberty Leaguers: cut relief and balance the budget. Garner, who spent the 1934 campaign hunting and fishing in Texas, predicted the usual mid-term loss of a few congressional seats back to the Republicans. Instead the Democrats picked up a startling number of new seats in both houses of Congress. The dispossessed had continued to vote with the Democratic party—but perhaps because there was no alternative but the Republicans who offered only retrenchment. Charles Beard commented that the 1934 election was "thunder on the left."

President Roosevelt, who was brilliantly sensitive to political forces, sensed fully the threat from the left. At the beginning of that crisis year 1935 he proposed in his annual message to Congress the enactment of a program to reinforce "the security of the men, women, and children of the nation" in their livelihood, to protect them against the major hazards and vicissitudes of life, and to enable them to obtain decent homes. In this increased emphasis upon security and reform, Professor Basil Rauch sees the beginnings of a second New Deal.

Certainly the pattern as it emerged in the next year was a brilliant one. Roosevelt neutralized Huey Long with the "soak the rich" tax, the "holding company death sentence," and with various measures directly of benefit to the poorer farmers of the South. Before an assassin's bullet felled Long, his political strength was already undercut. Similarly Roosevelt undermined the Townsend movement by pressing passage of the Social Security Act, which provided at least small benefits for the aged, at the same time that a congressional investigation disclosed how men around Townsend were fattening themselves on the nickels of millions of the aged. As for Father Coughlin, the Treasury announced that money from his coffers had gone into silver speculation at a time he had been loudly advocating that the government buy more silver at higher prices. More important, Coughlin had less appeal to employed workers after the new National Labor Relations Act raised a benign federal umbrella over collective bargaining. For the unemployed, a huge and substantial work relief program, the Works Progress Administration, came into existence.

Partly all this involved incisive political counterthrusts; partly it was a program Roosevelt had favored anyway. In any event, combined with Roosevelt's direct and effective appeal in radio fireside chats, it caused the dispossessed to look to him rather than to demagogues as their champion. Millions of them or their relations received some direct aid from the New Deal, whether a small crop payment or a WPA check. Millions more received wage boosts for which they were more grateful to Roosevelt than to their employers. Others through New Deal mortgage legislation had held onto their farms or homes. All these people, benefitting directly or indirectly, looked to Roosevelt as the source of their improved economic condition, and they were ready to vote accordingly. Roosevelt, who had been nominated in 1932 as the candidate of the South and the West, the champion of the farmer and the middle-class "forgotten man," after 1936 became increasingly the leader of the urban masses and the beneficiary of the growing power of organized labor.

What happened seems sharper and clearer in retrospect than it did at the time. Secretary Ickes, recording repeatedly in his diary during the early months of 1935 that the President was losing his grip, was echoing what many New Dealers and part of the public felt. They did not see a sharp shift into a second New Deal, and that is understandable. Roosevelt ever since he had become president had been talking about reform and from time to time recommending reform measures to Congress. He seems to have thought at the outset in two categories, about immediate or short-range emergency recovery measures to bring about a quick economic upswing, and also in terms of long-range reform legislation to make a recurrence of the depression less likely. Some of these reform measures like TVA had been ready for immediate enactment; others, like a revision of banking legislation and the social security legislation, he had planned from the beginning but were several years in the making. Frances Perkins has vividly described in her memoirs the lengthy task she and her associates undertook of drafting and selling to Congress and the public what became the Social Security Act of 1935.

Then Roosevelt had to face the additional factor that the emergency legislation had not succeeded in bringing rapid recovery. He had to think in terms of more permanent legislation with which to aim toward the same objectives. That meant he ceased trying to save money with a temporary program of cheaper direct relief, and switched instead to work relief (in which he had always believed) to try to stop some of the moral and physical erosion of the unfortunates who had been without employment for years.

In part the Supreme Court forced the recasting of some of his legislation. It gave a mercy killing in effect to the rickety, unwieldy NRA code structure when it handed down the Schechter or "sick chicken" decision of May 1935. On the whole the NRA had been unworkable, but it had achieved some outstanding results—in abolishing child labor, in bringing some order in the chaotic bituminous coal industry, and the like. Roosevelt was furious with the court, since the decision threatened to undermine all New Deal economic regulation. He charged that the justices were taking a horse and buggy view of the economic powers of the government. There followed six months later the court invalidation of the Triple-A processing tax, which for the moment threw out of gear the agricultural program.

The answer to these and similar Supreme Court decisions was Roosevelt's bold onslaught against the court after he had been re-elected in the great landslide of 1936. He had carried every state but Maine and Vermont; he considered himself as having a great mandate from the people to continue his program. Nor had he any reason to doubt his ability to push a court reform program through Congress, since the already bulging New Deal majorities had become still bigger. He was wrong; he failed. His failure came as much as anything through a great tactical error. He disguised his program as one to bring about a speedier handling of cases, when he should have presented it frankly as a means of ending the court obstruction of the New Deal. This obstruction was real. Many corporations openly flaunted the National Labor Relations Act, for example, they were so confident that the Supreme Court would invalidate it.

However laudable the end, to many a well-educated member of the middle class who had supported Roosevelt even through the campaign of 1936, Roosevelt's resort to subterfuge smacked of the devious ways of dictators. In 1937, Americans were all too aware of the way in which Hitler and Mussolini had gained power. It was not that any thinking man expected Roosevelt to follow their example, but rather that many objected to any threat, real or potential, to the constitutional system including the separation of powers. After Roosevelt, they argued, the potential dictator might appear. It may be too that times had improved sufficiently since March 1933 so that constitutional considerations could again overweigh economic exigencies. In any event, Roosevelt lost his battle—and won his war.

While the struggle was rocking the nation, the justices began exercising the judicial self-restraint which one of their number, Harlan F. Stone, had urged upon them the previous year. They surprised the nation by upholding the constitutionality of the National Labor Relations Act and the Social Security Act. In large part this eliminated the necessity for the New Dealers to make any change in the personnel of the court, and thus helped contribute to Roosevelt's defeat in Congress. Further, the fight had helped bring into existence a conservative coalition in Congress which from this time on gave Roosevelt a rough ride. Many old-line Democratic congressmen now dared proclaim in public what they had previously whispered in private. All this added up to a spectacular setback for Roosevelt—so spectacular that it is easy to over-look the enormous and permanent changes that had come about.

In the next few years the Supreme Court in effect rewrote a large part of constitutional law. The federal and state governments were now able to engage in extensive economic regulation with little or no court re-straint upon them. The limits upon regulation must be set for the most part by the legislative branch of the government, not the judiciary. Not only were the National Labor Relations Act and Social Security constitu-tional, but a bulging portfolio of other legislation.

These laws were not as spectacular as the measures of the Hundred Days, but in the bulk they were far more significant, for they brought about lasting changes in the economic role of the federal government. There was the continued subsidy to agriculture in order to maintain crop control—based upon soil conservation rather than a processing tax. There were all the agricultural relief measures which came to be central-ized in the Farm Security Administration. Although that agency has dis-appeared, most of its functions have continued in one way or another. There was a beginning of slum clearance and public housing, and a con-tinuation of TVA, held constitutional even before the court fight. There was a stiffening of securities regulation. There was a continuation of much that Roosevelt had considered beneficial in the NRA through a group of new laws usually referred to as the "little NRA." These per-petuated the coal and liquor codes, helped regulate oil production, tried to prevent wholesale price discriminations and legalized the establish-ment of "fair trade" prices by manufacturers. Most important of all, the Fair Labor Standards Act of 1937 set a national minimum of wages and maximum of hours of work, and prohibited the shipping in inter-state commerce of goods made by child labor. These are lasting contribu-tions of the New Deal, either substantial laws in themselves or the seeds for later legislation.

What then, is to be said of the recession and the anti-monopoly pro-gram? A Keynesian point of view is that public works spending, the other New Deal spending programs, and the payment of the bonus to veterans of the first World War (over Roosevelt's veto, incidentally), all these together had poured so such money into the economy that they brought about a substantial degree of recovery, except in employment, by the spring of 1937. At this point Roosevelt tried to balance the budget, especially by cutting public works and work relief expenditures. The result was a sharp recession. Roosevelt was forced to resort to renewed pump-priming, and in a few months the recession was over.

Even this recession experience did not convert Roosevelt to Keynesian-ism. Keynes once called upon Roosevelt at the White House and appar-ently tried to dazzle him with complex mathematical talk. Each was dis-appointed in the other. In 1939, after the recession when a protégé of

Mrs. Roosevelt's proposed additional welfare spending, Roosevelt replied by listing worthwhile projects in which the government could usefully spend an additional five billions a year. Then he pointed out that the deficit was already three billions, which could not go on forever. How, he inquired, could an eight billion dollar deficit be financed.

As for economists, many of them saw the answer in the enormous spending power which would be unleashed if the government poured out billions in time of depression. To most of them the lesson from the recession was that the only way to right the economy in time of upset was through spending.

As for businessmen, they could see in the recession only the logical outcome of Roosevelt's iniquitous tinkering with the economy. They had been especially angered by the protection the Wagner act had given to protective bargaining with the resulting militant expansion of organized labor. Roosevelt reciprocated the businessmen's feelings and blamed the recession upon their failure to co-operate. To a considerable degree he went along with a powerful handful of Progressive Republicans and Western Democrats in the Senate, like William E. Borah of Idaho and Joseph O'Mahoney of Wyoming, in attacking corporate monopoly as the villain. There are some indications, however, that the anti-monopoly program that he launched in the Department of Justice through the urbane Thurman Arnold was intended less to bust the trusts than to forestall too drastic legislation in the Congress. Roosevelt gave his strong backing to Arnold's anti-trust division only for the first year or two, and Arnold functioned for the most part through consent decrees. These in many instances allowed industries to function much as they had in the NRA days. The new program was in some respects more like a negative NRA than the antithesis of the NRA.

Thus from the beginning of the New Deal to the end, Roosevelt functioned with a fair degree of consistency. He heartily favored humanitarian welfare legislation and government policing of the economy, so long as these did not dangerously unbalance the budget. He preferred government co-operation with business to warfare with it.

Many of the New Dealers went far beyond Roosevelt in their views, and sometimes saw in his reluctance to support them, betrayal rather than a greater degree of conservatism. They had valid grievances some of the time when Roosevelt stuck to a middle course and seemed to them to be compromising away everything for which they thought he stood, in order to hold his motley political coalitions together. It is a serious moral question whether he compromised more than necessary, and whether at times he compromised his principles. It has been charged that his second four years in the White House represented a failure in political leadership.

In terms of gaining immediate political objectives, like the fiasco of the court fight, and the abortive "purge" in the 1938 primaries, this is undoubtedly true. In terms of the long-range New Deal program, I think the reverse is the case. These were years of piecemeal unspectacular consolidation of the earlier spectacular changes. It was many years before historians could say with certainty that these changes were permanent. By 1948 various public opinion samplings indicated that an overwhelming majority of those queried, even though Republican in voting habits, favored such things as social security and the TVA. The election of a Republican president in 1952 did not signify a popular repudiation of these programs. In the years after 1952 they were accepted, and in some instances even expanded, by the Republican administration. The only serious debate over them concerned degree, in which the Republicans were more cautious than the Democrats. The New Deal changes have even come for the most part to be accepted by the business community, although the United States Chamber of Commerce now issues manifestoes against federal aid to education with all the fervor it once directed against Roosevelt's proposals. The fact is that the business community in part bases its plans for the future upon some things that began as New Deal reforms. It takes for granted such factors as the "built-in stabilizers" in the social security system—something, incidentally, that Roosevelt pointed out at the time the legislation went into effect.

In January 1939 Roosevelt, concerned about the threat of world war, called a halt to his domestic reform program. What he said then, concerning the world crisis of 1939, is remarkably applicable to the United States more than two decades later:

"We have now passed the period of internal conflict in the launching of our program of social reform. Our full energies may now be released to invigorate the processes of recovery in order to preserve our reforms, and to give every man and woman who wants to work a real job at a living wage.

"But time is of paramount importance. The deadline of danger from within and from without is not within our control. The hour-glass may be in the hands of other nations. Our own hour-glass tells us that we are off on a race to make democracy work, so that we may be efficient in peace and therefore secure in national defense."

The new deal:
the third
American
revolution

Carl N. Degler

Twice since the founding of the Republic, cataclysmic events have sliced through the fabric of American life, snapping many of the threads which ordinarily bind the past to the future. The War for the Union was one such event, the Great Depression of the 1930's the other. And, as the Civil War was precipitated from the political and moral tensions of the preceding era, so the Great Depression was a culmination of the social and economic forces of industrialization and urbanization which had been transforming America since 1865. A depression of such pervasiveness as that of the thirties could happen only to a people already tightly interlaced by the multitudinous cords of a machine civilization and embedded in the matrix of an urban society.

In all our history no other economic collapse brought so many Americans to near starvation, endured so long, or came so close to overturning the basic institutions of American life. It is understandable, therefore, that from that experience should issue a new conception of the good society.

"HUNGER IS NOT DEBATABLE"

The economic dimensions of the Great Depression are quickly sketched—too quickly perhaps to permit a full appreciation of the abyss into which the economy slid between 1929 and 1933. The value of stocks on the New York Exchange, for example, slumped from a high of $87 billion in 1929 to a mere $19 billion in 1933. Wholesale prices dropped 38 per cent by 1933 and farm prices seemed almost to have ceased to exist: they were 60 per cent below the low level of 1929. Within less than three years, realized national income plummeted to almost half of what it had been in the last boom year; and the same was true of industrial production. The human cost of this catastrophic breakdown in the complicated industrial machine, *Fortune* magazine estimated in September, 1932, was 10 million totally unemployed or 25 million people without any source of income.

To worsen matters, the industrial stagnation was accompanied by a spreading fever of bank failures. First here and there, then all over the country, the banks began to close their doors in the faces of their depositors. By the beginning of 1933, the financial self-confidence of the nation reached a dangerously low level, requiring the new administration of Franklin Roosevelt, as its first official act, to order the closing of all banks. In all, more than 10,000 deposit banks failed in the five years after 1929. If the banks, the custodians of the measure of value, proved to be unsound, men might well wonder what was left to cling to as the winds of disaster gained in fury.

Unnerving as the failure of the banks undoubtedly was, for most people the Great Depression became starkly real only when unemployment struck. No one knew whom it would hit next; the jobless were everywhere—in the cities, in the towns, on the farms. Their helplessness, their bewilderment, were often written in their faces, reflected in their discouraged gaits, and mirrored in their run-down dwellings. John Dos Passos reported seeing the unemployed of Detroit in 1932 living in caves scooped out of giant abandoned sand piles. Though it was said that no one would be allowed to starve, *Fortune*, in September, 1932, suggested that some had already. The magazine counted the millions of the unemployed and told of families subsisting on a single loaf of bread for over a week or of going without food for two or three days on end. Discarded and spoiled vegetables or wild dandelions were the substance of meals for some families. Other reports in 1933 told of at least twenty-nine persons who died of starvation in New York City. Moreover, thousands must have died from diseases which gained an easy foothold in weakened and underfed bodies; but these unfortunates were never counted. Food, casually consumed in good times, suddenly became the focus of existence for thousands. In their desperation some urban folk actually tried to wring their food from the barren soil of the city. In Gary, Indiana, for example, 20,000 families were raising food on lots lent by the city; Robert and Helen Lynd reported that in Middletown in 1933, 2,500 of the town's 48,000 people eked out their food budgets with relief gardens.

The spreading unemployment generated new and deep-seated fears. When the unkempt veterans of the First World War camped in Washington in 1932, demanding a bonus to tide them over their joblessness, a fearful and unsure President had them dispersed by troops armed with tear gas. And when Congress in that same year voted a 10 per cent cut in government salaries, President Hoover sent a secret message urging that the enlisted men of the Army and the Navy be excluded from such decreases so that in case of domestic troubles the federal government would not be compelled to rely upon disgruntled troops.

Nor was it only the federal government that felt uneasy in the presence of the specter which was stalking the land. Malcolm Cowley, in an eyewitness account, described how the trucks bearing the disillusioned veterans out of Washington were quickly sped through town after town, the local authorities fearing that some of the unemployed veterans would jump off and become burdens on already overtaxed communities. Cowley tells of one citizen in Washington, not a marcher at all, who was hurriedly bundled into a truck by mistake and could not get off until he reached Indianapolis!

Driven by their desperation, some Americans began to talk of violence. Mutterings of revolution and threats to return with rifles were heard among the bonus marchers as they left Washington. Out on the farms, the dissatisfaction of the veterans was matched by sullen farmers who closed the courts and disrupted mortgage auctions to save their homes. The ugly turn which the discontent could take was revealed by the arrest of a man in Wisconsin in 1932 on suspicion of having removed a spike from the railroad track over which President Hoover's train was to pass. In that bleak year it was not uncommon for the President of the United States to be booed and hooted as he doggedly pursued his ill-starred campaign for re-election. To Theodore Dreiser, as the cold night of the depression settled over the land, it seemed that Karl Marx's prediction "that Capitalism would eventually evolve into failure . . . has come true."

Even for the Lords of Creation, as Frederick Lewis Allen was to call them, the Great Depression was an unsettling and confusing experience. "I'm afraid, every man is afraid," confessed Charles M. Schwab of United States Steel. "I don't know, we don't know, whether the values we have are going to be real next month or not." And in the very early months of the Roosevelt administration, Harold Ickes, attending a dinner of the Chamber of Commerce of the United States, could sense the pitiable impotence to which the nation's industrial leaders had sunk. "The great and the mighty in the business world were there in force," he rather gleefully noted in his diary, "and I couldn't help thinking how so many of these great and mighty were crawling to Washington on their hands and knees these days to beg the Government to run their businesses for them."

But it was the unspectacular, the everyday dreariness of unemployment that must have cut the deepest and endured the longest as far as the ordinary American was concerned. The simplest things of life, once taken for granted, now became points of irritation. "I forget how to cook good since I have nothing to cook with," remarked one housewife. Children lost their appetites upon seeing the milk and mush "that they have seen so often." Even the rare treat of fresh meat could not awaken an appetite long accustomed to disappointment and pallid food.

The routine entertainments of the poor were casualties to unemployment. "Suppose you go to a friend's house and she gives you a cup of tea and something," the wife of an unemployed worker told a social worker. "You feel ashamed. You think, now I got to do the same when she comes to my house. You know you can't so you stay home." Shifts in entertainment patterns among the unemployed were revealed in a study made of some 200 families in New Haven. Before the breadwinner lost his job, some 55 per cent went to the movies; once unemployment hit, however, only 16 per cent did. In the days when work was to be had, only 13 per cent found recreation in "sitting around the house," but now 25 per cent did so. With the loss of their jobs, 12 per cent of the men admitted they "chatted and gossiped" for recreation, although none of them did when they had work.

Unemployment's effect upon the family was often more profound and far-reaching. In recounting the case history of the Raparka family, one sociologist wrote that when Mr. Raparka "lost his job in the fall of 1933, he dominated the family. Two years later it was Mrs. Raparka who was the center of authority." Again and again social workers chronicled the alteration in the father's position in the family during a period of unemployment. Humiliation settled over many a father no longer able to fulfill his accustomed role in the family. "I would rather turn on the gas and put an end to the whole family than let my wife support me," was the way one unemployed father put it. One investigator found that one-fifth of her sample of fifty-nine families exhibited a breakdown in the father's authority, particularly in the eyes of the wife. For example, one wife said, "When your husband cannot provide for the family and makes you worry so, you lose your love for him."

Fathers discovered that without the usual financial power to buy bikes or bestow nickels, their control and authority over children were seriously weakened and sometimes completely undermined. In one family where the father was unemployed for a long time, his role was almost completely taken over by the eldest son. The father himself admitted: "The son of twenty-two is just like a father around the house. He tries to settle any little brother-and-sister fights and even encourages me and my wife." In the same family, a younger son who was working summed up his relationship to his parents in a few words. "I remind them," he said, "who makes the money. They don't say much. They just take it, that's all. I'm not the one on relief." In such circumstances, it is no exaggeration to say that the massive weight of the depression was grinding away at the bedrock of American institutions.

The ties of a home struck by unemployment were weak and the opportunities for fruitful and satisfying work were almost totally absent in 1932–33. *Fortune* reported in February, 1933, that something like 200,000 young men and boys were traveling around the country on railroad trains for lack of anything better to do. Tolerated by the railroads because of their obvious poverty and lack of jobs, the boys were often suffering from disease and malnutrition. The authorities in Los Angeles asserted, for example, that 25 per cent of those coming into the city needed clinical attention and 5 per cent required hospitalization. During a single season, one railroad announced, fifty such footloose boys were killed and one hundred injured. From Kansas City it was reported that girl wanderers, dressed in boy's clothing, were on the increase. To many such young people, now grown, the Great Depression must still seem the most purposeless, the most enervating period of their lives.

What Robert and Helen Lynd concluded for their study of Middletown in 1935 can be applied to America as a whole: ". . . the great knife of the depression had cut down impartially through the entire population cleaving open lives and hopes of rich as well as poor. The experience has been more nearly universal than any prolonged recent emotional experience in the city's history; it has approached in its elemental shock the primary experiences of birth and death."

THE END OF LAISSEZ FAIRE

Perhaps the most striking alteration in American thought which the depression fostered concerned the role of the government in the economy. Buffeted and bewildered by the economic debacle, the American people in the course of the 1930's abandoned, once and for all, the doctrine of laissez faire. This beau ideal of the nineteenth-century economists had become, ever since the days of Jackson, an increasingly cherished shibboleth of Americans. But now it was almost casually discarded. It is true, of course, that the rejection of laissez faire had a long history; certainly the Populists worked to undermine it. But with the depression the nation at large accepted the government as a permanent influence in the economy.[1]

Almost every one of the best-known measures of the federal government during the depression era made inroads into the hitherto private preserves of business and the individual. Furthermore, most of these new measures survived the period, taking their places as fundamental elements in the structure of American life. For modern Americans living under a federal government of transcendent influence and control in the economy, this is the historic meaning of the great depression.

Much of what is taken for granted today as the legitimate function of government and the social responsibility of business began only with the legislation of these turbulent years. Out of the investigation of banking and bankers in 1933, for example, issued legislation which separated commercial banking from the stock and bond markets, and insured the

[1] A complementary and highly suggestive way of viewing this trend away from laissez faire, of which the events of the 1930's are a culmination, is that taken in K. William Kapp, *The Social Costs of Private Enterprise* (Cambridge, Mass., 1950). Kapp observes that for a long time private enterprise had shifted the social costs of production—like industrially polluted water, industrial injuries, smoke nuisances and hazards, unemployment, and the like—onto society. The decline of laissez faire has, in this view, actually been a movement to compel industry to pay for those social costs of production which it has hitherto shirked.

bank deposits of ordinary citizens. The stock market, like the banks, was placed under new controls and a higher sense of responsibility to the public imposed upon it by the new Securities and Exchange Commission. The lesson of Black Tuesday in 1929 had not been forgotten; the classic free market itself—the Exchange—was hereafter to be under continuous governmental scrutiny.

The three Agricultural Adjustment Acts of 1933, 1936, and 1938, while somewhat diverse in detail, laid down the basic lines of what is still today the American approach to the agricultural problem. Ever since the collapse of the boom after the First World War, American agriculture had suffered from the low prices born of the tremendous surpluses. Unable to devise a method for expanding markets to absorb the excess, the government turned to restriction of output as the only feasible alternative. But because restriction of output meant curtailment of income for the farmer, it became necessary, if farm income was to be sustained, that farmers be compensated for their cut in production. Thus was inaugurated the singular phenomenon, which is still a part of the American answer to the agricultural surplus, of paying farmers for *not* growing crops. The other device introduced for raising farm prices, and still the mainstay of our farm policy, came with the 1938 act, which provided that the government would purchase and store excess farm goods, thus supporting the price level by withdrawing the surplus from the competitive market. Both methods constitute a subsidy for the farmer from society at large.[2]

Though the Eisenhower administration in the 1950's called for a return to a free market in farm products—that is, the removal of government supports from prices—very few steps have been taken in that direction, and probably very few ever will.[3] A free market was actually in operation during the twenties, but it succeeded only in making farmers the stepchildren of the golden prosperity of that decade. Today the farm bloc is too powerful politically to be treated so cavalierly. Moreover, the depression has taught most Americans that a free market is not only a rarity in the modern world but sometimes inimical to a stable and lasting prosperity.

Perhaps the most imaginative and fruitful of these innovations was the Tennessee Valley Authority, which transformed the heart of the

[2] On the day that the first AAA was declared unconstitutional, a Gallup poll revealed that, although the nation as a whole did not like the AAA, the farmers of the South and Midwest did. As a result, invalidation of the act by the Court did not mean the end of such a policy, but only the beginning of a search to find a new way of accomplishing the same end. Hence there were successive AAA's, whereas, when NRA was declared unconstitutional in 1935, it was dropped, primarily because neither business nor labor, for whose interests it had been organized, found much merit in its approach to their problems.
[3] As reported in the *New York Times,* July 2, 1958, forecasts for the fiscal year 1958–59 see government subsidies to agriculture reaching $6 billion—an all-time high.

South. "It was and is literally a down to earth experiment," native Tennesseean Broadus Mitchell has written, "with all that we know from test tube and logarithm tables called on to help. It was a union of heart and mind to restore what had been wasted. It was a social resurrection." For the TVA was much more than flood and erosion control or even hydroelectric power—though its gleaming white dams are perhaps its most striking and best-known monuments. It was social planning of the most humane sort, where even the dead were carefully removed from cemeteries before the waters backed up behind the dams. It brought new ideas, new wealth, new skills, new hope into a wasted, tired, and discouraged region.

At the time of the inception of the TVA, it was scarcely believable that the "backward" South would ever utilize all the power the great dams would create. But in its report of 1956, the Authority declared that the Valley's consumption of electricity far exceeded that produced from water sites: almost three-quarters of TVA's power is now generated from steam power, not from waterfall. In large part it was the TVA which taught the Valley how to use more power to expand its industries and to lighten the people's burdens. Back in 1935, Drew and Leon Pearson saw this creation of consumer demand in action. "Uncle Sam is a drummer with a commercial line to sell," they wrote in *Harper's Magazine*. "He sold liberty bonds before, but never refrigerators."

Measured against textbook definitions, the TVA is unquestionably socialism. The government owns the means of production and, moreover, it competes with private producers of electricity.[4] But pragmatic Americans—and particularly those living in the Valley—have had few sleepless nights as a consequence of this fact. The TVA does its appointed job and, as the recent fight over the Dixon and Yates contract seemed to show, it is here to stay. It, too, with all the talk of "creeping socialism," has been absorbed into that new American Way fashioned by the experimentalism of the American people from the wreckage of the Great Depression.

Undoubtedly social security deserves the appellation "revolutionary" quite as much as the TVA; it brought government into the lives of people as nothing had since the draft and the income tax. Social security legislation actually comprises two systems: insurance against old age and in-

[4] The extent of the intellectual change which the depression measures introduced can be appreciated by a quotation from President Hoover's veto in 1931 of a bill to develop a public power project in what was later to be the TVA area. "I am firmly opposed to the Government entering into any business the major purpose of which is competition with our citizens." Emergency measures of such a character might be tolerated, he said. "But for the Federal government deliberately to go out to build up and expand such an occasion to the major purpose of a power and manufacturing business is to break down the initiative and enterprise of the American people; it is destruction of equality of opportunity amongst our people; it is the negation of the ideals upon which our civilization has been based."

surance in the event of loss of work. The first system was completely organized and operated by the federal government; the second was shared with the states—but the national government set the standards; both were clear acknowledgment of the changes which had taken place in the family and in the business of making a living in America. No longer in urban America could the old folks, whose proportion in the society was steadily increasing, count on being taken in by their offspring as had been customary in a more agrarian world. Besides, such a makeshift arrangement was scarcely satisfying to the self-respect of the oldsters. With the transformation of the economy by industrialization, most Americans had become helpless before the vagaries of the business cycle. As a consequence of the social forces which were steadily augmenting social insecurity, only collective action by the government could arrest the drift.

To have the government concerned about the security of the individual was a new thing. Keenly aware of the novelty of this aim in individualistic America,[5] Roosevelt was careful to deny any serious departure from traditional paths. "These three great objectives—the security of the home, the security of livelihood, and the security of social insurance," he said in 1934, constitute "a minimum of the promise that we can offer to the American people." But this, he quickly added, "does not indicate a change in values."

Whether the American people thought their values had changed is not nearly as important as the fact that they accepted social security. And the proof that they did is shown in the steady increase in the proportion of the population covered by the old-age benefit program since 1935; today about 80 per cent of nonfarm workers are included in the system. Apart from being a minimum protection for the individual and society against the dry rot of industrial idleness, unemployment insurance is now recognized as one of the major devices for warding off another depression.

It is true, as proponents of the agrarian life have been quick to point out, that an industrialized people, stripped as they are of their economic self-reliance, have felt the need for social insurance more than people in other types of society. But it is perhaps just as important to recognize that it is only in such a highly productive society that people can even dare to dream of social security. Men in other ages have felt the biting pains of economic crisis, but few pre-industrial people have ever enjoyed that surfeit of goods which permits the fat years to fill out the lean ones.

[5] Characteristically enough, as his memoirs show, President Hoover had long been interested in both old-age and unemployment insurance, but always such schemes were to be worked out through private insurance companies, or at best with the states—never under the auspices of the federal government. "It required a great depression," he has written somewhat ruefully, "to awaken interest in the idea" of unemployment insurance.

But like so much else concerning industrialism, it is not always easy to calculate whether the boons it offers exceed in value the burdens which it imposes.

For the average man, the scourge of unemployment was the essence of the depression. Widespread unemployment, permeating all ranks and stations in society, drove the American people and their government into some of their most determined and deliberate departures from the hallowed policy of "hands off." But despite the determination, as late as 1938 the workless still numbered almost ten million—two thirds as great as in 1932 under President Hoover. The governmental policies of the 1930's never appreciably diminished the horde of unemployed—only the war prosperity of 1940 and after did that—but the providing of jobs by the federal government was a reflection of the people's new conviction that the government had a responsibility to alleviate economic disaster. Such bold action on the part of government, after the inconclusive, bewildered approach of the Hoover administration, was a tonic for the dragging spirits of the people.[6]

A whole range of agencies, from the Civil Works Administration (CWA) to the Works Progress Administration (WPA), were created to carry the attack against unemployment. It is true that the vast program of relief which was organized was not "permanent" in the sense that it is still in being, but for two reasons it deserves to be discussed here. First, since these agencies constituted America's principal weapon against unemployment, some form of them will surely be utilized if a depression should occur again. Second, the various relief agencies of the period afford the best examples of the new welfare outlook, which was then in the process of formation.

Though in the beginning relief programs were premised on little more than Harry Hopkins' celebrated dictum, "Hunger is not debatable," much more complex solutions to unemployment were soon worked out. The relief program of the WPA, which after 1935 was the major relief

[6] It was the misfortune of Herbert Hoover to have been President at a time when his considerable administrative and intellectual gifts were hamstrung by his basic political philosophy, which, instead of being a guide to action, served as an obstacle. Much more of an old-fashioned liberal than a reactionary, and deeply attached to the Jeffersonian dogma of the limited powers of the federal government, Hoover was psychologically and philosophically unable to use the immense powers and resources of his office in attacking the urgent threat of unemployment. Back in 1860–61, another President—James Buchanan—had been paralyzed in the midst of a national crisis by his limited conception of the federal power, but in that instance his inaction was palliated by the fact that his successor was to take office within less than three months. Hoover, however, wrestled with the depression for three years, and all during that trying period he stoutly held to his rigid intellectual position that federally supplied and administered relief would destroy the foundations of the nation. Never has an American President, including the two Adamses, defied overwhelming popular opinion for so long for the sake of his own ideals as Herbert Hoover did then; and never has a President since Buchanan fallen so quickly into obscurity as Hoover did after March 4, 1933.

agency, was a case in point. In 1937, *Fortune* magazine commented on "the evolution of unemployment relief from tool to institution"—a recognition of the importance and duration of relief in America. "In 1936, the federal government was so deeply involved in the relief of the unemployed," *Fortune* contended, "that it was not only keeping them alive, but it was also giving them an opportunity to work; and not only giving them an opportunity to work but giving them an opportunity to work at jobs for which they were peculiarly fitted; and not only giving them an opportunity to work at jobs for which they were peculiarly fitted, but creating for them jobs of an interest and usefulness which they could not have expected to find in private employment." The statement somewhat distorts the work of the WPA, but it sums up the main outlines of the evolution of the relief program.

The various artistic and cultural employment programs of the WPA are excellent examples of how relief provided more than employment, though any of the youth agencies like the Civilian Conservation Corps or the National Youth Administration (it subsidized student work) would serve equally well. At its peak, the Federal Writers' Project employed some 6,000 journalists, poets, novelists, and Ph.D.'s of one sort or another; unknowns worked on the same payroll, if not side by side, with John Steinbeck, Vardis Fisher, and Conrad Aiken. The $46 million expended on art—that is, painting and sculpture—by the WPA in 1936–37 exceeded the artistic budget of any country outside the totalitarian orbit —and there art was frankly propagandistic. *Fortune*, in May, 1937, found the American government's sponsorship of art singularly free of censorship or propaganda. The magazine concluded that "by and large the Arts Projects have been given a freedom no one would have thought possible in a government run undertaking. And by and large that freedom has not be abused." During the first fifteen months of the Federal Music Project, some fifty million people heard live concerts; in the first year of the WPA Theater, sixty million people in thirty states saw performances, with weekly attendance running to half a million. T. S. Eliot's *Murder in the Cathedral*, too risky for a commercial producer, was presented in New York by the Federal Theater to 40,000 people at a top price of 55 cents.

"What the government's experiments in music, painting, and the theater actually did," concluded *Fortune* in May, 1937, "even in their first year, was to work a sort of cultural revolution in America." For the first time the American audience and the American artist were brought face to face for their mutual benefit. "Art in America is being given its chance," said the British writer Ford Madox Ford, "and there has been nothing like it since before the Reformation. . . ."

Instead of being ignored on the superficially plausible grounds of the exigencies of the depression, the precious skills of thousands of painters, writers, and musicians were utilized. By this timely rescue of skills, tastes, and talents from the deadening hand of unemployment, the American people, through their government, showed their humanity and social imagination. Important for the future was the foresight displayed in the conserving of artistic talents and creations for the enrichment of generations to come.

The entrance of the federal government into a vast program of relief work was an abrupt departure from all previous practice, but it proved enduring. "When President Roosevelt laid it down that government had a social responsibility to care for the victims of the business cycle," *Fortune* remarked prophetically in 1937, "he set in motion an irreversible process." The burden of unemployment relief was too heavy to be carried by local government or private charities in an industrialized society; from now on, the national government would be expected to shoulder the responsibility. "Those who are on relief and in close contact otherwise with public matters realize that what has happened to the country is a bloodless revolution," wrote an anonymous relief recipient in *Harper's* in 1936. The government, he said, has assumed a new role in depressions, and only the rich might still be oblivious to it. But they too "will know it by 1940. And in time," they will "come to approve the idea of everyone having enough to eat."[7] Few people escaped the wide net of the depression: "Anybody sinks after a while," the anonymous reliefer pointed out. "Even you would have if God hadn't preserved, without apparent rhyme or reason, your job and your income." That the depression was a threat to all was perhaps the first lesson gained from the 1930's.

The second was that only through collective defense could such a threat be met. By virtue of the vigorous attack made upon the economic problems of the thirties by the government, the age-old conviction that dips in the business cycle were either the will of God or the consequence of unalterable economic laws was effectively demolished. As recently as 1931, President Hoover had told an audience that some people "have indomitable confidence that by some legerdemain we can legislate ourselves out of a world-wide depression. Such views are as accurate as the belief that we can exorcise a Caribbean hurricane." From the experience of the depression era, the American people learned that something could and ought to be done when economic disaster strikes. No party and no politician with a future will ever again dare to take the fatalistic and defeatist course of Herbert Hoover in 1929–33.

As the enactment of the Employment Act of 1946 showed, the preven-

---

[7] The providing of work relief instead of the dole did more than fill hungry stomachs; it re-established faith in America and in one's fellow man. "I'm proud of our United States," said one relief recipient. "There ain't no other nation in the world that would have sense enough to think of WPA and all the other A's." The wife of one WPA worker was quoted as saying, "We aren't on relief any more—my man is working for the government."

tion of depression now occupies top listing among the social anxieties of the American people. The act created a permanent Council of Economic Advisers to the President, to keep him continuously informed on the state of the economy and to advise him on the measures necessary to avoid an economic decline. And the Joint Committee on the Economic Report does the same for Congress.

Today political figures who indignantly repudiate any "left-wing" philosophy of any sort readily accept this inheritance from the depression. "Never again shall we allow a depression in the United States," vowed Republican candidate Eisenhower in 1952. As soon as we "foresee the signs of any recession and depression," he promised, ". . . the full power of private industry, of municipal government, of state government, of the Federal Government will be mobilized to see that that does not happen." Ignoring the fact that as a prospective federal official he had promised more than he could deliver, he innocently and accurately added, "I cannot pledge you more than that." Sensing the tremendous importance of the matter to the American people, Eisenhower made substantially the same statement three other times—at Yonkers, Peoria, and Pittsburgh. At Yonkers he said that he had "repeated this particular pledge over and over again in the United States" and that he and his associates were "dedicated to this proposition. . . ."

In the White House, Eisenhower continued to reflect this underlying and persistent fear that a depression would once again stride through the land. According to the account in Robert Donovan's semiofficial *Eisenhower: The Inside Story*, at session after session of the Cabinet during the recession of 1953–54, it was the President who stressed the urgency of the economic situation. It was he who constantly prodded Arthur F. Burns of the Council of Economic Advisers to prepare plans with which to forestall a serious drop in the economic indicators. Indeed as late as June, 1954, just after Burns had delivered an optimistic report on the condition and future of the economy, as Donovan tells it, "The President . . . was still concerned about whether the administration was doing enough. Even though it jarred the logic of some members of the Cabinet, he insisted, everything possible must be done to restore vigor to the economy. It was important, the President said, to produce results and to err on the side of doing too much rather than too little."

In the midst of the recession of 1957–58, Vice-President Nixon, speaking on April 24, 1958, specifically repudiated the Hoover approach of permitting the economy to right itself without government intervention. "Let us recognize once and for all," he told his audience, "that the time is past in the United States when the Federal Government can stand by and allow a recession to be prolonged or to deepen into depression without decisive Government action." Though Eisenhower was obviously worried that hasty measures might bring on further inflation, on May

20, in a public address, he agreed with the Vice-President that the government had "a continuing responsibility . . . to help counteract recession." In the same speech the President enumerated concrete measures already taken, such as extension of unemployment benefits, speeding up of defense and civilian procurement, acceleration of government construction projects, and the easing of credit by the Federal Reserve.

The Republican administration's evident acceptance of the new obligations of government in the economy is strikingly suggestive of the shock which the depression dealt conventional economic thought in America. . . .

WAS IT A NEW OR OLD DEAL?

One of the most enduring monuments to the Great Depression was that congeries of contradictions, naïveté, humanitarianism, realistic politics, and economic horse sense called the New Deal of Franklin D. Roosevelt. As the governmental agent which recast American thinking on the responsibilities of government, the New Deal was clearly the offspring of the depression. As we have seen, it was also more than that: it was a revitalization of the Democratic party; it was the political manifestation of that new spirit of reform which was stirring among the ranks of labor and the Negro people.

In their own time and since, the New Deal and Franklin Roosevelt have had a polarizing effect upon Americans. Probably at no time before Roosevelt has the leader of a great democratic nation come to symbolize as he did the hopes and the fears of so many people.[8] Not even Jackson, in whom Roosevelt himself recognized a President of his own popularity- and hatred-producing caliber, could rival him. Over a decade after Roosevelt's death, the mention of his name still evokes emotions, betrayed by the wistful look in the eye or in the hard set of the jaw. The election of 1956, moreover, demonstrated once again that the Old Guard of the Republican party still fights the dead Roosevelt while the Democratic party wanders leaderless in his absence. This too is a measure of the political revolution he led.

For the Democratic party, Roosevelt was like a lightning rod, drawing to himself all the venom and hatred of the opposition, only to discharge it harmlessly; nothing, it seemed, could weaken his personal hold on the affections of the majority of Americans. That something more was in-

[8] According to Harold Ickes, Roosevelt was profoundly struck by the adoration which was bestowed upon him by his admirers. During the 1936 campaign, the President told Ickes "that there was something terrible about the crowds that lined the streets along which he passed. He went on to explain what he meant, which was exclamations from individuals in the crowd, such as 'He saved my home,' 'He gave me a job,' 'God bless you, Mr. President,' etc." In May, 1936, Marquis Childs published an article in *Harper's*, entitled "They Hate Roosevelt," in which he described and tried to account for the unreasoning hatred for the President on the part of what Childs called the upper 2 per cent of the population.

volved than sheer popularity is shown by the example of Dwight Eisenhower. Though held in even greater popular esteem, Eisenhower has been unable to invest his party with his own vote-getting power; Republicans lose though Eisenhower wins. The difference between F.D.R. and Ike is that one stood for a program, a hope, and a future, while the other stands for himself as a good, well-intentioned man whom all instinctively trust and perhaps even admire. The one is a leader of a nation, the other a popular hero. Roosevelt is already a member of that tiny pantheon of great leaders of Americans in which Washington, Jackson, Lincoln, and Wilson are included; it is difficult to believe that Eisenhower will be included. His monument is more likely to be inscribed: "The best-liked man ever to be President."

In the thirties, as now, the place of the New Deal in the broad stream of American development has been a matter of controversy. Historians and commentators on the American scene have not yet reached a firm agreement—if they ever will—as to whether the New Deal was conservative or radical in character, though it does appear that the consensus now seems to lean toward calling it conservative and traditional.[9] Certainly if one searches the writings and utterances of Franklin Roosevelt, his own consciousness of conservative aims is quickly apparent. "The New Deal is an old deal—as old as the earliest aspirations of humanity for liberty and justice and the good life," he declared in 1934. "It was this administration," he told a Chicago audience in 1936, "which saved the system of private profit and free enterprise after it had been dragged to the brink of ruin. . . ."

But men making a revolution among a profoundly conservative people do not advertise their activity, and above all Franklin Roosevelt understood the temper of his people.[10] Nor should such a statement be interpreted as an insinuation of high conspiracy—far from it. Roosevelt was at heart a conservative, as his lifelong interest in history, among other things, suggests. But he was without dogma in his conservatism, which was heavily interlaced with genuine concern for people.[11] He did not shy away from new means and new approaches to problems when circumstances demanded it. His willingness to experiment, to listen to his

[9] For example, one of the most recent short evaluations of the New Deal, by a most knowledgeable historian, Arthur Link, concludes as follows: "The chief significance of the reform legislation of the 1930's was its essentially conservative character and the fact that it stemmed from a half century or more of discussion and practical experience and from ideas proposed as well by Republicans as by Democrats." *American Epoch* (New York, 1955), p. 425.
[10] It is significant that only once during the 1932 campaign, according to Ernest K. Lindley, did Roosevelt call for "a revolution"; and then he promptly qualified it to "the right kind, the only kind of revolution this nation can stand for—a revolution at the ballot box."
[11] When an economist suggested to F. D. R. that the depression be permitted to run its course and that then the economic system would soon right itself—as Frances Perkins tells the story—the President's face took on a "gray look of horror" as he told the economist: "People aren't cattle you know!"

university-bred Brains Trust, to accept a measure like the TVA, reveal the flexibility in his thought. Both his lack of theoretical presuppositions and his flexibility are to be seen in the way he came to support novel measures like social security and the Wagner Act. Response to popular demand was the major reason. "The Congress can't stand the pressure of the Townsend Plan unless we have a real old-age insurance system," he complained to Frances Perkins, "nor can I face the country without having . . . a solid plan which will give some assurance to old people of systematic assistance upon retirement." In like manner, the revolutionary NLRA was adopted as a part of his otherwise sketchy and rule-of-thumb philosophy of society. Though ultimately Roosevelt championed the Wagner bill in the House, it was a belated conversion dictated by the foreshadowed success of the measure and the recent invalidation of the NRA. In his pragmatic and common-sense reactions to the exigencies of the depression, Roosevelt, the easygoing conservative, ironically enough became the embodiment of a new era and a new social philosophy for the American people.

"This election," Herbert Hoover presciently said in 1932, "is not a mere shift from the ins to the outs. It means deciding the direction our nation will take over a century to come." The election of Franklin Roosevelt, he predicted, would result in "a radical departure from the foundations of 150 years which have made this the greatest nation in the world." Though Hoover may be charged with nothing more than campaign flourishing, it is nevertheless a fact that his speech was made just after Roosevelt's revealing Commonwealth Club address of September. Only in this single utterance, it should be remembered, did Roosevelt disclose in clear outline the philosophy and program which was later to be the New Deal. "Every man has a right to life," he had said, "and this means that he has also a right to make a comfortable living. . . . Our government, formal and informal, political and economic," he went on, "owes to everyone an avenue to possess himself of a portion of that plenty [from our industrial society] sufficient for his needs, through his own work." Here were the intimations of those new goals which the New Deal set for America.

Accent as heavily as one wishes the continuity between the reforms of the Progressive era and the New Deal, yet the wide difference between the goals of the two periods still remains. The Progressive impulse was narrowly reformist: it limited business, it assisted agriculture, it freed labor from some of the shackles imposed by the courts, but it continued to conceive of the state as policeman or judge and nothing more. The New Deal, on the other hand, was more than a regulator—though it was that too, as shown by the SEC and the reinvigoration of the antitrust division of the Justice Department. To the old goals for America set forth and fought for by the Jeffersonians and the Progressives the New

Deal appended new ones. Its primary and general innovation was the guaranteeing of a minimum standard of welfare for the people of the nation. WPA and the whole series of relief agencies which were a part of it, wages and hours legislation, AAA, bank deposit insurance, and social security,[12] each illustrates this new conception of the federal government. A resolution offered by New Deal Senator Walsh in 1935 clearly enunciated the new obligations of government. The resolution took notice of the disastrous effects of the depression "upon the lives of young men and women . . ." and then went on to say that "it is the duty of the Federal Government to use every possible means of opening up opportunities" for the youth of the nation "so that they may be rehabilitated and restored to *a decent standard of living* and ensured proper development of their talents. . . ."

But the guarantor state as it developed under the New Deal was more active and positive than this. It was a vigorous and dynamic force in the society, energizing and, if necessary, supplanting private enterprise when the general welfare required it. With the Wagner Act, for example, the government served notice that it would actively participate in securing the unionization of the American worker; the state was no longer to be an impartial policeman merely keeping order; it now declared for the side of labor. When social and economic problems like the rehabilitation of the Valley of the Tennessee were ignored or shirked by private enterprise, then the federal government undertook to do the job. Did private enterprise fail to provide adequate and sufficient housing for a minimum standard of welfare for the people, then the government would build houses. As a result, boasted Nathan Straus, head of the U.S. Housing Authority, "for the first time in a hundred years the slums of America ceased growing and began to shrink."

Few areas of American life were beyond the touch of the experimenting fingers of the New Deal; even the once sacrosanct domain of prices and the valuation of money felt the tinkering. The devaluation of the dollar, the gold-purchase program, the departure from the gold standard —in short, the whole monetary policy undertaken by F.D.R. as a means to stimulate recovery through a price rise—constituted an unprecedented repudiation of orthodox public finance. To achieve that minimum standard of well-being which the depression had taught the American people to expect of their government, nothing was out of bounds.

But it is not the variety of change which stamps the New Deal as the

---

[12] Social security is an excellent example of how, under the New Deal, reform measures, when they conflicted with recovery, were given priority. In siphoning millions of dollars of social security taxes from the purchasing power of the workers, social security was a deflationary measure, which must have seriously threatened the precariously based new economic recovery. For this reason and others, Abraham Epstein, the foremost authority in America on social security, denounced the act as a "sharing of poverty."

creator of a new America; its significance lies in the permanence of its program. For, novel as the New Deal program was, it has, significantly, not been repudiated by the Eisenhower administration, the first Republican government since the reforms were instituted. Verbally, it is true, the Republican administration has had to minimize its actual commitments to the New Deal philosophy, and it tends to trust private business more than the New Dealers did—witness, for example, its elimination of the minor governmental manufacturing enterprises which competed with private firms. But despite this, the administration's firm commitment to the guaranteeing of prosperity and averting depression at all costs is an accurate reflection of the American people's agreement with the New Deal's diagnosis of the depression. Nor has the Republican party dared to repeal or even emasculate the legislation which made up the vitals of the New Deal: TVA, banking and currency, SEC, social security, the Wagner Act, and fair treatment of the Negro. The New Deal Revolution has become so much a part of the American Way that no political party which aspires to high office dares now to repudiate it.

It may or may not be significant in this regard (for apothegms are more slippery than precise) but it is nonetheless interesting that Roosevelt and Eisenhower have both been impressed with the same single sentence from Lincoln regarding the role of government. "The legitimate object of Government," wrote Lincoln, "is to do for a community of people whatever they need to have done but cannot do at all or cannot do so well for themselves in their separate or individual capacities." Twice, in 1934 and again in 1936, F.D.R. in public addresses used this expression to epitomize his own New Deal, and Robert Donovan in his officially inspired book on the Eisenhower administration writes that this same "fragment of Lincoln's writing . . . Eisenhower uses time and again in describing his own philosophy of government." Between Lincoln and Eisenhower there was no Republican President, except perhaps Theodore Roosevelt, who would have been willing to subscribe to such a free-wheeling description of the federal power; in this can be measured the impact of the New Deal and the depression.

The conclusion seems inescapable that, traditional as the words may have been in which the New Deal expressed itself, in actuality it was a revolutionary response to a revolutionary situation. In its long history America has passed through two revolutions since the first one in 1776, but only the last two, the Civil War and the depression, were of such force as to change the direction of the relatively smooth flow of its progress. The Civil War rendered a final and irrevocable decision in the long debate over the nature of the Union and the position of the Negro in American society. From that revolutionary experience, America emerged a strong national state and dedicated by the words of its most hallowed document to the inclusion of the black man in a democratic culture. The searing ordeal of the Great Depression purged the American people of their belief in the limited powers of the federal government and convinced them of the necessity of the guarantor state. And as the Civil War constituted a watershed in American thought, so the depression and its New Deal marked the crossing of a divide from which, it would seem, there could be no turning back.

The new deal: radical and anti-business

Edgar E. Robinson

The financial crisis was real; no one could doubt it. The financial life of the nation was in a state of inanimate suspension. In the view of the outgoing administration, this condition was the result of the unwillingness of the incoming administration to co-operate in measures to restore confidence. The mass of the people were in a mood of despair. The millions of unemployed had yet to see any system of relief at the hands of the national government. For the able-bodied and the healthy there were no precedents for government aid.

President Roosevelt believed that the first of his problems was the restoration of confidence. His own words at the time embody his view of the necessity facing him.

Values have shrunken to fantastic levels; taxes have risen; our ability to pay has fallen; government of all kinds is faced by serious curtailment of income; the means of exchange are frozen in the currents of trade; the withered leaves of industrial enterprise lie on every side; farmers find no markets for their produce; the savings of many years in thousands of families are gone. . . . More important, a host of unemployed citizens face the grim problem of existence, and an equally great number toil with little return. Only a foolish optimist can deny the dark realities of the moment.

Yet a radio commentator had noted that on his way to the Capitol, Mr. Roosevelt looked "magnificently confident." According to his wife, the new President "believed in God and His guidance. He felt that human beings were given tasks to perform and with those tasks the ability and strength to put them through. He could pray for help and guidance and have faith in his own judgment as a result. The church services that he always insisted on holding on Inauguration Day . . . and whenever a great crisis impended were the expression of his religious faith."

From *The Roosevelt Leadership* by Edgar E. Robinson. Copyright 1955 by J. B. Lippincott. Published by J. B. Lippincott.

Mr. Roosevelt felt that the inaugural address contained all the elements in his program. It was the conviction of those who formulated this program that his addresses in the campaign had foreshadowed every important element in the New Deal. Viewed in perspective, no such pronounced result as emerged had in fact been envisaged.

As one of his closest advisers at the time saw it, "We stood in the city of Washington on March 4th like a handful of marauders in hostile territory . . . the Republican party had close to a monopoly of skillful, experienced administrators. To make matters worse, the business managers, established lawyers, and engineers from whose ranks top-drawer governmental executives so often come were, by and large, so partisan in their opposition to Roosevelt that he could scarcely be expected to tap those sources to the customary degree."

During the early phases of the first administration, conspicuous as personal advisers were Raymond Moley, Rexford G. Tugwell, Adolph Berle, Hugh Johnson, and of course Louis Howe and Henry Morgenthau, Jr. The work of each of these men in contributing to the determination of public policy deserves extensive examination. As the administration moved into its second year, the influence of Secretary Ickes became very important. The contribution of such close associates as Henry Wallace, James Farley, William Woodin and Frances Perkins had become well known. Harry Hopkins was in a different category than any other adviser, as events were to show. Not coming to Washington until May 22, he became almost at once—in the eyes of eager commentators—the embodiment of the New Deal as it related to relief.

It was not clearly apparent at the time, even though much public attention was fixed upon these men, how important they were in the emerging pattern of government in the "progressive" spirit. The people as a whole had voted to take over their own government. That was Mr. Roosevelt's view. But they had to have men in government to do this work. Experts, not elected to office, were to aid the President in his task.

To identify Franklin Roosevelt with the attitude of these experts who seemed, during the years 1933–1937, to speak for the nation, is to misunderstand him completely. It is possible that the time may come when a product of professional training in the social sciences will be elected to the Presidency. By inclination or experience, Mr. Roosevelt was not of such a group, however much he valued and used their services and however often, on occasion, he used their language. When he spoke of the American people he meant, as he visualized them, a people with somewhat the same attitude toward democracy, toward party, toward progress, toward reform, that he had. He conceived of reformers as men of action, rather than as men of thought. Roosevelt and the People were one.

Clearly, semi-dictatorial powers had been granted the President. The

Fascist press in Italy, commenting on the inaugural address, commended the cutting short of "the purposeless chatter of legislative assemblies. . . ."

The President had explained his point of view at his first press conference on March 8 and "delighted" the press with his candor. On Sunday evening, March 12, Mr. Roosevelt outlined the banking situation to the nation in a fifteen-minute radio address. The commentator Will Rogers wrote, "Well, he made everybody understand it, even the bankers." When the "Beer Bill," amending the Volstead Act, passed the House 316–97, Rogers was saying, "I don't know what additional authority Roosevelt may ask, but give it to him, even if it's to drown all the boy babies. . . . It just shows you what a country can do when you take their affairs out of the hands of Congress."

The response of the country to the new leadership was immediate, and on the whole favorable. The vigorous support in definite Congressional action was proof that the President had successfully asserted aggressive leadership.

President Roosevelt saw the nation's emergency as long in the making. In amplifying his view of this in 1934, he wrote:

After the World War, a wholly unplanned pyramiding of production and of speculation had left the country in such condition that methods of recovery used in previous periods of depression were useless.

He had seen it as

. . . an emergency that went to the roots of our agriculture, our commerce and our industry; it was an emergency that had existed for a whole generation in its underlying causes and for three and one-half years in its visible effects. It could be cured only by a complete reorganization and a measured control of the economic structure.

Yet, as he faced the tasks of the coming months, the country was still divided on his general policy as on no political issue since 1861. The proposals it was feared he would make were so divergent from the action of previous administrations and had been so lacking in development in his campaign utterances that the atmosphere of fear, in being dispelled, was followed by one of constant suspense and growing distrust. . . .

The New Deal that was . . . launched in the first hundred days of his administration was, as the President saw it, "a satisfactory combination of the Square Deal and the New Freedom . . . the fulfilment of the progressive ideas expounded by Theodore Roosevelt of a partnership between business and government and also of the determination of Woodrow Wilson that business should be subjected, through the power of government, to drastic legal limitations against abuses."

The President felt, furthermore, that:

In any event, the overwhelming majority of the business men in May, 1933, were entirely willing to go along with a great cooperative movement directed by the Government and working towards the elimination of the costly practices of the past.

There had been a swing of a large number of conservatives to the Roosevelt standard. They were being hospitably received and legislation of importance had been revised "in the light of the experience and opinion of men who work in the financial districts of the great cities." The boom support and stock market speculation of the twenties was thus in a way matched by the "risks" taken on the New Deal by the American people as a whole.

The financial and industrial groups were actually the first to be rescued by the New Deal, which in the perspective of history must stand as the substitution of "government inflation, risk, experiment, and, indeed, speculation, for almost complete private responsibility in this respect . . . substitution . . . initiated and progressively developed at the request, or with the connivance, of powerful leaders in banking, industry, agriculture, and labor organizations. . . ."

The battle over monetary policy was . . . launched early in the new administration. Disagreement among the President's advisers was particularly acute. "It was a battle not so much of men as of two conflicting schools of thought," commented James P. Warburg, one of the advisers, adding that the President acted "as a tireless, serene, and often amused referee."

"The President listened patiently to what I had to say" against further depreciation of the currency, said Mr. Warburg of a conference with Mr. Roosevelt on September 20, 1933, "but when I was all through, he smiled and told me that all that was very pretty, but meantime how were we going to keep prices advancing? How were we going to relieve the debt burden? What were we going to do about the farmers?"

Significant, in view of the fears expressed during the "interregnum," was the action of the President in this matter of currency manipulation. Although he felt justified in taking steps to control and direct what he perceived would be inevitable inflation in the hands of speculators, he said himself that the problem of the depression could best be solved by a policy that would encourage domestic inflation.

The first step in this process was the raising of commodity prices, but this was to be accomplished by raising the purchasing power of consumers by providing work for the unemployed. The cost of public relief, in the President's original plan, was to be met partly from diversion of funds allotted to the veterans' program, partly from taxes which would eventually be replaced by revenue from the sale of liquor, and partly by the issue of bonds to be paid off in the future.

When Mr. Roosevelt had asked for authority to obtain drastic retrenchment in government expenditure early in March, he had not contemplated "billions" for relief. The burden on the future came in time to be a heavy one, but in the first year of the New Deal emphasis was not on financing the program of relief, but rather on the machinery by which these benefits to the people might be distributed.

In his radio address of October 22, the President, reviewing the national situation for the fourth time during the year, announced:

When we have restored the price level, we shall seek to establish and maintain a dollar which will not change its purchasing and debt-paying power during the succeeding generation. . . .

The reader must conclude from the President's summary that, as far as he was concerned, traditional economics might well give way, under pressure, to experimentation.

The primary result of what his critics called "tinkering" with the currency was the furtherance of a "profound monetary revolution" by which, under cover of necessity, President Roosevelt was able to accomplish what radicals for generations had demanded. The devaluation of saved income, both of institutions and of individuals, Bryan had called for, as had the "silverites" up to 1930. Roosevelt's was revolutionary action under cover of law and was a blow intended to alter, in a fundamental way, the financial structure which had been built up by those who had hitherto dominated finance in the United States not only in private but in public life.

This, accomplished as part of the recovery program, was in fact an evidence that the reform purposes of the President and his liberal advisers were dictating the new national policy. Control of the nation would be taken out of the hands of the bankers and placed in the hands of those who had seized control of the government under cover of a general mandate from the people. The President, guided and advised by groups convinced of the necessity of remaking the financial structure of the nation and backed by subservient Congressional majorities, was in truth remaking by executive order this financial structure not only in his own time but for the future.

Yet it was argued twenty years later that President Roosevelt compromised too much in meeting the financial crisis of 1933. The nationalization of the banking system could have been tried, had not "practical" men opposed. Thus, the President compromised on "reform" in order to win "recovery." Mr. Warburg had remarked, shortly after the eventful period of President Roosevelt's first months in office that "Franklin Roosevelt will get more credit, when the final page is written, for having resisted inflation than for the steps he took in its direction. . . ."

As was natural, this extensive program of recovery and reform brought down upon the President charges of executive usurpation, of unconstitutional legislation, of stifling debts and taxation and, of course, certain national bankruptcy.

This brought into sharp focus the basic assumption of the President that the causes for maladjustment and weakening of democracy were to be found in the intention and philosophy of selfish groups who had ruled in the business and governmental life of the nation, and would do so again if the President were not upheld. These groups, in turn, made plain their opposition to his program of recovery and reform—even though they reluctantly accepted most of the measures for relief. Even these were preludes to socialism—in the eyes of most of his critics.

The heart of the opposition was found among the American business men who expressed more clearly than anywhere else in the world the view dominant among industrial and financial classes. The business man knew that he was no longer favored by a government that gave increased benefits to laborers in factory, farm, and mine. And unorganized labor was favored also because it was from its ranks that came the majority of the unemployed. If the purpose of the President was to bring into "better balance," as he so often said, agriculture, labor, and industry, then it was evident that he had succeeded—to the great advantage of wage earners and consumers—that is, if the capitalistic system could stand such transformation. . . .

The results of administrative action, facilitated by Congressional agreement in the first year of the new administration, thus produced varying response from the American people. Unquestionably a growing sense of assurance and of confidence activated the workers of the nation. This brought public realization, as well, of the vast number of the so-called underprivileged in so large a nation. Many of the would-be leaders had perceived a way out of their distress, and the extremists among them saw that perhaps this was the time to make fundamental changes not only in the political structure but in the social bases of American life.

At the same time, a revival of doubt as to the wisdom of much that had been done in 1933 was particularly evident among those who had been defeated in the Congressional elections of 1932. After all, many of these representatives of the people had been in power for a long time. They felt that they represented sections of the population that had led in the building of America. They represented now the gigantic power that rested in potential industrial and financial might.

Neither convinced followers of the New Deal nor those who had for a time acquiesced in it but were now convinced that it was filling but a temporary need, were much interested in the significant events taking place in western Europe. So concentrated upon the American scene was popular attention that most commentators agreed that the advocates of isolationism were expressing a deep and widely felt conviction of masses of the people.

As the campaign for members of the Congress developed in the late autumn of 1934, proposals for social security were an issue. The Democratic organization and most of the Democratic candidates actively supported administration proposals on this matter. Although the President was not personally a candidate, to an unusual degree the campaigning of 1934 was done in terms of the issues raised by his Presidential leadership. He was charged with unconstitutional action, with general usurpation of power, with a shifting policy on both taxation and debts, and with a general willingness to push the nation into later bankruptcy in his vigorous desire to build broader bases for political action through public expenditure.

It was remarked, as the campaign came to occupy general attention, that despite some significant state conflicts, no clear cut national decision was possible because the Congressional elections were, as usual, fought at random in terms of persons as well as issues. The outcome, nevertheless, strengthened the Democratic party in the Congress. This in turn, as usual, enlarged the problem of party control for the President, and decisions made by the Congress were, paradoxically, less clear cut.

As long as the President had loyal following in the Congress, the way of executive-legislative action was clear. Long-term results could not as yet be measured. Of course each new departure in legislation would in time be brought into the courts for judgment on Constitutional grounds. . . .

"That he is entitled to full credit for inducing recovery" could be said by Walter Lippmann in early 1934 as "demonstrably certain."

Yet a British critic observed that "In thus pinning their faith to the hem of the garments of a superman, the American people in 1933 were reacting to the World Crisis in somewhat the same fashion as their German and Italian and Russian contemporaries."

But an American publishing *The New Dealers* under the pseudonym of "Unofficial Observer" wrote with keener insight

The essence of the peaceful revolution which has begun under Roosevelt is that it is a new deal and not a free-for-all. . . .
For the New Deal is a laughing revolution. It is purging our institutions in the fires of mockery, and it is led by a group of men who possess two supreme qualifications for the task: common sense and a sense of humor.

It was said by the President that the people had nothing to fear but fear itself. This was primarily a call upon the individual to reassert his manhood. As the event proved, however, it was a suggestion that he might be saved by efforts other than his own. Presently he was assured that he *need* not fear, because his government would take care of him.

In this atmosphere of dependence, the American people easily gave over powers to the President. Millions were voted for the unemployed. Men co-operated in caring for themselves as they cared for their fellow citizens! This attitude of dependence—of itself working incalculable harm to the sturdy mind of America—was accompanied by cynicism and crass materialism. Much has been made of the iniquities of the industrial and financial world. Less has been said of the general attitude of distrust, envy, and disillusionment among the American people as a whole at this time. Too little, furthermore, has been said of the underly-

ing feeling that enabled a people emerging from serious financial crisis
to acclaim the repeal of the Eighteenth Amendment.

Whereas renewed confidence among those who were guiding the
destinies of the country came to be for the time being the mood in which
Congress resumed its function in January of 1935, many of the more extreme elements in the population still looked for drastic changes. Leaders representing these elements had wide appeal—particularly within a
half dozen states of the Union—and there were representatives in the
Congress as well.

The fact that the extremists were not satisfied with what the administration was doing is in itself clear evidence, if further evidence was necessary, that the President was succeeding in his role as conciliator of
the organized units of the American economy. Whatever may be thought
of his qualities in economic statesmanship, his program for labor, agriculture and industry, as well as for finance, indicated how easily in fact,
if not in appearance, he took the middle road. As long as the country felt
that it was returning to normal ways of living and working, such a middle road would have great appeal.

A considerable number of business men and industrialists had taken
the lead in the formulation of the National Industrial Recovery Act,
whereas the reforms proposed in dealing with agriculture and with labor
were reforms that had been foreshadowed in much of the agitation of
the previous fifty years.

Let it be repeated that, except for the first days of the administration,
there was continuous criticism of the actions of the President. This
was a natural outgrowth of the arguments that had been given free rein
in the campaign of 1932, and that had not abated to any considerable
extent in the period prior to the inauguration.

Moreover, this criticism was continually given new reason for existence by the increasing tendency of many, after the immediate crisis had
passed, to give fulsome credit to the leadership of the President. From
any point of view the center of the controversy was the conduct of the
President himself. There was disagreement, and will be for many years
to come, as to the extent of the President's influence in the formulation
of policies, bills, and pronouncements. Yet however diverse their origin
and even their written formulation, it was the President who took responsibility and was held responsible.

In one year of administration he had so completely held the center of
the stage that there was agreement by advocate and opponent alike that
he was in the line of "strong" Presidents. This was far from the expectation of friends and opponents alike when he had been elected. Thus, increasingly, the issue in politics was the President himself.

The fact that, as a result of the 1934 Congressional elections, the
Democratic party maintained its control in both House and Senate

meant that through that party organization the President would continue to work his will and that of his advisers. The party membership was of divergent view on the issues before them. It was noted as well that although the Republican membership was on party principle opposed to everything in the President's program, some Republicans in Senate and House were in reality supporters of the President's policies.

Had the President chosen, now that the crisis was past, to turn "right," in the phrase of the day, it is absolutely certain that no leadership existent in the Congress could have commanded a national following for a program of social reform or economic change. If the President did not push reform, no one in Congress would do so. There were aspirants for opportunity to *lead*, but none of real competence. No one, not even Huey Long, Senator from Louisiana, had the power.

Despite Mr. Roosevelt's apparent stand for a policy in advance of Mr. Hoover's, when the President now turned to dealing directly with the problem of insecurity in finance and the problem of social security, he found himself less eagerly followed.

The continuance of a program of government help for unemployment was apparently the most unorthodox of all his plans. It reflected the point of view and purpose of great numbers of social workers, but it certainly did not reflect the convictions of those who felt that government must pay its own way.

In due time, when all the materials are available and when years of research and analysis have carefully arranged the narrative of events, it will be possible to see with reasonable finality how the program of the New Deal was formulated, and why it was planned thus. At present this much can be said:

The President placed himself actively at the head of those who held that government is all-powerful; that it must act for the interests of the people as a whole; that it must convince them it so acts; and that the way to do this is to recognize divergent economic interests, and by arrangement, compromise, and even authoritarian control, to compel them to work together.

Such an approach ran counter to the view and action of the preceding administration; it ran counter, as well, to the prevailing economics of the American system. Within this system, by following an entirely different method of political action, remarkable results had been attained under free enterprise.

But the New Deal did embody a new force to meet a new emergency. It appeared to fulfill the general point of view which had been held by progressives and liberals and radicals in politics for a half-century.

In seeming, however, to follow a familiar road, that is, in retaining the outward appearance of unlimited private enterprise, the administration was assured of a popular backing. Just so, Mr. Roosevelt was assured of the active opposition of all those who still held to the view that the chief duty of government was merely to hold the balance for a competitive system of free enterprise.

Much has been made, and properly, of the weakness of Mr. Roosevelt's knowledge of economics. Fortunately, his primary task was not in the field of economics. It was in the field of politics. And here he was well informed and by nature interested. Information and interest, together with growing experience, gave him great power.

The President appeared to his fellow citizens in the years 1933–1935 as their symbol of recovery and of promise for the future. His pace of action and of utterance was vigorous. Everywhere he went and before many audiences, he appeared no longer as the advocate of a particular program. He appeared as a new kind of President, and he was given wide acclaim.

Most of his critics present his position unfairly. They condemn his policy because it does not fit into an economic theory, or because it does not give proper protection to some particular group. Yet he was faithful to his idea that he was acting for the American people as a whole. He wanted to protect their liberties and give them opportunities, and he chose measures and men to bring this about. . . .

Charges of dictatorship were made, arising out of the pressures exerted by Mr. Roosevelt upon the Congress, which were resented by many Congressmen. Such charges were naturally of interest to commentators, who were quick to see that although the formalities of the Constitutional system were being observed, the actualities were quite otherwise.

It must be said that an examination of the comments of the period reveals that the President's control of the patronage was an important factor in his influence upon individual members of the Congress. The forms of legislative enactment were observed. This was possible because the President unerringly chose and maintained the initiative. Buoyed up by unmistakable evidences of popular backing, advised closely by men who were experts in the matter of legislation, the President had a partisan control of the Congress. As has been seen, no Constitutional change had been asked, except for the preliminary steps that had led to the rescinding of the Eighteenth Amendment.

Even though the American system worked through a combination of popular support, Congressional acquiescence, and Presidential initiative, the great test would in the end be what is termed Presidential leadership.

The sessions of the Seventy-third Congress, which concluded in June of 1934, had made amply apparent to all who would see that two aspects of the legislative program associated with the New Deal were now coming to stand forth as all-important. One of these was full acceptance of the idea of vast federal expenditures contributing speedy recovery. The other was the growing satisfaction, at least among those in public office, at the large amount of patronage available and the increasing number of persons dependent upon federal subsidy.

The programs of relief and recovery would in the nature of things cost billions. Inasmuch as no steps had yet been taken to deal effectively with the tax structure, it was apparent that this method of conducting government must rest upon the broad basis of borrowing. The free acceptance of this fact, not of particular interest to the public as a whole, was of vital concern to all those engaged in private enterprise.

A sense of insecurity and uncertainty as to the future was of course particularly felt by those interests in the financial and industrial world concerned with public utilities. The program of the administration embodied in the T.V.A. and the explanations of its purpose clearly foreshadowed extension of governmental activity in this field.

Mr. Hoover repeatedly warned that the greatest danger in planning and regimentation lay in decline of the representative body and undue reliance on bureaucracy. "We cannot extend the mastery of government over the daily life of the people," Mr. Hoover contended, "without somewhere making it master of people's souls and thoughts."

It was clear by this time that the American people had set forth upon an unaccustomed and dimly discerned road to the future. . . .

In using the methods of the demagogue, Franklin Roosevelt was doing nothing new. In that sense, his revolutionary procedures were closely akin to those of a long line of American radicals. But *his* revolution consisted in making over the government itself: first, in a tremendous concentration of power in the Executive; second, in building up a vast system of bureaucratic control of private business; and third, by destroying the idea that much could be achieved for the people, by the government as umpire, through a careful adjustment of conflicting economic interests.

It is not possible to get at the heart of the Roosevelt revolution by confining attention to Mr. Roosevelt's wide support by masses of the population. The revolution consisted, rather, in a complete shift of the American view of the *role* of government. Government, and particularly the Executive, was to be all-powerful.

The defense of this—if there was a defense—was that the people freely and frequently could pass judgment upon it. As long as free elections persisted at stated times, no danger was embodied in such a government.

Protection against the action of a powerful government was assured by the strong weapon in American practice—free speech and the free press. Of course any suppression of absolute freedom would limit criticism.

It is perhaps significant that, like all popular leaders, the President was highly critical of those who freely criticized him. It is perhaps also significant that the masses did not fail to support him, and that except for a minority of extremists they failed to criticize him. Support based upon absence of criticism shelters the seeds of disaster. Had there been at any time a mere suggestion of suppression of the newspapers and commentators who vigorously opposed him, it would have been clearer to all how great a claim to absolute power the President's utterances and acts embodied.

To sum up the effect of Mr. Roosevelt's leadership at the time of his first re-election, it might be said that it was altogether "good" in arousing the public conscience to evils which had been observed by generations, but which had never moved any group in power to a comprehensive program of change. It might be added that it was "good" that he was able to formulate changes and to write them into law.

On the other hand, that his leadership aroused intense antagonism on the part of the more thoughtful members of society, was a direct effect of the basic *methods* used by the President. That is, in declaring that championship of a program on behalf of the people was in itself an indication of the virtue of the program, the President allied himself with the oldest enemies of democracy, in scorn of careful and sustained thought.

It cannot be said that in the long run the Roosevelt leadership was "good" in weakening greatly the powers of Congress. It must be admitted, however, that the events which followed the end of the Roosevelt years would tend to suggest that Congress has returned to somewhat the same position and function that it occupied prior to 1933.

It cannot be said that the attitude of the masses of the people on the Roosevelt leadership at this time was altogether healthy. That the place of careful planning was weakened is notable. In short, Mr. Roosevelt's experiments worked the greatest harm to the very people they were intended to benefit.

Yet, in the perspective of the intervening years, the emotional drive back of many of the violent charges against the President seems as unreal as the emotions of men a hundred or five hundred years ago. That Franklin Roosevelt was destroying private enterprise, was providing financial ruin, was substituting for a people's government a vast unmanageable bureaucracy; that there was in existence an electioneering agency that could not be beaten, that the administration was in fact socialistic and Communistic—criticisms that won plaudits from conservatives in 1936—seem unreal in 1955.

Mr. Roosevelt's conception of the Presidency, as he saw it in 1936, and the way he had functioned in the light of that conception during the first administration should be used as one basis for judging his influence upon the American system and his success in office.

Out of office and in an opposition party, his type of leadership would not have been at its best. In view of his record, it is difficult to think of

him as a minority leader year by year urging a forlorn hope. His participation as Vice-Presidential candidate in the campaign of 1920 is a case
in point.

Nor is it possible to envisage him providing patient and enduring leadership in a long campaign to present a particular program to an uninter-
ested and unresponsive voting population.

As a leader of the Congressional opposition, he would have been at a
disadvantage, lacking knowledge of economics and the technicalities of
legislation, and being unwilling or unable to co-operate with men of
equal responsibility.

But from the outset, the Presidency afforded him an opportunity to
govern and to lead, in his own way. His concept and use of this office is
clearly indicated by the kind of followers that composed his immediate
group of advisers. Perhaps more revealing still was the kind of opposition he incurred at each stage of his Presidency—never more clearly
than in the campaign of 1936.

Against a background of a generation of political history (1900–
1936), the American people returned to office a President who under the
slogan of "New Deal" and speaking for "The Forgotten Man," had provided a government in the pattern well recognized by radicals and progressives. This was a fact. No previous leader had done it—not even
Woodrow Wilson in the first year and a half of his administration.

Why had it been possible for Franklin Roosevelt to win confirmation
in 1936? Were the people convinced that they could turn back on the
road that led to national growth? Did they realize that Roosevelt's road
meant, by contrast, another way of life? Or had they re-elected Roosevelt
because they had been saved by him and were still frightened into believing his charges against the conservatives?

It is highly doubtful that, in the perspective of years, it will appear
that the American people had in 1936 decided upon so positive a change.
In the first place, a great minority—vocal, powerful, and long experienced—said "No!" This minority had been unable to make a clear-cut
campaign on the basic issues—as they could have done had they dared
to nominate Herbert Hoover.

On the other hand, the radicals were not convinced of the soundness
of Franklin Roosevelt's program, even though they praised it. They knew
it for what it was—the result of the planning of a combination of dis-
cordant elements that were bound to the party machines of the North as
well as to the ultra-conservatives of the South.

But, although opposed by the financial interests of the country, by the
conservatives of the South, and by the radicals of real conviction, Franklin Roosevelt and his heavy majorities in all parts of the nation were returned to complete control of the national government.

A comparison of the election results in 1936 with the outcome in 1932 is productive of real understanding of the meaning of this election. For the majority in 1932 had been made up in large part of rebels, insurgents, and those hitherto deprived of political power. In 1936 the majority were endorsing what their leaders with their support had been able to do. Yet no decision had been made in acceptance of any program except one—"Do not thwart the will of the People"—as expressed by President Roosevelt.

It followed that every issue was now to be fought anew—in the Congress and in the country. Turmoil, confusion, and incoherence were to characterize practically every discussion and prevent clear-cut decision on the most important issues. The country was to know no political peace. . . .

By 1937 it was clear that the leadership of Franklin Roosevelt had altered beyond easy recognition all existing political parties, including his own. It may be argued that he was but the victim of forces far beyond the control of even so successful a politician as he had proved himself to be. But it was his view as a personal leader who stood upon popular support with intention to further popular programs, that had taken the meaning out of Republican protest, out of splinter party appeal, and in the end out of Democratic party doctrine. If the political parties that had existed could have been barred from further activity, the real nature of the change would have been seen.

Could the President have gone to the country—without party support and not opposed by parties as such—it is probable that a majority of the electorate would have endorsed him and whatever program he offered at the time. The radicals saw this. It was a reflection not only of the mood elsewhere in the world, but in truth a reflection of many of the deeper currents of our own history that had been obscured by our natural aptitude for compromise rather than clear-cut decision.

The progressive tradition in American political feeling had an important part in determining the state of mind in which upholders of the President often met the charge that they were really Communists. The retort often on their lips was, We are "simply trying to improve the social order and give the underdog a chance."

Despite all that could be said—and was said repeatedly in press, on the radio, in pulpit, and in public forum—against the dangers of personal rule, a large section of the American public craved a dictator. The deepest wound that had been given the American practice of self-government had been given by its professed friends. Every argument, every program, every success on behalf of the American people made them less able to perform the functions of a self-supporting people. They asked security and were disposed to pay the price, whatever it was.

As has been seen, the fundamental divisions in American political feeling which had emerged during the first two terms of Franklin Roosevelt's Presidency were altered—for a time—by a new development in Europe. That the Nazi leader, Hitler, entered into a compact with the Communist leader, Stalin, could be easily comprehended by most Americans. Yet it shocked beyond measure the radicals in the United States, and led to a re-formation of political lines.

Russia was now linked with Germany as an enemy of democracy. It became clear that disagreements among radicals in the United States had roots in a misunderstanding of what communism really was. On the whole, the revelation of the pact and its meaning to the free world strengthened the hand and argument of all conservatives. And, as will be seen, this enabled the President to win many conservatives to his standard for the war in which the United States was about to engage.

Yet facts were facts. In six years of experimentation the national debt had been doubled. In every one of the years the administration had been in the eyes of the accountant "insolvent." "Private business" was still the basic interest of Americans in every walk of life. "Capitalism" had been saved because, with all the experimentation, the national government stood back of all "costs." So it was at last clear that not "Big Business" nor "Big Labor," nor "Big Farmers" would save the United States, but "Big Government."

SUGGESTIONS FOR FURTHER READING

The New Deal has already inspired more writing than many periods in American history, and most of it has been favorable. A balanced, general account, tightly packed and entertainingly written, is William E. Leuchtenburg, *Franklin Roosevelt and the New Deal* (New York, 1963). Leuchtenburg emphasizes the change in American life brought about by the New Deal, but not to the extent that Mario Einaudi does in The Roosevelt Revolution (New York, 1959). Arthur Schlesinger, Jr. has completed three volumes of his major study of The Age of Roosevelt (*The Crisis of the Old Order, The Coming of the New Deal, and The Politics of Upheaval [Boston, 1957, 1959, 1960]). Schlesinger writes exciting history and shows Roosevelt, the pragmatic-idealist, moving from cooperation with the business community early in his first term to a more critical attitude after 1935.

The best one-volume biography of Roosevelt is James MacGregor Burns, *Roosevelt: The Lion and the Fox (New York, 1956). Burns, like most historians, views Roosevelt as essentially conservative on political and economic issues. There is a great need for an intelligent evaluation of the New Deal from the right. Edgar Robinson, The Roosevelt Leadership, 1933–45 (Philadelphia, 1955), part of which is reprinted here, is better than John T. Flynn, The Roosevelt Myth (New York, 1948), but still is not adequate.

IX
THE ★
AMERICAN ★
CHARACTER ★

No question has intrigued Americans more than that asked by Michel-Guillaume de Crevecoeur during the Revolutionary War: "What then is the American, this new man?" Since that time literally thousands of Americans and foreign observers have asked that question anew. For, despite the efforts of perspicacious, sensitive commentators and highly trained specialists, the answer has been elusive.

The very fact that obvious and easily accepted American traits could not be found accounts, of course, for the fascination the question holds. Yet there is more to it than this. It might be just as difficult to describe and define the English character or the French character or the Italian character, but unlike Americans, Englishmen, Frenchmen, and Italians have given scant attention to the problem of trying to define what they were.

It is ironic that while Americans cannot agree on what an American is, they have devoted considerable attention to attempting to define what is un-American. Perhaps because we are so unsure of our identity, we constantly seek to set up certain rigid and mechanical standards to take the place of something we should all feel or take for granted. Or perhaps it is because we are so different and diverse, because we lack common characteristics which would arise from a long historical tradition, that we seek to set minimum standards. Maybe it is because we are so different that we must organize "Americanization" programs and search for "un-American activities" in our communities.

For whatever reason, Americans have been fascinated with the problem of discovering who they are. The reports and comments of thousands of visitors to our shores— Alexis de Tocqueville, Harriet Martineau, Charles Dickens, Frances Trollope, Lord Bryce, and Denis W. Brogan, to name but a few of the more insightful and better known —have been read eagerly in this country. Even those like Charles Dickens who heaped scorn upon us have been widely read. And the continued popularity of their works to the present day attests to the continued interest in the subject.

The search for an American character is a part of the consensus tradition in American history. Those who seek *the* American character have by the very definition of the problem accepted the notion of unity. Their premise (for which they feel no proof is required) is that there is *an* American character; their problem is to find *it*, describe *it*, and account for *it*. For such people there is something in the American environment and in the American experience which has molded a common American character. Thus there is not only a basic uniformity among Americans, but also a general continuity in American history: Certain relatively unchanging conditions have resulted in the creation of a relatively homogeneous population exhibiting basically common characteristics.

Not all of those who seek it find *an* American character; some find more than one. Accepting the argument that environment and experience create character, these people insist either that the American environment has changed so significantly over the years that there have been changes in the American character over time, or they argue that the environment at any given time is so diverse that different people experience different environments and hence have different characters.

In the first selection which follows, David M. Potter finds *an* American character stemming from the experience of economic abundance. Michael Harrington is also concerned with the affluent society, but he argues that there is a large part of the American population which does not experience economic abundance and hence does not share a common character with those who do. For Harrington there are really two Americas.

Frederick Jackson Turner looks at the matter in a very different way. For him the most important factor creating *an* American character was the frontier experience. Yet implicit in his entire argument is the suggestion that there would probably be a change, for he finds (writing in 1893) that for the first time in American history there is no longer a frontier. David Riesman is much more explicit. He finds that changes in the American society in the last hundred years have resulted in distinct and significant changes in the American character over this period.

Thus to answer Crevecoeur's question we must look back into American history and out into contemporary society. Were our experiences in the past similar enough to develop common characteristics which would set us apart from others? Was the American a "new man"? Or were our experiences so diverse that we must speak of several American characters? Have Americans changed over time? Has our society altered so fundamentally that we may speak of a changing American character? And what of today? Do businessmen and workers, Northerners and Southerners, Negroes and whites, urbanites and rural dwellers share a common character?

Abundance
and the
formation of
character

David M. Potter

Let us consider the situation of a six-month-old American infant, who is not yet aware that he is a citizen, a taxpayer, and a consumer.

This individual is, to all appearances, just a very young specimen of *Homo sapiens*, with certain needs for protection, care, shelter, and nourishment which may be regarded as the universal biological needs of human infancy rather than specific cultural needs. It would be difficult to prove that the culture has as yet differentiated him from other infants, and, though he is an American, few would argue that he has acquired an American character. Yet abundance and the circumstances arising from abundance have already dictated a whole range of basic conditions which, from his birth, are constantly at work upon this child and which will contribute in the most intimate and basic way to the formation of his character.

To begin with, abundance has already revolutionized the typical mode of his nourishment by providing for him to be fed upon cow's milk rather than upon his mother's milk, taken from the bottle rather than from the breast. Abundance contributes vitally to this transformation, because bottle feeding requires fairly elaborate facilities of refrigeration, heating, sterilization, and temperature control, which only an advanced technology can offer and only an economy of abundance can make widely available. I will not attempt here to resolve the debated question as to the psychological effects, for both mother and child, of bottle feeding as contrasted with breast feeding in infant nurture. But it is clear that the changeover to bottle feeding has encroached somewhat upon the intimacy of the bond between mother and child. The nature of this bond is, of course, one of the most crucial factors in the formation of character. Bottle feeding also must tend to emphasize the separateness of the infant as an individual, and thus it makes, for the first time, a point which the entire culture reiterates constantly throughout the life of the average American. In addition to the psychic influences which may be involved in the manner of taking the food, it is also a matter of capital importance that the bottle-fed baby is, on the whole,

better nourished than the breast-fed infant and therefore likely to grow
more rapidly, to be more vigorous, and to suffer fewer ailments, with
whatever effects these physical conditions may have upon his personality.

It may be argued also that abundance has provided a characteristic
mode of housing for the infant and that this mode further emphasizes
his separateness as an individual. In societies of scarcity, dwelling units
are few and hard to come by, with the result that high proportions of
newly married young people make their homes in the parental ménage,
thus forming part of an "extended" family, as it is called. Moreover,
scarcity provides a low ratio of rooms to individuals, with the consequence that whole families may expect as a matter of course to have
but one room for sleeping, where children will go to bed in intimate pro-
pinquity to their parents. But abundance prescribes a different regime.
By making it economically possible for newly married couples to maintain separate households of their own, it has almost destroyed the extended family as an institution in America and has ordained that the
child shall be reared in a "nuclear" family, so-called, where his only intimate associates are his parents and his siblings, with even the latter
far fewer now than in families of the past. The housing arrangements
of this new-style family are suggested by census data for 1950. In
that year there were 45,983,000 dwelling units to accommodate the
38,310,000 families in the United States, and, though the median
number of persons in the dwelling unit was 3.1, the median number
of rooms in the dwelling unit was 4.6. Eighty-four per cent of all dwelling units reported less than one person per room. By providing the ordinary family with more than one room for sleeping, the economy thus
produces a situation in which the child will sleep either in a room alone
or in a room shared with his brothers or sisters. Even without allowing for the cases in which children may have separate rooms, these
conditions mean that a very substantial percentage of children now
sleep in a room alone, for, with the declining birth rate, we have reached
a point at which an increasing proportion of families have one child
or two children rather than the larger number which was at one time
typical. For instance, in the most recent group of mothers who had
completed their childbearing phase, according to the census, 19.5 per
cent had had one child and 23.4 had had two. Thus almost half of all
families with offspring did not have more than two children throughout their duration. In the case of the first group, all the children were
"only" children throughout their childhood, and in the second group
half of the children were "only" children until the second child was
born. To state this in another, and perhaps a more forcible, way, it has
been shown that among American women who arrived at age thirty-
four during the year 1949 and who had borne children up to that time,

26.7 per cent had borne only one child, and 34.5 per cent had borne only two. If these tendencies persist, it would mean that, among families where there are children, hardly one in three will have more than two children.

The census has, of course, not got around to finding out how the new-style family, in its new-style dwelling unit, adjusts the life-practice to the space situation. But it is significant that America's most widely circulated book on the care of infants advises that "it is preferable that he [the infant] not sleep in his parents' room after he is about 12 months old," offers the opinion that "it's fine for each [child] to have a room of his own, if that's possible," and makes the sweeping assertion that "it's a sensible rule not to take a child into the parents' bed for any reason." It seems clear beyond dispute that the household space provided by the economy of abundance has been used to emphasize the separateness, the apartness, if not the isolation, of the American child.

Not only the nourishment and housing, but also the clothing of the American infant are controlled by American abundance. For one of the most sweeping consequences of our abundance is that, in contrast to other peoples who keep their bodies warm primarily by wearing clothes, Americans keep their bodies warm primarily by a far more expensive and even wasteful method: namely, by heating the buildings in which they are sheltered. Every American who has been abroad knows how much lighter is the clothing—especially the underclothing—of Americans than of people in countries like England and France, where the winters are far less severe than ours, and every American who can remember the conditions of a few decades ago knows how much lighter our clothing is than that of our grandparents. These changes have occurred because clothing is no longer the principal device for securing warmth. The oil furnace has not only displaced the open fireplace; it has also displaced the woolen undergarment and the vest.

This is a matter of considerable significance for adults but of far greater importance to infants, for adults discipline themselves to wear warm garments, submitting, for instance, to woolen underwear more or less voluntarily. But the infant knows no such discipline, and his garments or bedclothes must be kept upon him by forcible means. Hence primitive people, living in outdoor conditions, swaddle the child most rigorously, virtually binding him into his clothes, and breaking him to them almost as a horse is broken to the harness. Civilized peoples mitigate the rigor but still use huge pins or clips to frustrate the baby's efforts to kick off the blankets and free his limbs. In a state of nature, cold means confinement and warmth means freedom, so far as young humans are concerned. But abundance has given the American infant physical freedom by giving him physical warmth in cold weather.

In this connection it may be surmised that abundance has also given him a permissive system of toilet training. If our forebears imposed such training upon the child and we now wait for him to take the initiative in these matters himself, it is not wholly because the former held a grim Calvinistic doctrine of child-rearing that is philosophically contrary to ours. The fact was that the circumstances gave them little choice. A mother who was taking care of several babies, keeping them clean, making their clothes, washing their diapers in her own washtub, and doing this, as often as not, while another baby was on the way, had little choice but to hasten their fitness to toilet themselves. Today, on the contrary, the disposable diaper, the diaper service, and most of all the washing machine, not to mention the fact that one baby seldom presses upon the heels of another, make it far easier for the mother to indulge the child in a regime under which he will impose his own toilet controls in his own good time.

Thus the economy of plenty has influenced the feeding of the infant, his regime, and the physical setting within which he lives. These material conditions alone might be regarded as having some bearing upon the formation of his character, but the impact of abundance by no means ends at this point. In so far as it has an influence in determining what specific individuals shall initiate the infant into the ways of man and shall provide him with his formative impressions of the meaning of being a person, it must be regarded as even more vital. When it influences the nature of the relationships between these individuals and the infant, it must be recognized as reaching to the very essence of the process of character formation.

The central figures in the dramatis personae of the American infant's universe are still his parents, and in this respect, of course, there is nothing peculiar either to the American child or to the child of abundance. But abundance has at least provided him with parents who are in certain respects unlike the parents of children born in other countries or born fifty years ago. To begin with, it has given him young parents, for the median age of fathers at the birth of the first child in American marriages (as of 1940) was 25.3 years, and the median age of mothers was 22.6 years. This median age was substantially lower than it had been in the United States in 1890 for both fathers and mothers. Moreover, as the size of families has been reduced and the wife no longer continues to bear a succession of children throughout the period of her fertility, the median age of mothers at the birth of the last child has declined from 32 years (1890) to 27 years (1940). The age of the parents at the birth of both the first child and the last child is far lower than in the case of couples in most European countries. There can be little doubt that abundance has caused this differential, in the case of the first-born by making it economically possible for a high proportion of the population to meet the expenses of homemaking at a fairly early age. In the case of the last-born, it would also appear that one major reason for the earlier cessation of childbearing is a determination by parents to enjoy a high standard of living themselves and to limit their offspring to a number for whom they can maintain a similar standard.

By the very fact of their youth, these parents are more likely to remain alive until the child reaches maturity, thus giving him a better prospect of being reared by his own mother and father. This prospect is further reinforced by increases in the life-span, so that probably no child in history has ever enjoyed so strong a likelihood that his parents will survive to rear him. Abundance has produced this situation by providing optimum conditions for prolonging life. But, on the other hand, abundance has also contributed much to produce an economy in which the mother is no longer markedly dependent upon the father, and this change in the economic relation between the sexes has probably done much to remove obstacles to divorce. The results are all too familiar. During the decade 1940–49 there were 25.8 divorces for every 100 marriages in the United States, which ratio, if projected over a longer period, would mean that one marriage out of four would end in divorce. But our concern here is with a six-month-old child, and the problem is to know whether this factor of divorce involves childless couples predominantly or whether it is likely to touch him. The answer is indicated by the fact that, of all divorces granted in 1948, no less than 42 per cent were to couples with children under eighteen, and a very large proportion of these children were of much younger ages. Hence one might say that the economy of abundance has provided the child with younger parents who chose their role of parenthood deliberately and who are more likely than parents in the past to live until he is grown, but who are substantially less likely to preserve the unbroken family as the environment within which he shall be reared.

In addition to altering the characteristics of the child's parents, it has also altered the quantitative relationship between him and his parents. It has done this, first of all, by offering the father such lucrative opportunities through work outside the home that the old agricultural economy in which children worked alongside their fathers is now obsolete. Yet, on the other hand, the father's new employment gives so much more leisure than his former work that the child may, in fact, receive considerably more of his father's attention. But the most vital transformation is in the case of the mother. In the economy of scarcity which controlled the modes of life that were traditional for many centuries, an upper-class child was reared by a nurse, and all others were normally reared by their mothers. The scarcity economy could not support many nonproductive members, and these mothers, though not "employed," were most decidedly hard workers, busily engaged in cooking, washing, sewing, weaving, preserving, caring for the henhouse,

the garden, and perhaps the cow, and in general carrying on the domestic economy of a large family. Somehow they also attended to the
needs of a numerous brood of children, but the mother was in no sense
a full-time attendant upon any one child. Today, however, the economy
of abundance very nearly exempts a very large number of mothers from
the requirement of economic productivity in order that they may give
an unprecedented share of their time to the care of the one or two
young children who are now the usual number in an American family.
Within the home, the wide range of labor-saving devices and the assign-
ment of many functions, such as laundering, to service industries have
produced this result. Outside the home, employment of women in the
labor force has steadily increased, but the incidence of employment
falls upon unmarried women, wives without children, and wives with
grown children. In fact, married women without children are two and
one-half times as likely to be employed as those with children. Thus
what amounts to a new dispensation has been established for the child.
If he belongs to the upper class, his mother has replaced his nurse as
his full-time attendant. The differences in character formation that
might result from this change alone could easily be immense. To mention but one possibility, the presence of the nurse must inevitably have
made the child somewhat aware of his class status, whereas the presence of the mother would be less likely to have this effect. If the child
does not belong to the upper class, mother and child now impinge upon
each other in a relationship whose intensity is of an entirely different
magnitude from that which prevailed in the past. The mother has fewer
physical distractions in the care of the child, but she is more likely to
be restive in her maternal role because it takes her away from attractive employment with which it cannot be reconciled.

If abundance has thus altered the relationship of the child with his
parent, it has even more drastically altered the rest of his social milieu, for it has changed the identity of the rest of the personnel who
induct him into human society. In the extended family of the past, a
great array of kinspeople filled his cosmos and guided him to maturity.
By nature, he particularly needed association with children of his own
age (his "peers," as they are called), and he particularly responded to
the values asserted by these peers. Such peers were very often his brothers and sisters, and, since they were all members of his own family,
all came under parental control. This is to say that, in a sense, the parents controlled the peer group, and the peer group controlled the child.
The point is worth making because we frequently encounter the assertion that parental control of the child has been replaced by peer-group
control; but it is arguable that what is really the case is that children
were always deeply influenced by the peer group and that parents have
now lost their former measure of control over this group, since it is no

longer a familial group. Today the nursery school replaces the large family as a peer group, and the social associations, even of young children, undergo the same shift from focused contact with family to diffused contact with a miscellany of people, which John Galsworthy depicted for grown people in the three novels of the *Forsyte Saga*. Again, the effects upon character may very well be extensive.

Abundance, then, has played a critical part in revolutionizing both the physical circumstances and the human associations which surround the American infant and child. These changes alone would warrant the hypothesis that abundance has profoundly affected the formation of character for such a child. But to extend this inquiry one step further, it may be worth while to consider how these altered conditions actually impinge upon the individual. Here, of course, is an almost unlimited field for investigation, and I shall only attempt to indicate certain crucial points at which abundance projects conditions that are basic in the life of the child.

One of these points concerns the cohesive force which holds the family together. The family is the one institution which touches all members of society most intimately, and it is perhaps the only social institution which touches young children directly. The sources from which the family draws its strength are, therefore, of basic importance. In the past, these sources were, it would seem, primarily economic. For agrarian society, marriage distinctively involved a division of labor. Where economic opportunity was narrowly restricted, the necessity for considering economic ways and means in connection with marriage led to the arrangement of matches by parents and to the institution of the dowry. The emotional bonds of affection, while always important, were not deemed paramount, and the ideal of romantic love played little or no part in the lives of ordinary people. Where it existed at all, it was as an upper-class luxury. (The very term "courtship" implies this upper-class orientation.) This must inevitably have meant that the partners in the majority of marriages demanded less from one another emotionally than do the partners of romantic love and that the emotional factor was less important to the stability of the marriage. Abundance, however, has played its part in changing this picture. On the American frontier, where capital for dowries was as rare as opportunity for prosperous marriage was plentiful, the dowry became obsolete. Later still, when abundance began to diminish the economic duties imposed upon the housewife, the function of marriage as a division of labor ceased to seem paramount, and the romantic or emotional factor assumed increasing importance. Abundance brought the luxury of romantic love within the reach of all, and, as it did so, emotional harmony became the principal criterion of success in a marriage, while lack of such harmony became a major threat to the existence of the marriage. The statistics of divorce give us a measure of the loss of durability in marriage, but they give us no measure of the factors of instability in the marriages which endure and no measure of the increased focus upon emotional satisfactions in such marriages. The children of enduring marriages, as well as the children of divorce, must inevitably feel the impact of this increased emphasis upon emotional factors, must inevitably sense the difference in the foundations of the institution which holds their universe in place.

In the rearing of a child, it would be difficult to imagine any factors more vital than the distinction between a permissive and an authoritarian regime or more vital than the age at which economic responsibility is imposed. In both these matters the modern American child lives under a very different dispensation from children in the past. We commonly think of these changes as results of our more enlightened or progressive or humanitarian ideas. We may even think of them as results of developments in the specific field of child psychology, as if the changes were simply a matter of our understanding these matters better than our grandparents. But the fact is that the authoritarian discipline of the child, within the authoritarian family, was but an aspect of the authoritarian social system that was linked with the economy of scarcity. Such a regime could never have been significantly relaxed within the family so long as it remained diagnostic in the society. Nor could it have remained unmodified within the family, once society began to abandon it in other spheres.

Inevitably, the qualities which the parents inculcate in a child will depend upon the roles which they occupy themselves. For the ordinary man the economy of scarcity has offered one role, as Simon N. Patten observed many years ago, and the economy of abundance has offered another. Abundance offers "work calling urgently for workmen"; scarcity found the "worker seeking humbly any kind of toil." As a suppliant to his superiors, the worker under scarcity accepted the principle of authority; he accepted his own subordination and the obligation to cultivate the qualities appropriate to his subordination, such as submissiveness, obedience, and deference. Such a man naturally transferred the principle of authority into his own family and, through this principle, instilled into his children the qualities appropriate to people of their kind—submissiveness, obedience, and deference. Many copybook maxims still exist to remind us of the firmness of childhood discipline, while the difference between European and American children—one of the most clearly recognizable of all national differences—serves to emphasize the extent to which Americans have now departed from this firmness.

This new and far more permissive attitude toward children has arisen, significantly, in an economy of abundance, where work has called urgently for the workman. In this situation, no longer a suppliant, the workman found submissiveness no longer a necessity and therefore no longer a virtue. The principle of authority lost some of its majesty, and he was less likely to regard it as the only true criterion of domestic order. In short, he ceased to impose it upon his children. Finding that the most valuable trait in himself was a capacity for independent decision and self-reliant conduct in dealing with the diverse opportunities which abundance offered him, he tended to encourage this quality in his children. The irresponsibility of childhood still called for a measure of authority on one side and obedience on the other, but this became a means to an end and not an end in itself. On the whole, permissive training, to develop independent ability, even though it involves a certain sacrifice of obedience and discipline, is the characteristic mode of child-rearing in the one country which most distinctively enjoys an economy of abundance. Here, in a concrete way, one finds something approaching proof for Gerth and Mills's suggestion that the relation of father and child may have its importance not as a primary factor but rather as a "replica of the power relations of society."

If scarcity required men to "seek humbly any kind of toil," it seldom permitted women to seek employment outside the home at all. Consequently, the woman was economically dependent upon, and, accordingly, subordinate to, her husband or her father. Her subordination reinforced the principle of authority within the home. But the same transition which altered the role of the male worker has altered her status as well, for abundance "calling urgently for workmen" makes no distinctions of gender, and, by extending economic independence to women, has enabled them to assume the role of partners rather than of subordinates within the family. Once the relation of voluntarism and equality is introduced between husband and wife, it is, of course, far more readily extended to the relation between parent and child.

If abundance has fostered a more permissive regime for the child, amid circumstances of democratic equality within the family, it has no less certainly altered the entire process of imposing economic responsibility upon the child, hence the process of preparing the child for such responsibility. In the economy of scarcity, as I have remarked above, society could not afford to support any substantial quota of nonproductive members. Consequently, the child went to work when he was as yet young. He attended primary school for a much shorter school year than the child of today; only a minority attended high school; and only the favored few attended college. Even during the brief years of schooling, the child worked, in the home, on the farm, or even in the factory. But today the economy of abundance can afford to maintain a substantial proportion of the population in nonproductive status, and it assigns this role, sometimes against their will, to its younger and its elder members. It protracts the years of schooling, and it defers responsibilities for an unusually long span. It even enforces laws setting minimal ages for leaving school, for going to work, for consenting to sexual intercourse, or for marrying. It extends the jurisdiction of juvenile courts to the eighteenth or the twentieth year of age.

Such exemption from economic responsibility might seem to imply a long and blissful youth free from strain for the child. But the delays in reaching economic maturity are not matched by comparable delays in other phases of growing up. On the contrary, there are many respects in which the child matures earlier. Physically, the child at the lower social level will actually arrive at adolescence a year or so younger than his counterpart a generation ago, because of improvement in standards of health and nutrition. Culturally, the child is made aware of the allurements of sex at an earlier age, partly by his familiarity with the movies, television, and popular magazines, and partly by the practice of "dating" in the early teens. By the standards of his peer group, he is encouraged to demand expensive and mature recreations, similar to those of adults, at a fairly early age. By reason of the desire of his parents that he should excel in the mobility race and give proof during his youth of the qualities which will make him a winner in later life, he is exposed to the stimuli of competition before he leaves the nursery. Thus there is a kind of imbalance between the postponement of responsibility and the quickening of social maturity which may have contributed to make American adolescence a more difficult age than human biology alone would cause it to be. Here, again, there are broad implications for the formation of character, and here, again, abundance is at work on both sides of the equation, for it contributes as much to the hastening of social maturity as it does to the prolongation of economic immaturity.

Some of these aspects of the rearing of children in the United States are as distinctively American, when compared with other countries, as any Yankee traits that have ever been attributed to the American people. In the multiplicity which always complicates social analysis, such aspects of child-rearing might be linked with a number of factors in American life. But one of the more evident and more significant links, it would seem certain, is with the factor of abundance. Such a tie is especially pertinent in this discussion, where the intention of the whole book has been to relate the study of character, as the historian would approach it, to the same subject as it is viewed by the behavioral scientist. In this chapter, especially, the attempt has been made to throw a bridge between the general historical force of economic abundance and the specific behavioral pattern of people's lives. Historical forces are too often considered only in their public and over-all effects, while private lives are interpreted without sufficient reference to the historical determinants which shape them. But no major force at work in society can possibly make itself felt at one of these levels without also having its impact at the other level. In view of this fact, the study of national character should not stand apart, as it has in the past, from the study of the process of character formation in the individual. In view of this fact, also, the effect of economic abundance is especially pertinent. For economic abundance is a factor whose presence and whose force may be clearly and precisely recognized in the most personal and intimate phases of the development of personality in the child. Yet, at the same time, the presence and the force of this factor are recognizable with equal certainty in the whole broad, general range of American experience, American ideals, and American institutions. At both levels, it has exercised a pervasive influence in the shaping of the American character.

The
other
America

Michael Harrington

There is a familiar America. It is celebrated in speeches and advertised on television and in the magazines. It has the highest mass standard of living the world has ever known.

In the 1950's this America worried about itself, yet even its anxieties were products of abundance. The title of a brilliant book was widely misinterpreted, and the familiar America began to call itself "the affluent society." There was introspection about Madison Avenue and tail fins; there was discussion of the emotional suffering taking place in the suburbs. In all this, there was an implicit assumption that the basic grinding economic problems had been solved in the United States. In this theory the nation's problems were no longer a matter of basic human needs, of food, shelter, and clothing. Now they were seen as qualitative, a question of learning to live decently amid luxury.

While this discussion was carried on, there existed another America. In it dwelt somewhere between 40,000,000 and 50,000,000 citizens of this land. They were poor. They still are.

To be sure, the other America is not impoverished in the same sense as those poor nations where millions cling to hunger as a defense against starvation. This country has escaped such extremes. That does not change the fact that tens of millions of Americans are, at this very moment, maimed in body and spirit, existing at levels beneath those necessary for human decency. If these people are not starving, they are hungry, and sometimes fat with hunger, for that is what cheap foods do. They are without adequate housing and education and medical care.

The Government has documented what this means to the bodies of the poor, and the figures will be cited throughout this book. But even more basic, this poverty twists and deforms the spirit. The American poor are pessimistic and defeated, and they are victimized by mental suffering to a degree unknown in Suburbia.

This book is a description of the world in which these people live; it is about the other America. Here are the unskilled workers, the migrant farm workers, the aged, the minorities, and all the others who live in the economic underworld of American life. In all this, there will be statistics, and that offers the opportunity for disagreement among honest and sincere men. I would ask the reader to respond critically to every assertion, but not to allow statistical quibbling to obscure the huge, enormous, and intolerable fact of poverty in America. For, when all is said and done, that fact is unmistakable, whatever its exact dimensions, and the truly human reaction can only be outrage. As W. H. Auden wrote:

> Hunger allows no choice
> To the citizen or the police;
> We must love one another or die.

The millions who are poor in the United States tend to become increasingly invisible. Here is a great mass of people, yet it takes an effort of the intellect and will even to see them.

I discovered this personally in a curious way. After I wrote my first article on poverty in America, I had all the statistics down on paper. I had proved to my satisfaction that there were around 50,000,000 poor in this country. Yet, I realized I did not believe my own figures. The poor existed in the Government reports; they were percentages and numbers in long, close columns, but they were not part of my experience. I could prove that the other America existed, but I had never been there.

My response was not accidental. It was typical of what is happening to an entire society, and it reflects profound social changes in this nation. The other America, the America of poverty, is hidden today in a way that it never was before. Its millions are socially invisible to the rest of us. No wonder that so many misinterpreted Galbraith's title and assumed that "the affluent society" meant that everyone had a decent standard of life. The misinterpretation was true as far as the actual day-to-day lives of two-thirds of the nation were concerned. Thus, one must begin a description of the other America by understanding why we do not see it.

There are perennial reasons that make the other America an invisible land.

Poverty is often off the beaten track. It always has been. The ordinary tourist never left the main highway, and today he rides interstate turnpikes. He does not go into the valleys of Pennsylvania where the towns look like movie sets of Wales in the thirties. He does not see the company houses in rows, the rutted roads (the poor always have bad roads whether they live in the city, in towns, or on farms), and everything is black and dirty. And even if he were to pass through such a place by accident, the tourist would not meet the unemployed men in the bar or the women coming home from a runaway sweatshop.

Then, too, beauty and myths are perennial masks of poverty. The traveler comes to the Appalachians in the lovely season. He sees the hills, the streams, the foliage—but not the poor. Or perhaps he looks at a run-down mountain house and, remembering Rousseau rather than seeing with his eyes, decides that "those people" are truly fortunate to be living the way they are and that they are lucky to be exempt from the strains and tensions of the middle class. The only problem is that "those people," the quaint inhabitants of those hills, are undereducated, underprivileged, lack medical care, and are in the process of being forced from the land into a life in the cities, where they are misfits.

These are normal and obvious causes of the invisibility of the poor. They operated a generation ago; they will be functioning a generation hence. It is more important to understand that the very development of American society is creating a new kind of blindness about poverty. The poor are increasingly slipping out of the very experience and consciousness of the nation.

If the middle class never did like ugliness and poverty, it was at least aware of them. "Across the tracks" was not a very long way to go. There were forays into the slums at Christmas time; there were charitable organizations that brought contact with the poor. Occasionally, almost everyone passed through the Negro ghetto or the blocks of tenements, if only to get downtown to work or to entertainment.

Now the American city has been transformed. The poor still inhabit the miserable housing in the central area, but they are increasingly isolated from contact with, or sight of, anybody else. Middle-class women coming in from Suburbia on a rare trip may catch the merest glimpse of the other America on the way to an evening at the theater, but their children are segregated in suburban schools. The business or professional man may drive along the fringes of slums in a car or bus, but it is not an important experience to him. The failures, the unskilled, the disabled, the aged, and the minorities are right there, across the tracks, where they have always been. But hardly anyone else is.

In short, the very development of the American city has removed poverty from the living, emotional experience of millions upon millions of middle-class Americans. Living out in the suburbs, it is easy to assume that ours is, indeed, an affluent society.

This new segregation of poverty is compounded by a well-meaning ignorance. A good many concerned and sympathetic Americans are aware that there is much discussion of urban renewal. Suddenly, driving through the city, they notice that a familiar slum has been torn down and that there are towering, modern buildings where once there had been tenements or hovels. There is a warm feeling of satisfaction, of pride in the way things are working out: the poor, it is obvious, are being taken care of.

The irony in this . . . is that the truth is nearly the exact opposite to the impression. The total impact of the various housing programs in post-war America has been to squeeze more and more people into existing slums. More often than not, the modern apartment in a towering building rents at $40 a room or more. For, during the past decade and a half, there has been more subsidization of middle- and upper-income housing than there has been of housing for the poor.

Clothes make the poor invisible too: America has the best-dressed poverty the world has ever known. For a variety of reasons, the benefits of mass production have been spread much more evenly in this area than in many others. It is much easier in the United States to be decently dressed than it is to be decently housed, fed, or doctored. Even people with terribly depressed incomes can look prosperous.

This is an extremely important factor in defining our emotional and existential ignorance of poverty. In Detroit the existence of social classes became much more difficult to discern the day the companies put lockers in the plants. From that moment on, one did not see men in work clothes on the way to the factory, but citizens in slacks and white shirts. This process has been magnified with the poor throughout the country. There are tens of thousands of Americans in the big cities who are wearing shoes, perhaps even a stylishly cut suit or dress, and yet are hungry. It is not a matter of planning, though it almost seems as if the affluent society had given out costumes to the poor so that they would not offend the rest of society with the sight of rags.

Then, many of the poor are the wrong age to be seen. A good number of them (over 8,000,000) are sixty-five years of age or better; an even larger number are under eighteen. The aged members of the other America are often sick, and they cannot move. Another group of them live out their lives in loneliness and frustration: they sit in rented rooms, or else they stay close to a house in a neighborhood that has completely changed from the old days. Indeed, one of the worst aspects of poverty among the aged is that these people are out of sight and out of mind, and alone.

The young are somewhat more visible, yet they too stay close to their neighborhoods. Sometimes they advertise their poverty through a lurid tabloid story about a gang killing. But generally they do not disturb the quiet streets of the middle class.

And finally, the poor are politically invisible. It is one of the cruelest ironies of social life in advanced countries that the dispossessed at the bottom of society are unable to speak for themselves. The people of the other America do not, by far and large, belong to unions, to fraternal organizations, or to political parties. They are without lobbies of their own; they put forward no legislative program. As a group, they are atomized. They have no face; they have no voice.

Thus, there is not even a cynical political motive for caring about the poor, as in the old days. Because the slums are no longer centers of powerful political organizations, the politicians need not really care about their inhabitants. The slums are no longer visible to the middle class, so much of the idealistic urge to fight for those who need help is gone. Only the social agencies have a really direct involvement with the other America, and they are without any great political power.

To the extent that the poor have a spokesman in American life, that role is played by the labor movement. The unions have their own particular idealism, an ideology of concern. More than that, they realize that the existence of a reservoir of cheap, unorganized labor is a menace to wages and working conditions throughout the entire economy. Thus, many union legislative proposals—to extend the coverage of minimum wage and social security, to organize migrant farm laborers—articulate the needs of the poor.

That the poor are invisible is one of the most important things about them. They are not simply neglected and forgotten as in the old rhetoric of reform; what is much worse, they are not seen. . . .

Forty to 50,000,000 people are becoming increasingly invisible. That is a shocking fact. But there is a second basic irony of poverty that is equally important: if one is to make the mistake of being born poor, he should choose a time when the majority of the people are miserable too.

J. K. Galbraith develops this idea in *The Affluent Society,* and in doing so defines the "newness" of the kind of poverty in contemporary America. The old poverty, Galbraith notes, was general. It was the condition of life of an entire society, or at least of that huge majority who were without special skills or the luck of birth. When the entire economy advanced, a good many of these people gained higher standards of living. Unlike the poor today, the majority poor of a generation ago were an immediate (if cynical) concern of political leaders. The old slums of the immigrants had the votes; they provided the basis for labor organizations; their very numbers could be a powerful force in political conflict. At the same time the new technology required higher skills, more education, and stimulated an upward movement for millions.

Perhaps the most dramatic case of the power of the majority poor took place in the 1930's. The Congress of Industrial Organizations literally organized millions in a matter of years. A labor movement that had been declining and confined to a thin stratum of the highly skilled suddenly embraced masses of men and women in basic industry. At the same time this acted as a pressure upon the Government, and the New Deal codified some of the social gains in laws like the Wagner Act. The result was not a basic transformation of the American system, but it did transform the lives of an entire section of the population.

In the thirties one of the reasons for these advances was that misery was general. There was no need then to write books about unemployment and poverty. That was the decisive social experience of the entire society, and the apple sellers even invaded Wall Street. There was political sympathy from middle-class reformers; there were an élan and spirit that grew out of a deep crisis.

Some of those who advanced in the thirties did so because they had unique and individual personal talents. But for the great mass, it was a question of being at the right point in the economy at the right time in history, and utilizing that position for common struggle. Some of those who failed did so because they did not have the will to take advantage of new opportunities. But for the most part the poor who were left behind had been at the wrong place in the economy at the wrong moment in history.

These were the people in the unorganizable jobs, in the South, in the minority groups, in the fly-by-night factories that were low on capital and high on labor. When some of them did break into the economic mainstream—when, for instance, the CIO opened up the way for some Negroes to find good industrial jobs—they proved to be as resourceful as anyone else. As a group, the other Americans who stayed behind were not originally composed primarily of individual failures. Rather, they were victims of an impersonal process that selected some for progress and discriminated against others.

Out of the thirties came the welfare state. Its creation had been stimulated by mass impoverishment and misery, yet it helped the poor least of all. Laws like unemployment compensation, the Wagner Act, the various farm programs, all these were designed for the middle third in the cities, for the organized workers, and for the upper third in the country, for the big market farmers. If a man works in an extremely low-paying job, he may not even be covered by social security or other welfare programs. If he receives unemployment compensation, the payment is scaled down according to his low earnings.

One of the major laws that was designed to cover everyone, rich and poor, was social security. But even here the other Americans suffered discrimination. Over the years social security payments have not even provided a subsistence level of life. The middle third have been able to supplement the Federal pension through private plans negotiated by unions, through joining medical insurance schemes like Blue Cross, and so on. The poor have not been able to do so. They lead a bitter life, and then have to pay for that fact in old age.

Indeed, the paradox that the welfare state benefits those least who need help most is but a single instance of a persistent irony in the other America. Even when the money finally trickles down, even when a school is built in a poor neighborhood, for instance, the poor are still deprived. Their entire environment, their life, their values, do not prepare them to take advantage of the new opportunity. The parents are anxious for the children to go to work; the pupils are pent up, waiting for the moment when their education has complied with the law.

Today's poor, in short, missed the political and social gains of the thirties. They are, as Galbraith rightly points out, the first minority poor in history, the first poor not to be seen, the first poor whom the politicians could leave alone.

The first step toward the new poverty was taken when millions of people proved immune to progress. When that happened, the failure was not individual and personal, but a social product. But once the historic accident takes place, it begins to become a personal fate.

The new poor of the other America saw the rest of society move ahead. They went on living in depressed areas, and often they tended to become depressed human beings. In some of the West Virginia towns, for instance, an entire community will become shabby and defeated. The young and the adventurous go to the city, leaving behind those who cannot move and those who lack the will to do so. The entire area becomes permeated with failure, and that is one more reason the big corporations shy away.

Indeed, one of the most important things about the new poverty is that it cannot be defined in simple, statistical terms. Throughout this book a crucial term is used: aspiration. If a group has internal vitality, a will—if it has aspiration—it may live in dilapidated housing, it may eat an inadequate diet, and it may suffer poverty, but it is not impoverished. So it was in those ethnic slums of the immigrants that played such a dramatic role in the unfolding of the American dream. The people found themselves in slums, but they were not slum dwellers.

But the new poverty is constructed so as to destroy aspiration; it is a system designed to be impervious to hope. The other America does not contain the adventurous seeking a new life and land. It is populated by the failures, by those driven from the land and bewildered by the city, by old people suddenly confronted with the torments of loneliness and poverty, and by minorities facing a wall of prejudice.

In the past, when poverty was general in the unskilled and semi-skilled work force, the poor were all mixed together. The bright and the dull, those who were going to escape into the great society and those who were to stay behind, all of them lived on the same street. When the middle third rose, this community was destroyed. And the entire invisible land of the other Americans became a ghetto, a modern poor farm for the rejects of society and of the economy.

It is a blow to reform and the political hopes of the poor that the middle class no longer understands that poverty exists. But, perhaps more important, the poor are losing their links with the great world. If statistics and sociology can measure a feeling as delicate as loneliness . . . the other America is becoming increasingly populated by those who do not belong to anybody or anything. They are no longer participants in an ethnic culture from the old country; they are less and less religious; they do not belong to unions or clubs. They are not seen, and because of that they themselves cannot see. Their horizon has become more and more restricted; they see one another, and that means they see little reason to hope. . . .

. . . There is, in a sense, a personality of poverty, a type of human being produced by the grinding, wearing life of the slums. The other Americans feel differently than the rest of the nation. They tend to be hopeless and passive, yet prone to bursts of violence; they are lonely and isolated, often rigid and hostile. To be poor is not simply to be deprived of the material things of this world. It is to enter a fatal, futile universe, an America within America with a twisted spirit.

Perhaps the most classic (but still controversial) study of this subject is the book *Social Class and Mental Illness* by August B. Hollingshead and F. C. Redlich. Published in 1958, it summarizes a careful research project in New Haven, Connecticut. It is an academic, scholarly work, yet its statistics are the description of an abyss.

Hollingshead and Redlich divided New Haven into five social classes. At the top (Class I) were the rich, usually aristocrats of family as well as of money. Next came the executives and professionals more newly arrived to prestige and power. Then, the middle class, and beneath them, the workers with decent paying jobs. Class V, the bottom class, was made up of the poor. About half of its members were semiskilled, about half unskilled. The men had less than six years of education, the women less than eight.

As it turned out, this five-level breakdown was more revealing than the usual three-class image of American society (upper, middle, and lower). For it showed a sharp break between Class V at the bottom and Class IV just above it. In a dramatic psychological sense, the skilled unionized worker lived much, much closer to the middle class than he did to the world of the poor. Between Class IV and Class V, Hollingshead and Redlich found a chasm. This represents the gulf between working America, which may be up against it from time to time but which has a certain sense of security and dignity, and the other America of the poor.

Perhaps the most shocking and decisive statistic that Hollingshead and Redlich found was the one that tabulated the rate of treated psychiatric illness per 100,000 people in New Haven. These are their results:

Classes I and II	556 per 100,000
Class III	538
Class IV	642
Class V	1,659

From the top of society down to the organized workers, there are differences, but relatively small ones. But suddenly, when one crosses the line from Class IV to Class V, there is a huge leap, with the poor showing a rate of treated psychiatric illness of almost three times the magnitude of any other class.

But the mental suffering of the poor in these figures is not simply expressed in gross numbers. It is a matter of quality as well. In Classes I and II, 65 per cent of the treated psychiatric illness is for neurotic problems, and only 35 per cent for the much graver disturbances of psychoses. But at the bottom, in Class V, 90 per cent of the treated illness is for psychosis, and only 10 per cent for neurosis. In short, not only the rate but also the intensity of mental illness is much greater for the poor.

One of the standard professional criticisms of Hollingshead and Redlich is that their figures are for treated illness (those who actually got to a doctor or clinic) and do not indicate the "true prevalence" of mental illness in the population. Whatever merits this argument has in relation to other parts of the study, it points up that these particular figures are an understatement of the problem. The higher up the class scale one is, the more likely that there will be recognition of mental illness as a problem and that help will be sought. At the bottom of society, referral to psychiatric treatment usually comes from the courts. Thus, if anything, there is even more mental illness among the poor than the figures of Hollingshead and Redlich indicate.

The one place where this criticism might have some validity is with regard to the intensity of emotional disturbance. Only 10 per cent of the poor who received treatment are neurotics, yet the poor neurotic is the least likely person in the society to show up for treatment. He can function, if only in an impaired and maimed way. If there were something done about this situation, it is quite possible that one would find more neurosis in the other America at the same time as one discovered more mental illness generally.

However, it is not necessary to juggle with statistics and explanations in order to corroborate the main drift of the New Haven figures. During the fifties the Cornell University Department of Psychiatry undertook an ambitious study of "Midtown," a residential area in New York City. The research dealt with a population of 170,000 from every social class, 99 per cent of them white. (By leaving out the Negroes, there probably was a tendency to underestimate the problem of poverty generally, and the particular disabilities of a discriminated minority in particular.) The goal of the study was to discover "true prevalence," and there was interviewing in depth.

The Cornell scholars developed a measure of "mental health risk." They used a model of three classes, and consequently their figures are not so dramatic as those tabulated in New Haven. Yet they bear out the essential point: the lowest class had a mental health risk almost 40 per cent greater than the highest class. Once again the world of poverty was given definition as a spiritual and emotional reality.

The huge brute fact of emotional illness in the other America is fairly well substantiated. The reasons behind the fact are the subject of considerable controversy. There is no neat and simple summary that can be given at the present time, yet some of the analyses are provocative for an understanding of the culture of poverty even if they must be taken tentatively.

One of the most interesting speculations came from the Cornell study of "Midtown" in New York City. The researchers developed a series of "stress factors" that might be related to an individual's mental health risk. In childhood, these were poor mental health on the part of the parents, poor physical health for the parents, economic deprivation, broken homes, a negative attitude on the part of the child toward his parents, a quarrelsome home, and sharp disagreements with parents during adolescence. In adult life, the stress factors were poor health, work worries, money worries, a lack of neighbors and friends, marital worries, and parental worries.

The Cornell team then tested to see if there was any relationship between these factors and mental health. They discovered a marked correlation. The person who had been subjected to thirteen of these stress factors was three times more likely to be mentally disturbed than the person who had felt none of them. Indeed, the researchers were led to conclude that the sheer number of stress factors was more important than the quality of stresses. Those who had experienced any three factors were of a higher mental risk than those who had experienced two.

If the Cornell conclusions are validated in further research, they will constitute an important revision of some widely held ideas about mental health. The Freudian theory has emphasized the earliest years and the decisive trauma in the development of mental illness (for example, the death of a parent). This new theory would suggest a more cumulative conception of mental illness: as stress piles upon stress over a period of time, there is a greater tendency toward disturbance. It would be an important supplement to the Freudian ideas.

But if this theory is right, there is a fairly obvious reason for the emotional torment of the other America. The stress factors listed by the Cornell study are the very stuff of the life of the poor: physical illness, broken homes, worries about work and money, and all the rest. The slum, with its vibrant, dense life hammers away at the individual. And because of the sheer, grinding, dirty experience of being poor, the personality, the spirit, is impaired. It is as if human beings dilapidate along with the tenements in which they live.

However, some scholars have attempted to soften the grimness of this picture with a theory about "drift." The poor, they argue, have a high percentage of disturbed people, not because of the conditions of life in the urban and rural slums, but because this is the group that gets all the outcasts of society from the rest of the classes. If this thesis were true, then one would expect to find failures from the higher classes as a significant group in the culture of the poor.

Hollingshead and Redlich tested this theory in New Haven and did not find any confirmation for it. The mentally impaired poor had been, for the most part, born poor. Their sickness was a product of poverty, instead of their poverty being a product of sickness. Similarly, in the Midtown study, no evidence was turned up to indicate that the disturbed poor were the rejects from other classes. There are some exceptions to this rule: alcoholics . . . often tend to fall from a high position into the bitterest poverty. Still, current research points to a direct relationship between the experience of poverty and emotional disturbance.

And yet, an ironic point turned up in the Midtown research. It was discovered that a certain kind of neurosis was useful to a minority of poor people. The obsessive-compulsive neurotic often got ahead: his very sickness was a means of advancement out of the other America and into the great world. And yet, this might only prepare for a later crisis. On the lower and middle rungs of business society, hard work, attention to detail, and the like are enough to guarantee individual progress. But if such a person moves across the line, and is placed in a position where he must make decisions, there is the very real possibility of breakdown. . . .

The feelings, the emotions, the attitudes of the poor are different. But different from what? In this question there is an important problem of dealing with the chaotic in the world of poverty. . . .

Take the gangs. They are violent, and by middle-class standards they

are antisocial and disturbed. But within a slum, violence and disturbance are often norms, everyday facts of life. From the inside of the other
America, joining a "bopping" gang may well not seem like deviant behavior. It could be a necessity for dealing with a hostile world. (Once, in
a slum school in St. Louis, a teacher stopped a fight between two little
girls. "Nice girls don't fight," she told them. "Yeah," one of them replied,
"you should have seen my old lady at the tavern last night.")

Indeed, one of the most depressing pieces of research I have ever read
touches on this point. H. Warren Dunham carefully studied forty catatonic schizophrenics in Chicago in the early forties. He found that none
of them had belonged to gangs or had engaged in the kind of activity
the middle class regards as abnormal. They had, as a matter of fact, tried
to live up to the standards of the larger society, rather than conforming
to the values of the slum. "The catatonic young man can be described as
a good boy and one who has all the desirable traits which all the social
agencies would like to inculcate in the young men of the community."

The middle class does not understand the narrowness of its judgments. And worse, it acts upon them as if they were universal and accepted by everyone. In New Haven, Hollingshead and Redlich found two
girls with an almost identical problem. Both of them were extremely
promiscuous, so much so that they eventually had a run-in with the
police. When the girl from Class I was arrested, she was provided with
bail at once, newspaper stories were quashed, and she was taken care of
through private psychotherapy. The girl from Class V was sentenced to
reform school. She was paroled in two years, but was soon arrested again
and sent to the state reformatory.

James Baldwin made a brilliant and perceptive application of this
point to the problem of the Negro in a speech I heard not long ago. The
white, he said, cannot imagine what it is like to be Negro: the danger,
the lack of horizon, the necessity of always being on guard and watching. For that matter, Baldwin went on, the Negro problem is really the
white problem. It is not the Negro who sets dark skin and kinky hair
aside as something fearful, but the white. And the resolution of the racial agony in America requires a deep introspection on the part of the
whites. They must discover themselves even more than the Negro.

This is true of all the juvenile delinquents, all the disturbed people, in
the other America. One can put it baldly: their sickness is often a means
of relating to a diseased environment. Until this is understood, the emotionally disturbed poor person will probably go on hurting himself until
he becomes a police case. When he is finally given treatment, it will be at
public expense, and it will be inferior to that given the rich. (In New
Haven, according to Hollingshead and Redlich, the poor are five times
more likely to get organic therapy—including shock treatment—rather
than protracted, individual professional care.)

For that matter, some of the researchers in the field believe that sheer ignorance is one of the main causes of the high rate of disturbance among the poor. In the slum, conduct that would shock a middle-class neighborhood and lead to treatment is often considered normal. Even if someone is constantly and violently drunk, or beats his wife brutally, people will say of such a person, "Well, he's a little odd." Higher up on the class scale an individual with such a problem would probably realize that something was wrong (or his family would). He will have the knowledge and the money to get help.

One of the researchers in the field who puts great stress on the "basic universals" of the Freudian pattern (mother figure, father figure, siblings) looks upon this factor of ignorance as crucial. He is Dr. Lawrence Kubie. For Dr. Kubie, the fundamental determinants of mental health and illness are the same in every social class. But culture and income and education account for whether the individual will handle his problem; whether he understands himself as sick; whether he seeks help, and so on. This theory leaves the basic assumptions of traditional psychoanalysis intact, but, like any attempt to deal with the poor, it recognizes that something is different.

For the rich, then, and perhaps even for the better-paid worker, breakdowns, neurosis, and psychosis appear as illness and are increasingly treated as such. But the poor do not simply suffer these disturbances; they suffer them blindly. To them it does not appear that they are mentally sick; to them it appears that they are trapped in a fate. . . .

Out of all this, the research more and more suggests, there emerges the personality of poverty, the "typical citizen" of the other America.

This is how the Midtown researchers described the "low social economic status individual": they are "rigid, suspicious and have a fatalistic outlook on life. They do not plan ahead, a characteristic associated with their fatalism. They are prone to depression, have feelings of futility, lack of belongingness, friendliness, and a lack of trust in others." Translated into the statistics of the Midtown study, this means that the bottom of the society is three times more emotionally depressed than the top (36.2 per cent for the low, 11.1 per cent for the high).

A small point: America has a self-image of itself as a nation of joiners and doers. There are social clubs, charities, community drives, and the like. Churches have always played an important social role, often marking off the status of individuals. And yet this entire structure is a phenomenon of the middle class. Some time ago, a study in Franklin, Indiana, reported that the percentage of people in the bottom class who were without affiliations of any kind was eight times as great as the percentage in the high-income class.

Paradoxically, one of the factors that intensifies the social isolation of the poor is that America thinks of itself as a nation without social classes. As a result, there are few social or civic organizations that are separated on the basis of income and class. The "working-class culture" that sociologists have described in a country like England does not exist here, or at least it is much less of a reality. The poor person who might want to join an organization is afraid. Because he or she will have less education, less money, less competence to articulate ideas than any-one else in the group, they stay away.

Thus, studies of civilian-defense organizations during World War II showed that almost all the members were white-collar people. Indeed, though one might think that the poor would have more friends because they are packed densely together, there are studies that indicate that they are deprived in this regard, too. In one report, 47 per cent of the lower-class women said that they had no friend or no intimate friend.

Such a life is lonely; it is also insecure. In New Haven, Hollingshead and Redlich could find only 19 per cent of the people in the bottom class who thought that their jobs were safe. The Yale group described 45 per cent of the poor as "inured," and found that their motto was "We take what the tide brings in."

This fatalism is not, however, confined to personal experience alone, to expectations about job and family. It literally permeates every aspect of an individual's life; it is a way of seeing reality. In a poll the Gallup organization did for *Look* magazine in 1959 (a projection of what people anticipated in the sixties), the relationship between social class and political pessimism was striking. The bottom group was much more likely to think that World War III was coming, that a recession was around the corner, that they would not take a vacation in the coming year. As one went up the income scale, the opinion of the world tended to brighten.

This pessimism is involved in a basic attitude of the poor: the fact that they do not postpone satisfactions, that they do not save. When pleasure is available, they tend to take it immediately. The smug theorist of the middle class would probably deplore this as showing a lack of traditional American virtues. Actually, it is the logical and natural pat-tern of behavior for one living in a part of American life without a fu-ture. It is, sad to say, a piece of realism, not of vice.

Related to this pattern of immediate gratification is a tendency on the part of the poor to "act out," to be less inhibited, and sometimes violent. There are some superficial observers who give this aspect of slum life a Rousseauistic twist. They find it a proof of the vitality, of the naturalness of the poor who are not constrained by the conventions of polite society. It would be hard to imagine a more wrongheaded impression. In the first place, this violence is the creature of that most artificial environment the slum. It is a product of human density and misery. And far from being an aspect of personality that is symptomatic of health, it is one more way in which the poor are driven to hurt themselves.

If one turns to the family life of the other America, there is an almost summary case of the dislocation and strains at the bottom of society.

In New Haven, for instance, Hollingshead and Redlich found that in Class V (the poor) some 41 per cent of the children under seventeen lived in homes that had been disrupted by death, desertion, separation, or divorce. This, of course, has profound consequences for the personalities of the young people involved. (This would be an instance in which the traditional Freudian account of mental illness would be relevant to the other America. An unstable family structure, with a father or mother figure absent, would predict devastating personal consequences.)

Then, the types of family structure the Yale researchers found among the poor are important. Some 44 per cent of the children lived in "nuclear families," which unite father, mother, and children. But 23 per cent grew up in a "generation stem family," where different generations are thrown together, usually with a broken marriage or two. Under such circumstances there is the possibility of endless domestic conflict between the different generations (and this is exacerbated when the old people are immigrants with a foreign code). Another 18 per cent came from broken homes where one or the other parent was absent. And 11 per cent had experienced the death of a parent.

Another aspect of this family pattern is sexual. In New Haven the researchers found that it was fairly common for young girls in the slums to be pregnant before they were married. I saw a similar pattern in St. Louis. There, children had a sort of sophisticated ignorance about sexual matters at an early age. Jammed together in miserable housing, they knew the facts of sex from firsthand observation (though often what they saw was a brutalized and drunken form of sex). In this sense, they were much more sophisticated than the children in middle-class neighborhoods.

But the poor are never that really well informed. As noted before, along with a cynical version of the facts of life there went an enormous amount of misinformation. For instance, young girls were given systematic miseducation on the menstrual period. They were often frightened and guilt ridden about sex at the same time that they were sophisticated.

And finally, the family of the poor lives cheek and jowl with other families of the poor. The sounds of all the quarreling and fights of every other family are always present if there happens to be a moment of peace in one household. The radio and the television choices of the rest of the block are regularly in evidence. Life is lived in common, but not in community.

So it is that the adolescents roam the streets. For the young, there is no reason to stay around the house. The street is a moment of relief, relaxation, and excitement. The family, which should be a bulwark against the sheer physical misery of the poor, is overwhelmed by the environment. . . .

The emotional turmoil of the poor is . . . a form of protection against the turmoil of the society, a way of getting some attention and care in an uncaring world. Given this kind of "defense," it requires an enormous effort for these people to cross over into the great society.

Indeed, emotional upset is one of the main forms of the vicious circle of impoverishment. The structure of the society is hostile to these people: they do not have the right education or the right jobs, or perhaps there are no jobs to be had at all. Because of this, in a realistic adaptation to a socially perverse situation, the poor tend to become pessimistic and depressed; they seek immediate gratification instead of saving; they act out.

Once this mood, this unarticulated philosophy becomes a fact, society can change, the recession can end, and yet there is no motive for movement. The depression has become internalized. The middle class looks upon this process and sees "lazy" people who "just don't want to get ahead." People who are much too sensitive to demand of cripples that they run races ask of the poor that they get up and act just like everyone else in society.

The poor are not like everyone else. They are a different kind of people. They think and feel differently; they look upon a different America than the middle class looks upon. They, and not the quietly desperate clerk or the harried executive, are the main victims of this society's tension and conflict.

The significance of the frontier in American history

Frederick Jackson Turner

In a recent bulletin of the Superintendent of the Census for 1890 appear these significant words: "Up to and including 1880 the country had a frontier of settlement, but at present the unsettled area has been so broken into by isolated bodies of settlement that there can hardly be

From American Historical Association, *Annual Report, 1893* (Washington, D.C., 1894) ᴘp. 199–227. Reprinted by permission of American Historical Association.

said to be a frontier line. In the discussion of its extent, its westward movement, etc., it can not, therefore, any longer have a place in the census reports." This brief official statement marks the closing of a great historic movement. Up to our own day American history has been in a large degree the history of the colonization of the Great West. The existence of an area of free land, its continuous recession, and the advance of American settlement westward, explain American development.

Behind institutions, behind constitutional forms and modifications, lie the vital forces that call these organs into life and shape them to meet changing conditions. The peculiarity of American institutions is, the fact that they have been compelled to adapt themselves to the changes of an expanding people—to the changes involved in crossing a continent, in winning a wilderness, and in developing at each area of this progress out of the primitive economic and political conditions of the frontier into the complexity of city life. Said Calhoun in 1817, "We are great, and rapidly—I was about to say fearfully—growing!" So saying, he touched the distinguishing feature of American life. All peoples show development; the germ theory of politics has been sufficiently emphasized. In the case of most nations, however, the development has occurred in a limited area; and if the nation has expanded, it has met other growing peoples whom it has conquered. But in the case of the United States we have a different phenomenon. Limiting our attention to the Atlantic coast, we have the familiar phenomenon of the evolution of institutions in a limited area, such as the rise of representative government; the differentiation of simple colonial governments into complex organs; the progress from primitive industrial society, without division of labor, up to manufacturing civilization. But we have in addition to this a recurrence of the process of evolution in each western area reached in the process of expansion. Thus American development has exhibited not merely advance along a single line, but a return to primitive conditions on a continually advancing frontier line, and a new development for that area. American social development has been continually beginning over again on the frontier. This perennial rebirth, this fluidity of American life, this expansion westward with its new opportunities, its continuous touch with the simplicity of primitive society, furnish the forces dominating American character. The true point of view in the history of this nation is not the Atlantic coast, it is the Great West. Even the slavery struggle, which is made so exclusive an object of attention by writers like Professor von Holst, occupies its important place in American history because of its relation to westward expansion.

In this advance, the frontier is the outer edge of the wave—the meeting point between savagery and civilization. Much has been written about the frontier from the point of view of border warfare and the chase, but as a field for the serious study of the economist and the historian it has been neglected.

The American frontier is sharply distinguished from the European frontier—a fortified boundary line running through dense populations. The most significant thing about the American frontier is, that it lies at the hither edge of free land. In the census reports it is treated as the margin of that settlement which has a density of two or more to the square mile. The term is an elastic one, and for our purposes does not need sharp definition. We shall consider the whole frontier belt, including the Indian country and the outer margin of the "settled area" of the census reports. This paper will make no attempt to treat the subject exhaustively; its aim is simply to call attention to the frontier as a fertile field for investigation, and to suggest some of the problems which arise in connection with it.

In the settlement of America we have to observe how European life entered the continent, and how America modified and developed that life and reacted on Europe. Our early history is the study of European germs developing in an American environment. Too exclusive attention has been paid by institutional students to the Germanic origins, too little to the American factors. The frontier is the line of most rapid and effective Americanization. The wilderness masters the colonist. It finds him a European in dress, industries, tools, modes of travel, and thought. It takes him from the railroad car and puts him in the birch canoe. It strips off the garments of civilization and arrays him in the hunting shirt and the moccasin. It puts him in the log cabin of the Cherokee and Iroquois and runs an Indian palisade around him. Before long he has gone to planting Indian corn and plowing with a sharp stick; he shouts the war cry and takes the scalp in orthodox Indian fashion. In short, at the frontier the environment is at first too strong for the man. He must accept the conditions which it furnishes, or perish, and so he fits himself into the Indian clearings and follows the Indian trails. Little by little he transforms the wilderness, but the outcome is not the old Europe, not simply the development of Germanic germs, any more than the first phenomenon was a case of reversion to the Germanic mark. The fact is, that here is a new product that is American. At first, the frontier was the Atlantic coast. It was the frontier of Europe in a very real sense. Moving westward, the frontier became more and more American. As successive terminal moraines result from successive glaciations, so each frontier leaves its traces behind it, and when it becomes a settled area the region still partakes of the frontier characteristics. Thus the advance of the frontier has meant a steady movement away from the influence of Europe, a steady growth of independence on American lines. And to study this advance, the men who grew up under these conditions, and the political, economic, and social results of it, is to study the really American part of our history.

In the course of the seventeenth century the frontier was advanced up the Atlantic river courses, just beyond the "fall line," and the tidewater region became the settled area. In the first half of the eighteenth century another advance occurred. Traders followed the Delaware and Shawnese Indians to the Ohio as early as the end of the first quarter of the century. Gov. Spotswood, of Virginia, made an expedition in 1714 across the Blue Ridge. The end of the first quarter of the century saw the advance of the Scotch-Irish and the Palatine Germans up the Shenandoah Valley into the western part of Virginia, and along the Piedmont region of the Carolinas. The Germans in New York pushed the frontier of settlement up the Mohawk to German Flats. In Pennsylvania the town of Bedford indicates the line of settlement. Settlements soon began on the New River, or the Great Kanawha, and on the sources of the Yadkin and French Broad. The King attempted to arrest the advance by his proclamation of 1763, forbidding settlements beyond the sources of the rivers flowing into the Atlantic; but in vain. In the period of the Revolution the frontier crossed the Alleghanies into Kentucky and Tennessee, and the upper waters of the Ohio were settled. When the first census was taken in 1790, the continuous settled area was bounded by a line which ran near the coast of Maine, and included New England except a portion of Vermont and New Hampshire, New York along the Hudson and up the Mohawk about Schenectady, eastern and southern Pennsylvania, Virginia well across the Shenandoah Valley, and the Carolinas and eastern Georgia. Beyond this region of continuous settlement were the small settled areas of Kentucky and Tennessee, and the Ohio, with the mountains intervening between them and the Atlantic area, thus giving a new and important character to the frontier. The isolation of the region increased its peculiarly American tendencies, and the need of transportation facilities to connect it with the East called out important schemes of internal improvement, which will be noted farther on. The "West," as a self-conscious section, began to evolve.

From decade to decade distinct advances of the frontier occurred. By the census of 1820 the settled area included Ohio, southern Indiana and Illinois, southeastern Missouri, and about one-half of Louisiana. This settled area had surrounded Indian areas, and the management of these tribes became an object of political concern. The frontier region of the time lay along the Great Lakes, where Astor's American Fur Company operated in the Indian trade, and beyond the Mississippi, where Indian traders extended their activity even to the Rocky Mountains; Florida also furnished frontier conditions. The Mississippi River region was the scene of typical frontier settlements.

The rising steam navigation on western waters, the opening of the Erie Canal, and the westward extension of cotton culture added five frontier states to the Union in this period. Grund, writing in 1836, declares:

"It appears then that the universal disposition of Americans to emigrate to the western wilderness, in order to enlarge their dominion over inanimate nature, is the actual result of an expansive power which is inherent in them, and which by continually agitating all classes of society is constantly throwing a large portion of the whole population on the extreme confines of the State, in order to gain space for its development. Hardly is a new State or Territory formed before the same principle manifests itself again and gives rise to a further emigration; and so is it destined to go on until a physical barrier must finally obstruct its progress."

In the middle of this century the line indicated by the present eastern boundary of Indian Territory, Nebraska, and Kansas marked the frontier of the Indian country. Minnesota and Wisconsin still exhibited frontier conditions, but the distinctive frontier of the period is found in California, where the gold discoveries had sent a sudden tide of adventurous miners, and in Oregon, and the settlements in Utah. As the frontier had leaped over the Alleghanies, so now it skipped the Great Plains and the Rocky Mountains; and in the same way that the advance of the frontiersmen beyond the Alleghanies had caused the rise of important questions of transportation and internal improvement, so now the settlers beyond the Rocky Mountains needed means of communication with the East, and in the furnishing of these arose the settlement of the Great Plains and the development of still another kind of frontier life. Railroads, fostered by land grants, sent an increasing tide of immigrants into the Far West. The United States Army fought a series of Indian wars in Minnesota, Dakota, and the Indian Territory.

By 1880 the settled area had been pushed into northern Michigan, Wisconsin, and Minnesota, along Dakota rivers, and in the Black Hills region, and was ascending the rivers of Kansas and Nebraska. The development of mines in Colorado had drawn isolated frontier settlements into that region, and Montana and Idaho were receiving settlers. The frontier was found in these mining camps and the ranches of the Great Plains. The superintendent of the census for 1890 reports, as previously stated, that the settlements of the West lie so scattered over the region that there can no longer be said to be a frontier line.

In these successive frontiers we find natural boundary lines which have served to mark and to affect the characteristics of the frontiers, namely: the "fall line"; the Alleghany Mountains; the Mississippi; the Missouri where its direction approximates north and south; the line of the arid lands, approximately the ninety-ninth meridian; and the Rocky Mountains. The fall line marked the frontier of the seventeenth century; the Alleghanies that of the eighteenth; the Mississippi that of the first quarter of the nineteenth; the Missouri that of the middle of this century (omitting the California movement); and the belt of the Rocky

Mountains and the arid tract, the present frontier. Each was won by a series of Indian wars.

At the Atlantic frontier one can study the germs of processes repeated at each successive frontier. We have the complex European life sharply precipitated by the wilderness into the simplicity of primitive conditions. The first frontier had to meet its Indian question, its question of the disposition of the public domain, of the means of intercourse with older settlements, of the extension of political organization, of religious and educational activity. And the settlement of these and similar questions for one frontier served as a guide for the next. The American student needs not to go to the "prim little townships of Sleswick" for illustrations of the law of continuity and development. For example, he may study the origin of our land policies in the colonial land policy; he may see how the system grew by adapting the statutes to the customs of the successive frontiers. He may see how the mining experience in the lead regions of Wisconsin, Illinois, and Iowa was applied to the mining laws of the Sierras, and how our Indian policy has been a series of experimentations on successive frontiers. Each tier of new States has found in the older ones material for its constitutions. Each frontier has made similar contributions to American character, as will be discussed farther on.

But with all these similarities there are essential differences, due to the place element and the time element. It is evident that the farming frontier of the Mississippi Valley presents different conditions from the mining frontier of the Rocky Mountains. The frontier reached by the Pacific Railroad, surveyed into rectangles, guarded by the United States Army, and recruited by the daily immigrant ship, moves forward at a swifter pace and in a different way than the frontier reached by the birch canoe or the pack horse. The geologist traces patiently the shores of ancient seas, maps their areas, and compares the older and the newer. It would be a work worth the historian's labors to mark these various frontiers and in detail compare one with another. Not only would there result a more adequate conception of American development and characteristics, but invaluable additions would be made to the history of society.

Loria, the Italian economist, has urged the study of colonial life as an aid in understanding the stages of European development, affirming that colonial settlement is for economic science what the mountain is for geology, bringing to light primitive stratifications. "America," he says, "has the key to the historical enigma which Europe has sought for centuries in vain, and the land which has no history reveals luminously the course of universal history." There is much truth in this. The United States lies like a huge page in the history of society. Line by line as we read this continental page from West to East we find the record of social evolution. It begins with the Indian and the hunter; it goes on to tell of the disintegration of savagery by the entrance of the trader, the pathfinder of civilization; we read the annals of the pastoral stage in ranch life; the exploitation of the soil by the raising of unrotated crops of corn and wheat in sparsely settled farming communities; the intensive culture of the denser farm settlement; and finally the manufacturing organization with city and factory system. This page is familiar to the student of census statistics, but how little of it has been used by our historians. Particularly in eastern States this page is a palimpsest. What is now a manufacturing State was in an earlier decade an area of intensive farming. Earlier yet it had been a wheat area, and still earlier the "range" had attracted the cattle-herder. Thus Wisconsin, now developing manufacture, is a State with varied agricultural interests. But earlier it was given over to almost exclusive grain-raising, like North Dakota at the present time.

Each of these areas has had an influence in our economic and political history; the evolution of each into a higher stage has worked political transformations. But what constitutional historian has made any adequate attempt to interpret political facts by the light of these social areas and changes?

The Atlantic frontier was compounded of fisherman, fur-trader, miner, cattle-raiser, and farmer. Excepting the fisherman, each type of industry was on the march toward the West, impelled by an irresistible attraction. Each passed in successive waves across the continent. Stand at Cumberland Gap and watch the procession of civilization, marching single file —the buffalo following the trail to the salt springs, the Indian, the fur-trader and hunter, the cattle-raiser, the pioneer farmer—and the frontier has passed by. Stand at South Pass in the Rockies a century later and see the same procession with wider intervals between. The unequal rate of advance compels us to distinguish the frontier into the trader's frontier, the rancher's frontier, or the miner's frontier, and the farmer's frontier. When the mines and the cow pens were still near the fall line the traders' pack trains were tinkling across the Alleghanies, and the French on the Great Lakes were fortifying their posts, alarmed by the British trader's birch canoe. When the trappers scaled the Rockies, the farmer was still near the mouth of the Missouri.

Why was it that the Indian trader passed so rapidly across the continent? What effects followed from the trader's frontier? The trade was coeval with American discovery. The Norsemen, Vespuccius, Verrazani, Hudson, John Smith, all trafficked for furs. The Plymouth pilgrims settled in Indian cornfields, and their first return cargo was of beaver and lumber. The records of the various New England colonies show how steadily exploration was carried into the wilderness by this trade. What is true for New England is, as would be expected, even plainer for the rest of the colonies. All along the coast from Maine to Georgia the Indian trade opened up the river courses. Steadily the trader passed westward, utilizing the older lines of French trade. The Ohio, the Great Lakes, the Mississippi, the Missouri, and the Platte, the lines of western advance, were ascended by traders. They found the passes in the Rocky Mountains and guided Lewis and Clark, Frémont, and Bidwell. The explanation of the rapidity of this advance is connected with the effects of the trader on the Indian. The trading post left the unarmed tribes at the mercy of those that had purchased fire-arms—a truth which the Iroquois Indians wrote in blood, and so the remote and unvisited tribes gave eager welcome to the trader. "The savages," wrote La Salle, "take better care of us French than of their own children; from us only can they get guns and goods." This accounts for the trader's power and the rapidity of his advance. Thus the disintegrating forces of civilization entered the wilderness. Every river valley and Indian trail became a fissure in Indian society, and so that society became honeycombed. Long before the pioneer farmer appeared on the scene, primitive Indian life had passed away. The farmers met Indians armed with guns. The trading frontier, while steadily undermining Indian power by making the tribes ultimately dependent on the whites, yet, through its sale of guns, gave to the Indian increased power of resistance to the farming frontier. French colonization was dominated by its trading frontier; English colonization by its farming frontier. There was an antagonism between the two frontiers as between the two nations. Said Duquesne to the Iroquois, "Are you ignorant of the difference between the king of England and the king of France? Go see the forts that our king has established and you will see that you can still hunt under their very walls. They have been placed for your advantage in places which you frequent. The English, on the contrary, are no sooner in possession of a place than the game is driven away. The forest falls before them as they advance, and the soil is laid bare so that you can scarce find the wherewithal to erect a shelter for the night."

And yet, in spite of this opposition of the interests of the trader and the farmer, the Indian trade pioneered the way for civilization. The buffalo trail became the Indian trail, and this became the trader's "trace"; the trails widened into roads, and the roads into turnpikes, and these in turn were transformed into railroads. The same origin can be shown for the railroads of the South, the Far West, and the Dominion of Canada. The trading posts reached by these trails were on the sites of Indian villages which had been placed in positions suggested by nature; and these trading posts, situated so as to command the water systems of the country, have grown into such cities as Albany, Pittsburgh, Detroit, Chicago, St. Louis, Council Bluffs, and Kansas City. Thus civilization in America has followed the arteries made by geology, pouring an ever richer tide through them, until at last the slender paths of aboriginal intercourse have been broadened and interwoven into the complex mazes of modern commercial lines; the wilderness has been interpenetrated by lines of civilization growing ever more numerous. It is like the steady growth of a complex nervous system for the originally simple, inert continent. If one would understand why we are to-day one nation, rather than a collection of isolated states, he must study this economic and social consolidation of the country. In this progress from savage conditions lie topics for the evolutionist.

The effect of the Indian frontier as a consolidating agent in our history is important. From the close of the seventeenth century various intercolonial congresses have been called to treat with Indians and establish common measures of defense. Particularism was strongest in colonies with no Indian frontier. This frontier stretched along the western border like a cord of union. The Indian was a common danger, demanding united action. Most celebrated of these conferences was the Albany congress of 1754, called to treat with the Six Nations, and to consider plans of union. Even a cursory reading of the plan proposed by the congress reveals the importance of the frontier. The powers of the general council and the officers were, chiefly, the determination of peace and war with the Indians, the regulation of Indian trade, the purchase of Indian lands, and the creation and government of new settlements as a security against the Indians. It is evident that the unifying tendencies of the Revolutionary period were facilitated by the previous coöperation in the regulation of the frontier. In this connection may be mentioned the importance of the frontier, from that day to this, as a military training school, keeping alive the power of resistance to aggression, and developing the stalwart and rugged qualities of the frontiersman.

It would not be possible in the limits of this paper to trace the other frontiers across the continent. Travelers of the eighteenth century found the "cowpens" among the canebrakes and peavine pastures of the South, and the "cow drivers" took their droves to Charleston, Philadelphia, and New York. Travelers at the close of the War of 1812 met droves of more than a thousand cattle and swine from the interior of Ohio going to Pennsylvania to fatten for the Philadelphia market. The ranges of the Great Plains, with ranch and cowboy and nomadic life, are things of yesterday and of to-day. The experience of the Carolina cowpens guided the ranchers of Texas. One element favoring the rapid extension of the rancher's frontier is the fact that in a remote country lacking transportation facilities the product must be in small bulk, or must be able to transport itself, and the cattle raiser could easily drive his product to market. The effect of these great ranches on the subsequent agrarian history of the localities in which they existed should be studied.

The maps of the census reports show an uneven advance of the farmer's frontier, with tongues of settlement pushed forward and with indentations of wilderness. In part this is due to Indian resistance, in part to the location of river valleys and passes, in part to the unequal force of the centers of frontier attraction. Among the important centers of attraction may be mentioned the following: fertile and favorably situated soils, salt springs, mines, and army posts.

The frontier army post, serving to protect the settlers from the Indians, has also acted as a wedge to open the Indian country, and has been a nucleus for settlement. In this connection mention should also be made of the government military and exploring expeditions in determining the lines of settlement. But all the more important expeditions were greatly indebted to the earliest pathmakers, the Indian guides, the traders and trappers, and the French voyageurs, who were inevitable parts of governmental expeditions from the days of Lewis and Clark. Each expedition was an epitome of the previous factors in western advance.

In an interesting monograph, Victor Hehn has traced the effect of salt upon early European development, and has pointed out how it affected the lines of settlement and the form of administration. A similar study might be made for the salt springs of the United States. The early settlers were tied to the coast by the need of salt, without which they could not preserve their meats or live in comfort. Writing in 1752, Bishop Spangenburg says of a colony for which he was seeking lands in North Carolina, "They will require salt & other necessaries which they can neither manufacture nor raise. Either they must go to Charleston, which is 300 miles distant . . . Or else they must go to Boling's Point in Va. on a branch of the James & is also 300 miles from here . . . Or else they must go down the Roanoke—I know not how many miles—where salt is brought up from the Cape Fear." This may serve as a typical illustration. An annual pilgrimage to the coast for salt thus became essential. Taking flocks or furs and ginseng root, the early settlers sent their pack trains after seeding time each year to the coast. This proved to be an important educational influence, since it was almost the only way in which the pioneer learned what was going on in the East. But when discovery was made of the salt springs of the Kanawha, and the Holston, and Kentucky, and central New York, the West began to be freed from dependence on the coast. It was in part the effect of finding these salt springs that enabled settlement to cross the mountains.

From the time the mountains rose between the pioneer and the seaboard, a new order of Americanism arose. The West and the East began to get out of touch of each other. The settlements from the sea to the mountains kept connection with the rear and had a certain solidarity. But the over-mountain men grew more and more independent. The East took a narrow view of American advance, and nearly lost these men. Kentucky and Tennessee history bears abundant witness to the truth of this statement. The East began to try to hedge and limit westward expansion. Though Webster could declare that there were no Alleghanies in his politics, yet in politics in general they were a very solid factor.

The exploitation of the beasts took hunter and trader to the west, the exploitation of the grasses took the rancher west, and the exploitation of the virgin soil of the river valleys and prairies attracted the farmer. Good soils have been the most continuous attraction to the farmer's frontier. The land hunger of the Virginians drew them down the rivers into Carolina, in early colonial days; the search for soils took the Massachusetts men to Pennsylvania and to New York. As the eastern lands were taken up migration flowed across them to the west. Daniel Boone, the great backwoodsman, who combined the occupations of hunter, trader, cattle-raiser, farmer, and surveyor—learning, probably from the traders, of the fertility of the lands of the upper Yadkin, where the traders were wont to rest as they took their way to the Indians, left his Pennsylvania home with his father, and passed down the Great Valley road to that stream. Learning from a trader of the game and rich pastures of Kentucky, he pioneered the way for the farmers to that region. Thence he passed to the frontier of Missouri, where his settlement was long a landmark on the frontier. Here again he helped to open the way for civilization, finding salt licks, and trails, and land. His son was among the earliest trappers in the passes of the Rocky Mountains, and his party are said to have been the first to camp on the present site of Denver. His grandson, Col. A. J. Boone, of Colorado, was a power among the Indians of the Rocky Mountains, and was appointed an agent by the government. Kit Carson's mother was a Boone. Thus this family epitomizes the backwoodsman's advance across the continent.

The farmer's advance came in a distinct series of waves. In Peck's New Guide to the West, published in Boston in 1837, occurs this suggestive passage:

Generally, in all the western settlements, three classes, like the waves of the ocean, have rolled one after the other. First comes the pioneer, who depends for the subsistence of his family chiefly upon the natural growth of vegetation, called the "range," and the proceeds of hunting. His implements of agriculture are rude, chiefly of his own make, and his efforts directed mainly to a crop of corn and a "truck patch." The last is a rude garden for growing cabbage, beans, corn for roasting ears, cucumbers, and potatoes. A log cabin, and, occasionally, a stable and corn-crib, and a field of a dozen acres, the timber girdled or "deadened," and fenced, are enough for his occupancy. It is quite immaterial whether he ever becomes the owner of the soil. He is the occupant for the time being, pays no rent, and feels as independent as the "lord of the manor." With a horse, cow, and one or two breeders of swine, he strikes into the woods with his family, and becomes the founder of a new county, or perhaps state. He builds his cabin, gathers around him a few other families of similar tastes and habits, and occupies till the range is somewhat subdued, and hunting a little precarious, or, which is more frequently the case, till the neighbors crowd around, roads, bridges, and fields annoy him, and he lacks elbow room. The preëmption law enables him to dispose of his cabin and cornfield to the next class of emigrants; and, to employ his own figures, he "breaks for the high timber," "clears out for the New Purchase," or migrates to Arkansas or Texas, to work the same process over.

The next class of emigrants purchase the lands, add field to field, clear out the roads, throw rough bridges over the streams, put up hewn log houses with glass windows and brick or stone chimneys, occasionally plant orchards, build mills, schoolhouses, court-houses, etc., and exhibit the picture and forms of plain, frugal, civilized life.

Another wave rolls on. The men of capital and enterprise come. The settler is ready to sell out and take the advantage of the rise in property, push farther into the interior and become, himself, a man of capital and enterprise in turn. The small village rises to a spacious town or city; substantial edifices of brick, extensive fields, orchards, gardens, colleges, and churches are seen. Broadcloths, silks, leghorns, crapes, and all the refinements, luxuries, elegancies, frivolities, and fashions are in vogue. Thus wave after wave is rolling westward; the real Eldorado is still farther on.

A portion of the two first classes remain stationary amidst the general movement, improve their habits and condition, and rise in the scale of society.

The writer has traveled much amongst the first class, the real pioneers. He has lived many years in connection with the second grade; and now the third wave is sweeping over large districts of Indiana, Illinois, and Missouri. Migration has become almost a habit in the West. Hundreds of men can be found, not over 50 years of age, who have settled for the fourth, fifth, or sixth time on a new spot. To sell out and remove only a few hundred miles makes up a portion of the variety of backwoods life and manners.

Omitting those of the pioneer farmers who move from the love of adventure, the advance of the more steady farmer is easy to understand. Obviously the immigrant was attracted by the cheap lands of the frontier, and even the native farmer felt their influence strongly. Year by year the farmers who lived on soil whose returns were diminished by unrotated crops were offered the virgin soil of the frontier at nominal prices. Their growing families demanded more lands, and these were dear. The competition of the unexhausted, cheap, and easily tilled prairie lands compelled the farmer either to go west and continue the exhaustion of the soil on a new frontier, or to adopt intensive culture. Thus the census of 1890 shows, in the Northwest, many counties in which there is an absolute or a relative decrease of population. These States have been sending farmers to advance the frontier on the plains, and have themselves begun to turn to intensive farming and to manufacture. A decade before this, Ohio had shown the same transition stage. Thus the demand for land and the love of wilderness freedom drew the frontier ever onward.

Having now roughly outlined the various kinds of frontiers, and their modes of advance, chiefly from the point of view of the frontier itself, we may next inquire what were the influences on the East and on the Old World. A rapid enumeration of some of the more noteworthy effects is all that I have time for.

First, we note that the frontier promoted the formation of a composite nationality for the American people. The coast was preponderantly English, but the later tides of continental immigration flowed across to the free lands. This was the case from the early colonial days. The Scotch-Irish and the Palatine Germans, or "Pennsylvania Dutch," furnished the dominant element in the stock of the colonial frontier. With these peoples were also the freed indented servants, or redemptioners, who at the expiration of their time of service passed to the frontier. Governor Spotswood of Virginia writes in 1717, "The inhabitants of our frontiers are composed generally of such as have been transported hither as servants, and, being out of their time, settle themselves where land is to be taken up and that will produce the necessarys of life with little labour." Very generally these redemptioners were of non-English stock. In the crucible of the frontier the immigrants were Americanized, liberated, and fused into a mixed race, English in neither nationality nor characteristics. The process has gone on from the early days to our own. Burke and other writers in the middle of the eighteenth century believed that Pennsylvania was "threatened with the danger of being wholly foreign in language, manners, and perhaps even inclinations." The German and Scotch-Irish elements in the frontier of the South were only less great. In the middle of the present century the German element in Wisconsin was already so considerable that leading publicists looked to the creation of a German state out of the commonwealth by concentrating their colonization. Such examples teach us to beware of misinterpreting the fact that there is a common English speech in America into a belief that the stock is also English.

In another way the advance of the frontier decreased our dependence on England. The coast, particularly of the South, lacked diversified industries, and was dependent on England for the bulk of its supplies. In the South there was even a dependence on the Northern colonies for articles of food. Governor Glenn, of South Carolina, writes in the middle of the eighteenth century: "Our trade with New York and Philadelphia was of this sort, draining us of all the little money and bills we could gather from other places for their bread, flour, beer, hams, bacon, and other things of their produce, all which, except beer, our new townships begin to supply us with, which are settled with very industrious and thriving Germans. This no doubt diminishes the number of shipping and the appearance of our trade, but it is far from being a detriment to us." Before long the frontier created a demand for merchants. As it retreated from the coast it became less and less possible for England to bring her supplies directly to the consumer's wharfs, and carry away staple crops, and staple crops began to give way to diversified agriculture for a time. The effect of this phase of the frontier action upon the northern section is perceived when we realize how the advance of the frontier aroused seaboard cities like Boston, New York, and Baltimore, to engage in rivalry for what Washington called "the extensive and valuable trade of a rising empire."

The legislation which most developed the powers of the national government, and played the largest part in its activity, was conditioned on the frontier. Writers have discussed the subjects of tariff, land, and internal improvement, as subsidiary to the slavery question. But when American history comes to be rightly viewed it will be seen that the slavery question is an incident. In the period from the end of the first half of the present century to the close of the Civil War slavery rose to primary, but far from exclusive, importance. But this does not justify Dr. von Holst (to take an example) in treating our constitutional history in its formative period down to 1828 in a single volume, giving six volumes chiefly to the history of slavery from 1828 to 1861, under the title "Constitutional History of the United States." The growth of nationalism and the evolution of American political institutions were dependent on the advance of the frontier. Even so recent a writer as Rhodes, in his "History of the United States since the Compromise of 1850," has treated the legislation called out by the western advance as incidental to the slavery struggle.

This is a wrong perspective. The pioneer needed the goods of the coast, and so the grand series of internal improvement and railroad legislation began, with potent nationalizing effects. Over internal improvements occurred great debates, in which grave constitutional questions were discussed. Sectional groupings appear in the votes, profoundly significant for the historian. Loose construction increased as the nation marched westward. But the West was not content with bringing the farm to the factory. Under the lead of Clay—"Harry of the West"—protective tariffs were passed, with the cry of bringing the factory to the farm. The disposition of the public lands was a third important subject of national legislation influenced by the frontier.

The public domain has been a force of profound importance in the nationalization and development of the government. The effects of the struggle of the landed and the landless States, and of the Ordinance of 1787, need no discussion. Administratively the frontier called out some of the highest and most vitalizing activities of the general government. The purchase of Louisiana was perhaps the constitutional turning point in the history of the Republic, inasmuch as it afforded both a new area for national legislation and the occasion of the downfall of the policy of strict construction. But the purchase of Louisiana was called out by frontier needs and demands. As frontier States accrued to the Union the national power grew. In a speech on the dedication of the Calhoun monument Mr. Lamar explained: "In 1789 the States were the creators of the Federal Government; in 1861 the Federal Government was the creator of a large majority of the States."

When we consider the public domain from the point of view of the sale and disposal of the public lands we are again brought face to face with the frontier. The policy of the United States in dealing with its lands is in sharp contrast with the European system of scientific administration. Efforts to make this domain a source of revenue, and to withhold it from emigrants in order that settlement might be compact, were in vain. The jealousy and the fears of the East were powerless in the face of the demands of the frontiersmen. John Quincy Adams was obliged to confess: "My own system of administration, which was to make the national domain the inexhaustible fund for progressive and unceasing internal improvement, has failed." The reason is obvious; a system of administration was not what the West demanded; it wanted land. Adams states the situation as follows: "The slaveholders of the South have bought the coöperation of the western country by the bribe of the western lands, abandoning to the new Western States their own proportion of the public property and aiding them in the design of grasping all the lands into their own hands. Thomas H. Benton was the author of this system, which he brought forward as a substitute for the American system of Mr. Clay, and to supplant him as the leading statesman of the West. Mr. Clay, by his tariff compromise with Mr. Calhoun, abandoned his own American system. At the same time he brought forward a plan for distributing among all the States of the Union the proceeds of the sales of the public lands. His bill for that purpose passed both Houses of Congress, but was vetoed by President Jackson, who, in his annual message of December, 1832, formally recommended that all public lands should be gratuitously given away to individual adventurers and to the States in which the lands are situated."

"No subject," said Henry Clay, "which has presented itself to the present, or perhaps any preceding, Congress, is of greater magnitude than that of the public lands." When we consider the far-reaching effects of the government's land policy upon political, economic, and social aspects of American life, we are disposed to agree with him. But this legislation was framed under frontier influences, and under the lead of Western statesmen like Benton and Jackson. Said Senator Scott of Indiana in 1841: "I consider the preëmption law merely declaratory of the custom or common law of the settlers."

It is safe to say that the legislation with regard to land, tariff, and internal improvements—the American system of the nationalizing Whig party—was conditioned on frontier ideas and needs. But it was not merely in legislative action that the frontier worked against the sectionalism of the coast. The economic and social characteristics of the frontier worked against sectionalism. The men of the frontier had closer resemblances to the Middle region than to either of the other sections. Pennsylvania had been the seed-plot of frontier emigration, and, although she passed on her settlers along the Great Valley into the west of Virginia and the Carolinas, yet the industrial society of these Southern frontiersmen was always more like that of the Middle region than like that of the tide-water portion of the South, which later came to spread its industrial type throughout the South.

The Middle region, entered by New York harbor, was an open door to all Europe. The tide-water part of the South represented typical Englishmen, modified by a warm climate and servile labor, and living in baronial fashion on great plantations; New England stood for a special English movement—Puritanism. The Middle region was less English than the other sections. It had a wide mixture of nationalities, a varied society, the mixed town and county system of local government, a varied economic life, many religious sects. In short, it was a region mediating between New England and the South, and the East and the West. It represented that composite nationality which the contemporary United States exhibits, that juxtaposition of non-English groups, occupying a valley or a little settlement, and presenting reflections of the map of Europe in their variety. It was democratic and nonsectional, if not national; "easy, tolerant, and contented"; rooted strongly in material prosperity. It was typical of the modern United States. It was least sectional, not only because it lay between North and South, but also because with no barriers to shut out its frontiers from its settled region, and with a system of connecting waterways, the Middle region mediated between East and West as well as between North and South. Thus it became the typically American region. Even the New Englander, who was shut out from the frontier by the Middle region, tarrying in New York or Pennsylvania on his westward march, lost the acuteness of his sectionalism on the way.

The spread of cotton culture into the interior of the South finally broke down the contrast between the "tide-water" region and the rest of the State, and based Southern interests on slavery. Before this process revealed its results the western portion of the South, which was akin to Pennsylvania in stock, society, and industry, showed tendencies to fall away from the faith of the fathers into internal improvement legislation and nationalism. In the Virginia convention of 1829–30, called to revise the constitution, Mr. Leigh, of Chesterfield, one of the tide-water counties, declared:

One of the main causes of discontent which led to this convention, that which had the strongest influence in overcoming our veneration for the work of our fathers, which taught us to contemn the sentiments of Henry and Mason and Pendleton, which weaned us from our reverence for the constituted authorities of the State, was an overweening passion for internal improvement. I say this with perfect knowledge, for it has been avowed to me by gentlemen from the West over and over again. And let me tell the gentleman from Albemarle (Mr. Gordon) that it has been another principal object of those who set this ball of revolution in motion, to overturn the doctrine of State rights, of which Virginia has been the very pillar, and to remove the barrier she has interposed to the interference of the Federal Government in that same work of internal improvement, by so reorganizing the legislature that Virginia, too, may be hitched to the Federal car.

It was this nationalizing tendency of the West that transformed the democracy of Jefferson into the national republicanism of Monroe and the democracy of Andrew Jackson. The West of the War of 1812, the West of Clay, and Benton and Harrison, and Andrew Jackson, shut off by the Middle States and the mountains from the coast sections, had a solidarity of its own with national tendencies. On the tide of the Father of Waters, North and South met and mingled into a nation. Interstate migration went steadily on—a process of cross-fertilization of ideas and institutions. The fierce struggle of the sections over slavery on the western frontier does not diminish the truth of this statement; it proves the truth of it. Slavery was a sectional trait that would not down, but in the West it could not remain sectional. It was the greatest of frontiersmen who declared: "I believe this Government can not endure permanently half slave and half free. It will become all of one thing or all of the other." Nothing works for nationalism like intercourse within the nation. Mobility of population is death to localism, and the western frontier worked irresistibly in unsettling population. The effect reached back from the frontier and affected profoundly the Atlantic coast and even the Old World.

But the most important effect of the frontier has been in the promotion of democracy here and in Europe. As has been indicated, the frontier is productive of individualism. Complex society is precipitated by the wilderness into a kind of primitive organization based on the family. The tendency is anti-social. It produces antipathy to control, and particularly to any direct control. The tax-gatherer is viewed as a representative of oppression. Prof. Osgood, in an able article, has pointed out that the frontier conditions prevalent in the colonies are important factors in the explanation of the American Revolution, where individual liberty was sometimes confused with absence of all effective government. The same conditions aid in explaining the difficulty of instituting a strong government in the period of the confederacy. The frontier individualism has from the beginning promoted democracy.

The frontier States that came into the Union in the first quarter of a century of its existence came in with democratic suffrage provisions, and had reactive effects of the highest importance upon the older States whose peoples were being attracted there. An extension of the franchise became essential. It was *western* New York that forced an extension of suffrage in the constitutional convention of that State in 1821; and it was *western* Virginia that compelled the tide-water region to put a more liberal suffrage provision in the constitution framed in 1830, and to give to the frontier region a more nearly proportionate representation with the tide-water aristocracy. The rise of democracy as an effective force in the nation came in with western preponderance under Jackson and William Henry Harrison, and it meant the triumph of the frontier—with all of its good and with all of its evil elements. An interesting illustration of the tone of frontier democracy in 1830 comes from the same debates in the Virginia convention already referred to. A representative from western Virginia declared:

But, sir, it is not the increase of population in the West which this gentleman ought to fear. It is the energy which the mountain breeze and western habits impart to those emigrants. They are regenerated, politically I mean, sir. They soon become *working politicians;* and the difference, sir, between a *talking* and a *working* politician is immense. The Old Dominion has long been celebrated for producing great orators; the ablest metaphysicians in policy; men that can split hairs in all abstruse questions of political economy. But at home, or when they return from Congress, they have negroes to fan them asleep. But a Pennsylvania, a New York, an Ohio, or a western Virginia statesman, though far inferior in logic, metaphysics, and rhetoric to an old Virginia statesman, has this advantage, that when he returns home he takes off his coat and takes hold of the plow. This gives him bone and muscle, sir, and preserves his republican principles pure and uncontaminated.

So long as free land exists, the opportunity for a competency exists, and economic power secures political power. But the democracy born of free land, strong in selfishness and individualism, intolerant of administrative experience and education, and pressing individual liberty beyond its proper bounds, has its dangers as well as its benefits. Individualism in America has allowed a laxity in regard to governmental affairs which has rendered possible the spoils system and all the manifest evils that follow from the lack of a highly developed civic spirit. In this connection may be noted also the influence of frontier conditions in permitting lax business honor, inflated paper currency and wild-cat banking. The colonial and revolutionary frontier was the region whence emanated many of the worst forms of an evil currency. The West in the War of 1812 repeated the phenomenon on the frontier of that day, while the speculation and wild-cat banking of the period of the crisis of 1837 occurred on the new frontier belt of the next tier of States. Thus each one of the periods of lax financial integrity coincides with periods when a new set of frontier communities had arisen, and coincides in area with these successive frontiers, for the most part. The recent Populist agitation is a case in point. Many a State that now declines any connection with the tenets of the Populists, itself adhered to such ideas in an earlier stage of the development of the State. A primitive society can hardly be expected to show the intelligent appreciation of the complexity of business interests in a developed society. The continual recurrence of these areas of paper-money agitation is another evidence that the frontier can be isolated and studied as a factor in American history of the highest importance.

The East has always feared the result of an unregulated advance of the frontier, and has tried to check and guide it. The English authorities would have checked settlement at the headwaters of the Atlantic tributaries and allowed the "savages to enjoy their deserts in quiet lest the peltry trade should decrease." This called out Burke's splendid protest:

If you stopped your grants, what would be the consequence? The people would occupy without grants. They have already so occupied in many places. You can not station garrisons in every part of these deserts. If you drive the people from one place, they will carry on their annual tillage and remove with their flocks and herds to another. Many of the people in the back settlements are already little attached to particular situations. Already they have topped the Appalachian Mountains. From thence they behold before them an immense plain, one vast, rich, level meadow; a square of five hundred miles. Over this they would wander without a possibility of restraint; they would change their manners with their habits of life; would soon forget a government by which they were disowned; would become hordes of English Tartars; and, pouring down upon your unfortified frontiers a fierce and irresistible cavalry, become masters of your governors and your counselers, your collectors and comptrollers, and of all the slaves that adhered to them. Such would, and in no long time must, be the effect of attempting to forbid as a crime and to suppress as an evil the command and blessing of Providence, "Increase and multiply." Such would be the happy result of an endeavor to keep as a lair of wild beasts that earth which God, by an express charter, has given to the children of men.

But the English Government was not alone in its desire to limit the advance of the frontier and guide its destinies. Tidewater Virginia and South Carolina gerrymandered those colonies to insure the dominance of the coast in their legislatures. Washington desired to settle a State at a time in the Northwest; Jefferson would reserve from settlement the territory of his Louisiana Purchase north of the thirty-second parallel, in order to offer it to the Indians in exchange for their settlements east of the Mississippi. "When we shall be full on this side," he writes, "we may lay off a range of States on the western bank from the head to the mouth, and so range after range, advancing compactly as we multiply." Madison went so far as to argue to the French minister that the United States had no interest in seeing population extend itself on the right bank of the Mississippi, but should rather fear it. When the Oregon question was under debate, in 1824, Smyth, of Virginia, would draw an unchangeable line for the limits of the United States at the outer limit of two tiers of States beyond the Mississippi, complaining that the seaboard States were being drained of the flower of their population by the bringing of too much land into market. Even Thomas Benton, the man of widest views of the destiny of the West, at this stage of his career declared that along the ridge of the rocky mountains "the western limits of the Republic should be drawn, and the statue of the fabled god Terminus should be raised upon its highest peak, never to be thrown down." But

the attempts to limit the boundaries, to restrict land sales and settlement, and to deprive the West of its share of political power were all in
vain. Steadily the frontier of settlement advanced and carried with it
individualism, democracy, and nationalism, and powerfully affected the
East and the Old World.

The most effective efforts of the East to regulate the frontier came
through its educational and religious activity, exerted by interstate migration and by organized societies. Speaking in 1835, Dr. Lyman Beecher
declared: "It is equally plain that the religious and political destiny of
our nation is to be decided in the West," and he pointed out that the population of the West "is assembled from all the States of the Union and
from all the nations of Europe, and is rushing in like the waters of the
flood, demanding for its moral preservation the immediate and universal action of those institutions which discipline the mind and arm
the conscience and the heart. And so various are the opinions and habits, and so recent and imperfect is the acquaintance, and so sparse are
the settlements of the West, that no homogeneous public sentiment can
be formed to legislate immediately into being the requisite institutions.
And yet they are all needed immediately in their utmost perfection
and power. A nation is being 'born in a day.' . . . But what will become
of the West if her prosperity rushes up to such a majesty of power, while
those great institutions linger which are necessary to form the mind
and the conscience and the heart of that vast world. It must not be permitted. . . . Let no man at the East quiet himself and dream of liberty,
whatever may become of the West. . . . Her destiny is our destiny."

With the appeal to the conscience of New England, he adds appeals to
her fears lest other religious sects anticipate her own. The New England
preacher and school-teacher left their mark on the West. The dread of
Western emancipation from New England's political and economic control was paralleled by her fears lest the West cut loose from her religion.
Commenting in 1850 on reports that settlement was rapidly extending
northward in Wisconsin, the editor of the *Home Missionary* writes: "We
scarcely know whether to rejoice or mourn over this extension of our
settlements. While we sympathize in whatever tends to increase the
physical resources and prosperity of our country, we can not forget that
with all these dispersions into remote and still remoter corners of the
land the supply of the means of grace is becoming relatively less and
less." Acting in accordance with such ideas, home missions were established and Western colleges were erected. As seaboard cities like Philadelphia, New York, and Baltimore strove for the mastery of Western
trade, so the various denominations strove for the possession of the
West. Thus an intellectual stream from New England sources fertilized
the West. Other sections sent their missionaries; but the real struggle
was between sects. The contest for power and the expansive tendency

furnished to the various sects by the existence of a moving frontier must have had important results on the character of religious organization in the United States. The multiplication of rival churches in the little frontier towns had deep and lasting social effects. The religious aspects of the frontier make a chapter in our history which needs study.

From the conditions of frontier life came intellectual traits of profound importance. The works of travelers along each frontier from colonial days onward describe certain common traits, and these traits have, while softening down, still persisted as survivals in the place of their origin, even when a higher social organization succeeded. The result is that to the frontier the American intellect owes its striking characteristics. That coarseness and strength combined with acuteness and inquisitiveness; that practical, inventive turn of mind, quick to find expedients; that masterful grasp of material things, lacking in the artistic but powerful to effect great ends; that restless, nervous energy; that dominant individualism, working for good and for evil, and withal that buoyancy and exuberance which comes with freedom—these are traits of the frontier, or traits called out elsewhere because of the existence of the frontier. Since the days when the fleet of Columbus sailed into the waters of the New World, America has been another name for opportunity, and the people of the United States have taken their tone from the incessant expansion which has not only been open but has even been forced upon them. He would be a rash prophet who should assert that the expansive character of American life has now entirely ceased. Movement has been its dominant fact, and, unless this training has no effect upon a people, the American energy will continually demand a wider field for its exercise. But never again will such gifts of free land offer themselves. For a moment, at the frontier, the bonds of custom are broken and unrestraint is triumphant. There is not *tabula rasa*. The stubborn American environment is there with its imperious summons to accept its conditions; the inherited ways of doing things are also there; and yet, in spite of environment, and in spite of custom, each frontier did indeed furnish a new field of opportunity, a gate of escape from the bondage of the past; and freshness, and confidence, and scorn of older society, impatience of its restraints and its ideas, and indifference to its lessons, have accompanied the frontier. What the Mediterranean Sea was to the Greeks, breaking the bond of custom, offering new experiences, calling out new institutions and activities, that, and more, the ever retreating frontier has been to the United States directly, and to the nations of Europe more remotely. And now, four centuries from the discovery of America, at the end of a hundred years of life under the Constitution, the frontier has gone, and with its going has closed the first period of American history.

David Riesman

It is a difficult problem to attempt as in this series of lectures to link the psychological understanding of people to specific political and other social phenomena. In his paper Professor Parsons tried to show how individuals play roles in a society and how these roles within a social system may harness various types of personalities. To put it more specifically, you can get the same kind of political behavior, for instance, out of quite different human types. Although the behavior has different meanings for these people, the understanding of their differences and those different meanings may be quite irrelevant to their political and public role.

Nevertheless, and this is the topic of my discourse, it seems to me that personality does influence political behavior if we look at it in a sufficiently long-run historical view. Its influence is felt not in terms of specific behavior—in terms of explaining why somebody votes for Truman or Dewey or Wallace—but only in terms of what I like to call political style, the kind of attitude a person has towards the political cosmos: how he reacts to it, how he feels it reacting to him. If one is to speak as more than a spot-news analyst of political crisis, then he must be concerned with these long-run developments both in politics and personality.

In fact, I think there is a danger for the social scientist if he allows such a phrase as political crisis to make him try to be particularly relevant in talking about spot news, the atom bomb, or what not. Because curiously enough if the social scientist is any good he can't help being relevant. He lives in our society as a participant-observer and it is no problem for him to be relevant—he can't help it. If he isn't any good, and hence irrelevant, he is sometimes likely to compensate by grandiose ambitions; and when he tries to communicate about politics—to solve present crises—he is likely to say more about his own personality than he says about politics, ironically just because he is trying too hard to talk about politics.

That is at least my prologue for taking an excursion in this paper which will go back 100 years in American history. In this way we can take a look at the changes in American character and American political style as developing from the nineteenth century to the present. I know what I have to say is difficult, and I hope that in the discussion period the unanswered ambiguities in what I say can be brought up and threshed out.

Let me first present my dramatis personae. There are two types of character in the cast: one I call the inner-directed type and the other I call the other-directed type. And they orient themselves to the world in two political styles. I call the first, the style of the moralizers, and the second, the style of the inside-dopesters. And the scene on which these moralizers and inside-dopesters play their parts is in the changing power configurations of this country in the last decades. Naturally, the broad outlines of such a drama as this must be tentative, must be experimental.

Let me begin by describing what kind of people the inner-directeds are. In framing my character types, in trying to work with character types which have psychoanalytic depth and also historical relevance, I have focused on the problem of how conformity is assured; what these people conform to; what their society or their group in society expects of them. This, it seems to me, changes over historical time. In the nineteenth century—and still to a great extent in this century—it seems to me that conformity was assured by a mechanism which I call inner-direction, in which a person was socialized in an authoritative family group by impressive and often oppressive parents and in which he internalized his image of these parents. Freud's picture of the superego is a magnificent picture of this type. This was the typical American of the middle class of the last century, the parents and grandparents of most of us today. Some of us could still be called inner-directed.

Now, the inner-directed person is oriented early in childhood towards very clear goals in life. It may be money, fame, power, goodness, or any blend of these. And he is headed for these by the kind of intimate family socialization characteristic of his age. I like to use a metaphor to describe this mechanism. I speak of these people as gyroscopically-steered. The parents install a gyroscope in them and it stabilizes them all their life. They are less independent than they seem because the gyroscope keeps them on the course for which their parents headed them.

What is the kind of society in which such types will live and work? Theirs is a world in which the opening frontiers are the frontiers of production, discovery, science. We might call it the job-minded society—a society in which people are very much aware and interested in the malleability of the physical environment, the organizational environment, and in their social mobility, their ambitions. Their preoccupation is to harness themselves to fulfilling the tasks of the expanding society which needs a large physical plant, extensive social organization, extensive military preparation. In this kind of a job-minded society people are protected from too close resonance with each other by their concentration on these necessary and rewarding tasks.

It does not follow from this that the inner-directed man, concentrated on these tasks, is not concerned with people. People may be means to the ends of his gyroscopically-installed goal—people as voters, workers, soldiers. And he may be a pretty good manipulator of them for these ends. The point that is decisive in distinguishing him from the other-directed man is that he does not need anything from these peoples as ends in themselves. He does not look to them for approval. He does not look to them for warmth. He looks to them for usefulness and in other more specific and more tangible ways.

Obviously I am speaking in terms of contrast, and in order to do so I create what those who have sociological training would recognize as an ideal type—ideal not in the sense of noble, but ideal in the sense of abstract. There is no pure inner-directed man. Most of us are blends. We can make a judgment of the emphasis of these tendencies within given individuals or given social epochs.

In this job-minded society in which people oriented themselves early towards clearly defined goals, young people had clear models to follow. They might be very ambitious and hitch themselves to some star in the ancestral firmament. If they were going to be scientists, they might want to imitate Pasteur; or if painters, they might want to imitate Renoir. They thought in terms of great men. Maybe they thought their parents were great men; and they headed for that. They modeled themselves on these people. This was possible because the personal star developed in this way did not become obsolete but was good for a lifetime. In the case of the personality market, the market on which people sell themselves, there was a fair amount of stability so that a person who decided, when he was very young, that he wanted to be like, let us say, Henry Ford or Abraham Lincoln was not likely to find people calling him quaint by the time he was fifty—because others had gyroscopes too, spinning at about the same pace, moving in the same direction. People who had this type of character found themselves on the whole rewarded, found their lives unproblematical in the sense of concern with whether they fitted or not. To put the matter more generally, there was a certain fit between social structure and character structure.

Having said this, I think I have to stop at once and suggest that one should not get nostalgic about "life with father." As a play it may be amusing; but if he is your father, if he has hurt you, that may be a different matter. I think this nostalgia is actually an important social and political force in our time, and I want to come back to it later on.

Let me now introduce the next person in the dramatis personae, the other-directed. A new source of conformity is required, it seems to me, for the urban upper middle class in our big cities, a conformity for which gyroscopic adaption is not sufficiently flexible, not sufficiently resonant with other people. And for this new source of conformity I like to use the metaphor of the radar set. The other-directed child has a radar set installed, by which he can understand the interpersonal environment and see its signals around him. He is oriented very early in life, not to his ancestors, not to his parents or to his image of their exalted selves, but to his peers; that is, the other kids on the block, the other kids at school, the people who will do a great deal of the job of socializing him. In fact, those who are familiar with the work of Harry Stack Sullivan can see that he has become in a sense the analyst of this age because he was the person above all others who called attention to the importance of the peer group in the process of socialization.

One can see that the parents play a hand in this by their concern with whether the child is popular, how he is getting along with the other kids. One can see that the school also is concerned today more with morale than with morality—concerned with the social atmosphere. I speak now obviously of the progressive schools in the suburban and urban areas where the other-directed as a character type is emerging. The school puts a youngster in with the five-year-olds to see if he fits with the five-year-olds, not in terms of how much he knows, but in terms of how he gets along. And the parents are anxious and judge their success with their children by how the children get along, how popular they are; the parents act as chauffeurs and managers for the continuous stage performance of their children in the peer group.

It is important to see what the radar brings to the other-directed child. It brings direction; it brings a sense of what is worth having in life, what is worth experiencing, what is worth talking about, thinking about. And the goals obviously change with what the radar senses rather than being set for a lifetime as in the earlier epoch. Obviously I don't mean to imply that parents set about consciously to create little paragons who will fit into the society of 1950 or 1960 or 1970. They aren't that calculating, even if they would like to be. It is a long and complicated story and one, I am sure, many social investigators have worked on and thought about: how it happens that the parents, without actually being consciously aware of their role in this process, produce the children whom the next society makes use of. It is a story I cannot go into here. But I want to remark on just one of the changes from inner-direction to other-direction which might be called the change from bringing up children to bringing up father, for children may bring up parents in the other-directed society.

I think one might recognize, if he is interested in historical questions, that this does not sound so new. Perhaps the other-directed American is in a way the American as he appeared to the eyes of 150 years of European observation. The European always thought that the American was a person who cared more for what his fellows thought than any-thing else, that the American was more concerned with indiscriminate approval and with warmth, more dependent on his neighbors than the European was—or at least more than the European who came to Amer-ica to look around. And certainly there is very much in the way of social change and so on which helps to explain why it is we have a comic strip called "Bringing Up Father" in which the daughter as well as the mother cooperates.

Now, what is the kind of society in which the other-directed person moves? For him the frontiers are not the frontiers of production but the frontiers of consumption, the frontiers of much more abundant lei-sure and consumer goods. He moves in a society where—at least in his picture of it—the main productive job is done. The steel mills are built, the railroads are built, the mines are dug, the government organizations are set up. And his concern is to live as a consumer. Those who may be economists can recognize the touch of Keynesian economics in that. But I want to make clear that I am not talking about conspicuous consump-tion—I am not talking about keeping up with the Jonses. That is an older, perhaps a traditional pattern. As long as one is concerned only with what goods he is getting out of the society, out of its physical pro-ductiveness, he is still inner-directed. A person is other-directed only when his interest is not in the goods—he takes those for granted. After all, the middle-class family can have a car, a mink coat, good food, and so on. Consumption itself is no issue for most of these people. The prob-lem for the other-directed person is not the goods themselves, but the right attitudes about the goods. Is he having the right experiences vis-à-vis the wine he drinks, the car he drives, the girl he sleeps with, and so on? That is the problem. And he looks to others for guidance as to whether he is experiencing the right experiences on the frontiers of con-sumption. He takes more or less for granted that he has the where-withal, the ability to pay unremittingly to provide himself with the goods themselves.

This is another way of saying that in America we have moved from a job-minded society to a people-minded society in which one's concern is no longer with the malleability of the materiel but with the malleability of the personnel. It is a society in which people are no longer protected from each other by the objectivity of their workaday tasks and in which response from others becomes an end in life as well as a means.

In fact, I think it is quite interesting to look at specific individuals and see to what extent they may rationalize their need for warmth, their need for approval from others, in terms of, let us say, some sensible and easily rationalized goal such as money or security.

Think of Willy Loman, in the play, *Death of a Salesman*, as a man who looked to selling, not primarily for money—that too—but as a source of affection, a means of justifying himself, a *Weltanschauung*—all these things wrapped up in the job of the salesman. Incidentally, the play seemed quite incomprehensible to Londoners. They couldn't understand why anybody was that interested in selling and why people responded in terms other than cash. The English response showed that they didn't understand Americans. Obviously in such a society the old clear goals of ambition, the old stars of the heavenly firmament by which the inner-directed man guided himself no longer guide people.

Let me give an illustration. There was an interview with a thirteen-year-old girl about her comic-reading habits. She was asked what comics she preferred and she said Superman. Then she was asked why. "Oh, Superman can fly," she said, "and flying is very important." "Would you like to be able to fly?" the interviewer asked. "Oh, no, that would be kind of conspicuous," the girl said. Here one sees the fear of being conspicuous, the fear of being too ambitious, the fear somebody might say, "So you think you're big—so you think you're something." These are the fears which make it hard for people brought up in other-directed circles to have the same kind of sometimes fanatical and crushing ambition which was a characteristic of the middle-class man of an earlier epoch, a characteristic which still hangs on in this country because—obviously I am talking about trends—there are still men like Henry Ford.

I am talking about something that the investigator finds more among the young than the old, more in the upper middle class in the very large metropolitan areas than in the smaller cities and smaller towns. And this seems to me to be connected in subtle ways with the alteration of mobility channels. One no longer gets ahead in the society by making a better mousetrap but by packaging an old mousetrap in a new way and selling it by selling one's self first.

Those who know Erich Fromm's book *Man for Himself* will recognize the similarity of his marketing orientation to what I call the other-directed man. The man of the marketing orientation is concerned with how he is doing on the personality market of the large corporate enterprises, private, public, academic, and what not, of our society. And in order to succeed on the personality market he must be different but not too different; as different as Ford from Chevrolet—maybe as far different as Studebaker from Ford. And so he must always use his radar to find out: "Am I different enough to be recognized—to have a brand name, so to speak, for my personality—but not so different that I will be priced out of the market as an eccentric?" But even eccentricity can be made to pay in the right professions. Success comes in our society increasingly, it seems to me, through a person's ability to be malleable enough to fit into a cooperative network.

Adam Smith used the phrase "the invisible hand" to describe the economic organization of the free market. I think we have moved from the invisible hand to the glad hand and that today people in industry and the professions—particularly in medicine—are engaged in a cooperative network in which the esteem of colleagues is decisive for one's fate and in which to be known as a rate-buster would exclude one from the system. To be sure, there are survivals of the older age, but I am talking of the social character that seems to me to be emerging.

Let me now turn to the question of the political styles which seem to me in a rather indeterminate way to spring from these respective types of character. Yet first of all it must be recognized that the majority of Americans have no distinctive political style at all. There is very little traceable connection, it seems to me, between their character and their politics. Their politics depends on their situation, as I said at the outset, and not on their personality. Let me give an illustration.

If one takes a look at the book called *Southern Politics,* he will see that Professor Key interprets southern politics in America today as being dominated by what he calls the black-belt whites, the whites who live in the counties of large Negro predominance, and that their influence is, to a degree, based on the southern electoral systems as these have been inherited in several southern states. Now here is a situation in which—in order to understand this kind of southern politics—it would do very little good to interpret in idiosyncratic terms the character structure of the black-belt whites. To be sure, the fact that they are black-belt whites will reveal something about their character structure. But the situation and the electoral machinery in which the populace is caught matters much more than their character. Consequently, when I speak of style, I speak here only of those people in whom one can trace a connection between politics and character, and this limits me to those who are politically active either as political leaders and operators or as avid consumers of the political news of the day.

The first style I shall describe is the style of the moralizer—the political manifestation of inner-direction. However, not all inner-directed people are involved in politics; and they are not inevitably moralizers. Rather, this is the style which is politically compatible with their character. Their character gives them a slight push in the direction of being moralizers.

The moralizer is a person who views politics as a field of work and not primarily as a field of entertainment or consumption. To be sure, in the nineteenth century when the moralizer was in his heyday, there were torchlight parades, and politics was not entirely unamusing and unsportive. But on the whole politics was a field of work or, as many businessmen thought, interference with work. It was judged from the standpoint of work, from the standpoint of the harnessing of the resources of the society. The moralizer would never have attended a lecture with a title of *Personality and Political Crisis.* He would not have known what it meant, because for him politics stayed in its limited place. He thought of it in terms of government institutions, electoral machinery, and so on. Because he defined politics in a limited way, it helped him to view politics as a manageable domain—small, encompassable, not too complicated. He defined it in such a way as to leave it relatively uncomplicated. And correlatively his own relation to it was uncomplicated because he knew what he wanted. Because his goals were clear, he could decide where in politics his interests lay, either in terms of self-interest, or the interest of his group, his nation, or his god. The moralizer, by defining politics in a limited way, by defining his relationship to it in terms of a clear picture of his self-interest—often mistaken, but clear—did not feel overwhelmed. So many people today feel overwhelmed by politics, but to the moralizer, politics was masterable, was graspable. One had a vision—if one were inner-directed and a moralizer—of what was good work, what was a good political performance, and what was a bad political performance; and one could relate politics to these definitions.

The term moralizer is a little misleading in this connection. I don't mean that the moralizer was necessarily a moral man in the sense of having high morality or ethics. Rather, he was a person who clearly defined his relation to the political world, and since the discourse in this country in the nineteenth century was largely moralistic, he didn't have too much trouble in defending, let us say, a log-rolling job in moral terms.

But we must also think of the nineteenth century as a period in which enormous moralizing energies were harnessed in the political scene. To expand the school system, to do something about prisons and the insane, to free the slaves—all these issues provided a moralistic frame of reference in which people could take clear positions and feel relatively unfloundering in a narrowly-defined political ocean.

But this statement is an oversimplification of the nineteenth century. How much of an oversimplification? We can remind ourselves if we take a look at a very, as I think, exciting passage from Tocqueville who came over and took an unequalled brilliant look at this country in the 1830's. He wrote:

It is difficult to say what place is taken up in the life of an inhabitant of the United States by his concern for politics. To take a hand in the regulation of society and to discuss it is his biggest concern and, so to speak, the only pleasure an American knows. In some countries the inhabitants seem unwilling to avail themselves of the political privileges which the law gives them. It would seem that they set too high a value on their time to spend it on the interests of the community. But if an American were condemned to confine his activities to his own affairs, he would be robbed of one half of his existence. He would feel an immense void in the life he is accustomed to lead. His wretchedness would be unbearable.

One can see by this quotation some of the ambiguities of the use of politics as an agenda, as a way to get through the day, as a way to harness one's self in the nineteenth century.

It is awfully hard to say where the nineteenth-century American stood. Think of the people up in the State of Vermont who thought the country was engulfed in a masonic conspiracy. Think of the people who thought that Phi Beta Kappa was a subversive organization. But on the whole the moralizer's picture of the world was a pretty clear picture, and the Know-Nothing and so on of that day was rather the forerunner of what I like to call the bewildered moralizer of today—the person whose world has vanished and who turns into a curdled indignant when he contemplates the political scene. He no longer understands it—politics refuses to fit into its narrow compartments. Much of the outcry against the welfare state and so on comes from people who say, "Politics ought to stay where I put it." And it won't stay. Then the self-interest of a person no longer seems clear.

What way does self-interest lie today in politics? What way does morality lie?

While the conflict between public and private moralities is an old one, the network of publics to be considered makes the discussion of moral issues today ever more complicated, ambiguous, and equivocal. The bewildered moralizer, the curdled indignant, reacts negatively to this. The world doesn't make sense to him. And one thing that facilitates this development is the fact that he lives in a society increasingly other-directed, in which the mass media of communication bombard him with messages which he can't understand.

What is the small-town curdled indignant to make of Billy Rose's accounts of love and life at Lindy's? What is he to do about network radio, about the sophisticated pace of A-budget movies? He can't follow them. But there is one place where he can follow. He can follow politics because he can make politics obey him. The editoral writer, the political campaigner appeal to the curdled indignant with an old familiar tune. They tell him that after all his world would make sense if only a few bad people, these smooth city slickers, these other-directed men, were to be thrown out. Then the world would go back to where it could be run by the invisible hand.

This brings me to the inside-dopester, the political manifestation of the other-directed. He is socialized in a setting where he can't be too conspicuous, where he learns to hold his emotional fire, and where he learns to bring certain skills to bear which are chiefly skills of consumption, skills of the consumer.

A short time ago I was talking with some friends of mine who have two children, aged four and five. They told me the children could look at the cars in the street and tell which is a '50 Pontiac and which is a '49 Oldsmobile. As very young children they have become members of the consumers' union. And when they become a little bit older, they bring this consumers'-union skill to bear on politics. They may bring it to bear in one of two ways. First, the inside-dopester may try to manipulate others, in which case he will interpret politics as a problem of being able to get the right man on the telephone. But if he is less close to the switchboard, if he is less close to the politically-operative group, then he is likely not to be able to manipulate others. In this case he will choose the second way: he will harness his manipulative energies solely to himself, in order to make sure that he has the right reactions to the political news.

Many people have doubtless observed, if they have been in government service—or indeed anywhere—that politics is a form of office gossip in which to have the right reaction is all that is required of one. The goal of the inside-dopester is never to be taken in by any person, cause, or event; that is, to be a sharp member of the consumers' union. It is interesting to trace these developments, even in radical left-wing politics. A generation ago the young Communist, for instance, had to have a working knowledge of Marxism, had to be able to handle the dialectic, had to make noises like a Marxist. Today all he has to do is know how to get Marcantonio elected. It is no longer necessary for him to be able to have a stance on principle, at least in the political scene.

I think one can say in general that the inside-dopester sees politics as a field of mood engineering. Sometimes the only moods he can engineer are his own and those of his small peerage. At other times he can try to engineer the mood of a nation. This is his way of coping with the growing complexity of politics, the complexity which no longer submits to the simplifications of the moralizer.

One other way of tracing this development is to ask one's self: In any social setting, who are the people who make a living by scaring businessmen or government officials? In the nineteenth century the people who made the best living in this way were lawyers, and they frightened businessmen and government officials about their standing with two very limited publics—judges and legislators. The scare was not great because often the judges and legislators could be managed for cash on the barrelhead. In this rather simple picture the businessman might be a little frightened by the pictures his lawyer drew for him, but after all he knew what the lawyer was describing; and the lawyer himself was a fellow who knew the institutional structure, knew how to talk to judges and legislators.

Today it is my impression that the dependence of the lawyer has lessened and it is the contact man who frightens businessmen and government officials about a whole range of publics which are as likely to disappear on inspection as did the Cheshire cat. These are all those publics who may say nasty things about the businessman, if, for instance, he does not do the right thing or make the right public-relations move. In this amorphous sea of contacts the businessman no longer knows what his interests are and he has to ask his public-relations advisor not only what publics to propitiate but what interest he has in propitiating them. Of course, this work may still be done by lawyers —that is, members of the bar who have not had this attitude trained out of them by their education.

It may be said, in fact, that whereas the moralizer's gullibility about politics was often based on limiting his definition of politics, the inside-dopester's gullibility about politics is often based on the delusion, basic to his whole character and basic to his attitude, that there is somebody somewhere—maybe Kiplinger, maybe the people who write the *Newsweek* "Periscope," maybe a private eye of some sort—who sees all and knows all. But actually—and this is part of the ambiguous development of our society—the inside-dopester *does* know more than the moralizer. He is better informed; his range is wider; he is able to see both sides. There are very few innocents left to go fight city hall.

Another facet in this development which has moved us from morality to morale is the necessity of the political consumer today to be ready for rapid changes of line. His political attitude, his political style might be obsolete in a moment if he did not have his radar set in good working order. And this is part of the increasingly fast pace with which our society makes obsolete automobiles, people, and ideas. One interesting way of tracing this empirically—of course in a very tentative way—is to study public opinion polls. And there we see, interestingly enough, that the middle class—that is, the group in which these tendencies are far more manifest than in the working class—shifts its political attitudes much more rapidly and readily. It is true about their opinion on the last war and on Russia.

I have been struck by Machiavelli's observation—contrary to all the political observers of his day and many since—that the masses are far less fickle than the rulers. And I think public opinion polls show this to be true. "Fickle" may be the wrong word, too biased a word, because the readiness of the middle class for rapid changes of line is connected with the actual changes in the situation; with the greater reality-orientation vis-à-vis politics which many inside-dopesters have.

The problem is that the inside-dopester's motive for political consumption, for political operation, is not to secure a reality-orientation. For him politics is a means of group conformity, if he lives in a group where it is fashionable to be up on the political news of the day. In other groups (and, to a degree, in the same group) one might be up on the sporting news.

These are the compelling motivations that keep the inside-dopester political in spite of the evaporation of his political emotions. It is an interesting problem: the inside-dopester is a person who is not committed, who does not bring to politics a clear notion of his own self-interest or clear principles—yet he follows politics. I think he follows politics because he lives in a group which follows politics. Then one might ask, why does the group follow politics? This is a question that I cannot get into here. I would just mention one paradox. Where the group to which the inside-dopester belongs is a moralizing group, he will look like a moralizer, sound like a moralizer, feel himself to be a moralizer.

I want to get into a more fundamental paradox; namely, the fact that the word "morale" conceals a moral judgment. I think we in the Western society have changed our style in hypocrisy. The Victorian hypocrite was a person who concealed bad actions under the high-sounding cloak of good ones. But ever since Freud and a number of other people, the hypocrite has concealed his good actions under the cloak of solid self-interest. This hypocrisy makes it possible to disguise, under such a term as morale, one's morality.

A student working with me has been doing a number of interviews in the community outside Chicago called Park Forest, a newly-developing suburb which has been built by the American Community Builders, a large real estate operation. This student went out there in the early days of this development and he asked people what they thought about the American Community Builders, what they thought about their community, and what their political attitudes were. Many had grievances about their homes, lawns, roads, and so on. But from many of those people with grievances he got this answer: "The American Community Builders has bad public relations." They emphasized no grievance as much as that. What does that mean if you try to analyze it for latent meaning? The respondent seems to be saying: "The trouble with the stupid people who run this town is that they haven't made me like it." Or he might not even be saying that. He may be saying: "They haven't made those other fellows like it." He conceals any judgment based on principle, on his own experience, on his own life, under the cover of the bad mechanics, the poor mood engineering on the part of the operators.

I will cite another illustration. Some of my associates and I did some interviews before the last election. We asked people about the candidates. And we found many people who said, "Well, Truman is sincere and Dewey is insincere." We tried to think what that meant. Why did they use this word? And I was reminded of the fact that in doing interviews on popular music a student came across the same expression. He played a record for people and then asked, "Well, did you like the record?" "Oh, yes, I like Dinah Shore. She's so sincere." Or, "I like Frank Sinatra. He's so sincere." What does this judgment mean? I don't know all the answers to that question. I think we would understand a lot if we knew. I have some hunches about it. I think for one thing this judgment on the basis of sincerity is a moral judgment; that is, "This man can manipulate me because he involves himself in his performance. He sends me. And I allow him to send me because he is sending himself too." But there is more to it than that. This is a judgment in terms of personality—at least in the field of politics and I think also in the field of popular music—and it is not one of personality only. Using the criterion of sincerity may be an avoidance of the judgment of performance. Is Dinah Shore a good singer? Has she got the right vocal equipment? Is the political candidate able to deliver? Judgment on the basis of answers to these questions is ducked by focusing on an issue of mood which in many political situations is of little importance. If the moralizer thought that he wanted a government of laws and not of men, the inside-dopester think he wants a government of men and not of laws. Both have unattainable ideals.

I have said that there were concealed moral judgments—repressed morality—in the reaction of the inside-dopester. The psychiatrist knows, I think, that people often end up being what they play at being. And since the inside-dopester has given up trying to find out what he wants in politics, he is more and more apt to tolerate what is wanted of him, provided it is put in a nice way.

I want to turn now to the stage on which these characters play, and ask what are the changes in the political configuration of this country that may evoke and reward either inner-directed or other-directed tendencies within people—thus, in turn, encouraging or repressing one or another political style. In my opinion it is of decisive importance both for political style and for character that we no longer have a clear social-class hierarchy in America.

Let me put the problem this way. Who runs the country? This was a relatively easy question to answer in 1896. The people like Morgan were at the top of the prestige ladder; they were models for ambitious youth, whether in the Horatio Alger stories or in the *Saturday Evening Post*. They were the focus of attention. These were the captains of industry, and they dominated the country fifty years ago.

Who runs the country today? It's a hard question. Who ranks whom at a dinner party? Is an Army colonel superior to a doctor at the Washington School of Psychiatry? How about a college professor, the head of an oil company, the head of a big advertising agency, Jack Benny? Which way is up? Who are the models for youth? The answer to these questions as stated in the mass media—see the brilliant study made by Leo Lowenthal of the popular magazines, *Saturday Evening Post* and *Colliers*—is that the focus of attention is no longer on the captains of industry but on what I like to call the captains of nonindustry: a Hollywood star, a golf pro, a cafe-society boy. Take a look at the men-of-distinction ads and tell me who runs the country!

It seems to me that what we have today is a situation in which the older hierarchy has crumbled and has been replaced by a lot of smaller hierarchies which I like to call the veto groups; that is, the lobbies. And whereas the political leader in 1896 had a clear relationship to his public, the political leader today is found within the lobby, within the Farm Bureau, the trade associations, the American Jewish Congress, the American Medical Association, and so on, endlessly. They are veto groups because they have a much better opportunity to stop action than to start it. Their concern is chiefly with prevention. But with this change in hierarchy comes a change in the type of attitude one has to have to operate in politics and understand politics. The lobbyist within one of these veto groups is concerned with the veto subgroups within his own group down to the last veto group of one. It may be a recalcitrant farmer who will not conform with the Farm Bureau's policies. It may be a recalcitrant who holds out on the union leader. And when the lobbyist is operating with other co-equals who are heads of other veto groups his concern is that each of them has a "reasonable" and just slightly expanding cut of the political pie. In today's politics there are a great many ins and very few outs. And the leader, therefore, in the older sense is virtually disappearing. What we see instead as the so-called leader is either the man who can placate the veto groups and operate within this framework of coalitions—as Roosevelt did so capably—or the man who tries to deal with the few unorganized wretches who have not yet invented their group. But obviously this leads to a situation in which there is a constant elaboration of the publics with which leaders are concerned. The need to see and propitiate these publics can be rationalized in terms of public relations.

One sees a very interesting thing in the discussion of the atom bomb and the hydrogen bomb today which I might put in terms of the old cartoon "Who's excited?" Everybody is concerned with everybody else's mood and asking that question in regard to all these various publics, whether or not these publics have any actual power to affect the course of events. In fact, actual ignorance of who has power is in some ways an asset if one is to be a veto-group leader because it permits one to propitiate still other publics in terms of the fact that they might have power. Let me give an illustration: If a college professor writes a book attacking business, he makes a lot of jobs for his students in the business world, for business must answer him. The businessmen want to be told that there are some people who don't like them and whom they need to propitiate, whether or not the professor's book sells any copies or has any weight.

In this situation of complex and tenuous interpersonal webs within the lobbies and among the lobbies, obviously it takes a man with the gifts and the social skills more nearly like those of the inside-dopester to get along rather than those skills associated with the moralizer. Thus the skills of the inside-dopester are in demand.

Of course, many people still assume we have a ruling class in this country. But I think one of the reasons they assume this is that they need to justify their own propitiation. They can't tell themselves that they need to be liked; therefore they have to assume somebody has power. I think another reason, perhaps more basic, is the feeling of discomfort if there is nobody in charge. Everyone likes to think that there is someone in charge, even if the person in charge does not represent him.

Plainly, these emotional ideas of the inside-dopester are not the only ones current in politics. I have left aside for a moment the curdled indignant—the bewildered moralizer who feels that the world doesn't make sense to him. Mood engineering on the part of the inside-dopester is a red flag to the curdled indignant. What the latter responds to is the appearance of impiety, violence, on the part of a Pegler or the *New York Daily News* or Branch Rickey; that is, the very mood engineering which the inside-dopester attempts as a way of propitiating publics may be just the thing which makes the curdled indignant feel most bewildered and most angry. So he falls back, as I indicated earlier, to a more familiar style, a style of the *political* indignant, of the leader who is able to say: "There are a few bad men around and all we have to do is get rid of them." But even the other-directed man, just because he doesn't know what he wants, just because of his concern with the plethora of publics, has a tendency to call on older types when the going gets rough. When the glad hand is rebuffed, the inside-dopester may even wish *not* to reach an agreement, whereas earlier he would have given anything for someone to say: "Let's agree to disagree." So it is that the inside-dopester is in some ways unfit for conflict. In fact, "conflict" is a word he avoids. He prefers the words "tension," "low morale," or "poor communications."

All this may delay the triumph of morale over morality. But little hope lies in that delay. I think it should be clear, from what I have said, that neither the style of the moralizer nor the style of the inside-dopester is adequate to politics. The former sees politics in too limited a context. And the latter fails to bring to politics the very humanity which would let him react as a human being; as a result, he often fails to see the potentialities which lie underneath the "reality" to which he is so passionately attached.

Now we might ask, What changes in American political structure and what changes in American character structure might bring new motives into play in the political arena and thus reward the development of a more mature political style?

People today are asked to participate and involve themselves in politics for motives that seem to me inadequate. They are asked to involve themselves by appeals to self-interest—as if we were still living in the days of the moralizers when everyone knew what his interests were.

They are asked to involve themselves by appeals to group conformity—often snob appeals to be active politically and belong to the PTA or the DAR or what not. Or they are appealed to on behalf of a Sincere Candidate who will decide all the questions for them.

It is probably not possible to decide how to appeal to other motivations and get results. But at least it is necessary to raise the question of whether the trouble lies always with the people, or whether it might not be found in the politics. Is the American political scene so dull or uninteresting that there is no reason why people should be interested for good motives? Might it not make more sense to improve the political wares that are offered to the American people, rather than to spend energy on asking Americans to participate in, to be concerned about, to be less apathetic about politics? Are there not other political packages that Americans can buy?

I think that a beginning can be made on this problem by concentrating on evoking more political imagination. Why not indicate more alternatives to the American people, especially in the domestic scene? For instance, it might be pointed out that there is a wider range of choice in the kinds of lives people might lead, if they wished. But this is only possible if in such an attempt a more experimental attitude is assumed: Americans need not always be satisfied with denouncing the political show, as curdled indignants; or with trying to alter the mood of the show or their own mood towards it, as inside-dopesters.

SUGGESTIONS FOR FURTHER READING

David Riesman's evidence for a changing American character may be followed in more detail in his *The Lonely Crowd* (New Haven, 1961). Henry Steele Commager finds a significant change in the American character in his *The American Mind* (New Haven, 1950). Vance Packard argues that the American character is changing because of our great wealth in *The Waste Makers* (New York, 1963).

Alexis de Tocqueville studied Americans during his visit in 1831–32. His report, *Democracy in America* (in numerous editions; also in paperback), described an American character which seems very much up to date today. As Turner found the westward movement, and Potter, the availability of wealth, to be experiences which all Americans shared, de Tocqueville found the democratic experience to be that which Americans shared and which consequently shaped their character. Numerous other visitors to our shores attempted to describe the American they met. A convenient collection is Henry Steele Commager, *America in Perspective* (New York, 1947).

A valuable study reviewing the evidence relating to the question of a changing American character is Clyde Kluckholm, "Have There Been Discernible Shifts in American

Values during the Past Generation?" in Elting E. Morrison, ed., *The American Style* (New York, 1958), pp. 145–217. Michael McGiffert has brought together a collection of readings on the question of American character and has also assembled a full bibliography in *The Character of Americans* (Homewood, Ill., 1964).

General Bibliography

Those interested in pursuing the theme of conflict and consensus further should begin with the three giants of American historiography who reshaped the writing of American history in the twentieth century— Charles Beard, Vernon Parrington, and Frederick Jackson Turner. The best approach to Beard is through Charles and Mary Beard, *The Rise of American Civilization* (New York, 1927, 1930), a lively and interesting interpretation of the whole course of American history with an emphasis on class and economic conflict. Parrington's one important book, *Main Currents in American Thought* (New York, 1927, 1930) complements Beard's work and deals with the relationship of literature and ideas to society and social movements. Turner wrote very little but had an immense influence. A convenient introduction to Turner, his critics, and his supporters is George Rogers Taylor, ed., *The Turner Thesis Concerning the Role of the Frontier in America* (Boston, 1956). Turner's essays may be found in *The Frontier in American History* (New York, 1920) and *The Significance of Sections in American History* (New York, 1932). See also his *Rise of the New West, 1819–1829* (New York, 1906).

The best general introduction to the consensus interpretation (which in a sense is an attack on Parrington, Beard, and Turner) can be found in Louis Hartz, *The Liberal Tradition in America* (New York, 1955), and Daniel J. Boorstin, *The Genius of American Politics* (Chicago, 1953). Both men see a uniform and essentially harmonious tradition in American politics that has made debate and disagreement mere shadow boxing. Some of the implications of the rise of the consensus interpretation are explored in two provocative essays: John Higham, "The Cult of the American Consensus," *Commentary*, XXVII (February, 1959), 93–100; J. Rogers Hollingsworth, "Consensus and Continuity in Recent American Historical Writing," *South Atlantic Quarterly*, LXI (Winter, 1962), 40–50.

Many of the younger American historians have adopted a consensus approach, but there are still many followers of Beard, Parrington, and Turner. For a discussion of recent trends in American historiography, including the problem dealt with in this book, see John Higham, ed., *The Reconstruction of American History* (New York, 1962). Several discussions on a theme closely related to the problem of conflict and consensus are brought together by John A. Braeman, Robert H. Bremner, and Everett Walters, eds., *Change and Continuity in Twentieth Century America* (Columbus, Ohio, 1965).

459